The Mighty Eighth

The Mighty Eighth

Units, Men and Machines

(A History of the US 8th Army Air Force)

Roger A. Freeman

With colour drawings by
John B. Rabbets

**Doubleday and Company, Inc.
Garden City, New York**

Doubleday and Company edition

First published 1970

Third impression revised 1972

MADE AND PRINTED IN GREAT BRITAIN

Contents

Introduction

When heavier-than-air machines first took the air, at the start of the century, few dreamed of the far-reaching consequences of this achievement, particularly in the military field. In little more than a decade the British had created a new military service entirely devoted to aerial warfare, and within another thirty years air power had become a decisive factor in war and a deterrent enforcing the peace.

The Wright brothers, who made the World's first powered flight in December 1903, were United States citizens but their countrymen were slow in appreciating the significance of their achievement. During the 1914-1918 conflict it was the European powers, Britain, France, and Germany who developed the aeroplane as an effective instrument of war, and when the US Air Service aviators came to the Western Front in 1918 they flew, initially, aircraft provided by their allies.

At first a vehicle for observation of the enemy's activities, the aeroplane had been quickly developed for offensive roles; the dropping of bombs as an extension of artillery range, the direction of artillery by aerial observation and combating the machines of the enemy in the air. If the contribution of the duelling fragile machines above the trenches did not greatly affect the course of the war, at least the possibilities of the aeroplane as a weapon had made itself plain by the end of hostilities. It was this potential that inspired the leaders of the American flying units to seek an independent air arm following a precedent already set in 1918 by the Royal Air Force; the General Staff of the US Army, however, could see little reason for aircraft other than for the support of ground forces. The political climate at the time was govered by a return to the Monroe Doctrine, and by pursuing this isolationist policy any entanglement in any future war outside the American continent was not foreseen. Conversely, if others outside the Pan-American sphere menaced the USA, even the air bombing advocates did not see prospects of inter-continental strikes by aircraft. In any case the very limited military funds authorised by Congress in the immediate postwar years did not allow for such revolutionary schemes as those for which the air leaders clamoured. Reduced in strength to just over a score of squadrons, the Air Service continued as part of the US Army while the US Navy continued to keep its own flying units.

But the leaders of the Army Air Service continued to propound their theories of an independent air arm constituting a major portion of national defence. One, the voluble General "Billy" Mitchell who had commanded an American air element in France, was particularly impressed with the possibilities of the bombing aeroplane. He nourished the visionaries' ideas of aircraft able to bomb and destroy industry and installations vital to the support of an enemy's armed forces. To prove the value of the bomber aeroplane as an instrument of national defence, Mitchell succeeded in using the simple machines of the period to successfully sink disused naval vessels during tests staged in 1921 and 1923. Canvassing his ideas with such fervour that he overstepped his military office, he incurred the antagonism of the traditional forces, eventually leading to his court-martial. His quest to obtain autonomy for the Army Air Service was however, not without effect, for in 1926 the Service was raised in status. By becoming the Army Air Corps representation was gained on the General Staff, while at the same time a programme of expansion was authorised.

Americans who believed air power, tended to look on an offensive by bombardment as the main facet of that power. Little practical encouragement was forthcoming as their country was committed to an isolationist policy and only defensive weapons qualified for a share of the limited military appropriations. However, in spite of persistent opposition, not only did a reasonably clear-cut method for such bombardment evolve, but by devious means much of the equipment to give it credibility came into the hands of the Air Corps long before their doctrine came to be accepted by higher authority.

By 1931 some agreement had been reached with the Navy on the subject of coastal defence and the right of the Air Corps to engage in certain specified reconnaissance and bombardment activities to seaward. The way was then open for the procurement of a long-range aircraft that could fulfil this defence commitment, for which a range of 5,000 miles, bomb load of 2,000 lbs and a top speed of 200 mph were advocated, ostensibly for this purpose. But the Air Corps would also have in such an aircraft the ideal vehicle to further its beliefs in offensive air power. Of the resulting designs put forward by manufacturers to meet this proposal, that of the Boeing Company was selected and ordered.

The Boeing prototype, the first all-metal four-motor monoplane designed specifically as a bomber to take to the air, first flew on July 28th 1935. Its rather prominent gun emplacements engendered a press description "flying fortress"; although hardly appropriate at the time, the name caught on. The Air Corps wanted 65 of these "Flying Fortresses": the War Department allowed an order for 13. With the military designation Y1B-17 (i.e. the 17th bomber type with the Y1 prefix denoting service test models) these were delivered by Boeings during 1937. The recipients were confident that they now had a bomber which could prove their theories.

In the early 'thirties the performance of Army Air Corps' bomber aircraft had approached that of their fighters. The vision of a bomber possessed of sufficient speed and armament to take care of itself in any conflict with enemy fighters was conceived. With the advent of the B-17 bomber—which had a top speed in excess of the standard Air Corps fighter—this was feasible. Thinking also centred upon operations at high altitude where the danger of pursuit and anti-aircraft fire would be further limited. To fly really high, crews would need oxygen and to bomb accurately from such altitudes a precision bomb-sight was imperative. Both these requirements could be met, for as early as 1928 a new liquid oxygen system for airmen at high altitudes had been successfully tested, and a precision bomb-sight had been under development since 1932. The latter, originally designed by Mr C. L. Norden for the Navy, was adopted by the Air Corps. This fine instrument became one of the most highly guarded items of secret equipment in the Air Corps armoury, and little wonder, for its precision was such that Fortress bombardiers could time and again drop bombs within 50 ft of a practice target from the rarefied atmosphere, four miles high, above the dry lake at Muroc, California. Visibility was ideal and the hundred-foot aiming circle on the range far below could be easily distinguished; but that such conditions might not prevail elsewhere were facts overlooked by the uncautioned exponents of these achievements who talked of "pickle-barrel accuracy". Thus a popular legend was born: that American Army aviators could drop a bomb into a pickle-barrel from four or five miles above the earth.

Two other items of equipment already commonplace on American military aircraft became important features of the high altitude precision bomber. Much attention had already been paid in America developing superchargers to obtain better aero-engine performance at high altitude, by forcing compressed air into the carburettors. Superchargers fitted to an experimental "Flying Fortress' gave it a top speed of over 300 mph at operational heights. And if American warplanes had deficiencies in defensive armament, then it was in quantity rather than quality. Unlike the air arms of other powers, standardised on a .303 rifle calibre machine gun for both fighters and bombers, the Air Corps had made use of the .50 calibre machine-gun. This "Point Fifty" fired "half-inch diameter" bullets with greater range and higher velocity due to the increased charge. With the exception of a .303 gun in the nose, the B-17 used the larger gun for defensive firepower.

The year the "Flying Fortress" first took to the air, the Air Corps had achieved another major step towards autonomy by the establishment of a special headquarters to concentrate the bomber and fighter flying units under a single head, instead of under the command of a US Army formation. If the idea of air power was becoming more acceptable to the Army General Staff and War Department, nevertheless, they were soon to retract their favours. Once more Air Corps fortunes waned when, in 1938, restrictions were placed upon the ranging of their recently acquired "heavy bombers". The persistent attempts of air leaders to foster their belief in an offensive capability by an independent arm as a method of defence still went very much against the grain: official policy decreed that the role of the Air Corps was Army support in national defence, even though there were by then ominous signs from Europe of what air power alone might achieve.

The wind of change came with President Franklin D. Roosevelt who had other views. He foresaw that the United States, despite her avowed policy of non-intervention, might eventually be drawn into a war that seemed imminently likely to engulf Europe. Roosevelt also believed that the military aeroplane would play a great part in winning such a war. So it came about that those who had so recently put the Air Corps in its place were faced with much re-thinking, on the lead given by none other than the President. Plans for American rearmament went ahead and a vast expansion for the Air Corps was scheduled. It would be wrong to suggest that the doctrine of offensive bombardment was accepted over-night, even though henceforth it became the dominating feature of American air planning. The critics were many.

The yardstick in planning an expansion of the Air Corps was by the number of Groups. A group was usually composed of three or four squadrons—the basic and traditional flying units. From the 14 groups of December 1938, the total rose to 67 by the date the United States entered the Second World War and correspondingly the number of Air Corps personnel rose from 21,000 to 354,000. To match this growth, the American aircraft industry had mushroomed, also producing aircraft for Britain and France. This demand so strained the aircraft industry that shortages in aircraft and equipment affected air units long after America entered the war.

When Hitler had sent his armies into Poland, an event obliging Britain and France to declare war on Germany, the Army Air Corps had but 23 B-17s on its inventory. But these Army aviators would not have to do battle until two more years had passed. Time was allowed to prepare.

On June 20th 1941, the Army Air Force was created which co-ordinated the activities of all US Army air elements, representing another hard-won concession on the road to autonomy. Major General H. H. Arnold, previously head of the Air Corps, remained as chief; he had watched the development of the air war in Europe with intense interest. The British and the Germans had come to grief with their attempts to carry out aerial bombing in daylight and both had turned to night operations. The method of bombardment advocated and developed by the Air Corps was essentially a daylight method, yet there was little discouragement at this juncture. The American doctrine was based on technical achievements and a mode of attack far removed from that practised by British and German bombers in the early years of the war.

Early in 1941 when a score of the latest B-17s, the B-17C model, were acquired by Royal Air Force Bomber Command, their use in a number of small attacks upon enemy targets was closely watched by the Americans. The experience was discouraging for little if any effective damage was done to enemy installations and eight Fortresses were written off as operational losses. The British considered the aircraft well constructed and good to fly but at that their admiration finished. When their own four-motor night bombers could carry a bomb load of 10,000 lbs they considered the 4,000 lbs the Fortress accommodated to be insufficient. Self-sealing fuel tanks and armour protection, both vital necessities, were lacking. Further, it hardly lived up to its name, as defensive armament proved wholly inadequate. As far as the RAF were concerned, the American ideas of daylight bombing showed no more signs of success than their own. But the outcome still had little effect upon the faith of Arnold and other enthusiasts of high-altitude daylight precision bombing. They could point to many weaknesses in the RAF's employment of the Fortresses, besides technical failings in the aircraft. The B-17 was already undergoing radical redesign and many of the improvements suggested by the experience of the RAF were embodied in a new model.

Another American four-motor bomber of similar size, weight and performance to the Fortress was also under development. This was the Consolidated Aircraft Corporation's B-24 Liberator of more recent design, the prototype having first flown in December 1939. Superior to the B-17 in bomb load capacity and range, it showed promise to the RAF who received some of the early production models. These early deliveries, however, were not used for bombing European targets, for their flight endurance made them ideal for anti-submarine use, to combat the serious menace of the U-boats to Atlantic shipping in 1941.

Months before the Axis powers went to war with the United States, in December 1941, the Roosevelt administration had planned for their country's eventual involvement in the European war, with Britain as their chief ally. The possibility of war with Japan at the same time was acknowledged, but Germany, as the principal Axis power, would have to be dealt with first. Hitler's forces, having overrun the continent of Europe would be brought to battle, but first it would take considerable time to build an invasion force strong enough to breach the continental defences from the sea. While such a force was prepared, American air forces would join those of the British in a sustained air offensive to weaken the enemy's military power.

For the air leaders of the US Army who had struggled so long to assert their belief in airpower, this was their opportunity. With the British Isles as a base, the way was open for a programme of aerial bombardment of specific enemy industrial and other vital installations whose destruction would cause the maximum disruption of the enemy's war effort. And if such targets could be successfully destroyed to bring about a weakening of ability to wage war—and perhaps a complete breakdown—there was a chance that the task of the invading army would be no more than that of occupation. Thus was the concept of strategic bombing. The US Army Air Forces went to the United Kingdom with its doctrine of high-altitude daylight precision bombing, to help fight the Nazis who had the best part of Europe in their grip. They partnered the RAF, also believers that airpower had a vital part to play in winning the war. Arnold and his team knew that if their system of bombing worked, and they could destroy vital industry in the enemy's home land and bring him to his knees, air power would become the dominant military force. And if that happened who could deny them the full autonomy of a United States Air Force?

The Boeing B-17 Flying Fortress *Stric Nine* takes off from the 91st Bomb Group base in Bassingbourn, England en route to bomb enemy installations in Europe.

Chapter 1: A Winged Eight

On a dull February day, a Douglas DC-3 transport crossed the south-west coast of England after the long and dangerous over-watér flight from Lisbon. In that year of 1942, Luftwaffe long-range patrol aircraft from French bases frequently searched the Bay of Biscay in the hope of intercepting traffic to and from Britain. The travellers who that day successfully eluded enemy patrols included a group of seven United States Army Air Force (USAAF) officers who had come to arrange for the reception of American combat flying units, soon to be based in England, for operations over Hitler's "Fortress Europe". Their leader was no stranger to Britain having spent many weeks in previous years studying the Royal Air Force's operations. He was Brigadier General Ira C. Eaker, an ardent believer in the USAAF's concept of strategic bombardment as a war-winning facet of air power. He was to head an American bomber command to work alongside that of the British; but whereas the RAF bombers flew by night, the USAAF would operate by day.

Eaker knew the British were generally sceptical of these American ideas, having already seen proof of high losses from daylight operations. Nevertheless, the USAAF was determined to put their theories to the test and the British, though doubting the chances of success, were more than willing to help their new Allies in every possible way. So, on February 20th 1942, the seven officers in civilian clothes arrived at Hendon and were warmly greeted. In addition to Eaker, they were, Lt Col Frank A. Armstrong Jr, Major Peter Beasley, Captains Fred Castle and Beirne Lay Jr, Lts Harris Hull and William Cowart Jr. Ahead of them lay the tedium of much desk work.

Initially, Eaker and his staff were stationed at RAF Bomber Command Headquarters, near High Wycombe, Buckinghamshire, where they could closely study RAF procedures and make recommendations to incoming American units. The USAAF drew heavily upon the RAF's two and a half years experience in operating against the enemy, and which was still building up its own strategic bombing offensive against Germany. Eaker based the organisation of his own command as close as possible to that of the RAF's to facilitate co-operation.

A name for the new force was a matter for early consideration. The American Air Staff had assented to a bomber force in the UK known simply as the projected Army Air Force in Great Britain. In the United States at the time, the Force consisted of four separate air forces, located in geographical regions and designated by numbers, First to Fourth. Early in 1942 a new air force was formed to provide the air element of a task force being assembled for a projected invasion of North-West Africa. When inaugurated on January 2nd, 1942 it was known as the "Fifth" Air Force but four days later this title was changed to "Eighth" Air Force under revised plans to incorporate units in American overseas possessions and protectorates into the Fifth, Sixth and Seventh Air Forces. The US Eighth Army Air Force was officially born on January 28th 1942 when a headquarters was activated at Savannah Army Air Base in Georgia. No sooner had its first units assembled in the training area than the build-up for the North African invasion was cancelled in order to meet pressing demands in the Pacific war areas. The Eighth Air Force, commanded by

Colonel Asa N. Duncan, then found itself without a mission four weeks after its inception.

Designated for over-all command of the Army Air Force in Great Britain was Major General Carl Spaatz, veteran pilot of combat in the First World War, with a fine following record in the Army air organisations, and now one of Arnold's foremost commanders. Spaatz suggested to Arnold that the infant Eighth Air Force could provide the nucleus for the build-up in the United Kingdom. This was accepted and Eaker learned early in April that he was preparing the way for an "Eighth Air Force".

To the USAAF, the Eighth Air Force, to be symbolised by a winged eight insignia, constituted an opportunity of promoting and testing their doctrine of high-altitude daylight precision bombing. However, the US War Department had no plan for a strategic bomber offensive against Germany except as a preliminary to an amphibious invasion of Europe, provisionally planned for mid-1943.

Meanwhile, the advance party of USAAF personnel busied themselves in England. The British Air Ministry had appropriated a country mansion not far from RAF Bomber Command HQ and on April 15th Eaker's staff moved into these sumptuous premises. This was Daws Hill Lodge, High Wycombe, once the seat of English nobility and more recently part of the evacuated Wycombe Abbey Girls' School.

The planned strength of the Eighth Air Force in the United Kingdom was put at 60 combat groups, made up of 17 heavy, 10 medium and 6 light bomber; 7 observation, 12 fighter and 8 transport groups—a strength of some 3,500 aircraft to be available in the United Kingdom by April 1943. This great force, larger than the combined total of all combat units of the home-based RAF, had to be found airfields and base installations in the UK. Fortunately, even before Pearl Harbor, consultations had taken place between Britain and America over the possible establishment of American forces in Britain, if the United States became involved in the war, and the problem of airfield accommodation had been considered. The British Air Ministry at this stage put into effect its airfield building programme.

The area selected for basing the first US bomber units was centred on the county of Huntingdonshire, roughly halfway between London and the coastal indentation called The Wash. Airfields in this area were already under construction for a new RAF Bomber Command formation which was then disbanded, so that the installations could be made available.

The RAF normally based two bomber squadrons on one airfield and as an American bomber group consisted of four squadrons it was assumed that one group would occupy two airfields. It was foreseen that a total of 75 airfields would be required by the Eighth Air Force. The majority were to be sited in the eastern coastal bulge of England known as East Anglia. A small group of airfields were to be provided in Northern Ireland and these were eventually allocated to training and "logistics" (maintenance and supply). The airfield requirements were increased as the months went by to meet revised assessments of the number of combat units likely to form this American force.

The standard British bomber airfield consisted of three runways, within a perimeter track edged with aircraft dispersal

This fuel bowser and Oxford communications aircraft were two of the many items supplied to the Eighth by the RAF.—(IWM)

points; these were of concrete with bituminous surfacing. Administrative buildings, living accommodation, maintenance facilities were normally dispersed in the neighbouring countryside to minimise damage in the event of an enemy air attack.

The problem of maintenance and supply was a most exacting task. A force on the scale planned would consume prodigious quantities of ordnance, fuel and lubricants and parts to keep the aircraft operational, besides the needs of administrative staffs and the domestic requirements. Some action had also been taken the previous year to plan for maintenance and supply facilities. Arnold had sent one of his officers to the UK to discuss this problem and come to some arrangement with the British on setting up depots for major repairs and overhauls. Two sites were selected. The first, in Northern Ireland, was a large country estate named Langford Lodge where construction commenced in February 1942. The Lockheed Aircraft Corporation, already operating an assembly plant for the RAF at Speke, near Liverpool, was co-opted to staff and operate this depot; although it was planned eventually to have it operated entirely by military personnel when they were suitably trained. The other site, at Warton, Lancashire, in a highly industrialised area was not far from the west coast port of Liverpool. An existing airfield was to be enlarged and depot facilities provided.

Since neither of these major depots would come into operations for many months more immediate facilities for heavy repairs had to be provided. Fortunately at Burtonwood, not far from Warton, the Ministry of Aircraft Production had a repair depot already handling American aircraft for the RAF and an agreement was reached for the transfer of this establishment, with its staff of British technicians, to the repair of USAAF aircraft and components at an early date; US technicians eventually took over most of the work from the British. Small depots, nearer the combat airfields had also to be established as essential links in the chain of maintenance and supply. Additionally, much storage space had to be provided.

Although the USAAF sought to be functionally independent it was only prudent that it should adopt certain systems and procedures proven by the British. For communications and air traffic control a unified system was essential, and the efficient RAF operating procedures were adopted.

This contact with the RAF highlighted some deficiencies in USAAF operational techniques and equipment. Intelligence in particular had been neglected and the RAF undertook to train American intelligence officers in its schools. At first, all relevant target and enemy defences information was readily provided from British sources.

The adoption of many RAF operating procedures and reliance on special British equipment meant additional training for USAAF personnel. Newly arrived aircrews needed to be familiarised and special units, known as Combat Crew Replacement and Training Centers (CCRC) were arranged initially with RAF instructional staff. Conveniently sited a few miles north-east of Eaker's Headquarters was Bovingdon airfield, then in an advanced state of completion for the RAF. The Air Ministry agreed, however, to lease this base, and its satellite at Cheddington, to the USAAF for training purposes. It was further agreed that any extension of training facilities should utilise bases in Northern Ireland, which could be better spared than those in eastern England.

The first unit of the Eighth Air Force to leave America was the 689th Quartermaster Company. They sailed on the *SS Cathay* on April 22nd 1942. The one officer and fifty men of the 689th formed part of the 2nd Air Depot Group of which the major portion, in company with advance parties of Eighth Air Force HQ, the VIII Bomber, Fighter and Base Commands, and the 15th Bombardment Squadron, sailed on the *SS Andes* from Boston five days later. The *Andes*, with 1850 officers and men arrived first, docking at Liverpool on May 11th.

The command staffs journeyed to High Wycombe, while the 2nd Air Depot went to Molesworth airfield in Huntingdonshire and the 15th Bomb. Sqdn. to the airfield at Grafton Underwood, near Kettering. The 689th Quartermaster Company set foot on British soil at Newport, Monmouthshire on May 14th and from there travelled to Wickstead Park, near Kettering. Lt W. T. Fairbanks, the commanding and only officer, confined his men to camp for the first evening and busied them about settling into their new home. He was somewhat taken aback to see a large crowd of "natives" had gathered outside the fence lining the adjoining road. Curiosity at what these "Yanks" were like was obviously too much for the traditionally reserved local inhabitants and it was some days before the evening audiences subsided. With a few hundred officers and men the Eighth was an entity in the UK; even though there was yet little semblance of an air force. If the aeroplane was the symbol of such status it could at least boast one, an Airspeed Oxford trainer loaned for courier purposes by the RAF.

A bombing offensive being the keynote of USAAF plans, the heavy bomber dominated the schedules for the Eighth Air Force. Two four-engined types were currently in production in the USA. One, a new version of the Fortress, the B-17 model "E", included refinements in the light of experiences with earlier models. The rear section of the fuselage and the tailplane featured a complete redesign, with a tail gun position to enhance rearward firepower and larger tail surfaces giving better stability at high altitudes. Production of the B-17E was soon superseded by the B-17F, embodying further refinements. Although Fortresses would be the backbone of the bomber force for at least a year, it was planned to concurrently produce the B-24 Liberator, a design of the Consolidated Aircraft Corporation of San Diego, California. Although a far less shapely machine than the B-17, the B-24 possessed greater flight endurance and bomb-carrying capacity. It was scheduled for production on an even larger scale than the Fortress. The mighty Ford Motor Company built a vast factory especially for producing Liberators. All told, five American plants would be devoted to final assembly of B-24s and three to B-17s. But early in 1942 B-24 production was only just getting under way and the first complete B-24 group was still in training.

As mentioned, the formation known as the group, rather than the squadron, had become the component by which the USAAF measured its strength. The squadrons forming a group were usually activated with the parent group and were rarely separated. Bombing operations were usually conducted on a group basis, and this had led to some loss of individual squadron identities. A bomb group in the spring of 1942 was composed of a Headquarters and four combat squadrons, each having establishment for 8-10 aircraft.

When the US entered the war many of the 67 groups in being were little more than a nucleus of men awaiting training. Thirteen of these groups were designated as "heavy bombardment" although few had either aircraft or crews to substantiate the title. With the huge expansion programme projected for 1942, most of the groups that were equipped with B-17s and B-24s, and not actively engaged against the Japanese, were allocated to training new heavy bomber groups. By coincidence, on the day the Eighth Air Force was officially made active at Savannah, the War Department sanctioned the constitution of twenty new heavy bombardment groups, designated by the USAAF 88, 90 to 100 and 301 to 308 (the large numbering gap took account of a traditional ruling that numbers in the 101-300 range should be reserved for units of the National Guard, State territorial organisations.) These new groups were soon earmarked for the Eighth; four became training organisations and remained in the States, five were diverted to other theatres of war, and the remaining eleven eventually became the original, and some of the most distinguished, heavy bombardment groups to operate from England.

Fighter groups assigned to the Eighth Air Force were intended primarily for a bomber support role. In the spring of 1942 the best American fighter for such work was deemed to be the twin-engined Lockheed P-38F Lightning, a beautifully streamlined machine of unusual configuration with a performance far superior to any other American production

fighter of the day. However, the Lightning's advanced design brought teething troubles that delayed its entry into combat groups until the winter of 1941-1942—and then only in small numbers.

Another fighter selected for service in England with the Eighth was the Bell P-39D Airacobra, then currently equipping a fair proportion of the thirty or so pursuit groups. This too was a novel design, its conventional appearance belying the fact that the engine was placed mid-fuselage, behind the pilot's cockpit. The prototype, flown in 1938, had promised a good performance, but Service models by 1942, laden with combat equipment, could only give their best at low altitudes.

The RAF had shown an interest in both types. After putting the Airacobra in service with No. 601 Squadron in late 1941 they found its performance too poor for operations across the English Channel and the type was withdrawn in March 1942. In the case of the Lightning, American security restrictions of that time permitted only a low-powered version to be made available to the British. The RAF, not inspired with this model, offered the bulk of their order back to the USAAF.

First of the heavy bombardment groups constituted in January 1942 to be made ready for a combat theatre was the 97th Bombardment Group flying B-17Es. Assigned to the Eighth Bomber Command in May it moved to the overseas staging area in the north-east tip of the USA from where the aircraft and crews proceeded by air across the North Atlantic ferry route to the UK, while the ground personnel travelled by sea.

The Eighth was also assigned the 1st and 31st Fighter Groups, the first units to have received P-38s and P-39s. The 1st was the oldest and most distinguished group in the USAAF having originated in the First World War. The 31st, formed in 1940, had newly assigned squadrons, its original units having been transferred to the south-west Pacific, just prior to commitment to the UK. A shortage of shipping space and the delay in moving fighter aircraft by sea had some bearing on the ambitious plan formulated for the 1st and 31st Groups to fly their aircraft to the UK, with B-17s of the 97th as navigational guides. These two fighter groups moved into the staging area in May to prepare for the long overwater flights, with the movement date set for June 1st or as soon as possible thereafter.

At the end of May, however, a new Japanese threat in the Pacific caused the movement to be postponed. The 1st with its P-38s and the 97th with its B-17s were switched to the west coast of the US on a defence emergency from which the last aircraft did not return to Maine until the middle of June. Meanwhile, any misgivings on the advisability of flying the single-motor P-39s to the UK were settled by the absence of the B-17s to guide the fighters. The 31st pilots were therefore sent by sea, leaving their planes behind.

Early in June, the 60th Transport Group had been added to

Pilot of 14th FG P-38F 41-7651 stretches his legs after the flight from Iceland to Scotland.—(IWM)

the Eighth Air Force's strength and moved to the staging area. The first fully-equipped Douglas C-47 Skytrain (RAF Dakota) transport group to complete its training and be allocated for overseas service, the 60th was to be used initially to provide logistical support for the Eighth, and its Skytrains carried stores and equipment on their flight eastward.

With the return of the 97th and 1st Groups, the air movement could go ahead and on June 18th the first units were ordered to the airfield on Presque Island, at the extreme north-east tip of Maine, in preparation for the first leg of the flight, 569 miles to Goose Bay in Labrador. A minimum of twenty B-17s were needed to escort the eighty P-38s of the 1st Group and those not required for escort were sent on ahead. At 16.25 hrs on June 26th the first fifteen B-17Es reached Goose Bay. Refuelled, they took off about three hours later for the Bluie West 1 landing-ground on the southwest tip of Greenland, 776 miles distant. The visibility on approach was so poor that they were unable to land. Faced either with a return to Goose Bay or an alternative landing ground 400 miles along the Greenland coast, eleven Fortresses returned to Goose Bay after fourteen hours in the air, and one went on to land at Bluie West 8. The remaining three machines, hopelessly lost, were forced down out of fuel on the Greenland coast; luckily all crews were saved. This first experience underlined the difficulties in ferrying along this route, particularly the weather hazards.

The following day the first P-38s began their movement, usually with one B-17 leading an element of four Lightnings. This time the flight went smoothly and on July 1st the first USAAF manned combat aircraft reached Britain when B-17E 41-9085 of the 97th Group, touched down at Prestwick, Scotland. On July 18th the final flight of eight P-38s left Presque Island led by two B-17s carrying the VIII Fighter Command commander and his staff. Their Headquarters had been responsible for the direction of the Eighth's first air movement overseas, from a temporary station in New Hampshire. On July 27th this flight arrived at Prestwick, completing the ferrying of the 180 aircraft of the 1st, 60th and 97th Groups. The 2,965 mile route from Presque Island, via Goose Bay, Bluie West 1, Reykjavik, to Prestwick had been negotiated with the loss of 5 B-17s and 6 P-38s, although all crews were saved. Two of the B-17s and the P-38s were supposedly the victims of misleading directional broadcasts put out by the Germans.

Rumour was part of everyday life in wartime English villages, so it was not surprising that when Americans were said to have been seen on the local airfield at Polebrook, Northamptonshire, speculation was rife. Rumours were soon given some substance in June when a troop train pulled into the little country station at nearby Oundle and disgorged several hundred men clad in olive drab, speaking English with accents that most of the locals associated with the cinema. On July 6th native curiosity was roused still further when large four-engined aircraft marked with a white star on a blue disc background landed at Polebrook. The B-17s had arrived. By coincidence, it had been at Polebrook in the previous summer that the RAF had chosen to base the early Fortresses for their experimental daylight bombing raids. With Headquarters and two squadrons at Polebrook, the other two squadrons of the 97th went to the nearby satellite field at Grafton Underwood.

On July 25th the first C-47s of the 60th Group arrived at Chelveston, also in Northants, and five days later the last of their 48 machines had come in. Perhaps the greatest interest was engendered by the Lightnings when part of the air echelon of the 1st Group landed at Goxhill in Lincolnshire, on July 9th. Only two of the 1st's squadrons were destined to complete the journey to England at this time. Its 27th Fighter Squadron was ordered to remain at Reykjavik, Iceland for defensive patrols in view of possible German air attacks on the island.

41-7787, N, of 60th TCG wings low over an English town.—(Odhams)

While the initial air movement of American units to the UK were in progress, the white star insignia had also begun to appear on Spitfires at Atcham airfield, near Shrewsbury, in the west of England. The 31st Group, whose personnel had reached England early in June, was there training on the famous British fighter which the RAF insisted was superior in performance to the P-39s the Group had flown in the US. Thus, the 31st could claim to be the first complete USAAF group established in England: the first of the many. For another group, the 52nd, trained to fly P-39s and already on its way, it was arranged that their equipment should be left behind in favour of equipping with Spitfire Vs on arrival.

Between the Bomber Command and the combat groups a formation organisation was required for the more detailed planning and direction of combat operations—the wing. Two of the original wings that dated from early US Army Air Service days, the 1st and 2nd, were established; the former at Brampton Grange, hub of the complex of eight airfields selected as the first heavy bomber bases, and the latter at Old Catton in Norfolk, where a number of bomber fields were nearing completion. The Headquarters of VIII Fighter Command, under Brigadier General Frank O'D. Hunter, appropriately a distinguished fighter pilot of the First World War, was set up at Bushey Hall, near Watford, close to its RAF counterpart at Bentley Priory. It was to lean heavily on RAF Fighter Command HQ in these formative days. A new fighter wing, the 6th activated in the States, was on its way to afford operational control for the Eighth's fighter groups.

With the arrival of Major General Carl Spaatz in London on June 18th, the Eighth Air Force was officially located in Britain. A few thousand men with no more than 200 aeroplanes, its test in battle was awaited with much interest on

Peggy-D a 97th BG B-17E flies over England. Skull and bombs design on rear fuselage was part of 342nd BS badge.—(IWM)

both sides of the Atlantic and presumably with apprehension in the Third Reich. The British were pleasantly surprised by the determination of the US airmen to come to grips with the enemy, a feeling neatly reflected in the following comment overheard in an RAF officer's mess at that time: "Not a bad lot of chaps; damned eager; but little idea—the war, I mean, not the other."

Famous British Fighter in Uncle Sam's colours: a Spitfire V of 308th FS, with pilot and ground crew.—(USAF)

Chapter 2: Damned Eager

The first unit of the Eighth Air Force destined to enter combat was not governed by the bombing methods the USAAF was eager to put to the test over Europe. In fact, the 15th Bomb. Sqdn. (Light) was originally ordered to the UK for defensive, not offensive, purposes. While America lacked a night fighter force, the RAF had successfully adapted the American Douglas DB-7 light bomber for night fighting as their Havoc. Following this lead similar modifications were made on a USAAF version designated the A-20. An A-20 squadron was sent to Britain for instruction in the use of airborne search-lights as used by the RAF's Havocs. The squadron selected, the 15th, was separated from its parent organisation, 27th Group, and sent to England with the first shipment of troops for the Eighth Air Force.

Meanwhile, the RAF had discarded this system for night fighting in favour of airborne radar, so the 15th Bomb. Sqdn. found after arrival its role changed. Having moved from Grafton Underwood to Molesworth in Huntingdonshire, prior to the arrival of the 97th Group's Fortresses, the 15th was placed under the guidance of No. 226 Squadron RAF. This squadron flew the Boston III (RAF name for the bomber version of the Douglas DB-7) and as the 15th had no aircraft of their own they borrowed from their mentors. The British instructed the American crews in flight procedures and their methods of light bomber attack on enemy targets.

Towards the end of June 1942, No. 226 Squadron's commander considered his charges proficient enough to conduct combat operations. The first combat sortie by a USAAF crew was a somewhat unofficial initiation when on June 29th AL743, one of twelve RAF Bostons sent to bomb Hazebrouck marshalling yard, was flown by Captain Kegelman, Lt Bell, T/Sgt Robert Golay and Sgt Bennie Cunningham. American Independence Day, July 4th, was obviously a propitious date to formally commence operations and plans were made accordingly. Six American crews were notified to join No. 226 Squadron crews in a low-level attack on four Luftwaffe airfields in the Low Countries.

At 07.11 hrs on the appointed day, the twelve Bostons, all bearing RAF roundels, commenced take-off from the small grass airfield at Swanton Morley. They assembled into four flights of three aircraft; each flight with at least one experienced RAF crew, was assigned a different target. Flying low over the North Sea to avoid detection by enemy radar, the formation headed out towards Holland. Unfortunately enemy vessels were sighted in the distance and it is possible that these gave warning to the German defences for, on reaching the Dutch

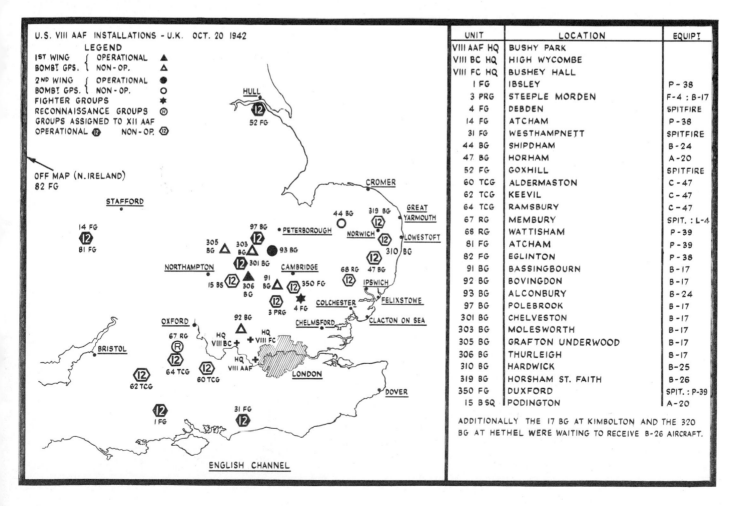

U.S. VIII AAF INSTALLATIONS - U.K. OCT. 20 1942

LEGEND

	OPERATIONAL	▲
1ST WING BOMB'T GPS.	NON-OP.	△
2ND WING BOMB'T GPS.	OPERATIONAL	●
	NON-OP.	○
FIGHTER GROUPS		★
RECONNAISSANCE GROUPS		®
GROUPS ASSIGNED TO XII AAF OPERATIONAL ⑫	NON-OP.	⑫

OFF MAP (N. IRELAND)
82 FG

UNIT	LOCATION	EQUIPT
VIII AAF HQ	BUSHY PARK	
VIII BC HQ	HIGH WYCOMBE	
VIII FC HQ	BUSHEY HALL	
I FG	IBSLEY	P-38
3 PRG	STEEPLE MORDEN	F-4 : B-17
4 FG	DEBDEN	SPITFIRE
14 FG	ATCHAM	P-38
31 FG	WESTHAMPNETT	SPITFIRE
44 BG	SHIPDHAM	B-24
47 BG	HORHAM	A-20
52 FG	GOXHILL	SPITFIRE
60 TCG	ALDERMASTON	C-47
62 TCG	KEEVIL	C-47
64 TCG	RAMSBURY	C-47
67 RG	MEMBURY	SPIT. : L-4
68 RG	WATTISHAM	P-39
81 FG	ATCHAM	P-39
82 FG	EGLINTON	P-38
91 BG	BASSINGBOURN	B-17
92 BG	BOVINGDON	B-17
93 BG	ALCONBURY	B-24
97 BG	POLEBROOK	B-17
301 BG	CHELVESTON	B-17
303 BG	MOLESWORTH	B-17
305 BG	GRAFTON UNDERWOOD	B-17
306 BG	THURLEIGH	B-17
310 BG	HARDWICK	B-25
319 BG	HORSHAM ST. FAITH	B-26
350 FG	DUXFORD	SPIT. : P-39
15 BSQ	PODINGTON	A-20

ADDITIONALLY THE 17 BG AT KIMBOLTON AND THE 320 BG AT HETHEL WERE WAITING TO RECEIVE B-26 AIRCRAFT.

coast and splitting up to attack their assigned targets, the two flights veering north immediately ran into anti-aircraft fire.

The flight approaching De Kooy airfield met with intense fire. The leading RAF Boston escaped, but the American-manned AL677 piloted by 2nd Lt F. A. Loehrl was hit and crashed in flames, near the target. The other aircraft AL750, piloted by Captain Charles C. Kegelman, received a direct flak hit in the starboard engine, causing the propeller to fly off and flames to appear from under the cowling. Under momentary loss of control, the right wingtip touched the ground and the rear of the fuselage scraped the surface of the airfield as Kegelman wrestled to keep airborne. Crippled as it was, the Boston continued to fly and after jettisoning bombs and a brief exchange of fire with a flak tower, Kegelman regained the coast. Luckily the flames in the disabled engine went out and the other engine succeeded in bearing the crew safely back to Swanton Morley.

Bergen/Alkamaar airfield was not fully identified until anti-aircraft guns opened up. Because of this the Bostons attacked in line astern instead of line abreast as planned. Lt Lynn's crew (AL741) dropped their bombs but anti-aircraft fire claimed them before they could clear the target. At Haamstede Captain Odell and two RAF Bostons attacked without loss. The remaining flight could not locate their target and returned to base without bombing. In addition to the two American manned Bostons lost, one of the RAF's failed to return.

The performance of the US crews was impressive enough for the award of three American DFCs and, to Kegelman, the second highest US decoration for bravery, the DSC—the first of 226 awarded Eighth AF airmen. If this baptism of fire had resulted in the loss of one third of the American force engaged for practically no hurt to the enemy, there was some consolation in that No. 226 Squadron veterans considered the raid one of the most strongly contested they had ever experienced. But the raid had great morale value to the Allied cause. The Stars and Stripes had been well and truly waved: the Americans were active in the air war over Western Europe.

The 15th was sent out again on July 12th, led by Captain Odell. This time Abbeville/Drucat airfield was bombed from medium altitude—8,500 ft—to minimise the effects of flak. Again manning RAF Bostons, the six crews returned safely, although two machines were slightly damaged by ground fire. The Eighth Air Force then procured some Bostons from the RAF to equip the 15th Bomb. Sqdn. and after this second mission it stood down temporarily to make them ready. In future the squadron would fly aircraft marked with the white star.

While these may have been the first airmen of the USAAF to go into action from the UK, they were certainly not the first Americans to fly in combat against the Germans in the Second World War. Since hostilities began American citizens had been volunteering for the RAF. The first in action was Pilot Officer W. M. L. Fiske who fought and died in the Battle of Britain. By the time the United States entered the war, Americans were flying in practically every branch of the RAF, along with volunteers from a dozen other nations.

It was always fighters that caught the fancy of adventurous young men and by the time the Eighth Air Force arrived in Britain, three Spitfire fighter squadrons were operational with American pilots. It was hoped to absorb these "Eagle Squadrons" into the USAAF where their experience would be invaluable to the embryo VIII Fighter Command. But before this transfer was completed, the first fighter groups from the US were operational.

The 31st Group, the first complete American group to be established in the UK, had made steady progress training on Spitfire Vs at Atcham. Some of their officers had gained operational experience flying with RAF squadrons on cross-channel sweeps. By mid-July RAF advisers considered it combat-worthy and on August 1st its three squadrons were

CO of 309th FS, Major Harold Thyng, named his personal Spitfire V *Mary-James* for his wife and young son. At dusk on 9 Aug. 1942 he was involved in VIII FC's first combat when he attacked and damaged a Ju 88 over the Channel.—(USAF)

each moved to different south-coast airfields for operations under the guidance of RAF fighter wings. The first sorties were on July 26th when six pilots, including the three squadron commanders, joined a Canadian squadron of the Biggin Hill Wing in a sweep over Gravelines, St Omer and Abbeville areas of France. The result was rather discouraging, for Lt Col Albert P. Clark of Headquarters was shot down and taken prisoner.

The pilots of the 31st had some difficulty in getting the "feel" of the narrow tracked Spitfires after the robust tricycle undercarriage of their Airacobras. Atcham saw a few wrecks

Brig Gen Hunter, CG VIII FC, decorates 2/Lt Sam Junkin with the DFC for his exploits of 19 Aug. 1942. Junkin was still in hospital, recovering from wounds, at the time.—(USAF)

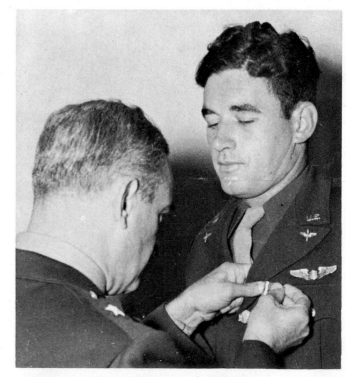

as a result of this. The pilots were considered in need of further training additional to theatre indoctrination.

From August 5th, the 31st's squadrons flew feint and practice sweeps plus a few defensive patrols; on one of the patrols two Spitfires made an inconclusive attack on an enemy aircraft. On the 18th the sweeps, still as part of RAF operations, were no longer feints, and next day, the date of the combined landing operations at Dieppe, the 31st came well and truly to grips with the enemy with 123 sorties. To Lt Samuel S. Junkin went the credit of achieving the USAAF's first victory over an enemy aircraft in Europe, when he shot down an FW190 during one of the frequent air battles that raged over the assault forces. Junkin, however, was then shot down himself, but survived his dip in the Channel. The 31st Group had much to learn, for eight of its Spitfires went down in the battle.

Although the P-38F Lightnings to equip the 1st Group had begun to arrive early in July, there was some delay in getting this US fighter into action. It was necessary to modify the radio sets to conform with the United Kingdom control system. The British had pioneered the very high frequency (VHF) communications for aircraft enabling ground controllers to give directions over distances of several hundred miles. The design for VHF sets was given to the US early in 1941, but production was slow getting under way and in consequence most of the fighter aircraft arriving in 1942 still had the somewhat inferior high frequency (HF) US Army sets. Apart from this, and other technical modifications, it was necessary for the Lightning pilots and the 1st's operations officers to undergo a period of indoctrination. For this the RAF had established at major USAAF installations in the UK, a small liaison team of technical and administrative personnel. They provided information on both non-operational and operational flying, with particular attention to notifying British gun zones and balloon defence areas. The vital art of aircraft recognition was another weakness the RAF instructors sought to remedy. Some Group personnel were sent on detachment to various RAF schools to receive instruction in subjects that would be necessary to the smooth functioning of the Group under the established air traffic control system.

At the end of July, the Group Commander of the 1st, Colonel John Stone, flew his P-38F to the Royal Aircraft Establishment at Farnborough to match it against a captured FW190A. The results showed the twin-engined Lockheed to come up well in turns and manoeuvres at lower altitudes, but unable to achieve the 190's rate of climb or acceleration.

In August, Goxhill was handed over to American tenancy and "Old Glory" flew from the mast outside station headquarters. The chief change noted by the RAF liaison team was that under the new regime afternoon tea was abolished— but as one member explained, "the CO was a humane man and set aside a small room near his office, where the British officers could congregate and brew themselves a cup about 4 o'clock. In fact, it was not unusual for the commanding officer to drop in for a cup himself!"

HQ 1st FG and the 71st Ftr. Sqdn. were based at Goxhill, while the 94th Ftr. Sqdn. was 18 miles away at RAF station Kirton-in-Lindsey. This station housed No. 303 (Polish) Squadron, RAF, under whose guidance the 94th flexed their wings.

The Group's other squadron, the 27th, had remained in Iceland to fly defensive patrols. On August 14th, two of its P-38s were engaged in mock combat with a P-40 of the 33rd Ftr. Sqdn. (an American unit based in the island for the past year) when an FW200, German four-motor aircraft, was spotted. In the following engagement the P-40 got in shots and the P-38 flown by Lt Elza K. Shahan succeeded in finishing off the enemy to gain for the 1st Group its first victory of the Second World War.

The chief concern of the Eighth Air Force leaders was, not unnaturally, to get their heavy bombers into action. But the USAAF plan for a daylight air offensive against Germany was meeting with scepticism in many quarters, particularly in Britain. Therefore, the sooner the plans and equipment were put to the test the better. As with the fighter units, it was found that crews of the 97th Group's Fortresses were insufficiently trained—particularly in those duties upon which the success of the bombing plans depended. Pilots had done little flying at high altitude and on oxygen, neither had they practised much formation flying. Particular short-comings in crew training were with air gunners, some of whom had never operated a turret in the air, let alone fired at aerial targets. The general standard of shooting was poor. Radio operators too were lacking in many respects, some could neither send nor receive Morse code! These deficiencies resulted from the urgency of mobilisation. The 97th, in common with other groups being hastily formed and despatched to Europe, had to accept partly trained men to complete its complement. Bomber crews had, in some cases, only trained together for a few weeks before being sent overseas.

Again the RAF was able to help, for if the British doubted the American bombing technique they were nonetheless exceedingly willing to assist their Allies in mounting their venture. Bombing and gunnery facilities as well as target towing aircraft for air to air gunnery practice were provided. Items of equipment that were still outstanding from shipments from the States, particularly transport, were obtained for the 97th. As with other groups, personnel were detached for courses at RAF schools on various subjects and aircrews were drilled in ditching technique. Above all, it was necessary for Colonel Frank A. Armstrong (one of Eaker's original 'septet', who had assumed command of the Group on July 31st) to give his crews an intensified flying programme. To this end, the first few days of August saw constant activity around Polebrook and Grafton Underwood as B-17s came and went. The hitherto rare spectacle of a score of four-engined aircraft in tight formation became commonplace, as did the throb of a multitude of Wright Cyclone engines high above the English countryside. With RAF fighters as mock enemies, defensive tactics were evolved and the same fighters also supplied experience in escort co-operation. It had already been agreed that RAF squadrons would provide the bulk of the fighter escort for the Eighth's heavies on the early raids, where penetration would be within range of Spitfires.

Perhaps the most difficult obstacle encountered was the English weather. The British Isles, subject to rapidly fluctuating areas of high and low pressure from the Atlantic, undergo frequent changes with predominantly cloud-covered skies.

To the exponents of high-altitude precision bombing, it became obvious that the number of days when weather conditions would permit successful bombing would be limited. The ragged skies of western Europe were a far cry from the conditions prevailing back at Muroc where precision bombing trials had met with such success. It was not only bomb aiming that would be hampered. To assemble a formation of heavy bombers at altitude needed much skill in fair conditions. With heavy, banked cloud and poor visibility the danger of collisions arose. It was the weather that frustrated the Eighth's first heavy bomber mission and inflicted the first casualties.

With many crews of the 97th judged combat-worthy, an order was received at Polebrook during the evening of August 9th for a combat mission to be flown next day. Excitement ran high as preparations were mounted, but the weather changed and the mission was cancelled. Two days later B-17E, 41-9098 of the 340th Bomb. Sqdn. was wending its way through clouds when it flew into the Berwyn Mountains in Wales, killing all on board. The weather hazard was to dog the Eighth throughout its stay in Britain.

The base was alerted for operations on August 12th, but

again the mission was scrubbed. On the 16th the elements showed signs of being set fair and Spaatz and Eaker alerted the 97th for action on the morrow. The target selected was the Rouen-Sotteville marshalling yards, not far inland from the French coast. This time the weather held.

At 15.12 hrs on the 17th, six B-17Es began take-off from Polebrook and climbed up over the golden harvest fields. In separate flights of three aircraft from 340th and 341st Bomb Sqdns., they flew east and south respectively. The 340th's aircraft rendezvoused with a strong force of Spitfires over the distinctive point near The Naze, where the estuaries of the rivers Stour and Orwell meet to form a jagged arrowhead pointed at the heart of Europe, and headed down-Channel towards Dunkirk. The 341st made for Portland Bill and then Alderney. Ten miles from France both Forces turned about and headed back, for they carried nothing sinister in their bomb-bays and were used as a feint to draw Luftwaffe fighters eastwards, away from the main bomber force which took off from Grafton Underwood fifteen minutes later.

The main formation, bound for Rouen, consisted of eleven Fortresses from the 342nd and 414th Bomb. Sqdns., and one from the 340th. They took an hour to gain altitude and assemble. The leading aircraft of the first flight of six, *Butcher Shop,* carried the group commander, Colonel Armstrong, in the pilot's seat. The co-pilot, Major Paul W. Tibbets, was destined to be at the controls of a bomber making an even more historic mission in three years time—to Hiroshima with the Atom Bomb. The lead aircraft of the second flight, appropriately named *Yankee Doodle,* carried the Commanding General of VIII Bomber Command, Ira Eaker. That Spaatz had allowed him to take part in the operation, was certainly a gesture of faith in the ability of the Fortresses to take care of themselves.

Over the Channel, four RAF squadrons of the new Spitfire IXs were contacted and gave close cover to the target. As the B-17s crossed the French coast, a British monitoring post heard the German defence controller announce over his radio network that "12 Lancasters" were heading inland.

Visibility proved good and bombardiers were able to see the target 10 miles away and from 23,000 ft they unloaded 36,900 lbs of General Purpose bombs. One element carried nine 1,100 lb bombs intended for a locomotive workshop, while the other aircraft carried 600 pounders—all of British manufacture—for rolling stock repair shops. The bombing was reasonably accurate with about half the bombs falling in the general target area—fortunately a large one.

If the damage to rolling stock, track and buildings was insufficient to cause the enemy much concern, it did point the way to what might be achieved by a larger force. Anti-

General Eaker poses at the door of *Yankee Doodle* after a quick change of dress on return from Rouen.—(USAF)

aircraft fire was meagre although two B-17s sustained slight damage. The escort kept enemy fighters at bay with an exchange of two for two in losses. One Me109 ventured within range of the Forts and received a spraying from the ball gunner of *Birmingham Blitzkrieg,* the trailing aircraft of the formation.

By 18.22 hrs all the diversion aircraft had landed safely at Polebrook, although while coming in one hit a pigeon which shattered the plexiglass nose causing slight cuts to the navigator and bombardier. At Grafton, General Spaatz and high-ranking American and British officers awaited the return from Rouen. Shortly before 19.00 hrs a watcher on the control tower shouted that he could see specks approaching from the west. All strained to make a count and with relief all twelve were soon observed. It was an elated Eaker who stepped from Fortress 41-9023 to be greeted by his staff—no loss in life or machines and relatively good bombing.

The thirty-odd pressmen who had assembled to report the occasion were quick to notice the nickname on the nose of Eaker's Fortress. Nicknaming of machines was not new and was in vogue with the RAF. Even so, no such brazen examples as the 97th's had been seen before. They gave an individuality to the B-17s that otherwise had little to distinguish them separately, except for a serial number painted in yellow across the tail fin. So it was, that when the story of the raid appeared in the London and New York papers next day, Eaker was reported as having gone to Rouen not so much in a Fortress, as in *Yankee Doodle.* Perhaps it was this nickname that inspired Air Marshal Harris, C-in-C, RAF Bomber Command to say in his congratulatory message to Eaker—"Yankee Doodle certainly went to town and can stick another well-deserved feather in his cap."

With the success of the mission to give renewed vigour to their faith in high-level precision bombing, the Eighth's commanders could hope for stronger formations in the near future. For next day into Prestwick came the B-17Fs of the 326th Bombardment Squadron after a non-stop flight from Gander, Newfoundland. This unit, part of the 92nd Group

Col Frank Armstrong led the Rouen mission in *Butcher Shop.*—(USAF)

Ball turret gunner on *Birmingham Blitzkrieg*, Sgt Kent West (centre) enjoys a meal after debriefing. He was at first credited with destroying an Me 109. *Birmingham Blitzkrieg* had minor damage from flak fragments in eleven places.—(USAF)

whose other three squadrons eventually followed on this 2,119 mile hop without incident, opened up an alternative route on the North Atlantic crossing. Earlier in the month another Fortress group, the 301st, also flying the improved B-17F model had reached the UK. Like the 97th, they came via the Greenland-Iceland route to Prestwick shepherding P-38 fighters; their last aircraft arrived on August 16th and they underwent indoctrination at Chelveston. The 60th Troop Carrier Group, formerly at this airfield, had moved south to Aldermaston the previous week. First used for hauling supplies between Air Depots and combat bases, training with the 2nd Battalion 503rd Paratroop Infantry Regiment followed and while the outcome of the Rouen raid was awaited, ten C-47s of the Group carried a company of paratroopers for their first practice jump over England.

A second troop carrier group, the 64th, crossed from the US at the same time as the 301st and its C-47s were based at Ramsbury, Wiltshire. At the same time the new P-38 group, the 14th, was taking up station at Atcham; one of their squadrons, the 50th, was left in Iceland to relieve the 1st Group's 27th Ftr. Sqdn. which then went south to rejoin its parent organisation.

Thus, on August 18th, the Eighth Air Force seemed assured of three heavy bomber groups; the 97th operational, the 301st in pre-combat training and the 92nd arriving or en route; supported by four fighter groups, the 31st operational with Spitfires, the 1st (P-38s) and 52nd (Spitfires) in an advanced state of training, and the 14th arriving with P-38s. There was also the separate 15th Bomb. Sqdn. (Light) and the two C-47 groups, although the latter were not so directly connected with the air offensive against Germany. It could be said that Spaatz now had the semblance of a strategic air force and some evidence that the offensive planned was feasible. Alas, in the matter of build-up, the fortunes of the Eighth were destined to wane, for while the B-17s had pounded the Sotteville rail yards, it was being charged with a new, albeit temporary, mission.

In mid-1942 the Allies had decided that an invasion of the Continent would not be practicable that year or the next. The plan for a landing in North-West Africa, for which the Eighth had originally been formed, was revived and scheduled for the autumn. The strategic bombing offensive, let it be understood, to which Arnold and other exponents of the USAAF's heavy bombardment tactics were committing the Eighth Air Force, had no place in American war plans except as a preliminary to an invasion of Europe. The forces for the North African landing were partly assembled in the UK and

these had prior claims on air units available. The task of furnishing a nucleus for the American element of the air striking force fell to the Eighth which, although not committed by name, had much of its personnel and equipment sent to North Africa as part of a new air force formed especially for this venture. Physically, the Air Force was at first an off-shoot of the Eighth which was further charged with its organisation and training. In addition to combat groups already in the UK, the new air force would receive other medium bomber, observation and fighter groups being readied in the US. The Twelfth Air Force was headed by Brigadier General James Doolittle, of first Tokyo raid fame. He was currently commanding the 4th Bombardment Wing, due to arrive in England during August.

It was not only the North African invasion that had priority over men and machines of the Eighth Air Force. Pressure from home demanded a more substantial air support in the Pacific, forcing the AAF to divert fifteen groups scheduled for the UK. Although it appeared the Eighth Air Force would have to be completely rebuilt for its strategic bombing role, they pressed ahead with their campaign before the Twelfth took the experienced groups to Africa. In any case, it was desirable that the four fighter groups to be transferred to the Twelfth Air Force should not only be thoroughly trained, but battle tried before being committed to a new campaign.

31st FG Spitfire V, EN799, taxies out at Merston, late Aug. 1942.-
(Holmes)

The 31st Group engaged in intensive activity during August although there were no further contacts with enemy aircraft after the Dieppe raid. At first operating individually with RAF fighter wings, the three squadrons usually flew formations of twelve aircraft on sweeps and the occasional bomber escort. Sometimes small elements were sent on such diverse tasks as protecting air-sea rescue Walrus flying boats or to intercept reported hostile raids. At this time the RAF's offensive day fighter role in Europe was chiefly confined to operations across the Channel coast, with the purpose of drawing the Luftwaffe into combat to relieve pressure on the Russian Front. When Hitler had turned his forces east, the Luftwaffe had left two Jagdgeschwadern (Fighter regiments) guarding the Channel coast area. These, with about 100 aircraft each, were led by some of the Luftwaffe's outstanding commanders and included some of the most experienced German fighter pilots. Jagdgeschwader 2 (J.G.2) covered the area from the Brest peninsula to Paris, while Jagdgeschwader 26 (J.G. 26) was based in the Pas de Calais area of France and Belgium. The strength of a Jagdgeschwader fluctuated, but normally these two each comprised three Gruppen with three Staffeln each. The Staffel was a unit basically the equivalent of an RAF Squadron.

The introduction of the Focke-Wulf 190 in the spring of 1941, gave the Luftwaffe the edge over the RAF's Spitfire Vs. However, the Spitfire IX, with a more powerful Merlin engine, was the answer to the FW190, but this improved model was only just reaching Fighter Command in the summer of 1942. The majority of RAF fighter squadrons at this time still flew the Mk V, which also equipped the USAAF squadrons.

Spitfire V, QP: V of 2nd FS, taxies out against the sun: Kenley, Sept. 1942.—(USAF)

The US fighter units were trained in the mode of air warfare practised by RAF Fighter Command and, until a sizeable force could be built up, came under the operational control of this experienced organisation. RAF operating techniques and procedures were followed and adopted, and although the Americans later developed these to suit their particular needs, the pattern of VIII Fighter Command followed closely that of its British counterpart.

By August 24th the 52nd Group pilots were considered proficient and with operational status, its 2nd and 4th squadrons moved to southern England from Northern Ireland, leaving the 5th Ftr. Sqdn. behind at Eglinton to continue training with defensive coastal patrols. The 2nd went first to Kenley and the 4th to Biggin Hill where they worked in conjunction with an RAF wing. The Spitfires of these squadrons took part in sweeps and patrols but did not see action or experience any combat losses while flying from England.

The 1st Group meanwhile had moved south on the 24th, to Ibsley, Hants, where five days later two P-38s of the 94th Ftr. Sqdn. initiated their first war sorties from the UK when "scrambled" to intercept enemy aircraft reported approaching the coast. No contact was made and later that day two more sorties by the 94th were equally unrewarding.

Eager to give the Lightning pilots some combat experience before they were transferred to the growing Twelfth Air Force, VIII Fighter Command despatched 32 fighters on a sweep on the first day of September. Throughout September and October the Lightnings set out on escorts, sweeps and patrols, only to return without coming to grips with the enemy.

By October 2nd, the 14th Group had also begun flying practise sweeps in co-ordination with RAF units. Using Ford and Westhampnett, their Lightnings continued on offensive operations until October 25th, without engaging the enemy. Evidently the Germans had no desire to engage these un-orthodox American fighters. The sudden increase in air activity in recent months had brought numerical disadvantage to the Luftwaffe and the Channel coast Jagdgeschwadern were not to be provoked into action. Even the battle-blooded 31st added but one more victory to their record while based in England—and that a sneak raider caught off the south coast.

During this time there was some concern among pilots at the behaviour of the Lightning in certain manoeuvres, par-ticularly dives. One high altitude dive had resulted in non-recovery with fatal results. Shortly afterwards this happened to another Lightning but this time the pilot managed to get out. He was actually torn out from the cockpit by the slip-stream, breaking both legs—but he lived. He reported that once speed had built up, the aircraft would not respond to the controls.

At this time little was known about compressibility in high speed flight, but it was assumed that this had some bearing on control surfaces in such dives. This was a problem for the technical staffs. One of the technical staff officers who had arrived with General Hunter on July 27th, was 36-year old Lt Col Cass Hough (pronounced Huff). Intent on finding out

for himself what went wrong, he took a P-38 up to 43,000 feet to experiment. He eventually discovered that in high speed dives a vacuum built up aft of the centre section, starving the elevators of air and affecting their function. By using a degree and half of tail heavy trim he was able to effect recovery, but the aircraft rocketed straight up for about 7 or 8,000 feet before it could be levelled out.

To prove his case, Hough dived the P-38 from 43,000 feet near Bovingdon on September 27th 1942 during which a speed of 525 mph was indicated at 35,000 feet; this was the longest terminal velocity dive successfully undertaken at that time.

During September preparations were underway to transfer the three RAF Eagle Squadrons to a specially activated group, designated the 4th. There had been a 4th Group in France during World War I, and the number had since been used by a composite organisation in the Philippines before those islands fell to the Japanese. The new 4th, however, had no lineal connections with these predecessors. Established at Debden

Lt Col Cass S. Hough, the man behind much of VIII FC's technical superiority.—(USAF)

on September 12th, the "Eagles" transferred from the RAF with an official ceremony on the 29th in which Spaatz and Hunter were joined by Air Chief Marshal Sir Sholto Douglas of RAF Fighter Command to witness Nos. 71, 121, and 133 Squadrons, RAF, becoming the 334th, 335th and 336th Fighter Squadrons of the USAAF. The commander was 38-year old Colonel Edward Anderson who had come over from the States with the P-38 groups; flying command was vested in Wing Commander Duke-Woolley, RAF, until an experienced American flying commander was available.

The Spitfire Vs that had served them so well went with the pilots, in fact the only immediate visible change was the replacement of roundels by white star insignia. The three squadrons had a combined total of 73½ aerial victories, of which the oldest, No. 71, was responsible for over half. The comparatively new No. 133 had just suffered a disaster. Three days previous eleven pilots in new Spitfire IXs had been lost over the Continent when caught up in bad weather. Only

The Stars and Stripes is run up at the ceremonial transfer of the three Eagle squadrons. Several pilots who would later earn fame are amongst the squadron personnel lined up on the wet parade ground at Debden. —(IWM)

Plt Off Beaty had come back to crash-land at Kingsbridge. Since Spitfire IXs were in short supply, what remained of No. 133 reverted back to Mark Vs.

RAF ground crews remained to service the Spitfires until American personnel had been trained. However, a nucleus for this task existed in the ground personnel of the 50th Fighter Squadron of the 14th Group who until now had languished at Atcham awaiting their pilots and Lightnings, when it was learned that the air echelon would remain in Iceland permanently for defence purposes.

While the Eagle pilots were generally pleased to become part of the USAAF, their attachment to the traditions and ways

Cpt Don Willis flew and fought with the Finns and Norwegians before joining RAF's 121 Squadron and transferring with it to 4th FG. In Apr. 1944 Willis had to bail out of a P-38 while acting as observer for 67th FW during the first Droop Snoot mission.—(USAF)

of the RAF distinguished them among their fellow nationals for months to come. Indeed, it can be fairly said that such was the pride in their origin that the squadrons of the 4th went out of their way to preserve and foster these connections. As a fighting unit, the 4th was immediately on operational status.

Apart from those pilots of the Eagle Squadrons, the RAF had many other US nationals in training. Some with Spitfire qualifications were sent to increase the experience levels in the 31st and 52nd Groups or reinforced the 4th. Others joined the new 350th Group at Duxford, Cambs., formed early in October by VIII FC primarily for the purpose of absorbing the surplus P-39 pilots and adding a useful army support fighter unit to the Twelfth Air Force. It was equipped mainly with Airacobras, sent to the RAF and earmarked for shipment to Russia, plus a few Spitfire Vs.

During September and October many new groups had arrived from America to prepare for the North African invasion, tentatively fixed for early November 1942. A third Lightning group, the 82nd, landing in Northern Ireland, had gone to Eglinton and Maydown in the first week of October. Yet another P-38 trained fighter group, was following by sea later that month. The 3rd Photographic Group came into Membury early in September, as did the 67th Observation Group. Both lacked equipment, though the 3rd eventually mustered a few camera-carrying Lightnings and B-17Fs while the 67th was equipped with a variety of types from British sources. Two squadrons and detachments of the 68th Observation Group reached Wattisham (which the Twelfth Air Force had made its first UK station on September 12th) and on October 4th commenced training with Airacobras. The third troop-carrier group to fly in via the North Atlantic ferry route was the 62nd which settled at Keevil close to the other two C-47 bases.

A P-400 Airacobra with long-range tank installed for the flight to North Africa. Because of mechanical trouble this one was left behind in the UK until 1943.—(USAF)

In East Anglia, four twin-engined bomber groups had assembled for training; the ground echelons of the 47th, 310th, 319th and 320th having arrived by sea in September, were sent to Bury St Edmunds, Hardwick, Shipdham and Hethel respectively, although early in October the 47th moved to Horham and the 319th to Horsham St Faith. The aircraft and crews flew the Newfoundland, Greenland, Iceland, Prestwick route. They were not as fortunate as earlier travellers for winter was setting in. Most of the 310th Bomb Group's B-25 Mitchells made the crossing safely by mid-October but the A-20 Havocs of the 47th and the B-26 Marauders of the 319th suffered some accidents due to weather conditions, so bad that the B-26s of the 320th were re-routed to Africa via the South Atlantic. As it was, the last aircraft of these groups did not reach East Anglia until December.

The Eighth Air Force was committed to train all these freshman groups and then send them on their way once suitable airfields had been secured in North Africa. Although this considerable task would severely sap the strength of the Eighth, it did relieve it of any immediate support commitments for landings in Europe. Thus, Arnold hoped it would still be possible to build up a strategic bombing force in the UK to test the AAF's doctrine.

Meanwhile, Spaatz and Eaker were determined that VIII Bomber Command should gain as much operational experience as possible before it lost its two original B-17 groups. The small raid by the 97th on Rouen was no criterion; weather conditions had been ideal, fighter and anti-aircraft defences had been ineffectual, and the raid had necessitated only shallow penetration of enemy territory. To gain priority in men and materials to establish a strong force capable of dealing crippling blows to the enemy's war potential, it would be necessary to show substantial proof of the Eighth's ability in the face of opposition. Many theatres of war had call for air support, and there was still an authoritative body in the US military hierarchy unconvinced of the value, or advisability, of strategic bombing. Thus, further missions were scheduled.

For its early missions, Eighth Air Force target selection was carried out by VIII Bomber Command in co-ordination with RAF Bomber Command. Target priorities changed but generally fell under the headings: Submarine building and port facilities, aircraft factories, repair depots and other key munitions establishments and lines of communication.

Two days after the Rouen mission, the Dieppe landings were carried out and a 97th Group formation was sent in support. This time six B-17s from each of the four squadrons were despatched to bomb Abbeville/Drucat airfield in France, the home of Gruppe II/J.G. 26—the legendary "yellow-nosed Messerschmitts" acknowledged by the RAF as the elite of German fighter units. The FW190s were evidently too busy over Dieppe to pay attention to the Fortresses and again all the 97th's aircraft returned safely, having left 89 fresh holes on or around the landing field and one hangar in ruins. Only 22 aircraft had attacked, two having "aborted"—a term signifying a failure, either in equipment or personnel, causing a return to base before completing an assigned task. Next day, the Polebrook Fortresses and their Spitfire escort went to Amiens/Longueau marshalling yards where all but one of the twelve bombers despatched bombed. Again all came back. Morale in the 97th was high, the crews were confident—perhaps over confident. To them it seemed the case for high-altitude day bombing was already proven. The commanders were pleased, but cautious, knowing full well that—as Eaker had put it after Rouen—"one swallow doesn't make a summer". Neither did three, for on the morrow the 97th received a taste of unpleasant things to come.

Twelve B-17Es from 342nd and 412th Bomb. Sqdns. set out from Grafton Underwood on the dewy morning of August 21st. The formation, slow in assembling, did not rendezvous with the escort at the appointed time of 10.15 hrs. The escort of three Spitfire squadrons—including 308th of the 31st Group—orbited for 16 minutes before the errant B-17s hove in sight. In consequence the Spitfires had only enough fuel to escort their charges half-way across the North Sea before having to withdraw. The Forts droned on and reached the Dutch coast at which point VIII BC recalled them by radio.

The German fighter controller had not been idle and finding the bombers without escort, vectored a score of interceptors to the area. The FW190s coming out of cloud on to the formation found the massed firepower of the Fortresses somewhat of a shock and the German pilots refrained from closing in with their attacks. Instead, five concentrated upon the lone *Johnny Reb*, caught lagging behind the main formation. One of their 20 mm cannon shells, exploding on one side of the cockpit windscreen, mortally wounded the co-pilot, 2/Lt Donald A. Walter, and burned the hands of 2/Lt Richard F. Starks the pilot, who then relinquished control

to 2/Lt E. T. Sconiers, the bombardier. With the top turret inoperative after firing only a single burst and with two engines damaged, the Fortress limped across the Norfolk coast to put down at Horsham St Faith, just north of Norwich. Its gunners claimed to have shot down three enemy fighters and those in the rest of the formation four more.

After interrogation, the Group was credited with a reduced score of 2 destroyed, 5 probably destroyed and 6 damaged— or 2-5-6, to use the form of record then in use. The heavy bomber crews had suffered their first combat fatality but had successfully fought off 20 to 25 Focke-Wulfs, destroying two. Hitherto, such an encounter by bombers would in all probability have been disastrous and some RAF officers were inclined to question the strength of the opposition on this occasion. The estimation of aircraft numbers in a fast moving action was a very difficult task and often resulted in an exaggerated figure. In retrospect, it appears that no more than five or six enemy fighters actually fired at the Fortresses. Nevertheless, all the bombers had returned.

On August 24th, 27th, 28th and 29th, the 97th was despatched to shipyards and aircraft targets in the Low Countries and France with an escorted force of never more than a dozen B-17s. Sometimes the bombing was promising, sometimes poor, but on each occasion the bombers returned without challenge from the Luftwaffe.

Meanwhile, the 301st Group was progressing with its combat training and the 92nd Group had completed its move to the UK; the latter however was earmarked for training. A fully functional Combat Crew Replacement and Training Center was now essential to the force and its establishment was hampered by lack of both personnel and bomber aircraft. This deficiency could be temporarily resolved by utilising one of the newly arrived combat groups, and the 92nd Group was selected; for nearly eight months it fulfilled at Bovingdon an operational training unit role as the 11th CCRC. This group, however, was equipped with the new improved B-17F. Outwardly identical to the B-17E, except for a frameless plexiglass nose-piece, it nevertheless incorporated over 400 design changes affecting most of the major components. Although a thousand pounds heavier than the B-17E, it was a far more combat-worthy version of the Fortress. Therefore VIII BC ordered the 97th to take over the 92nd's B-17Fs in exchange for their faithful B-17Es.

On September 5th, the Eighth Air Force's bombers set out to revisit the Rouen marshalling yards. The leading formation of 25 of the 97th with their new B-17Fs, was followed by twelve from the 301st Group, now making their first mission. Heavier damage was caused than on the first raid but unfortunately some bombs from the inexperienced 301st, fell outside the yards causing, according to reports, the death of 140 French civilians—a happening the Allies were most anxious to avoid, and one which played into the hands of German propagandists. Once again all the Forts came home.

Next day, the effort was again increased when the 92nd took fourteen B-17Es along to gain themselves combat experience. Trailing the 97th, the eight machines that stayed the full trip added their bomb loads to those of the 22 Fortresses of the lead group. In spite of a fighter escort, the yellow nosed FW190s this time made a determined attack on both groups on their return. Near Flasselles B-17F 41-24445 of the 97th, piloted by Lt Lipsley, went down apparently under control; four parachutes were seen to open. Badly damaged, 41-9095 of the 92nd lost altitude and never regained the English coast: a search revealed no trace of the crew or aircraft.

Air gunners on this Rouen mission were credited with four enemy aircraft destroyed plus many damaged and probables, but this did little to alleviate the loss of the first two Fortresses. Insignificant by comparison with losses in later battles, it understandably dampened the spirits of returning crews. To VIII BC statisticians, it was loss percentage of the total force

The P-38F packed a heavy punch: a 20 mm cannon and four .50 mgs. This is 1st FG's 41-7622 at Colerne, Sept. 1942. Figures are factory serial (small) and early plane-in-group number.—(H. W. Rued)

involved in a combat mission, balanced against the results achieved, that gave the measure of success. However, a 10% loss was considered prohibitive whatever the results.

September 6th brought the first attack on two targets by diverging B-17 forces. The 97th and 92nd bombed Meaulte while the 301st was returning from a diversion mission to St Omer/Longuenesses airfield. Two of the thirteen B-17Fs sent, mistook and bombed St Omer/Ft Rouge for the assigned target. Shortly before the B-17 attacks the 15th Bomb. Sqdn. (L) was in action again by a strike of twelve of its A 20s at the home of II/J.G. 26 at Abbeville.

Next day the 97th and 301st were despatched to Rotterdam-Wilton shipyards, but bombing was poor. Once again the Luftwaffe was waiting, but all the B-17s returned safely with

Bombs from 15th BS Bostons explode near a quay at Le Havre, 2 Oct. 1942. This was the last mission the squadron would fly from Britain.—(IWM)

gunners—mostly from the 97th which had met the majority of attacks—claiming 12-10-12. There followed a period of unsuitable weather when haze obscured targets. A large effort was planned for the 26th and over 70 aircraft were airborne including a P-38 escort, but with deteriorating weather conditions all B-17s returned without bombing.

Although operating under the auspices of the Eighth Air Force, the 97th and 301st Groups were now assigned to the Twelfth Air Force for administrative control having been transferred together with the four fighter and two troop-carrier groups on September 14th. During this month and October, six other heavy bombardment groups were en route from America and the building up of a combat trained force had to begin again. Fortunately, Eaker was able to retain some of his experienced commanders who stood him in good stead.

On September 5th, the *Queen Elizabeth* dropped anchor at Greenock with the ground echelons of two of the new groups among her complement, the 93rd and 306th for Alconbury and Thurleigh respectively. The liner's arrival coincided with the departure from New York of her sister-ship the *Queen Mary* carrying the ground personnel of the 91st, 303rd, and 305th Groups which were destined for Kimbolton, Molesworth and Grafton Underwood. To ensure accommodation and facilitate administration, all four squadrons of a bomber group were now based on one airfield, the 342nd and 414th squadrons of the 97th consequently joined the other squadrons and Group Headquarters at Polebrook. Four of the new groups had Fortresses and these flew via Greenland and Iceland. The 93rd Group flew B-24 Liberators, and two of their squadrons made the first non-stop formation flight direct from Gander to Prestwick.

A fine day on October 2nd enabled the Fortresses to return to Meaulte aircraft factory where they had suffered their first losses. Eighteen from the 97th and 25 from the 301st were sent out while six more 97th aircraft attacked St Omer and the 92nd flew a diversion along the coast. Over enemy territory the FW190s appeared and were hotly received with gunners being credited with 4-5-1 for no B-17s lost.

This time the 301st received most attacks and one of the B-17s in the rear of its formation, *Phyllis* piloted by Lt Charles W. Paine Jr, demonstrated the damage a Fortress could sustain yet remain airborne. The upper turret was hit and the gunner badly wounded, then on the starboard wing the outboard engine 'ran away' and defied control while the inboard engine was put out of action. Hits aft had damaged control wires to the tail and the machine rose in an uncontrolled climb, requiring the efforts of both pilots to regain level flight. Meanwhile, failure of part of the oxygen system had caused two of the crew in the radio room to pass out and a lower altitude had to be sought. The starboard wing was so badly damaged it needed almost full left aileron to keep level. After limping across the Channel *Phyllis* was brought down for a wheels-up landing on the first airfield seen—Gatwick. For a moment it appeared that the disabled Fort was going to crash into a hangar and it did in fact catch a wingtip on a building. On coming to rest, it was found that 16 cannon shells had penetrated or exploded against her and there were some 300 small calibre bullet holes in wings, tail and fuselage.

At dusk the same day, a tragic and gruesome accident occured to B-17F 41-24492 on a practice mission 24,000 ft over the Wash, when a waist gunner had trouble with his oxygen supply and passed out. To gain denser air quickly, the pilot dived the aircraft some nine thousand feet. The pull-out was apparently too violent, for control cables snapped, and part of the wing with the starboard engine broke away and the aircraft caught fire. The bomb bay doors broke away and one struck the rear fuselage with such force that it completely severed part of the tail with the tail gunner's compartment. The tail gunner tried desperately to free himself from the falling section as it twirled over and over. He hammered at the windows, but they would not give. Finally, he kicked a hole in the torn side of his compartment only to get his shoulders wedged while trying to wriggle through. When a bare thousand feet from the ground he finally got clear, his parachute opening just in time to land him safely near an anti-aircraft gun site some three miles south east of Spalding. The major portion of the B-17 crashed in flames only 100 yds away, but the intensity of the fire kept rescuers from the wreck. One other crew member managed to escape by parachute, but he was injured. This harrowing experience had such a disturbing effect on the tail gunner that he developed a phobia about flying, and subsequently—after gallantly facing a number of missions—he was grounded. Flying accidents were an ever present possibility and every group in time, experienced such tragedies. For the unit concerned this time; the 367th Bomb. Sqdn. of the 306th Group, it was an early incident in a bitter history of losses.

The most notable Eighth Air Force mission in the autumn of 1942 was undoubtedly that of October 9th to the Fives-Lille steel works in Belgium. A record total of 108 heavy bombers, plus seven on diversion, were despatched, a figure not to be surpassed for another six months. The heaviest opposition so far encountered, and the largest claims by gunners, highlighted this mission.

In addition to the 97th and 301st, the 92nd provided a small force and two of the new groups, the 306th and 93rd, made their maiden missions. Early in the morning the Fortresses began climbing into a clear October sky. The 306th Group with its commander, Colonel Charles Overacker, commenced take-off at 08.30 hrs. At Alconbury, Colonel "Ted" Timberlake prepared to lead his crews. The Liberators were to bring up the rear of the bomber stream. A heavy force of RAF and USAAF fighters, including the three P-38 Squadrons of 1st Group, supported the bomber formations from mid-Channel, but Luftwaffe tactics were to avoid the escort where possible and tackle the heavies.

The inexperience of the 306th and 93rd led to a poor bombing pattern, many bombs landed outside the target area causing civilian casualties. A B-17 of 306th Group dropped over France, so did one of the 93rd's B-24s. Two other Fortresses came down in the sea, where their 92nd and 301st Group's crews were duly picked up by British rescue launches. For this loss of four, opposing claims of 56-26-20 were allowed; but as this constituted the total German fighter force believed participating, its validity was in doubt.

The British Press hailed the raid as a great victory for the American bombers; even so, there was implied disbelief at the numbers of enemy planes claimed as shot down. To many Britons it was viewed as another case of "Yankee big-talk", for at that time gross exaggeration was generally believed to be a regular facet of the American national character! The bomber gunners, however, claimed in good faith. The speed of air combat was such that an attacking fighter might only be visible to a gunner for a few seconds and tricks could easily be played on straining eyes. Flame and smoke from an exhaust could be mistaken for an engine on fire or gun flashes seen as explosions. And, inevitably, when a score of gunners all fired at the same fighter, each was convinced it was *his* bullets that caused the enemy to fall. To eliminate overlapping claims, VIII BC devised various procedures, even so the totals were still exaggerated. A revision of the Lille claims finally gave credit for 21-21-15, but this was too high if German records are accurate—and there is reason to believe they are incomplete in this instance. These show only two fighters lost through enemy action and no others damaged.

The performance of the Liberators on their first mission was generally poor. Fourteen had turned back or failed to attack due to various mechanical and crew failures, and the bombing of the ten that reached the target was generally ineffectual. Their baptism of fire was not gentle, for ten

Sgt Ernest Kish, tail gunner of *Teggie Ann*, first Eighth AF B-24 to penetrate Hitler's Festung Europa. On 9 Oct. 1942 Kish suffered frost-bite when he removed his gloves to free frozen guns: similar troubles were all too common during early missions.—(USAF)

returned with some form of damage. Perhaps the worst hit was 41-23722 of the 328th Bomb. Sqdn., with approximately 200 holes of various sizes. The ground crew chief, M/Sgt Charles A. Chambers, on seeing his ward so damaged, forgot all respect for rank and reportedly assailed the pilot with: "Goddamit, Lieutenant—What the hell you been doin' to my ship!" Repair offered a problem as many B-24 components were not available in the UK. A solution was seen in the write-off of the most damaged bomber to "cannibalise" it for the parts needed by others. Eyes turned upon "722", but Sgt Chambers backed by its pilot, Lt John Stewart, indignantly refuted the idea with such vigour, that the maintenance men relented and "722", alias *Bomerang* (pronounced Bomber-ang), lived to fly again and Chambers' and Stewart's faith in this battle-scarred Liberator eventually paid rich dividends.

The other freshman group had fared little better. Anti-aircraft fire was both intense and accurate inflicting many shrapnel hits and forcing the formation to spread out. The leading Fortress of the rear squadron (423rd) with a feathered airscrew, lost speed and the other machines slowed to remain with it. Lagging behind the rest of the 306th, the 423rd drew the attentions of FW190s whose attack resulted in damage to nearly every B-17 but all managed to return to England. One 306th aircraft from the same squadron that experienced the accident near Spalding, the 367th, went down after a direct flak hit. Repair crews were presented with their greatest task to date; in addition to the ten B-24s, 36 B-17s were damaged —four severely.

In retrospect, the Lille mission does not appear in the same profitable light as it did at the time. Then, dispersed bombing was partly off-set by the large number of enemy aircraft believed destroyed. The mission had shown that heavy bombers could penetrate enemy territory in daylight and survive a determined fighter attack with moderate losses; this added to the optimism of Eighth Air Force commanders.

Inclement weather restricted further operations until October 21st, when the heavies made their only other attack of that month—although 11 missions had been initiated and cancelled at an early stage due to weather changes.

This time the submarine base at Lorient was the objective, resulting from a new directive, issued the previous day, placing submarine facilities as top priority for the Eighth's bombers.

A long over-water route was planned to avoid interception by enemy fighters until the last possible moment, but of 66 B-17s of the 97th, 301st and 306th and 24 B-24s of the 93rd setting out, only the 97th attacked. The rest turned back early, as heavy cloud obscured the target. However, the 97th's formation found a cloudbreak, dropped through to 17,500 ft and prepared for a bombing run. As they crossed the coast they were set upon by FW190s closing in quickly, firing and breaking away. These vicious attacks upon the rear elements of the formation, sent three B-17s down, and damaged another six. In spite of this fifteen Fortresses were able to place 21 of the thirty 2,000 lb bombs dropped, within a thousand yards radius of the aiming point. Five concrete submarine shelters were hit, though these could withstand such punishment; the dockside machinery was more vulnerable.

It was a depleted 97th that put down at south coast airfields in England and a sobering blow to aircrew who had tended to underate the opposition. The gunners could scarcely be elated at four enemy aircraft destroyed being allowed, when their group had sustained the heaviest loss of any group to that date. As it was, this proved the 97th's last mission with the Eighth, for on November 9th it began flying out to North Africa, to be followed by the 301st on the 26th.

The departure of the two most experienced and oldest bombardment groups left VIII BC a half dozen others which, for the best part, were insufficiently trained due to the haste to get them to Europe. Another Liberator group, the 44th, had arrived at Shipdham in Norfolk, and together with the 93rd and the four Fortress groups, 91st, 303rd, 305th and 306th, would constitute the complement for further experimentation with high-altitude daylight precision bombing.

A few questions had already been answered but the case had by no means been proven. The future of the Eighth Air Force, and indeed of the USAAF's plans for strategic bombing, rested largely on the outcome of operations during the next few months. Millions of dollars and manhours were expended in putting a bomber force in the air; VIII Bomber Command had to justify such expenditure and effort by the destruction of installations vital to the enemy's war effort. It would not be settled by a few missions under fairly favourable circumstances. The exigencies of the North African venture, plus the unfavourable weather that could be counted on in the North-West European winter, were added difficulties. If the B-17s and B-24s showed signs of succeeding in their task, their numbers would be increased tenfold; if they failed the American heavy bombers would in all probability be relegated to tactical missions at a later stage. The fate of the Eighth Air Force was in the balance.

Chapter 3: The Pioneers

For six months, from November 1942 until the following May, the American day bomber offensive from England was carried out largely by four B-17F Fortress groups. Two B-24D Liberator groups were also assigned to the Eighth Air Force, but diversions and detachments resulted in rarely more than a score of these bombers being available during much of this period. Only the Fortresses comprised a force large enough for VIII Bomber Command to prove the USAAF's bombing doctrine.

Each bomber squadron had an average strength of nine aircraft upon arrival in the UK, and with four squadrons to a group it gave the command a potential total strength of around 140 B-17s. But due to the embodiment of modifications, repair and servicing difficulties, less than two-thirds could be actively employed on any one combat mission. It was, as General Eaker later put it in a letter to Arnold, "a piddling little force" with which to conduct so important an experiment.

The most experienced of the four Fortress groups was the 306th at Thurleigh, although it had only completed one mission by the time the next group, the 91st, was sent out for the first time. The 91st, under Colonel Stanley Wray, moved down to Bassingbourn in Cambridgeshire in mid-October when Kimbolton runways were found in need of strengthening. Their new base was a pre-war RAF station that offered the men of the 91st luxurious accommodation compared to the wartime structures housing the other groups. London was more readily accessible from Bassingbourn and the GIs made good use of this facility; it was not long before one 91st B-17F sported the sobriquet *Piccadilly Commando* in recognition of the hazards to be faced in the big city! War correspondents covering Eighth Air Force activities, often preferred to visit Bassingbourn, than risk the unsignposted route (signposts had been removed in 1940 as an anti-invasion measure) to the more remote airfields. The image of life at an Eighth Air Force bomber base presented on paper and screen in later years, owes much to observations made at this base.

In spite of being insufficiently trained, the 91st Group weathered its first two missions without loss. After its maiden trip to the U-boat port of Brest on November 7th, it flew a diversion raid over Abbeville/Drucat next day while the main force attempted to improve on its bombing at Lille. On their third mission the 91st suffered their first experience of a heavy flak barrage as the Fortresses flew over St Nazaire. The Germans had over fifty heavy anti-aircraft guns and were in the process of bringing in more to this U-boat base; in the months ahead, St Nazaire became notorious for its deadly flak.

Following accurate bombing achieved by the 97th Group at Lorient the previous month, VIII BC was encouraged to experiment with attacks from lower altitudes. To avoid detection by German radar, the 47 bombers set off for St Nazaire at 500 ft over the sea, skirting the Brest peninsula, and then climbing to 7,500 ft or more before making a sharp turn onto the target. The 91st, leading at 10,000 ft, ran into an intense barrage and every aircraft but one received some damage. Twelve Liberators of the 44th and 93rd Groups, flying at around 18,000 ft, were above the barrage and returned practically unscathed. The trailing 306th Group— even lower than the 91st, at around 7,500 ft—lost three Forts in succession.

On leaving the target the B-17 formations were widely dispersed and exceedingly vulnerable to fighter attack. Fortunately the Luftwaffe failed to appear. The battered 306th put into Portreath, an RAF station on the south western tip of Britain, where the badly shaken crews cast off their tension with an impromptu party in the mess, which from all accounts did not endear them to their Allies.

No further missions were made at such low altitudes. Anti-aircraft fire was far too effective and disrupted bombing. Henceforth, St Nazaire and other well defended targets were to be attacked from four miles high where, so far, flak had proved fairly ineffectual.

The 303rd Group operating from Molesworth made its debut on November 17th when sixteen of its B-17Fs set forth on another Eighth Air Force strike at St Nazaire. Seven hours later, the Group returned with full bomb-bays having been unable to locate the target due to cloud conditions. Once again intense anti-aircraft fire met those groups that did bomb, but this time all aircraft returned to England. Next day, when the 303rd tried again, their navigation was not all it might have been—to say the least. Nineteen B-17s bombed what was taken to be the briefed target, La Pallice, but which turned out to have been St Nazaire—100 miles away! Over Lorient four days later the 303rd did better, for eleven of their B-17s were the only bombers to attack, of 76 despatched by the Command. The other groups were unable to find gaps in the thick cloud that shrouded the French coast.

Since the first mission to the submarine bases along the occupied Atlantic coast, the bombers had seen little of the Luftwaffe. The long, four to five hundred mile over-water routes were planned to give the Germans the minimum of time to react. The Eighth was not so lucky on November 23rd when 58 B-17s set out again for St Nazaire.

The Luftwaffe unit entrusted with defending the U-boat ports, was Gruppe III of J.G. 2, commanded by the redoubtable Oberstleutnant Egon Mayer, a distinguished fighter pilot and canny tactician. Mayer had a healthy respect for the firepower of a Fortress formation having already led his Gruppe against these "mad Americans". The recognised method of bomber interception was to approach from the rear, but with the Fortresses the number of heavy calibre machine-guns that could be brought to bear on a fighter approaching from this quarter made such action very dangerous indeed. Experiments to find an approach angle which lessened the danger from defensive fire had been tried, but when the bombers maintained a tight formation little success was achieved. Soon the Germans discovered that the nose area of the Fortress with few guns was thus the weakest spot. Head-on attacks, however, were considered impracticable: a closing rate approaching 600 mph made sighting difficult apart from the danger of collision. To Mayer, however, the advantages outweighed the disadvantages. The Fortress's frontal area offered opportunities of hitting engines and the vital cockpit area where they lacked good armour protection. There was also the possibility of visual effects which might cause bomber pilots to take evasive action and break up the formation.

Mayer's chance to initiate a frontal assault came on the 23rd when the German raid reporting system warned of bombers approaching St Nazaire. Incessant cloud and generally bad weather caused many aircraft from the 91st and 306th groups to turn back and by the time the target

1/Lt Riordan makes the Indian war cry that was the nickname of his B-17. Badly shot up on one of 306th BG's early raids she was salvaged. —(USAF)

was reached their formations were reduced to 5 and 4 aircraft respectively. It was on these that III/J.G. 2 made their attack with flights of three bearing down on the Forts from dead ahead, firing well-aimed bursts with their cannon. Two 91st B-17s tumbled out of the sky and two others were badly hit; one, trying to reach Bassingbourn, crashed near Leavesden, Herts, killing three of the crew. *Quitchurbitchin*, piloted by 1/Lt Charles 'Red' Cliburn, was the only Fortress able to make its base.

It was a bad day for the 91st Group for none of its bombs were delivered on target and the aircraft shot down carried the commanders of the 322nd and 323rd Bomb. Sqdns., the Group's navigator, bombardier and gunnery officers. The 306th's diminished force, from the 367th Bomb. Sqdn., also came in for fighter attack, particularly the Fortress piloted by Captain Robert C. Williams, lagging behind after being hit by flak. *Banshee*, commanded by 2/Lt William "Wild Bill" Casey, then deliberately dropped back to add its guns to those of its beleaguered squadron mate. During the twelve minutes that the two bombers fought off the attack, gunners in Casey's aircraft claimed seven enemy fighters. William's B-17 limped home with a dead gunner and Casey's aircraft returned safely.

A fourth Fortress lost on this raid was the 303rd's *Lady Fairweather* shot down in flames near the target. Mayer's head-on tactics had resulted in the Luftwaffe's most successful interception so far. Only the 305th Group from Chelveston returned unscathed from this, its first bombing mission.

The USAAF had earlier appreciated the deficiencies in forward-firing armament and some extra nose guns had been provided. B-17Es left the factory with four off-centre sockets in their nose pieces, through which a flexible mounted .300 calibre machine-gun could be fired by the bombardier, but the field of fire was extremely limited whichever socket was used. Prior to overseas movement, enlarged windows were installed in staggered positions either side of the B-17E's nose, and through each was fitted a flexible .50 Browning for the navigator's use. Although these increased forward firepower, there was still a blind spot straight ahead which neither nose guns, nor those of the dorsal and ventral turrets, could cover. The B-17F was, if anything, worse, having only two nose sockets for the .300 machine-gun. It too, had extra .50 guns installed in ports after manufacture.

The Liberator's nose armament was little better; although it had .50 "cheek" guns, the single .50 projecting through the lower part of the perspex nose, could not be elevated above the horizontal plane resulting in a blind spot dead ahead. It was possible, and came to be frequently practised, for B-17s

and B-24s to manoeuvre in a slight diving turn to allow the "cheek" guns and the upper turret to be brought to bear on fighters making frontal attacks. Apart from being undesirable on a bombing run, such action presented the attacker with a slightly larger area.

An obvious remedy was a power-operated gun turret in the nose of the heavies, and this was being developed in the US, but it was many months before it could be introduced on production. More immediate remedial action to counter frontal attacks was to uncover blind spots and provide more effective hand-held guns. Since the .300 gun in the B-17's nose had proved of little value, various agencies in the Eighth Air Force set about installing a .50 gun in its place. The initial modifications, carried out at airfields by group personnel, was a somewhat difficult task, for the B-17F's perspex nose piece was not stressed to support a .50 machine gun. Special support framing had to be manufactured and fitted carefully so as not to impede the bombardier at his bombsight. The four groups contrived some skilful adaptions. In many B-17s two .50s were fitted in the nose, rigged to fire and be sighted together although on a few they were operated independently.

The arrangements if somewhat unwieldy, did give extra firepower where it was most wanted. Fortresses fitted with twin nose guns were then usually flown in leading or exposed

One swivel socket in the plexi-glass nose of this early B-17F had been modified to take a .50 gun. Other upper socket still holds the removable .30 gun. Spent cases have collected in bottom of nosepiece. Still secret bomb sight was covered before this picture was taken.—(USAF)

positions of a combat formation. However, a single .50 with a fair field of fire proved a better proposition. During December 1942 an armourer and welder in the 306th's 367th Bomb. Sqdn., S/Sgts James C. Green and Ben F. Marcilonis, spent much of their spare time devising and constructing a mount for a single .50. This had many commendable features and its manufacture and installation were taken up by VIII Air Service Command. The single .50 nose mount of this type became a standard fitment on most B-17Fs modified at Honington in following months. But before these armament changes had been fully effected, further operations were scheduled.

Romilly-sur-Seine, lying some sixty miles up river from Paris, was the site of a major Luftwaffe servicing base. Here much aircraft repair work was carried out and reserve machines prepared for units in Luftflotte 3, a command organisation covering much of France and the Low Countries. Romilly was an ideal VIII Bomber Command target, being easy to locate and offering an opportunity to deliver a costly blow to the Luftwaffe. On the other hand, this target lay a hundred miles further inland than any previously attacked by the Eighth's bombers. The prize being considered worth the risk, and with five groups operational (half the B-24s were detached to Africa), Romilly became the object of attention for VIII BC during the greater part of December.

The mission, scheduled for December 10th, was cancelled due to unfavourable weather. The forecast was favourable two days later, but by the time ninety bombers had assembled and crossed the French coast, cloud conditions had become so bad that the formations had to turn back. The 306th and 303rd turned right on to a secondary target, the Rouen marshalling yards. Only the latter bombed and for their perseverance were harassed by enemy fighters both to and from the target, losing two B-17s while others suffered damage. This again showed the vulnerability of a small formation alone over enemy territory. One of the missing Fortresses, *Wulf Hound*, touched

Wulf Hound in her new guise. She was chiefly employed in the development of fighter tactics to be used against her kin.

down in a French field with little damage, thus presenting the Germans with what is believed to be their first flyable example of this type. Not until the 20th did the weather allow the next attempt on Romilly-sur-Seine, when VIII Bomber Command mustered 101 bombers, the largest force despatched since the Lille raid in October. Twelve squadrons of RAF and USAAF Spitfires supported the penetration, but not until the Spitfire IXs turned back near Rouen did the Luftwaffe choose to appear. Then at 11.50 hrs, aircraft of J.G.26 approached the 91st Group with frontal attacks and claimed two of their B-17s. After fifteen minutes the FW190s, running low on fuel, broke off the battle; but at the same time some 50 others from J.G.2 arrived and kept up the attacks until the first bombers were nearing the target at 12.40 hrs. Thereafter, relays of enemy fighters—presumably those engaged in the early stages of the battle had refuelled—harried the American formations, breaking off just before seven squadrons of RAF Spitfires arrived to provide withdrawal escort. The 306th Group then bore

the brunt of the attacks. Having lost one B-17 just before bombing, two more were stricken near Paris and a fourth crashed into the sea approaching the English coast. Two other bombers of the Command crash-landed at Fletchling and Bovingdon on return, while of 29 damaged, some were written off as salvage. The sixty B-17s and twelve B-24s that bombed dropped 153 tons of high explosive and 12 tons of incendiary bombs, causing a fair amount of destruction among buildings and aircraft at Romilly, although the estimate of results was inclined to be optimistic.

The mission proved that a sizeable force could penetrate a hundred miles into enemy held territory and survive continuous fighter attack without crippling losses. Gunners claimed 53 enemy aircraft but as this constituted about half the enemy force known to have been available in the area, this figure was obviously exaggerated. Eventually, VIII BC lowered these claims to 21 destroyed plus another 31 probably destroyed. It is now known that the true German losses were no more than 5.

At times when weather conditions did not allow a combat mission, the bombers were up practising formation flying and co-operation with fighters. Each group evolved measures to improve combat ability from engine starting to touch-down and, understandably, defensive tactics received most attention. Effective resistance to fighter attack depended largely upon the strength and compactness of a formation. The massed firepower of a group of B-17s or B-24s presented a formidable obstacle to an interceptor but, to achieve the maximum field for their weapons, it was essential for bombers in a formation to be carefully spaced. Throughout the war the basic element of Eighth Air Force heavy bomber formations was usually the 3-plane "V" flight. On early missions the B-17s flew in separated squadron formations of two flights each. This allowed good manoeuvrability for bomb sighting, but aircraft were spread out over a wide area leaving some vulnerable to fighter attack. During the late September missions, to improve their defensive system, two or three squadrons were flown together to form a stepped-up group formation of 18 aircraft. Thereafter, this grouping was used extensively in varying forms. Although an improvement it had many shortcomings, particularly in the face of the head-on assaults the enemy fighters employed so effectively.

From the beginning, bombing had been carried out on the individual sightings of each bombardier while formation was maintained within squadrons. The problems of defence and bombing accuracy were unavoidably linked, in that any move to improve the firepower of a formation might present new obstacles to the bombardiers; alternatively, a move to further success on the bomb run might be detrimental from a defensive standpoint.

It was this aspect of the many tactical problems that became the obsession of Colonel Curtis LeMay and his staff at Chelveston. The commander of the 305th Group was a stocky 35-year old whose terse manner and seemingly cold attitude earned him the title 'Iron Ass' from his men. Nevertheless, those who worked with him soon came to appreciate his intent will and perceptive mind. The early missions of his Group were not auspicious, for on three occasions most aircraft had been unable to bomb and air discipline was not all it might have been.

LeMay, experimenting with formations to find the best form for staving off fighter attacks, finally favoured staggered 3-plane elements within a Squadron, and staggered squadrons within a group positioned to give a compact, yet easily manoeuvrable, "box" formation. But such an arrangement could complicate the bombing, with risks of confusion, if each aircraft attempted to manoeuvre for accurate aiming. This, LeMay decided, could be avoided if every machine maintained position in formation, and bombed on a signal from the leading aircraft of a group. While an error by the bombardier in the lead aircraft could cause all bombs to be wasted, the antithesis held that accurate sighting would ensure a highly concentrated pattern of strikes on the target area. By selecting the best bombardiers to fly with a highly trained lead crew, the chances of success for a group 'dropping on the leader' were improved. Thus was the gist of LeMay's reasoning and experiments. Brigadier General Kuter, who took command of 1st Wing early in December, encouraged LeMay's ideas, as did his successor, Brigadier General Hansell.

When on December 30th weather permitted the B-17s to resume attacks on the Lorient submarine-pens, the 305th Group tried a revised formation. At the target, the bomb run was made into the afternoon sun, from which glare hindered the gunners when the Luftwaffe made another of their head-on attacks. A 91st bomber went down taking yet another squadron commander, this time from the 401st. A 306th aircraft, flying with the 305th, turned away from the formation after leaving the target and immediately fell victim to enemy fighters. A 305th aircraft that had pulled out, to aid it with its firepower, was also shot down, demonstrating the futility of such action and the relative safety of a close knit formation. Another of this Group's Fortresses heavily hit, Captain Clyde B. Walker's *Boom Town,* fell behind and was considered lost, but it managed to limp to St Eval with one dead and two wounded among the crew.

The first mission of 1943 was to the notorious St Nazaire, on January 3rd. The 305th Group led the 85 bombers involved and Brigadier General Hansell went along to witness the effectiveness of some of LeMay's new tactics. To attain good bombing results a long, straight run-in was made with the formations ranged between 20,000 and 22,000 ft. While exceptional visibility and absence of cloud afforded good sighting, a sub-stratosphere gale nearly doubled the time planned for the bombing run. Hitherto, German anti-aircraft fire had generally proved ineffective above 20,000 ft, but the gunners at St Nazaire were becoming more proficient. For the first time a predicted barrage was put up in the path of the oncoming heavies. The official communique of VIII Bomber Command described these measures as ''Intense, heavy and accurate''. One veteran pilot considered it the most disturbing sight he had encountered on a dozen missions. For over nine minutes the bombers were exposed to the barrage as they lumbered on their straight path, and in the teeth of the gale, towards the target. Two B-17s were seen to sustain fatal hits and a third aircraft that failed to return was presumed another victim of the flak. Most airmen preferred to face fighters than flak—at least they could fight back. Over half the returning planes had received damage from shell fragments or actual hits. Bomber men came to talk of St Nazaire as ''Flak City''.

Four B-17s fell to fighters on this mission, but one at least, *Son of Fury,* a 306th machine piloted by Lt Charles Cranmer, was previously crippled by ground fire. With two engines feathered, and a gaping hole where the underside of the nose had been blasted away taking navigator and bombardier with it, the Fortress lagged behind on the return. Once out to sea the formation reduced altitude to 500 ft to escape radar tracking and avert interceptions from below, but Cranmer dare not bring his crippled charge down too close to the sea and trailed along at 1500 feet some distance behind his group. Forty miles north-west of Brest, six FW190s caught up with the straggler and its fate was observed by Sgt P. D. Small who was tail gunner in *Banshee,* one of the rearmost B-17s in the 306th's formation. As the enemy fighters made their first pass, he saw four parachutes blossom out as men jumped from *Son of Fury.* The battered Fortress then went down steadily, as if Cranmer still had control, and settled in the water. Then, as the icy waters rose around the upper turret, Small observed that firing continued at the Focke-Wulfs that appeared to be strafing their sinking victim. In thirty seconds the Fortress had disappeared. Thus were the deeds of T/Sgt

Arizona Harris, the man who went to a watery grave still firing his guns, witnessed. He was posthumously awarded the DSC, the second highest award for heroism. Many felt he deserved his country's highest honour.

Most of the 342 x 1,000 lb bombs that went down on St Nazaire that day were well placed and the first use of the 'bombing-on-leader' technique showed considerable promise. The long run-in may have aided the bombardiers, but the dangers of a flak barrage made it a dubious proposition over such a well defended target. The VIII Bomber Command had sustained its heaviest loss so far, with 70 men missing aboard the 7 bombers shot down, plus 2 killed and 7 wounded in some of the 47 aircraft with battle damage. Even this was not the full tally, for on return to England two formations went off course and short of fuel had to seek emergency fields. Crash-landings claimed two more bombers with further loss of life.

There was rarely an occasion when a commanding General or Colonel did not fly on these pioneering missions. Although ''Top Brass'' were no more immune to the perils of air combat than others, not once was a group or wing commander lost during the experimental period up to May 1943. The services of Laurence Kuter being needed in North Africa, 1st Wing's new commanding General, Haywood Hansell, officially took over a few hours before his flight on the costly St Nazaire mission. He was in the lead 305th Fortress on the 13th when the Eighth made for another familiar target, the Fives loco-motive works at Lille. This day, all four B-17 groups flew the staggered 18-plane group formations with the chief architects of the technique in a leading position. The B-17 carrying Hansell was *Dry Martini II,* a name derived from her regular pilot—Captain Allen V. Martini, but on this occasion flown by the 364th Bomb. Sqn. Commander, Major T. H. Taylor; Martini had been grounded for the day through illness. Over Lille the yellow-nosed Focke-Wulfs pulled their now familiar tactic of hitting the lead group on the bomb run, with the object of upsetting their aim. The lead plane was an obvious choice of target, and one cannon shell exploded in the cockpit of *Dry Martini II* killing Major Taylor.

The staggered formations presented the attacking fighters with a much warmer reception. Against the one 305th bomber lost the Group's gunners claimed 29 victories, a figure later reduced to 6 destroyed and 13 probables or damaged. As for Fives-Lille, the bombing appeared to have wrought more damage than any of the previous raids. At least, VIII Bomber Command never returned to this target again.

Two other B-17s that failed to return were believed to have collided over Belgium. Both were from the 306th's 369th Bomb. Sqn. which was to become known as the 'Fitin' Bitin' '' squadron. One fatality was not the work of the enemy. When the tail-gunner of a Fortress did not respond to a call over the inter-phone, a member of the crew was sent back to discover why. He found the gunner dead with a failed oxygen system.

While Lille had been a ''Milk Run'' for the 303rd, they were

Werewolf begins her take-off run on the improvised runway at Daw-lish.—(USAF)

not so lucky when, after nine days respite, the Fortresses once more set out for the French coast submarine-pens. The Luftwaffe had tried a new technique by making simultaneous attacks on a formation from each side and above, presumably to cause confusion and dispersion of the defensive fire. They succeeded in sending down five of the 303rd's B-17s. Flak nearly claimed another; this was *Werewolf* which limped home with engines faltering until only one was still operative by the time the south coast of England was reached. Lt George J. Oxrider ordered his crew to bale out, before making a successful landing in a small field of greens at Dawlish. Instead of the usual lengthy job of dismantling and hauling away, VIII AF Service Command decided to fly it out. While three engines were changed, a team of US engineers cleared trees, walls and hedges to make a 2,250 ft runway. Two weeks later, *Werewolf* was flying again and eventually returned to Molesworth.

While the Eighth strove to perfect the art of daylight precision bombing, the value of these raids was still questioned in both British and American circles. During January Allied leaders conferred on war plans at Casablanca where the British again expressed their belief that the US heavy bombers would be better employed in aiding the RAF on night assaults. General Arnold had Eaker flown down from England to put the case for continuing daylight raids. This Eaker appears to have done most effectively, for one of the results of the conference was a policy directive calling for a day and night strategic bomber offensive in which the RAF and USAAF would combine. Not until the late spring of 1943 were detailed plans for such an offensive completed and put into operation; meanwhile, the Eighth Air Force's bombing campaign continued to be regarded as on probation by Allied planners.

The basic question after VIII Bomber Command's thirty operations was still—could the Eighth's bombers make effective attacks without prohibitive losses?

So far, the B-17s and B-24s had shown a lower loss rate than the RAF on night raids. But, it was on the night bomber that the Germans had been concentrating their defensive efforts, due to their belief that large bombers were too vulnerable for daylight operations. They had been caught off guard when the US formations appeared. Nevertheless, the Luftwaffe had been quick to rally, for whereas 3.7% of the attacking bombers had fallen to enemy fighters in November, the figure had risen to 8.8% in December.

Bombing results appeared to vary from good to very bad. In any case, the effect of the early missions upon the German war effort can hardly have been more than a matter of extreme irritation, for owing to the small force of bombers the amount of damage created was readily repaired. Even so, the Eighth's commanders looked for better bombing results as their tactics improved, for it had been as much a case of finding the best methods of attack, as actually attacking.

In seeking to prove the worth of the US bombing doctrine the Eighth was beset with many other problems; the greatest was undoubtedly weather conditions. The essential good visibility for precision bombing was seldom available in the winter months. Cloud had constantly to be reckoned with, for a cloudless or near cloudless sky occurred on the average only about once every 20 days during the winter of 1942-1943. This was the factor conditioning the slow pace of operations. Even on a day that started with a clear blue sky, such was the variable nature of the weather that a complete overcast could develop within hours. During October only three missions were possible while eleven planned had to be cancelled because of excessive cloud. In November and December half the bombers forced to return from a mission without bombing, did so because of bad weather conditions. Often the bombers would be airborne when deteriorating weather over the Continent caused the abandonement of a mission; a frustrating and morale dampening occurrence for the crews, yet one which came to be a regular feature of operations.

Mounting a mission was a hectic and laborious task that began hours before the bombers commenced take-off and entailed meticulous staff planning. As soon as the alert was received at a bomber base, engineering sections would ready the aircraft, checking and testing most of the night. The ordnance and chemical men who handled the high explosive and incendiary bombs would begin loading while it was still dark; ammunition was put aboard and turrets given a final go-over by armourers. Radios were checked by technicians, the still closely guarded bombsights were installed, oxygen bottles replenished, cameras for strike photos loaded and set, and fuel tanks topped up, plus a variety of essential tasks. Meanwhile, the combat crews would be wakened and cooks would prepare breakfast to fit into a schedule that would allow a briefing period by intelligence officers and give time to prepare their flying equipment. Transport would have been arranged to carry them to briefing and to their aircraft. A number of specialist tasks had to be fitted in—the medical team made last minute check-ups, navigators would have to study routes and schedules, bombardiers their targets, pilots their formating instructions and any particular problems of the mission, while gunners checked their weapons.

As the minutes ticked by and the crucial moment of take-off approached nearly every man on the base played his part in preparing for a mission, each knowing that at any time from the Field Order coming in on the teletype machine, to the Group's formation approaching the enemy coast, the mission could be cancelled—or "scrubbed" to use the idiom of the day. To the crews under pre-combat tension this was no relief, for it meant they had to face the same procedure again before they could cross another mission from the 25 each was usually expected to fly. To the ground men it meant that bombs, guns, bombsights, cameras and other equipment had to be removed and fuel drawn off each bomber. And perhaps a few hours after this had been completed the whole process might begin again. A scrubbed mission was the most morale sapping problem of the Eighth's first winter.

The English winter also hindered operations in another way. Dampness affected the functioning of aircraft, for moisture and wet that found its way into components on the airfield would turn to ice at 15,000 ft. At combat altitudes gun-actuating, turret and bomb-door mechanisms and trimming tabs, failed to operate due to lubricants freezing, while often superchargers could not be worked because of congealing oil in the regulator lines. New oils with anti-freeze elements eventually solved most of these problems. The original US oils proved unsatisfactory and British products were used pending the supply of new types from America. It was necessary for guns to be completely covered with oil to ensure their operation at high altitude. The sub-zero conditions at extreme altitude were also responsible for landing lights burning out and the glass covers cracking through sudden changes of temperature. Aircrews suffered much during this first winter. Oxygen masks had a nasty habit of becoming stiff with ice. The electrically heated shoes were particularly inadequate and many times airmen returned with frost-bitten feet.

Another major factor influencing VIII Bomber Command's rate of operations was the demands of "Junior"—as the Twelfth Air Force was dubbed. Apart from training units and supplying personnel, the Eighth had parted with 75% of its stocks of aircraft spares and servicing equipment. The cupboard was indeed bare and there was little hope of replenishment in the near future, for the North African campaign continued to have priority on the limited shipments from the USA. The situation would have been even worse had it not been for British assistance in providing transport, servicing equipment, tools, bombs, dinghies and flying clothes, not to mention items for base and personnel use. The transport included several thousand cycles, personal transport for Colonels down

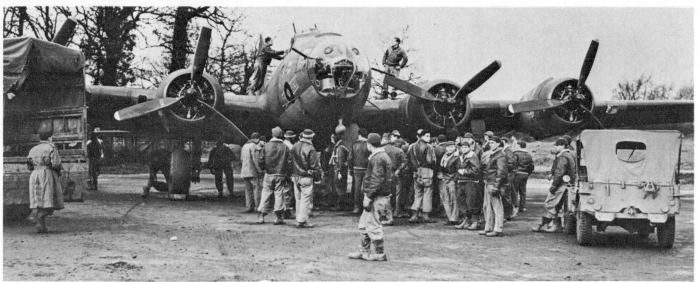

The *Eight Ball* comes to rest on her Molesworth hardstand after the first raid on Germany, 27 Jan. 1943. Ground crew men gather round to hear how it went from 1/Lt Harold Stouse and his crew.—(USAF)

to privates. Much of this equipment was counted a poor substitute, yet some was retained in preference long after deficiencies were made up from the USA. Above all, the few aircraft and crews reaching the Eighth in the closing months of 1942 were inadequate to replace operational losses. In consequence combat crews saw their units visibly shrinking with every mission, a situation not conducive to good morale.

All thirty missions so far undertaken by VIII Bomber Command were to targets in enemy occupied territories. There had long been a desire amongst all ranks of the Eighth Air Force to attack targets in the enemy's homeland. Apart from wishing to be on equal terms with the RAF whose bombers raided Germany almost nightly, the bombing of enemy targets in France and the Low Countries had often resulted in casualties among the local civilian population, occurrences that German propaganda agencies were quick to exploit. Inevitably bombs went astray and it was understandable that aircrews preferred this to happen over Germany. Additionally, the first offensive action by Americans against the enemy homeland would bring badly needed publicity to the Eighth's efforts.

Submarine building yards were number one priority on the target list and the officers in the Wycombe Abbey war room had long shown interest in a particularly promising target at Vegesack, situated on the Weser some thirty miles from its North Sea estuary. Here they planned to send their first bombers to Germany in a maximum effort. With a chance of suitable weather in the area on January 27th the Field Order, with the significant word "Germany", was sent out to Thurleigh, Molesworth, Chelveston, Bassingbourn, and Shipdham. Led by the 306th, oldest operational group in the Command, 64 B-17s set off soon after dawn. In the leading aircraft was Colonel Frank Armstrong who had flown in the lead plane on the B-17s first venture to Rouen the previous August. Because of his experience, Armstrong had been retained by Eaker when the 97th Group was sent to Africa. Early in January he had been sent to Thurleigh to command and shape up the battle-sore 306th.

To minimise the chances of interception the bombers' route was planned to take them far out into the North Sea, to avoid skirting the enemy coast. After turning towards Germany and climbing to bombing altitude, weather conditions deteriorated, and by the time the enemy coast was reached it became evident that cloud conditions inland would prohibit bombing. Frustrated, the force then turned for the secondary target, the port of Wilhelmshaven, which was only thinly veiled with cloud. At precisely 11.10 hrs, flying at 25,000 ft near the

island of Baltrum, the Fortresses crossed the coastal threshold of the hostile house of Germany for the first time. The honour of being first over Germany was disputed by returning crews. It appears that the B-17 piloted by 1/Lt Edward J. Hennessey may have been the first, as this flew on the extreme right of the 306th formation and swung in over the coast before the lead plane flown by the Colonel and the Group Executive, Major Putnam. Gaps in the thin cloud did allow 58 B-17s to bomb, though sighting was further hindered by a smoke screen. The resulting bomb patterns were spread over the dock area and damage to installations was not extensive. Two Fortresses unable to drop on Wilhelmshaven, unloaded over Emden on the return journey. Opposition was surprisingly ineffective. Flak was light and inaccurate, while the estimated 50-75 enemy fighters intercepting on the way home did not press their attacks with the skill and determination of the Luftwaffe units encountered over France. Additional to Me109s and FW190s, twin-engined fighters were reported for the first time, but they did not approach the bombers. Losses amounted to one B-17, and two B-24s of a small force which made an abortive attempt to bomb the same target. Gunners were credited with 22 victories; the Germans actually lost seven fighters which still amounted to a considerable success for the attackers.

The fortresses did not escape so lightly in their next raid on Germany. Even more ambitious than the plan to attack Vegesack was that to hit the important rail marshalling yard at Hamm, deep in the stoutly defended Ruhr. After two false starts the bombers were first despatched on February 2nd but bad weather caused them to return. Two days later they were briefed for the same destination and 86 bombers set out on the long haul over the North Sea intent on striking down to the Ruhr area from the North German coast, thus shortening the period that they would be over hostile territory. Once again heavy cloud was found over north-west Germany and again the raid was abandoned. Over Emden 39 B-17s unloaded and others aimed for a convoy just off the coast. The somewhat straggling formations came under heavy attacks from fighters, including twin-engined machines, which pursued the Fortresses well out to sea and accounted for 4 of the 5 missing that day. An FW190 collided head-on with a 305th Group Fort. The 91st Group, led by Colonel Wray and Captain R. Morgan in *Memphis Belle*, experienced a new Luftwaffe trick when twin-engined aircraft dropped fragmentation bombs on the formation. 1/Lt James A. Verinis, described the experience: "As we started home over the North Sea, we began to see explosions high above us. We first thought it was flak, then reasoned that impossible as there was sea and no guns beneath us. Finally we saw a Heinkel two thousand feet above. We could see bombs falling. They apparently were time bombs set to explode at our altitude. We dived out of range." While this innovation did no damage, it warned of new German attempts to break up the formations.

Foul weather kept the Eighth's bombers from operating until the 14th, and then cloud conditions foiled another attempt to bomb Hamm, for the force turned back at the enemy coast.

Back in a Molesworth hangar Donald Stockton takes a close look at the damage wrought by an FW 190's fire. Six foot, four inch tall Lt H. E. Miller sits in the hole.—(USAF)

Two days later, weather prospects were brighter in Western France and 89 heavies left for 'Flak City'. This notorious target lived up to its evil reputation: six B-17s were crippled, while the performance of the Luftwaffe interceptors confirmed crews' opinions that J.G.2 and J.G.26 constituted the most dangerous opposition so far encountered. The aiming point was the U-boat basin locks, but though these were missed the preliminary report of the bombing used the word "excellent". A rather exaggerated verdict, particularly as bombsight trouble caused the 305th Group to fail completely. One of thirty damaged Fortresses, the 303rd's *Joe Btfsplk* flown by 1/Lt Donald E. Stockton, came home with a cannon fire hole as big as a household door in the fin.

Over North-West Germany on February 26th it was the same familiar story; a heavy undercast was found to be obscuring the area of the primary objective and the B-17s were forced to return without bombing, or find an alternative target. As with the first venture into Germany, almost a month before, Wilhelmshaven was visible. This port received some 150 tons of high explosive originally intended for Bremen. The Luftwaffe reception committee dealt severely with the invaders, particularly the 305th Group which suffered half of the US losses incurred during air combat, plus the sole flak victim of the day. Led by Major J. J. Preston, who had played a big part in developing the new bombing techniques, the Group considered this the strongest fighter opposition so far encountered. Enemy bombing was again reported, plus a new parachute mine put up by guns in the path of the bombers.

Southern Comfort was the name of a 305th BG aircraft that led an eventful career. When the Group was badly mauled by Me109s of JG1 on 26 Feb. 1943, she came home alone on three engines and with considerable battle damage.—(USAF)

From one of the missing bombers S/Sgt Lee C. 'Shorty' Gordon parachuted from his ball turret. A survivor of many 'scrapes' he escaped three times from POW camps, the last time successfully to reach Allied territory exactly a year and a day after this event. He was the first US airman awarded the Silver Star for escaping.

In contrast, a trip to Brest next day saw no losses to enemy action. The Germans, however, employed another tactic with success; one flight of bombers turned back when almost to the target, upon receiving a bogus recall radio signal. The absence of the Luftwaffe was put down to the "excellent quality" of the RAF Spitfire escort.

The VIII Bomber Command groups were in need of a "milk run", for during February aircraft losses had amounted to 22 of the average effective strength for combat of 84 aircraft and 74 crews. The aircraft situation reflected the seriousness of the repair position for there were approximately an equal number unserviceable in combat units. In the case of air crews, these were being lost faster than replacements were assigned. Most of the Eighth's commitments to the Twelfth Air Force had been met, but the promised strengthening of its own forces had yet to materialise.

Five times the Eighth's bombers had set out to make a reasonably deep penetration into North-West Germany, only to be frustrated by the vicissitudes of the elements. So far attacks on the enemy homeland had all been on coastal ports. On March 4th the Fortress crews were again briefed for the Hamm marshalling yards and although they took off into a grey dawn, fair conditions had been forecast ahead. Once more the familiar route out across the Norfolk coast, then steering north-east over the North Sea in the hope that detection by the enemy would cause him to think his coastal ports were endangered. Some fifty miles out from England, the formations turned south-east to head across Holland to the target. A dense haze hung off the sea and at times crews had less than a thousand yard visibility; as there seemed little sign of improvement the leading groups elected to turn back. The 305th formation led by Major J. J. Preston, and the 303rd led by Lt Col George L. Robinson, turned south and finding clearer skies were able to bomb the last-resort target at Rotterdam. The 306th abandoning the mission, brought its bombs back to Thurleigh.

While the winter weather, it seemed, had again cheated the Eighth of its first stab into the German hinterland, there occurred one incident that could have little direct effect on the course of the war, yet was worth much in morale to the unit involved and, indeed, to the promoters of the day bombing doctrine. Above the "soup", fifteen B-17Fs of the 91st Group, out of visual contact believed the other formations to be still ahead due to dense contrails that marked the sky. Approaching the Continent, visibility began to improve and the vapour trails disappeared. Major Paul Fishburne, a youngster of 22, leading in *Chief Sly II*, scanned the sky ahead in vain for a sight of the other groups. It was the moment for decision; the 91st formation, apparently alone, would have been quite justified in turning back but Fishburne chose to go on. As

With hydraulics shot out *Stormy Weather* wouldn't stop at the end of the Bassingbourn runway. She went through bushes and barbed wire to repose partly on a road and partly on a manure heap. She had returned from the first mission into the Ruhr.—(USAF)

the 91st droned over Friesland towards the borders of the Reich, the haze was clearing rapidly. German fighter controllers were evidently confused by the various bomber tracks that morning, for not until the Group was half an hour off its objective did the Luftwaffe appear. Even so, neither their attacks, nor a flak barrage, disrupted an excellent bombing run that planted the Group's bombs right in the rail yards. By then the enemy's defence system was well alerted and opposition increased on the home trip. For an hour, single and twin-engined fighters harried the gallant band, mostly attacking from above. Their Fortresses were the first of the Eighth's Fortress units that Luftwaffe pilots could recognise in action; for while the other three groups painted their recognition lettering in grey, this Bassingbourn "outfit" used a distinguishing yellow. Such a small force could not hope to come through without loss, and before the coast was reached three B-17s had gone down. A fourth, *Excalibur,* with three engines crippled, was unable to make the North Sea crossing. In ditching, the bomber was put down into the swell instead of parallel to it, with the result that it broke into four parts. Seven of the crew, excluding the pilots and ball gunner, were picked up later by a British minesweeper.

The 91st gunners claimed 13-3-4 but the cost was high; four bombers lost, one damaged beyond repair and some damage to all the rest; 33 men missing, 1 dead and 5 seriously wounded. The effect of the bombing probably tempered any misgivings higher command may have had over such a small force "going it alone", deeper into Germany than ever before. The 91st, though sorely hit, had a pioneering mission all to itself and one which did much for unit pride. In fact, the Hamm raid is the earliest action by an Eighth Air Force unit to earn a Distinguished Unit Citation, although the award was not made until two years after the war, reflecting perhaps command fears that if the heroics of such an action were over-emphasized other formations of inadequate strength might attack rashly with disastrous result. Nevertheless, in April, Paul Fishburne received the DFC for his leadership on this mission and from none other than the "Father of the RAF"—Lord Trenchard.

Having struck an important marshalling yard in Germany, the Eighth turned attention to one at Rennes in Brittany, France, through which supplies flowed to the submarine bases. Brigadier General Hansell flew with the 305th, led by Major Preston, to review formation developments and in turn witnessed excellent bombing which severed lines halting traffic for three or four days. Bomb dropping in unison with the group or squadron leader had become the standard form of attack, and was to remain so for visual bombing until the end of hostilities.

Experiments with formation and sighting procedures continued and constant variations were tried in the search for better results. Analysts of VIII Bomber Command evaluated a unit's bombing pattern on the basis of its relation to the mean

point of impact (MPI), i.e. the planned centre of a bomb concentration. The percentage of hits within 1,000 ft and 2,000 ft circles from the MPI were the bombing criteria. The ideal to make the 'pickle barrel' dreams come true, was for group dropping within the 1,000 ft circle. At this time, when bombardiers and lead crews were gaining experience and experimenting with new techniques, there was little hope of such overall precision. All the same, there were occasions when some groups came near to the perfect strike. On March 18th at Vegesack, the 305th managed to place 76% of its bombs within 1,000 ft of the MPI in what proved to be the most precise piece of bombing so far turned out by the B-17s.

After two further missions to other French railyards without loss, the Force revisited to Germany. In perfect visibility 73 B-17s and 24 B-24s dropped 268 tons of high explosive squarely on Bremer Vulkan Schiffbau, the submarine yards at Vegesack that had also been the briefed target for the first raid on the Reich back in January. From the evidence of reconnaissance photographs, seven submarines were assessed

Rarely was visibility as good as the day 1st Wing hit Lorient for the sixth time. Heavy flak had stopped by the time 305th BG turned off target: 6 Mar. 1943.—(IWM)

as severely damaged and two thirds of the shipyard buildings and much of the plant appeared to have been demolished. This was the sort of result Eaker, and for that matter Arnold, needed to convince the sceptics. For the loss of two bombers a major U-boat yard had been devastated and put out of action for at least two months. Indeed, this mission was later said to have proved the case for high-altitude precision day bombing, and its success doubtless influenced those US war leaders who sought evidence to justify the direction of a goodly part of the US war effort to creating a strategic air force.

The mission to Vegesack followed the usual over-water route to North Germany. Near Heligoland the fighters of J.G.1 put in an appearance and made sporadic passes all the way to the target. Heading the task force that day were 22 303rd aircraft under the command of Lt Col George Robinson, the Group Executive Officer. On the bomb run the Group encountered heavy and accurate flak, and at one point the low squadron, the 359th, was bracketed by bursts. Bombing was to be done by squadrons and in *The Duchess*, lead plane of the 359th, 24,000 feet above the earth, 1/Lt Jack Mathis had his eye to the Norden sight. Less than a minute from the release point, a shell exploded near the right side of the nose; shrapnel shattered part of the plexiglass hurling Mathis back some nine feet to the rear of the nose compartment. Though mortally injured—his right arm was nearly severed above the elbow and there were deep wounds in his side and abdomen —he somehow managed to drag himself to his bombsight to

When this photo was taken some weeks later the only signs of the grim incident that took place within the nose of this aircraft are the two flak patches; one below man on left and the other just forward of nude's right leg. The men who kept *The Duchess* flying are: l. to r. Sgt Joe Worthington, T/Sgt Jim Wilson, Sgt R. Raubach, Sgt Francis Gallant, and Sgt Sid Jackson.—(USAF)

release the bombs on time. The navigator, also knocked over by the explosion, was unhurt and did not realise Mathis's plight until the gallant bombardier collapsed over his bomb-sight in the act of reaching out to operate the switch closing the bomb-bay doors. Whether or not Mathis realized the extent of his wounds in those few seconds of consciousness can only be conjectured, he knew the other aircraft in the squadron depended upon his sighting to release. As it was, the Group's bombing was highly accurate.

The only B-17 lost on the mission was from the 303rd; *The Duchess* was brought safely home by pilot Captain Harold Stouse. This Fortress was to survive all the Eighth's bitter air battles of 1943 and complete 59 missions before being retired. In that time the only casualty to her many crews was Jack Mathis, whose conduct over Vegesack that March day brought the posthumous award of his country's highest decoration for bravery, the Medal of Honor, the first to go to an Eighth Air Force flier.

The mission was notable for the first successful use of automatic flight control equipment (AFCE) with which LeMay's group had been experimenting. Coupled in on the bomb run, AFCE allowed the bombardier to fly the aircraft by linking up with the automatic pilot. In earlier trials this equipment was found wanting, but modifications had effected improvement and AFCE was later installed in most group lead bombers, although its reliability was never assured.

Record claims of 52-20-23 were put in by gunners. As the enemy fighters engaged probably numbered no more than sixty from I and III/J.G.1, this again reflects the confused nature of such air battles. The standard of gunnery was still far from good, particularly among men using the hand-held guns in nose and waist positions. Manipulating a reverberating .50 gun, weighing 64 lb, in a 200 mph slip-stream, was no easy task. Nor were the holes found in some bombers always made by enemy missiles for waist gunners, attempting to track an enemy aircraft too far, sometimes fired into the tail surfaces of their own aircraft.

To improve markmanship, gunnery training flights were made regularly over British coastal ranges for aerial target practice. Target-towing was not without its risks. On one occasion gunners fired at a drogue before the cable was fully paid out from the ex-RAF Boston used by the 305th for this

purpose. It received some of the bullets, one shattering the right shoulder of the pilot, Captain Henry MacDonald, causing him to lose control. The two other crew members managed to right the Boston and MacDonald made a successful landing using his left hand and chin!

Not until after the war, when the Allies had access to German records, was it known how far in excess of the true losses gunner claims were. At the time, intelligence circles appreciated some overstatement, but not to the degree now apparent. The bomber crews, however, were convinced that they were inflicting crippling defeats on the enemy fighter force. In part, this belief helped to counter the shock of their own losses and the notion of "giving him more than we get" helped in sustaining morale. By VIII Bomber Command assessments, some prodigious scores had been run up by the groups. Highest total claims were made by the 91st at Bassingbourn—102 destroyed! Next came the 306th with 68 credits, and then the 303rd with 65.

It was often suggested that the lot of bomber crews was much better than that of infantrymen. Yet there were no fox holes in the sky; only an aircraft's thin alloy skin lay between crews and any shell splinters or bullets that came their way. It gave a very naked feeling. In the autumn of 1942 an analysis of wounds sustained by aircrew showed that 70% were caused by missiles of a relatively low velocity. Colonel Malcolm C. Grow, chief surgeon of the Eighth Air Force, instituted research into the possibility of a lightweight body armour to prevent or lessen such wounds. On British advice, Grow approached the Wilkinson Sword Company of London, a firm which had been making body armour off and on for 300 years. The outcome was the so-called Flak Suit, a jerkin formed of 2 inch square, 1/16th inch thick, laminated manganese steel plates, overlapping 3/8th inch on all sides. A quick release mechanism was fitted and the whole suit weighed 20 lbs. An initial order for 300 was given to Wilkinson's and as the suits became available they were issued to ten crews at Bassingbourn for combat trials by the 91st Group. During March and April 1943

Original design flak suits, displayed by two members of *Oklahoma Okie's* crew. Later battle armour was more flexible and less weighty.—(USAF)

The 91st BG waits to move onto the runway: Bassingbourn, 22 Mar. 1943, destination Wilhelmshaven. Lead plane is *Invasion II*, piloted by Capt Oscar O'Neill. Next in line is *Bomboogie* followed by *Bad Egg*.

the suits proved their worth on a number of occasions and further suits were ordered both in Britain and America.

After Vegesack came further missions to Wilhelmshaven and Rouen, and on the last day of March the bombers visited the Rotterdam shipyard. On both the latter missions the Luftwaffe intercepted over the Channel and in one case followed to within sight of the English coast.

The first mission of April brought more evidence of the value of the bombardment campaign when Fortresses left the Renault motor vehicle works at Paris a smoking ruin; it took six months to resume full production, denying the enemy 3,075 military lorries. The star performer that day was again the 305th, the mission leader. For of 251 tons dropped most of the 81 tons that landed on the factory were from the LeMay group. Led by Major McGhee, eighteen B-17s took off from Chelveston shortly after 11.00 hrs and assembled under broken cloud at 5,000 ft. Two hours were needed for the four groups to assemble battle formations and gain the necessary altitude. A total of 97 B-17s departed Beachy Head and made landfall on the French coast near Dieppe flying at 25,000 ft. A Spitfire escort was provided for much of the penetration and there was still no sign of the Luftwaffe in the cloudless sky when the bombers reached Paris. The target was picked out in spite of industrial haze that shrouded much of the city and the leaders commenced their run through moderate, and comparatively inaccurate, flak at 22,000 ft. Bombs from the 305th's Fortresses struck at least 19 factory buildings, sending a column of smoke up some 4,000 ft. The accuracy of the trailing groups was, unfortunately, not so high and many bombs fell outside the target area causing civilian casualties.

Allen Martini (third from right) with some of the crew of *Dry Martini 4th*. A photo taken later—13 May 1943—when 1st Wing CO, Brig Gen Hansel flew with them to Meaulte.—(USAF)

Five minutes after turning off the target, the Luftwaffe arrived and an estimated 50 to 75 FW190s attacked for 50 minutes. As usual, their attention was mainly devoted to the exposed elements of the leading group. Heading in for frontal passes, with four or six aircraft at a time, the enemy staged the intervals between attacks so that B-17s manoeuvring to meet one flight of Focke-Wulfs, had no time to re-position before the next flight attacked. *Dry Martini 4th,* leading the low unit (364th Bomb. Sqdn.) attracted successive attacks. By quick evasive action of the pilot, Captain Allen Martini, and able shooting by his gunners, the Fortress survived. The ten "Jerries" credited to the crew as destroyed was a record for a bomber on a single mission, being half the 305th's total score for the day. Three of the squadron's B-17s went down before the Luftwaffe left. Of one of these, *Available Jones,* it was said that the navigator had a premonition his bomber would not return and he pocketed his shaving kit; ten parachutes were seen to open from the doomed bomber, so perhaps he needed it!

The 306th led a charmed life during the greater part of March, flying six consecutive missions without loss. Men of the Thurleigh group were beginning to hope their ill luck was something in the past when, on April 5th, came a mission to Antwerp. Then, all five B-17s failing to return were from the unfortunate 306th who received head-on attacks by J.G.26's FW190s just before reaching the target. Gunners claimed five enemy fighters destroyed. The validity of these claims is unknown but the commander of III/J.G.26, Hauptmann Fritz Geisshardt, credited with 100 victories, died of wounds received during this battle. One bomber struck by cannon fire carried Brigadier General Frank Armstrong, an ex-306th Commander elevated to 1st Wing Staff, who was flying as an observer with Major James Wilson, Group Executive. This Fortress limped back to England.

On this day, T/Sgt Michael Roscovich achieved the ambition of every man in VIII Bomber Command—to successfully complete his operational tour. By the law of averages an airman did not stand to survive 20 missions over *Festung Europa* at this time. Roscovich was the first man in the Eighth to complete the 25 missions. Possessed of an incredibly happy disposition, and known as the 'Mad Russian' for his outlandish jokes, Roscovich delighted in such pranks as taking along suitably inscribed items of hardware to drop on targets, or cutting off the neckties of fellow crew members about to go "on pass". Roscovich did not go home. Instead, he took a commission and became a gunnery officer at another station, adding more missions to his log before finally deciding to return to America. This man; who survived 33 missions against the best of Hitler's flak and fighters, tragically lost his life when the aircraft taking him home crashed in Scotland.

The American day bombers had obviously caused the Germans mounting concern during the first few months of

1943. There was evidence that the number of fighters were being increased with units transferred from other fronts to bolster the heavily taxed J.G.2 and J.G.26, and to a lesser degree J.G.1. Tactics were being improved and new weapons tried out. While head-on attacks resulted in some success for the Luftwaffe and still predominated, considerable skill was required. The 91st Group led by Major Haley Aycock encountered the original promoters of this technique when the Group approached Lorient on the Eighth's next mission, April 16th. Only one of the 59 B-17s bombing failed to return from this raid, while a small force of B-24s attacking Brest lost three to rear interceptions by FW190s believed to be elements of J.G.26. Accurate precision bombing was demonstrated, particularly by the 305th Group, and a dock power station was badly damaged despite an extensive smoke screen. But the fiercest battle yet fought by the four Fortress groups came the following day. It was a day of records; one giving ominous signs that the Fortresses were more vulnerable to a determined fighter attack than their advocates were inclined to believe.

The first record was that a larger force was despatched than on any previous mission. In all, 115 B-17s set off for Bremen that morning from Bassingbourn, Chelveston, Molesworth and Thurleigh. Instead of submarine yards, the Fortresses sought the Focke-Wulf factory producing the fighters that had been their chief antagonists for so long. Since March the situation of replacement aircraft and crews had steadily improved, enabling squadron strengths to be built up to average 12 aircraft and 10 crews apiece; even so, the days of impoverishment were far from over.

Expecting strong opposition, the striking force assembled in two combat wing formations, each consisting of three group boxes of 18 to 21 aircraft, flying one above the other with the centre group forward of the other two. This idea had arisen during the winter months, primarily as a method of bringing the maximum firepower to bear on enemy fighters attacking head-on. In general, the larger and more compact a bomber formation, the better its defensive capability. On the other hand, there were serious disadvantages for the actual bombing and it was a matter for compromise. At first group boxes had been staggered upwards and backwards, with the disadvantage that enemy fighters nearly always attacked the most exposed position—the low squadron of the lowest and leading group. Better protection for the lowest group was effected by leading with the middle group, placed above and ahead of the lowest group. Thus, enemy fighters attacking the latter head-on, had to fly through the fire from the leading group. Nevertheless, the low group was still the most vulnerable in the formation and crews dubbed its role "Purple Heart Corner" (The Purple Heart is the US decoration given to all men wounded in action). There was little enthusiasm for flying in this position, and a system of squadron rotation was instituted.

Leading the first combat wing on April 17th was the 91st Group, with the 306th below and a composite group on top of the so-called "vertical wedge". The Molesworth and Chelveston groups flew a similar set-up in the second combat wing. This was the first occasion that these formations had been flown on such a scale and the mass of aircraft with 3,000 ft between lowest and highest elements was not easy to control. Over the North Sea the bombers had the misfortune to be spotted by a Luftwaffe reconnaissance aircraft which wirelessed a warning almost an hour before the German coast was reached. The Luftwaffe Controller, alerted so well in advance, called in the first fighter interceptions after the B-17s passed the Friesian Isles. But not until the bombing run did the Germans unleash two Gruppen of J.G.1 that had been sent to deal with the invaders. Wave after wave of Focke-Wulfs came head-on at the first combat wing boxes, then separated and in trail for bombing. An intense flak barrage, some half mile in depth, was thrown up over Bremen. Yet so determined were the enemy fighters to press home their attacks, that they

appeared to pay no heed to the barrage. The 91st and 306th managed to release their bombs with considerable accuracy, but such was the tenacity of the enemy attack that fifteen B-17s went down from this leading wing, mostly in the target area; another was lost to direct flak hits. The following, more compact, formations went unharmed. Six of the bombers lost were from the 91st, in fact its entire low squadron, the 401st, while the unhappy 306th, which had suffered badly earlier in the month, was decimated by the loss of ten of its 16 aircraft. Captain Youree's B-17F, severely hit by cannon fire, was brought home with parachute harness tied to severed control cables. It was a black day for Thurleigh. The loss of 16 B-17s was a 50% jump over any previous figure for one mission of VIII Bomber Command. Additionally, 48 B-17s were damaged to some degree.

Focke-Wulf Flugzeugbau had been hit by a good proportion of the 531 x 1000 lb bombs dropped and according to a German estimate half the factory was destroyed. However, FW190 assembly had stopped six months earlier under a production dispersal plan. Gunners returned claims for 63 fighters shot down which, although suspect, served to indicate the intensity of the battle. Post-war German records reveal ten Luftwaffe fighters as the maximum that could have justifiably been claimed.

The luckless 306th again sustained the major losses in a May Day mission to St Nazaire. First 7/10th cloud foiled the attack and limited the bombing attempts, then a navigational error by the 306th brought the Group's return course nearer the French coast than planned. Land sighted through the murk was assumed to be Land's End and the formation began to descend, to be greeted with well aimed flak from the Brest Peninsula.

A 423rd Squadron Fortress (42-29649), piloted by 1/Lt Lewis P. Johnson, received several hits, starting fires in both the tail wheel housing and radio compartment. The ball turret gunner, S/Sgt Maynard "Snuffy" Smith on his first mission,

Lt Bob McCullum (born in Scotland) was one of the men 'up front' in 42-29649 on 1 May 1943. Here he takes a look at the hole burnt through the side of the radio-room. This Fortress never flew again.— (IWM)

emerged from his turret as its power-operated rotating mechanism had ceased to function. Seeing the two waist gunners and the radio operator, all veterans of action over Europe, take to their parachutes he might have been expected to follow suit. What motivated him to stay in the apparently doomed plane is not clear. At the time there was no way of telling if the men forward were preparing to jump, for the raging fire in the radio room isolated them. Wrapping a sweater around his face to filter air in the acrid smoke, Smith fought the fire with a hand extinguisher. As the B-17 maintained formation, he assumed that there must be somebody in the cockpit. Momentarily turning attention to a minor fire in the rear, he found the tail gunner had not jumped with the other men and was lying badly wounded outside his compartment. After rendering first aid, Smith returned to fight the radio room fire. Focke-Wulfs were now attacking the formation and he occasionally fired the waist guns between fire-fighting and keeping an eye on the wounded gunner. Escaping oxygen fanned the flames to intense heat. Ammunition boxes stored near the radio began to explode and Smith heaved these through the gaping hole burnt in the fuselage side, or moved them away from the flames. For ninety minutes he fought the fires. Having used the last extinguisher he tried smothering the flames with clothing and, as a final gesture, urinated on the smouldering wreckage. Nearing the English coast, Smith threw out all items of equipment he could in order to lessen the strain on the rear of the fuselage. Fire had so weakened the structure there was a real danger that it might break up on landing. Fortunately the fuselage held when Johnson landed it safely at Predannack, near Land's End.

The fire had been so intense that some metal parts of the camera, radio and gun mounts had melted. The aircraft also had a damaged propeller and engine nacelle, its oxygen and inter-communication systems were wrecked, the top turret, nose, flaps and a wing fuel tank had been hit and damaged, and the tail wheel well had been burnt out.

A few weeks later, the slight, 32-year old ball turret gunner received his country's highest decoration for this action. The fuss attendant upon the award of the first Medal of Honor to a living member of the Eighth apparently had an adverse effect on Smith's conduct on the ground. Dubbed a "difficult character" he was taken off operations after four more missions and given a ground job. Regardless of any subsequent failings, "Snuffy" Smith's gallantry on his first mission undoubtedly saved the aircraft and possibly the lives of those with whom he flew. His feat is unique in the annals of Eighth Air Force history.

On May 4th 79 B-17s of the four groups set out for the Ford and General motor works at Antwerp, escorted by twelve squadrons of Allied fighters. That there were no losses, says much for the presence of the escort. Six squadrons were composed of the Eighth's new P-47 Thunderbolts flying their first combat escort. The raid was also significant in that it was to be the last occasion on which the 91st, 303rd, 305th and 306th had to "go it alone". The expansion programme at home was bringing forth reinforcements. In April, four new B-17 groups had arrived and the 92nd Group was now relieved of its training commitments to receive new crews and aircraft to resume combat. Additionally, another seven Fortress groups were scheduled to arrive within the next two months giving VIII Bomber Command four times its previous striking force.

The expansion heralded a new phase in which VIII Bomber Command expanded its sphere of operations. The past six months had been primarily a period of experimentation during which the feasibility of daylight precision bombing under the prevailing conditions had been proved. The contribution of the 50 to 120 Fortresses despatched on missions during these months of trial had little direct effect on the enemy's war effort, but was of paramount importance in determining what were to become Standing Operating Procedures in VIII Bomber Command. As for the bombing by the four pioneering groups, it was not until March that the Fortresses began to achieve telling results. Most missions had been against objectives connected with the anti-submarine campaign. Although bombing often appeared to cause extensive damage, and was at the time held responsible for some of the decline in U-boat activity, post-war studies have revealed that the Nazi-submarine campaign was hardly affected. For one thing, the Germans had built reinforced concrete shelters over U-boat docks, with roofing up to twelve feet thick, that could withstand hits from any bombs then in use by the Allies. Then, when B-17s and B-24s appeared on the scene, the Germans soon moved dockside plant essential to the repair and turnround of their submarines under the concrete pens. The most effective bombings had been against more vulnerable targets such as the rail yards at Rennes, the Renault motor factory in Paris and the Focke-Wulf factory at Bremen.

By January the Germans were well aware that they had underestimated the defences of the US bombers and their bombing techniques. The Luftwaffe felt confident that given time, they would be able to master the closely knit formations of Fortresses, inflicting such high losses that the campaign would be too costly for the Americans to continue. Over Bremen there had been signs that their confidence was not misplaced. When the Eighth began operations in the fall of 1942, the Luftwaffe had some 200 interceptors strung out along the coastal areas of occupied France, plus 60 in North-East Germany. By May preparations were in hand to double this number and anti-aircraft installations were being strengthened at many likely targets.

From the American side, the attrition presumed suffered by the Luftwaffe fighters in engagements with the Fortresses, added to their conviction of the success of the winter experiments. Even revised figures for the period allowed the four groups a total of nearly 450 enemy fighters destroyed in combat. Had the truth been known, that the Luftwaffe's losses were no more than 50, some of the enthusiasm in the Command would undoubtedly have been dampened. But however strong the opposition encountered, it was a fact that not once had a bomber mission been turned back by the enemy, although on some raids the small force engaged had sustained more than a 10% loss—the figure at which losses were considered prohibitive. The 91st, 303rd, 305th and 306th Groups had lost a total of 99 bombers, excluding four crashing in the UK, since their first missions, and over 100 others received some form of battle damage. The losses in B-17s amounted to two-thirds the strength in crews and aircraft that the four groups had originally brought to England. While many of the losses were replacement crews and planes, it nevertheless became evident to crews that their chances of survival were remote: one bomber lost for every 20 effective sorties, theoretically gave no man a chance of reaching the 25 missions usually demanded to complete a combat tour. In reality, some 25% survived their tours, which gave the surviving original crews from six to ten months of combat strain to endure. By the end of February 1943 most of the original crews were considered in need of replacement due to operational fatigue, known as "War Weariness": this was not possible without ceasing effective operations, due to the acute shortage of properly trained replacements. Prior to February losses had been three times in excess of replacement rate, only 20 new crews had been received in the Eighth to that date. Thereafter the position improved, but not until May and June were the original 1st Wing veterans retired.

Of the four groups, the 306th had suffered heaviest losses with 45 B-17s lost in action. Their 367th Bomb Sqdn., *The Clay Pigeons*, had created a record for losses while by some quirk of fate its sister squadron, the 369th, *Fitin' Bitin'*, had not lost a crew to the enemy since January. In the 91st their 401st Bomb Sqdn. had 115 men killed or missing yet had a strength

The men who commanded the four 'pioneer' groups listen to Group Captain H. Dawes as he reads the citations upon the award of British DFCs. L. to r. Brig Gen Frank Armstrong, Col Curtis LeMay, Col James Wallace, and Col Stanley Wray.

of only 90 aircrew upon commencing operations in November!

Nevertheless, morale was generally good, although the tensions that built up over a period of several months put these young men under considerable strain. To most, the uncertainty prior to a mission was the most unbearable part. One gunner claimed to have attended 65 briefings yet flown only 15 missions, due to operations being "scrubbed".

Under such circumstances command of a bomber unit was an exacting task. Apart from being administrator and combat leader, a group commander, in particular, became the figurehead of his base. At the time, security regulations forbade the mention of group designations. The extensive press organisation, eager to tell the American public of the exploits of their airmen over Germany, were able to circumvent the regulations by using the names of Commanders. Thus the 91st was alluded to as "the Wray Group", the 303rd as "Colonel Marion's outfit", and so on. As with all military organisations the Commanding Officer was responsible for the conduct of his unit. If he was considered lacking in some qualities, or earned the displeasure of his superiors, he was replaced; although this by no means meant he was a failure. Changes in command were often occasioned by the need for battle experienced officers in staff posts. Group commanders often flew on operations, usually picking the "toughest" missions. So far all had survived; but in the months ahead many groups would lose their commanders in combat. Two of the original leaders of the four pioneer groups remained by May 1943, Stanley Wray of the 91st and Curtiss LeMay the brilliant tactician of the 305th. Both were soon to be relieved and given higher command.

Publicity also focussed on particular aircraft, where nicknaming gave an individual identity, so that some B-17s became better known than their crews. The most renowned in the 91st was Captain Robert Morgan's *Memphis Belle,* subject of a colour film on the Eighth Air Force being made by a team under William Wyler (a distinguished post-war Hollywood producer). This aircraft had completed 23 sorties by the second May mission, more than any other in the Group and on many occasions had led both its group and squadron. *Invasion II,* captained by Captain Oscar O'Niel, had held the record for operations until it went down over Bremen in April; *Delta*

Rebel II was another with more than twenty missions. Other Bassingbourn bombers of repute were *Bad Penny, The Careful Virgin, The Eagle's Wrath, Jack the Ripper, Our Gang,* and *Quitcherbitchin.* In the 303rd at Molesworth, Captain Irl Baldwin's *Hell's Angels* had flown 24 missions without once having turned through any malfunctioning. Other famed Fortresses at Molesworth were *The Duchess,* in which Jack Mathis was killed, *Eight Ball, Jersey Bounce, Satan's Workshop, Yardbird* and *Thumper.* At Chelveston the B-17F with the most "hash marks" on its nose was *Wham Bam* with 20 missions. *Dry Martini 4th* flown by Captain Allen Martini and his "Cocktail Kids" (previous Dry Martini's had been well and truly shot up and retired), *Carter's Little Liver Pills* which could only be crewed by Captain J. W. Carter and "his little liver pills", *Sunrise Serenader, Boom Town* and *Lucky Strike,* all featured in memorable incidents. Another 305th Fort' that courted trouble was *Southern Comfort;* after her final brush with the enemy the crew were forced to abandon her over Essex. Twenty years later, gardeners at Great Totham were still digging up her fragments. The 306th had Captain Rip Riordan's *Wahoo II* with 20 missions to its credit; its predecessor *Wahoo* had been inspected by King George VI when he visited Thurleigh in December. This and *Nemesis, Joan of Arc, Geezil II* and *Piccadilly Commando* (there were several Fortresses of this last name) were of the fortunate 369th Squadron; some of its aircraft were transferred to make up deficiencies in the other squadrons, where they were lost, such as the famous *Banshee* piloted by "Wild Bill" Casey. *Impatient Virgin, Sweetpea, Chennault's Pappy* and *Little Audrey* were other B-17s that graced the hardstandings at Thurleigh. Nicknames were no longer confined to neat inscriptions only readable from a few yards; by the spring of 1943 many bombers had personal decorations that spread over most of their nose area. The preferred subject was the female form and the artistry in VIII Bomber Command was quite amazing.

For some of the surviving bombers of the veteran groups greater fame lay ahead. Many of the airmen who had flown and fought the early missions would come to command other units in the Eighth. New men would fill the ranks at the four stations. Yet the 91st, 303rd, 305th and 306th would always have a unique claim to pride of place—they were the pioneers.

Chapter 4: The "Circus" and the "Eightballs"

In the Eighth Air Force's early combat history, Liberators were in a minority whose exploits were frequently over-shadowed by those of the more numerous Fortresses. Even in later months when numbers equalised, the Liberator never quite achieved the same prominence as its team-mate. The Fortress was bestowed with a certain romanticism due to the very nature of its development as the prime weapon of Air Corps pre-war bombardment plans: the Liberator had no such background; neither could it compete visually with the gracious curvy lines of the refined Boeing. Characterised by two large vertical stabilisers and a deep slab-sided fuselage, it brought forth such derogatory sobriquets as "Pregnant Cow" or "Banana Boat" from the Fortress men. Liberator men retorted with "Glamour Girl" and "Medium Bomber" for the B-17; they did not themselves find their charges lacking in aesthetic qualities and were quick to point out the advantages of being able to fly faster, further and with a much heavier bomb load than the vaunted Fortress, facts that made the B-24 the most sought after aircraft on the American inventory by late 1942.

The first true Liberator group was the 44th which, having mastered the new bomber, was given the task of forming and training other groups. Its first offspring went to the Middle East, the second eventually found its way to the United Kingdom and the third was despatched to the Pacific. Thereafter the 44th was relieved of training duties and sent to England were its protégy, the 93rd, had already entered combat. Not until September 1943 were more Liberator bomber groups to join the 44th and 93rd in operations from the UK for others, originally scheduled to arrive earlier, were diverted to the Pacific fronts and a good proportion of new aircraft were diverted to an anti-submarine role.

In the early days, the two UK-based groups were as distant in their careers as in their fortunes. The 44th followed the Fortresses over Northern Europe and suffered severely, so that even the B-17 men referred to them as "the jinx B-24 outfit". Conversely, the 93rd had the lowest operational loss rate of all six groups in VIII Bomber Command. This group took its turn across the Channel, hunted U-boats in the Bay of Biscay, experimented with "blind bombing" techniques, and also 'wintered' in Africa. Diverse activities and locations earned the Group the title "Ted's Travelling Circus". The 44th dubbed itself "The Flying Eightballs" and was unique in the Eighth Air Force for a group design painted on the noses of its aircraft.

After an initial baptism of fire and loss over Lille on October 9th 1942, the 93rd fared comparatively well. Sent out on eight further occasions up to December, no B-24s were lost by enemy action although some of these missions were not without incident. Only small forces were despatched for on November 25th the Group's 330th Bomb Sqdn.was ordered to Holmsley South, Hampshire, for anti-submarine patrols under the direction of RAF Coastal Command. The 409th Bomb Sqdn. was similarly detached, but after aiding in the fruitless search for a 97th Group Fort that had disappeared while carrying Brigadier General Asa Duncan (the Eighth's first commander) to Africa, it was withdrawn from Holmsley South after a brief stay and returned to Alconbury. The 330th's task during the crucial stages of the North African landings was to assist in convoy protection and for a month their aircraft scanned the Bay of Biscay, in flights of up to twelve hours endurance. Although opportunities to attack enemy shipping did not

arise, sighting reports were sent in on a U-boat and five enemy surface vessels. Skirmishes with hostile aircraft occurred twice during November, the most spectacular on the 21st when a B-24 piloted by the Squadron Commander, Major Ramsey Potts, was confronted with five Ju 88s. It did not prove the easy kill the enemy apparently anticipated, for their somewhat clumsy approach resulted in two being shot down and a third damaged before the Liberator escaped. While no loss was sustained through enemy action on patrol work, one B-24 on a routine flight crashed at Porlock Bay, Somerset on October 30th, killing the crew.

During his first visits to Eighth AF stations on 14 Nov. 1942, King George VI met the crew of *Teggie Ann* at Alconbury. Here he talks to Cpt C. A. Culpepper. Behind him is Col 'Ted' Timberlake.—(USAF)

Although currently committed to training the air units for North Africa, the Eighth's 2nd Bombardment Wing, located in Norfolk, was selected to control all Liberator groups and early in November it was announced that the 93rd would soon transfer to this organisation. While still at Alconbury on November 13th, King George VI paid the first of his many visits to Eighth Air Force stations and Colonel Timberlake showed His Majesty around *Teggie Ann,* then regarded as the Group's "lead ship".

Two days after the 330th returned from Coastal Command, the 329th was packed off to Hardwick in Norfolk for special duties. The USAAF was 'extremely interested in the various British radio devices for bombing in overcast, and in October 1942 VIII Bomber Command came to an agreement whereby eight Liberators would be fitted with 'Gee' and trained in its use for bad weather intruder raids.

Gee was a navigational aid by which computations based on the time lag in signals received from two widely spaced transmitting stations, would give an exact position. Originally plans were to equip a squadron of the 44th Group but the final choice was the 93rd's 329th Bomb Sqdn., although crews were selected from all squadrons of the 93rd and placed in the 329th. After a week at Hardwick the Squadron began moving to the satellite field near Bungay and by December 16th was ready for individual intrusions, or "Moling" as it was termed. The chief object was to alert enemy raid warning systems to disrupt work in industrial areas. Because of the vulnerability of a single heavy bomber, times of maximum cloud cover were essential; added to this, British concern that the secret equipment might fall into enemy hands, made only bad weather conditions suitable for these sorties. Strangely enough, and to the amazement of the Americans who were convinced that the weather was never anything but bad, such conditions proved more difficult to find than a clear sky for a visual bombing!

The first Moling mission was on January 2nd 1943 when four Gee-equipped B-24Ds set out independently for various parts of the Ruhr, but as they neared their targets diminishing cloud forced them to return without bombing. Liberators of the 329th again set out from Bungay on January 11th and 13th in what seemed ideal Moling weather, but on both occasions conditions improved sufficiently to jeopardize their safety. Of four further attempts made up to March 28th, the few aircraft engaged had to return due to improved weather and lack of cloud, and thereafter Moling was abandoned. The project was not entirely barren for the squadron personnel had gained valuable experience in blind bombing, a technique entirely new to the USAAF, and in later months some of the men involved were taken to form the nucleus of a pathfinder unit charged with the use of radar devices.

The 329th had also engaged in normal day bombing towards the end of its "Moling" assignment. With secret equipment removed, a few B-24s joined those of the 44th Group on operations. The reason for teaming with this, and not its own

Group, was the absence of the three other squadrons, constituting the 93rd, overseas.

Early on December 5th, Colonel "Ted" Timberlake had received telephoned orders from General Eaker to take the air echelon of his Group—less the 329th—on a "ten day" detachment to North Africa, where long range bombers were urgently needed to disrupt Axis supply ports. The following morning 24 Liberators left Alconbury for Portreath, Cornwall, to refuel there for the long over-water flight to Oran. To service them a few ground crews were carried, while the rest of the ground echelon remained in England and began the move from the 1st Wing base at Alconbury to the 2nd Wing base at Hardwick.

Heading south at dawn on December 7th, the air echelon left England; but while the 328th and 409th Bomb Sqdns. reached Tafaroui airfield without incident, the 330th ran into difficulties. Three of its aircraft strayed off course and were fired at by batteries along the Spanish Moroccan coast; another crashed into a mountain south of Tafaroui with the loss of all aboard.

Africa, conjuring up visions of heat and sunshine brought disillusionment. Alconbury, their first English home had been found wanting, but at this North African airfield base facilities were non-existent, runways were dangerously short, and mud abounded. Three times missions were scheduled and then abandoned due to the persistent rain making taxying well nigh impossible. The XII Bomber Command, under whose orders the Group was flying, impatient to make use of the B-24s ordered a mission on December 12th in spite of Timberlake's view that conditions were still too dangerous to attempt take-off. Justification for the Colonel's views came when the nose wheel of Lt W. Williams' *Geronimo* collapsed and the aircraft buried its nose in the boggy ground. After this, the mission was cancelled.

Drying weather allowed the ground to harden and on the next two days missions were flown to Bizerte harbour, following which the Group was alerted to move. Though the "ten days" were nearly up, the course was further east, not west. At midnight on December 15th 1942, the Group took off and flew across enemy territory to LG 139, Gambut Main where IX Bomber Command held sway. Gambut in comparison

Geronimo with nose in the ground after the rains had passed, 14 Dec. 1942. The GI debate probably concerned how best to effect her removal but in any case she was condemned as salvage.—(USAF)

was dry, too dry; dust storms played havoc with engines and were a constant discomfort to the crews. Nevertheless, seven missions were flown against the enemy's North African ports and then, early in January, the 93rd joined with IX Bomber Command's own two B-24 groups in attacks to support the British Eighth Army, mainly by attacking Italian supply centres across the Mediterranean. Operations continued with a frequency never attained in England and when on February 18th orders were received to return, a total of 22 missions had been flown. A final attack on Cretone, Italy on February 22nd rounded off the 93rd's African Expedition and shortly thereafter the Group departed the Libyan wastes. One officer of Group Headquarters, Lt Col K. K. Compton, was left behind to command a IX Bomber Command group, the 376th.

During its African operations the 93rd had dropped 530 tons of bombs on enemy airfields, ports and shipping—sinking at least seven merchant vessels. The average time for these missions worked out at 9 hours, 38 minutes, the longest having been 11½ hours. The cost was five Liberators to flak and enemy fighters, while air gunners claimed ten enemy aircraft destroyed. There were some narrow escapes. Over Bizerte *Big Dealer* found the flak near to the St Nazaire standard and came back with 320 holes in her skin. *Shoot Luke,* with Captain John Murphy's crew, was heavily hit over Sousse on January 18th, but with flames streaming from an engine and seven wounded men on board she managed to make Malta—the first US Liberator to land on that beleagured Isle. All told, eight B-24s did not return from Africa, including one that encountered bad weather on the return trip and made an emergency landing in Spanish Morocco.

The "ten days" had grown into 81 days by the time the advance elements of the air echelon arrived back at Hardwick. Two weeks later all four squadrons of the Group were reunited and ready to resume work for VIII Bomber Command; participation in the famous Vegesack mission being first call. Near Heligoland the Liberators attracted the Luftwaffe's attention and one 93rd bomber went down.

Word of the return of the 93rd filtered through to news agencies and press men, sensing a bomber story with a different twist, made haste to Hardwick. *Stars and Stripes,* the US Forces newspaper, ran an article on "Ted's Travelling Circus" and *Yank* followed suit a few days later. This lauding met with cool comment at Shipdham, home of the Eighth's only other B-24 group. "The Flying Eightballs" were unconvinced that weathering the discomforts of the African desert was more worthy of publicity than enduring the bitter cold and superior opposition encountered at 20,000 feet over Northern Europe. During the three-month absence of the 93rd, the 44th Group had incurred the highest loss/sortie ratio in the Eighth with their 67th Bomb. Sqdn., all but annihilated in the course of a score of missions, yet for all the mention their efforts had received the Group might not have existed. The Press were interested in triumphs not tribulations. Already bitter that the Fortress men got practically all the credit, it was even more galling when the 93rd returned to so much acclaim. The 44th had little love for the Hardwick Liberators.

The 44th Group had experienced an unfortunate history. Depletion had started even before leaving the States when the fourth squadron was diverted to the Aleutians where further Japanese encroachment was feared. With no time to train a replacement before the move to England, Colonel Frank Robinson brought the remaining 27 B-24Ds of the air echelon across the Atlantic early in October. The one Liberator forced to turn back from the ocean flight earned the nickname *Lemon Drop* for its reluctance to leave America; however, in combat, this bomber was to endure long after her apparently more willing contemporaries had come to grief.

While the aircrews received theatre indoctrination, their aircraft were given the modifications deemed necessary for operations over Europe by engineers at Langford Lodge.

Shortages in staff and facilities curtailed work and six weeks passed before their Liberators were ready. Modifications included the installation of scanning windows in the nose compartment, fitting of British IFF equipment and alterations to defensive stations and armament, notably replacing by belt feed, the ammunition cans on hand-held guns. The cans, containing three dozen rounds, would have had to be changed in flight, whereas with belt feed several hundred rounds of automatic fire was possible. By the summer of 1943 the Langford Lodge list of possible B-24 major modifications had grown to 43, but in these early days a good deal of improvisation was carried out at Shipdham, an example being the fitting of two .50 guns on flexible mountings in the nose of some B-24Ds, much after the fashion of the installation on Fortresses.

On November 7th the Group was placed on limited combat status and eight aircraft were despatched on a diversion flight while other bombers of the Command went to Cape de la Hague. General Hodges, commanding the 2nd Bombardment Wing, went along on what was also his own formation's first operation. On return, his Liberator, lost in cloud became separated from the rest and put down on the partly completed Great Ashfield airfield in Suffolk.

An even smaller force from the 44th joined the 93rd in bombing St Nazaire two days later and from this, and three non-bombing missions later in the month, the "Flying Eightballs" were much troubled by frostbite; flying clothes were not adequate for the freezing conditions of high altitude winter flying.

By early December the 67th Bomb Sqdn., whose aircraft were the last to return from modification, was ready for action, and on the 6th the first full Group mission was flown from Shipdham. Nineteen B-24s set off to bomb Abbeville/Drucat as a diversion; but as they neared the enemy coast a recall signal was sent out. This was received by the 66th and 67th Bomb Sqdns. who returned, but the six aircraft of the 68th continued. Soon after bombing, they were attacked by some thirty FW190s; every B-24 was hit and one, piloted by Lt Dubard, went down in flames over the Channel. A 20-mm cannon shell exploded in the cockpit of another, wounding both pilots and the first DFC for the Group went to Lt W. T. Holmes for successfully landing this Liberator, though badly injured in the head and shoulders.

The loss of their first aircraft and crew had a sobering effect. Like their fellows in other Eighth Air Force units the young men of the 44th could not then comprehend the magnitude of VIII Bomber Command's objective, nor that they were very much "guinea pigs" in its attainment. Many were, for some unfathomable reason, convinced that their unit would return to America after a few missions.

After an abortive attempt to hit Abbeville/Drucat again, the Shipdham Liberators followed the Fortresses to Romilly-sur-Seine a few days later. For his leadership of the Group on this mission, 66th Bomb Sqdn's commander, Major Algene Key, later received the DSC. Key was an aviator of repute, having helped set a world endurance record in 1935 with a flight of 653 hours, 34 minutes. All the B-24s returned from Romilly, but a direct shell hit killed a crewman and wounded two others.

Abortives in this raid were high, for only 12 of the 21 Liberators despatched actually bombed. Equipment failure due to freezing conditions was the major reason for early returns—as with the Fortresses. Another not infrequent cause was supercharger failure at high altitude. This was eventually traced to improper relation of supercharger settings to throttle openings and not to a mechanical breakdown.

Learning by experience was the way of things at this time and the ordered chain of command of military establishment became less evident in these circumstances. Colonels sought the views of 2nd Lieutenants on tactical problems which "the book'' did not mention, let alone provide a ruling. Indeed, military manuals had little bearing on life or operations undertaken by the Eighth at this time.

The 44th Group had only the brief experience of the 93rd Group to aid it in the many aspects of combat flying with the B-24 and when the 93rd departed for North Africa the three squadrons at Shipdham, each with nine aircraft, constituted the entire B-24 force in Europe for normal daylight bombing. The operational employment of this small number of Liberators in conjunction with Fortresses posed many problems, due mainly to the differing performance of the two aircraft. As a result of the high aspect Davis wing the B-24's optimum cruising speed was some 20 mph faster than the B-17's with similar loadings at 20,000 feet, thus creating difficulties in maintaining station in related formations. The Liberator was the more difficult of the two types to fly in formation due to its higher wing loading, and not being a very stable aircraft was prone to fall away violently in propeller wash. The Fortress in comparison could attain a more closely knit formation; and it was found expedient to place the Liberators at the rear of the bomber stream and at a slightly different altitude. Nevertheless, Liberator groups did remarkably well considering that their aircraft were, relatively, very heavy on the controls, and kept the tight formation so imperative to ensure adequate defensive fire. In the Eighth, a group came to be judged by the formation it kept.

To alleviate some of the disparities the 44th's Liberators had restricted fuel loads, considered ample for the task, when they set out for St Nazaire on January 3rd. By the time the Brest peninsula was crossed only eight aircraft remained, others having been forced to return early. Surviving the flak barrage at the target, these B-24s followed a Fortress group on the return course which took them out over the Atlantic, to give a wide berth to enemy fighters. Unfortunately, the B-17 group proved to be off course, for the south-western coast of England failed to appear through the growing haze at the scheduled time. After a while, land was faintly discerned to the east and the Liberator men now realised they had missed Land's End and were flying up the Irish Sea.

Fuel supplies did not allow for a navigational error of such magnitude and tanks were very low. The 44th turned east, and in deteriorating weather and gathering darkness the formation split up to seek the sparsely situated airfields along the Pembrokeshire coast. A few aircraft were successful but others searched in vain until fuel exhaustion forced them into wheels-up landings in pastures. *Texan* of the 67th Bomb Sqdn. piloted by Lt R. Long, found Talbenny airfield only to have its last engine fail just prior to touch-down, the machine was wrecked in the ensuing crash and the crew were lucky to escape without major injury. Not so fortunate were two others completely wrecked when what appeared to be small hedges turned out to be lichened stone walls, resulting in three men being killed and others injured. Censure from above on these tragedies, partly due to fuel shortages, took the familiar form —a new Commanding Officer. Colonel Leon Johnson, one of the original staff officers of the Eighth Air Force, found that his new command did not readily warm towards him, particularly as his predecessor had been a popular man.

After another trip to the submarine pens in France, the 44th was alerted for a maximum effort to Germany. While the Fortresses made for Vegesack, 27 B-24s were briefed to hit Wilhelmshaven; it so transpired, that it was the Fortresses that bombed Wilhelmshaven while the Liberators found only trouble. Through a combination of bad weather and poor navigation they blundered over Friesland, unable to locate their target; Unfortunately the Luftwaffe located the 44th. In the ensuing battle one B-24 was shot down over Terschelling while a FW190, hit by defensive fire from the formation, crashed into another bomber bringing both down. The 44th's gunners despatched another fighter which was literally shot

When General George Stratemeyer, Arnold's Chief of Air Staff, visited Alconbury he was taken out to see *Suzy Q.* Here he talks with Leon Johnson, Howard Moore and Lt R. I. Brown.—(USAF)

to Hell—crashing in a Dutch village of that name! Next day the British and American press devoted much space to the Eighth's first mission to Germany; there was hardly a mention of the Liberators' part in taking much of the opposition from the Fortresses. Spirits ran low at Shipdham.

Scrubbed missions punctuated the early weeks of February, then on the 15th a maximum effort was ordered for an attack on the German raider *Tojo*, reported in dock at Dunkirk. Led by the 67th Bomb Sqdn. under its commander, Major D. W. MacDonald, 22 B-24s crossed the English coast at 15.30 hrs and began a long straight run in towards Dunkirk to ensure accuracy. At 15.40 hrs bombs were dropped as soon as the leader's release was observed and simultaneously the formation became blanketed by flak. 2/Lt W. Cameron, co-pilot in *Little Beaver*, watching the lead aircraft, wrote, ''Suddenly and without warning the entire nose section of Major MacDonald's bomber disappeared, the bombardier and navigator with it. The skeleton fragments of the metal ribs which framed the plexiglass windows of the nose compartment remained and these, protruding forward from the cockpit area, seemed ringed with fire. I could scarcely credit my eyes. The cockpit, however appeared intact. For long moments we were confronted with the spectacle of a noseless B-24 leading us forward towards Dunkirk. Then it slowly rolled off and down to our right. The two inboard engines were also crippled and going into a steep dive the right wing came off, followed by an explosion.'' Debris struck a bomber following but this made a crash landing on Sandwich Flats at the English coast without hurt to the crew.

Flak also hit another aircraft of the squadron which was finished off by fighters. The German anti-aircraft gunners were probably alerted by an RAF Boston raid, earlier in the day, and no doubt used the formation's long, straight-in, bomb run to make accurate computations of height and speed with telling results. Worse still, the *Tojo* survived.

Next day Colonel Johnson mustered enough B-24s to follow the B-17s to St Nazaire. On this mission a temporary loss of control by the pilots of one Liberator, resulted in collison with an aircraft below; after exploding, the remains of the two B-24s fell through a Fortress formation below.

Ten days later, on a mission to Wilhelmshaven the 44th fell foul of Messerschmitts of J.G.1 and two more B-24s were lost. In some quarters there was reference to ''that hard luck group'' and speculation as to whether the Liberator was good enough for the European Theatre. True, there were indications that the B-24 was more susceptible to superficial damage and appeared to have a greater fire hazard than the B-17, but for the most part their misfortunes could be put down to in-experience and disparity in numbers. Fortress men chided: "The B-24s are our best escort. When they're along Jerry leaves us alone". This grim jest had a ring of truth, particularly after March 8th when sixteen B-24s were despatched to bomb the Rouen railyards while the main force of B-17s made a successful attack on Rennes. Several squadrons of RAF Spitfires plus two of the 4th Group were to provide escort for the Liberators all the way in and to the 44th it looked like a "milk run". The Luftwaffe's tactics, however, made a rout of the mission. While the B-24s droned towards Rouen, a force from J.G.26 deliberately engaged the escort; with the Spitfires thus embroiled, a Gruppe of FW190s went for the bombers on their target run. The B-24 crews had assumed the specks in the sky ahead to be part of their escort, but within a few seconds these became enemy fighters swiftly approaching with guns flashing. In that single head-on pass the Focke-Wulfs shot down two bombers, one being Captain Price's lead aircraft which plunged in flames shortly before bomb release. Disrupted by the absence of both leader and his No. 2, bombs were scattered far and wide, some ten to fifteen miles from the target as the 44th turned for home in defeat. Both losses were from the ill-fated 67th Bomb Sqdn. whose original complement of nine crews and aircraft were now reduced to three of each; five had been lost in action, one destroyed in a crash, and one crew had been broken up through illness. Not a single replacement in men or machines had been received. Of seven American Press correspondents allowed to fly on this mission, only the *New York Times* representative who alone chose to fly with the Liberators, failed to return.

When on March 18th the 67th's new commander, Major Moore, set off in *Suzy Q* to lead the 44th to Vegesack, the accompanying 93rd Group made it the largest B-24 force thus far despatched. Trailing some 2,000 feet below the B-17s, they again proved a greater attraction for the enemy but the only B-24 lost that day was from the 93rd, although the Shipdham Group came in for strong fighter attacks and the gunners on *Suzy Q* claimed six destroyed. The opposition was even stronger on March 22nd. Colonel "Ted" Timberlake in *Teggie Ann* had a 20-mm cannon shell shatter his plexiglass window and miss his head by barely six inches. While fate

was kind to the 93rd's commander, it was not to the 44th's unfortunate 67th Bomb. Sqdn., for near Wilhelmshaven flak claimed another of its bombers leaving only two of the originals—Major Moore and his *Suzy Q* and 1/Lt Phillips with *Little Beaver*. But at long last replacements were forthcoming and a new squadron, the 506th, arrived at Shipdham to give the Group its full complement of four squadrons.

A mission to Paris early in April brought more trouble to *Suzy Q*, for on return her nose wheel collapsed while taxiing to dispersal. She had sustained more battle damage than any other bomber at Shipdham, making her skin a mass of patches. This battered veteran, much in need of a complete overhaul, was flown to Langford Lodge after temporary repairs.

During April the 44th engaged chiefly in rebuilding its depleted ranks; a dozen new B-24s arrived but trained crews were virtually unobtainable. In an effort to remedy the situation, experienced co-pilots were elevated to first pilots and given new crews. The bottom of the replacement crew barrel having long ago been scraped bare, "new crews" were formed in a most unorthodox manner. They included Americans transferred from the RAF, "rejects" from B-17 units, while a number of the Group's ground crew were sent to train as air gunners. Even so, there were more aircraft than crews for a while.

From the outset, with only small numbers of Liberators available, Eaker had endeavoured to use these to meet the demands of other agencies so as not to impair the efforts of the Fortresses. After ocean patrol work and the African episode came a plan for them to join with RAF Coastal Command in an all-out attack on German naval forces operating along the Norwegian coast. Then, at the end of April, the 2nd Bombardment Wing was directed to prepare for night operations. The 44th had sustained further losses by the enemy and the 93rd was also reduced to a low operational state and perhaps because of this, and the 329th Squadron's experience in blind flying, this Group was selected for night missions. A dual day and night role was impracticable by virtue of the specialist equipment and modifications required. One technicality was the need for exhaust flame dampers and the effect on performance was such that they would be unsuitable for operations by day alongside others not so equipped. Thus, on May

Special jack-trolleys and stands were required to position bombs under the low bomb bay of a Liberator. These ordnance men are moving 1,000 pounders at Shipdham, Nov. 1942.—(USAF)

A strike photo taken by a 306th BG Fortress far above, shows six B-24s of the beleaguered 44th BG over Kiel. Variation in camouflage blotching can be clearly seen.—(USAF)

3rd, the 93rd was withdrawn from operations to train for the new assignment. For the time being, policy decreed that the 44th would remain on combat status to undertake diversion missions for VIII Bomber Command, and when opportunity allowed to train in night flying. Once again the "Flying Eightballs' were to "go it alone"—and the mission of May 14th was in no way a diversion.

The Force had not hauled incendiary bombs to enemy targets since late the previous year. Now the strategists wished to reintroduce the weapon, planning to add them to 300 tons of high explosive earmarked for Kiel shipyards. A complete group was to be loaded with incendiaries and the choice fell upon the 44th's Liberators and thus 19 B-24s of the 66th, 67th and 506th Bomb Sqdns. followed in the wake of over a hundred 1st Bombardment Wing Fortresses.

Fighter attacks commenced at the enemy coast and were concentrated on the exposed 44th, flying below the low group of the second combat wing. The shorter trajectory of incendiaries meant holding the bomb run for some two miles after the B-17s had released, as well as opening formation to avoid incendiaries from the leading bombers striking those following. By the time the release point was reached, five of the B-24s had been shot down; another was lost on the return journey. The effective bombing of Kiel did little to alleviate the blow to the 44th.

Bringing up the rear of the formation had been three B-24s of the 67th; none returned. One was flown by the only replacement crew, another by the late co-pilot of *Suzy Q* with her usual crew, and the third was Lt Phillip's *Little Beaver.* The only crew left to the squadron was that recently formed for Lt Cameron after he vacated the co-pilot's seat of *Little Beaver.* Major Moore and Lt Cameron had just returned from three days leave as the aircraft set out. They found that all that was left of 90 airmen that came to Shipdham seven months before were a few stragglers from other crews who had been indisposed or on leave when their planes were lost. Of the nine original B-24Ds only *Suzy Q*, reposing at Langford Lodge, remained. The 67th Bomb Sqdn. had been all but annihilated by its operations.

The 44th Group arrived at Shipdham with 27 aircraft. The tally after Kiel was 20 lost in action and 7 aircraft written off

in crashes or scrapped as beyond repair; in comparison the 93rd Group had 10 missing in action and 8 lost by other causes. Besides men lost on operations or killed in crashes, several others had been wounded, yet in spite of this attrition a fair morale was sustained. The airmen accepted that nothing could be done about the situation and realised that the chances of survival were slim, yet their attitude to life was far from one of hopelessness. Some did break down, became ill, or even refused to fly, but they were very few. The 44th's esprit de corps was partly sustained through acrimony: bitterness towards the B-17 groups and the 93rd who eclipsed them in the public eye; bitterness towards their Command whom they believed used them as a bait to draw the Luftwaffe from the Forts and towards those who said the "Flying Eightballs" were a jinx unit.

A week after the 93rd had been taken off operations for night training, revised plans allowed part of the Group to return to combat and bolster the 44th on diversion missions. The Kiel battle was only 48 hours old when all combat-worthy Liberators from the two groups were secretly flown to Davidstowe Moor in Cornwall. The following morning, May 17th, twenty-one 44th Group and eighteen 93rd Group B-24s were despatched to bomb Bordeaux while the B-17s hammered Atlantic U-boat bases. A 700 mile course, mostly at 2,500 feet, was planned to keep the Liberators beyond the range of coastal detection in an endeavour to obtain surprise. Aborts were to be expected and four bombers had turned back by the time the groups began the climb to bombing altitude.

Leading the 44th was none other than the rejuvenated *Suzy Q,* piloted by her own Major Moore with Colonel Johnson in the co-pilot's seat and General Hodges on board as an observer. In spite of four new engines *Suzy Q* could not maintain the required speed, one engine failing during the climb and in consequence the formation began to lag. To meet this situation Lt "Mike" Mikolowski set a new course inside the curve of the original. The Group had not hitherto been renowned for its standard of navigation, but on this occasion the skill of the lead navigator was evident in that the Group arrived at 22,000 feet over Bordeaux almost exactly at the briefed time. Bombardier Jim DeVinney made an accurate bomb release and the resultant damage from the Group's pattern was the best work of the day. Harbour lock gates were shattered and extensive damage created in the port area. A few bursts of anti-aircraft fire and a single hostile fighter was the only opposition encountered. One B-24, developing serious mechanical trouble just short of the target, limped to neutral Spain. A waist gunner was the only casualty of the mission when, somehow, his parachute released in the fuselage and the slipstream drew him out of a waist window.

This raid was followed by another success without loss to La Pallice docks on May 29th, following which the "Travelling Circus" and "Flying Eightballs" were mysteriously taken off operations. Then, much to the delight of small boys and to the misfortune of farm animals, high altitude Liberator bombers were seen skipping across the East Anglian landscape as low as 150 feet during the warm June days—and then they disappeared from their East Anglian airfields. Around the Fortress bases it was rumoured that "top brass" had finally realised that the B-24 was no match for the flak and fighters of the enemy and had sent them to a less demanding battle front. In truth, the Liberators were destined for one of the most important and heavily defended targets in Europe.

The Circus on a practise mission over England in May 1943.—(USAF)

Chapter 5: Fledgeling Fighters

When the last of the four fighter groups committed to accompany the Twelfth Air Force to North Africa were taken off operations on October 26th 1942, the only fighter group remaining under VIII Fighter Command on a permanent basis was the 4th at Debden. But even the proud "Eagles" had not gone untouched by the demands of TORCH (Allied code name for North African invasions) and personnel had been transferred to raise the experience level of the other Spitfire-equipped American fighter groups.

The VIII Fighter Command intended to use the 4th as the nucleus for rebuilding fighter strength. The planned establishment of the Command was fifteen groups in three wings, although it was generally rumoured at Bushey Hall that it would eventually be in the region of 26 groups. For the immediate future it appeared that the demands of the North African venture would allow little headway to be made in establishing this force, moreover, the initial successes of the Eighth's heavy bombers in penetrating the enemy's defences with only a 3% loss, lent weight to a belief in some quarters that daylight bombardment missions could continue without fighter escort.

The 4th was still very much the "Eagle Squadrons" in spite of American uniforms and the star insignia on their aircraft. RAF personnel still remained at Debden, chiefly to help the American ground crews become proficient in maintaining the Spitfire VBs. The gradual, but inevitable, replacement of RAF trained pilots by those from the States would tend to mellow the British influence in the 4th. The Group was, however, tenaciously proud of its early associations and throughout the war, long after the original members had departed home or been lost in action, it clung to things that would mark its genesis and distinguish it from the Eighth's other fighter groups. There was no modesty with the 4th; they were the first of the Americans to fly against the Luftwaffe and they did not let VIII Fighter Command forget it. They objected loudly to many of the moves that threatened their heritage with an impertinence that did not endear them to some of the regular Army officers faced with the task of administration. The most bitter blow to their morale was the news that their beloved Spitfires were to be replaced by a new American fighter. So far as they were concerned there just wasn't an American fighter!

The 36 Spitfires that the 4th could muster for action continued under the operational control of the RAF sector, and operations for this small force were planned in conjunction with RAF Fighter Command. Wing Commander Duke-Woolley continued as flying leader until relieved by Major Chesley G. Peterson, a famous commander of 71st Eagle Squadron, who had just spent some weeks in the US with the AAF's Material Planning Council. During the winter of 1942-1943, rarely did the Debden Spitfires fly support missions to the Eighth Air Force heavies: more often they escorted RAF Bostons or accompanied British Spitfire squadrons on cross-Channel sweeps.

The first examples of the new American fighter for VIII Fighter Command arrived in Britain as deck cargo on December 20th 1942, and by Christmas Eve that organisation possessed one Republic P-47C Thunderbolt. Compared with other single-engined contemporaries, the Thunderbolt was massive and at nearly 15,000 lbs gross it was far more than twice the weight of a Spitfire or Me109. In fact it looked more like a dive bomber than a fighter. Power was provided by a 2,000 hp radial engine fitted with turbo-supercharging for maximum performance at high altitude. Armament consisted of eight fixed .50 machine guns in the wings compared to the Spitfire's eight .303s. Hitherto, a weakness of American fighters had been an inability to fight at altitude and the P-47 seemed to be a step in the right direction. It was, however, a new and untried design, with no performance data on the model supplied.

To remedy the lack of data, General Hunter called on Cass Hough to conduct flight tests: the results showed the aircraft's inclination to dive very fast, but it needed coaxing to climb. On February 27th Hough dived a P-47C from 39,000 to 18,000 ft reaching speeds equal to those attained with his P-38F.

The first P-47 arriving at Debden in January 1943, met with a determined bunch of critics. Its size and weight engendered the most caustic comments from pilots of the sleek Spitfire. The blunt nose, housing the air-cooled radial engine, gave a fuselage shape which its beholders likened to a milk bottle. Thus to the men of the 4th the P-47 had little to commend it. They conceded points to the widely spaced undercarriage legs and the roomy cockpit, but to do battle in this monstrosity, passed off as a fighter, was considered suicidal. The quip that pilots were to be ruthlessly sacrificed, produced another name for the Thunderbolt—'Juggernaut', soon to be shortened to 'Jug' which became the colloquial term for this Republic fighter.

As with the P-38F, so with the P-47C, it was pitted against the RAF's captured FW190A. At high altitude the Thunderbolt acquitted itself well, but below 15,000 feet the Focke-Wulf showed better acceleration suggesting that the Thunderbolt would be at a disadvantage if involved in a dog-fight at low altitude. The FW190's rate of climb was superior although the

Lt Col Chesley Peterson was rescued from the Channel twice by Walruses of RAF's 276 Sqdn. Here he hands a $100 cheque, subscribed by Eighth AF personnel for the Squadron's comforts funds, to Wing Co R. C. Wilkinson. Col Peterson is receiving a model Walrus from Wing Co Anthony Linney, as the Squadron thought he would be safer to carry one all the time. The lady is Mrs. Peterson.—(USAF)

Thunderbolt's performance could be improved if its diving momentum was used prior to a climb. The outcome of the comparison can be summed up as—Above 20,000 feet, maybe; below 15,000 feet, never!

On January 11th, the personnel of the 56th Fighter Group disembarked from the *Queen Elizabeth* at Gourock, Scotland. The 56th, formed two years previously, had received in June 1942 the first production Thunderbolts—P-47Bs—to come from Republic's Long Island factory. The exigencies of war precluded a long development period prior to quantity production and the 56th's job amounted to one of 'bug finding' and the Thunderbolt had its share with 190 unsatisfactory reports submitted. Most serious of all, sharp manoeuvres resulted in the buckling of tail control surfaces, sometimes causing part of the tail to break away; the substitution of metal for fabric covering on elevators and rudder cured this. Its weight proved too great for the main tyres causing a number of bursts on take-off and landing—tyres with rayon weave and increased plies solved this trouble.

The accident rate was high with a number of fatalities and there might have been more, but for the rugged construction of the aircraft. In many crash landings, completely wrecking the aircraft, pilots were able to walk away shaken but unharmed. This was largely due to the depth of fuselage where the pilot sat, above ducting connecting engine and supercharger. In a severe belly landing this ducting, and not the pilot's legs as in many other fighters, took the force of the impact.

In spite of losses and malfunctioning the men of the 56th grew to like the Thunderbolt and few had qualms about taking it into action when they arrived in England. But then they were an elite unit, with many pilots who were among those selected pre-war when there was intense competition to enter the AAF and only the best were selected. Furthermore, they had the advantages of the thorough pre-war training.

To lead the first Thunderbolts the 28-year old Major Hubert Zemke was selected. Commissioned in 1937, his ability as a pilot coupled with a ready appreciation of technical and tactical problems led to his being sent to England to demonstrate the Curtiss P-40 Tomahawk and study British methods. In June 1941 he went to Russia to supervise the assembly and testing of these Tomahawks when the British decided to pass them on. Prior to leading the 56th, Zemke had trained Chinese pilots in handling the P-40—mostly with the aid of sign language!

A month before the arrival of the 56th, VIII Fighter Command had received another P-38F Lightning group, the 78th, and installed it at Goxhill for theatre indoctrination. The P-38s were shipped over and assembled at Speke, with the intention that the Group should have its full quota by mid-January and begin working up for its operational debut the following month. However, by this time the losses and unserviceability among P-38s sent to North Africa were so great that General Arnold ordered the aircraft and most of the pilots of the 78th to Africa as replacements. The P-38 was a complicated aircraft to build and production was unable to meet both the demands of attrition and equipment for new units.

Since it appeared that the Eighth heavy bomber campaign could progress without prohibitive losses, Arnold gave other theatres of war call upon the P-38s during the early months of 1943. As for the 78th, they received Thunderbolts and pilots trained in their use, in lieu. Only fifteen of the original pilots remained after the exodus of the P-38s. These included the Commanding Officer, Lt Col Arman Peterson, his deputies, the three squadron commanders, operations officers, and flight leaders. Peterson, a most capable officer, had moulded the raw 78th into a most promising outfit; P-38 training had progressed well and in January some of the aircraft had gone to Chelveston to practise escorting with the B-17s of 305th Group. He and his staff were understandably bitter at the loss of their air echelon

and the necessity to commence training a fresh set of pilots in theatre procedures. The P-47 was considered a poor substitute for the P-38: one officer commented that it was like changing from 'thoroughbreds to plough horses'. Ground crews of the 78th Group, however, soon found maintenance of the P-47 somewhat less arduous than with the P-38.

The VIII Fighter Command planned to have the first P-47 group, the 4th, operational by March 1st, the 56th a fortnight later and the 78th before the end of the month. While pilot training was a regulating factor, it was soon apparent that the P-47C still had teething troubles. Nevertheless, after modifications to radios and other equipment it was decided to attempt operations and fourteen of the 4th's Thunderbolts left on a sweep off Walcheren on March 10th.

Led by the Group's flying executive, Lt Col Chesley Peterson, with Colonel Anderson flying as his wingman, the 4th Group took off from Debden, climbing for altitude over the Essex countryside. At over 30,000 feet and with battle speed the 2,000 hp engines caused radio interference to such a degree that inter-communication was virtually impossible. The pilots, already apprehensive of duelling with FW190s in their heavy mounts, grew even more uneasy—fortunately the enemy were not encountered.

Although VIII Fighter Command had become used to Debden complaining about the P-47, it was obvious that it could not be sent into combat while the radio trouble persisted. Both American and British experts worked on the problem but a month passed before the Thunderbolts were again operational. The source of the interference was magnetos, generators and sparking plugs. An immediate remedy was largely the idea of Major Charles E. Lee of Air Service Command. Utilising the simple principle of basic electricity to suppress the noise, he installed brass rings in the distributors to give a perfect bonding between the distributor and the metal casing enclosing sparking plug leads. Engine troubles, particularly with the turbo-supercharger, persisted, but this did not restrict operations.

Deficiencies in gunnery training were apparent and during March elements of the three groups were sent to RAF ranges for air-to-air firing. Some members of the 56th were uneasy about the possibility of having inadvertently despatched the target-towing Lysander that did not return to base after a sortie from Llanbedr on March 27th. Those pilots of the 78th who had flown the nose-armed P-38, were faced with the more complicated gunnery problems that came with wing guns.

Prior to their operational debut the 56th and 78th were moved south to airfields in East Anglia, nearer to their operating area. The RAF had earmarked well-drained grass surfaced airfields for US fighter units. A number of these were pre-war stations with good facilities and had centrally heated, brick built barracks. Both groups found themselves at stations comparable to the "Eagle's nest" at Debden. The 78th left "Goat Hill" (Goxhill) for "The Duckpond" (Duxford) on April 3rd and two days later the 56th began moving into Horsham St Faith.

By the first week of April all three fighter groups had sufficient modified P-47s and qualified pilots to commence initial operations. On April 1st the 4th Group flew fourteen sorties with Spitfires on coastal patrol and then paid the valiant little fighter a reluctant goodbye—it would appear that they were allowed to retain one machine as a 'hack', Command evidently pandering to their vanity. Since their first mission as the 4th Fighter Group on October 2nd 1942 the "Eagles" had run up a score of $11\frac{1}{2}$ enemy aircraft destroyed and two probables, for five Spitfires missing in action.

The great day was April 8th. In all, 24 P-47s were scheduled to take off from Debden for a sweep over the Pas de Calais at 30,000 ft. The experienced 4th Group led the aircraft that finally flew out over the English coast including flights of both

The 4th FG sets off with its 'flying milk bottles' to sweep the Dutch coast, May 1943. Taking-off in pairs (SOP) are aircraft of 336th FS while in the foreground 335th FS awaits its turn.—(USAF)

the 56th and 78th. There was no sign of flak or enemy aircraft and all machines returned safely. Not until the 13th were the P-47s sent out in force again; then shortly after noon, three squadrons totalling 36 P-47s were airborne. One squadron of the 78th (composed of the 82nd and 83rd Ftr. Sqdns. pilots) led by Lt Col Arman Peterson, joined two squadrons of the 4th and proceeded to sweep over inland to St Omer. Once again there were no signs that they were over enemy occupied territory as the Americans cautiously edged in at 30,000 ft. The flight was not without incident, for over the French coast the Thunderbolt piloted by Lt Col Joseph E. Dickman, the 78th's Executive Officer, suffered engine failure. Forced to bale out, Dickman landed in the sea some twelve miles north-east of Calais but was quickly picked up by the RAF Air Sea Rescue service.

These first missions were intended chiefly to give group, squadron, and flight commanders experience. Four members of the 56th with their aircraft were despatched to Debden and flew with the 4th Group. A second force was despatched in the evening along a similar route. This time twelve aircraft from each group made up the formation that assembled over Debden. Zemke and the other 56th pilots at Debden took off to link up with eight P-47s that had come from Horsham St Faith. The 78th Group flew its 82nd Squadron. Zemke was forced to turn back with oxygen regulator trouble and his deputy, Major David Schilling, commanding the 62nd Ftr. Sqdn. took over. Once again the enemy failed to put in an appearance though he did give many of the P-47 pilots their first view of flak bursts. Near Dunkirk, on withdrawal, the engine of a 56th aircraft failed. The pilot, Captain Dyar of the 63rd Ftr. Sqdn., turned out of formation in an attempt to glide across the Channel and successfully 'bellied in' near Deal. A British anti-aircraft battery apparently mistook the P-47 for a hit-and-run Focke-Wulf and assumed that the few rounds they unleashed were responsible for the resulting crash-landing—which happily they were not. Each of these sweeps had been in company with a strong force of RAF Spitfires, that for some weeks would sally forth in support of the largely inexperienced Americans.

Two days later the Thunderbolts were out again; 12 aircraft from the 4th and 24 each from the 56th and 78th, and this time the Luftwaffe rose to the challenge. It was an evening mission with the sun in a favourable position for the P-47s. Shortly after crossing the enemy coast the force was warned by ground. VHF control to look out for hostile aircraft coming from the east. Soon, the 56th were startled to see a large formation heading from that direction. They immediately manoeuvred but confusion arose and squadrons became separated. The approaching formation, however, had the white recognition bands of Thunderbolts and turned out to be from the 4th and 78th. Ten of the 4th Group aircraft heading the sweep that day (two had been forced to return early) were led by Major Donald Blakeslee, an old hand at air fighting, formerly with No. 133 (Eagle) Squadron RAF and now in command of the 335th Ftr. Sqdn. USAAF. Blakeslee spotted three FW190s flying about 10,000 feet below him and took his flight down to attack. He opened fire and followed one aircraft as it dived away. Overhauling the Focke-Wulf, Blakeslee got in a finishing burst to send it out of control into the outskirts of Ostend. Meanwhile the rest of the 4th's formation had been involved in combat with other FW190s resulting in claims of two more destroyed while one P-47 had been shot down. Unhappily two other Thunderbolts failed to return to base; engine failure was the cause.

The fact that they could claim three victories (one was later assessed as a 'probable') did little to pacify the "Eagle's" uneasiness about their aircraft. It was often quoted in Eighth Air Force fighter circles that after this mission Blakeslee had countered a congratulatory remark about catching his quarry in a dive, by observing that the P-47 ought to dive since it certainly couldn't climb. The pilots had to concede that the P-47 showed promise in turning and top speed, particularly as the combat had ranged far below the altitude at which it was considered advantageous for it to fight. The occasion marred chiefly by the loss of two aircraft through engine failure, was probably due to blown cylinder heads resulting from too high a manifold boost and incorrect manipulation, necessitating modifications to the turbo-superchargers and the fitting of inter-connected controls. The fault was not easily traced or rectified and engine failure dogged P-47 operations for many weeks to come.

Five further fighter sweeps were carried out during April and the last of these, on the 29th, saw the three groups operating three 12-plane squadrons each. The 4th and 78th returned without encountering the enemy but the Luftwaffe sprang a trap for the 56th. The 61st Ftr. Sqdn. was then flying top cover for the 62nd and 63rd which were at 28,000 ft. Having penetrated to Woensdretch and turned north, two

Staffeln of FW190 dived on the two lower squadrons which turned to meet them. During the ensuing melee one P-47 was shot down and another so badly damaged that the pilot had to abandon it at the Dutch coast. Major Schilling, leading the group, called on the top cover for help but in vain as his radio was not functioning properly above 20,000 ft. Two for nothing—in the enemy's favour—was not a very auspicious beginning to the 56th's contact with the Luftwaffe.

Allied fighter sweeps were primarily intended to provoke the German fighters into combat, but the enemy had no intention of being drawn, preferring to conserve his forces for intercepting American day bomber raids. The Luftwaffe generally ignored the frequent Allied fighter incursions over the Pas de Calais and Low Countries, rarely intercepting unless in a favourable position. Nevertheless, it was not always possible for their warning system to distinguish between impending bomber or fighter raids, a predicament the Allies exploited to advantage. The German Air Force was still confident that the daylight Fortress raids could be made too costly for the Americans to continue and to this end the reinforcement of Jagdgeschwadern in the West was under way. The total strength of J.G.1, J.G.2, and J.G.26 was approximately 350 Me109 and FW190 in January 1943. By June the figure was nearly 600, largely achieved by transferring Gruppen from the Eastern and Mediterranean Fronts.

The Thunderbolts first escort mission was flown on May 4th when the 4th and 56th Groups accompanied B-17s attacking Antwerp, while the 78th flew with a diversionary force feinting towards Paris. So far as bomber protection went the Antwerp raid was a success for all the B-17s returned safely and the only P-47 lost, a 4th Group machine, was apparently another victim of engine failure. The 4th and 56th Groups both made contact with the enemy and Lt George Carpenter of the former's 336th Ftr. Sqdn. shot down an FW190.

It proved another unhappy day for the 56th on withdrawal support. Near Walcheren what was taken to be an Me109 was attacked and shot down. The victim later proved to have been an RAF Spitfire but in fairness it must be recorded that units had not been briefed to expect any likelihood of Spitfires in the area. Aircraft recognition was, however, a subject in which many American pilots were sadly lacking at this time.

The 78th's 48 P-47s, now with sufficient aircraft to enable each squadron to fly four four-plane flights returned to Duxford without incident. P-47 squadrons had commenced operations with an average assigned strength of 18 aircraft each but by mid-May this had been raised to 25. It soon became standard operational procedure for a group to despatch three squadrons of 16 fighters each, although the actual number crossing the enemy coast would vary depending on 'early returns' due to mechanical or other trouble.

The next combat with the Luftwaffe came on May 14th when 118 P-47s gave general support to another B-17 raid on Antwerp. Led by the recently promoted Colonel Arman Peterson, the 78th Group had its first action when about twenty red-nosed FW190s were encountered at between 20,000 and 24,000 feet in the vicinity of the bomber's target. The Germans had the better of the battle and three P-47s went down for two FW190s. Major James Stone, commanding the 83rd Ftr. Sqdn., claimed one of the Focke-Wulfs, and the other victory was credited to one of his flight leaders, Captain Charles London. On the following day's sweep, the same group lost a pilot who was forced to bale out over the Channel when his Thunderbolt's engine cut. A sweep on the 16th gave Colonel Petersen his first victory when the 78th Group met the Luftwaffe for the third day running.

Almost daily activity by the Thunderbolts continued throughout May, but the enemy usually failed to be drawn unless bombers participated. In the first two months of operations 2,279 individual sorties were flown by the Eighth's Thunderbolts during which they were credited with the destruction of 10 enemy fighters, the probable destruction of 7, and 18 assessed as damaged. Against this 18 P-47s were 'missing in action' though at least 5 were known to have been the victims of engine failure. The victories were divided between the 4th and 78th, the groups who had been least enthusiastic about the Thunderbolt, while its advocates, the 56th, had nothing to show for their loss of 3 P-47s but some inconclusive combats and the unfortunate incidents involving their Allies. That Zemke's group had the poorest showing could be put down in part to ill luck and inexperience. Fighter pilots were not made in a day, and while the Americans were eager to do battle, eagerness was no substitute for experience.

By June contact with the Luftwaffe averaged about once in every five missions. Sweeps were usually uneventful but on June 12th two sweeps did bring actions. On the first the 78th fought Focke Wulfs and made claims of 3-0-2 for the loss of two while on the second, Captain Walter V. Cook of the 62nd Ftr. Sqdn. shot down an FW190 to give the 56th Group its first confirmed victory. It seemed things were looking up for the Zemke Group for on the morrow it despatched three more 190s and damaged others without loss to itself. At 09.00 hrs the Group had commenced take-off from Horsham St Faith for a sweep over Gravelines, Bailleul, Aeltre and Knocke. East of Bruges at 27,000 ft some twenty FW190s were sighted 7,000 ft below and climbing north west from the direction of Ypres. Colonel Zemke, leading the 56th, immediately took the seven P-47s, constituting the first section of the 61st Ftr. Sqdn., into a dive to attack a four-plane flight of the enemy. The Colonel approaching the rearmost No. 4 enemy aircraft apparently undetected from astern, started firing at 200 yds range and a second later the Focke-Wulf burst into flames. He then opened fire on the No. 3 in the formation and noted strikes on a wingtip. The surprised German immediately dived away placing Zemke directly astern of the next man in the enemy formation. Another burst exploded this aircraft. Meanwhile 1/Lt Joe Curtis fired at another FW190, damaging it and 2/Lt Robert S. Johnson of the 61st, who had spotted the German fighters at the same time as Zemke, took it upon himself to break away from his flight and dive upon the leader of the enemy formation. For breaking one of the cardinal rules of air discipline Johnson was severely reprimanded on return, but the fact that the enemy plane had been destroyed undoubtedly tempered Zemke's wrath.

On June 22nd the three groups were despatched to give support to B-17s attacking Antwerp, a satisfactory mission resulting in the 4th and 78th claiming 7 enemy fighters with no loss to themselves. Captain E. D. Beatie of the 4th emulated Zemke's earlier action by destroying two.

That the German fighter units were generally well trained and able to inflict severe punishment on pilots still relatively new to air combat was demonstrated on June 26th. In the evening the 56th was giving withdrawal support for B-17s bombing Villacoublay. Using Manston as a forward base to increase their range, the 49 P-47s took-off at 18.12 hrs. Contact was made with the bombers near Forges where they were under attack from a strong force of fighters. During the ensuing battle that raged half-way across the Channel the Group managed to shoot down two Focke-Wulfs. But it was a badly trounced 56th that returned. Four Thunderbolts were missing—believed shot down, another was so crippled it was abandoned over the sea, four were badly damaged and two had minor damage.

The Johnsons of the Group, unrelated but both of the 61st Ftr. Sqdn., were featured prominently in the day's incidents. One of the enemy became the first victory of Gerald Johnson and 2/Lt Robert Johnson, who had jumped formation to destroy a Focke-Wulf earlier that month, very nearly fell victim to a distinguished German pilot. With his aircraft badly shot up and difficult to fly, Johnson was being followed home

Gerald Johnson's P-47D was 'bought' with bonds by the people of Jackson County. It proved a good investment. 56th FG.

by an FW190 which luckily for him had exhausted its cannon ammunition, and could only pepper Johnson's HV-P (appropriately named 'All Hell') with the remaining machine gun ammunition. When this was exhausted, the enemy pilot flew along-side and judged that the ailing Thunderbolt would be unlikely to make the English coast. A somewhat shaken Johnson was able to bring his aircraft safely down at Manston. Later it is said, an enemy radio station broadcast an interview with Oberst Egon Mayer of J.G.2, who told how he shot down three P-47s on the Villacoublay raid, including one marked HV-P! 1/Lt Ralph Johnson was also attacked and his aircraft too, returned in an extremely battered condition. Only one undercarriage leg would come down and once down remained jammed in that position. Johnson flew on to his home base at Horsham St Faith where Colonel Zemke took-off to make an aerial inspection of the cripple and radio suggestions to Johnson on various manoeuvres that might shake down the other leg. It proved impossible and as a crash-landing would be suicidal with part of the undercarriage in the down position, Johnson was ordered to fly out to sea and parachute down. The Air Sea Rescue service was alerted and retrieved Johnson from the sea just north of Yarmouth.

During a dog fight over Schouwen, Holland on July 1st, the 78th claimed a 4 for 1 victory, but that one was the P-47 flown by Colonel Arman Peterson, the Group's popular commander who went down with his fighter near Ouddorp. At the time the 78th had the best record of the three P-47 "outfits" and this was undoubtedly due to his endeavours. It

Ground men listen to a radio relay of Lt Ralph Johnson's conversation with the Horsham St. Faith's control prior to baling out.—(USAF)

was also the 78th that fought the Luftwaffe on the next occasion Thunderbolts and Focke-Wulfs clashed. While escorting Fortresses attacking Amiens/Glisy airfield, a 3 for 3 engagement resulted. Lt August DeGenaro, wounded in this action and with his aircraft damaged and losing altitude, prepared to crash-land at the English coast, but his landfall was over the town of Newhaven. Unable to nurse his stricken machine clear of the town he turned back over the sea and baled out. Happily a fishing boat was at hand to rescue this wounded 82nd Ftr. Sqdn. pilot, who later received the DSC for his consideration in directing his aircraft out to sea rather than risk it falling on a populated area.

The Thunderbolt had acquitted itself well during the first three months of combat but VIII Fighter Command was only just beginning to get the best out of their weapon. In battle, the P-47 proved at least equal to the Focke-Wulfs and Messerschmitts and though the scores stood about even there were occasions when the Thunderbolt had proved very much the victor. US fighter tacticians soon appreciated that the P-47 could not only outdive both the Me109G and FW190A, but could usually overhaul them in level flight. It seemed well able to turn with the enemy at altitudes above 15,000 feet and a superior rate of roll allowed it to execute escape manoeuvres that the enemy fighters could rarely follow. The weight which gave the Thunderbolt high speed in a dive could also

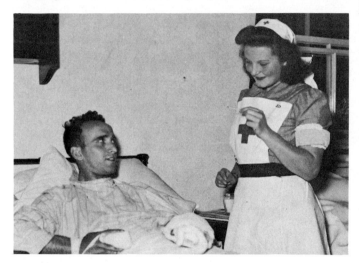

Lt DeGenaro about to have his temperature taken by Nurse Alex Wolfe-Barry. After seeing this picture members of DeGenaro's squadron voted Newhaven the place they would most like to bail out over.—(USAF)

compensate for the poor rate of climb in the hands of a skilful pilot using diving momentum to augment a climb. The armament of eight .50 machine guns appeared to offer far superior fire-power to that of the German fighters. Firing 800 rounds per minute per gun, a well-aimed burst, lasting a fraction of a second, was often sufficient to have a crippling effect on an enemy machine. Incendiary, tracer, and armour-piercing ammunition was included in the 425 rounds maximum carried for each gun. Poor acceleration, the Thunderbolt's chief weakness, had the attention of Republic's engineers. The 2,000 hp Pratt & Whitney engine was extremely thirsty and the 305 gallons of fuel carried in the fuselage tanks of the P-47C were consumed on a combat mission at the average rate of approximately 100 gallons per hour. This gave a radius of action of about 175 to 190 miles varying with the type of mission flown. This contrasts with the Spitfire IXs 100 gallons used at a rate of approximately 45 gallons per hour and giving a combat radius of 150 miles, extended to 180 with the use of a jettisonable auxiliary fuel tank.

The first examples of a new Thunderbolt model, the P-47D, had been assigned to the squadrons early in May. This differed

A 4th FG P-47C tries its paces against an RAF captured FW 190A.—
(USAF)

from the C model in only minor respects and was identical in appearance.

Once again, taking a lead from the RAF, VIII Fighter Command set out to analyse almost every aspect of its operations. These enquiries played a considerable part in improving equipment, tactics, and the ability of the P-47 pilot to vanquish his foe. The urgency of getting the P-47 operational had seen the majority of pilots enter combat with insufficient gunnery practise, which had some bearing on the fact that during the first months of combat two thirds of the enemy aircraft attacked escaped without damage. By a careful analysis of pilot's reports, the films of combat from cameras that functioned when guns were fired, and the counts of ammunition expended, VIII FC statisticians were able to establish that pilots were generally underestimating the range of an enemy aircraft when firing. Frequently, the enemy fighter was twice as far ahead as the pilot estimated, opening fire at between 400-600 yds believing their adversary to be only 300 yds away. In consequence much ammunition was wasted while the range was closed. A victory was usually assured with a well-aimed, one-second burst at 250 yards.

Control procedures, battle formations, and the basic tactics of the Thunderbolt groups were largely inherited from the RAF. But, performances of different fighter types varied and in the light of comparisons, VIII Fighter Command had to decide how best to use the P-47 to advantage. For escort, the procedure evolved of flying the three squadrons of a group above the bombers with the centre squadron 2-3,000 ft above the others which in turn flew 3-4,000 ft higher than the bombers. The centre and highest squadron acted as 'top cover' protection for the lower squadrons whose job it was to intercept enemy fighters making for the bombers. In this event, the German fighters had to pass below the P-47s and the American fighters were in a position to make fast diving attacks on the enemy and then climb back to the safety of their own formations. The Luftwaffe was, therefore, faced with running the gauntlet of the escort unless it chose to engage this first, which it rarely did.

Hard pressed though the Luftwaffe fighter arm was, in the early summer of 1943, it possessed the strength to deal severely with the fledgling American fighter groups. Rather than take direct action while the Americans were "green", they chose to concentrate their forces and use their ingenuity against the bombers; seldom did they make deliberate efforts to engage the American escorts. Often they withheld their assaults until fuel limitations caused the P-47s to turn back and then they concentrated on the bombers. The result was that the American fighter pilots gained both confidence and experience, and in the P-47 they had an aircraft capable of operating at higher altitudes than the Spitfire Vs of which the Luftwaffe had the measure. Some brilliant air leaders were emerging whose ideas on team-work and tactics were shaping the future of VIII Fighter Command. Equally significant, were the technical improvements that were taking place. The Luftwaffe fighters, instead of tackling the issue at the outset, allowed themselves to be steadily out-paced.

Chapter 6: Second Wind

Ira Eaker recorded that May 13th 1943 was a great day for the Eighth Air Force. With the English spring had come more drab shaded American war planes to perch on the many new airfields carved from the green landscape of East Anglia. Judged ready for the fray, the six new bombardment groups doubled the strength of VIII Bomber Command overnight. Five groups were equipped with the B-17F Fortress, the other with the B-26B Marauder medium bomber. Technically, one of the Fortress groups was not new to combat, though the level of aircrew experience was such that it could be considered so; this was the rejuvenated 92nd Group that had served as the Eighth's bomber OTU throughout the winter months. Early in January the 92nd had moved to Alconbury leaving its 326th Bomb Sqdn. as the main flying element at the Bovingdon CCRC. Depleted in personnel and with only a few obsolescent B-17Es to fly, the Group was unable to assume a combat guise until the influx of fresh crews and aircraft towards the end of April. During the inactive period many of the remaining crews were taken to fill the gaps in combat units and two were lost in action. When returned to operational status the 92nd was only at half strength as a bombardment organisation with a score of B-17Fs in two squadrons. The third squadron at Alconbury, the 327th, was equipped with twelve YB-40s a secret, experimental version of the Fortress, intended for a formation defence role.

The plan to adapt heavy bombers as destroyer escorts that could fly in exposed position formations had been effected during the late summer of 1942. Both B-17 and B-24 versions were originally called for but only the former was taken beyond the prototype stage. Vega Aircraft Corporation did the initial work and in August 1942 converted a B-17F into the XB-40. After satisfactory preliminary tests, thirteen experimental models were ordered between November and March. These Vega-built B-17Fs were turned into YB-40s at the Douglas modification centre at Tulsa, by installing two additional power turrets, one amidships over the radio room and the other, a neat, remotely controlled installation, under the nose, and gun positions in waist windows. These gave the aircraft a total of fourteen .50 machine guns against nine for the standard B-17F.

On the YB-40 a prodigious amount of ammunition (some 12,400 rounds) was allowed for and much armour plate added at crew stations. Their crews were trained under 4 officers and 9 enlisted men detailed from the Eighth Air Force.

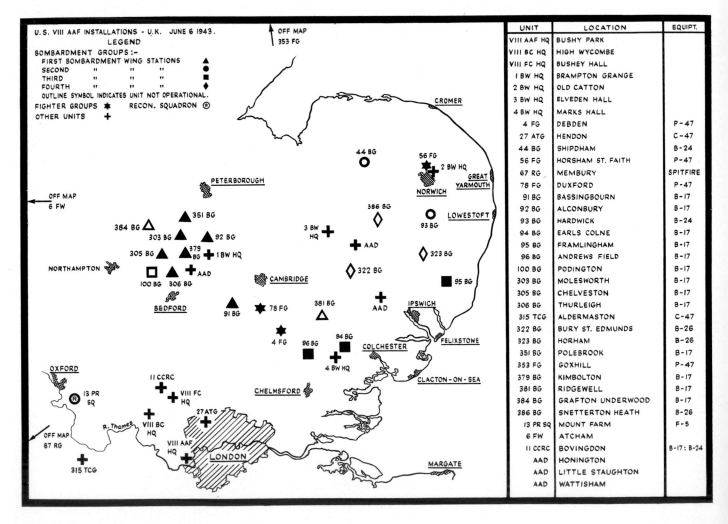

UNIT	LOCATION	EQUIPT.
VIII AAF HQ	BUSHY PARK	
VIII BC HQ	HIGH WYCOMBE	
VIII FC HQ	BUSHEY HALL	
I BW HQ	BRAMPTON GRANGE	
2 BW HQ	OLD CATTON	
3 BW HQ	ELVEDEN HALL	
4 BW HQ	MARKS HALL	
4 FG	DEBDEN	P-47
27 ATG	HENDON	C-47
44 BG	SHIPDHAM	B-24
56 FG	HORSHAM ST. FAITH	P-47
67 RG	MEMBURY	SPITFIRE
78 FG	DUXFORD	P-47
91 BG	BASSINGBOURN	B-17
92 BG	ALCONBURY	B-17
93 BG	HARDWICK	B-24
94 BG	EARLS COLNE	B-17
95 BG	FRAMLINGHAM	B-17
96 BG	ANDREWS FIELD	B-17
100 BG	PODINGTON	B-17
303 BG	MOLESWORTH	B-17
305 BG	CHELVESTON	B-17
306 BG	THURLEIGH	B-17
315 TCG	ALDERMASTON	C-47
322 BG	BURY ST. EDMUNDS	B-26
323 BG	HORHAM	B-26
351 BG	POLEBROOK	B-17
353 FG	GOXHILL	P-47
379 BG	KIMBOLTON	B-17
381 BG	RIDGEWELL	B-17
384 BG	GRAFTON UNDERWOOD	B-17
386 BG	SNETTERTON HEATH	B-26
13 PR SQ	MOUNT FARM	F-5
6 FW	ATCHAM	
II CCRC	BOVINGDON	B-17: B-24
AAD	HONINGTON	
AAD	LITTLE STAUGHTON	
AAD	WATTISHAM	

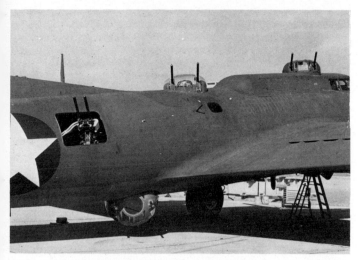

Twin-gun installations on the YB-40 could bring heavy fire to meet a beam attack, but in practise this was of little value as the majority of fighter passes were at the tail or nose areas.—(Lockheed)

That the crews of the 92nd's 327th Bomb Sqdn. came to be chosen to test the YB-40 in battle, was not by chance. Late the previous year some highly ingenious surgery was carried out on one of Bovingdon's ailing B-17Es. Eventually 41-9112 appeared with large B-24 type power-operated turrets in nose and tail. The displaced bomb aimer had a special "bath tub" housing beneath the nose. While not a pretty sight and lacking in speed, 41-9112 offered some practical ideas on what could be achieved to improve firepower. As it happened, this monster came to be the perfect blind for the YB-40s by being mistaken for such on its frequent trips around UK airfields. The moving force behind this conversion was apparently Major Robert Reed of the 327th. His enterprise reportedly earned him an advisory job on the YB-40. He was followed to the States by another 92nd Group officer, Major Robert B. Keck, who took command of the thirteen aircraft and their crews.

In the first week of May, Keck brought his charge to Britain across the North Atlantic, but YB-40 42-5732, somehow went off course on the last leg from Iceland and as fuel tanks ran dry her pilot elected to make a wheels up landing on what turned out to be a peat bog. By May 8th, Keck's aircraft had reached Alconbury and, although secreted away in a far corner of the field, became a source of curiosity. At that time, in addition to the 92nd, Alconbury held the air echelon of the 95th Group, first of the "new" groups to arrive from the US. Its ground echelon, delayed in America, through shipping shortages, eventually reached the UK two days before the aircrews commenced operations. Other bombardment groups were similarly affected, the aircraft and crews flying over were preceding ground personnel by about a month.

B-17Fs of the 96th Group came into Grafton Underwood

YB-40 UX: O lands at Alconbury. Despite the second upper turret the censor identified the aircraft as a B-17. The picture was released for publication when the YB-40 was still secret but apparently was never used.—(USAF)

on April 14th. A few days later Fortresses of the 351st and 94th Groups put down on airfields in the 1st Wing area. Training facilities at Bovingdon were overwhelmed and the four novices had to be aided by the "pioneer" groups where possible. Group and squadron commanders obtained their first taste of combat flying introductory missions with the 1st Wing veterans.

The newcomers came in war-winning, perhaps over-confident mood. Although the enemy's calibre was never underrated during Stateside training, personnel were apt to be influenced by sources, such as the US press, which presented a somewhat inflated picture of Eighth Air Force successes. The veterans of the winter experiment were wont to curb their exuberance. The arrival of the new groups also coincided with a stiffening of Luftwaffe opposition and heavier losses.

There was no long period of kindergarten missions for the 94th, 95th, 96th and 351st. Suitable weather dictated the numbers to be despatched for any mission. In any case the standard of training in the new groups was superior to that of the units who had arrived the previous autumn. Gunnery, navigation and pilotage were good, and crews were already versed in many techniques that the veterans had been forced to work out for themselves. Tight formations were flown—in some cases too tight for flight safety; circling for landing at Polebrook on May 6th, a B-17 hit turbulence, lost control and struck another Fortress. Parts of the falling wreckage brought down a third aircraft. A tragic prelude to operations.

With the prospect of further new Fortress groups in the next two months, Eaker instituted another wing headquarters, the 4th, initially embracing the 94th, 95th and 96th Groups. All three had late production B-17Fs with 'Tokyo tanks', additional fuel cells near the wing tips providing for another 1080 gallons, adding considerably to their range. The new Wing, commanded by Brigadier General Fred L. Anderson, was established at an old Elizabethan mansion, Marks Hall, near Colchester; a district where several new airfields were nearing completion.

For its combat initiation the 4th Wing was sent on May 13th to the long-suffering airfields at St Omer. The three groups despatched 72 B-17s. Bombing by 31 aircraft of the 94th and 95th added more pock marks to the flying field. The 96th Group, late in assembly, did not complete the mission; one of their Fortresses getting into trouble on the way out ditched in the Channel, but the crew were saved. The following day while General Anderson led the 94th and 95th to Antwerp, the 96th joined the 1st Wing's untutored 351st in bombing Courtrai airfield. At the time the bombing by these novices was considered fairly ineffective. Later it came to light that the attack caused such damage to facilities that the tenants, III/J.G.26 were forced to move elsewhere.

Meanwhile the veterans of 1st Wing, having battled with the Luftwaffe over Meaulte the previous day, went to Kiel for the first time in the longest and farthest mission so far. The 92nd Group re-entered the arena on this occasion with a meagre force of seven, one of which failed to return. Bombing at Kiel created extensive damage to shipyards.

May 14th, 1943 was a milestone for the Eighth. For the first time over 200 heavies were despatched and the debut of the B-26 Marauder brought total VIII Bomber Command sorties to 236. Another notable occurrence that day was the completion of 25 missions by the Molesworth Fortress *Hells Angels*. Not once had it had to turn back due to mechanical failure and only one bullet hole and a few flak patches bore witness to its hours in hostile skies.

There were now sufficient bombers to attack a number of widely spaced targets in one day, timed to cause the maximum confusion to the German defences. The duration of the enemy fighters, up to 90 minutes dependent on model and auxiliary tankage, was a prime consideration in planning routes and timing operations. Penetration routes were frequently planned to conceal the ultimate destination from the enemy for as long as possible. In this way a proportion of his fighter force might be reserved for fear of another attack in another sector. Feints and diversions played a big part in the scheme of things: a successful ruse could save bombers and thereby lives.

On May 15th, for the third day running, the Eighth used its new-found strength. The new groups graduated to accompanying the veterans to Germany. The 4th Wing went to Emden but a cloud carpet, offering few gaps for sighting, brought erratic bombing. Colonel "Dinty" Moore's 94th Group trailed the formation with the first loads of incendiary bombs that Fortresses had carried since the previous autumn. A 95th Group aircraft, disintegrating from a direct flak hit, was the only loss from the 59 bombing. The 1st Wing had been briefed for Wilhelmshaven, but finding unbroken cloud the Fortresses turned for targets of opportunity at Heligoland, Dune and Wangeroog Island. Here III/J.G.54 fell upon them and a vicious air battle ensued and five of their B-17s did not return, but the enemy lost at least 8 Me109s.

The 365th Bomb. Sqdn., 305th Group, included a B-17F 42-29673 nicknamed *Old Bill* in honour of the famous cartoon character of World War I trenches created by Bruce Bairnsfather, the British artist who currently contributed cartoons to the US Army newspaper *Stars and Stripes*. This aircraft returned from Heligoland bearing witness of the severest battering a Chelveston aircraft had received and survived. The Luftwaffe had commenced a series of head-on passes at the 305th, as it prepared to unload over Heligoland. In *Old Bill* oxygen lines were hit and shell fragments entered pilot 1/Lt William Whitson's leg. Co-pilot 2/Lt Harry L. Holt, without oxygen, took over while Whitson went aft to fetch emergency bottles. Holt was almost unconscious when the pilot returned. Revived, he took over the controls again to allow the pilot to have his wounds dressed. Cannon fire from a subsequent attack shattered the plexiglass nose and

The face of Captain Bruce Bairnsfather, who created the famous Great War character *Old Bill*, shows solemn mood after he surveyed the damage to Watson's aircraft. Ground men working on wrecked nose have covered damaged bomb sight with coat. The Norden was still secret at that date.—(USAF)

mortally wounded navigator 2/Lt Douglas Venable, manning the nose guns, while Bombardier 1/Lt Robert W. Barrall, partly shielded by the bomb-sight, suffered minor injury. Cannon shells also struck the top turret, leaving gunner Albert Haymon bleeding profusely from a head wound and damaging the operating mechanism. Haymon continued to operate the turret by hand cranking until it jammed. Cannon fire again found its mark in a further head-on fighter pass and Bombardier Barrall, manning the nose cheek guns, was again wounded. Then a 20-mm shell, exploding against the pilot's window, greviously wounded Harry Holt. Despite their wounds, Haymon and Barrall took turns at the controls while pilot and co-pilot were given first aid. The rear of the aircraft had also been riddled with bullets and shrapnel, particularly the radio compartment where the operator, Sgt Fred Bewak, received wounds. Left waist gunner Homer Ramsey had also been hit, but was able to give first aid to the radio man. Only two of the eleven on board (a photographer was present) were unharmed, the tail and right waist gunners.

With a 200 mph slipstream coming through the open nose, a buckled right wing and defunct hydraulics, *Old Bill* struggled back to Chelveston where emergency systems enabled the gallant crew to make a successful wheels down landing without brakes or flaps. The crew later became the most decorated in the 305th. Whitson and Barrall collected DSCs for their part; eight Silver Stars and seven Purple Hearts also went to the crew for this action.

Following a day's respite, VIII Bomber Command despatched 159 bombers to the French Atlantic coast where 2nd Wing Liberators made a spectacular attack on Bordeaux, while the two Fortress wings hit Lorient. First Wing aircraft were briefed to hit the Karoman submarine shelters, where three B-17s from the leading 305th Group were lost to enemy fighters. Once again a head-on attack was met during the bomb run. Fifteen minutes later the 4th Wing bombed the port area and U-boat basin, gaining hits on the power house. Flak and the Luftwaffe accounted for another two B-17s. The bomber in which 95th's Commander flew was crippled, but limped to an emergency landing at Exeter. Crews of the 94th Group reported one of the intercepting FW190s as painted yellow/gold all over.

A day of inaction and then 123 B-17s flew north east to U-boat yards at the other extremity of the Nazi's western seaboard. The 4th Wing went to Flensburg where 55 bombers performed their most acurate work to date and returned without loss. The brunt of the enemy defence was delivered, as expected, against 1st Wing's return from Kiel. The 305th Group's penchant for accurate bombing resulted in its spearheading the mission with Lt Col De Russy as air commander. Again the lead group came in for chief attention and lost four of the six bombers failing to return from this wing. The 1st Wing's freshman 351st Group now regularly accompanied its more experienced associates, on this occasion being led by its Commander, Colonel Hatcher, flying in the pilot's seat of 1/Lt W. E. Peters' *Snowball*, a Fortress from Major Clinton Ball's 511th Bomb Sqdn. It was, incidentally, this squadron commander's name that inspired a naming series for the unit's Fortresses— *Cannon Ball, Screwball, Speedball, Highball, Spitball, Foulball* and *Spareball*. The Major's bomber was *Linda Ball*, after his baby daughter. The "Ball Boys" seemed to roll into more trouble than the other three Squadrons of the 351st. 2/Lt Meli's *Spareball* went first, going down over Holland on May 15th. On this second Kiel raid *Fireball* at 26,000 ft had the oxygen supply hit and rendered inoperative. In the confusion one crew member baled out, releasing his parachute too quickly so that it fouled the rear fuselage door. At lower altitude other crew men tried unsuccessfully to haul the half-opened 'chute and trailing airman back into the bomber. The slipstream was too strong and not until *Fireball* reached the Norfolk coast were they able to retrieve the gunner

Major Ball waves from the cockpit of *Linda Ball*.

who was found to be dead. 2/Lt W. R. Smith brought the plane down at Sculthorpe.

On May 21st 1/Lt Donald Norris's *Foulball* was in trouble. Her ball-turret gunner, S/Sgt Hoy Embree later received the DSC for his conduct that day when the Luftwaffe took the main honours. Their persistent frontal attacks upon leading groups during the target leg paid off. The 1st Wing, with the 91st Group leading had gone to Wilhelmshaven while 4th Wing made for nearby Emden where it had fruitlessly visited 6 days previous. At both targets the German fighter controller was able to muster a Gruppe of fighters as the leading elements of the bomber formations neared the IP. Sections of 4 or 8 FW190s kept up frontal passes through the Fortresses and so disrupted the formations that bombing was erratic. At Emden the target was completely missed when the 96th Group received the strongest opposition from fighters it had so far encountered. The Group's gunners received credit for 15 of the 21 fighters claimed by the Wing. Five 4th Wing and seven 1st Wing B-17s were lost. One of the latter was 306th Group's *La Mersa Lass* piloted by 1/Lt Robert H. Smith. Seven gunners on this lady were credited with shooting down 11 fighters, a record surpassing that of *Dry Martini 4th* crew in April. *La Mersa Lass* was ditched in the North Sea and their crew rescued by an RAF launch. On this day the first definite reports of enemy fighters launching air-to-air rocket projectiles was received from the Wilhelmshaven force, although no damage was reported by this means. The Germans had already attempted to break up B-17 formations from beyond the range of defensive fire by air-to-air bombing and other devices, the air launched rockets looked like the answer to their quest once greater accuracy was achieved. Nevertheless, this new threat was of some concern, albeit a development anticipated by the Eighth's technical advisers.

Not only battle took its toll; at approximately 20.30 hrs on May 27th the Huntingdonshire countryside was rocked by a shattering explosion. At Alconbury a rising column of smoke marked the spot where 18 men were killed, and 21 seriously (one of whom died) and 14 slightly injured when several 500 lbs of bombs had inexplicably detonated. At the dispersal area allotted to the lodging 95th Group, ground personnel were loading 500 lb bombs into Fortress 42-29685 in preparation for the morrow. In a flash, a relatively peaceful

scene transformed into one of carnage and destruction. Four B-17s were completely wrecked and eleven others damaged. This accident dealt the freshman 95th Group a blow heavier than it had received in any of its six missions against the enemy.

Two days after the Alconbury tragedy weather conditions, which had brought a lull in the offensive, improved sufficiently for the Eighth to despatch a record 279 bombers—1st Wing to St Nazaire and La Pallice and 4th Wing to Rennes marshalling yard. the 4th Wing's mission was to inflict disorder upon the important rail centre serving the Atlantic coast U-boat ports, where earlier damage wrought by the Eighth's bombers had been repaired. Primarily a diversion force preceding the 1st Wing, its 72 Fortresses were to be escorted in by two P-47 groups, and another P-47 group with ten Spitfire squadrons were to cover their withdrawal. But the wily Luftwaffe fighter controller kept his interceptors away from the Allied fighters. When fuel shortage forced the P-47s to turn for home, Me109s and FW190s cruising in the vicinity, succoured by auxiliary fuel tanks, were brought into action. In a series of brief but vicious attacks, direct hits on a 95th Group squadron commander's Fortress caused it to loop uncontrolled into collision with another aircraft of the formation. The 94th Group, taking the heaviest onslaught, had three of its bombers shot down. Again this Group's gunners reported an all-yellow FW190 prominent in the battle. All told, six Fortresses were lost before Spitfires arrived upon the scene. Neither did the Rennes raid save the 1st Wing bombers from the Luftwaffe's attentions for, with tanks replenished, FW190s and Me109s attacked as they returned across the Brest peninsula. A painful introduction to the war over Europe was given to the 379th Group from Kimbolton which lost three B-17s, two to the infamous guns of "Flak City".

May 29th was also the occasion of the YB-40s debut when seven were sent out with leading elements of the St Nazaire force. Their performance was not a success. Shortcomings had been evident soon after arrival at Alconbury; before they could be flown in combat it was necessary to install ammunition feed chutes to eliminate the manhandling of ammunition to some positions. But the most troublesome aspect of the YB-40 was its flying characteristics, particularly its tendency to fly tail heavy due to the added weight in the rear section. On this

An aerial shot of the 95th BG dispersal area shortly after the explosion that killed 18 men. *Passion Flower*, QW: W, with a single mission to its credit, would fly again. The spot where the B-17 that exploded stood can be seen beyond the wreck of QW: Q.—(USAF)

first mission they flew in leading positions, but after the B-17s had bombed the YB-40s, still laden with ammunition, could not keep pace, thereby forcing the whole formation to reduce speed.

The air echelons of the three 4th Wing groups had been reunited with their ground organisations prior to this mission. The 94th was at Earls Colne, the 95th at Framlingham, and the 96th at Andrews Field (Gt Saling) the first UK airfield constructed by the US Pioneer Corps. However, plans were in hand for another move, a juxtaposition of 3rd and 4th Wings. After initial setbacks to Marauder medium bombers on operations the decision was made to transfer them to VIII Air Support Command and to place them within closer range of the Continent than their bases in the north Suffolk area. An exchange of bases commenced on June 10th when the newly-arrived 386th Group took its Marauders from Snetterton Heath to Boxted in north Essex; the 96th Group moving into the vacated base next day. The shuttling of B-26 and B-17 groups continued for three days. The 3rd and 4th Bomb Wing headquarters also exchanged premises, the Fortress organisation now being established in Elveden Hall a country mansion in the Suffolk countryside.

Another week of inclement weather passed and not until June 11th were conditions favourable for precision bombing. Even then cloud and haze were encountered and obscured the primary target Bremen. The task force then turned for Wilhelmshaven where conditions were better. Flak encountered on the bomb run put both Nos 1 and 2 engines of Colonel Marion's bomber, in the leading 303rd Group, out of action causing it to yaw and lose way. Groups closely following had to manoeuvre violently and reduce speed to avoid collision. As a result formations became scattered just as the Luftwaffe made its usual move of meeting the leading bombers head-on; the brunt of these attacks was met by the 379th Group flying in the high group position. Seven of the eight B-17s lost were from the leading combat wing, six of these from the Kimbolton group, making nine (a complete squadron strength) losses in its first two missions. A further eighteen men of the 379th sustained wounds and most of its returning aircraft was

damaged. B-17F *Dangerous Dan* received a well placed burst from an enemy fighter in the cockpit. Co-pilot Bersinger was knocked unconscious by shell fragments, while a bullet went through pilot Lt W. Jones's mouth and out by his shoulder. Top turret gunner Cliff Erikson took over the controls and made his first ever landing successfully with directions from the wounded pilot.

The Luftwaffe tactics had brought success in further disrupting the formations and upsetting the aim of the already handicapped lead bomber. So intent were the enemy fighters on pressing home attacks that three collisions were only narrowly avoided and one such disaster did occur when an FW190's wing hit the nose of the 303rd Fortress *Pappy*.

There was little elation at VIII Bomber Command that night: a mission involving 252 B-17s had produced a largely negative result. But the next mission, to the North German ports, was an even unhappier affair.

June 13th marked the three 4th Bombardment Wing groups' first month of combat operations, a bitter initiation that had

Memphis Belle goes home, 9 Jun. 1943. First B-17 in the 91st BG to complete 25 missions, she was also the first in VIII BC to be returned to the USA with her crew.

cost them over 200 airmen and a score of bombers in eight missions. The two groups regularly involved in trouble and sustaining most of the losses were the 94th and 95th; this day, the occasion of their ninth mission, was the blackest in their eventful histories.

The target was Kiel, the submarine yards which had received their first visit from the Eighth a month before when incendiary-carrying Liberators had suffered so cruelly. In anticipation that enemy opposition would be strong, the Command plan called for two separate forces to hit the submarine yards at Bremen and within minutes of one another, thus splitting the German fighter opposition. The 4th Wing B-17s took off early that Sunday morning to assemble in four combat boxes (one a composite). For the 94th Group, it was their last take-off from Earls Colne; the Group was moving north to Bury St Edmunds where the bombers would land on return from the mission. Leading the task force were 18 Fortresses of the 95th Group with a command aircraft piloted by Captain H. A. Stirwalt, carrying Brigadier General Nathan Bedford Forrest as an observer. The 38-year old General had only recently been designated to command a new provisional combat Wing.

The King and Queen met the crew of *Memphis Belle* shortly before the aircraft set off on a 'bond tour' of the USA. Here they talk to Col Wray.—(USAF)

The bombers had no sooner reached the enemy coast to begin their target run towards Kiel when the first fighter attacks were made. The onslaught came as usual against the spearhead formation and the attack left the General's aircraft with one engine trailing smoke and evidence of strikes in the cabin area. It began to drop back, but presently regained its position to lead the 95th over the target. Then it was again riddled with cannon fire as a further fighter attack developed. Falling away, it was last seen spiralling down with an engine in flames and much of the tailplane shot away. General Forrest, later presumed killed in action, was the first US General to become a combat casualty in Europe. Also on board was squadron commander Major A. W. Wilder and the Group navigator. Such was the ferocity of the enemy attacks that 7 or 8 of the 95th's B-17s had gone down by the time the coast was regained. One uncontrollable bomber smashed into another Fortress. Only six of the sixteen 95th aircraft in the leading group (two had aborted early) struggled back to England—and one of those to a crash landing. The rest of the 4th Wing also encountered strong opposition but not of the same intensity. During the long haul back over the North Sea, some gunners in the 94th Group formation, assumed that the Luftwaffe had been left far behind, started cleaning and dismantling their weapons—a post-mission chore. But when only 20 or 30 miles off the Norfolk coast, a dozen black Ju88 night

fighters appeared and in a matter of minutes, shot nine of the bombers into the sea. The remnants of the 94th eventually found their way to their new home. A moving day well remembered.

Gunners of the 4th Bombardment Wing claimed 39-5-14. Two victories were the work of S/Sgt D. W. Crossley a 94th gunner, flying in *Easy Aces* who was earning a reputation as a marksman. Actual German fighter losses were at least eight, including the Commander of III/J.G.26 who lost his life when his parachute failed to open.

Bombing at Kiel was suspect, only 16 aircraft having dropped in the harbour area. Many other bombs were scattered on the U-boat basin and various targets of opportunity. USAAF hailed the second Kiel mission as their "greatest single air battle of the war" and Brigadier General F. L. Anderson of 4th Wing said—"Not only did we hit the important U-boat yards at Kiel, but we also drew practically all the enemy aircraft in the area so that the other formation was able to do a job at Bremen with little opposition".

The 102 Fortresses of 1st Wing had, in fact, done a mediocre job of bombing, although a proportion of the tonnage caused serious damage to shipyard installations. Flak and a smoke screen had made accuracy difficult. In all, 26 B-17s were lost that day—a new high—22 of them from 4th Wing.

A sense of shock pervaded the bases of the 94th and 95th Groups that evening. The 95th had hardly recovered from the tragedy of the Alconbury explosion a fortnight before. By these harrowing experiences the boisterous youngsters of a month previous, or rather those who remained, reached a state of psychological disquiet far quicker than the airmen of the pioneering groups the previous winter. After only nine missions nearly half the original crews and aircraft were gone, and many a young airman at Bury and Framlingham could see no future beyond the next few missions: morale was but a word. With the object of giving a boost to confidence, the commanders of the two groups were given posts in higher command and their places taken by two gifted officers from Eaker's headquarters. To Horham—where the 95th had moved after Kiel owing to the uncompleted state of base facilities at Framlingham—came Colonel John Gerhart, one of the original officers assigned to the Eighth Air Force on its activation in January 1942. To the ailing 94th, Eaker sent Colonel Frederick Castle. Castle, a personal friend of Eaker, had re-enlisted in the USAAF at the latter's request. As Assistant President of the Sperry Corporation he had been deeply concerned with the instrument on which the precision bombing programme largely depended—the Norden bombsight. A member of Eaker's

Lt Weitzenfeld brought *Old Ironsides*, LL: Y home to Bassingbourn minus a stabiliser, which had been knocked off over Bremen by a 1,000 lb HE from another 91st BG B-17. Bombing accidents occurred on a number of occasions throughout the Eighth's campaign.—(USAF)

"original seven" he had long hankered after the opportunity to see action and had finally forced Eaker's hand. The task before Gerhart and Castle was an unenviable one. Staff work was not the kind of background calculated to command the respect of battle fatigued airmen. As was usual, the removal of a proven commander was resented.

Three days prior to the disastrous Kiel mission, the Eighth Air Force had received a new bombing directive. Resulting from decisions made at the Casablanca Conference to mount a Combined Bomber Offensive (CBO), the new plan listed as primary objectives, German submarine yards and bases, aircraft industry, ball-bearings and oil. Secondary objectives were synthetic rubber and military motor transport vehicles. However, the CBP planners recognised that the increasing strength of German fighter defences was the over-riding factor affecting the success of the offensive. Heavy combat losses and impaired tactical efficiency could render both night and day bombing highly unprofitable. The directive therefore concluded that "German fighter strength must be considered as an Intermediate Objective second to none in priority".

Even the most optimistic exponents of the "go it alone" bombing campaign now had to concede that daylight bombing could not hope to succeed unless Luftwaffe opposition was neutralised. The immediate means to this end lay in bombardment of enemy airfields, depots and plants.

The first missions fulfilled under the new directive was the disruption of the synthetic rubber plant at Huls, in which 235 Fortresses of both wings participated on June 22nd. Although the Eighth's first large-scale penetration of the Ruhr, the most heavily defended area of the Third Reich at that time, the mission resulted in the most effective bombardment of a strategic target so far achieved. Cut off from supplies of natural rubber, Germany relied upon a synthetic product. As Chemische Werke, Hüls produced some 30% of the nation's total output, its destruction was bound to be felt. Just under one quarter of the bomb tonnage dropped, exploded within the factory area rendering the plant inoperative for a month. Full production was not resumed for six months.

Bearing testimony to the good bombing was a huge column of acrid smoke that rose over Hüls, it may also have given added incentive to the fighters. Attacks materialised as expected with the main effort directed against the leading group—this time the veteran 91st from Bassingbourn which lost five aircraft. All told sixteen Fortresses failed to return, one being a YB-40 hit by flak; another 170 B-17s received some form of damage. Attempting to avert Luftwaffe interception, Command planners had contrived a number of deceptive moves. The Hüls force had been despatched on the

Smoke Billows up from Hüls (bottom left) as 42-3051, KY: M of the 305th BG pulls off target.—(IWM)

well flown North Sea route as if once again bound for the North German ports. After a hundred miles these bombers turned south-east across Holland where enemy fighters were refuelling after engaging an earlier raid by RAF medium bombers. At this point, a smaller force of Fortresses, escorted in strength by RAF and US fighters, planned to attack the Ford and General Motor works at Antwerp to draw Luftwaffe interceptors. Unfortunately the B-17s arriving over Antwerp were late and without fighter support. This was in part due to take-off delays, non-reception of radio messages, and the inexperience of units. There were three newcomers on combat status this day, of which the 381st Group at Ridgewell and the 384th at Grafton Underwood, last of 1st Bomb Wing's quota of the "new" Fortress groups, made up the Antwerp force. The raid did succeed in drawing some of the enemy interceptors away from the Hüls mission but the circumstances were not as intended. With no Allied fighters on hand to protect the novices the vectored FW190 reception committee from II/J.G.26 flashed head-on through the 41 bombers with guns blazing and two B-17s from each group went down. The enemy force did not appear again, and the disarrayed bomber formation having survived a flak barrage went in peace. Two 384th Group aircraft, badly damaged themselves —earning nicknames *Salvage Queen* and *Patches*, kept formation with a crippled B-17 as it went down under control towards the sea. The pilots, not realising the cripple was beyond help, did not excuse the tactical error for which they were duly admonished. Breaking formation to add protective fire to a wounded comrade had long ago proved an extremely dangerous practice.

The third new Fortress group was the 100th based at Thorpe Abbots, assigned to the 4th Bombardment Wing. The group had been detailed to fly a diversionary 21 aircraft over the North Sea in a further attempt to draw the enemy's attention from the main task force, but ground mists and other delays nullified their effect.

All the "new" groups arriving during the spring and early summer of 1943 suffered grievous combat losses; but for the three groups entering the arena on June 22nd ill fortune was all too frequently in attendance. Two of these three, in months to come, came to be considered the unluckiest in the Eighth, and for one the jinx persisted until the last days of the war.

Cloud, frequently the obstacle to precision bombing, foiled missions to Luftwaffe air depots next day and was also responsible for the costly fiasco over N.W. Germany on June 25th when 18 B-17s were missing in action. Hamburg was the primary target, but conditions encountered during penetration were so bad that the bomber stream was broken and some formations scattered among the towering banks of cloud. With no prospect of bombing Hamburg, groups either picked out targets of opportunity or hauled their bombs home. Enemy fighters engaging the ragged formations of the new groups were able to shoot down many Fortresses. One third of the total loss was sustained by the 379th (Kimbolton) Group— the second occasion this newcomer had lost heavily within a fortnight. Gunners claimed 62 victories in the numerous battles.

Weather conditions continued to mar the chances of accurate bombing over Germany during the rest of June and early July. To avoid a repetition of the Hamburg affair, Command despatched bombers on shallow penetrations, for the most part Luftwaffe installations in France, particularly the major air depot at Villacoublay serving fighter bases in the Paris area.

On June 26th 246 B-17s were sent to Villacoublay, but tiered layers of cloud so interfered with target location that only a dozen B-17s bombed. The freshman 384th Group from Grafton Underwood incurred the total losses of the Eighth that day when FW190s cut down five of its B-17s near Paris. To avoid the cloudbound North, the Fortresses revisited St

A cannon shell exploded in the waist gun positions.

Nazaire on June 28th, taking out the only serviceable lock entrance to the U-boat basin. Major Glenn Hazenbuch, leading the 303rd Group, said it was one of the best jobs of precision bombing he'd seen in his 24 trips. This proved to be the Eighth's last major raid on "Flak City", the proving ground for much of its tactics.

An almost complete overcast persisted, causing two of the three bomber forces sent to attack French air depots on the late June missions to bring their bombs back to jettisoning in mid-Channel. Only the 4th Wing were able to see their target, although few of the bombs they dropped caused hurt to the Gnome-Rhone aero engine plant at Le Mans.

Independence Day 1943 marked the first anniversary of Eighth Air Force bomber operations from the UK. The occasion was marked by a three-pronged assault in force with 192 1st Wing Forts visiting aircraft works at Le Mans and Nantes while 83 from 4th Wing went down to La Pallice. One of the Fortresses raiding the S.N.C.A. aircraft factory at Nantes was *Ruthie* of the 326th Bomb. Sqdn. which was a unit recently re-established in the 92nd Group after acting as the bomber CCRC nucleus. Just after bombing, this Fortress was hit by cannon fire puncturing two fuel tanks and wrecking the hydraulic system and flaps. A 20-mm cannon shell, piercing the floor between the two waist gunners, exploded in the radio toom wrecking equipment. Another shell hit the ball turret seriously wounding Sgt Richard O. Gettys in the groin, chest and face. The turret was still partly serviceable and though failing in strength Gettus continued firing his guns until he collapsed. The tail gunner was also wounded. 1/Lt Robert L. Campbell flew *Ruthie* (named after his wife) home to Alconbury. An SOS was flashed by lamp to the formation leader asking him to notify base of *Ruthie's* difficulties. Campbell said afterwards, "When I started to land I discovered

The pilot of 94th BG B-17F, 42-3190, QE: W, managed to put her down in a French wheat field on 14 Jul. 1943. Luftwaffe officers survey the damage done by cannon shells.—(H. Holmes)

we had a flat tyre. I held her on the runway as long as I could and then whirled her around in front of the control tower, but she stayed up." *Ruthie* was only fit for salvage. They gave ball gunner Gettys the DSC and Campbell another Fort on which he bestowed the name *Ruthie II*. This Fortress was destined to become the vehicle of one of the most heroic actions in the annals of the Eighth Air Force.

Cloud, and still more cloud persisted. A chance blow at Villacoublay was made six days later but came to nought. Two groups unloaded over coastal airfields and the rest deposited their wares in the depths of the Channel. The Fortresses finally got to Villacoublay on Bastille Day, July 14th, and wrought considerable havoc. Le Bourget and Amiens/Glisy airfields were also attacked with creditable results. A Fortress *T.S.* (ostensibly Tough Stuff but generally having a more purposeful if unprintable meaning) of the 381st Group was on its fifth mission as part of the force sent to Amiens/Glisy. The Ridgewell group was attacked head-on and one FW190, either hit by defensive fire or through pilot error, struck the *T.S.* with a wing. The impact knocked the propeller from the Fort's No. 3 engine, amputated the Focke-Wulf's wing as it slashed almost halfway through that of *T.S.*, and caused the enemy machine to cartwheel over the Fortress disintegrating as it went and tearing away part of the bomber's fuselage skin and fin. *T.S.* wallowed around the sky, but somehow held together and, under the watchful eye of eight Duxford Thunderbolts, lurched into Manston for a wheels up landing. From its battered fuselage the crew emerged without a scratch. One of the Focke-Wulf's gun barrels was found embedded in the wall of the radio room.

The debut of the 385th and 388th Groups (4th Wing) allowed Eaker to despatch a record 332 B-17s to targets in N.W. Germany on July 17th. The weather however, deteriorated and most of the bombers turned back. The only Fortress to fall foul of the Luftwaffe was one of the Polebrook "Ball Boys". *Snowball*, on her 13th mission, sustained damage from a near flak burst which put out two engines. Lagging behind the rest of the Group the straggler was jumped at the enemy coast by Me109s which took out a third engine. 1/Lt William E. Peters piloting, put the B-17 down into the sea near the Dutch coast where the crew were picked up by an RAF rescue launch. Ball turret gunner on *Snowball* was T/Sgt Thomas Dye who that day claimed two enemy aircraft. He had originally trained as a radio operator, but volunteered to become a ball turret gunner—such gunners were scarce during 1943, chiefly due to the necessary limitations in stature. After five missions and two victories credited, he was sent to a gunnery school for a "refresher course", not having before attended a gunnery school as he "picked up" the art. Here, he failed the course! However, the crew of *Snowball* had no qualms about his ability and on return to his unit he was promptly back in the ball turret. On completion of his tour, Dye had credit for the destruction of 8 enemy aircraft the highest score in his Group and one of the highest in the Eighth for bomber gunners.

The last of the "Second wind" groups was coming into Framlingham early in July. This group, the 390th, had benefited from being the first to go through the USAAF's recently established School of Applied Tactics at Orlando, Florida, where the fruits of operational experience were embodied in a comprehensive training curriculum. The 390th appeared to have slightly more polish than its predecessors. It was also distinguished by an unusual pet. Since the first of the "new" groups arrived in April no less than 30 pets had been smuggled into the UK by their air echelons. Dogs, naturally, predominated but there were also parrots and monkeys. The 390th, or rather one squadron, went one better by bringing in a honey bear which frequently escaped into the Suffolk countryside to confront many an incredulous native. Authority had hitherto shown a blind eye but for fear that competition might arise

Aircraft of the 'new' 385th BG display group identification markings. 42-30263, N, has the early yellow letter on dulled white square device, 42-3422, Y, the standard insignia blue letter on dulled white square.

and pet mascots might get out of hand, immigration precautions were tightened.

The sultry days of July passed in England while Continental Europe lay blanketed with intermittent cloud. Meanwhile, the Fortresses droned over England practising their arts. On the evening of July 22nd 1/Lt Harry Joho took off from Knettishall with the crew of *Joho's Jokers*. Although he had never done so before, gunner Sgt Elias Thomas decided to wear his parachute in the ball turret, which was just as well, for as the B-17 cruised peacefully in the summer evening, the back fell out of the turret and Thomas with it. Thomas made a safe, but somewhat shame-faced, parachute landing.

At VIII Bombardment Command many wondered if there would ever be a settled period of weather to permit a major strike at priority targets in the Reich. Spring and summer in 1943 had so far produced few days when conditions were ideal for precision bombing. Apart from the mission to the Hüls synthetic rubber plant the bombers had achieved little in the way of strategic bombing since the "new" groups began operations. In terms of bombing results, the Eighth's contribution to victory during May, June and early July was not very inspiring, particularly in view of the effort expended. While cloudy weather continued to be the primary obstacle, the Luftwaffe's opposition to the US daylight raids had increased threefold. Aware of the impending build-up of US bomber strength in the UK, the Germans bolstered their defences in the West. On April 1st 1943 the fighter force guarding the N.W. German seaboard, J.G.1, had been split to make a new Jagdgeschwader. Designated J.G.11 and equipped with FW190s and Me109s the new organisation was based in the north of central Germany. At the same time some Luftwaffe units were withdrawn from the Soviet and Mediterranean fronts. III/J.G.54 (Me109s) became operational in N.W. France in April, and I/J.G.27 (Me109s) followed at the end of May. Late in July II/J.G.51 and II/J.G.27 redeployed from Sardinia and Italy and all three Gruppen of J.G.3 (Me109s) from South Russia moved to the Low Countries. All told the strength of the Fighter Force in North West Germany, France and the Low Countries rose from 270 in April 1943 to 630 by August, most of the increase being in Me109s. In Germany plans were afoot to reform two Zerstörer wings. The Eighth now had some 580 B-17s in 16 combat groups of which approximately 400 could be counted on to be airworthy for any one mission.

For both the Eight Air Force and the Luftwaffe the mode of battle had changed little; each side was aware of the tactics and devices the other would be likely to employ, though both were apprehensive of some new device or technique. Planners at VIII Bombardment Command strove to outwit the enemy's fighter defences by feints, diversions and divided missions timed to play upon the limited flight duration of enemy fighters. Often the scale of losses hinged upon how well these plans worked. German defence controllers were, however, not easily fooled and fighter opposition was an expected hazard of every mission. The Fortress squadron personnel whose lot it was to fly in "purple heart corner" of the low group in the leading wing of a deep penetration, knew the grim prospects to be faced. The repetitive Luftwaffe tactic of frontal assault against the leading B-17 boxes, usually during the crucial period of the bomb run, was effective as both sides appreciated. The Americans still tended to over-estimate the effectiveness of their defending gunfire. The picture of the German fighter force being defeated in the air by the Eighth's bombers, was the general impression of the public in Britain and the US, and to a certain degree this view was held by many of the men engaged in the bitter conflict five miles above the soil of Europe. Many of the second wave groups had also suffered particularly heavy losses from contact with enemy fighters. This was in part due to inexperience and in part to ill fortune. But from these initial battles was kindled a fierce unit pride that in future did much to sustain a group in times of adversity. Each group, usually set down on remote airfields in the English countryside, became very much an individual entity, the very nature of their existence creating an introvert atmosphere. A group that had flown but a half dozen missions of dubious value, while incurring the loss of a quarter of its original bombers and personnel, elected to be "the finest damn bomb outfit in the ETO". To the unprejudiced observer this esprit de corps often appeared a greater motivation to get to grips with the enemy than any thought of vanquishing the Nazis.

Early in July, the Eighth Air Force introduced a means of group identification on B-17s that became an emblem zealously prized and proudly sported in the months to come. Hitherto, only an aircraft's squadron could be identified by the markings carried. Now, after trials to find the best visual form, each bombardment wing was given a white symbol containing a blue letter displayed on the tail fins. Fortresses of the 1st Bombardment Wing had a triangle symbol, those of the 4th Wing a square; a different letter within these symbols identified the particular group. Henceforth, the 91st Group at Bassingbourn was known to friend and foe as the Triangle A, the 92nd as the Triangle B, and so on.

On July 23rd 1943, RAF meteorologists reported that the frequent weather "lows" that had lurked over N.W. Europe for the better part of three months were giving way to a "high". With the promise of clear skies VIII Bombardment Command prepared to launch a sustained offensive in accordance with the terms of the CBO. A Fortress Blitz.

Chapter 7: Martin's Maligned Madame

The twin-engined medium bomber is not generally associated with the US Eighth Army Air Force. Medium bombardment units did, however, serve operationally with the Eighth for a period during 1943; their story being very much the story of a controversial aeroplane—the Martin B-26 Marauder.

The Glenn L. Martin Company was a firm of long standing for the supply of bombers to the US Forces. The B-26 Marauder, born of the Air Corps expansion prior to Pearl Harbor, promised to uphold their tradition. The prototype's maximum speed of 315 mph and ability to haul a 3,000 lb bomb load to a target 500 miles distant at 265 mph; was an impressive performance for that time. Whereas bombers tended towards plain functional configurations, the Marauder was strikingly streamlined. Its beautiful cigar-shaped fuselage was practically devoid of projections except for Martin's own compact twin-gun power-operated turret. Two powerful Pratt and Whitney Double Wasps were encased in streamlined nacelles that also contained the main wheels of a tricycle undercarriage.

The Marauder looked good and carried a useful bomb load at fair speed, but initially did not handle well. For its time the aircraft had a high wing loading further increased by armour plate and other paraphenalia deemed essential in the light of air warfare over Europe. Thus laden, the Marauder needed longer take-off runs to become airborne. Stalling speed advanced, necessitating faster touch downs which the undercarriage, coupled with the added weight, was not wont to withstand. Added to this the early Double Wasps were prone to malfunction and at critical speeds loss of engine power meant loss of control. Unless the B-26 was quickly retrimmed when an engine failed, the torque of the other engine could roll the aircraft over and into a spin. On occasions, the propeller pitch control mechanism went wild too. All these troubles brought a soaring accident rate among first production models which, in the urgency to get the type into service, had been ordered "off the drawing board". A combination of malfunctioning and pilot inexperience, brought frequent crashes and many fatalities in training units. Rumours grew and the tale soon spread around AAF bases that the new Martin ship was a killer—a widow maker. Some wit, remarking on the lack of wing area said the aircraft had "no visible means of support" leading to damning epithets such as "Baltimore Whore" and "Flying Prostitute".

Command concern was such that the USAAF considered abandoning development and concentrating instead upon the B-25 Mitchell, that by contrast was ungainly but vice free. However, work by Martin's corrected many of the troubles and design improvements were put in hand. The first two B-26 groups were sent to the South-West Pacific where they acquitted themselves well in support of operations in New Guinea and Guadalcanal before being withdrawn due to range limitations.

Since it was in Europe that aerodrome facilities and target ranges were more suited to the B-26's ability, three B-26 groups were ordered to move to England during the autumn of 1942. Ground complements crossed by sea and aircraft were flown on the North Atlantic ferry route. In September the 319th Bomb Group set out but bad weather and malfunctioning resulted in aircraft and crews being scattered along the route. The other groups were then re-routed across the South Atlantic by which time the North African invasion had commenced and all B-26s were committed to the Twelfth Air Force for that campaign. The 319th, gathering its strength at Horsham St Faith and Attlebridge, both near Norwich, and flying on low altitude training missions over the English countryside, was soon ordered to Africa.

On November 12th a flight set off from the south coast led by the Group Commander, Colonel Rutherford. But what was to have been an oversea transit flight to North Africa, brought the Marauder into its first appearance over occupied Europe. Bad weather and poor navigation brought the formation over Cherbourg where two, including the Commander's aircraft, were shot down. A third B-26, badly shot up, turned back to England to crash-land at Warmwell.

Three weeks later the ground complement of another Marauder group arrived in the UK, the first of four groups specifically assigned to the Eighth Air Force for medium bombardment operations from the UK. The Marauder force was established under the 3rd Bombardment Wing, already with headquarters installed at Elveden Hall and controlling several airfields in Suffolk and south Norfolk. While the ground personnel of the newcomer, the 322nd Group, acclimatised themselves to the damp conditions at Rattlesden and Bury St Edmunds airfields, the flying crews trained and awaited combat planes 4,000 miles away in the sub-tropical climate of Florida.

The staff at Elveden Hall knew of the unfortunate affair involving the 319th, and the history of the Marauder's teething troubles. Whilst there may have been some misgivings in the staff about the aircraft scheduled to equip the wing, among lower echelons, where rumour flourished, the prospect was far from pleasing. Distorted stories of a mission over Cherbourg from which none returned, found their way to the recent arrivals at Bury and Rattlesden. Not the sort of advance publicity likely to inspire confidence in a controversial bomber yet to be battle proved in Western Europe.

Training of B-26 squadrons at home was under the auspices of III Bomber Command. The mode of attack practised was low-level target approach with the object of obtaining maximum surprise advantage. Fighter interception was always difficult at "zero" altitude, radar detection impossible, ground fire minimised, and a high degree of bombing accuracy attainable. So reasoned the advocates. In the Pacific such tactics had met with success and AAF Headquarters saw no reason why this form of attack could not be equally effective against selected targets in occupied Europe. It was too early to establish a precedent from experience with the B-26 in North Africa, besides that, neither the Pacific nor Africa presented circumstances comparable with attacking targets across the English Channel.

The British had practised low-level attack with considerable success and bearable losses. The RAF emphasized that speed and surprise were essential to success. The question was—had the Marauder sufficient speed? The RAF used Boston and Mosquito light bombers at low levels preferring to send its mediums, Venturas and Mitchells, over well defended targets at medium heights (10,000 to 15,000 ft). The VIII Bomber Command did not enthuse over the idea, but prepared to investigate the feasibility of low level missions integrated with the heavy bomber campaign.

On a low-level practice mission, Marauders of 322nd BG streak across Crowfield, Suffolk; Mar. 1943. 41-17750 is an early B model formerly of 319th BG.—(Mallon)

Not until March 7th 1943 did the first of the 322nd Group Marauders put down on Bury St Edmunds. These were from the 450th Bomb Sqdn. Approximately a month was to pass before the next Squadron (452nd) arrived. The Americans, hitherto fervent advocates of a high altitude offensive, now went to the other extreme. Mediums skipped across the East Anglian plain at levels frightening to observe. One Marauder pilot, suddenly faced with overhead power cables, went under them! Pilots found the slight time lag in control response made such flying extremely hazardous, resulting in some narrow scrapes with tree tops and cables. Nevertheless, there was no serious mishap until April 26th. On that day a B-26, practising evasive action, lost part of its tail and ran into the ground near Cambridge, killing the crew of five. Accidents happened in most units, whatever their mission or equipment, and investigation of this tragedy was not allowed to hinder training, then in an advanced stage.

By the second week in May both squadrons were considered ready for action. An electrical generating plant near Ijmuiden on the Dutch coast was the target selected for the May 14th premiere. By no means an "easy" target,, the German Navy had made the port an E-boat base and installed substantial anti-aircraft defences—to which the RAF could testify from experience during two earlier raids that month. It was planned to send twelve Marauders, each loaded with four 500 lb British delayed action bombs. Major Othel Turner, commander of 450th Squadron was to lead with Group Commander Colonel Stillman, and Brigadier General Brady of the 3rd Wing flying in following aircraft.

Shortly after 09.50 hrs on May 14th, the first Marauder was airborne from the airfield on the hill above Bury St Edmunds—a city steeped in English history where, six centuries before, it is said the barons met and drew up Magna Carta, first deed of democracy.

The 322nd formation set out in two-plane elements, flying a few feet above the North Sea to avoid radar detection. Landfall was made near Leiden, amongst some well directed ground fire which silenced the left engine of *Too Much of Texas* and tore away a sizeable portion of her rudder. For a few seconds the aircraft was in jeopardy as her pilot, Lt R. C. Fry, strove to keep control, turning away from the formation to jettison bombs in the sea. This accomplished, Fry was then faced with the prospect of nursing the Marauder home across 120 miles of sea on one engine. As it happened, he was no stranger to this situation having on three previous occasions been forced to fly and land a B-26 on one engine.

The other Marauders, having turned north, followed a canal and railway track leading to Ijmuiden, where the air-raid alarm sounded at 10.57 hrs. Three minutes later the eleven aircraft were over the target and away. Ground fire of varying intensity followed the formation from the coast and every aircraft but one received some damage, chiefly from small calibre weapons. On regaining the Suffolk coast Fry had put down at Gt Ashfield and another damaged B-26 made for Honington, while a third was so badly crippled that Lt John J. Howell ordered his crew to bale out near their home base. Before Howell could himself jump the aircraft crashed out of control at Rougham. Some of the heaviest damage had been sustained by the aircraft of the 452nd's Squadron Commander, Major G. C. Celio. Finding one main undercarriage leg would not lower, due to hits on the mechanism, the Major circled his airfield for eighty minutes while hydraulic pressure was restored. Altogether some 300 holes were counted in his aircraft. Major Turner in the leading B-26 was one of seven men wounded during the raid.

Though executed much as according to plan the returning crews were understandably not particularly enthusiastic about low-level attack. On the other hand, they felt confident that a good job of bombing had been done: their confidence, however, was soon shattered. Two days later Colonel Stillman attended a meeting at Elveden Hall where he was told his bombers had missed the target and that a return visit was planned next day. Stillman did not like the idea of going back to Ijmuiden so soon and said so. His protest was considered but Command did not think it valid, particularly as the raid had been planned as an integral part of extensive operations over Europe next day and target alterations were not desirable at such a late hour. Those who participated in the first mission, could not believe the objective was missed. They conjectured that the Germans had removed some of the delayed action bombs. Long afterwards the truth was known; all bombs, though near, had failed to hit the plant.

The Field Order that came through to the 322nd Group Operations Staff on the night of May 16th called for twelve aircraft loaded as before. This time the force was to split after crossing the enemy coast, one half going to Ijmuiden and the other to another generating station at nearby Haarlem. With many aircraft still under flak damage repairs, Stillman could only muster eleven serviceable B-26s from the two squadrons. A third squadron, the 451st, had just flown in but its aircraft were still in need of ETO modifications.

Tensions preceding combat missions were made all the worse by the apprehension of returning to Ijmuiden. Take-off commenced at 10.56 hrs and once assembled the formation soon disappeared eastwards in the bright spring sunshine. Sometime after noon one Marauder returned. The pilot reported that he had been forced to turn back some thirty miles off the Dutch coast on discovering that his generators were not functioning. As the return time (12.50 hrs) for the bombers passed, an uneasy feeling grew with General Brady and others waiting at the control tower. Then came the moment when fuel would have been exhausted and the aircraft could no longer be in flight. Some cherished the hope that the Marauders had put down on another airfield, but checking soon showed this not to be the case. At VIII Bomber Command, the force was listed 'Missing in Action, cause unknown'.

A reconnaissance revealed no evidence that bombing took place. In the meantime, it was found that the aborting Marauder had climbed to 1000 ft on turning back. While gaining altitude was normal safety procedure in such circumstances, at over 1000 ft the aircraft had been clearly visible on RAF radar screens and presumably on the enemy's as well. Thus, it could be assumed the German defences were forewarned. Then, five days after the raid, a Royal Navy destroyer came upon two exhausted airmen huddled in a dinghy some miles off the East Anglian coast. The two were Sgts George Williams and Jesse Lewis, tail and turret gunners, and sole survivors of a B-26 that had come down in the sea. From their stories and information later received from intelligence sources much of the disaster was reconstructed.

From the outset the formation had blundered, through a wrong heading or a gross navigational error, so that landfall occurred some thirty miles south of the point planned. The formation then crossed the mouth of the Maas, one of the most heavily defended areas of Holland, where Colonel Stillman's bomber was hit and crashed out of control into sand dunes at Rozenburg. A minute later flak claimed another B-26 which fell into the Meuse near Maasluis. The remaining Marauders survived the hail of small arms and light flak and in some confusion continued north-east on a heading that would take them 25 to 30 miles east of their objectives. The leader of the second element accelerated to assume the command position, but in so doing collided with Stillman's wingman, causing both B-26s to crash at Bodegraven. Debris from the collision or flak damage received earlier, caused another bomber to ''belly in' a few miles on.

Hopelessly lost, the 'remaining Marauders blundered into the defences of Amsterdam, bombed a gas holder and headed west. Four were so badly damaged that they got little further than the coast and fell into the sea. The remaining Marauder had progressed fifty miles on the homeward journey when it was attacked head on by three Me109s. After a second pass by the fighters, it went into the sea, sinking in 45 seconds. This was the bomber from which the two gunners survived. Of the 62 airmen who came down in enemy territory, twenty survived as prisoners of war. Lt Col Purinton, group executive and leader of the Haarlem attack, was rescued with his crew from the sea by an enemy boat, while from the mangled wreckage of Stillman's bomber the Germans extracted the 322nd's Commander and two gunners alive but badly injured.

Monday May 17th 1943 was a black day for 322nd Group, the gloom thereof persisted, and indeed deepened, in the weeks to come. Lt Col Glenn Nye, a staff officer at 3rd Wing who had been mentor to the group prior to Stillman's arrival from the US, was given command of the 322nd. He informed the Group that operations would cease for the time being although training for low-level attack would continue. The situation was not helped by another fatal accident on May 29th when a

S/Sgt Jesse Lewis and S/Sgt George Williams, only survivors of the disastrous 17 May 1943 mission to return to the 322nd BG.—(IWM)

Marauder practising violent evasive action at low altitude, lost part of its tail and crashed into one of the Bury hangars. After that few could doubt that the barrack room cynics were right— one had no chance of survival in a B-26 unit, if the enemy didn't get you the plane would! Surely, some asked, no further proof was needed, the Marauder was unsafe to fly let alone fight in. Many confidently predicted the group would now convert to another type of aircraft. The irony of the situation was that on that very airfield stood two Marauders, untried in combat, and as yet identified only by their numbers, 41-31819 and 41-31773, that would in time have considerable bearing upon establishing the worth of their kin.

The gloom had spread to the 322nd's two other squadrons recently arrived, and to some extent to a new group, the 323rd that came into nearby Horham. However, the emotional solutions aired around the Marauder bases were not compatible with those soberly contrived by higher command.

Two more B-26 groups (386th and 387th) were due to arrive in England within a month giving the Eighth over 250 mediums. While Command would have been happier if these had been B-17s, in the circumstances there was nothing to be done but find some profitable means of employing the B-26. Although dogged by a series of mechanical troubles and not the easiest of aircraft to fly, it was also a fact that current Marauders, handled by properly trained crews, were incurring

Col Carl Storrie brings the 387th BG to the UK. This is his personal aircraft, *Bat Outa Hell II*, on arrival.—(IWM)

an accident rate no greater than with other bomber types. Furthermore, the last two squadrons of the 322nd to arrive and those of following groups were all equipped with late production models incorporating numerous improvements, in particular a six feet increase in wing span, larger tail surfaces and greater fuel capacity.

Eaker decided that since VIII Bomber Command was fully committed to furthering the strategic bombing campaign, to which the Marauder units could apparently add little weight, the mediums would be placed under VIII Air Support Command, an organisation primarily devoted to the support of ground forces and hitherto a quiet backwater of the Eighth's operational activity. Whether there was more to this decision than meets the eye is a matter for conjecture, for it could have been an implied suggestion to Washington that the Marauder was not suitable for bombing operations in the ETO. The change of command was accompanied by the movement south of the 3rd Wing and its units from Suffolk to Essex which, apart from bringing the mediums nearer to the Continent, placed them in an area where it was planned to establish a US tactical air force for the coming invasion of the Continent. In reality, the move was an interchange of bases with the 4th Wing Fortresses. The first group into Essex was the 386th which, after a few days sojourn at Snetterton Heath, moved into uncompleted Boxted airfield near Colchester. The 322nd moved to Andrews Field near Braintree, the 323rd to Earls Colne and the 3rd Bomb Wing traded one mansion for another—although Elizabethan Marks Hall was not quite so luxurious as their former residence. Towards the end of the month the 387th Group arrived at Chipping Ongar from America. Like its predecessors it, too, was trained for low-level attack.

In North Africa the USAAF had ceased to employ B-26s on low-level strikes early in 1943 preferring operations at medium altitude well out of range of light anti-aircraft fire. It was, therefore, logical that VIII ASC should decide to explore the feasibility of using British-based Marauders in similar fashion. The RAF were consulted, particularly on the matter of providing fighter cover, and planning eventually centred on tight formations of 18 bombers operating at 12,000 ft. But as aircrew had been trained for low-level attack, a new training programme had to be instituted. Initially only the 323rd Group, under Colonel Thatcher, was instructed to practise for medium altitude bombing. Technical complications were many: Norden bombsights had to be procured and installed in place of the D8 type, as did strike cameras and downwards firing rear hatch guns. This, in company with more minor modifications deemed necessary to bring the Marauder to an acceptable combat standard, took time. Two whole months

The 323rd BG had mostly B-26Cs as original equipment. 41-34953, YU: S seen taking off from Earls Colne is a C-15 model with Martin-Bell power operated tail turret. Many early B-26Cs were scrapped in 1944 when structural failure was discovered.—(USAF)

Mechanics replace the power turret plexiglass on a 323rd BG B-26C-5. The aircraft has the earlier hand-held tail guns. Most activity on this Earls Colne hardstand appears to be concerned with the personal GI transport provided by the British—bicycles.—(USAF)

passed before the 323rd Group was ready for operations. On July 16th, 18 Marauders were scheduled to fly from Earls Colne to attack the marshalling yards at Abbeville. Sixteen actually unloaded over the target and, weathering a fair amount of flak, returned safely to base. In anticipation, flak suits were worn by participating crews. Several squadrons of RAF Spitfires were in attendance and drove off enemy aircraft that appeared. Bombing was pathetic, but this apart things had gone smoothly. Even before this raid the decision had been taken to train the other three groups in medium altitude attack; the 322nd ceased its hedge-hopping activities.

An intervening week of inclement weather made it the 25th before the 323rd operated again at medium altitude. This

View from the pilot's (left) and co-pilot's (right) seats in a 322nd BG Marauder heading for Rouen, 27 Aug. 1943. Aircraft on right side of pilot's view is *Mild and Bitter* which was to become the first B-26 in England to fly 100 missions.—(USAF)

time the objective was Ghent coke ovens in Belgium. Again bombing was poor and the coke ovens survived as did the thirteen Marauders involved—thanks to several squadrons of Spitfires fighting off enemy interceptors at a cost of four missing for one Me109 claimed destroyed. Next day the 323rd sent eighteen B-26s to the much harried airfield at St Omer/Longueness. Bombardiers, beginning to get the hang of things, left the field well cratered. And again the following day Marauders rose from Earls Colne with full bomb bays, for another enemy airfield—Tricqueville. Seventeen bombed and returned to base while their protectors fought another battle with Focke-Wulfs claiming nine destroyed for the loss of one Spitfire, whose pilot was saved from the sea. In brilliant sunshine on July 28th the 323rd continued its activities with a visit to Zeebrugge coke ovens, following this next day with a trip to the other St Omer airfield. Five days in a row the 323rd penetrated hostile air space, making nearly a hundred Marauder sorties, without one loss. It seemed too good to be true.

During the 323rd's series of missions the 322nd and 386th had been flying diversions, both for the 323rd and B-17s. On July 30th the 386th at Boxted commenced operations. The group was commanded by Colonel Lester Maitland, whose rotund appearance belied his ability as an aviator. In 1927 Maitland was one of two men in a Fokker C-2 trimotor transport to make the first flight from the US to Hawaii. The 386th had watched the previous days' missions with relief and found new confidence in their aircraft as a viable weapon. What the 323rd could do, they could do also. But the 386th was born under a different star. Of 21 aircraft despatched only 11 bombed the target, Woensdrecht airfield, although with fair results. But the mission was decidedly "rough"; the Luftwaffe made a determined effort to deal with the mediums and a number of FW190s evaded the Spitfire escort. They shot down B-26C 41-34706 belonging to 553rd Bomb Sqdn. and damaged seven others, while the 386th gunners claimed 6-5-1 and were allowed 3-2-2.

The last day of July the ill-fated 322nd resumed operations, flying its first medium altitude mission against Tricqueville, with poor bombing results. FW190s attempting to intercept lost one of their number to a gunner, S/Sgt C. S. Maddox, whose claim a Spitfire pilot confirmed. Slight small arms damage to three aircraft was all the 322nd suffered. On the same day VIII ASC also sent out another B-26 mission, the 386th Group visiting the notorious Abbeville/Drucat airfield.

The pattern of two separate missions a day was followed regularly for some weeks, and from August 2nd three-squadron, 36 aircraft, formations became the usual operating strength. This was the maximum number for which the RAF could provide sufficient fighter escort and gave each force a potential delivery of fifty tons of high explosive with a good chance of causing substantial damage.

Blazing Heat leads B-26s of the 386th BG past the Boxted crew rooms in the Aug. morning sunlight. The cannibalised remains of 384th BG's *Patches* (see chapter 8) can be seen third from the left, in the distance.
—(IWM)

Flak, in varying degrees, became a feature of Marauder missions. Over targets it was usually unavoidable; but adherence to a well conceived flight plan, avoiding known flak areas en route, plus co-ordinated evasive action, could considerably reduce the hazard. On August 2nd the 323rd and 386th Groups experienced the heaviest anti-aircraft barrages so far encountered by Marauders when visiting French airfields. Many aircraft suffered extensive damage. A direct hit on one of the 386th's, painfully wounded pilot Lt R. P. Sanford who insisted on remaining at the controls to reach the objective (St Omer), and back to base where he made a successful landing.

Bombing from medium altitudes had so far brought indifferent results. When 33 aircraft of the 322nd attacked Le Trait shipyards two days later the pattern was declared excellent, for strike photos showed heavy damage to installations in the yard. All but a few bombs had fallen in the 330 x 650 yd target area. On the 9th, the 322nd and 386th went back to St Omer/Ft Rouge but clouds prevented good results being attained. Aircraft became separated in the poor flying conditions and when noses were counted back at base, another 386th aircraft was missing. This was the victim of one of those tragic accidents that not infrequently occurred; the Marauder, discovered by two Spitfires in an area where only enemy aircraft were expected, was mistakenly identified and shot down.

Enemy airfields predominated on target lists in a policy aimed at forcing the Luftwaffe to withdraw fighter units from the coastal belt and so reduce their effectiveness against the heavies. On August 12th it was Poix Nord; Abbeville and

Enemy fighter fields were a frequent target for the Marauders. Here the 386th BG turns away after bombing a landing ground at Bryas-Sud, near St. Pol, 17 Aug. 1943. 41-34949, AN: H, pictured here had to 'belly in' at Boxted on return. Fuselage blister window was a modification carried out in the UK.—(IWM)

Woensdrecht again on the 15th, while 387th Group joined the act with an appearance over St Omer/Ft Rouge. Bernay/St Martin and Beaumont Le Roger on the 16th, Bryas/Sud and Poix on the 17th, Woensdrecht and Lille/Vendville where the 322nd went astray and hit the wrong airfield on the 18th and Bryas/Sud and Amiens/Glisy next day. Flak peppered the B-26s, men were wounded, but all bombers came back. Many of these were targets which a few months before would have brought strong opposition from the Luftwaffe and targets where many B-17s had fallen. True, the enemy fighter force, though enlarged, was sorely pressed to meet all RAF and USAAF raids. Then there was the formidable and constant escort of RAF Spitfires who, as the Marauder men were first to acknowledge, did a masterly job in keeping enemy interceptions to a minimum. Whatever the reasons, the Marauders were now turning in the lowest loss per sortie ratio in the Eighth.

The enemy did hit back at the 386th in an unexpected way on the night of August 17th when Boxted was bombed; a 500 lb bomb falling on a living site killed 2 men and wounded 29.

The 386th, the group which had suffered most of the losses since medium altitude bombing began, met trouble again on August 22nd. Seemingly it had magnetic qualities for drawing enemy flak and fighters and this was soon displayed over Beaumont Le Roger. Shortly after the bomb run the formation was attacked by FW190s. *Pay-Off*, piloted by Lt Wilma T. Caldwell, was hit in one engine and the bomb bay, where fire took hold threatening to engulf fuel tanks. Caldwell strove to keep the aircraft in a controlled glide while his crew jumped, but after four men were seen to leave the tanks exploded breaking the machine in two. For his sacrifice Caldwell was awarded the DSC, the highest decoration to reach a 386th man. From another Marauder in the formation, *Honey Chile*, the tail gunner, Sgt John L. Dorton, was credited with destroying a Focke-Wulf.

Eleven more missions were flown by B-26s during the remainder of August to bring the tonnage delivered by the mediums during the month to 908 tons of high explosive in 679 sorties. The cost was 4 Marauders missing in action (flak claimed a 322nd machine on the 25th and the 387th's *King Bee* on the 31st) but gunners were awarded claims of 4-2-3 enemy fighters. It was obvious that on current standing, aircrew chance of survival in a B-26 was relatively high. There was now a noticeable quiet among dissenters around

Marauder bases: the aircraft had also ceased to be a butt for jokes of B-17 crewmen.

Although the operation of medium bombers posed special problems, 3rd Wing tacticians could, to some extent, adopt many procedures employed by the heavies. Marauder defensive formations, flak measures and so on, were in the first instance not dissimilar to those of the B-17s. As with the Fortresses, the prime consideration was to find means of achieving higher degrees of bombing accuracy. Results were improving and on September 2nd this was taken a step further with 386th Group's initial use of a revised formation 'drop-on-leader' technique that achieved a well concentrated bomb pattern—the Mazingarbe power station and chemical plant was put out of action by the severe damage inflicted. The technique held such promise that it was later adopted by the other 3rd Wing groups.

Early September brought the B-26 units their busiest period of the year. STARKEY, the great Allied ruse to make the Germans suspect a full scale invasion, involved concentrated efforts against communication centres and airfields near the Channel coast. For eight days in succession the four groups worked away, sometimes flying two missions each a day. Fighter opposition was met, but once again countered by the Spitfire escort. The inevitable flak brought most troubles and there were many incidents, the 386th again taking a share.

Incendiary Mary, the Marauder whose red haired nude decor had been considered a little too revealing by a Senate investigating committee, was one of a formation headed for Rouen marshalling yards on the 6th. She became victim of engine failure forty miles into enemy territory and still with a full bomb load. The cynics held that there was little hope of return in these circumstances: nursing a Marauder carefully along on one engine required skill under the most favourable circumstances; in hostile airspace such a handicap would render the aircraft victim of flak or fighters. But the pilot, Captain Don Weiss, proved one more point in the Marauder's favour. He related: "We were well into France and just about

Major Sherman Beaty, CO of 555th BS, does his best to look like the *Son of Satan* motif on his aircraft. General Eisenhower was to inspect this bomber in the spring of 1944.—(USAF)

at the point where we were to start our bomb run when the right engine quit. We had to get rid of our bombs to lighten the ship, so I decided to make a run on one engine. By losing about 200 feet of altitude and turning inside the main formation, I managed to keep pretty well up with them as we went over the target. We had no bombsight so it was necessary to keep up with the formation if we were to do accurate bombing''.

Bombardier/navigator Lt David Meserow calculated the bomb release point by estimating *Incendiary Mary's* distance below and behind the main formation. Having unloaded, Weiss turned towards the coast. They were now down to 7000 ft—nearly half the usual height—and an inviting target for flak, being well within the range of the lighter 7.9 mm guns. The shells came fast and thick. Controlling a B-26 with one engine feathered was not an easy task: evasive action in such circumstances might mean loss of control and was hitherto untried. Weiss had no option and *Incendiary Mary's* girations were such that she came through unscathed. For nearly 200 miles the aircraft flew on one engine and came back to make a perfect landing at base.

Incendiary Mary was an aircraft of the Group's 555th Bomb Sqdn., and, indeed, her fiery tag was in keeping with many other nicknames painted on the unit's aircraft. The squadron badge embodied a red devil motif, from which the

The fixed forward firing armament was designed to further the B-26's strike power in the low-level attack role. When this was abandoned the fixed armament had little value and the single .50, to the right side of the plexiglass nose, was eventually removed. Lt F. W. Harris's *Rat Poison* was to fly 121 missions with the 386th BG before being retired and used as a Group transport.—(USAF)

8 Sept. 1943; the 386th BG regains the Channel after passing through a flak barrage. The aircraft trailing smoke got home. *Margie*, rapidly losing height, is the speck within the propeller arc of the B-26 on the left.—(IWM)

be precise, a total of 219 B-26s were despatched of which 202 bombed, timed so that a formation went over the targets every fifteen minutes for two hours. This activity brought three losses, one each from the 322nd, 386th and 387th Groups, from very intense flak. Many aircraft were damaged, the 322nd having 19 in need of patching.

Like the crews of other groups participating those of the 387th had been told no more at briefing than that Allied Fleets were in the Channel. For all they knew this could have been a prelude to a landing on the French coast and their

Idiot's Delight II was shot up by FW 190s on 27 Aug. 1943. Flares in the nose caught fire and filled the aircraft with smoke, impairing vision. For some time F/O Frank Remmele could only judge his flight attitude by reference to the cumulus cloud undercast.—(IWM)

satanic inspiration was drawn. Major Beaty, Commanding, named his aircraft *Son of Satan*—others were *Hell's Angels*, *Hell's Fury*, *Hell's-a-poppin*, *Hell's Bells* and *Nemo*. A compromise was the ingenious *Perkatory* derived from that 'half-way place' and the pilot's name—Lt Perkins.

Margie of a sister squadron, the 552nd, was not as fortunate two days later when an engine failed over the target. Flak shrapnel was the suspected cause. With a Spitfire flight as close escort, 2/Lt Romney Spencer turned *Margie* for the coast only to have the remaining engine start running erratically. The pilots were able to restart the engine, but it refused to function for long. Eventually loss of altitude made a ditching inevitable. Spencer let the rear fuselage strike first to slow the aircraft, even so, when the nacelles touched *Margie* was immediately swamped. All but one gunner managed to escape, when it sank within thirty seconds. Soon a Spitfire of the Air Sea Rescue service arrived overhead to drop a life raft and then a launch arrived to make the first ASR pick-up of Marauder crew members.

Next day, September 9th, was to be the busiest day of all for the Marauders during their Eighth Air Force service. The four groups each contributed 18 aircraft formations to three separate missions against coastal defences near Boulogne; to participation vital to its success. Their airfield, Chipping Ongar in the Thames basin, was shrouded with early morning mist extending up to 400 ft, reducing ground visibility to 100 yards or less. Despite the conditions—justifying postponement or abandoning the mission, the 387th took off. One B-26 did crash off the end of the runway and only the tail gunner lived, but 55 B-26s successfully flew off "blind", a not insignificant feat for pilots with only a limited experience of instrument take-offs; a feat the cynics would not have believed possible in the Marauder.

Thereafter the weather broke and cloud hindered operations. On September 11th it caused a diversion to a secondary target and on the 14th conditions deteriorated so much that the force was recalled. The following two days saw renewed and successful activity, only for bad weather to take command again on the 18th when the majority of the 162 Marauders despatched during the day were frustrated by clouds. The 19th was very much a repetition of the previous day.

Clouds allowed only part of the 322nd to join the 387th in bombing the Beauvais/Tille dispersal area on the 21st. A 387th bomber went down but the 322nd despatched an FW190 that had attacked them and killed a crewman in one aircraft. For seven consecutive days the Marauders were despatched to repeat hits on enemy airfields whose names were becoming familiar to the airmen of 3rd Wing.

The Luftwaffe used cloud cover to avoid the Spitfires and came to grips with the Marauders, but it did them little good, for thirteen of the enemy were claimed shot down by gunners and all seven B-26s lost were victims of flak. The seven were lost in 1,897 effective sorties over enemy territory. Losses might have been greater, but the B-26 was showing that the Fortress was not the only aircraft that could take heavy punishment and still fly. The 323rd's *Double Trouble* was brought home by Lt Richard Ulvestad with one engine on fire, *Idiot's Delight II* had its empennage blasted and control surfaces wrecked yet kept flying, and there were many others.

The first mission of October had to be abandoned. On return one B-26 trying to land at North Weald, over-shot and crashed into the officers' mess. Weather conditions were better on the 3rd when the defences of Amsterdam/Schipol

opened up on the B-26s for the first time. On this raid, *Flak Happy* was severely shot up; her pilot, Captain George Watson had been co-pilot of the most bullet-riddled B-26 that returned from the 322nd's first low level raid back in May.

On October 8th the 322nd and 386th Groups were despatched to Lille/Vendeville and Chievres airfields, and on the following day the 323rd and 387th Groups flew the Marauders' last operation with the Eighth. As of October 16th 1943, the four groups were transferred to the Ninth Air Force, newly established in the UK charged with building up US tactical air power for the Allied invasion of Europe. The 3rd Wing and VIII Air Support Command went with them, although these designations changed with their passing.

The transfer of the Marauder units received little attention. Yet their's was a remarkable success story that few would have believed possible earlier in the year. In three months the reputation of the Martin bomber had been redeemed and the acid terms "Flying Prostitute" and "Baltimore Whore" were no longer heard. The Marauder was still not the best of warplanes to fly, a pilot had to know her well to handle her successfully. She was indeed a madame, but a much maligned one. In ninety medium altitude missions involving some 4000 sorties the enemy had claimed only thirteen and then only one through fighter action, in effect a 0.3% loss rate with bombing results equal to those of the heavies.

*　　*　　*　　*　　*　　*　　*

Preserved in the Smithsonian museum, Washington D.C., is a drab twin-engined aeroplane from World War Two. It bears the name *Flak Bait*, has 202 hand-painted symbols for bombing missions in a hostile sky and visible signs of repair. No other USAAF bomber completed so many operations over Europe. This Marauder, 41-31773, flew with the 449th Bomb Sqdn. of the ill-starred 322nd Group. It had been one of the aircraft parked at Bury St Edmunds in late May 1943, when few believed the Marauder worthy of flying one combat mission—let alone 200.

Chapter 8: Blitz Week

The sustained attacks during the last week of July 1943 became popularly known as "Blitz Week" when Eaker, seizing the opportunity created by predominately cloudless skies, sent his bombers far and wide in their heaviest onslaught on the German war machine so far.

It began on 24th July, when the Fortresses first went to Norway. Three hundred and twenty-four took off into the overcast, all but 15 rendezvousing on time. Cloud cloaked England and extended across the North Sea that morning, but clear skies ahead were predicted. Hitherto, overcast conditions at take-off had presented difficulties in assembling a formation, at times causing a mission to be scrubbed, and though a hazard remained, it was lessened by a new standard technique introduced on this occasion. Use was made of Splasher beacons, British medium frequency radio stations situated at intervals across the East Anglian countryside, the bombers taking off, climbing on instruments and assembling into group formation above the overcast around the Splasher signal, and by utilising three such beacons combat wing assembly was also affected.

Destination of the 1st Bomb Wing was Heroya, some 600 miles distant, where the Germans had just completed a new nitrate factory. The 4th Wing, having Fortresses with extra wing tankage, were assigned Bergen and Trondheim harbours, 950 miles away. Both forces crossed the North Sea at 2,500 feet to obtain optimum fuel economy, climbing to around 16,000 ft and 20,000 ft respectively for bombing. At Heroya 167 Forts stopped nitrate production for 3½ months and caused adjoining unfinished aluminium and magnesium plants to be abandoned. The moderate flak barrage crippled but one bomber, the 381st Group's *Georgia Rebel*, which limped into

Swedes gather round *Georgia Rebel* after she was crash-landed at Vännacka.—(T. Olausson)

neutral Sweden and successfully crash-landed in a bog at Vaannacka. All others returned safely. The 4th Wing hit Trondheim, but Bergen was cloud covered and bombs were brought back to England. Apart from Ju88s sent to find the bombers on the return flight, opposition was negligible suggesting the Luftwaffe had been taken off guard by this northerly thrust.

Early afternoon the day following, Fortresses were to be seen outward bound over Cromer, favourite routing point for bombers making for N.W. Germany. One combat wing from the 1st Bomb Wing made for Kiel, the others to Hamburg, and the 4th Bomb Wing to an aircraft works at Warnemunde beyond Kiel. Only the Kiel force fulfilled its assignment, elsewhere unexpected cloud conditions caused many groups

Second mission for Knettishall's 388th BG was Bergen harbour in Norway but cloud covered the target. Where the terrain was visible it looked none too inviting from 20,000 ft.—(IWM)

Knock Out Dropper over smoke haze at Hamburg. The bird's foot-like markings are medium green camouflage blotches. This B-17F later become one of 303rd BG's most distinguished aircraft.—(USAF)

to seek targets of opportunity. A pall of smoke some 15,000 ft high hung over Hamburg marking the previous night's visit of the RAF and hindered the sighting of shipyards and a diesel engine works. As it was, only the first formation was able to bomb before cloud intervened. The price was high, 19 Forts lost, of which five were claimed by anti-aircraft fire. Once again, low groups were in trouble and the 384th Group flying in that position in the leading wing lost seven bombers—all those in Purple Heart Corner.

In spite of loss and damage, VIII Bomber Command was again able to despatch over 300 bombers within 24 hours, but heavy overcast disrupted their assembly in spite of the new techniques and groups delayed were recalled. As a result some formations dropped on targets of opportunity along the German coast and the briefed targets at Hamburg and Hanover were attacked by only two combat wings each. Nevertheless, the 92 B-17s attacking the Continental Gummi Werke at Hanover, a synthetic rubber plant and major tyre factory, achieved considerable success. Damage resulting from 21

Hamburg was still burning from the RAF's attack the previous night when VIII BC arrived on 25 Jul. 1943. This photo taken by a 381st BG B-17 'caught' an FW 190 diving to attack three 4th Wing aircraft.— (USAF)

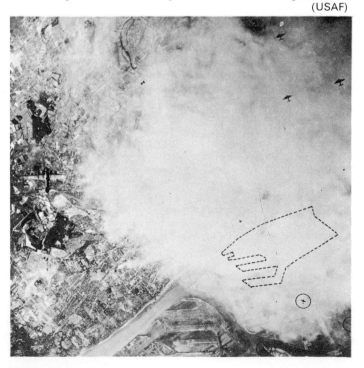

direct hits on buildings caused production losses of almost one quarter for weeks thereafter. Fires and explosions produced a huge column of smoke that rose to 22,000 ft, just below the bombers—although some groups attacked from the unusually high altitude of 31,000 ft on this occasion. Enemy defensive measures were on a par with those usually experienced with missions to this area of Germany and concentrated fighter attacks were launched at leading Fortress formations on penetration.

From the many stories of ordeal under fire that emerged that day, one ranks high in the annals of the Eighth, indeed it has become legend. One of 17 B-17Fs in the 92nd Group formation (there were also two YB-40s) was *Ruthie II*, piloted by 1/Lt Robert L. Campbell. This replacement for *Ruthie I*, written off after the Independence Day mission to Nantes, was again named after the pilot's wife. Close to landfall, the 92nd was subjected to a frontal attack by FW190s. A bullet struck Campbell, splitting his skull. He collapsed forward over the control column, clasping his arms tightly around it so that the co-pilot, Flying Officer John C. Morgan, had to use brute force to work the controls on his side and keep the bomber on course. Morgan, a Texan, had volunteered and flown for the RCAF for seven months before transferring to the Eighth. Like many other transferees from the RAF and RCAF he had helped to make up the shortage in combat crews. A striking red-haired, six-footer Morgan needed all of his 200 lbs to overcome the crazed strength of the dying pilot. Finding no response over the interphone, Morgan concentrated as best he could to keep the pilot from disrupting control. He reasoned that keeping within the protection of the formation gave the best prospects for a return to base, besides there was good reason to believe the bombs could yet be delivered at Hanover. The same burst of fire that mortally wounded Campbell, also struck the top turret severing S/Sgt Tyre C. Weaver's left arm just below the shoulder. Weaver slid down into the rear of the nose compartment and slumped on the floor behind the navigator, 2/Lt Keith J. Koske, who immediately went to his aid. Unsuccessful in giving a morphine injection because the needle was damaged, and also unable to apply a tourniquet because the arm was off too close to the shoulder, Koske realised that unless medical aid was forthcoming, Weaver would bleed to death. He made a quick decision; adjusting Weaver's parachute he placed the ripcord ring in his right hand, opened the nose door and proceeded to push him out into space. Unfortunately Weaver, suffering from shock, immediately pulled the cord causing the pilot 'chute to release. This Koske managed to bundle up under Weaver's right arm and then pushed him clear. The ball gunner reported seeing the parachute open and weeks afterwards word reached England that Weaver was alive and well in a German hospital.

Ruthie II was then about 25 miles west of the target at over 24,000 ft and Morgan's ordeal in the cockpit was unknown to other crew members. Hearing no defensive fire from the rear, Morgan assumed the gunners had baled out. In fact those in the waist, radio room and tail were unconscious due to the oxygen lines having been shattered. As the aircraft kept level, except for what was taken to be evasive action, the two men in the nose assumed all to be well and it was not until the Fort was fifteen minutes out from the enemy coast on the way home, that Koske left his navigator's table and gun to see how things were with the rest. He found Morgan flying the bomber with one hand while keeping the still struggling Campbell off the controls—as he had been for the past two hours! The co-pilot's windscreen was shattered so badly that Morgan had to move to the pilot's seat to have a clear view for landing. Koske, with Morgan's aid got Campbell into the nose where the bombardier held him to prevent his slipping through the open hatch. The plight of the gunners was discovered and when revived they were found to be

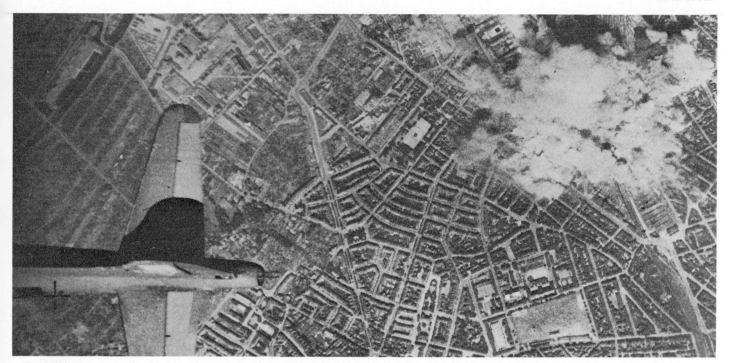

In addition to the main attack on Continental Gummi-Werke, a small force of Fortresses bombed the Vahrenwalder-Strasse plant at Hanover on 26 Jul. 1943. This is the target, shown in this photo, some five miles beneath the tail of 95th BG's QW: V.—(USAF)

badly frost bitten. Soon after the coast of Norfolk came into view, Morgan brought the aircraft in to land at RAF Foulsham. Keeping formation was never easy, a fact that made Morgan's feat the more remarkable, and no doubt influenced the decision to award him the Medal of Honor, the third to go to the Eighth Air Force.

Although fair, predictions did not appear certain enough for a mission on the 27th, thus affording crews a well earned rest. This interlude was but brief, for at dawn next day VIII Bomber Command launched its most ambitious attack yet in an attempt to destroy factories building fighters for the Luftwaffe. Taking the familiar North Sea route 1st Wing Forts planned to press inland to the Fieseler components works at Kassel, while 4th Wing formations made the deepest penetration so far, to an assembly plant at Oschersleben. The 182 aircraft despatched to Kassel came up against old bugbear of cloud, resulting in limited and generally ineffective bombing. Returning to meet fighter escort on the Dutch border, one formation was suddenly attacked by Me109s firing rocket projectiles. Each Messerschmitt appeared to carry a pair of launching tubes, one under each wing and released the time-fused at around 1000 yards range. Although many of the missiles exploded amongst the Fortress formation—the 379th Group—none made a direct hit, suggesting limited accuracy. Nonetheless, fragments of rocket casing were blasted around when the war-head exploded and several aircraft received some minor damage in this way. One, *The Sack,* was struck just below the top turret by a large fragment that exploded oxygen bottles and blasted quite an imposing hole.

Lead of the Oschersleben force was given to the 94th Group at Bury St Edmunds. To many of the airmen at briefing that morning, leading on the deepest penetration of Germany so far attempted by the Eighth, looked like a ticket to extinction on the strength of recent experiences. Anticipating the understandable apprehension of the crews, Colonel Fred Castle chose to take the 94th to Oschersleben personally on what he too expected to be a "hot mission". Plans called for the bombers to feint towards the Hamburg-Kiel area before turning south-east for the target, but the 120 4th Wing bombers were soon confronted with adverse weather causing dispersal. J.G.1 made contact almost at the coast and their

FW190s scored against the bombers, some of which had strayed towards Denmark. One stricken B-17, crashing into two others, brought all three down. From engagements, chiefly in the Heligoland area, fifteen 4th Wing bombers failed to return making this mission a most unprofitable venture but for the endeavours of two groups. While other formations turned back in some confusion, the 94th plus a few machines of the 96th forged ahead into Germany Riding in *Sour Puss,* Castle realised that the Group's chance of making a successful attack depended on finding a break in the clouds below at the right time and place; having come so far he considered the chance worth taking. Even in fine visibility the aircraft factory would have proved difficult to locate for there were no significant features like rivers or mountains as landmarks in the vicinity. However the 94th were lucky, for when only a few miles from the objective a gap in the undercast allowed the lead bombardier to recognise a crossroads a few miles from his aiming point. Quickly calculating the time from target, he released his bombs by estimation and 14 other Forts dropped by this signal, while

It appears incredible that the blast that made this hole did not injure the engineer/gunner or pilots of *Sack.*—(USAF)

Calamity Jane was aptly named, for soon after arrival at Framlingham she was wrecked in a taxying accident. She became 390th BG's first 'hangar queen', supplying parts for other B-17s. In the background the wreckage of 306th BG's GY: L (which crashed on the base) is being loaded on to a "Queen Mary" transporter.—(USAF)

13 from the 388th Group in a following formation was also able to make a successful strike. Photo reconnaissance next day revealed an excellent concentration of bombs on the plant, causing an estimated loss of a month's production—about 50 FW190s.

Amazingly, the 94th returned to Bury St Edmunds that day without having lost a single aircraft in combat, although the opposition encountered had been intensive enough to produce claims of 21 destroyed. Castle summed it all up rather grandly for the PRO: "When the boys who had caught hell for months were given the responsibility and honor of heading the entire formation of a crucial mission, they didn't flinch. Practice and disheartening experience paid rich dividends". The Oschersleben mission re-kindled the flame of esprit de corps at Bury St Edmunds. The reproach that greeted Castle's taking of command after the Kiel fiasco in June was gone: "Any man would fly to hell and back with him". Leading one of the 94th's squadrons on the raid had been Captain Franklin Colby; nearing his 42nd birthday, he was the oldest operational pilot in the Command. In an air force where the average age of a combat airman was around 20, Colby was looked upon as a really old man.

Barely had engines had time to cool, before being readied for further action. But the pace and opposition were beginning to tell on men and aircraft, for no longer could the same strength of attack be maintained. The 4th Wing set off for Warnemunde, which it had made an abortive attempt to hit four days previously. This time half the force were able to do excellent bombing, destroying 18 of the 27 buildings at the Heinkel assembly plant engaged in FW190 production. The 1st Wing went to Kiel and unloaded 767,000 propaganda leaflets with 207.9 tons of bombs over the shipyards. Two of the B-17s lost on this occasion were from the 369th Bomb Sqdn. members of the 306th Group, one being the squadron lead plane with the "Fitin Bitin" insignia on its nose. This loss ended a remarkable record run up by this squadron over the past six months, during which it had not had one aircraft or crew listed 'Missing in Action'—and this through one of the periods of fiercest combat for the Eighth. Five B-17s had been lost before the record began in January and the squadron had to this date flown on all but two of the 56 missions made by 'the Thurleigh group. If this good luck record had been broken there was some consolation in that the notoriously heavy losses suffered by a sister squadron, the 367th, were no longer being perpetuated.

At dawn on July 30th both B-17 wings took off for Kassel. The sky, clear all the way, permitted good bombing, and Thunderbolts flying further in than ever before to meet the returning bombers, by virtue of drop tanks, encountered the enemy opposition at its height. This time only 186 Fortresses were sent out and of those reaching enemy airspace, 12 did not return, and a few that did never flew again. One that ended its days was *Patches* of the 384th Group who had earned its nickname from troubles on the Group's first mission in June. On the Kassel raid, in the hands of Lt William Harry and crew, trouble was experienced with the oxygen system and the aircraft dropped out of formation to seek safety in a lower altitude. This soon attracted enemy fighters but Harry put *Patches* through violent evasive manoeuvres, and eventually managed to escape the antagonists. But that it still flew seemed incredible. There were more than a thousand holes from bullets and shrapnel, most of one elevator was gone and a large piece had been shot out of the rudder: the throttles were jammed and six of the ten men aboard were wounded including Lt Harry. Just before noon *Patches* crossed the English coast, wallowing in the warm blue summer sky as her pilots sought an airfield. Finding Boxted the battered Fortress was weaved down towards this field while red warning flares were fired. A flat tyre did not help matters, but Harry with co-pilot Rice managed to put it down safely albeit askew to the runways. *Patches* was eventually canabilised while her crew recovered to fly again.

The last day of July was also fine but the German radar screens were denied the familiar pattern of a gathering bomber raid. The reason was primarily that the battle-weary Fortress groups were in no position to fly another large scale mission to Germany without a short period of recuperation to rebuild their effective strengths in men and machines. Thereafter the elements enforced a lull in operations during the opening days of August with storm clouds again blanketing much of Western Europe.

Blitz week had proved the most intensive period of operations so far, tiring both flying and ground crews. When the bombers had set out to Norway the fifteen B-17 groups had approximately 330 aircraft and crews ready for operations; within a week that effective strength was reduced to below 200. Approximately 100 B-17s had been lost during operations, or scrapped as a result of extensive damage, and the equivalent of some 90 crews were either missing, killed or wounded during the same period. Additionally nearly half of the bombers participating sustained some form of damage. However, the replacement aircraft position had considerably improved, but the availability of trained crews was the limiting factor—understandably so as the CCRCs had to find the equivalent of the flying complement of nine squadrons due to the casualties in Blitz Week alone.

Chapter 9: The Mounting Cost

For two weeks the Fortresses stood on their hardstanding among the golden harvest fields or flew practice missions over Britain. While the crews rested, Eighth Air Force staffs were recasting the most ambitious and cleverly conceived strike plan of the year. Neutralising the Luftwaffe opposition was still, of necessity, a prime aim, with the destruction of fighter aircraft plants at the heart of the scheme. The main production of Me109s and 48% of all German fighters was at Regensburg and Wiener Neustadt, 525 and 725 miles respectively from East Anglia. A flight to and from these targets would entail many hours in a hostile sky, allowing the enemy ample time to deploy his defensive forces in strength. To avert this, a new plan called for the B-17s to fly on to Allied bases in North Africa, thus confusing the enemy who would expect the bombers to return to the UK. As many 1st Wing B-17s did not have Tokyo tanks it was decided that the Wiener Neustadt mission would be flown from North Africa by the Ninth Air Force's two B-24 groups and the three from the Eighth then on detached service in Libya. The two targets were to have been attacked on the same day to cause maximum confusion and saturation to enemy defences. August 7th was the date set, but on this and succeeding days the weather was not good enough to allow the Regensburg force to be sent from England. A revamping of the plan then allowed each force to attack its assigned target as opportunity presented; the Liberators finally visited Wiener Neustadt on the 13th, while the way to the Eighth's objectives continued to be barred by cloud.

In the meantime every opportunity was taken to continue the daylight bomber offensive from England and August 12th offered a chance of hitting targets in the Ruhr. The VIII Bomber Command put up 330 bombers including, for the first time, those of its newest member the 390th Group from Framlingham. This mission was again thwarted by clouds

Clark Gable poses after a flight in *Delta Rebel No. 2*. This 91st BG B-17F failed to return from the first Schweinfurt mission a few days later.—(USAF)

intervening between sights and target, and only two groups unloaded over their assigned objective. The enemy, making good use of smoke screens, even foiled some formations that found gaps in the cloud. Targets of opportunity were then sought, and in the general confusion the Luftwaffe reaped a rich harvest: 25 heavies failed to return, a figure surpassing all previous losses for one day apart from that of June 13th. The 1st Wing groups met particularly heavy opposition near Gelsenkirchen, the 384th Group losing five aircraft—the third occasion on which this "new group" had suffered heavily. Leading Fortress of the Gelsenkirchen force, piloted by Major Theodore Milton of the 351st Group, carried Captain Clark Gable who took films of the proceedings for use in a gunnery training film.

From the beginning of the third week in August, the Eighth's heavies participated in the STARKEY deception plan aimed at making the Germans think invasion of the Pas de Calais coast was imminent in order to halt troop movements to Russia and Italy. In most cases these attacks were against airfields and thus furthered the campaign against the German Air Force as well as promoting STARKEY. The bombing of airfields in France and the Low countries on August 15th and 16th were comparatively easy operations, serving as introductory missions for the many replacement crews that had reached the groups during the past week or two.

Only twice during STARKEY were major missions made to the Reich, the first on August 17th 1943, was the anniversary of the beginning of VIII Bomber Command's operations from England. With weather favourable both over Europe and Mediterranean the ambitious "Shuttle" mission, striking the Regensburg Messerschmitt factory and flying on to bases in North Africa was launched. The task fell to the 4th Wing with its longer ranged Fortresses, and in order to confuse and split enemy defences the 1st Wing undertook a parallel mission to bearing factories at Schweinfurt with a return to England. German manufacture of ball bearings, essential to the machines of war, was concentrated in the Schweinfurt area. In view of the importance of the targets and the distances to be flown, Command anticipated a major air battle: they were not mistaken.

The seven groups of 4th Bomb Wing, which had been reserved from action on the 16th, were not surprised when late that evening crews were alerted for a mission next day. They were however, puzzled, to say the least, when told to pack canteen and cutlery, razor and toilet articles, underclothing and a blanket. Not until the small hours briefing did they learn the reason for this strange order; they would spend the next night on another continent! Although the mission had all the signs of being 'tough' its novelty engendered excitement and enthusiasm. Each group would fly a 21-plane formation with extras accompanying as far as the enemy coast to take the places of any abortives; in all 147 B-17s, mostly carrying 5000 lbs of bombs each. A dawn take-off was scheduled but the summer morning mists affecting visibility at most bases caused the bombers to be held back. The Regensburg force could not be delayed more than ninety minutes if it was to reach North Africa in daylight. For a while it looked as if Command might cancel the mission, but gradually the mist over Suffolk and Norfolk thinned and the 4th Wing was ordered off. Some groups, having difficulty in rendezvousing in the cloud conditions prevailing, caused formations to drone above the East Anglian countryside for over two hours; again it appeared the mission might have to be 'scrubbed'. Fuel was the critical item and failure to assemble the task force in time would leave insufficient reserve fuel for the flight. Fortunately the errant groups found their positions just in time and by 09.35 hrs the leading combat wing was heading out over Lowestoft towards the Continent.

Meanwhile, the 1st Wing bombers remained grounded, the mist being far thicker inland and still defying the sun's efforts to disperse it. The delay posed a crucial problem. All four operational P-47 groups had been assigned to give maximum escort to the 4th Wing penetration which was expected to draw most of the enemy interceptors, and then leave them little time to refuel and meet the on-coming Schweinfurt force. With the 1st Wing bombers still at their bases, this advantage was jeopardised, and Command were finally forced to hold back the Schweinfurt mission until the P-47s had returned and could be refuelled to provide another escort. Thus, the chance to split and confuse enemy defences by a two-pronged thrust was lost.

By 10.00 hrs the 4th Bombardment Wing bomber column bound for Regensburg was crossing the Dutch coast. The three combat wing formations were well formed but with too much distance between each for the satisfaction of the Wing commander, Colonel Le May, flying in a bomber of the leading 96th Group from Snetterton Heath. The other groups in the first formation were the 388th and 390th flying the low and high positions respectively; the latter was on its third mission and still without experience of an air battle. The following combat wing was led by Castle's 94th Group with Vandevanter's 385th flying low, while the last formation, carrying incendiaries, was also composed of two groups—the 95th leading and the 100th in the unenviable low position. Stepped up from 17,000 ft the bombers found fair weather with unlimited visibility and only an odd wispy patch of high cloud disturbing the deep blue backcloth of the sky.

Two groups of P-47s to escort the Fortresses to the German border should have arrived at this juncture; one group did, taking up station over the leading boxes, but the other group miscalculating time, left the rearmost bombers unguarded. The enemy were not long in taking advantage of the situation, fifteen minutes after crossing the coast, 20 miles south east of Brussels, Focke-Wulfs made for the last combat wing that trailed far behind and out of sight of the ministering Thunderbolts—some 15 miles separated the leading and trailing bomber groups. At 10.25 hrs the battle was joined in earnest with pairs of FW190s attacking head-on through the two rear groups. True to form, most of their attacks were directed at the low squadron of the low group, from which two 100th bombers went down, one exploding, while a stricken 95th Fort began to drop out of formation.

Up in front, the time had come for the Thunderbolts to withdraw and as they turned back at 10.32 hrs over Eupen they could see some of the first B-17s going down, but with their fuel reserves at a minimum there was nothing they could do. As the Fortresses headed into Germany the enemy opposition grew in intensity; no sooner had one fighter Staffel attacked, than another took its place. The 100th Group continued to be the chief object of attention and as bomber after bomber fell away the possibility of complete annihilation must have loomed in the minds of surviving crews. Along 150 miles FW190s and Me109s pressed home attacks, singly, in pairs, or in waves of four or more, chiefly at the last combat wing. The battle moved over Germany at 180 mph, its course marked by flashes, flames, smoke, the debris of disintegrating aircraft, parachutes and men; the noise indescribable. Lt Colonel Beirne Lay, one of Eaker's "original seven" riding as an observer in the 100th's *Piccadilly Lily*, said "The sight was fantastic; it surpassed fiction". Past Mannheim the attacks by

single-engined fighters dropped off as they exhausted fuel and ammunition. Their place was taken by twin-engined Me110 Zerstörers and Ju88 night fighters that harried the bombers from the rear, some releasing rockets. Then, shortly before the target was reached fighter attacks virtually ceased, giving the Fortress gunners their first respite for 1½ hours. During that time 17 Fortresses had gone down, 13 from the last combat wing, but several enemy fighters had also been destroyed and others damaged. Navigation to Regensburg had been good and in perfect visibility the Messerschmitt works could be easily picked out nestling in a bend of the Danube. To obtain a high degree of accuracy the force was ordered to bomb from between 17,000 and 19,000 ft. The concentration was in fact excellent and Le May later cabled London from Africa: "Objective believed totally destroyed". Also unbeknown to Allied intelligence the raid destroyed most of the

96th BG scales the Alps after Regensburg.—(USAF)

fuselage jigs for a secret jet fighter, the Me262. The 129 bombers that left the factory enveloped in smoke and flame met further opposition from a few twin-engined fighters; but 30 minutes after bombing opposition ceased. The Germans were evidently not prepared for the bombers south western course now taken, and besides their attention was then occupied by an even larger raid developing from England.

Le May led his force over the Alps and across Italy and then descended to an altitude suiting maximum fuel conservation over the Mediterranean. At 17.28 hrs, over 11 hrs after take-off, the first Fortresses put down in North Africa. Dust storms, exhausted fuel and unfamiliar terrain caused B-17s to be scattered along the Tunisian coast; the majority, however, made Bone and Telergma. Of the 24 aircraft missing, fuel exhaustion and engine failure were responsible for five ditchings in the Mediterranean, one had crash-landed in Northern Italy, and two (from 100th and 390th Groups) in Switzerland—the first battle-damaged USAAF warplanes to seek sanctuary in that neutral country; the remaining casualties lay scattered across the Reich. From the leading combat wing only the 390th Group had suffered serious attrition, six bombers being lost to fuel shortage and attacks by twin-engined fighters near the target. The Framlingham group, 'baby' of the VIII Command had nevertheless excelled in bombing accuracy, producing the best of all seven groups—58% within 1000 ft of the aiming point and 94% within 2000 ft. In the second combat wing, the low 385th Group had lost three of its number and a waist gunner in one of its Forts was killed by a 'friendly' bullet. The trailing combat wing had suffered most with 14 B-17s missing of which ten were from the 100th Group. While every B-17 group entering combat during the summer of 1943 faced bitter experiences, there were those groups on which particular misfortune was apt to dwell. Hitherto, the 100th had not ranked as one of these

Lt Oakes of 100th BG managed to bring the damaged 42-30080, EP: F down in Switzerland.—(Birdsall)

unfortunates, but from Regensburg attack onwards their misfortunes became a legend.

At roughly the same time as the 4th Wing reached Africa, 1st Wing bombers were coming back over the Suffolk coast. Their experience had been no less epic, the scattered formations that passed over Ipswich with individual Fortresses putting down on the first airfields they could find, gave evidence of hard battle.

A force of 230 B-17s had been despatched to Schweinfurt in four combat wings, the extra wing being built up with composite groups—squadrons from different bases combining to make a group box. The first combat wing had the veteran 91st Group in lead position with the 381st low. Like his counterpart in 4th Wing, Brigadier General Robert B. Williams had chosen to fly with his men on this important mission, riding in a 91st bomber as task force commander. In the lead Fortress of the 91st Group flew its commander Colonel Wurzbach with Colonel Gross another officer of the wing.

The bombers had followed much the same route as the Regensburg force, but near Mannheim they turned north-east to make for their target. Against this force the enemy vectored the greater part of his single-engined fighters in the west, even bringing Gruppen of J.G.1 and J.G 11 down from the North German seaboard, some 250 miles. Approximately 200 enemy aircraft made interceptions commencing near Antwerp and continuing intermittently to the target and back to the coast. Every trick and device was contrived by the Luftwaffe; attacks were delivered from all quarters, with those in the region of nose and tail predominating. A frequent method was to dive

from the sun firing at a high squadron and continue through a group to strike the low squadron as well.

The Luftwaffe reversed tactics against this force but they attempted to obliterate the formation heading the bomber column. This they very nearly succeeded in doing, hammering at the unfortunate low group and then the leading 91st. Bombing at Schweinfurt, while not as effective as that at Regensburg, was still very good, but the cost was high; over 370 airmen and 36 B-17s missing, plus many dead and wounded in returning bombers. The unfortunate 91st and 381st groups contributed nearly a third each to these figures having lost 10 and 11 bombers respectively. The senior officers survived to reflect on the mounting cost of daylight strategic bombing.

These first anniversary raids occupy a prominent place in the history of the Eighth Air Force for a number of reasons, not least of which was the loss of 60 bombers (the previous high was 26 on the June 13th raid). Against this gunner claims ran to an even more staggering figure of 288 enemy aircraft destroyed—nearly the entire force actually involved in interception! These claims were later reduced to 148 with nearly another hundred damaged or probables which, if true, was still a crippling blow to the Luftwaffe. Combat crews and many of the Eighth's senior officers genuinely believed these figures bore some relation to the truth, and as such contributed nearly as much to the demise of the Luftwaffe as the destruction wrought by bombing two key industries. To a large degree the morale factor hinged on these claims, and the true German losses of 27 fighters would never have been accepted at the time. In history, the American claims serve to indicate the intensity of the air battle, a battle which had few equals in the Second World War.

During the remainder of August and early September VIII Bomber Command was chiefly occupied with missions to the Channel coast in furtherance of the STARKEY ruse. Cloud, present in varying degrees for the better part of six weeks following Regensburg/Schweinfurt, prevented any major strikes at German targets. An attempt to bomb Dutch airfields later the same week was largely abortive due to overcast. On this occasion 4th Bomb Wing had been able to send out a small formation formed with crews and aircraft that had not made the Shuttle trip, for not until a week after that famous

Regensburg a few hours after the attack. Major damage to two-thirds of the workshops is visible in this photograph. Completed Me 109s that escaped damage can be seen on flying field near hangars.—(USAF)

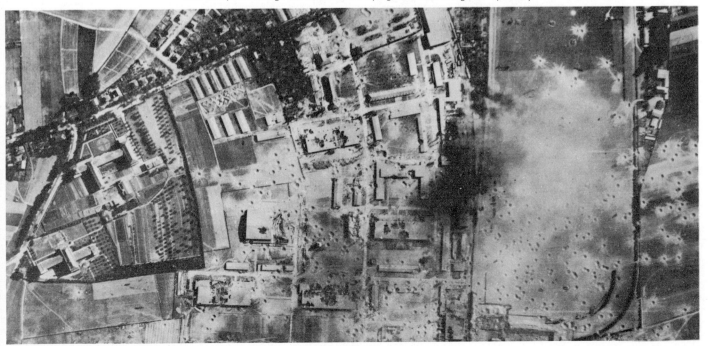

event did the participants return. Sixty of the 115 Fortresses that reached Africa were deemed airworthy for return to the UK with the job of bombing Bordeaux/Merignac airfield during passage across France. The flight was comparatively easy, malfunction being the prime factor in the failure of three B-17s to gain the English coast. One of these, *Lulu Belle*, lead ship of 385th Group on Regensburg and other missions, had to put down in the sea off Land's End. Major Preston Piper, group executive, and seven on board were rescued but two others were drowned trying to swim to a life raft dropped by the RAF and another two died of exposure. These losses reflected the pitifully inadequate maintenance facilities available in North Africa, lack of replacement parts and servicing equipment, delaying the return of many B-17s for some weeks. It influenced VIII BC in the decision to refrain from further shuttle missions, at least until this situation had been remedied. The most notable souvenirs brought back to England from North Africa were a couple of donkeys, both named Lady Moe by their respective owners at Thorpe Abbots and Snetterton Heath.

While crews attending briefing on the morning of August 27th were relieved to find the day's missions would take them no further than the Pas de Calais, there was considerable curiosity as to the nature of the targets described as "special aeronautical facilities". These concrete structures were approached at altitudes as low as 14,000 ft to ensure accurate bombing. The 368 2,000 lb bombs dropped by the 187 B-17s caused much more harm than seemed apparent, the raid being well-timed while a great deal of the concrete was still wet. Aircrew opinion reckoned the structures part of the coastal defences and not until much later was the true purpose of them revealed—launching bases for Hitler's secret V-weapons. This mission was the first of many under the code name CROSSBOW, the Allied counter to V-1 sites.

On the last day of the month there seemed to be a good chance of attacking Luftwaffe depots and aircraft component factories around Paris. Heavy cloud permitted only the 1st Wing to bomb—a last resort target—while 4th Wing brought

In good formation, 306th BG B-17s encounter gathering cloud on the way to Stuttgart.—(USAF)

Lady Moe takes a look at England from the waist window of 96th BG's *The Miracle Tribe* supported by S/Sgt L. Klinchak and Sgt E. C. Mathews. The North African donkey cost the men 400 francs.—(USAF)

their bombs home again. Much the same occurred two days later when only two small formations of a force of 300 plus bombers could find gaps in the cloud. Next morning, it was a case of third time lucky when the weather improved to enable 1st Wing to wreck the aircraft park at Romilly-sur-Seine and 4th Wing to blast aircraft component among other factories in the Paris area.

Without doubt, throughout the summer of 1943, cloud afforded German industry its best defence against attack from the American bombers, both by blanketing targets and dispersing the closely-knit formations. Perhaps the most disastrous occasion on which cloud baulked a major mission was September 6th, 1943, when what was to have been an important strike primarily against a Stuttgart factory making instrument bearings, and for the first time involving over 400 bombers (Liberators recently returned from Africa were to fly a diversion), turned into the biggest fiasco of the year—surpassing that of the June mission to Hamburg. A force of 338 B-17s assembled, but cloud became heavier as they advanced across France and by the time the leading formations reached Stuttgart it became clear the missions should have been abandoned. German fighters made only a few spasmodic attacks en route, an ominous sign where a deep penetration was intended. The German controller had obviously been marshalling his forces and when the leading 4th Wing groups reached their target these fears were realised. Several Gruppen of Me109s and FW190s began an assault in the now familiar pattern, flying out two or three miles ahead of the bombers, turning to meet them on the same level and coming in from 11 and 12 o'clock positions, one after another, at about 20-second intervals. Around 300 yards from the bombers each fighter would commence to roll and then fire. The 388th Group was taking its turn in the low position and these vicious and concentrated attacks brought the Knettishall group its severest losses of the war; one of its 21 Fortresses went down before the release point and ten more soon thereafter. The 563rd Bomb Sqdn. on this trip, occupying Purple Heart Corner was completely wiped out.

Only one combat wing succeeded in seeing their objective, following formations could find no such view through the broken cloud and enemy smoke screens. Brigadier General Robert Travis, Air Commander of the 1st Wing, orbited the area with his leading formations but all in vain. The bomber column already disorganised turned for home seeking targets of opportunity on the way, and 233 unloaded in this fashion. Meanwhile, the Luftwaffe sought to punish where it could. South-west of Paris they caught the 100th Group preparing to attack airfields; four of the five bombers 4th Wing lost on the previous mission had been from the 100th and on this occasion another three failed to return.

The 100th Group might have lost one more but for the skill and tenacity of 1/Lt Sumner Reeder, piloting *Squawkin' Hawk II* which dropped out of formation with several cannon shells placed in the nose and control cabin, fatally wounding the co-pilot and seriously wounding two men. Reeder, shocked and bleeding, realised their perilous position and dived to seek the protection of the squadron below. But he was forced to leave the formation completely as the oxygen system had been partly destroyed and the crew were in danger of anoxia. This quest for denser air brought more German fighters in its wake and the only chance for the crippled bomber lay still further below the cloud. Diving at nearly 300 mph *Squawkin' Hawk* dropped some 14,000 ft successfully gaining the sanctuary of the clouds where a cat and mouse game with enemy fighters ensued until the Channel coast was reached. With only radio headings as a navigational aid Reeder brought the bomber back to England, putting down at an RCAF fighter airfield. After repairs—apart from a large hole in the nose and others in fuselage and wings, a fuel tank was punctured and hydraulics damaged—*Squawkin' Hawk II* went back on operations and by the following spring had become the first Fortress in the 100th to survive fifty missions, thereafter being retired to the States. Reeder rose in rank to Major and command of his squadron, the 349th, only to lose his life in an aircraft accident after returning to the US.

Some of the groups on the September 6th mission overshot Stuttgart and those of the 1st Wing were faced with another danger, diminished fuel supplies. Aircraft forced by cloud to climb above the set altitude, to take evasive action and make two or three target runs, imposed a heavy drain on fuel tanks, and red warning lights were showing by the time the Channel coast was regained. Before long rescue services were inundated with 'Mayday' calls for altogether twelve Fortresses ditched short of fuel. Mercifully the sea was calm and brilliant work by RAF launch crews rescued every crew, 118 men in all. At airfields along the south coast other Fortresses were putting down in haste and two were wrecked in crash landings. *The Sweater Girl* of the 379th Group nearly suffered the same fate: while circling an R.A.F. airfield preparatory to

making a landing all her engines, starved of fuel, stopped. Hectic action by the pilots Lts W. L. Hawkins and D. G. Barnes just managed to bring the gliding bomber down on the runway, where the other members of the crew learned from two rather unnerved pilots that it had not been the normal landing it had seemed. When the tally was taken, 45 bombers were missing or known lost from this mission, almost half directly or indirectly to fuel shortage, human error and equipment troubles which, in turn, arose from unfavourable weather conditions. Five wandering or damaged B-17s turned up in Switzerland; *Raunchy* from the 100th Group attempted a ditching on Bodensee lake during which ball-turret gunner Joe Moloney was killed, the first American airman to die in Switzerland but by no means the last.

The British and American Press told the Stuttgart mission in terms of much heroism and another vital blow at Nazi Germany. The cold facts facing Eaker and his staff were far from impressive and highlighted the familiar weaknesses in the daylight bombing concept. Those British and American planners who advocated the Eighth's participation in night bombing as an alternative had gained some hearing, resulting in small scale trials within VIII Bomber Command. One of the B-24 groups was originally selected for this purpose but with the despatch of the Liberators to the Middle East the choice fell on a Fortress unit, the 422nd Bomb Sqdn., which was already earmarked for dropping propaganda leaflets although its first ten months in the ETO were spent in normal daylight missions with its parent 305th group. With a minimum of special equipment the 422nd put in many practice night flights during the late summer of 1943 and on September 8th five of its B-17s accompanied an RAF force bombing coastal defences near Boulogne. Another seven missions were undertaken during the next four weeks when the squadron's aircraft (usually numbering five) were despatched to targets with the RAF. The experiment was then discontinued, for while the Fortress presented no problems in night operation its use was considered uneconomical apart from difficulties in training crews if the programme was to be extended. Proficient in night flying, the 422nd was set to hauling newsprint over occupied countries and the Reich during hours of darkness.

Meanwhile, VIII Bomber Command pressed on with

On 2 Sept. 1943, General Arnold, on a visit to the UK, was taken by 4th Wing officers to see a severely shot up B-17F at Hethel. This was 379th BG's 42-3154, LF: B which ran into enemy fighters on the 12 Aug. 1943 mission. L. to r. Eaker, Arnold, Le May and Col Fred Castle.—(IWM)

daylight operations at every opportunity. The day after Stuttgart the Fortresses had ventured over the French and Belgian coasts, 1st Wing attacking Brussels/Evere airfield while the 4th Wing made the second CROSSBOW mission— against a large structure at Watten. Heavily escorted, every bomber returned. The culmination of the STARKEY raids came on September 9th with over 200 Fortresses engaging in the bombardment of nine airfields in N.W. France; fleet activity at sea and the erection of dummy P-47s and other aircraft types on English south coast airfields did not apparently fool the Germans who refrained from being drawn into air battles with superior numbers of Allied fighters.

During September there were some changes to the command structure of VIII Bomber Command, when an organisation known as an Air Division was introduced between Command and the Wings. Designed to regularise the Provisional Combat Wings that had tactical operational control over two or three groups apiece it amounted to little more than changes of designation for existing organisations. The 1st, 2nd and 4th Bombardment Wings were renamed 1st, 2nd and 3rd Bombardment Divisions respectively, and the Provisional Combat Wings became Combat Bombardment Wings while taking the numbers of regular established wings. All organisations continued to function in much the same fashion, from the same bases and with the same commanders, although where a man had been both group and provisional combat wing commander on a base, he now relinquished the former assignment. The term combat wing remained in use for the battle formation flown composed of two or three group boxes.

French airfields continued to receive the attentions of the Fortresses for most of September while conditions were suitable for visual bombing. Several times missions to Germany had been planned only to be cancelled when skies became overcast. When the Forts went to Romilly on September 15th some 1st Division machines carried two externally slung bombs in addition to a regular bomb load. These 1000 pounders were attached, one each, to wing racks between the inboard engines and the fuselage, allowed full advantage to be taken of the B-17's lifting power on short haul missions.

The flight plans for missions on September 16th were reminiscent of those frequently flown during the previous winter, as they led the bombers far out over the Atlantic round the Brest peninsula. The 1st Division was sent to Nantes to bomb port installations, provoking several Staffeln of Focke-Wulfs in the process. The 3rd Division's "Tokyo tank" air fleet went further south to aircraft works at Bordeaux, with a small force visiting Cognac airfield. As the primary target was lying

Under-wing shackles on 385th BG's *Piccadilly Queen* support a 2,000 lb H.E. Shackles were rarely used due to range limitations with heavy bomb loads.—(USAF)

beneath an overcast, the Bordeaux force turned for targets of opportunity, chiefly La Pallice U-boat docks.

The Cognac force, composed of the new 4th Combat Bombardment Wing had better luck—at least the leading 94th Group did for its 21 aircraft found and bombed the target. This represented the longest round trip so far undertaken by B-17s from England, 1,600 miles taking over 11 hours flying time. On the return trip the formation descended to 2,000 ft to minimise radar detection and conserve fuel, although a few enemy aircraft found and attacked them. Warned by radio of a cloud front ahead that extended to 6,000 ft, the Group was able to climb and maintain formation eventually arriving over Bury St Edmunds in darkness. In the next half hour the 94th

S/Sgt James Jones (21), the 388th BG tail gunner who 'fell out' of a Flying Fortress and lived. This picture also shows the linked sight and tail guns of early B-17s.—(IWM)

executed its first operational night landing, to round off a day without loss or mishap and add another feather to the cap of the particular Yankee Doodles watched over by Colonel Castle.

Many of the other groups were not so fortunate. In half light and darkness B-17s were forced to put down on airfields in S.W. England. Unfamiliarity with the terrain led to a number of crashes into high ground. The 390th Group's *Ascend Charlie* flew full tilt into a Welsh hill while the 388th Group lost two bombers in similar circumstances and in one, B-17F 42-5904, tail gunner James F. Jones had a most remarkable escape. The group formation had been dispersed by flying into a storm front which had the effect of putting radio altimeters about 1000 ft out. Also some searchlights, placed in valleys, gave pilots a false impression. While trying to locate an airfield the aircraft in which Jones flew scraped a hilltop near South Molton, the impact throwing Jones against the escape door with such violence that it gave way. The bomber was still airborne (it crashed 3 miles away) and Jones, not realising the impact had been due to contact with the ground, pulled his rip-cord. The parachute had just started to release when Jones' revolving body came into contact with the ground after which he remembered no more until waking to see a red flare in the sky. On striking the ground he had rolled for nearly 100 yards, the partly opened parachute winding around him as he went. Although unconscious for two hours, Jones had only a slightly sprained leg and bruises to show for his experience. He became something of a curiosity back at Knettishall; to fall out of an aeroplane moving at nearly 200 mph and live to tell the tale was little short of a miracle. Another B-17 from that station came down in the sea near Seahouses, Northumberland. With radio gone and complete loss of bearings it had been in the air for 13 hours!

Nantes was revisited a week later, the two divisions making attacks separated by some hours and experiencing difficulty

42-5793 with H2S 'bath tub' under nose, flies a practise mission over cloud tops on 25 Aug. 1943.—(USAF)

with cloud. Cloud forestalled a mission to the Paris region on September 26th causing most B-17s to haul their bombs back to base. No planes were lost to the enemy, but two from 385th Group collided over West Horndon when returning, an all too common occurrence in poor visibility and close formation.

The weather forecasters were all important in the scheme of things for, on their pronouncements, decisions to launch a mission largely depended. While every depression on the weather chart meant frustration for Eaker and those Command planners endeavouring to pursue the CBO directive, B-17 crews would cheerfully admit that a cloudy day held better prospects of being alive on the morrow than a clear day: it usually meant the difference between a fighter-escorted short range mission and a deep go-it-alone strike into Germany. The Eighth Air Force had conducted its first 12 months of operations through a year with an unusually high pre-ponderance of cloud, and while it was true the promoters of

'Stinky' B-17F PC: X at Alconbury. The RAF also operated Fortresses with similar H2S installations.—(USAF)

the US daylight precision bombing campaign had initially been primed with data on the limitations of weather in the theatre, it had so far proved to be a far greater obstacle to operations than anticipated. An obvious solution was some locator device that would allow accurate bombing through over-cast and it was to the British that the USAAF turned for this assistance.

A number of blind bombing and navigational aids had already been developed by the British, the first of these adopted by the Eighth being Gee in the unsuccessful B-24 Moling sorties earlier in the year. Gee was primarily a naviga-tional aid and as such was being installed in most B-17s and B-24s by October. RAF night bombers were making good use of two other radio/radar aids in bombing: Oboe, a short range precision device which, like Gee, made use of signals received from ground stations, and H2S, an airborne radar scanner which gave a crude impression of terrain below on a cathode ray tube in the aircraft. Oboe had so far been employed chiefly by RAF Mosquitoes where speed and cover of darkness

lessened the chances of this useful device falling into enemy hands. There was some reluctance in letting the Eighth use this in its more vulnerable aircraft, besides which, in common with H2S, production was as yet on a limited scale and equipment very scarce. Trial installations of both were eventually arranged and additional production of the more attractive device, H2S, was sought in the USA. Fitting Oboe equipment in a B-17 presented few difficulties, compared with H2S where the scanner must extend clear beneath the aircraft. Original H2S installations were made in the nose compartment, with the scanner encased in a large plastic cover that gave the B-17Fs so fitted the appearance of having a bath tub slung under the nose.

The complexity of these radar bombing devices necessitated the formation of a special unit and in August 1943 the 482nd Group (Pathfinder) was brought into being at Alconbury for this purpose, the first and only US heavy bomber group raised in England. Three squadrons, two equipped with B-17 and one with B-24 were planned, the first to take shape being the 813th Bomb Sqdn. earmarked to employ British H2S and Oboe. A nucleus of personnel for this organisation was provided by the handful of men trained to operate Gee earlier in the year, plus some personnel from two anti-submarine Liberator squadrons disbanded when the US Navy took over this work in Britain.

The method of employment devised for H2S called for the B-17 so equipped to fly lead position in a combat wing with all bombers dropping on its release. British smoke marker bombs were to be used to mark the release point for following formations. When such a trial was carried out over North Sea ranges on September 23rd, the resulting bomb pattern was most promising. On the 27th Eaker launched the first mission in which H2S aircraft were to act in a pathfinder role if visual bombing was not possible. The objective for the 305 B-17s was the port of Emden where the contrasting reflections of land and water would show more distinctly on the instrument. As the intricate H2S (to become familiarly known as Stinky) often failed to function properly, another 813th aircraft was detailed to fly with the leading elements of the 1st and 3rd Divisions, a necessary precaution for on arrival at Emden only one set in each formation was still operative. There was some confusion in manoeuvring above the overcast at the target approach but the lead combat wing successfully dropped in unison with the Pathfinder from 22,000 ft, the second wing dropping on the smoke markers, while the third found no trace of markers and sought to find worthwhile targets else-where. Much the same happened to the three 3rd Division wings except that the second found a gap in the cloud and dropped visually. Subsequent photo reconnaissance returned evidence to show that only the H2S-assisted formation had achieved a fair concentration on Emden, while other bomb patterns had wandered as much as five miles from the city. Radar was still supposed to be very much a secret and all Brigadier General Fred Anderson would volunteer for the press was: "Our bombardiers dropped their bombs through 9/10 cloud".

Led by General Travis, a larger force of B-17s paid a second visit to Emden on October 2nd. The two H2S aircraft des-patched both bombed but one release was too early resulting in many bombs dropping short of the target. On top of this winds carried the marker smoke away disrupting the aim of following formations. Two strange B-17s were reported along-side observing the US formations perhaps indicating enemy interest in this new development. There was obviously much room for improvement of technique in H2S bombing although the device held much promise as a means of extending the Eighth's offensive on cloudy days. Of first importance was the need to obtain more pathfinder aircraft and trained crews so that eventually each group formation could have a blind bombing leader. Many months would pass before this could

'Yank' hospitality was well known in England. This 'Kiddies Party' was held at Kimbolton on 2 Oct. 1943. The 'Flying Fortress' children are looking over is actually a retired YB-40. Three machine gun symbols on the nose tell its operational record.—(USAF)

be brought about and even in that event radar bombing could only be looked upon as a poor substitute for visual attacks.

A month was to pass before Command would resort to H2S again. In the first place, 482nd Group had insufficient aircraft and crews to participate in a major mission and, secondly, there were several days on which conditions were suitable for visual attack over Western Germany. On the two radar missions bomber losses had been small, for they had been conducted within the range of P-47 escorts using large capacity drop tanks and the Luftwaffe's single-seat fighter pilots, ill-trained for blind flying on instruments, had difficulty in making interceptions through overcast.

However, the five visual missions of October were to meet with the heaviest and most concentrated opposition since the Regensburg and Schweinfurt missions of August 17th. The Nazis, slow to accept the US daylight attacks as a threat to their war industry, had preferred to believe Luftwaffe forces on hand would make these raids too costly, but the many successful bombings of spring and summer 1943 brought home the urgency of the situation. In consequence, the numbers of single-engined fighters facing the Eighth rose from approximately the 300 mark in April to nearly 800 in October (about 65% of German fighter strength), achieved largely by withdrawing units from other fronts. By early October only the six Gruppen of J.G.2 and J.G.26 remained based in France and the Low Countries, the bulk of the defence force—the equivalent of 19 Jagd Gruppen were concentrated in Germany. These were J.G.1, 3, 11 and 300 in full and some Gruppen from J.G.5, 27, 51 and 54. Additionally, there were now 60 twin-engined fighters available in two Zerstörer Geschwader—Z.G.26 and the newly formed Z.G.76, while 16 night fighter Gruppen could also be called upon in an emergency. The German fighter force (Jagdverbände) had developed a high degree of mobility through the use of expendable fuel tanks and on occasions units had travelled 250 miles from base to join battle. Such movements were usually carried out at low altitude to avoid detection by British monitoring posts. Improved armament and armour on both FW190 and Me109s were also proving effective. Extra 20-mm and 30-mm cannon were added to new models specifically for "killing Boeings". The 21-cm rocket missile was also employed more extensively and in addition to its use by FW190s of J.G.1 and J.G.26 the Me110 Zerstörer had been found an excellent launching vehicle. This weapon was about 4 ft long, with an 80 lb time-fused explosive warhead occupy-

ing just over a foot of the length and propellent mixture in the remainder.

The October battles began on the 4th when weather fronts foiled most attacks on primary objectives for the 361 heavies despatched, although visual bombing was accomplished at other targets. Strong opposition was encountered and, but for good fighter support, losses would have undoubtedly been much higher than the 16 lost including four B-24s surprised on a diversion flight. Gunners claimed 56 enemy aircraft destroyed and those on board the 351st Group's *Murder Incorporated*, "tail-end Charlie" in the last formation over Frankfurt, contributed 11 of these; although this new high in claims for an individual crew was later whittled down to 3-2-6 by interrogators. S/Sgt Crossley, tail gunner on 94th Group's *Brass Rail Boys*, was credited with an FW190, his 12th officially confirmed victory in 22 missions and ultimately to prove the highest score for an Eighth Air Force gunner. In the light of true German losses, the validity of the confirmation is open to question, but it reflects the frequency of fighter interception experienced by one man in five months of combat. Crossley was apparently one of the few natural marksmen; and only a small minority of the gunners were accomplished in the art of deflection shooting. The majority used what was officially referred to as "the zone system" of aiming: in plain fact this amounted to simply pointing the gun in the direction of the enemy aircraft and filling that area of sky with bullets. Hitting the enemy was therefore a matter of chance to say nothing of the gross expenditure of ammunition.

A new Fortress model began to reach squadrons as replacement aircraft during September. Similarly powered, it was heavier, reducing performance slightly, but it had its compensations. This was the B-17G featuring a Bendix remotely controlled "chin" turret, as introduced on the YB-40 and found invaluable for forward defence. Some late production B-17Fs were also fitted with this turret, but the majority of 'F' models soldiered on in their original form until claimed by battle or retired. In spite of the ravages of battle (the average life expectancy of an Eighth AF Fortress in late 1943 was only 11 missions) over a dozen original B-17Fs of the pioneer groups survived. The 303rd still had seven, three currently vying for the honour of being the first Fortress to fly 50 missions. One, *Hell's Angels* that had been the first B-17 of the Eighth to reach 25 missions, had by 4th October completed 43. At this time the lead was taken by *Knockout Dropper* which had participated in 45 raids. The third Fortress which carried

M/Sgt Fabian Folmer adds another bomb symbol to *Hells Angels*.—
(USAF)

its squadron's "Bug's Bunny" insignia on the nose as the only personal adornment, was 41-24613 which had completed 42 raids.

The air battles of October 4th were soon overshadowed by those during the three-pronged attack on Bremen on the 8th. The 3rd Division planned to approach from the north-west over the North Sea, while the 1st made a more direct approach across Holland. The 2nd Division, with 55 Liberators, was to take another North Sea route and descend to attack Vegesack. Withdrawal for all B-17s was to be across Holland, while the B-24s returned by much the same route as they had come, far out in the North Sea. This plan, with shrewd timing, did not prevent the enemy controller from having both the B-17 divisions met by substantial forces. Once the first P-47 escort had turned back, FW190s from Leeuwarden and Me109s from Schipol appeared and began the familiar pattern of attack on the leading elements of 1st Division. This was 1st Wing whose groups had led the Schweinfurt raid and suffered

so highly in August, and once again the luckless 381st Group was taking its turn in low group. A comparable disaster was in store as the FWs flew to within 100 yards before breaking away. The attacks continued almost to the rendezvous point with Thunderbolts about a half hour from the target, by which time the 381st had lost 7 of its 18 bombers (over half the divisional loss) including the lead aircraft, and all its remaining bombers received some damage resulting in 2 men being killed and 2 wounded. One of these was the pilot of *Tinkertoy*, an original B-17 of the group that had several times returned from missions with dead and wounded and was now looked upon as the 'jinx' ship of the Ridgewell group. This remarkable Fortress had even gained a part in a Hollywood movie at her birth—location work at the Vega factory for the Deanna Durbin film "Hers to Hold" had resulted in this Fortress appearing in the background.

The Third Bomb Division also received a hot reception, and again paralleling the August 17th mission the unfortunate 100th Group sustained the heaviest loss. It flew lead in the third combat wing and as a result of losing its leader and his deputy to a well placed flak barrage, was so disorganised that another Group in the Wing took over. Seven of its B-17s—also half the division loss—failed to return and its lead Fortress, although returning to Ludham, was written off in a landing collision with a Norfolk oak. One 100th bomber, *Miss Carriage*, returned with three engines and the crew's oxygen system defunct. Only two propellers would feather yet Lt E. G. Stork (once a loco fireman) was able to achieve the incredible by nursing the ailing plane 400 miles to England on one engine—and even that had been hit by flak. The flak at Bremen, of the intensity of that found over the French Atlantic Ports, and of such accuracy, inflicted damage of varying seriousness on two thirds of the B-17s going over the target.

Attempting to minimize flak damage, the Eighth Air Force adopted another British radio device, code-named "Carpet", which caused interference to gunlaying radar. Forty B-17s of the leading 3rd Division groups (388th and 96th) used this equipment over Bremen with apparent success as they suffered least of the Division's formations in the barrage. "Carpet" was gradually installed in many other bombers during the months ahead.

Tinkertoy, 'jinx ship' of 381st BG, after the 8 Oct. 1943 mission. Men point to holes made by 20 mm cannon shells which decapitated pilot.—(USAF)

Despite battle damage sustained by this record force, the Command could still send out 378 heavies next morning. This availability resulted from marked improvements in the supply of replacement crews and aircraft; permitting squadron aircraft complements to be increased from 9 to 14 plus spares. Allied with good planning and fair weather, this brought the most spectacular bombing of the year. The 41st and 1st Wings set out with 115 B-17s to attack the Arado aircraft component works at Anklam, a target far beyond the previous area of day bomber activity, along the Baltic coast. Even so, it was selected primarily as a diversionary target to draw the enemy's attention while 100 B-17s of the 4th and 13th Wings made for the important Focke-Wulf factory at Marienburg many miles further east. The 40th and 45th Wings were to attack Gdynia on the Polish border with the 14th Wing B-24s, while the 2nd Wing Liberators went to Danzig.

At 09.30 hrs Brigadier General Travis with the 303rd Group, leading the eight combat wings, passed over Cromer at 1000 ft—an altitude chosen to delay detection by enemy radar. However, British interception of Bremen defence area control HF radio messages (apparently ground communications had been put out of action by RAF raids the previous night), indicated that the Germans were aware that three sizeable forces were forming. From the general route taken by the US bombers, the enemy expected attacks in the north-west and vectored additional fighters to the area. By 10.30 hrs the bombers were approaching the Danish coast and the German control was in a better position to judge their destination. It is possible they believed the whole force to be making for the Anklam area for only here was there opposition in strength. Having turned south-east, but still several miles from the target, the Anklam force made contact with enemy fighters. It was not until after bombing, as the Fortresses headed back across the Danish peninsula, that the Luftwaffe appeared in force and pressed attacks. A furious battle ensued and while the 41st Wing was not without casualties, the trailing 1st Wing took a severe mauling for the second day running, 14 of its aircraft failing to return and many others suffering heavy damage. Rockets were used with some success; the 351st Group's *Speedball* came back from Anklam with part of one, measuring 14 x 4 in and weighing 11 lb, wrapped around the end of a wing.

At Gdynia and Danzig heavy smoke screens proved so effective that the B-24s completely missed their targets. The

The 'bombing of the year'. 94th BG turns away as the Marienburg Focke Wulf plant burns.—(IWM)

B-17s were also confused and some undertook a second run to obtain a sighting which achieved direct hits on ships in the harbour, notably the liner *Stuttgart*.

The "bombing of the year" was carried out by 4th and 13th Wings at Marienburg, home of a factory accounting for nearly half of FW190 production at that time. Led by the 385th Group with 4th Wing commander, Colonel Russ Wilson, the force had a comparatively charmed life losing only two bombers, one of these being a 385th aircraft that developed engine trouble and crashed in Denmark. Photographs showed that the 96 B-17s attacking placed 58% of their bombs within 1,000 ft of the aiming point and 83% within 2,000 ft. This was achieved in part by reducing the bombing altitude to between 11 and 13,000 ft, as anti-aircraft defences were known to be almost non-existent. A new type of incendiary was introduced on this raid, the M-47A2 which was basically a 100 lb jellied oil device.

That such achievements depended largely upon good leadership of a well co-ordinated team of pilot, navigator and bombardier, was appreciated in the late summer when directives ordered the establishment of special lead crews at each station. Two crews formed in each squadron underwent intensive training for the task of acting as group or squadron

Fortresses lined up at the Honington air depot: Sept. 1943. Two are late B-17F's with chin turrets, and at the far end is the 'war weary' B-17, used for transport duties, with all camouflage paint removed. The six B-17s in the foreground were all destroyed within a few months. The two 100th BG aircraft at Bremen and Münster in Oct., one 388th BG machine at Bremen in Nov. and the other at Brunswick in Jan. 1944; the far 385th BG machine was classified salvage early in Jan. while the Fort nearest the camera, *Dragon Lady* was lost the following month.—(Rust)

lead crews on combat missions—and they were only to participate in combat in this capacity. Further, two aircraft in each squadron were equipped with every approved device to aid location and accurate bombing of a target, and would be flown only as lead bombers. The rear gunner's position in a "lead ship" was invariably occupied by an officer pilot who could advise the pilot on the state of the formation. The Germans had long been conscious of the special position occupied by lead aircraft and expected the most experienced crews to fly in the van of every bomber formation. Their sharp reaction against the first formation of a bomber force became a standardised tactic, of which a prize example occurred when for the third day in succession a Fortress raid was launched against the Reich.

Münster, the destination for 274 B-17s, was a rail junction handling much of the traffic into the industrial Ruhr, and though offering many targets for precision bombing the 3rd Division was directed to drop on the city itself with the planned intention of disrupting the working population. That they were deliberately being sent to kill and make homeless civilians apparently did not produce any moral qualms amongst the airmen: it is recorded that some cheered this news at briefing; their own sufferings having bred bitterness.

The leading 13th Wing, composed of the 95th, 100th and 390th in lead, low and high positions respectively, had good reason to expect trouble, but a fairly direct route was planned allowing a degree of fighter escort all the way. The 56th Fighter Group, tasked to fly directly to a point near the target to cover the leading bombers was late in picking them up due to a slight navigational error. This lapse was quickly exploited by the enemy well in command of the situation for when the penetration escort turned back near the IP, the heavies being still nine minutes from Münster, a sizeable force of German fighters was on hand for battle. Concentrating on the lead wing, some 200 plus enemy aircraft attacked for about 45 minutes. At 14.53 hrs pairs of FW190s, in quick succession, commenced hitting the ill-fated 100th Group (flying at 23,000 ft) with straight and level frontal attacks, closing in to 50-75 yds before breaking away. The lead bomber was ignited by a rocket and as it peeled away five other bombers followed it down splitting the formation in two. Within two minutes the 100th was broken up as bombers went down out of control and others manoeuvred to avoid them. After seven minutes, when the Group had been completely dispersed, attention was switched from the low to the high group. Between Saerbeck and Gronau twin-engined aircraft (identified as Ju88s) fired rockets into the 390th from 100 yds astern; one Fort blew up and another hit amidships broke in two, part of the wreckage crashing into another bomber and taking that down with it. In *Norma J* a rocket projectile entered a waist window and lay smoking on the floor; Gunner George T. Rankin quickly grabbed with his gloves and threw it overboard—the warhead appeared intact. Meanwhile other enemy formations were finishing off the remaining aircraft of the 100th Group and pressing the low squadron of the lead group.

During the six minute bomb run, a heavy anti-aircraft barrage was experienced as fighter attacks fell off. The 95th Group kept good formation; its release brought the best concentration around the MPI for the mission. Fighters soon returned and at times it appeared that they would completely annihilate the lead wing. The action became so involved that surviving aircrew found it difficult to recall time or order of events. Me110 and Me410s were reported firing projectiles from positions under their wings and then closing in with cannon fire. A new feature was the appearance of Do217 bombers flying parallel with the B-17s and firing projectiles from their sides.

By the time the P-47 escort appeared the 100th Group had disappeared from the sky, nearly half the 390th's formation (one bomber lost was piloted by 1/Lt John Winant, son of the

US Ambassador to Britain who was later reported a POW) and a quarter of the 95th Group had also gone. Troubles were by no means over for on return to England many Suffolk airfields were found to be shrouded with late afternoon mists making it doubly difficult for damaged bombers to land. A crippled 384th Group Fortress crashed near Eye after seven of the crew baled out near Ipswich. Statistics told a grim tale for the 13th Wing. Of the B-17s missing, 29 were from the 3rd Division and 25 of those from the lead wing. Of those which reached the IP the 95th lost 5 from 19, the 390th 8 from 18, and 100th 12 out of 13! On the other hand, many groups never saw a German fighter that day: the excellent Thunderbolt escort was undoubtedly the deterrent.

In fact the battle had not been a one-sided affair, Eighth Air Force gunners claimed 183, the 3rd Division's share being 180 and the 13th CBW's 105. In being credited with 62 victories the 390th Group set a record unsurpassed through the war for bomber claims by a single group on one mission. The gunners on board *Cabin in the Sky* were credited with 11 enemy fighters destroyed. Tongue in cheek, pilot Captain Robert D. Brown afterwards commented "The Germans were queuing up for us. You didn't have to aim, just stick your gun out the window and pull the trigger." *Cabin in*

Ohio Air Force sports 14 swastikas and 12 mission symbols. Bomber ground crews often nicknamed individual engines of their charges: hence *Bern.* Yellow propeller bosses identified this B-17F as a member of 549th BS.

the Sky's figure was surpassed, however, by 2/Lt John Rickey's crew who claimed 12 in defending *Ohio Air Force*, a 385th Group bomber in the last formation of the 3rd Division. The supposed destruction wrought by the B-17 gunners was a useful antidote to the enemy's vicious sting: battle weary aircrews were convinced they were dealing out as severe a punishment as they took, and to the last days of the war the 390th Group looked upon Münster as more a great victory over the Luftwaffe than a near disaster. German records reveal that 22 fighters were destroyed and 5 damaged, but many of these must have fallen to US fighters. Nevertheless, the 13th Wing's trial of fire at Münster was probably the most concentrated air battle fought by a B-17 wing.

For the unhappy 100th Group, Münster was another black chapter to add to an already grim book. Coming as it did, two days after the heavy loss at Bremen, it was a stunning blow and no amount of bravado could conceal the gloom which descended upon Thorpe Abbots with the autumn mists. Only Lt Robert Rosenthal and his crew survived the ordeal in *Rosie's Riverters* and that came back on two engines with two badly wounded waist gunners. The Group had lost 20 bombers and over 200 men missing or killed in a week—including two squadron COs. Some were convinced the Luftwaffe singled out the Square D marked Fortresses for special attention, or that a German unit was pursuing a personal vendetta against the 100th because on some past mission one of its planes had dropped its wheels as a signal of surrender but when enemy fighters came alongside to escort the Fort to a landing, gunners on board opened fire and shot down the fighters. This same story, however, was later told about a half-dozen different groups. Other rumours thrived: an enemy plane had been seen over the 390th base when the groups had prepared for take-off. It did not take much imagination to connect this report with a spy signalling details of the mission to this aircraft. In truth, it was simply bad luck that the 100th on several occasions flew the position that bore the brunt of Luftwaffe attacks. As no news travels like bad news, the 100th's fortunes were soon known at other bases where the Thorpe Abbots group was often referred to as a "jinx outfit". The course of events was to change the "a" to "the" and bring a telling epithet, known beyond the confines of the Eighth Air Force.

The 100th Group could only find 8 battleworthy bombers for a maximum effort mission to Schweinfurt on the following Thursday. Command had hoped to send 360 B-17s and 60 B-24s but this figure was not met and due to weather difficulties the total number actually despatched to attack the ball-bearing plants was less than 300. Weather over Norfolk hampered B-24 assembly and the 29 that did make formation presented too small a force for a long mission in hostile skies. Instead, these bombers made a diversionary feint. The 149 1st Division B-17s with Colonel Peaslee, task force commander flying with the 92nd Group, crossed the Dutch coast at Walcheren, while 30 miles south the 96th Group headed the 3rd Division's force of 142. While 1st Division took a more or less direct route, until the P-47 escort turned back near Aachen, 3rd Division made an abrupt turn south, a successful deceptive move for not until a 90 degree turn east over Luxembourg were enemy fighters encountered and then not in numbers until well into Germany.

The 1st Division on the other hand, encountered opposition as soon as the escort departed and though sporadic on the Coblenz and Frankfurt leg, thereafter it grew in intensity. Things had not gone well for the Division from the beginning; overcast had hindered assembly over England and the 305th Group failed to appear in position as the low group of the lead wing. Instead, and unbeknown to the task force commander at the time, it had joined as low to the 1st Wing whose 351st and 381st Groups ended up flying a combined high formation. With only two groups which would have been too vulnerable a force to continue in the lead position, the task force commander ordered his following combat wing (the 1st) to take the lead while his wing formation manoeuvred to take up a position high on the left and almost level with the new leading wing, in effect, forming a five group wing. This change found the 91st Group (Lt Col Theodore Milton in command) leading to Schweinfurt as it had done before. Memories of what had befallen their group as leaders of that first mission must have caused dismay to many 91st men.

The enemy's reaction could be predicted with some accuracy and as the battle unfolded it was seen to be running to the familiar pattern. The first attacks on 1st Division were frontal from the 11 to one o'clock sector, 190s and 109s rolling as they fired and violently "split-s'ed" away to avoid the defensive fire. Past Frankfurt, Me110s appeared astern and began lobbing rockets. For the 305th Group, in the vulnerable low position, it was to be very much a repeat performance of what had befallen the 100th at Munster. On the target run only 3 of the 18 bombers despatched were still to be seen (another 3 had aborted). Major G. G. Y. Normand leading, in one of the three, elected to join the also depleted 92nd formation above for bombing. Soon, only two 305th aircraft were left. The 306th Group, flying high to the 92nd, fared little better, losing ten aircraft before the target: all told 27 B-17s of the 40th CBW groups—half the starting force—were gone at this point.

Three of the five bearing plants at Schweinfurt were targets and all were heavily hit. Best overall results in the 1st Division were obtained by the 91st Group, while Captain H. D. Wallace, a squadron bombardier for part of the 351st Group force in the leading wing, placed all bombs within 1,000 ft of the MPI. But the best group bombing of the day went to the Eighth's youngest group, the 390th, when all 15 aircraft sent put 51% within 1,000 ft of the MPI in spite of the lead aircraft's auto-pilot being inoperative and complicating the bombing run.

After leaving the target the bombers turned to take a westerly route home, some miles south of that followed on penetration; yet another attempt to confuse the enemy and stretch the range of his fighters. The predicted low cloud on the coastal approach served as a refuge for stragglers, but there was no slackening of the Luftwaffe's assault. Gruppen from J.G.3 and J.G.51 were now based near Munich, added to which twin-engined and night fighter forces were available from the Stuttgart and Metz areas; aircraft from the former units appeared on the scene as the 1st Division came off target, giving attention chiefly to the trailing combat wing. A group of FW190s set upon the lead 379th Group fatally crippling 3 Forts in their first pass. Another bomber was lost in collision with a fighter and both went down. Inevitably, persistent attacks were also made against the low group of this wing, the 384th Group from which several bombers fell. Past Metz and across France the attacks against 1st Division fell off; for them the battle was over.

First bombs from the 3rd Division fell six minutes after those of the last 1st Division groups, by which time smoke obscured much of the targets and made it difficult for bombardiers to pick out their aiming points. Fighter attacks against this division had not commenced in earnest until some miles from the IP and only the leading 96th had taken losses by the time Schweinfurt was reached, thereafter single-engined fighters made a heavy assault on this Group, considered by many veterans to be the worst to befall the 96th. The battle was at its peak for the 3rd Division on the flight home and instead of friendly fighters, Focke-Wulfs met the bombers near the Channel coast and inflicted further punishment—the P-47s had been kept on the ground by the half-fog over their bases. Shortly after 17.00 hrs the first bombers were reaching Beachy Head and soon damaged B-17s or those with wounded on board were putting down on the first available airfields. Few RAF stations along the south coast did not have American visitors that evening. *Paper Doll*, a 96th Group Fortress that landed at Ford, was brought home largely by the efforts of navigator Lt Miles McFann when the pilot was killed and co-pilot wounded. Next day McFann met Winston Churchill who visited Ford to watch RAF manoeuvres. As the mists thickened into dusk on that damp October Thursday the Eighth took stock. Sixty B-17s were missing, 5 had crashed in England due principally to battle damage, 12 others were written off in crash landings or so badly damaged as to be fit only for scrap, and 121 needed repairs; 600 men were missing and 5 dead and 43 wounded airmen were taken from returning bombers. These losses were on a par with those of August 17th. Only one group in VIII BC suffered neither casualties nor aircraft loss—the "hard luck" 100th.

In Britain and America the second Schweinfurt raid was acclaimed an air victory of considerable magnitude, the laying waste of three bearing factories and the destruction of 288 enemy fighters surely being a staggering blow to the enemy, dreadful though the cost had been. Allied leaders enthused over the achievement and General Arnold was moved to say " . . . the opposition isn't nearly what it was and we are wearing them down". Even the normally reserved British waxed enthusiastic, Portal, then Chief of the Air Staff, pronouncing: "The Schweinfurt raid may well go down in history as one of the decisive air actions of this war, and it may prove to have saved countless lives by depriving the enemy of a great part of his means of resistance". Indeed, Thursday, October 14th 1943 proved to be a decisive air action but not, one thinks, in the way meant by the Air Marshal. For under the veneer of propaganda lay hard and unpleasant facts which presented a very different picture.

While few could question estimates based on photographic intelligence of Schweinfurt damage—six months before the plants could return to full production and an immediate 50% fall in total German bearing output—the destruction of 288 fighters was not so easily accepted. Even when this figure was later whittled down to 186 it still meant that in the five major air battles of October over 700 destroyed and 300 probable and damaged claims had been allowed, amounting to the total annihilation of the known German fighter force! It would have been difficult to persuade the men who survived Schweinfurt that the opposition encountered was the last desperate effort of a beaten force. Air Ministry intelligence had at all times fair knowledge of Luftwaffe combat units and they could find only a strengthening and expansion of the Jagdverbände during this period. Indeed, this was the true picture for although the German fighter force was extremely hard pressed and suffering a high rate of attrition, it was far from being demised. On the contrary Anklam, Münster and Schweinfurt demonstrated its growing ability to break up the tightly knit bomber boxes and inflict severe punishment; still

a hazardous task for the German fighter pilots, but the formula of mass concentration on one bomber formation at a time, dispersing it by firing rockets from beyond the effective range of defensive guns, and then repeatedly pressing attacks with single-engined fighters, brought successes.

The loss incurred on October 14th amounted to more than double the 10% of force figure that Eighth Air Force considered prohibitive to operations. Morale at bomber bases was at a low ebb and little wonder when the Fortress crews were currently incurring a casualty rate higher than any other branch of the US Forces. Even with the undeniable good bombing results achieved on many occasions the price was becoming too high to pay. The situation could best be resolved by more and longer ranged fighter escorts. The value of fighter support had been plainly demonstrated on many occasions and it had gradually been elevated to a position of paramount importance in planning future missions. So far as the Eighth was concerned, the USAAF's self-defensive bomber formation doctrine was dead. Curtis LeMay summed up the feelings pervading command when he said; "The more Fortresses we have here the shorter the war is going to be and the more fighters we have to protect the Forts the smaller the losses will be". The future of the daylight strategic bomber had come very much to depend on the presence of the long range escort fighter.

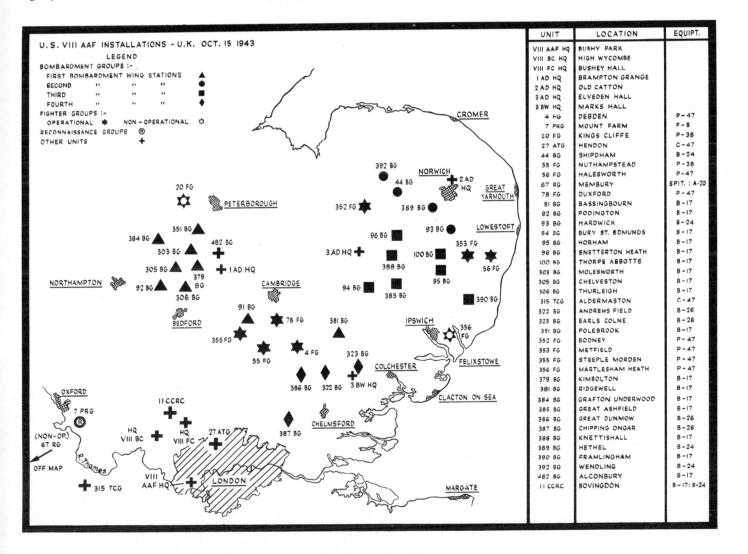

UNIT	LOCATION	EQUIPT.
VIII AAF HQ	BUSHY PARK	
VIII BC HQ	HIGH WYCOMBE	
VIII FC HQ	BUSHEY HALL	
1 AD HQ	BRAMPTON GRANGE	
2 AD HQ	OLD CATTON	
3 AD HQ	ELVEDEN HALL	
3 BW HQ	MARKS HALL	
4 FG	DEBDEN	P-47
7 PRG	MOUNT FARM	F-5
20 FG	KINGS CLIFFE	P-38
27 ATG	HENDON	C-47
44 BG	SHIPDHAM	B-24
55 FG	NUTHAMPSTEAD	P-38
56 FG	HALESWORTH	P-47
67 RG	MEMBURY	SPIT. : A-20
78 FG	DUXFORD	P-47
91 BG	BASSINGBOURN	B-17
92 BG	PODINGTON	B-17
93 BG	HARDWICK	B-24
94 BG	BURY ST. EDMUNDS	B-17
95 BG	HORHAM	B-17
96 BG	SNETTERTON HEATH	B-17
100 BG	THORPE ABBOTTS	B-17
303 BG	MOLESWORTH	B-17
305 BG	CHELVESTON	B-17
306 BG	THURLEIGH	B-17
315 TCG	ALDERMASTON	C-47
322 BG	ANDREWS FIELD	B-26
323 BG	EARLS COLNE	B-26
351 BG	POLEBROOK	B-17
352 FG	BODNEY	P-47
353 FG	METFIELD	P-47
355 FG	STEEPLE MORDEN	P-47
356 FG	MARTLESHAM HEATH	P-47
379 BG	KIMBOLTON	B-17
381 BG	RIDGEWELL	B-17
384 BG	GRAFTON UNDERWOOD	B-17
385 BG	GREAT ASHFIELD	B-17
386 BG	GREAT DUNMOW	B-26
387 BG	CHIPPING ONGAR	B-26
388 BG	KNETTISHALL	B-17
389 BG	HETHEL	B-24
390 BG	FRAMLINGHAM	B-17
392 BG	WENDLING	B-24
482 BG	ALCONBURY	B-17
11 CCRC	BOVINGDON	B-17 : B-24

U.S. VIII AAF INSTALLATIONS - U.K. OCT. 15 1943

LEGEND

BOMBARDMENT GROUPS :-
FIRST BOMBARDMENT WING STATIONS ▲
SECOND " " " ●
THIRD " " " ■
FOURTH " " " ◆

FIGHTER GROUPS :-
OPERATIONAL ✶ NON - OPERATIONAL ✩
RECONNAISSANCE GROUPS Ⓡ
OTHER UNITS ✚

Chapter 10: The Babies

The range problem of escort fighters had been in General Hunter's mind long before the Thunderbolt became operational. On January 24th 1943 he directed the Air Technical Section of VIII Fighter Command to investigate the possible use of jettisonable tanks and the engineering problems involved. The drop-tank—as it was called—was by no means a new innovation. For some time the RAF had been using such tanks to extend the range of its Spitfires on cross-Channel sorties. Both the P-38 Lightning and P-39 Airacobra had been fitted with tanks slung externally to facilitate ferrying over long distances. Republic Aircraft also produced a version for ferrying the Thunderbolt, but as the first P-47Cs to arrive in the UK had come by sea examples of the ferry tank were not available.

The Air Technical Section, based at Bovingdon, Herts, was commanded by Colonel Ben S. Kelsey who, before the war, had earned fame as test pilot of the prototype Lockheed Lightning. His deputy, the resourceful Cass Hough, entrusted with investigating the use of auxiliary tanks, immediately requested a supply of P-47 ferry tanks from the States but it was March 1st before they arrived at Bovingdon. Having a capacity of 200 (sometimes quoted as 205) gallons these tanks were made of resinated paper and attached to the belly of the Thunderbolt at four suspension points. They proved unsatisfactory, chiefly because fuel could not be drawn from them above 23,000 ft due to atmospheric pressure. They also leaked badly if fuel was left in them for several hours and had poor aerodynamic qualities causing some loss of speed. In view of the limited use to which these 200 gallon ferry tanks could be put—they could not be pressurised—Hough sought the manufacture of a more suitable tank in the US, while at the same time seeking similar help from the British. Andre Rosseau and Tom O'Reilly had designed tanks for the RAF and their assistance was recruited along with that of production engineer A. A. Richards. These three Britishers joined Hough and his assistant Lt Robert Shafer on the project, which ultimately became of major significance in sustaining the Eighth's offensive.

At altitudes over 20,000 feet pressurisation was necessary in order to maintain a sufficient head of fuel to the engine driven pump. USAAF regulations did not cater for the carrying of aviation spirit under pressure—not that this was a major obstacle when so much depended on the outcome. The engineers ingeniously set about harnessing the air pressure going to waste in the exhaust of the vacuum pump—a standard component on the P-47 and most aircraft of the day. A control valve was obtained from British sources to meter the pressure at varying altitudes and maintain a given pressure differential between the inside of the tank and the outside atmosphere. It was necessary to maintain a pressure of 15-17 psi for the aircraft's fuel pump to function properly.

Air Service Command designed, and delivered on May 20th, the prototype of a fully pressurised metal tank of approximately 100 gallons which proved completely successful and would adequately supply fuel up to 35,000 ft. Production was arranged in Britain but, due to an acute shortage of sheet steel, delivery could not commence for an estimated 90 days. The imperative need to improve range then led ATS to consider the British-made paper tank that had been offered. Originally developed for the Hawker Hurricane, this cylindrical tank

had an approximate capacity of 108 gallons. Hough's team, reinforcing it to withstand the required working pressure, tested it during the first week of July. Quick deliveries could be promised and production examples began to arrive on July 12th. There were, however, snags—'The buggeration factor' as Hough put it—to contend with and quantities sufficient for large-scale operational use did not appear until September.

Meanwhile, by early July over 1,100 examples of the American unpressurised 200 gallon ferry tank were in Britain; Hough suggested these could be used by Thunderbolts at least to climb from their bases to the enemy coast, providing certain limitations on engine power were observed and an altitude of over 23,000 ft was not exceeded while drawing fuel from the tank. Since an estimated extra 75 miles to the radius of action could result, VIII Fighter Command adopted the suggestions and by July 28th the 4th and 78th Groups were ready.

The two groups put up 105 P-47s into a clear morning sky to act as withdrawal support, but considerable trouble was experienced with the belly tanks from the outset and two actually dropped off Debden P-47s before the aircraft were airborne. Some pilots reported difficulty in drawing fuel and at least one tank failed to release. Although the 'belly tanks' were only filled with 100 gallons of fuel—sufficient to take them to the enemy coast—there was some slight instability on turns and assembly over base took about five minutes longer than usual. The 4th, scheduled to make the deepest penetration, greatly surprised a group of enemy fighters outside the accepted Allied fighter range. Near Emmerich, on the Dutch/German border, the 4th found the returning Fortress formation under heavy attack by Me109s and FW190s. In the ensuing engagement the Group claimed 9-1-6; only one P-47 failed to return. Leading was Major G. Halsey (335th Fighter Squadron) but also flying with the 4th was its CO, Colonel Edward Anderson. A fighter pilot was considered old at 25 but age did not handicap the 39-year old Colonel in shooting down two of the enemy on this occasion. Although the pilots and ground crews did not like the troublesome tanks, there was no doubt that they had allowed the Group to venture over 260 miles from England, 30 miles deeper than Thunderbolts had ever been before.

The 78th Group on a shallow penetration met no opposition. Two days later on one of the most memorable operations in the 78th's history, the worth of the tanks, leaky and cumbersome as they might be, was proven. Crossing the German border to meet returning B-17s near Haldern, the 78th was soon engaged. Major Eugene Roberts, commanding the 84th Fighter Squadron, shot down 2 FW190s and an Me109 to become the first US fighter pilot to be credited with three victories on a single mission. Meanwhile, Captain Charles P. London added two more victories to his score to receive the accolade of acehood—the first fighter pilot of the Eighth to destroy five enemy planes. The Group returned to Duxford with 16 victories, the highest score of a single mission to date. Unfortunately the battle deprived them of their second commanding officer, for one of the three P-47s failing to return was that of Lt Col McNickle, who had taken over when Peterson went down. He was taken prisoner.

Yet another 'first' occurred—although its significance for

Cpt Charles London's *El Jeepo* in which he claimed the five victories that made him VIII FC's first ace.—(London)

the Thunderbolt was yet to be appreciated. Lt Quince L. Brown having lost altitude in the engagement decided to make for home 'on the deck'. In so doing, he took the opportunity to shoot up an enemy locomotive and a belligerent gun position west of Rotterdam. The Thunderbolt had done its first ground strafing; a year later it would be considered the best aircraft available for this work.

The 107 P-47s that day made a record claim of 25-4-8 against the Luftwaffe for a loss of 7. The 56th claimed four destroyed and lost two, and the 4th, five for two. The Thunderbolts had fought units of I and III/J.G.1, III/J.G.11 and J.G.26; all experienced organisations. Enemy concentration on the Fortresses had allowed many P-47 squadrons to make surprise attacks, diving on the Me109s and FW190s and then 'zooming' away. The standard evasive manoeuvre of the German fighters was to roll over and dive. While this had worked very well with the light Spitfire, against which it had been developed, it did not provide escape from the Thunderbolt. Yet Luftwaffe pilots continued to practice this manoeuvre, to their cost, and on this occasion the German pilots had obviously not expected to find Allied fighters so far inland and mistook them at first for their own formations.

A sweep carried out by P-47s on August 9th was primarily for the benefit of a new fighter group, the 353rd, flying its first mission over enemy held territory. They had arrived in England in June, but a shortage of P-47s kept them languishing at Goxhill for almost two months before being moved to their first combat station at Metfield, Suffolk on August 3rd. This new airfield was not far from the 56th's new home at Halesworth and it fell chiefly to the 56th to shepherd the new group through its early missions. On this occasion 16 P-47s from the 353rd accompanied 32 from the older group on a sweep over Holland and Belgium. It became policy for new units to first gain experience either by flying as part of the formation

200 gl. unpressurised tank on a 56th FG P-47C at Horsham St. Faiths. Some examples were without the central rib.—(Forward)

of an established group, or by being led by an experienced commander from such an outfit.

The 56th's turn to use the awkward 200 gallon belly tanks came on August 12th, when all the 131 P-47s of the three groups sent on bomber escort were so equipped. Four days later another belly tank mission was run in support of B-17 raids on German air depots in France. Escorting 1st Bomb Wing B-17s towards Le Bourget, the 4th Group actively engaged elements, believed of J.G.2, endeavouring to attack the bombers, resulting in the most resounding defeat for the Luftwaffe fighters so far. Eighteen Me109s and FW190s were destroyed, for the loss of a single P-47. Of even greater importance, all the bombers returned safely. Much of the success was credited to the capable leader of the 4th Group's formation, Major Don Blakeslee, who showed remarkable skill in his direction of the air battle. No enemy aircraft were shot down by the other P-47 groups that day although the 353rd had its first contact with the enemy, being involved in some wary sparring with yellow nosed FW190s. The 353rd's CO, Lt Col Joe Morris, led his flight down in a steep dive on a single FW190 heading for the bombers. The outcome was uncertain as other Focke-Wulfs intervened and when the

When these visitors to Bovingdon posed before Cass Hough's P-47, they could not have guessed the significant part the drop tank they had inspected would eventually play in the Eighth's campaign. This was the prototype pressurised 108 gl. 'paper' tank. Note the special mounting.—(Hough)

First two-seat adaption of the Lightning in the ETO was this P-38F 41-7552. Cass Hough with S/Sgt Olsen (crew chief) in rear seat prior to take-off; 12 Aug. 1943.

rest of the flight pulled up again the Colonel's P-47 was nowhere to be seen. The CO as their first loss over enemy-held territory was a hard blow for the 353rd.

The following day, August 17th 1943, was the occasion of the first attacks on Schweinfurt and Regensburg and the 'shuttle' to North Africa. Though remembered chiefly for the violent air battles involving the Fortresses, this date also witnessed a change in the fortunes of the hitherto unspectacular 56th Fighter Group for, of 19 enemy aircraft claimed, 17 fell to their guns. The Group had flown with the inbound Regensburg force early in the day, making little contact with the Luftwaffe. In the afternoon at 15.20 hrs, 51 of their aircraft had set off again, this time to meet the bombers returning from Schweinfurt. It was usual to release belly tanks on crossing the enemy coast, regardless of fuel remaining, for a 'bounce' by the enemy while still encumbered might be disastrous. On this occasion the 56th retained its tanks for an additional ten minutes, facilitating penetration to 15 miles past Eupen to rendezvous with the Fortresses at 16.21 hrs.

Positioned above the bombers, the 56th did not have to wait long before Staffeln from J.G.26 appeared and started to make head-on attacks on the B-17s. Zemke had waited for such an opportunity and with splendid team work the 56th fought off the enemy aircraft until relieved by RAF Spitfires in the vicinity of Antwerp. Major Wilhelm Galland, brother of the famous Luftwaffe General and victor of 55 combats, was in one of the German fighters that went down that day. Captain Gerald Johnson flying *Jackson County Fighter* claimed 2 Me109s and an Me110, while Lt Glen Schiltz of the 63rd Ftr. Sqdn., flying UN-Z also destroyed three in this, his first combat action. Two FW190s were credited to Captain Walker Mahurin; a redeeming act on his part for on August 8th he had been involved in a collision that completely wrecked his aircraft. On a training flight over England he had spotted a B-24 Liberator—at the time not a particularly common aeroplane in English skies. While flying formation with the bomber he took his Thunderbolt (41-6334) a little too close resulting in the empennage being slashed off by the Liberators propellers. Mahurin came down by parachute, his P-47 disintegrated in an English field and the Liberator made a successful landing having sustained only minor damage. Thunderbolts, costing $104.258 each, were still in short supply and Mahurin's folly did not endear him to the authorities.

The 56th claimed all the fighter scored victories two days later, while supporting 1st Wing B-17s attacking Gilze Rijen airfield. The enemy rose to meet this attack perhaps thinking another deep penetration was in the offing. Again Luftwaffe losses exceeded those of the Thunderbolts, mechanical failure being the cause of the only 56th aircraft to go down. Captain

2/Lt Robert Brower, of 82nd FS, swung off course during take-off on 19 Aug. 1943 and demolished the Duxford windsock. The P-47C (41-6179, MX: E) struck the ground with such force that the engine was wrenched off and left some 40 yards behind the rest of the plane. All Brower suffered was singed eyebrows.—(IWM)

Gerald Johnson shot down an Me109 to become the second Thunderbolt ace in England and the first in the 56th.

The ratio of German to American fighter losses was better than 6 to 1 in August. The 56th claimed 29 victories, the 4th 21, the 78th 7 and the 353rd 2.

The Duxford Group, which had played a prominent part in the previous month's actions, had lacked opportunity. It was the 'luck of the draw' that had placed the 4th and 56th at a time and place where the Luftwaffe had chosen to be; but the outcome of the battles of August 16th and 17th had much to do with team work and tactics, under the leadership of Blakeslee and Zemke.

So far as the bombers were concerned, the Regensburg and Schweinfurt missions brought convincing evidence that the

31 Aug. 1943; Maj Eugene Roberts indicates the two kills that made him VIII FC's second ace.—(USAF)

cost of such unescorted daylight raids was prohibitive. The advantages of long range fighter escort were already proven for bomber losses, it was estimated, were reduced by half when Spitfires and Thunderbolts were around. The vital factor was how far could escorts be extended? Much then depended on the outcome of experiments at Bovingdon.

A quantity of 75 gallon tanks had arrived from the States and Cass Hough made the first test of a pressurised version on August 17th. This metal tank was of neat, teardrop shape and though known as the 75 gallon tank its actual capacity was 85 gallons. Air Technical Section made the necessary modifications to allow for the pressurisation system already operating for the 108 gallon tank. The 75 gallon tank had been originally designed for ferrying P-39 and P-40 fighters, but by a change from four to two-point suspension shackles enabled its use by the P-47D. Conversion sets for the two-point gear (known as the B-7) were made available and the 4th and 56th Groups were first to fit these shackles—one squadron at a time—and by the end of August were carrying the 75 gallon tank on missions. The P-47s could now attain a higher altitude before dropping the tanks and the quantity of fuel carried was about equal to that of the unpressurised 200 gallon tank which it was not practicable to fill with more than 75 to 100

Pressurised metal 75 gl. 'tear drop' tank on Maj Eugene Roberts' *Spokane Chief*.

gallons. Drag, only an estimated 12-15 mph with an almost negligible effect on flying qualities, prompted air leaders to consider retaining the tanks until they were empty or until the enemy was sighted.

During early September the first locally produced metal tanks were available to VIII Fighter Command. These were reckoned at 108 gallon capacity, the same as the British made paper tanks that were being delivered in steadily increasing, if still small, quantities. About 10,000 of the 75 gallon tanks were being shipped from the US and this type would be the mainstay until larger quantities of British produced tanks were forthcoming.

With one exception, September brought the Eighth's fighter groups no large claims against the Luftwaffe. Most of the actions were small and frequently involved the 56th Group.

On the 9th and 14th, two more P-47D groups flew their first combat missions; they were respectively the 352nd commanded by Lt Col Joe L. Mason based at Bodney, and the 355th under Lt Col William Cummings Jr based at Steeple Morden. Both had reached England early in July but their initiation had been retarded through shortage of aircraft. Like the other groups they were given time to 'flex their wings' in sweeps and short range escorts for the first few missions.

Another three fighter groups were in training. The 356th, at Goxhill, had arrived in late August. Some of their P-47Ds were flown across the Atlantic by the northern ferry route. The other two groups, the 20th at King's Cliffe and the 55th at Nuthampstead, had arrived in late August and early September, respectively. Both were P-38 Lightning groups hurriedly sent to the UK to provide escorts with the additional range. The shortage of P-38s was even more acute than that

General Arnold meets the aces at Duxford. With him are, l. to r. Gen Kepner, Eugene Roberts, Gerald Johnson and Charles London.— (IWM)

of P-47s and this Lockheed 'plane, requiring more man-hours to build, was the most sought US fighter in all American battle areas. The 20th acquired some P-38H models but, as the 55th had more experience of the P-38, these aircraft were turned over to the Nuthampstead group.

The Eighth's bombers had flown two missions into Germany during September. The first to Stuttgart on the 6th gave the P-47s little opportunity for combat as the Luftwaffe fighter Staffeln kept out of the way of the American escorts. Their radio talk was regularly monitored by British listening posts and from the tone of these messages it had been evident for some time that the Luftwaffe fighter pilots were reluctant to approach the bombers if Allied escort was present. On this day the listeners in England heard among the combat warnings— 'Achtung, Thunderbolts kommen!' and 'Achten auf dem Führer!'

The other raid, on September 27th, was a milestone for VIII Fighter Command aircraft. For the first time Thunderbolts were despatched to escort the B-17s right to the target area in the German homeland. Emden, the target, meant that the fighters faced a 200 mile journey over the North Sea. The plan

3 Sept. 1943. Work in progress at Halesworth on Major Schilling's P-47D after it had been shot up. Olive drab surfaces were waxed to produce better performance.—(USAF)

was that the first task force of B-17s would be met by the 4th and 353rd Groups off the Frisian Islands, escorted to the target and on withdrawal as far as fuel supplies allowed; the 56th and 78th Groups were to shepherd the second task force of bombers in a similar way. The 4th used 108 gallon tanks and the other units the 75 gallon tanks, while the 'tankless' 352nd and 355th groups were to carry out sweeps over Holland in support of the operation. The weather was bad with considerable cloud but the 4th and 353rd both rendezvoused with the bombers as scheduled and the latter inflicted a 7-0-4 loss and damage score on a greatly surprised defending fighter force. The weather had deteriorated by the time the 56th and 78th arrived but the latter, though unable to take up position as planned, was soon engaged in their best days fighting since July; 10-0-2 being claimed for no loss. The 56th did not rendezvous on time and did not pick up its bombers until they were withdrawing. The 63rd Ftr. Sqdn. had 5 victories and it was from this squadron that the only P-47 missing on the raid went down. The Thunderbolts had flown 400 miles, nearly all of it over water, to inflict a resounding 21 for 1 defeat on the enemy. A full month previous no-one would have thought this possible—least of all the Luftwaffe.

On October 2nd, when the bombers went back to Emden, the German fighters were disinclined to give battle. Only five of the enemy were caught, one falling to the 56th's leader, 29-year-old Hubert Zemke, to make him the Group's second ace. Two days later the 56th, led by Major Schilling, the deputy commander, observed in the course of a maximum penetration escort for a Fortress raid on Frankfurt, forty twin-engined Me110s preparing for a surprise attack on the last box of bombers. The surprise was on the crews of the Zerstörer

One of the greatest fighter leaders of the war: Hubert Zemke.—(USAF)

Gruppe who suddenly found Thunderbolts bearing down on them. The heavy and unwieldy Messerschmitts, which could lob rockets into a Fortress formation from outside the range of its victim's guns, were no match for the single-seater fighters. Within minutes, fifteen had been shot down in the vicinity of Düren without the loss of a single P-47. Captain Walker Mahurin, who had two victories on August 17th, raised his score to five: he and Lt Vance Ludwig both claimed three apiece.

The 108 gallon tanks and prudent use of engine had allowed the 56th to travel a record 750 miles! Other fighter groups added four more victories to make the day's total 19 for 1. On the 8th the 56th's share of twelve VIII Fighter Command victories was 5. Near Nordhorn there was a fight with FW190s: one that went down in flames took Obstlt Hans Philipp, commander of J.G.1 and victor of 213 combats, to his death. The 10th saw the Group take 10 of the 21 that fell to American fighters on the Munster mission. Once again the diving attack-and-climb ploy brought victories without loss. This day saw Major Dave Schilling and Lt Robert Johnson reach 'ace' status and Captain Gerald Johnson increased his score to 7, the highest in the 56th. The 78th's second ace, Major Eugene Roberts, was credited with 2 victories and with a total of 8 he now led the Eighth's aces. The 353rd also had an up and coming ace in Captain Walter C. Beckham, nick-named 'Turk', who destroyed three enemy planes on the Münster mission; he had only scored his first victory on September 23rd and now had six in only 6 missions.

In a matter of weeks the Thunderbolt's radius of action had been extended by over 100 miles. By holding onto their 108 gallon tanks until empty, it was possible to reach up to 375 miles from base and with the 75 gallon type, 340 miles. Exactly how far, depended on the type of mission undertaken. Continuous escort, where the P-47s had to weave in order not to pull ahead of the bombers, substantially reduced penetration. Maximum range could only be achieved by flying straight to a prearranged rendezvous point.

As the new groups became more proficient VIII Fighter

Command was better able to employ the relay system of escort that had been initiated in September. Every escort had to be carefully worked out and the Command was not yet strong enough to give the bombers continuous protection except on short range targets. Luftwaffe leaders, originally confident that the day bomber raids would come to nought, were faced with a situation they had not allowed for; fighter escort over the very borders of the Reich. With the approach of winter, it was thought that weather conditions of Northern Europe would hamper these escorts, considered to have reached the practical limit of penetration. Realising that it could, in any case, no longer afford to disregard or avoid the American fighters, the Luftwaffe turned to the obvious solution of engaging the P-47s on landfall, forcing them to release their belly tanks and thereby limiting their value as escorts.

Anticipating the move, VIII Fighter Command instructed the fighter groups to take on the enemy at the point of interception and make him pay dearly. For, even if the escort had to be abandoned, a number of enemy fighters would be so involved that they would be prevented from harassing the bombers. It so happened, that the Luftwaffe only made this move on about six occasions and on only three did it gain any substantial dividends. Moreover, the German forces assigned to this task were often small, and one Thunderbolt squadron was often sufficient to keep them engaged while the rest of the group continued with its escort.

The Luftwaffe had tried this tactic on October 14th, on the second costly Fortress mission to Schweinfurt. The 353rd Group, when going in with the bombers over Walcheren, was suddenly attacked by 20 plus FW190s and Me109s. Numerous dog fights ensued from which the P-47 emerged without loss and claims of 5 German fighters. A good portion of the Group was able to continue to the Sittart area of Holland before withdrawing and having a further engagement in which six Focke-Wulfs were claimed for a P-47 shot down. Some of the Thunderbolts were damaged and in the deteriorating weather had difficulty in reaching base. Two crash-landed in England and one pilot was killed. Foul weather conditions of thick cloud and fog prevented many of the fighter groups taking off or making contact with the bombers. The 56th was the only other group to see action and claimed 3 of the enemy on its escort in as far as the Aachen area.

On October 15th both the 55th (P-38s) and 356th (P-47s) Groups reached operational status, the latter having moved down to Martlesham Heath, near Ipswich. Both indulged in the usual pattern of preparatory sweeps, although there was considerable urgency in making the Lightnings available for escort at the earliest opportunity. The twin-engined Lockheed with drop-tanks promised a radius of action of some 450 miles. Word went around the fighter groups that a new version of the Mustang single-seater was to be seen down at Green-ham Common Air Service Command base in US colours—'A real hot ship with some range', rumour said. It also had a

'Gabby' Gabreski buzzes the 100th BG at Thorpe Abbots.—(Preston)

Re-enter the Lightning. P-38Hs of 55th FG ready to roll for their second mission from Nuthampstead; 16 Oct. 1943. Aircraft in foreground is Lt Col Jack Jenkin's *Texas Ranger* in which he made VIII FC's first 'kill' with a Lightning.—(USAF)

Merlin engine similar to that powering the Spitfire. Merlin was a sweet word to the veterans of the 4th, who had never really come to accept the Thunderbolt. The P-51 Mustang came to be a frequent topic of conversation at Debden.

On November 5th 1943 the 56th Fighter Group became the first Eighth Air Force fighter group credited with 100 enemy aircraft destroyed—nearly twice as many as its nearest rival, the 4th. Lt George Hall claimed the 100th victory—an Me210 type—one of six German fighters the Group brought down that day to make the total 101. The 56th's successes had started to mount in August and by the end of September it had overhauled the 4th. It was not simply a question of good fortune, although that had played its part. Much was due to the leadership of Hubert Zemke, a brilliant tactician, intent upon analysing mission results to find better ways of outwitting and defeating the Luftwaffe. Once a green and luckless organisation, the 56th was now a highly efficient fighting machine. The pilots were capable, confident and aggressive; morale was high. They now looked upon themselves as hunters of Messerschmitts and Focke-Wulfs in addition to being defenders of the bombers. Someone said the Thunderbolt pilots of the 56th hunted like a pack of wolves—as the 'The Wolf Pack' they became known and the Group continued to prove its validity.

At November 1st the record of the Thunderbolt groups stood at 237 for 73—better than 3 to 1. There were also 34 probably destroyed credits and 123 cases of damage inflicted to take into account. Unlike the claims of the bomber gunners, the majority of fighter claims allowed were backed by gun camera film. It was not mere wishful thinking; there was tangible evidence in celluloid. That assessments from combat films was sometimes faulty is true, but when German records became available at the end of the war the claims of American fighter units were found to approximate the actual losses sustained by the Luftwaffe.

To the Eighth Air Force, more important than the number of Luftwaffe aircraft brought down, was the marked reduction in bomber losses when P-47s were present. In the light of the costly B-17 missions into Germany early in October, the continuation of the Eighth's offensive depended largely on developing fighter support still further. But there were many sceptics—not least, the Luftwaffe!

Chapter 11: Summer Fortunes of the Liberators

Early in June 1943 the men 'on the line' at Hardwick and Shipdham became aware that their charges were to be employed in yet another role, low altitude attack. Orders had been received to remove the coveted Norden bomb sights from some Liberators and instal in their place a low altitude type—actually a modified gunsight. Singly, or in small formations, these aircraft were despatched on cross-country training missions, flying at a few hundred feet to bomb a specially allotted target range in the Wash. The object was obscured by the usual secrecy, the inevitable rumours were rife, the most prevalent was that an attack on a German battleship in a Norwegian fjord was planned. Those who did know the truth were very few and Group Headquarters knew little beyond a connection with a project code-named STATESMAN. Speculation increased; first by an order to transfer a dozen B-24s from Shipdham to Hardwick to replace those 93rd Group had modified for night flying and leaflet dropping operations, then by the preparation of bomb bay fuel tanks for at least 25 aircraft in each group. Heavier nose armament was also hurried along suggesting that strong opposition was anticipated.

One of the few men in 2nd Bomb Wing in the know was Colonel Ted Timberlake, the 93rd's original commander, now heading the 201st Provisional Combat Wing that planned and co-ordinated operations of the Liberator groups in the Eighth Air Force. The necessity to prevent the slightest hint of the target name from reaching the enemy was particularly important, for although the Germans appreciated the possibility of an attack, they also knew it would be difficult to effect and was thus most unlikely. Therefore, the strange name Ploesti was absolutely taboo.

Oil had long commanded the attention of Allied planning but oil targets were widely dispersed and not easily reached with bombers operating from the U.K. The most important area, the Ploesti complex of refineries, in the Rumanian oil fields, was well out of range—but it could just be reached by heavies staging at North African bases. This plum target was reckoned to be producing 60% of Hitler's oil and destruction of a proportion of the installations resulting in reduced capacity, could have an important effect on the duration of the war: so mused the strategists, who had asked for a study of the possibilities.

A round trip of some two thousand miles would be entailed, a large part over hostile territory exacting maximum endurance from the longest ranged Allied bombers available and thereby allowing enemy forces ample time to intercept. The odds were great, but so was the prize.

There had been a precedent. In the summer of 1942 a few American Liberators had flown in darkness in an attempt to bomb Ploesti, but none found the target. This initial taste without loss, served to whet the appetite of those who sought to demolish this vital Axis installation; the idea of a major attack persisted and was given substance in the following spring. The Liberator was obviously the tool for the job with North Africa as the launching point. Final plans called for a force of 200 from both Eighth and Ninth AAFs, to combine in a low-level attack against seven installations in the Ploesti complex. The operation would be under the auspices of the Libyan-based Ninth Air Force which would provide its two B-24 groups while the rest of the task force would move temporarily from the UK. A new Liberator group was scheduled to join the Eighth Air Force in June 1943 and would accompany the veterans to Africa for the mission.

Colonel Jack Wood and the vanguard of 389th Group arrived at Hethel, Norfolk on June 11th to be followed by the remainder of the air echelon during the next fortnight. Meanwhile, the ground staff still waited at New York for the *Queen Elizabeth* to ferry them across the Atlantic and with the urgency of giving the group maximum training in local procedure, prior to departure for Africa, men from the 44th and 93rd were detailed to provide a temporary ground echelon. Perhaps the 389th airmen were even more perplexed than the veterans of Shipdham and Hardwick at the form of flight training, for versed in high altitude attack and assigned to a theatre where this was heavy bomber standard operating procedure, the hedge-hopping to which they were now applied did not make sense. During low-flying activity over East Anglia, it was the Hethel newcomers that came to grief with two Liberators colliding and only two of the twenty men surviving.

In the last week of June the Liberators made for North Africa via Portreath, the 93rd departing late on the evening of the 25th, the 44th following two days later and the 389th on the 31st. All told 124 B-24s were sent; an influx of new planes and crews had built up the depleted "Eightballs" and "Circus", enabling them to provide 41 and 42 bombers respectively.

In Libya the three groups came under the operational control of IX Bomber Command with the 44th being located at Benina with that Command's 98th Group, while the others occupied sites in the Benghazi area. Many of the 93rd's personnel were familiar with the discomforts of the desert, from their previous sojourn during winter—infinitely more bearable than the intense heat and discomforts of full summer. Frequent dust storms made aircraft maintenance most difficult for ground crews. Relations with the two Ninth Air Force groups were not particularly happy; the men from England considered their desert companions generally lax and absorbed in their own welfare. The 44th lodged uneasily with the 98th particularly after accusations that the latter's cooks (who fed

Mechanics are sheltered from the heat of the Libyan sun by the wing of *Buzzin Bear*.—(Cameron)

Conditions were primitive; but at least it didn't rain! A 44th BG mechanic cleans a .50.—(Cameron)

both) were deliberately withholding rations . . . the others thought the UK gunners made rash claims and the crews generally cocky and undisciplined.

The attack on Ploesti was not immediately undertaken, the Liberators were first required for another campaign. The Allied invasion of Sicily was being mounted and the arrivals from England were quickly involved in bombing Italian targets to 'assist' the campaign. On July 2nd the 93rd and 44th were sent to bomb airfields from normal altitudes and found the enemy equally attentive as over northern Europe. One "Eightball" aircraft was shot down over the target and another ditched in the Mediterranean. For a fortnight the Eighth's Liberators accompanied those of the Ninth in a series of attacks chiefly aimed at airfields and marshalling yards, the 44th and 93rd flying ten missions apiece while the 389th flew six. The new group entered combat on the 9th when 28 of its aircraft bombed Maleme, Crete. It proved an uncomfortable debut, for a Staffel of Me109s made repeated attacks, shooting down a Liberator. Bombing missions over the "boot" of Italy were often flown at single group strength without fighter support, frequently tantalising enemy interceptors who, though few in numbers, were generally tenacious.

The "Flying Eightballs" still seemed to possess a fatal attraction for the Luftwaffe and more often than not it was this group that tangled with the enemy. Even so, some of the star characters continued to maintain and add to their standing. The 67th Squadron's redoubtable *Suzy Q* and her pilot Major "Pappy" Moore were about due to part, but not without furthering their legend. Many 44th Group crewmen, following an old movie the previous evening in which the quotation "see Naples and die" appeared, found themselves next day bound for that very city, behind the *Suzy Q* in lead position carrying Moore on the final mission of his tour. One engine failed on the way, but *Suzy Q* carried on maintaining her position over the target with a feathered prop and weathering fighter attacks on the way home.

Two aircraft were missing from this raid. One was *Buzzin' Bear* with Captain W. R. Cameron, the only other pilot survivor from the 67th Bomb Sqdn's. original complement. However, *Buzzin' Bear* had not come to grief and two days later alighted at Benina Main well stocked with vino. Leaving Naples, Cameron had been forced to shut down the badly damaged No. 3 engine with the result that the bomber lagged behind the group formation. Concern over the rapidly diminishing fuel supply caused a decision to head for Malta and when that island loomed up sooner than expected, the bomber was brought down to 1,500 ft while radio contact was attempted and eventually established with an airfield on Malta. Before a bearing could be obtained another engine faltered and seeing

an airstrip in the distance, Cameron put down without waiting for radio instructions, not that they would have been of any help—as the island was Sicily! The Comiso fighter airstrip, on which they had alighted, was close to the front line and in receipt of regular attention from German dive-bombers. Since *Buzzin' Bear* was a large and inviting target, it was imperative to replenish her tanks and fly her out quickly. The only aviation spirit on the site was in 5-gallon cans, so the crew formed a human chain and spent several hours passing up 600 gallons to the wing tanks. A take-off was accomplished that night and the real Malta was reached for temporary repairs.

Major Moore took *Suzy-Q* on the last flight of his tour on July 18th. The aircraft's ground crew chief, Sgt Marion Bagley, waiting for her return, saw that from around 1,500 ft *Suzy-Q* began a rather steep approach. Bagley then became aware that all four props were feathered! The veteran bomber failed to reach the edge of the runway, and momentarily disappeared from view behind a rise in the ground a quarter of a mile short. The rending crash feared did not come and to his amazement *Suzy-Q* reappeared, hurtling towards the airfield barely clearing scrub and small boulders, vaulting a four-foot ditch, before finally coming to rest none the worse for her experience. Bagley enquired of a slightly unnerved Major Moore, "That was your last one wasn't it?" "Sarg, you never spoke truer words!" came the emphatic reply. A few hours after this parting gesture to "her" pilot *Suzy Q* was leading the 44th in the first USAAF bombing raid on Rome, with Captain Cameron at the controls. She behaved impeccably.

Major Kenneth Caldwell leading the 389th Group confessed to some apprehension over Rome when he found his formation confronted with thousands of shimmering particles. It transpired that what appeared to be a new type of flak, was really leaflets dropped by preceding aircraft.

This attack on railyards was the last mission undertaken by the Liberator groups in support of the Sicilian campaign, in fact they had already continued for a week longer than planned. Now came a period of training and maintenance for the major strike at the Ploesti oilfields.

"We expect our losses to be 50%, but even though we should lose everything we've sent, but hit the target, it will be well worth it."—those words of General Brereton, Commanding General of the Ninth Air Force, and in overall control of the attack were cold comfort to the participating airmen. There was little doubt that the raid could be a most costly business yet the sporadic enemy opposition in this theatre lent hope to some that it might turn out to be a milk run.

After twelve days of maintenance and practice against a mock Ploesti in the desert wastes, the mission was called for Sunday August 1st. The Ninth's 376th Group led the bomber

The Eightballs being briefed for Ploesti.—(Cameron)

As the B-24s set course for Ploesti, smoke from one that crashed on take-off at Benina Main casts a dark shadow on the desert.—(Cameron)

best bombing of the raid was accomplished here resulting in destruction that put the refinery out of action for the duration of the war. Turning away, both columns of the 44th were engaged by fighters.

The 389th Group's target involved the longest planned flight and was given to this group because its B-24Ds were late models fitted with extra integral tankage. These aircraft were also heavier, particularly those with ball turrets, and in consequence they were slightly slower and more vulnerable to ground fire on the target run. Campina was believed only lightly defended in this respect and hence another good reason for assigning the 389th to this target. Led by Colonel Wood in an aircraft piloted by Major K. M. Caldwell, the Group found and totally destroyed the Campina refinery although there were some anxious moments during the approach when a turn was made down the wrong valley.

German Me109s and Rumanian IAR-80s attacked some 44th and 93rd Liberators after bombing in the neighbourhood of Ploesti and on the return flight over the Ionian Sea. It was ground fire, however, that took the major toll of the 52 bombers listed as lost from the 179 despatched. The three Eighth AF groups contributed 30 and 103 respectively to these totals although six of the former (2 from each group) came down in Turkey where the crews were interned.

Ploesti was the scene of many individual acts of heroism and brought the unprecedented award of five Medals of Honor for a single operation; four went to Eighth Air Force personnel. The 44th's commander Colonel Leon Johnson was one recipient and that irrepressible *Suzy-Q* was the bomber in which he earned the award. Chosen as command plane for the "Eightball's" effort, *Suzy-Q* had shown trouble during the pre-flight run-ups, a broken spark plug in the master cylinder of No. 2 engine was diagnosed to be the trouble but hasty action on the part of M/Sgt M. Ulosovich and his ground crew had her ready just in time. Major William Brandon piloted her with Colonel Johnson in the co-pilot's seat acting as formation commander. On the target run Johnson found his assigned target already burning and the defences alerted. Instead of turning away he decided to go on and bomb any unscathed plant to be seen. Brandon took *Suzy-Q* through the smoke and flame collecting more severe damage to her already well patched frame. By the time *Suzy Q* had regained the Mediterranean and was on a heading for base only one

stream followed by the Eighth's 93rd, then the 98th Group of the Ninth, and finally the 44th and 389th Groups. During the long flight the two leading groups became separated from the others. On approach to the target the 376th mistook the IP (Floresti), and turned south too soon. The 93rd Group followed, but realising their mistake, made another turn, back towards Ploesti and in so doing positioned the group ideally to attack some targets, assigned to other groups. First to bomb, the 93rd faced intense AA fire and was also intercepted by enemy fighters. Meanwhile the trailing groups had reached the check point Pitesti, where the 389th Group veered north-east for its target at Campina, 18 miles N.W. of the main refinery complex. Some confusion had arisen between the 44th and 98th as to which formations were ahead and which trailing, but eventually both reached the correct IP (Floresti) for the turn south-east to the targets. The large force of 44th aircraft had two briefed targets and while Colonel Johnson took sixteen B-24s to one, Lt Col James Posey led the remaining 21 to the other; Johnson's target had already been attacked by the 93rd some 20 minutes before, but Posey's was untouched and the

44th BG Liberators skip over the Balkans en route to Ploesti. A photo taken by 389th BG which overtook them.—(USAF)

The pilot of *Buzzin Bear,* Cpt Bill Cameron took this picture of *Suzy Q* returning from Ploesti. Note damage to starboard rudder.—(Cameron)

other aircraft of the group remained with her—*Buzzin' Bear* with Cameron, last of the 67th originals, flying a voluntary mission after completing his tour. A few days before, while talking with British anti-aircraft gunners on the field at Benia, the Captain had asked which aircraft in a low flying formation they would aim at. He was told the highest. This Cameron remembered and took *Buzzin' Bear* down over Ploesti as low as he dare. The two Liberators were the only ones of the 17 from the 66th and 67th Bomb Sqdn's, who managed to return to Benina that day, having been airborne for 13 hours 40 minutes. The others were either missing or had landed elsewhere.

Two Medals of Honor were awarded posthumously to the pilot and co-pilot of the leading 93rd aircraft, *Hell's Wench.* Having followed the errant 376th Group in a turn at the wrong IP, Colonel Addison Baker and Major John Jerstad were soon to rectify the mistake by making a turn in the opposite direction and putting the 93rd on a completely different target approach to that planned. In their path lay the heaviest ground defences in the area which opened up in force destroying many aircraft of the 93rd. When still three miles from the refineries *Hell's Wench* appeared to receive a heavy shell hit in or against the nose which started a fire. Bombs were immediately jettisoned but instead of making a belly landing in the fields below the Liberator continued leading the formation towards the refineries. Her fuselage engulfed in flames, *Hell's Wench* reached the target and went into a climb that observers said would have needed two men's strength on the controls to achieve. Some men were seen to parachute before the lead bomber fell away and crashed in a field, even so there were no survivors from the ten men on board. Captain Walter Stewart, group deputy leader, flying *Utah Man* the only surviving aircraft from the lead flight, glimpsed this drama while fighting to keep control. *Utah Man* stayed in the air despite 365 holes and touched down nearly 14 hours after departure. Last B-24 to return from the mission was K. D. McFarland's *Liberty Lad* which limped in on two engines having been airborne 16 hours. The 93rd suffered the loss of nine aircraft in the target area, two by collision returning in cloud. One that rode out the holocaust without much hurt was *Bomerang,* the same threatened with cannibalism after the Eighth's very first Liberator mission.

The other Medal of Honor was also a posthumous award. Lt Lloyd D. Hughes was piloting the 389th Group's "753" when the fuel tanks were holed by ground fire and escaping petrol streamed back past the waist windows. In spite of the imminent danger of fire, Hughes was apparently determined to see that his bombs reached the target. The aircraft was, in fact, ignited by flames from the burning refinery. Hughes appeared to attempt a landing in a river bed, pulled up over a bridge, but the burning right wing touched a ground obstruction and the machine crashed. Even so two gunners and the navigator escaped, although the latter died of injuries.

The foregoing brief outline hardly does justice to the Eighth Air Force effort. The low level Ploesti mission is probably the best chronicled of USAAF air actions and need not be enlarged upon here. Any survivor of the Americans and one

Briton who flew on this raid, whatever his part, has never ceased to be regarded with some awe.

Replenished in men and aircraft, the three Eighth Air Force B-24 groups had another important mission to undertake before returning "home" to England; a strike at Wiener Neustadt, Austria, centre of Me109 production. The mission was originally scheduled for August 7th to coincide with B-17 raids against Regensburg from the UK; the unfavourable trend of weather over Europe caused this plan to be abandoned and the B-24s set out at the first suitable opportunity.

In company with the two Ninth AF groups, the Liberators were despatched at 07.00 hrs on August 13th, with Colonel Ted Timberlake of the 201st PCWB in command and flying with the leading 389th Group. The route needed careful planning for like Ploesti it stretched the B-24s range to the maximum and even with two bomb bay tanks it was not considered advisable for the bombers to attempt to return to their Libyan bases but instead to nearer Tunisian airfields.

Sixty-nine of the 101 bombers were from Eighth Air Force groups. The trailing elements, a composite Ninth AF formation, abandoned the mission while over the Adriatic, so the operation became a completely Eighth AF affair. In contrast to the vicious reception over Ploesti, this raid was met with only meagre and inaccurate anti-aircraft fire. The only attempts at interception, confined to a Staffel of FW190s over Austria and another of Me109s on the return over southern Italy, were made ineffectively against the "Eightballs". Evidently this 12-hour mission was not anticipated by the Germans and the target, though thinly veiled with cloud, was thought to have been hit effectively. Timberlake said on return—"I think we had a good day. As we turned away, I could see innumerable bursts on the target". In fact two of four assembly shops received major damage and Me109 production fell from 270 in July to 184 in August.

Return to England was further delayed as once more the attention of the Liberators was requested in support of the final Allied advance in Sicily. Three missions were flown from which the 389th had no operational losses, the 93rd one, but the 44th eight. This further debacle for the "Eightballs" occurred on August 16th when a mission was sent to Foggia. A surprise and skilfully executed attack by Me109s near the Italian coast brought the end to a legend—for *Suzy-Q*, last original aircraft of the 67th Bomb Sqdn. and seemingly indestructible, was one of those that fell; a new crew was lost in her pyre on an Italian beach. *Buzzin' Bear* was lost too, but Cameron, promoted to Squadron Commander, had not gone along; the mission was expected to have been an easy one and thus a number of new and "green" crews were sent.

During the last week of the month the groups finally received orders to return to Norfolk. The "Sky Scorpions"— as the 389th had dubbed themselves—had comparatively few wounds to show for their two months of operations from the desert. The "Travelling Circus" had suffered severely at Ploesti but escaped any catastrophies on other missions. In the case of the "Flying Eightballs", it seemed the jinx still stuck, for the second time the group had come near to obliteration.

From May until early September 1943 the 2nd Bomb Wing had no tactical units available for operations from England. A few B-24s left behind at the Norfolk airfields were utilised for training purposes and on two occasions flew Air-Sea Rescue patrols to aid in the search for Fortress crewmen down in the North Sea. However, during August another Liberator group arrived from the US bringing the first B-24Hs to the UK. Among other refinements this new model had a power-operated nose gun turret, a retractable turret amidships as on later B-24Ds and greater ammunition storage capacity. The aircrew of the 392nd Group received these aircraft just before leaving America and the majority of the maintenance crews, already embarked on the *Queen Elizabeth,* did not have experience of these machines until reuniting with the airmen at Wendling airfield. So, while aircrew attended the usual theatre indoctrination classes and Gee instruction, the ground men had to undertake additional training on the B-24H.

Initiation of the 392nd Group came on September 6th when a North Sea diversion for the infamous Stuttgart mission was flown by all four B-24 groups. Next day the 44th and 389th Groups set off for Leeuwarden but cumulus cloud turned them away to another Dutch airfield which was also partly obscured. Three 389th aircraft unloaded their Group's first contribution to the Eighth's campaign, while other aircraft dropped on a convoy of a dozen ships, sighted off Texel. On the 9th the Liberators joined in the STARKEY deception raids with indecisive attacks on the famous Luftwaffe fields at Abbeville and St Omer.

The mission to Chartres six days later was despatched in the late afternoon and the return to base was in darkness. Only eighteen aircraft of the 93rd Group bombed the primary target and intercepting night fighters claimed one bomber. The 389th Group had difficulty in following proper landing procedures but all returning aircraft eventually put down safely. The following morning airmen of the 44th, 93rd and 389th Groups were somewhat astounded to receive orders for another detachment to North Africa, this time to furnish additional support to retrieve the situation of the ground forces in the Salerno beachhead.

During the brief period in the UK the groups had received many replacement crews and aircraft, the latter mostly nose-turreted models. These Liberators were received with some misgivings by old hands. Never an easy plane to fly at altitude, the weight increases made the newer models less speedy and responsive. Another complaint about the B-24H, was the ineffectual padding round the nose turret which allowed icy draughts to add to crew discomfort.

Previously devoid of any distinguishing unit marking, the groups of 2nd Bombardment Division (as the original 2nd Bombardment Wing had been renamed) now carried the white disc or circle of this organisation on tail fins, each with a group identity code letter thereon. Thus adorned, the three groups set out on the third "African Expedition".

The crisis at Salerno had, in the meantime, passed; the B-24s were therefore directed to bombing Italian targets that had some bearing on the land campaign. Docks at Leghorn and Bastia, and Pisa marshalling yards, were successfully

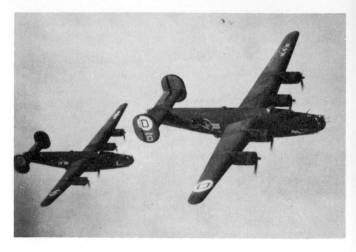

B-24Hs of 392nd BG.—(USAF)

attacked on September 21st and 24th respectively, but thereafter the weather over Italy proved as difficult as that encountered over Northern Europe and several missions had to be abandoned or cancelled. Another attack on the Wiener Neustadt Messerschmitt factory was the only other mission undertaken of many planned, and even this was accomplished in far from satisfactory conditions. General Hodges led 73 B-24s only to find that overcast persisted from the Adriatic to Austria. Luckily a small gap was found in the clouds and though inadequate for a good bomb-run, photographic evidence later showed many hits on the target.

Unlike the previous mission to Wiener Neustadt this was strongly opposed. An accurate flak barrage was encountered: a shell exploding beneath *Bomerang* was said to have pitched her violently upwards for several feet. A strong force of enemy fighters (mostly Me109s) with heavy calibre machine guns and rockets intercepted at the IP. The brunt of this assault was once again borne by the "Eightballs", last in line, who were assailed by wave after wave of fighters. The intensity of the air battle is reflected in the 44th gunners claims of 43-3-6. Fourteen B-24s were listed lost on this mission, 10 from Eighth Air Force groups including eight from the 44th. Another 41 of the Eighth's Liberators sustained damage of some degree,

389th BG hits shipping at Bastia, Corsica on 21 Sept. 1943. Recently added group marking, Circle C, can be seen on the right wing.—(IWM)

and eight of the 44th's crash-landed so that they had to be left behind when the Group returned to England two days later. The "Eightballs" had cherished a belief that their run of catastrophies must cease, that the law of averages must allow an evening out in the punishment accorded their profession. Yet, having sustained double the losses of the 93rd during this African detachment, it became even harder not to believe in the jinx.

Back in England the 392nd had bitter experience of the Luftwaffe's prowess. In the absence of the other groups, training continued and experience was gained by flying decoy missions over the North Sea. The first three of these were fighter escorted and without incident; the fourth, on October 4th, unescorted, met thirty-plus enemy fighters. In the ensuing mêlée four Liberators went down with 43 men, and eleven men were wounded in the many damaged surviving bombers. After that the Wendling group was pitchforked into the offensive with the experienced groups, once more established at their home bases. On October 8th it accompanied the 93rd and 389th to Vegesack (the 44th was recovering from its recent debacle) to bomb shipyards. Little damage was done to the primary target. Next day all four groups took part in raids along the Baltic coast, the 93rd and 389th making for Danzig and the 44th and 392nd, Gdynia. Heavy smoke screens foiled their efforts.

During the remainder of October weather prevented the Liberators from carrying out any further missions. Sixty aircraft were scheduled to go with the B-17s to Schweinfurt but only the 93rd and 392nd managed to assemble for a diversion flight out to sea. The Liberators were back in the "Big League" but their numbers were still too small for deep, unescorted penetrations into enemy territory.

The future at least looked more promising. Five American factories were now producing Liberators at a 150 per week rate, while training schools were turning out a good flow of crews to meet the AAF share of the production. The 2nd Bomb Division was scheduled to double its group strength by the end of the year, additionally new techniques and new equipment were becoming available.

A year had seen many changes in the oldest units, original crews not lost had completed tours and gone home; a handful remained in administrative posts or to command. Leon Johnson now headed a combat wing composed of the 44th

Lt Gen Spaatz, assisted by Col Jack Wood, fixes the DUC streamer to the 389th BG's colours at a ceremony at Hethel.—(USAF)

and 392nd Groups, Lt Col James Posey had taken command of the "Eightballs" and a newcomer, Lt Col Leland Feigel, took over the 93rd after Addison Baker was killed at Ploesti.

A few of the original aircraft endured: Shipdham still had *Lemon Drop*, noted for her reluctance to leave America when the 44th moved to England; also *V-Victory* in which Posey and Diehl respectively had led the 68th and 506th Bomb Sqdns to Ploesti. At Hardwick there were half a dozen veterans; *Bomerang* was still going strong and just to prove the worth of the reprieve after that first raid, the anniversary date was marked by flying a round trip of 1,600 miles to Poland.

The contribution of the Liberators during their first year of war was of necessity small due to lack of numbers. They had been the stop-gap on many occasions, sop to the calls for air power from the Middle East. Very much the Cinderella force, they had come to have their day in undertaking one of the most spectacular air attacks of the war. The lot of the B-24 men had often been hard, yet a fierce pride distinguished the veterans of Hardwick and Shipdham. As often happened, an ill-fated minority gained high morale through comradeship in adversity.

Chapter 12: "Little Friends"

At the time of its appearance in 1939, the Lockheed P-38 Lightning was both brilliant in its concept and promising in its performance. Such an advanced and unorthodox design was not quickly developed and the first combat worthy models did not reach USAAF squadrons until 1942. These were P-38Fs, sent first to England where pilot indoctrination and modifications to radios had left little time for combat missions before the units concerned were moved down to Africa: how the P-38 would fare over Northern Europe had yet to be discovered. A generally good performance and particularly useful range made it the object of demand from many theatres of war. During the winter of 1942-1943 and the following spring, the limited numbers available went mainly to the South-West Pacific and North Africa where they proved very valuable in what were chiefly tactical operations. The three Lightning groups in North Africa (1st, 14th, and 82nd) suffered heavy losses in the early months of that campaign but the aircraft showed up well in combat with FW190s and Me109s. At low and medium altitudes, where combat most frequently took place the P-38F, in spite of its large comparative size, was able to turn with the enemy aircraft, could usually out-climb them, and had a faster top speed. Although the attrition rate was high the P-38 proved its worth in North Africa against the Luftwaffe equally as well as it had fared against the Japanese in the South-West Pacific.

By November the Germans had approximately 800 fighters ranged in the west to meet the Eighth Air Force bombers and there was every sign that the enemy force was being rapidly expanded. The Combined Bomber Offensive plan had given high priority to gaining air superiority over the Luftwaffe; it was now, more than ever, apparent that if the bombers were to continue their task they would have to have increased protection from the mounting German fighter assaults. The long-range fighter was the only immediate answer, one that had already brought notable success both in protecting the bombers and inflicting severe losses on the enemy fighters. The Thunderbolt was not the "flying brick" many had assumed; it could more than hold its own with Luftwaffe fighters. The P-38 Lightning with drop tanks offered at least another hundred miles of protection for the bombers and General Arnold gave priority to the P-38 Lightning for the Eighth Air Force during the autumn of 1943.

Two groups trained to fly Lightnings had arrived in England in August with the improved P-38H model; the first to become operational was the 55th on October 15th. On that date 36 of its aircraft flew an uneventful sweep along the Dutch coast— ten days short of a year since Lightnings last operated from England. For the next five consecutive days, the 55th flew sweeps and limited heavy bomber support missions while on two further October days it operated as escort for Marauder medium bombers. Mechanical difficulties were much in evidence during this period and were the suspected reason for the failure of one P-38 to return from an early mission.

Then on November 3rd came the Group's first deep penetration, acting as target support for 40th Wing B-17s bombing Wilhelmshaven. That evening the Group's Air Executive recorded the event in his diary: "As someone yelled 'bombs away' I looked over and saw thousands of bombs falling on a flare marker dropped by the lead bomber. About that time flak hit one B-17 in the third box and he rolled over and spun earthward. Some of the boys say he exploded shortly after being hit. A second later, I saw two FW190s attacking the rear of this box. I took my flight in and closed in on one Hun, firing all guns. He burst into flames and spun downward. I claimed him as destroyed. I started home 'driving' along the boxes. Towards the front I noticed another box being attacked by two Me109s. I closed in on one, fired two long bursts and he burst into flames, rolled over and baled out. We joined up and came home without further incident. All our lads returned safely. We claimed 6 destroyed (only 3 allowed) and several damaged. Morale is sky high and the mechanics are going wild!"

Two days later the three squadrons of the 55th, despatched from Nuthampstead, were accompanied by eight aircraft of the 20th Group all being flown by 79th Ftr. Sqdn. pilots. Not long after take-off some Lightnings experienced mechanical troubles and were forced to abort, leaving 47 to climb up through the overcast towards their rendezvous with Liberators bound for Münster. These became separated in the bad visibility, and —50° temperature at 25,000 ft caused further aircraft to turn back with engine trouble. At the rendezvous point they found no sign of the bombers and only one squadron, the 38th, finally contacted them—near the target at about the same time as a strong force of Me109s and rocket-carrying Do217s launched an attack. Outnumbered, perhaps three to one, the sixteen remaining Lightnings led by Major Milton Joel set about breaking up the enemy attacks. Most combats were inconclusive as pilots did not let themselves be drawn away from the bombers. Even so, claims of 5-3-4 were made on return to Nuthampstead, for no loss to the 55th. Their escort value was also evinced by only three of the B-24s failing to return from the mission.

The Lightnings were not always so fortunate in combat. In another, two days later, the 55th was assigned to escort Marauders bombing Melun airfield in France. Here Focke-Wulfs slipped out of the cloud and attacked elements of the 20th Group that had gone along. One Lightning was severely damaged, the pilot baling out over the Channel and another failed to return to base, its fate unknown.

The 13th was certainly an unlucky day for the 55th. In typical English November weather, damp and overcast, forty-eight P-38s set out to escort bombers on the target leg of a mission to Bremen; one turned back before the enemy coast was crossed and two more aborted later. At 26,000 ft over Germany pilots shivered in bitterly cold cockpits; flying conditions were unusually bad, and the probability of mechanical troubles at that temperature did not help. Again outnumbered, the 55th was heavily engaged near the target as it strove to defend the bombers, for which it paid dearly. Seven P-38s fell, five to enemy fighters and the others to unknown causes; it was suspected that engine troubles might have made some of the P-38s lost easy prey for enemy fighters. Sixteen returned with battle damage: one, pitted with over a hundred small calibre bullet holes and ripped from five cannon shell bursts, came back on one engine. The Group had sustained grievous losses, but there was some consolation to be found in the protection they had afforded the bombers which, after all, was their object. Worse was to follow.

On the 29th the 55th Group again set forth to Bremen, with elements of the 20th Group bringing up the rear. Just after

55th FG pilots who distinguished themselves in the early battles between P-38s and the Luftwaffe. Lt Col Jack Jenkins, Group Executive (top left); Cpt Joe Myers with ground crew and personal P-38 *Journey's End*; Cpt Jim Hancock with ground crew of *Repuls-ive*; and Major Mark Shipman, 38th FS CO.—(Jenkins)

crossing the Dutch coast at 31,000 ft, Me109s of III J.G.1 pounced on the Lightnings in a surprise attack evidently designed to entice the Americans into releasing their drop tanks prematurely. Another seven P-38s failed to return to base although three of the enemy were definitely shot down.

During November, eighteen P-38s were lost on operations and four others written off in crashes on return to England, amounting to almost a third of the 55th Fighter Group's strength. The P-38, supposedly a proven fighter, had been dogged with mechanical failure on these first missions. The extremely low temperatures encountered at altitudes above 20,000 ft was the primary cause of the engine trouble. At —50° lubricating oil became sluggish and the sudden application of full power, particularly in a climb, could cause piston rod bearings to break up with dire consequences. Above 22,000 ft the Allison engines would also begin to throw oil, in fact, oil consumption rose from an average 1 to 2 quarts an hour at lower altitudes, to 4 to 8 above 22,000 ft. This reduced engine life to average 80 odd hours—almost half normal operating time at lower altitudes. Turbo-supercharger regulators also gave trouble, eventually traced to moisture from

the vapour trail, gathering behind the engine exhaust stubs, getting into the balance lines and freezing. The vapour trails were also a tactical handicap for they marked the passage of a Lightning through the upper air by distinctive twin trails, that could be discerned up to 4 miles away. Whereas Luftwaffe pilots could not distinguish between the single trails made by Spitfires or Thunderbolts, or their own 109s and 190s, they were able to recognise Lightning formations in this way.

Lightning pilots faced considerable physical discomfort, at times amounting to agony. Their hands and feet became numb with cold and in some instances frost-bitten; not infrequently a pilot was so weakened by conditions that he had to be assisted out of the cockpit upon return. Cockpits had warm air ducted from the engines, but this heating system proved quite inadequate for high altitude flights over North-Western Europe during winter months. The Lightning had not previously operated on any scale from England in winter, but experience with the few photographic reconnaissance versions had revealed shortcomings in cockpit heating, but improvements were still awaited. As an immediate solution extra and better protective clothing was sought locally by the 55th and arrangements were made to procure electrically heated flying suits, gloves and spats.

In actual combat, what had proved to be the case in Africa was found to apply—below 18,000 ft the P-38 was a better machine in most respects than the Me109G and stood up well against the FW190A. Above that its performance fell off and it could neither pursue an enemy with much chance of success above 28,000 ft, nor out-dive the Messerschmitts and Focke-Wulfs at such heights. Once the fight was brought down to 18,000 ft then the tables were turned in these respects. The rate of roll was also poor at high altitudes, but in maximum speed in level flight the P-38 had the edge over enemy interceptors at most altitudes. But for its escort work it was expected to operate with the bombers at heights up to 33,000 ft. Quite plainly the P-38H had neither the high altitude performance to match operational requirements of the theatre, nor was it mechanically suited to operate in the prevailing cold and damp conditions of North-West Europe.

Shipments of Lightnings enabled the King's Cliffe Group to fully equip in December. Having operated since November 5th as a fourth squadron to the 55th Group, the 20th flew its first full group mission on December 28th under the leadership of the 55th's experienced deputy, Lt Col Jenkins. The 20th's new Lightnings were P-38Js, distinguished from P-38Hs by a flat panel windscreen and deep radiator intake housings just behind and below the propeller spinners. Performance of the 'J' differed little from late 'H' models of the 55th having the B-33 Type turbo-supercharger. Their chief advantage was in endurance. The deeper air intake held the inter-cooler radiator in addition to the oil radiators, the former having been re-positioned from inside the leading edge of the wing to allow a 55 gallon fuel tank to be substituted each side. The first Js, however, arrived without these extra tanks which followed late in December and were installed in January. These increased the radius of action by approximately 125 miles.

Both types used drop tanks. The 150 gallon drop tank was the type normally used by P-38s in England and with two the 'H' could theoretically reach 520 miles from base, and the 'J' about 640 miles. But these distances were rarely obtainable in practice. Support for fifteen minutes in the target area, reduced the P-38J's mileage to under 400 and if close escort entailed weaving to stay with the bombers then 300 miles was about the limit. Even so, the Lightning had a substantial range advantage over the Thunderbolt and continued to provide target leg escort and support on deep bomber penetrations.

Both Allies and enemy, anticipated some limiting of VIII Fighter Command operations with the onset of winter. Between London and Berlin storm conditions averaged a predicted twice a week. Such weather making even the flying

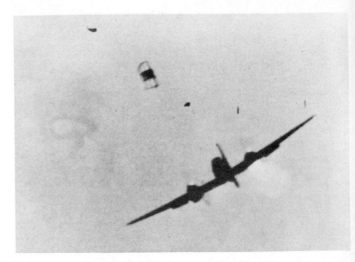

Canopy and pieces hurtle back from a crippled Me 410 as 353rd FG's Lt Richard Stearns gives it another burst. Right engine is in flames. 5 Nov. 1943.—(IWM)

of a multi-engine bomber difficult, affected to a much greater degree the small and control sensitive single-seat fighters, causing temporary loss of control and even collisions. Layers of cloud, sometimes extending from 300 to 29,000 ft, necessitated long spells of instrument flying and prolonged climbing through overcast and occasionally caused a pilot to fall victim to vertigo. Separated from his formation in the murk, he could fail to sense his flight attitude and get into a fatal spin. Nevertheless, VIII Fighter Command fighters went out in appalling weather conditions to rendezvous with bombers after a two to three hundred mile journey over continual cloud; which says much for the high standard of navigation. None were more appreciative of this effort than the bomber men, who drew much confidence from the sight of "Little Friends" —their familiar term for Allied fighters—even over Germany itself. That the majority of these long and difficult sorties were flown in the single-engined Thunderbolts was also significant.

The P-47 had a remarkably high standard of reliability once the early engine troubles had been successfully cured. By November substantial quantities of P-47Ds were arriving in the UK and VIII Fighter Command progesssively increased group establishments so that aircraft strength reached at least 100 and numbers of enlisted men rose by about 30 to around 280-285. There was, however, a shortage of fully trained pilots and it was some weeks before this deficiency could be remedied. One of the first groups to have its aircraft complement increased was the 78th at Duxford. On November 5th it had sufficient strength to fly two separate formations known as 78th 'A' & 'B' Groups, each having three 12-plane squadrons and operating independently of one another on the day's mission. This became general practice by the spring of 1944, with most experienced groups flying two formations on escort and support missions.

The VIII Fighter Command had considered so called fighter-bomber sorties with P-39s back in the autumn of 1942 but this idea was shelved when the aircraft were transferred to the Twelfth Air Force. Thereafter, the Command was fully involved in establishing its small force of P-47 Thunderbolts in the escort fighter role. As the winter of 1943-1944 set in and unsatisfactory weather caused many days of inactivity by the heavies, the fighter-bomber idea was revived. The shackle which held the long range tank to the belly of the Thunderbolt was designed for alternative 500 or 1,000 lb bomb loads, but little guidance was available on the best techniques—dive or skip bombing. The former seemed to offer greater accuracy but as the P-47 was inclined to build up high speeds in a dive with consequent difficulties in pulling out at low altitudes, some experimentation was necessary. This task was given to

Cpt Walter Beckham's gun camera film shows pieces flying off the FW 190 he claimed on 11 Nov. 1943.

the 353rd Group because there the Group Executive Officer, Major Glenn Duncan, and a notable pilot, Captain Walter Beckham, had previous experience of this form of bombing with P-39 and P-40 fighters.

Captain Beckham and four other members of the 351st Ftr. Sqdn. thus took their Thunderbolts from Metfield to Llanbedr, Wales, where a small off-shore islet presented a suitable target. This outcrop, measuring approximately 150 x 50 ft, the pilots had difficulty at first in hitting. It proved a simple matter of practice and at the end of the trials all had become quite accomplished at blasting the unfortunate rock. Best results appeared to be obtained by starting a 60° dive from 10,000 ft, pulling out at 4,000 ft. On November 25th, nearly two and a half months practice in this technique was put to the test when sixteen Thunderbolts of the 351st Ftr. Sqdn., each carrying a 500 lb bomb slung beneath its belly, took off to attack the St Omer/Ft Rouge airfield, not far from the French Channel coast. Escort was provided by the 78th Group and other squadrons of the 353rd. Approaching the target heavy ground fire was encountered and the leading plane, *Cookie* flown by the Group CO, Colonel McCollom,

Loren McCollom. Photo taken before he left 56th FG.—(Holmes)

received a near or direct hit which tore away a large area of under-fuselage skin, and fired a fuel tank. McCollom managed to bale out and was captured by the Germans, to spend the rest of the war as a prisoner. Another P-47 was forced, through mechanical difficulties, to jettison its bomb, leaving 14 to bomb. The results were poor with few hits on the airfield causing little worthwhile damage.

While the 353rd carried out the first Thunderbolt dive-bombing attack, the 56th Group experimented with another fighter-bomber technique against the nearby airfield of St Omer/Longuenesse. Escorted by the Martlesham Heath based 356th, fifty bomb-laden P-47s of the 56th Group flew at 24,000 ft in tight formation with a B-24 Liberator which was to sight on the target for them: an application of VIII Bomber Command's "drop-on-leader" technique extended to fighters. Unfortunately, a failure of the B-24's release mechanism delayed the dropping and caused most of the 500 lb bombs carried by the P-47s to overshoot. No 56th aircraft were lost, but some suffered damage from the intense flak barrage put up. One of the disadvantages of this form of fighter-bombing was the relative speeds of the P-47 and the B-24 used for sighting. No more high-level missions of this type were run in 1943 but the 353rd continued to develop the dive-bombing technique, following up with attacks on the Dutch airfield at Gilze Rijen on 4th and 23rd December. In January other Thunderbolt groups took to bombing; the 356th made its bombing debut on the 23rd, and the 78th—after cloud had foiled an attempt

Hugging one of the new 108 gl. paper tanks 42-8400, WR: E of 355th FG scales the clouds.—(USAF)

on the 25th—on the 31st. On both occasions Gilze Rijen was the target, being in easy reach of P-47 bases and the approach flight less heavily defended than appeared to be the case with the French airfields.

The day following their first venture in a bombing role, VIII Fighter Command groups achieved their largest victory so far, by trouncing the Luftwaffe 36 for 4 during escort and support on a mission to Bremen. Once again the top honours went to the 56th which had one of its most successful days of the war. Contact with the heavy bombers was made just after the first wave had left the target. The rear box of bombers was being attacked by 50 to 60 enemy aircraft, mostly Zerstörer Me110s and Me410s with a screen of single-engined fighters. Captain Mahurin who had a penchant for intense action shot down three Me110s, and repeating his performance of October 4th. With a total of 11 victories, he was then the highest scoring fighter ace in the Eighth. Six pilots of the Group claimed two enemy aircraft each: Lt Col Schilling, Majors Gabreski and Craig, Captains Cook and Ralph Johnson, and Flying Officer Velenta. All told 23 destroyed and 2 probably destroyed were the credits awarded after return to Halesworth, 18 of the victims being twin-engined fighters. One Thunderbolt was lost but the pilot, Lt B. Morrill of the 62nd Ftr. Sqdn. had baled out over Holland. The same mission also brought the first victories to the 352nd Group from Bodney. A flight of its 487th Ftr. Sqdn., while returning to England spotted a straggling B-24 about to be attacked by a number of Me109s. Having the advantage, Major John Meyer led his P-47s into the attack shooting down one Messerschmitt himself while other pilots destroyed another and drove off the rest.

November 29th—the day the 55th's P-38s suffered so heavily—saw VIII Fighter Command lose 16 fighters for 15 claims. Of these claims 6 were made by the chief exponents of the Thunderbolt, the 56th, and 5 by the 356th which had its first major clash with the enemy. Led by its new CO Lt Col Einar Malmstrom, a noted "barnstormer" of pre-war days, the Group took off from Martlesham at 13.45 hrs and headed out to rendezvous with the bombers that had been despatched to Bremen. Two and a half hours later the pilots were urgently calling for homings on their radios. Bad weather and battle with the enemy had separated the flights and taxed fuel supplies severely—as yet the Group could only carry 75 gallon drop tanks. Five Thunderbolts failed to return to base, most suspected victims of the elements.

During November 1943, Lt Col Donald Blakeslee, deputy CO of the 4th Group, was sent to Boxted airfield near Colchester to gain experience in flying the new P-51B Mustangs of a recently arrived Ninth Air Force group. Blakeslee was probably the most experienced American fighter pilot in Europe having a prodigious number of flying hours "under his belt" from 120 sweeps with the RAF and a year's missions with the ex-Eagles. He was, moreover, an excellent air leader and it was to be his lot to lead the new group, the 354th, on its early raids until its own commanders had the experience to take over. If Blakeslee found the Mustang lacking in any respect, he was still sure of one thing—it was far and away the best fighter for long-range work he had ever flown.

The Mustang was by no means a new design, having been used by the RAF for some time. The P-51B Model was, however, a completely revitalised version far surpassing the performance of its predecessors of the same name; the most significant improvement was a Packhard-built version of the Rolls-Royce Merlin 61 engine in place of the low-altitude rated Allison. The Merlin gave the P-51B an excellent all-round performance with high top speed and a good rate of climb. Further, the aircraft appeared to fulfil VIII Fighter Command's quest for a fighter that could accompany the bombers to distant targets. With a fuel consumption approximately half that of the P-47 and P-38, the P-51B carried 184 gallons in internal wing tanks, sufficient to take it 300 miles from base and back. Already plans were afoot to add another tank of 85 gallons capacity in the fuselage behind the pilot, raising the radius of action on the internal supply to 475 miles —a hundred miles further than the Thunderbolt could go even with the addition of a 108 gallon drop tank. The P-51B was also fitted with racks which would hold a 75 gallon drop tank, one under each wing, and this promised the then amazing radius for a single-engine fighter of 650 miles. Like the Thunderbolt, the Mustang needed an air pressure system to draw fuel from drop tanks at high altitude and Air Technical Section did a similar satisfactory plumbing job for the new North American fighter as that developed for the Republic fighter.

The extraordinary position was that these nimble and long-legged escorts were assigned to groups in the newly-arrived Ninth Air Force, a purely tactical organisation charged with local support to Allied armies in the Field during the forthcoming invasion of the Continent. To understand this situation it is necessary to take into consideration the environment of the Mustang. Designed in 1940 specifically to British needs, it evoked little interest from the Army Air Corps who considered the P-38 and P-47 designs capable of meeting its future requirements. Even reports on two specimens tested at Wright Field were singularly unenthusiastic. The RAF put the Mustang into service during 1942 but as the Allison engine rated for low altitude operation made it unsuitable for fighter sweeps it was used in a tactical reconnaissance role. The USAAF eventually procured a number and rigged them out in a ground support role and even as "attack" bombers. Meanwhile the RAF had married the Mustang airframe to a Rolls-Royce Merlin 61 series.

At this point Lt Col Tommy Hitchcock, on the American Embassy staff in London, encouraged by the Ambassador, J. G. Winant, advocated interest in the development of the Mustang with the Merlin as a long-range fighter. Eventually such conversions were made both sides of the Atlantic. In the spring of 1943, two British conversions were tested at Bovingdon and Cass Hough gave his opinion: "They were good, and very fast but the directional stability was poor". North American improved the flight characteristics and put it into production. AAF planners, however, had still seen the P-51B (the first Merlin version) as a tactical fighter. Thus, the first production batches sent to England were for three groups of the tactical Ninth Air Force. The VIII Fighter Command, whose needs for such an aircraft had since become urgent, were dismayed by this assignment, but a reversal of policy was not easily obtained and in any case the Ninth Air Force were loth to part with their prodigy. The Eighth had a strong case and in late October 1943 a compromise was reached, whereby the Ninth's Mustangs would furnish support and escort for the Eighth's heavy bombers until further notice. Eventually, the Eighth secured an adjustment of fighter allocations to give it priority on Mustangs.

Thus the first Merlin-engined Mustang group commenced operations under the control of VIII Fighter Command though assigned to IX Fighter Command, a policy that also embraced the Ninth's first P-47 units. Few of the 354th pilots had flown Mustangs before they arrived in England during October. Training and equipment problems delayed the first operational mission until December 1st, when Lt Col Blakeslee and Colonel K. R. Martin (Group CO) led 23 aircraft on a sweep over the Knocke area on the Belgian coast. The first escort duty came on the 5th when Blakeslee again led: the Group flew as far as Amiens on an uneventful mission. On the 11th a deeper penetration was made flying support for 1st Division Fortresses attacking Emden: enemy aircraft were seen but they evaded. The enemy fighter force was more willing during the December 16th bomber escort to Bremen and an engagement with Me109s and Ju88s brought the 354th a victory. Four days later the Mustangs were nearly attacked by Thunderbolts, whose pilots mistook them for Messerschmitt Me109s. Breaking in the Mustang took time and the aircraft was hampered by "bugs", in addition the extra fuselage fuel tank and wing drop tahk system were being installed during December, all helping to limit the scope of these early missions.

As the year waned the established Thunderbolt units still remained the chief contestant of the Luftwaffe's fighter defence. The ubiquitous *Wolfpack* performed yet another of its brilliant attack manoeuvres on the December Emden mission. Once again twin-engined fighters were caught preparatory to launching an attack on the rear of a bomber box. Thirty Me110s believed to have been units from Z.G.26, were seen just off Spiekeroog Island. The 61st Ftr. Sqdn. following Major Gabreski, bore down on these in a mass dive with a turn into the attack which brought fourteen Zerstörers down. Captain R. Lamb, Lieutenants P. Conger and D. Smith all sent down three apiece. The official report of the 56th's activities, that brought a total of 17 victories, ran:

Group crossed enemy coast, Texel Island 1151 hrs 30,000 ft. Group in battle formation, Squadrons line abreast with 62nd on right flank, 63rd in center and 61st on left flank and with Yellow Flights of the flanking squadrons acting as scouts. In vicinity east coast Zuider Zee, 8 to 12 Me109s observed approaching Group from east at 35,000 ft. E/A continued towards Group positioned up-sun on 62nd Sqdn and launched attacks in elements of twos and threes on rear of 62nd Sqdn. E/A tactics were to initiate attacks with one or two elements, retaining top cover. As a result, all but Blue Flight, 62nd Sqdn, were engaged. This flight continuing on to R/V with bombers. After this engagement three flights, 62nd, being short of gas, proceeded to patrol Leeuwarden area to limit of endurance. As originally reported, 25/30 E/A were involved in the bounce on 62nd Sqdn but approx 20 A/C now believed to have been friendly P-47s of another Group which became engaged in

Death of a rocket-carrying Me 110. 56th FG's Lt Paul Conger destroyed this and two others that he and his wingman caught on 11 Dec. 1943.—(IWM)

Aircraft flown by Eighth AF's two top air aces. Gabreski's HV: A and Bob Johnson's HV: P, "Lucky", on dispersal points at Halesworth late 1943.

the melee. 61 and 63 Sqdns continued to R/V area with 61st effecting R/V with leading box of B-17s approx 8 miles N Langeroog Island, 30,000 ft, 12.16 hrs, and 63rd making R/V Essens-Hugh area. Bombers given escort from 8 miles N Langeroog Island to target and approx 20 miles NW Terschelling Island by 16 A/C 61st Sqdn, and 4 A/C 62nd Sqdn and 11 A/C 63rd Sqdn. As a result of combats, Group considerably broken up into flights and elements making a given time and place of landfall out impossible. 61st Sqdn reports 100 plus E/A between R/V and target area, 30 T/E which were following close astern first box B-17s and 70 S/E A/C. Combats by 61st Sqdn were mostly in R/V area from 27,000 ft down. Yellow Two (Lt Strand) and Yellow Four (Lt Kruer) collided in a cross over manoeuver as they were preparing to bounce. Both planes exploded and one empty chute was seen. It is not believed that either pilot survived. Six Me109s flying parallel to bombers at same level coming from N in R/V area observed by 63rd Sqdn. Three FW190s were flying at 15,000 ft apparently attempting to draw flight down. One box of bombers seen approaching R/V flying S of brief course apparently attempting to make up time. It appeared that enemy was concentrating on B-17s as T/E A/C were flying behind Forts, and Liberators appeared unmolested. Evidently enemy's tactics were to send two or three A/C down retaining top cover and then attacking planes would zoom up and change places with top cover. Reports indicate that apparently the new Me209 was encountered as this S/E A/C out-turned, out-climbed and out-ran the P-47 at 27,000 ft. Some of these

were painted white. New FW190 with longer wing span reported. No facts available as to performance. Me109s had markings some with wide yellow stripes on wings, others with white bellies, solid white, and some with red stripes on fuselage. E/A were at very high altitude and would retain bouncing position and when turned into would again seek safety in climbing advantage and in sun. Smoke seen over target. One B-17 seen to crash in sea and explode N Baltrum Island. A second B-17 went down 10 miles past target, 6 chutes observed. Moderate inaccurate flak over target, Leeuwarden and Friesian Islands. Four M/V in Ems Basin. Intense radio jamming. Several attempts made to contact bombers without success. Weather: 8/10ths increasing to 10/10ths halfway across North Sea, from this point decreasing to about 1/10 over target, top 8,000 ft.

This report, primarily intended for the evaluation of the mission by Command staff, touches on some interesting points. The Me209 and Macchi 202 (Italian) types which were reported by fighters on a number of occasions during December, were in all probability FW190D models, the long nosed version of the Focke-Wulf that was then undergoing operational trials with J.G.3. The colours and markings of enemy aircraft were reported for identification of units and any tricks that might be afoot to confuse Allied aircrews. The average fighter pilot's assessment of colours and markings was not to be relied upon: an impression gained during high speed combat was often by a trick of light or mind.

German ground stations made a regular practice of jamming Allied fighter pilot's radio transmissions. It took the form of a whine of varying intensity and during the summer of 1943 communication between pilots had become extremely difficult. Measures were continually in hand to counter this disturbance and while it could be subdued, it was not eliminated. Radio links between fighters and the heavy bombers enabled the latter to call for help when attacked. It also allowed fighter leaders to pass on pertinent information, available to them through their more extensive radio facilities.

Radio was very much the fighter pilot's lifeline and a major factor in a safe return to England when weather conditions, combat with the enemy, or a mis-calculation, caused pilots to lose their way. When fuel supplies were low, ground control "homings" gave the pilot the nearest emergency base, as occurred on December 30th when the 56th Group was flying on withdrawal support for B-17s returning from Ludwigshafen. The relieving group, apparently late in taking over, caused the 56th to remain until fuel gauges bordered on the danger mark. The P-47s made emergency landings at a dozen different airfields along the Essex and Suffolk coast. One, flown by 2/Lt Fred J. Christensen Jr (destined to be one of the 56th's foremost aces), had faulty gauges to make matters worse, and just after crossing the coast the P-47 ran completely out of fuel. Christensen attempted a "dead stick" landing on Leiston airfield, but the plane's glide was insufficient to reach the runway and it crashed just short. True to its fashion, the rugged Thunderbolt, though severely damaged, let the pilot walk away unharmed. Some were not so lucky: others even luckier.

On a long haul to the Bordeaux region the following day—longest mission so far for Eighth fighters—cloud conditions prevailed with variable cirrus over the Channel up to 25,000 feet and 6 to 7/10s cumulus over France at 6,000 ft. The Lightnings, staying a little too long, were desperately short of fuel on return; some force-landed, others just managed to reach airfields along the south coast of England from Exeter to Ford. Lt Harold Bauer of the 55th Group did not get that far. At 14,000 ft, 15 miles off Lizard Point, his fuel gauges registered empty and he knew that in a few seconds his P-38's tanks would run dry. Bauer tried giving the "Mayday" air-sea rescue call but his radio transmitter was apparently inoperative. As he prepared to bale out he knew he had little chance of surviving long in an icy mid-winter sea below. At that moment he caught sight of an RAF rescue launch and decided to put his aircraft down on the water as close to it as possible. No-one had yet ditched a Lightning and lived to tell the tale, but although his fighter went under quickly Bauer managed to scramble out onto the wing. He was wearing extra heavy flying clothes, occasioned by the P-38s cold cockpit problem, yet the Mae West like jacket kept him afloat until the launch crew retrieved him, four minutes later, not much the worse for his experience.

Two more P-47 groups started operations on December 13th and 20th; the 359th based at East Wretham and the 358th at Leiston. Another, the 361st, arriving at the end of November and was working up at Bottisham, near Cambridge, proved to be the last group of P-47s to join VIII Fighter Command. Twelve fighter groups were now on hand (10 P-47 and 2 P-38), 3 short of the Command's total planned strength. The last of the three fighter wings, the 67th at Walcott Hall, near Stamford, became fully operational in December; the 66th Fighter Wing at Sawston Hall, seven miles from Cambridge, having achieved this status during the previous month. Each wing would ultimately control five groups.

Combat unit strength of VIII FC had trebled during the last quarter of 1943 and aircraft complements of many were double that of the previous spring. Now able to fly a force of 550 fighters, an escort of one for one could be given the heavies, whose maximum strength on missions was then around the same figure. However, the influx of new bomber groups during the opening months of 1944, would soon upset this balance. Also, the numbers of Luftwaffe fighters in the West had now risen, to approximately 1,500, as new Jagdgeschwader were being formed and others strengthened. While the Luftwaffe had achieved notable successes against the US bombers during recent months by improved tactics and new weapons, its effort against the far-ranging escort was generally feeble and unrewarding. For despite its growing numbers, the enemy showed a marked reluctance to enage the American fighters, preferring to concentrate on such bombers as were unescorted or had weak escort. The USAAF was now painfully aware that the bombing of industry likely to affect aircraft production and the attrition presumed to have been wrought in air battles, had not weakened the opposition to the day bomber raids. Indeed, Allied intelligence agencies could supply fairly conclusive evidence of the build up of Luftwaffe fighter forces in Germany and the West. The Allies had yet to achieve air superiority, vital to the forthcoming invasion as it was to the continuation of the American strategic bombing campaign. When General Arnold sent a New Year's message to the Eighth Air Force he underlined what its commanders knew was their immediate task: "Destroy the Enemy Air Force wherever you find them, in air, on the ground and in the factories".

Chapter 13: Build Up to Big Week

During the gruelling operations of the early autumn of 1943, both Generals Arnold and Eaker appeared optimistic as to the success the Eighth's attacks were achieving. It was genuinely believed that irreparable harm was being done to German industry and a high attrition rate wrought on the Luftwaffe in the air. Intelligence had yet to learn that air gunner's claims were so far removed from the truth, and that bombing results were being over-estimated while German powers of recuperation were under-estimated. In spite of its presumed heavy losses, the Luftwaffe's ascendancy had been painfully obvious for some time and it was the early battles of October as a whole that brought final realisation that the AAF's original concept of daylight bombardment was no longer valid. The vulnerability of the Fortresses to improved enemy defences had been clearly demonstrated, as for that matter had the benefits of Thunderbolt escort. More and longer ranged fighters was the obvious solution. Schweinfurt was the last major mission into Germany where the bombers were sent a considerable distance without support from long range fighters, and as such can be regarded as a milestone in the fortunes of the Eighth Air Force. Nevertheless, there was no definite order to discontinue deep penetrations: the opportunity did not occur again during the remainder of the year by which time the first really long range escort was available.

The winter weather in North Europe, with almost continuous heavy cloud conditions, was the principal reason for limiting the offensive against POINTBLANK (Attack on German fighter forces and the industry upon which they depended) targets. This also influenced a far-reaching decision affecting the Eighth Air Force—to transfer a large part of its bomber group allocation to another theatre. Arnold and his planners, apparently impatient with the slow pace of operations from the UK, had come to consider as an attractive proposition the establishment of another strategic air force in the Mediterranean area. Not only did the climatic conditions of southern Europe appear to offer better opportunities for visual bombing, but such a force could attack targets in Germany and eastern Europe beyond the range of British-based bombers. Further, the enemy would be forced to split his air defences in countering the new threat. Other advantages were more daylight hours in winter and some relief to the crowded air space over England.

Although Eaker and most RAF commanders were loth to see the diversion of heavy bombers destined for the UK, the plan was quickly implemented and the new Air Force, the Fifteenth, activated on November 1st. Combat bases were to be established around the recently captured Foggia area of Italy and the initial complement of heavy bomb groups came from the Twelfth Air Force (which had absorbed the two B-24 groups of the Ninth) and by the following March it was to receive thirteen Liberator and two Fortress groups originally earmarked for the Eighth. In consequence, a number of bomber airfields under construction in East Anglia never received their intended tenants and others in the planning stage were abandoned. In practice, the advantages claimed for the establishment of the Fifteenth Air Force were hardly justified. The weather proved as great an obstacle as in England, the Alps proved a formidable barrier to returning aircraft in trouble and base and repair facilities were poor and

took time to improve. The Fifteenth also suffered grievously at the hands of the Luftwaffe in its early raids.

Even with this reduction its proposed ultimate strength would still leave the Eighth as the largest of the AAFs. Between October 1943 and June 1944 the number of units would double as well as unit establishments being increased. It was planned to enlarge the first line squadrons already in the UK and the number of heavy bombers in each was raised from nine to twelve in October. Trained crews, however, continued to be scarce until the following spring. In building the Eighth into the mightiest air striking force of the Second World War, the AAF's leaders were still pursuing their beliefs in the war winning role of the strategic bomber. Unaware of the true facts, they talked as if the German Air Force was within an ace of being defeated. To the men on the bomber stations there were few signs of the neutralisation of the Luftwaffe as winter intervened in the campaign.

Seemingly, a constant cloud blanket shrouded North-West Europe during the latter half of October. Four days after Schweinfurt, VIII Bomber Command attempted to launch a mission to Düren but had to abandon it after several accidents in the course of take-off and assembly. Another four days were to pass before a mission to this city of non-ferrous metal industries was completed. Little else was achieved: the Pathfinder 813th Bomb Sqdn. on this trip attempted its first Oboe strike but, either through an electrical fault or human error, its signal caused a premature release by a combat wing. Some formations were confronted with cirrus stratus extending to 30,000 ft and only a little over half the force was able to drop on or near the target.

Pathfinders led each of the seven B-17 combat wings when 555 heavies set out over unbroken cloud on November 3rd. Two were H2S-equipped B-17s, while nine had H2X, which the 812th Bomb Sqdn. was scheduled to introduce on operations. H2X was a US development of the British H2S; it used a new and shorter microwavelength claimed to give a sharper picture of the ground than the British apparatus. Such was the urgency in obtaining radar bombing equipment that, prior to output from production, a dozen sets of components were built up and sent to Alconbury for installation in late production B-17Fs. Their scanners were housed in a retractable radome situated just aft of the chin turret; in the extended position these gave the Fortresses an unorthodox double-chinned appearance. Since this rather cluttered crew positions

One of twelve B-17s with 'hand built' H2X installations. Radome is extended in this picture.—(USAF)

in the nose, production installations on B-17Gs arriving early in the new year, had the ball turret omitted and the retractable radome installed in its place; the radar operator was then situated in what was normally the radio operator's position.

The target for this first use of H2X (cover name—Mickey Mouse, later shortened to Mickey) was the port of Wilhelmshaven, not an important target in the CBO plan but ideally suited for attack with this equipment, as land and water produced well defined distinctions on the operator's screen. Escorted all the way, with P-38 Lightnings on the target leg, the bombers had little trouble from the Luftwaffe. Over 500 bombed, a record number of Liberators bringing up the rear having to aim on the parachute flare target markers of the preceeding Fortresses. The resulting strike pattern was widely spread but with a significant concentration within the port area. Command were tempted to expect great things on the results of this first use of H2X.

Both Oboe and H2X were used two days later when 374 Fortresses, sent to Gelsenkirchen, were led by five Oboe-equipped pathfinders but the results were not very encouraging. The hundred-odd Liberators, going to Münster, followed B-17 pathfinders and when one was hit by flak on the bomb run some formations attempted to bomb visually through cloud breaks. This was, in any case, an unsatisfactory arrangement as the disparity of the relative operating speeds of the two bomber types was increased by the drag caused by the additional radome. Losses were not heavy, but there were some narrow escapes. Two B-17s had tortured journeys back to England after half their crews had baled out. Another nearly crashed into the centre of an East Anglian town. This aircraft of the 351st Group's Ball squadron, *Lucille Ball* named after the film actress, was progressing steadily on automatic pilot when suddenly the bomber started to dive steeply into the clouds. On breaking through, 1/Lt Donald Gaylord and his co-pilot found their errant charge heading for the centre of Ipswich and initially resisting their attempts to bring her back under control. Further frantic work with the controls enabled them to pull *Lucille Ball* out of her dive at around 2,000 ft and make an emergency landing at nearby Ipswich airport.

Equipment failures and inexperience had so far brought little success to the Oboe pathfinders. When this technique was tried again on November 7th against Düren, an estimated one thousand bombs scattered for a hundred miles along the border of Holland and Belgium bore witness to yet another failure. Even H2X was not repeating its early promise, principally due to persistent equipment failures. When this happened,

2/Lt Donald Gaylord takes a close look at the tangled clutter of wires and hydraulic lines to the cockpit controls of *Lucille Ball*. B-17 nose compartment was lined with insulating material against noise and cold.—(USAF)

The aptly named 359th BS Fortress that became the first in VIII BC to complete 50 missions.—(USAF)

427th BS's 'Bugs Bunny' emblem on 41-24619, GN: S, is touched up by M/Sgt Fred Kuhn. This aircraft was a contender for the 'first B-17 to complete 50 missions' title. She was lost on 11 Jan. 1944.—(USAF)

as in one instance over Bremen on the 13th the bombers resorted to unloading on a flak concentration, presuming the city to be below. It was a matter of guessing and negated the effect of the 12-plane sections flown on this occasion in an effort to improve the bomb pattern.

Each day VIII Bomber Command planners looked to the weather men for the promise of a target that could be viewed through a Norden sight but during November this was denied in the Eighth's usual area of operations. The only missions launched with visual bombing intent were to Norway. On the 16th, 1st Division Fortresses attacked the Knaben molybdenum mines and those of the 3rd Division a generating plant at Rjukan believed to be connected with German nuclear experiments. Opposition was negligible and some formations spent an hour and a half seeking a bomb run through the clouds. The two B-17s failing to return were probably both victims of engine strain on the long flight. A 390th machine caught fire and ditched in the sea near some fishing boats while one of the 92nd Group's with an engine out of control was abandoned by its crew over Norway. This day was one of some excitement at Molesworth for the returning 303rd Group formation brought the veteran *Knockout Dropper* back from its 50th mission, a feat no other Eighth Air Force Fortress had yet achieved. This B-17 was one of three original bombers of the group that were competing for the honour: *Hell's Angels* had completed 47 missions and a nameless 427th Bomb Sqdn. aircraft, S for Sugar, had run up 47. *Hell's Angels* had never once had to turn back for mechanical reasons on a raid, whereas the champion had been plagued with such trouble.

The Liberators had also been despatched to Norway but being unable to bomb their primary, an aircraft repair depot at Oslo, they were sent back two days later. Attacking from 12,000 ft, the bombing appeared accurate and the force of nearly one hundred made tracks for home. The Norwegian coastline had hardly disappeared below the horizon when the Luftwaffe suddenly arrived in the form of a Staffel of Me109s and some Ju88s. In the ensuing action six B-24s were shot down. Three other Liberators that failed to return, had taken refuge in Sweden when damage and mechanical failure made the long over-water return a dubious proposition.

Twisted propellers were thrown some distance from 41-29161, H during Lt Griffith's spectacular crash-landing at Shipdham.—(IWM)

The *Eightballs* had five aircraft missing. Another came home on three uncertain engines and only one undercarriage leg would come down when this bomber arrived over Shipdham. With fuel diminishing, the control tower wirelessed orders for the bomber to be put on a seaward heading and the crew to jump. As a gunner was badly wounded and in no condition to parachute the pilot, Lt R. C. Griffith, elected to attempt a crash landing after seven men had jumped. Making this even more hazardous, the starboard rudder and flaps were inoperative. After a good approach Griffith touched down on the runway on the one main wheel and by sheer strength managed to hold the Liberator level for about four hundred yards. Then, loss of speed allowed the left wing to drop and drag the stricken aircraft round shedding pieces as it went. Luckily there was no fire and Griffith and the wounded man suffered no further harm. On examination, the supposedly one good engine was found to have an unexploded 20-mm shell in it.

Two days after the Norwegian interlude the heavies were once again sent to scale the cloud banks over Germany and dispense high explosive and incendiary on the advice of the "magic boxes". Oboe still wasn't producing the correct magic and the bomber stream flew far to the north of its objective,

Gelsenkirchen, and 127 bombers had no option but to drop on targets of opportunity or haul their loads home. At least there were no losses to enemy action, again underlining the enemy's inability to mount an effective interception through heavy overcast. But the clouds were broken enough a week later for the enemy to inflict the severest punishment since Schweinfurt. Conditions brought many difficulties for the bombers, particularly the Liberators which had to be taken up to well over 25,000 ft to surmount it, far above their usual domain. Areas of clear sky were forecast over France and with the possibility of a visual attack 128 3rd Division Fortresses went to Paris, only to return with their bombs when the forecast proved wrong. A record force of 633 heavies were despatched this day, the numbers being swelled by the B-17Gs of the 401st Group which followed the main force and pathfinders to Bremen. The maiden mission for this "first of the flood" group saw one man missing in action under extraordinary circumstances. A Fortress out of control collided with 1/Lt Scribner Dailey's *Fancy Nancy* causing severe damage and knocking off most of the ball turret. The unfortunate occupant was a waist gunner who had just entered the turret to right a gun fault that the ball-turret gunner had been unable to do. *Fancy Nancy* brought the rest of her crew back to Detling where she was later condemned as salvage.

The cold on this mission was intense—as it had been on most missions of the month—the temperature at operating height descending to—50° Fahrenheit of frost and caused ice formations nearly two inches thick on windows. Frost bite struck in a matter of seconds if gloves were removed, oxygen masks iced and made breathing difficult and the icy gale sweeping open gun positions made the rear gunners' lives particularly miserable. Already special gun windows enclosing the waist positions on B-17s were in production although it was the New Year before these aircraft started to arrive at combat bases. It was the extreme winter cold and the need for extra clothing that led airmen to wear their "flight jackets" under furlined flying clothes and electric suits. The so-called "flight jackets" were by themselves quite unsuitable for the extreme conditions of the ETO winter and were generally used as casual wear at bases, often decorated with the personal insignia of the bomber in which a man usually flew. A harmless enough fad—until the Bremen raid. Following this, the German press carried pictures of Lt Kenneth Williams wearing a flight jacket emblazoned *Murder Incorporated*. An accompanying report purported this to be an official slogan carried by each individual member of a bomber squadron on the back of his clothing, and claimed it tantamount to an American admission that they deliberately engaged in terror

The flight jacket bearing the *Murder Inc.* inscription worn by Lt Kenneth Williams. Pictures that appeared in German newspapers.—(Zwanenburg)

bombing of residential areas. Lt Williams, a bombardier, was one of three men, wearing similarly marked jackets, who parachuted from a crippled Fortress before it crash-landed near Eggese on the 26th. The Germans also claimed that the name was to be seen on the bomber, but this was not so for that morning *Murder Incorporated* had developed engine trouble and her crew, under 1/Lt Orville Castle, took another B–17 on the mission. The sinister inference German propaganda drew from this incident was of some embarrassment to the Eighth Air Force authorities who ordered group headquarters to look for any similar ill-chosen inscriptions on jackets and aircraft.

Inflatable jacks under each wing proved the best and quickest method of raising a "bellied in" bomber. When *Devil's Daughter* was lifted, 17 Dec. 1943, the undercarriage was lowered and the aircraft towed from the Horham runway.—(USAF)

At 26,000 ft the 92nd BG heads for Cologne; 1 Dec. 1943. Higher contrails are those of P-38 escort.—(Havelaar)

For the more discriminating commanders who had been a little concerned about the double-meaning names and doubtful illustrations that adorned the aircraft on their stations, this proved to be an ideal excuse for instigating a general censorship campaign. It is said that in some groups suggestive slogans and nude decor were forbidden, the latter having to be decked out with the necessary garments if they were to remain on an aircraft. This attempt at censorship was short lived and rarely effective, for, as a contemporary put it, "crews skirted the regulations rather than the ladies". It did not need much ingenuity to provide a clinging form of swim suit or negligé.

After returning to Bremen on November 29th, missions were flown to Solingen on the last day of the month and the first of the new. Both took their toll in men and machines, particularly the last, and little recompense showed in later reconnaissance photos to justify the expense in terms of strategic achievement. On December 5th, 546 heavies flew into French airspace and two hours later, less a few, flew out again with their loads, having found no sight of the airfields they were to bomb. Back to the North German ports on December 11th, radar operators peered into their scopes for the image that was Emden and then for the much troubled Bremen on the 13th, 16th and 20th of the month. On the second of these operations the legendary *Bomerang*, nearly consigned to the scrap heap after the Eighth's first Liberator operation, came back to Hardwick having completed its fiftieth mission. Flak had scratched the painting on her nose but this was nothing in comparison with some of the batterings it had taken in fourteen months of combat, to set this record for an Eighth Air Force B-24. On the last of these operations *Tinkertoy*, the 381st Group's "jinx ship", went out true to form in a spectacular way—a head-on collision with an enemy fighter. Due to high winds some of the bombers were flying thirty minutes late and off the briefed course that day, and but for the excellence of the fighter support they would undoubtedly have sustained a much heavier loss than the 27 missing. The crew of one, the 303rd's *Jersey Bounce Jr*, were rescued by a passing coaster after

ditching east of Cromer. Interrogation of the crew brought the radio man, T/Sgt Forrest Vosler, the Group's second Medal of Honor.

Hit by flak over the target and dropping behind the formation, *Jersey Bounce Jr* had soon attracted enemy fighters. Vosler, wounded in the thighs and legs by a 20-mm cannon shell exploding in the radio-room, continued to fire his gun at the attackers. Then another shell exploded nearby. Splinters lodged in his chest and face, and both eyes were hit impairing his vision so that he could only distinguish blurred shapes. His face bathed in blood, he declined first aid and cheerfully continued to carry out his duties. The radio had been damaged but between lapses into unconsciousness he managed to repair it, working entirely by touch. When the crippled Fortress

401st BG's *Nasty Habit* comes back to Deenethorpe from Kiel, 13 Dec. 1943. Hangar is standard T2 type that graced most airfields constructed for the USAAF. Checkered runway control caravan was provided by the RAF.—(USAF)

had to ditch, Vosler scrambled out onto a wing unaided and held another badly wounded crewman to keep him from falling off until others could help them into a dinghy. Vosler's wounds were such that he was discharged from the Service after ten months in hospitals.

The Bremen missions also served as an introduction to combat for two Liberator groups, the 445th and 446th, and a third newcomer, the 448th, joined them on the Osnabruck raid of the 22nd, where each contributed two losses to the 13 their Division suffered that day. A fourth group—the 447th (B-17s)—became operational during December and joined the Command's first NOBALL mission, to the Pas de Calais on Christmas Eve. NOBALL targets were the V-weapon launching and assembly sites, storage and manufacturing centres, of which some seventy sites had by then been identified by British Intelligence. The exact nature of the weapons that the Germans were deploying was still obscure, but the effort expended on constructing these sites gave rise to concern. "Barrack-room intelligence" soon decided that the enemy had a secret weapon in store; rockets were mooted and soon the Pas de Calais became known as "the rocket coast". This speculation, as it transpired, was not all that far removed from the truth. On this occasion, 22 of the ski-shaped launching sites were in receipt of 1,700 tons of high explosive with what was termed excellent results.

The last two days of 1943 brought long and difficult missions to the south. On the 30th nearly 650 heavies, bombing through the overcast, failed to damage oil installations at Ludwigshafen. On the following day when there were signs of weather improvement over Southern France, a slightly smaller force hit several airfields along the Atlantic seaboard. In spite of P-38s and the new P-51s being in attendance, these two operations cost 23 and 25 bombers respectively, figures which though high (they had been approached or exceeded on six other occasions during November and December) had to be considered in relation to the much stronger forces sent out. Although the total of heavies missing from December's operations was nearly as great as that for the blackest month of 1943, October, as a percentage of sorties flown it was one of the best. The missing in action figures were not the complete story, as they only referred to bombers failing to return to England. Crippled machines that reached home and then crashed, or returned safely to earth but were too badly damaged to be worth repairing, were assessed differently.

There were many losses for which the enemy had no part. Collisions in cloud or crashes on landing often occurred during assembly or on return. December 31st was such a day; the long eight-hour mission brought many aircraft back in gathering darkness and heavy cloud. No less than 18 were written off in England, some having sustained battle damage. During the early morning take-off, a B-17G of the 306th Group crashed in darkness on a railway line near Stevenage. A B-17F lost in cloud made a belly landing at Sywell, hit a parked Wellington and ended up minus parts of its tail and right wing. Another lost Fortress, landing there soon afterwards, skidded through the perimeter hedge. Near Peterborough, a 384th Group Fortress crashed killing the co-pilot while another from the same group bellied in elsewhere. Two 401st Group Fortresses were abandoned by their crews (Scribner Daily and his men parted company with their second *Fancy Nancy*) when fuel ran out while searching for a landing place. A B-24D was also abandoned, its crew parachuting down near Hastings. Two

389th Group Liberators were wrecked in crash landings in Kent due to fuel shortage, crews escaping without injury. Because difficult flying conditions had strained fuel reserves American aircraft were putting down on airfields all along the south coast upon return. So many reports of parachutes were received by ARP (the civil Air Raid Precaution organisation) authorities in Kent that there was some concern for a while that an airborne invasion might be underway.

Mechanical faults took toll as well, on occasions to an extent not fully appreciated by VIII Bomber Command. A prevalent cause was failure of propellers to feather. The variable pitch propeller allowed a pilot to alter the "bite" in flight to increase or decrease thrust as the action or altitude demanded while maintaining a constant engine speed. The intricate constant speed unit, actuated hydraulically on both the B-17 and B-24, drew oil from the engine lubricating system. If the engine itself was out of action, or shut down in flight, it was essential to feather its airscrew, i.e. turn the blades so that no rotating force acted upon them to prevent the propeller from "windmilling"—over-running and causing excessive and dangerous vibration. But loss of oil in a crippled engine also deprived the mechanism of its hydraulic power and the blade pitch could not be altered or feathered. This was particularly so in B-17s, which did not have an auxiliary supply system. At least a score of B-17s and B-24s had been lost directly or indirectly to failure of feathering mechanisms during November and December, no less than seven of the 23 bombers missing in action on December 30th and another six of the following day's total. This was unknown at the time and only after debriefing repatriated and evading aircrew was this trouble manifest. Not until the autumn of 1944 did B-17s—which had double the B-24 incidence of failures—receive an engine sump standby pipe designed to give an auxiliary oil supply.

One aircraft that fell victim to feathering trouble on the final mission of 1943 was 92nd's B-17F 42-3186, whose No. 4 engine "ran away". Oil was leaking and the engine began to vibrate violently. The Fortress began to drop out of formation and lag behind the other bombers and, because of the run away engine, could not be turned except by cutting both port engines and giving full rudder. Being several hundred miles out over the Atlantic, the crew decided that their chances of regaining the English coast were remote, so they elected to head in towards France, flying on automatic

500 lb and 1,000 lb HE bombs stacked on a Framlingham hardstand prior to completion of bomb dump. British contractors often hauled bombs to airfields. Mound at left is 'shooting-in' butts. B-17F in picture, 42-30320, was lost a few days after this photo was taken.— (USAF)

pilot. Suddenly, the shaft of the errant propeller apparently broke loose, for after a tremendous bang it windmilled faster than ever. The aircraft lost height rapidly but managed to gain the French coast and make a crash landing.

It was engine failure that in the majority of cases led to the feathering trouble. Apart from failure due to battle damage, VIII BC was at this time faced with a growing incidence of engine failures on B-17s for other reasons, chiefly overstrain. Many Fortresses were aborting with blown cylinder heads due to engine over-heating during their climb to altitude. The Air Technical Section at Bovingdon had been primarily concerned with fighter problems, but had recently been expanded to include bomber activities and this problem was handed to them. Cass Hough and his men studied the rash of reports on aborting B-17s to find that in the majority of cases the pilots concerned were replacements fresh from the States. This suggested that the trouble was human rather than mechanical; further enquiries revealed that, by a lapse in technical training, these pilots tended to open the engine cowling flaps prematurely, increasing drag and slowing down the aircraft and, in turn, required more power to stay in formation. The remedy lay in new instructions to pilots and amendments to type handbooks.

Some extraordinary accidents occurred from time to time. During the first mission of 1944, T/Sgt Fred Wagner fell from the open bomb bay of a 384th Group Fortress as it was leaving Kiel. He had gone into the bay to release some stuck bombs when his oxygen supply failed and he lost consciousness, slipping out. Reviving at a lower altitude, he was able to let out his parachute in time. The following day to the same target a 305th Group Fortress, *Boeing's Best*, was struck by a bomb bay tank falling from a higher aircraft. Hitting No. 2 engine, it bounced across the top turret and hit the fin, leaving a trail of damage in its wake. Nevertheless, the aircraft continued on its bomb run before limping home. This visual attack, produced a good concentration on the docks of this important naval port. The same day other bombers had flown to the other extreme of the German-controlled seaboard, hitting airfields and associated targets in south-west France. For the Bassingbourn-based 91st Group it was the 100th time that its Fortresses had violated hostile airspace, a total unsurpassed by any other group. This occasion proved comparatively uneventful but in reaching its century the "Ragged Irregulars" had also incurred a heavier loss in men and machines than any of its compatriots.

The mission of January 5th—recorded as Mission No. 176 for VIII BC—was the last under this famous title. A major reorganisation of the US Air Force in Europe was effected at the turn of the year. With the establishment of the Fifteenth Air Force in Italy, an overall headquarters to formulate and

379th BG leader Lt Col Louis Rohr (centre) gives an account to Group CO Col Maurice Preston (rt.) after returning from Kiel on 5 Jan. 1944.

co-ordinate policy embracing both the Eighth and the new strategic air force was deemed advisable. This new organisation, eventually known as United States Strategic Air Forces in Europe (USSTAF), was brought into being at Bushey Park and initially was little more than a redesignation of the original Eighth Air Force Headquarters. At the same time, a new Eighth Air Force HQ was established from the disbanded VIII Bomber Command at High Wycombe. The official date of redesignation was not until the middle of February, but in practice the changes were considered effective at the time of the appointment of new commanders on January 6th. General Carl Spaatz and Lt Gen James H. Doolittle, who once commanded the Eighth's 4th Wing, were brought back from North Africa to take over USSTAF and the Eighth respectively, while General Eaker was given a new overall command in the Mediterranean. Possibly Eaker would have preferred to continue in command of the force he had brought to England and watched grow from a handful of men and aircraft to a thousand bomber fleet. Arnold apparently considered the changes appropriate. While the departure of Eaker was regretted at most levels, Doolittle came with a reputation that made him acceptable.

The operational pattern of January and the first half of February 1944 was similar to that of the closing weeks of 1943; principally pathfinder bombing through overcast on German ports and industrial areas, with few opportunities for visual sighting. In fact only two missions featured visual bombing of German industry and one of these was a chance attack by a small formation. The only major visual operation occurred on Tuesday, January 11th, when the weather in Central Europe, expected to be fine, offered one of the first opportunities for three months to strike important aircraft manufacturing plants deep in Germany.

A maximum effort of over 650 bombers was laid on to attack five plants in the Brunswick area; the leading 1st Division was despatched to Oschersleben's FW190 factory, principal production centre for this most successful of German fighters since the destruction of the Marienburg plant in October, and the Junkers plant at Halberstadt; three combat wings went to the former and two to the latter. Third Division B-17s were next in the bomber stream with the 2nd Division's Liberators bringing up the rear, both divisions dividing their seven combat wings amongst the three other Brunswick targets. Plans decreed that if weather prevented visual bombing the task force was to use the pathfinder technique on Brunswick city. To this end fifteen 482nd Group aircraft were in attendance including, for the first time, four H2S-equipped Liberators.

As the bombers droned aloft for two hours, gaining altitude and assembling into battle array through heavy rain clouds, Command watched the weather with mounting concern; for, as frequently happened, conditions were gradually deteriorating as the day wore on. Abnormally high cloud extended all the way across the Channel and Holland, and also began closing in on the clear area over the objectives, but there was still a chance and the force set out. When the first aircraft were well into Germany and the remainder strung out across Holland, Command became aware that weather conditions would deny the bombers full fighter support. The two P-38 groups and sole P-51 fighter group capable of providing support in the target area, had entered the overcast soon after take-off, to find that it extended to 22,000 ft. Some P-38s, not breaking through at 24,000 ft upon reaching the Dutch coast, returned to base. With the chance of visual attack fading, and the escort already depleted, a recall went out to the 2nd and 3rd Divisions; the 1st, at this time less than 100 miles from its targets, was allowed to proceed. The leading combat wing of the 3rd Division (the 4th CBW) was also near to its objective and as there seemed a good chance that the target would be visible, the leader of this formation elected to continue. The

experienced. The 303rd Group, heading the 1st Division force, lost ten B-17s in this onslaught. *The Eight Ball,* carrying task force commander, General Robert Travis, survived, but not the precious H2X pathfinder. Groups of the 1st and 94th Wings also suffered severely; the seven losses sustained by the 351st Group brought to an end a most extraordinary record. Until this mission the Group's 509th Bomb Sqdn., which was commanded by Lt Col LeDoux, had not had a single B-17 missing in action since June 13th, a period which had seen the heaviest air fighting of the war. All told 34 Fortresses were lost from the 174 bombers sent to Oschersleben and this figure might have been higher had it not been for the activity of the two score Mustangs that made valiant efforts to ward off enemy fighters in the target area until fuel shortage forced them to turn away. One pilot, Major James Howard, distinguished himself by going to the aid of the 401st Group and single-handed fighting off Me110 rocket attacks. The other two combat wings of 1st Division (40th Wing and a composite) bombing nearby Halberstadt were less troubled. The bombing, particularly at Oschersleben, was good with considerable damage done to factory buildings. First Division's performance on this day later brought a Distinguished Unit Citation for all its groups.

Brig Ben Robert Travis (left) flew with 303rd BG's Lt Col William Calhourn in *The Eight Ball* to Oschersleben. Back at Molesworth, smiles for the camera conceal harrowing experience.—(IWM)

rest of the 3rd Division and all the 2nd turned back, some finding targets of opportunity en route.

Only one squadron of P-38s finally made contact with the bombers and it was left to 49 P-51s to provide what protection they could in the target area. For while the cloud was gradually spreading in these, the weather conditions had been sufficiently good in the East for the Germans to assemble one of the largest defensive fighter forces since the October battles. All day fighter units were alerted and also at least three night fighter Geschwader. The brunt of the Luftwaffe effort was directed, as anticipated, against the leading formations flying without escort. They were subjected to some of the most concentrated rocket attacks by twin-engined aircraft so far

Until recovered by the R. Neth. AF, this photograph lay for 24 years in the Zuider Zee. It was in the strike camera of 42-3486, the 482nd BG H2X B-17F which led the 1st Division. The sun glints on a lower 303rd BG Fortress at 'bombs away'.—Zwanenburg)

303rd BG under attack; 11 Jan. 1944. *Flying Bison* passes smoke from an exploded B-17 as an FW 190 wheels away (top left).—(IWM)

Meanwhile, the solitary 3rd Division wing had put up an even more impressive performance. Under the command of Lt Col Louis Thorup, air executive, the 94th Group in lead position had been 25 miles from their target, the Me110 assembly plant at Waggum, five miles outside Brunswick, when the recall signal was received. Unable to verify the order and realising there was every chance of making a visual attack, Thorup decided to go on. The objective could not be clearly identified during the initial approach so Thorup took the lead box through a 360° turn making a fresh run after the other two boxes had bombed and turned away. The twenty aircraft of the 94th, in spite of being under more or less continuous fighter attack, managed to place 73% of their bombs within 1,000 ft of the assigned aiming point, and all within 2,000 ft. The 447th also bombed very accurately and placed 74% within 1,000 ft. Extensive damage was caused and every major installation was hit.

S/Sgt Jerome Bajenski, radio man on B-17 *Sick Call,* was convinced of the flak vest's value after 11 Jan. 1944. A 20 mm incendiary (he holds the remains) exploded over his heart but only knocked him breathless! This is one of the later types of armoured vest.—(USAF)

On withdrawal speed was reduced by a 90 mph headwind. Seven 94th B-17s never returned and all but one of their other aircraft was damaged. There might have been an eighth loss for when *Frenesi* went out of control with hits in the tail, wings and an engine, and with the oxygen and inter-com systems failed, the crew could be excused giving it up as lost. Five crew and a photographer baled out leaving the pilot and co-pilot with three wounded gunners. One gunner, unable to find his parachute, crawled forward to report his predicament to the pilots. But by that time 1/Lt William Cely had *Frenesi* under control and headed for home. For its part in the mission the 94th was awarded a Distinguished Unit Citation and Thorup a Silver Star. This officer had flown with the Group since the early summer and had been in one of the B-17s

A rocket caused this damage to *Nine Yanks and a Rebel* on 11 Jan. 1944. Lt Hahn brought her home safely.—(USAF)

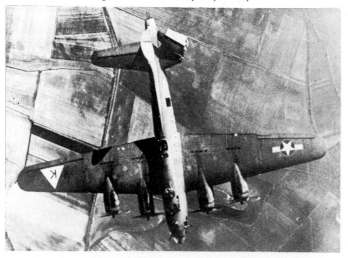

brought down in the North Sea on that black day in June when the Group had been surprised by enemy fighters just off the English coast.

The scale of air fighting on January 11th reached epic proportions. Over 400 individual attacks were reported by the 1st Division in 3½ hours and these, plus the gunner's permitted claims of 210 destroyed and 127 damaged or "probables", are significant indications of the intensity of battle. While true Luftwaffe losses appear to have been 39 of the 207 fighters that made contact, their claims of 150 heavies were also exaggerated. The 60 bombers actually missing in action put the cost on a par with the Schweinfurt mission, again emphasising the perils of deep penetration by unescorted or poorly escorted heavies. To those anticipating a decline in Luftwaffe opposition resulting from the prolonged bombing of aircraft plants and attrition in the air, there was cold comfort. The facts were that the enemy was still expanding his defences.

At this time the Luftwaffe had 25 Gruppen of single-engined fighters in the Reich and the West (approximately 750 aircraft), plus 7 Gruppen of twin-engined Zerstörer fighters (about 180) aircraft. The twin-engined day fighter force, due to its recent successes with air-to-air rockets, had been revived. Me110 units had been brought back from Russian, Mediterranean and Biscay areas during the autumn of 1943 and a new unit had been formed with this type, but long-range US fighters had soon confined their employment to the central and southern areas of the Reich.

The Germans were continually experimenting with new devices and B-17 crewmen on the Oschersleben mission reported a Ju88 ahead of their formation attempting to winch

Pilot 2/Lt William Cely and co-pilot 2/Lt Jabez Churchill survey the perforations in *Frenesi* as she stands on her dispersal point at Bury St. Edmunds.—(USAF)

out an explosive charge on the end of a long cable. A decline in air-to-air bombing was noticed with the introduction of air-to-air rockets. Ground-to-air rockets were first reported in January 1944; upon detonation, five small incendiary bombs on parachutes were released to drift through the path of the bombers. Each bomb burned for about a minute, but their accuracy and intensity were never enough to cause much concern.

In fighter tactics, the Germans still found frontal attacks on a large formation yielded the best results, and this had become the standard method in most front rank Geschwadern. Attacking in Staffel strength of eight at a time in line abreast each formation turned into the attack from three to five miles ahead of the bombers. After delivering the attack, the normal procedure was to dive away beneath the bombers and continue on to the next formation in the bomber column to repeat the performance. In this way time was not lost in manoeuvring for a second strike on the original formation and this made the maximum effective use of a fighter's limited duration. Closing in at Staffel strength had the advantage of saturating defensive fire from the bombers but frontal attack still required considerable skill and was generally unpopular because of the difficulty of training sights at the fast closing speed.

The most effective counter-measures against these tactics, evasive action, was precluded by the close formation, essential for concentrated defensive fire; the vital importance of keeping station had been installed in pilots from the earliest days of their combat training. This held them in good stead in general, but in frontal assault to have been able to 'jink' would have had its advantages. Many German pilots testified that, because of the high closing speed, their aim was invariably spoilt when a bomber engaged in evasive flying. On the other hand, they considered evasive action rarely helped a bomber under attack from the rear as a fighter then closed much less speedily and could be manoeuvred to a position where a bomber presented a very large target. In any case, defensive fire from the tail gunners deterred this mode of attack. The Luftwaffe's success in mass frontal attacks on the heavies led, in December, to the creation of a special unit charged with developing the technique of storming bomber boxes. Major v. Kornatzki, an able pilot and tactician, headed this Staffel, fore-runner of the dreaded Sturmgruppen which would appear on the scene in the months ahead.

During the remainder of January 1944, B-17s and B-24s flew several missions to V-1 sites in the Pas de Calais plus three large pathfinder missions to German cities. The NOBALL missions were generally considered "milk runs" as they entailed very little time over hostile territory; nevertheless, anti-aircraft defences had been substantially reinforced and usually took their toll of a bomber or two. Very occasionally the Luftwaffe put in a surprise appearance, as it did on January 21st when a sharp engagement occurred between a few Focke-Wulfs and the Liberators of the 44th Group which were searching for a cloud break to locate their target. Five B-24s failed to return and the "lead ship" crashed at the English coast due to heavy flak damage. When a single B-17 was the only other heavy lost by the Eighth that day, such a blow was harder to take—not that the "Eightballs" were unaccustomed to disaster.

The 44th featured in a happier episode nine days later when the Eighth despatched a record 778 bombers to attack Brunswick by pathfinder methods. The combat wing, composed of 44th and 392nd group aircraft, became separated from the main force en route and near Hanover chanced upon a large break in the clouds. Through this the lead crew caught sight of the synthetic rubber plant (scene of that most successful piece of precision bombing in June 1943) and decided, in the circumstances, to take advantage of a visual run on this worthy target of opportunity. Forty B-24s dropped,

First PFF B-24s of 814th BS had retractable dustbin shaped radome in position normally occupied by ball-turret. 42-7644, D, still retained the tail marking of 44th BG when she led 93rd BG to Frankfurt on 29 Jan. 1944.—(IWM)

scoring several hits on factory installations, and returned safely to Norfolk.

Following an operational test of Gee-H on the January 5th mission to Kiel, a NOBALL mission of January 31st saw the first use of Gee-H pathfinders. The 329th Bomb Sqdn., a component of the 93rd Group, which had been concerned in the Eighth's original Gee experiments back in 1942, was the unit specialising in this technique. For this mission it provided a lead B-24 for each of four groups going to the Pas de Calais.

February weather at first conditioned a continuation of the pattern of pathfinder missions over the cloud tops to cities and ports in the Reich and, when conditions along the Channel coast offered visual opportunities, visits to NOBALL targets. Originally the bombing of V-sites was carried out at the comparatively low altitude of 12,000 ft, but the increasing incidence of flak made this a somewhat dangerous procedure so bombing heights were raised to around 20,000 ft. Thirteen of the 29 missions during January and February were to CROSSBOW targets, which apart from the direct objective of denying or delaying the use of these installations to the Germans, were useful for the combat initiation of new crews and the trial of new techniques.

On February 19th an extensive high pressure area appeared to be moving south-east across Central Germany bringing the prospect of that all too rare essential for precision bombing, good visibility and a clear sky. To the generals at USSTAF, long since conditioned to the exasperating vagaries of the weather in Europe, this seemed to be the opportunity to unleash the long planned series of concentrated attacks against aircraft factories in Germany, an over-riding priority for the CBO. It transpired that the clouds were not completely banished from the scene, but for a week the weather was fair

Dinah didn't. 452nd BG suffered heavily during its early operations. *Dinah Might* was put down on a polder near the Zuider Zee, 10 Feb. 1944 on what is believed to have been her first mission—(Zwanenburg)

enough for the Eighth to mount an almost continuous offensive.

Sunday morning, February 20th, was bleak and cold in Eastern England. Heavy cloud hung over much of the land and snow showers sprinkled the runways at many airfields. Into the dark of this winter's morn a thousand bombers were despatched to form 16 combat wings to assail twelve different targets deep in the Reich. The largest force consisting of 1st Divisions B-17s and 2nd Divisions B-24s set out in ten combat wings for Central Germany; as this column was likely to encounter the stiffest opposition in the air, it was assigned all long-range fighter support. To aid the fighter escort, the flight plan called for the bomber stream to make for a point just west of Brunswick where each wing would then proceed to its specified target, bomb and reassemble in force for withdrawal.

The sky over Germany was not so untroubled by clouds as the weather men had predicted, but visual bombing was possible at several of the briefed targets with some excellent results. Spearheading the bomber stream was the 401st Group, youngest of 1st Division's groups yet one which had achieved a high operational standard since its debut in late November. These Deenethorpe Fortresses, led by their CO, attacked one of the Leipzig plants engaged in Me109 production and put down the best bomb pattern of the day with many hits on important buildings. The Luftwaffe attempted to break up the leading formations but Allied fighter support, in spite of bad weather en route, helped to mitigate the severity of the attack although a few sharp encounters were experienced by several groups. The Fortress carrying the deputy leader of the 401st had one engine disabled and another damaged when attacked by Me109s. Forced out of formation, this aircraft was put into a spiral in the hope of bluffing the enemy fighters intent on making a "kill". This apparently had the desired effect as enemy fighters left after following the Fortress down for some distance. Levelling out at around 2,000 ft, the pilots decided that they could best escape the attention of the Luftwaffe at lower altitudes so Lt A. H. Chapman flew *Battlin' Betty* all the way back to the UK, over Germany and occupied territory, at around this height. Luckily heavy anti-aircraft installations were avoided and the long and dangerous lone flight was safely completed.

Other bombers limping home alone were not so fortunate. Turning away from the target, the 305th Group's formation received a sudden head-on pass from enemy fighters. One bomber, that had been unable to release its load because the rack activating mechanism was frozen, received a cannon shell in the cockpit. The co-pilot was killed and the pilot, 1/Lt William R. Lawley, was badly wounded in the face; another seven crew members were wounded and an engine was set on fire. The aircraft had dived steeply out of control but Lawley, recovering from the initial shock, quickly forced the co-pilot's body off the controls with his right hand, while pulling the bomber out of the dive with the other. A broken and blood-spattered windshield obscuring forward vision, added to his difficulties. With the full bomb load aboard and imminent danger of an explosion if the blazing engine fire spread, Lawley gave the order to bale out. Immediately one of the waist gunners reported that two other gunners were so severely injured that they could not leave the aircraft. Lawley then tried to bring the Fortress down safely for a crash landing. Crew members, who had the option of baling out, all stayed. The engine fire was put out and there seemed a good chance of bringing the ailing bomber home, until another fighter attack was experienced. Using skilful evasive action, Lawley managed to lose his new tormentors although not before another engine had apparently been hit and later caught fire; in time, this too was successfully extinguished. Meanwhile the bombardier, 1/Lt Harry G. Mason, had managed to free the racks and jettison the bombs. On the slow long journey home, loss of blood and shock brought Lawley to a state of collapse, and Mason took over the controls until he revived. Over the English

coast one engine spluttered as it ran out of fuel. The first airfield seen was Redhill and as Lawley made his approach one of the damaged engines again burst into flames. With only one sound engine and the risk that an error in judgment could precipitate a stall, Lawley skilfully brought the crippled Fortress in for a crash-landing without further hurt to his crew.

A cannon shell exploding in a cockpit brought about another dramatic return. It happened to a 351st Group Fortress among the leading waves of the Leipzig force. A shell smashed through the starboard windscreen killing the co-pilot and gravely injured the pilot who lost consciousness. The bombardier of the floundering aircraft, assuming it doomed, called the crew on the interphone with orders to bale out, and jumped himself. In spite of the carnage in the cockpit, some of the crew hesitated to abandon the bomber. Sgt Archie Mathies, ball turret gunner and engineer, made his way to the cockpit, leant over the mutilated bodies and succeeded in regaining control. He was joined by the navigator, Walter Truemper, and other members of the crew. Although a freezing blast of air assailed them through the fractured windscreen, they elected to attempt the flight back to England. They had difficulty in first extracting the dead co-pilot from the cockpit and while they attempted this Mathies and Truemper took turns in flying the bomber, crouched down between the pilots' seats, using ailerons and elevators only. When finally they had removed the co-pilot's body, Mathies—who had the most though very limited experience of piloting—took the co-pilot's seat. From time to time he became so numbed with cold that Truemper and others had to relieve him for spells. Having reached a lower altitude and escaped from hostile air space, Mathies continued on his own but as neither he or Truemper had any experience of landing aeroplanes they decided to make for their home field and radio the tower of their predicament. In view of the condition of the still unconscious pilot, Mathies and Truemper volunteered to attempt a landing while other members of the crew were ordered to parachute out over the base. Meanwhile, Colonel Eugene Romig, Commanding the 351st, had taken off in another Fortress with the idea of giving Mathies and Truemper stage-by-stage advice on landing as he flew along side. Unfortunately, radio contact could not be established between them so Romig then tried to fly close in to try some means of visual instruction but the damaged B-17 flew too erratic a course to allow this. By then there were many anxious eyes watching the drama above Polebrook as the two aircraft orbited the field. Romig radioed the control tower to tell Mathies and Truemper to head the bomber out to the coast, abandon it and parachute to safety, as he did not think they had the necessary experience to bring a crippled bomber in successfully. The two men replied that the pilot was still alive and they would not desert him while there was a chance of landing the bomber. They were then given permission to try and an officer in the tower radioed stage-by-stage instructions. The first approach was too high, so was a second. Tragically it was not a case of third time lucky for on the next approach the bomber stalled and crashed in a field killing both men. The pilot whom they had tried to save was still alive when rescuers reached the wreck but, mortally wounded, he died a little later.

Overall losses had been surprisingly light. Due chiefly to the enemy vectoring most of his fighters to meet the northern thrust, only twenty-one of nearly a thousand bombers that crossed the enemy coast were missing in action. It also appeared to be one of the best day's work the heavies had achieved with considerable damage wrought at vital aircraft factories where visual attacks had been made. But in terms of epic experience and bravery February 20th has another claim in the annals of the Eighth Air Force; it was to be the only day for which more than one award of the Medal of Honor was made to men flying from Britain—to William Lawley and posthumously to both Archie Mathies and Walter Truemper.

Off the runway but showing little sign of damage in this photo, *Bag O'Bolts* returned to Seething 21 Feb. 1944 with 400 extra holes. Hit by flak and attacked by fighter she was 'hedge-hopped' home. Two men were wounded and one man bailed out over Germany when he apparently thought *Bag O'Bolts* doomed.—(USAF)

On the strength of another favourable forecast the Eighth scheduled an almost equally strong force of heavies the following day. Principal targets were aircraft factories at Brunswick but cloud, having the better of the weather men, obscured the city which had to be bombed by pathfinder means. Important airfields and aircraft depots were other briefed targets and of these only Diepholz air depot received well aimed concentrations. Many other formations were foiled by cloud and sought targets of opportunity. Once again losses were light considering the number of sorties.

That afternoon, as Fortresses from Great Ashfield made landfall near Yarmouth and were letting down through the overcast, one emerged from cloud at 3,000 feet in a side slip and smashed its tail into the starboard wing of the flight leader. Both bombers plummeted down into the bleak Reedham marshes before anyone on board had a chance to escape: 21 men died instantly. Captain Hutchinson and crew in the lead Fortress had just completed the 25th and last mission of their tour. Incidents such as this did more to sicken an airman's soul than any losses in combat.

The Eightballs turn away from Diepholz air depot, 21 Feb. 1944 after another highly accurate Big Week bombardment. In foreground is *Greenwich*

When, for the third day running, the heavies were despatched to continue the assault on the enemy's aircraft industry, they again faced foul flying conditions to reach the fair weather predicted for Germany. Clouds extended up to thousands of feet and in these blind conditions more collisions occurred as the bombers attempted assembly. The 3rd Division was particularly troubled and General Le May ordered this force to abandon the raid. A good deal of confusion arose among the air leaders of this Division as to whether or not the recall message was correctly received. The 2nd Division bomber column was so badly strung out that they too were recalled while over the Low Countries. Some Liberators found targets of opportunity and one, unfortunately, bombed England. A bomb, accidentally released from a recalled aircraft as it passed over Tibenham airfield, exploded in a living site killing two servicemen and a woman in a nearby house. One of the targets of opportunity also brought tragedy. A B-24 Group bombed Nijmegen in error for a German town and caused 200 Dutch civilian deaths.

Five combat wings of the 1st Division comprising 289 B-17s, struggling through dense contrails and bitter cold, continued on their way to Oschersleben, Aschersleben, Halberstadt and Bernburg. The cloud extended further than anticipated, hiding much from view and allowing only 99 bombers to drop on their primary targets. The best bombing was the work of two of the old 'pioneer' groups. At Aschersleben the 303rd Group, aided by a few B-17s from the 384th caused such damage at the Junkers works that production was cut by half for two months. At Bernburg, the 306th Group making a good run created considerable destruction among installations at another factory engaged in Junkers Ju88 production.

After bombing, the 306th Group was attacked intermittently, but at times fiercely, by enemy interceptors on the 200 mile return trip to the Dutch coast; seven of their bombers were lost while all the remaining 23 received varying degrees of battle damage.

For the 1st Division the mission was reminiscent of that to the same area on January 11th, as bad weather over England had again hindered escort operations and for much of the time the Fortresses were on their own. Every group had taken some punishment, many severe. Despite the sending of a small force of 92nd Group B-17s to bomb an airfield in Denmark and operate radar jamming devices en route as a diversion, and the Fifteenth Air Force's attack on Regensburg from the south, the Germans were still able to concentrate their defences and

No Balls At All makes her last journey—on a German salvage wagon to the smelting works. This 351st BG B-17F was originally named *Eight Ball* until a propeller flew off No. 2 engine and sliced away part of the nickname painted on her nose. When repaired it was deemed appropriate to signify this severing experience with a new name. *No Balls At All* was brought down near Amsterdam, 22 Feb. 1944.—

ASSIGNMENT OF BOMBARDMENT GROUPS TO COMBAT BOMBARDMENT WINGS

Final plan early 1944

1 BD	2 BD	3 BD
91 BG	389 BG	94 BG
1 CBW—381 BG	2 CBW—445 BG	4 CBW—385 BG
398 BG	453 BG	447 BG
92 BG	44 BG	95 BG
40 CBW—305 BG	14 CBW—392 BG	13 CBW—100 BG
306 BG	492 BG	390 BG
303 BG	93 BG	96 BG
41 CBW—379 BG	20 CBW—446 BG	45 CBW—388 BG
384 BG	448 BG	452 BG
351 BG	95 CBW—489 BG	92 CBW—486 BG
94 CBW—401 BG	491 BG	487 BG
457 BG	458 BG	34 BG
	96 CBW—466 BG	93 CBW—490 BG
	467 BG	493 BG

inflict far heavier punishment on the British based bombers than during the previous two days: 41 were missing, 38 from the 1st Division.

The bombers were grounded on the 23rd, principally because weather conditions over Germany were doubtful but also due to the need to catch up on repairs to the large number of damaged aircraft. Many of these were ready to join the scheduled 800 plus force next day when, as on the previous Sunday, the 3rd Division was to fly north-east unescorted and attack targets near the German and Polish Baltic coasts, while other divisions went to Central Germany. The 3rd's bombers again found their objectives veiled, so resorted to a radar bombing of Rostock and returned home having encountered little opposition. Of the forces going into Central Germany, 1st Division's Fortresses bombed Schweinfurt from a blue sky and although causing heavy damage to anti-friction bearing factories, heavy smoke caused bombs from the rear group to hit a jam factory, a gelatine plant and a malt works, none of which could be deemed to further the strategic bombing campaign. It was the Liberators that made the most spectacular bombing and who also incurred the fiercest and most pro-longed opposition from the Luftwaffe that they had so far encountered.

Gotha's Me110 factories were the destination of 2nd Division. Eight groups—a ninth, the 458th, became operational that day and flew a diversion over the North Sea—assembled in three large combat wing formations, each group force numbering approximately 25 to 30 bombers. These unusually large combat wings, though difficult to manoeuvre, were deemed advisable for defence, and set off below and ahead of the 1st Division. The 2nd Wing groups composed the lead force, 14th Wing the middle and 20th Wing brought up the rear. When still 80 minutes from Gotha the leading B-24 wing, flying well ahead of schedule, due to a different wind velocity and direction to that forecast, met persistent fighter attacks that continued to the target. Some confusion arose at the IP where the lead aircraft of 389th Group suffered oxygen failure, veered off course, and released its bombs when the bombardier collapsed over his sight and tripped the release switch. The rest of the group too, then bombed. The 445th Group, recognising the error in time, continued to the target alone. Having bombed, this lone group was given special attention by the Luftwaffe and for an hour on the homeward journey enemy aircraft whittled down its formation. Of its 25 B-24s thirteen were shot out of the sky and nine others suffered battle damage. The 389th Group which had bombed

While servicing was in progress after dark on 23 Feb. 1944, this 379th BG Fortress 42-29889, became enveloped in flames before fire fighters could reach her. She had flown on the Group's first mission in May 1943.—(USAF)

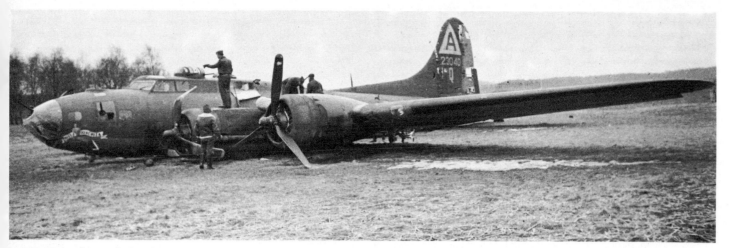

Major Heinz Baer, a Luftwaffe ace with more than a hundred victories, looks at another of his victims, the 91st BG's *Miss Quachita* lost 22 Feb. 1944. Baer was shot down no less than 18 times between Sept. 1939 and Apr. 1945, but was credited with 220 victories.

in error also suffered heavily bringing a total loss of 19 for the lead wing.

The second combat wing experienced heavy fighter opposition soon after crossing the Dutch coast by the Germans pulling every trick out of the bag, including air-to-air bombing, cable bomb towing and rockets. At the IP the leading 392nd Group, not following the diverging groups ahead, executed a correct and highly accurate bomb run resulting in 98% of the bombs exploding within 2,000 feet of the aiming point. The 44th Group, making up the rest of this wing, also achieved an extremely accurate pattern. Almost every building was damaged and as a result an estimated six to seven weeks production lost. The 392nd Group also took heavy punishment losing seven B-24s and having thirteen with battle damage in varying degrees.

It had been a costly day with 49 heavies missing due to fortuitous circumstances for the Luftwaffe and a repeat of tactics employed on the previous mission. Instead of concentrating their attacks on the bombers just prior to the target when wing formations had to be broken for bombing, the

446th BG B-24s leave the burning Gotha factory; 24 Feb. 1944. A great many aircraft can be seen parked on the snow covered airfield.—

Fragmentation Bombs

enemy fighters engaged early during penetration when escort was often weak.

A total of 830 heavies were scheduled for the fifth day of the week to continue the strikes against enemy fighter plants. The 1st Division was to divide its forces between Augsburg and Stuttgart. The Liberators were to hit Fürth and the 3rd Division Regensburg, scene of its most spectacular mission the previous year. Regensburg Messerschmitt factories were also scheduled to be attacked by Fifteenth Air Force B-17s an hour before the Eighth arrived. An almost clear sky with good visibility allowed good to excellent bombing at all targets, especially at Regensburg where damage retarded production for four months, and Augsburg where some 30 buildings were destroyed and a third of the machine tools damaged; the cost was 31 heavies missing in action. The concession by the elements was short-lived for on the morrow weather fronts moved in on Western Europe and cloud held sway for many days thereafter.

The week 19th-25th February was the most concentrated period of operations so far for the Eighth, contributing 3,300 bomber sorties and 6,000 tons of bombs to the 8,148 sorties and 19,177 tons total of the combined USSTAF-RAF Bomber Command effort during this period. The resulting devastation gave good reason to believe the objective of the CBO plan was nearing attainment. The "Big Week" campaign un-doubtedly deprived the Luftwaffe of many badly needed fighter aircraft but Allied estimations of the extent of this curtailment in production were over-optimistic. By February the German dispersal programme, initiated after the great raids of July/August 1943, was having a cushioning effect. Moreover, the small size of HE bombs carried by the American bombers were not powerful enough to destroy vital machine tools which the Germans were often able to retrieve from the tangled ruins of their factories and use again. Nevertheless, German fighter production took a plunge after "Big Week" and the following month's total was less than half that planned. In its efforts to stop the bombers the Luftwaffe had been sorely harassed in the air by the growing preponderance of Allied escort fighters, yet had taken toll of half the 400 Allied bombers lost. In terms of heroics no other week ultimately brought so many high decorations for the Eighth's bomber men: three Medals of Honor and four Distinguished Unit Citations.

With the participation of two new bomb groups in the final mission of "Big Week", the Eighth Air Force reached another milestone; it had outgrown RAF Bomber Command in the matter of aircraft and crews available for operations. Thirty operational heavy bombardment groups also made it the giant of the US Army Air Force.

Chapter 14: Big B

Having dealt what was assumed to be a crippling blow against German fighter aircraft manufacturing plants, USSTAF was eager to maintain the pressure on the Luftwaffe by bringing it to battle at every opportunity. Thus in target selection some consideration was given to provocation of the enemy fighter force. The Luftwaffe, faced with overwhelming numbers of escort fighters appeared to be conserving forces and joining battle only under advantageous circumstances. It was reasoned that the one place the Luftwaffe was most likely to defend, regardless of circumstances, was the Reich capital. Berlin offered important strategic targets but it was also very much one of prestige: to the man in the street in Britain and America it was the ultimate in German targets; bombing Hitler's capital was akin to piercing the heart of the Nazi machine. The RAF had been to Berlin many times, when and how the Americans would make their first visit had long been speculated, not least among those who were most likely to be involved.

The first briefing for Berlin—"Big B" as it became familiarly known in the Eighth—had been on November 23rd 1943 but the mission was scrubbed before take-off. Now, USSTAF was intent on attacking Berlin at the first opportunity, which appeared to be presented on March 3rd. Take-off was ordered and some formations did get as far as the Schleswig-Holstein coast before leaders decided to turn back when faced with unusually high cloud. Other formations consumed too much fuel during the difficult assembly so the whole mission was abandoned. Next day it looked like being a repetition when cloud piled up at an increasing rate while the heavies assembled. First Division cancelled the raid at this stage and in the bitterly cold winds and snow flurries brought its Fortresses back to their bases. The recall signal went out to the 3rd Division force which was well on its way but one combat wing composed of two 95th Group squadrons and one from 100th Group in the high slot reported it did not receive the message and continued towards their objective. Realising that not all its formations were responding to the signal, Eighth Air Force let some of the escort continue on to the

Berlin area where their support would soon be needed by the thirty-one Fortresses scaling the cloud tops.

At some fourteen minutes from the capital, a few Me109s intercepted, concentrating on the 100th Group section. Top turret gunner of *Rubber Check,* T/Sgt Harold Stearns, sighting on one coming in from 12 o'clock high and level, opened fire at a range of 400 yards and saw it dive away smoking. Other members of the crew reported seeing this fighter spin down in flames, confirming the first claim for the B-17s in the air battle for Berlin.

95th BG CO in congratulatory pose with Lt Col Harry Mumford, leader of 4 Mar. 1944 Berlin raid. In the background 1/Lt A. H. Brown and crew of *I'll Be Around* in which Mumford flew.—(USAF)

The leading elements of the formation were the 95th Group and in the command bomber, *I'll Be Around,* rode Lt Col Harry Mumford. He said afterwards: "Going in wasn't tough; the weather was pretty bad; clouds were broken. And it was cold— damn cold—down to 55 degrees below zero. As we got near to the city the clouds were still broken. We caught some ground checks, even though we were nearly five miles up. My navigator—and believe me he deserves all the credit (1/Lt Malcolm M. Durr)—saw enough ground points to set us up for a visual bomb run. But the clouds closed in again and the bombing was done through clouds. I'm sure we hit the place". So it was left to the leading 482nd Group radar aircraft, piloted by 1/Lt William V. Owens, to make the release; at 13.42 hrs twenty-nine B-17s unloaded the first American bombs on Berlin when bombardier 2/Lt Marshall J. Phixton touched the switch. More fighter opposition was encountered on the return journey, mostly flown through cloud as the formation had to descend to lower altitudes due to diminishing oxygen supplies. The 95th lost four bombers and the 100th one, but the lone venture did much to boost spirits. At Horham it became the proud boast that Fortresses with the Square B marking were first over Berlin.

During the following twenty-four hours Allied news agencies made much of this first American raid on Berlin. Behind the propaganda value, the effort of a solitary wing that missed a "raid abandoned" signal and continued on to scatter

T/Sgt Harold Stearns (rt.) at interrogation after 4 Mar. 1944 mission.— (IWM)

6 Mar. 1944. This picture was taken in the Polebrook briefing room as Col Eugene Romig announced the target and the curtain concealing the route map was drawn back. Who knows what emotion these faces conceal at the dawn of the bloodiest day Eighth AF was to know. In the event the 351st was lucky and lost no aircraft to the enemy.—(IWM)

a few bombs through the clouds was no great military achievement. The German radio refuted US claims although saying there was proof US formations had orders to attack Berlin but were unable to carry them out. It was well known to the Germans that if the Americans were denied an opportunity of hitting a target through bad weather they would usually return at the first opportunity. Thus, when the Würzburg radars gathered echoes from a large number of aircraft over East Anglia at the dawning of March 6th, the Luftwaffe had ample time to concentrate its forces to defend the capital. As the Fortresses and Liberators set course to fly the direct route to Berlin the Luftwaffe deployed its forces and set the scene for the most costly mission the Eighth was ever to fly.

Nearly 800 crews had been taken to their bombers as light snow blew across the darkened airfields. From this wintry scene 730 were finally despatched towards the enemy coast to be watched over by 796 fighter pilots from nineteen Eighth and Ninth Air Force groups and two RAF Mustang squadrons. The 1st Division led the way to the primary objective, the Erkner bearing plant, its five combat wings strongly escorted in anticipation of enemy reaction. Dummer

Lake, a landmark from the air where enemy fighters concentrated, produced the first interceptions and despite excellent cover by the escort, Focke-Wulfs and Messerschmitts were so numerous that they were able to give the two leading combat wings a rough time, shooting down several B-17s from the 91st, 92nd and 381st Groups. Even so, there were many airmen in other 1st Division groups who never saw an enemy aircraft that day.

Following its usual tactic of concentrating on the van, in this case the 1st Division, the Luftwaffe then contested the 3rd Division's progress in an unexpected way. When these B-17s were nearly halfway, the German ground controller became aware that the combat wing in the middle of the sixty mile long column was without escort. Small forces of interceptors were sent to engage and involve the US fighters flying with the head and tail of 3rd Division, while about a hundred set upon the unshielded formations in the centre. It was the two groups that had made the first Berlin mission two days before, the 95th and 100th, that caught most of this thirty-minute onslaught by successive Staffeln of Me109s and FW190s. As a result no less than 23 B-17s from these groups were shot out of the sky or so damaged that they did not return. Flying as an observer in one of the surviving 100th Group bombers was the CO of one of the new B-29 Superfortress groups then forming in the United States. What he observed left him in no doubt that the B-29 could not withstand such opposition.

The 3rd Division commander, Brigadier General Russell Wilson, flew in an H2X-equipped B-17 with the leading 385th Group, which was to open the bombing on the Bosch electrical factory. Also in this bomber was 1/Lt John C. Morgan whose ordeal in the battered cockpit of a B-17 the previous July had earned him the Medal of Honor. The leading wing had not encountered any serious fighter opposition but over the precincts of Berlin heavy flak was put up directly in the path of the command aircraft. Apparently taking more than one direct hit the aircraft continued on its bomb run although one engine was on fire. Then it began to lose altitude and the pilot, Major Fred A. Rabo, gave the order to abandon. Seconds later the bomber exploded killing eight of the twelve men aboard. One of the survivors was Morgan. Subsequently recalling his miraculous escape, he said, ''I was just conscious of something terrific happening and I had a faint idea of a lot

6 Mar. 1944. Fortresses of the 303rd BG ride through flak.—(IWM)

Two that did not come home from Berlin. Sole 445th BG B-24 lost on 6 Mar. 1944 was 42-7566, Q +. 390th BG's *Phyllis Marie* went down on 8 Mar. 1944. Her pilots made a wheels down landing in a large field but ran into a ditch. Repaired, she was flown by the Luftwaffe and found intact on a Bavarian airfield in May 1945.—(Holmes)

of metal tearing at me and then I was falling, I don't think I ever lost consciousness. I had my 'chute under my arm when we blew. I kept trying to get it on. When I was falling feet first the pressure kept pushing it up too high, and when I was falling head first it kept pushing it past my chest. I guess I was on my back when I finally got it fastened on. . . . I think you think clearer when you're so damned near dead. Three or four seconds after the 'chute popped open I landed in the top of a tree. I fell out if it—about 30 ft—and landed on my feet. I felt like I'd busted every bone in me. What a jolt!" Morgan was taken prisoner by soldiers from a flak battery.

Doolittle had gone down to Kimbolton to await the return of the 379th BG formation from the Erkner target. While Doolittle and some of his staff were on the control tower watching the bombers land one Fortress with a feathered propeller, firing red emergency flares, broke into the feathered propeller, firing red emergency flares, broke into the

A falling bomb is believed to have knocked the tail off 384th BG's *Silver Dollar* over Berlin on 9 Mar. 1944.—(Havelaar)

pattern and came straight down on the runway. This was *Dragon Lady* with four of her crew wounded by Berlin flak. Coming in too close behind another Fortress at the point of touch down, she caught propwash and was thrown out of control. Careering off the runway straight for the control tower, it appeared for a moment that the life of the Eighth's commander was in jeopardy but pilot Frederick Sommer gave the aircraft full throttle and just managed to lift her up, clearing the tower by a few feet.

The 2nd Division, bringing up the rear, met comparatively little air opposition on this mission as their claims of only five enemy aircraft shot down indicate. Nevertheless, when the day's expenditure in men and aircraft was totted up sixteen B-24s were missing due to the combined causes of enemy action, malfunction and accident. With 18 B-17s from 1st Division and 35 from the 3rd this amounted to a record loss of 69 heavies. Another three bombers were only fit for scrap and 102 had major damage. This was a fearful price to pay in the quest for air supremacy, particularly as partially overcast conditions forced the majority of bombs to be deposited over a five mile stretch of Berlin's suburbs without damage to any primary targets. On the other hand the Luftwaffe had certainly been brought to battle and many of its aircraft fell that day. Nevertheless the figures claimed by the Americans were on the exaggerated side: 93-44-66 by bomber crews and 82-9-32 by the US fighters. The Germans claimed 140 US aircraft destroyed; the true figure being 80. Fifteen of these had been B-17s of the 100th Group, the highest loss for a single group and also for one squadron, the 350th Bomb Sqdn. which lost ten. These losses by a group whose formations had come near to annihilation on the first Regensburg and Münster missions, gave fresh impetus to "the jinx outfit" assessment of barrack and bar talk. Now a grim sobriquet arose and spread—"The Bloody Hundredth".

Spaatz and Doolittle apparently remained unshaken, for a little over thirty-six hours after the last bomber had returned to base on the 6th, B-17s and B-24s were again preparing for take-off to Berlin. It says much for the support echelons of the Eighth that it could launch 600 heavies so soon after such a costly mission. This time the sky over Berlin was generally fine and clear, offering good prospects of visual bombing. The 3rd Division was first over the enemy coast with its 45th Wing leading and the 100th Group at the head of 13th Wing, next in line. For the surviving 100th Group crews, the announcement that they were returning to Berlin came as a shock.

Again taking advantage of a lapse in escort cover, the enemy controller cleverly vectored his fighters to hit the leading wing as it reached the IP and in a sharp encounter several B-17s went down. Having lost its leaders, the 45th Wing became confused and in reorganising its formation took an incorrect heading for the target. The commander of the 100th Group recognising the error, made the turn correctly so that the 100th led the whole Eighth Air Force into Berlin.

Under visual conditions bombing was heavy and accurate with some 75 direct hits wrecking the Erkner bearing plant (actually 16 miles south-east of the city). Although weather conditions were perfect, little fighter opposition was encountered other than the initial attack on the first wing. Most of the 37 bombers missing were from the 3rd Division—groups in the 45th Wing contributed fifteen—but the 100th Group, in spite of its exposed position, lost only a single aircraft that had first been forced to leave the formation through engine trouble.

The B-17s and B-24s were back over Berlin again next day and as 10/10ths cloud blanketed their intended targets, a radar bombing of the city ensued. The Luftwaffe did not appear and while it was known that lack of blind flying training handicapped German fighter pilots, it appeared that on this occasion the enemy was conserving his badly mauled forces knowing

On a mission to Augsburg, 16 Mar. 1944, 390th BG was attacked by Me410s. After firing rockets which burst ahead of the bomber formation (note smoke from bursts in picture) they made a head-on pass firing cannon. Two B-17s went down and 390th gunners claimed 22 Me410s. —(USAF)

the Americans would be unable to make a precision attack. The German radio claimed nine aircraft had been shot down by flak on the 9th, a figure that tallied with US admissions.

On such deep penetrations effective fighter escort was imperative and this called for good flight conditions if the rendezvous was to be on schedule and losses kept to a minimum. Most of the heavy attacks on bombers during the Berlin raids had come when the escort was missing. After the 9th, good weather deserted North-Western Europe despite the prospect of spring. Another major attack on Berlin was hardly prudent under such circumstances so the heavies returned once again to the familiar pathfinder missions to Münster and Brunswick, plus visits to the NOBALL sites. Meanwhile Command studied the meteorological reports for a forecast of open skies in some part of *Festung Europa*. Such an opportunity appeared in Southern Germany on March 16th and about 500 Fortresses and 200 Liberators left England to bomb aircraft factories. Their long flight was made only to

Rocket attack blasted open radio room of 42-31968, LN: D on the Lechfeld mission of 18 Mar. 1944. Despite damage the aircraft was brought safely back and landed at Raydon.—(USAF)

find that the weather men had been wrong again, although the bombers did find good secondary targets in the clear. Opposition fell chiefly upon the spearhead of the 3rd Division whose groups suffered three separate onslaughts chiefly from Zerstörer units with rocket-firing Me110s and Me410s. It cost eighteen B-17s while the B-24s got off comparatively lightly. Seven of the bombers failing to return managed to reach the sanctuary of neutral Switzerland.

Two days later prospects for a visual attack in Southern Germany again seemed good and a similarly sized force had better luck in finding targets. Six primary targets, plus two secondaries and five of opportunity were bombed; these provided the first visual attacks on aircraft factories since 'Big Week'. But in spite of good visibility, Friedrichshafen had to be attacked by pathfinder technique. Anticipating the objective, the Germans enveloped the city with a heavy smoke screen partly achieved by sending smoke floats out on Lake Constance. Enemy fighters, again very active and well directed, were responsible for most of the 43 heavies lost—this time sixteen came down in Switzerland. Airmen whose lives were daily in jeopardy took a morbid interest in loss assessments. This was another black day for the unlucky units. Over half the bombers missing were from one combat wing, the 14th, composed of the ill-starred 44th Group, and the 392nd Group. It would seem that the "Eightballs" jinx extended to their partners in the Wing, the Wendling group having taken some pretty hard knocks during its few months of action; but the second Friedrichshafen mission was to rank as the hardest knock of all. Little opposition was encountered on penetration and it was over the target that trouble really began when the Wing ran into a flak barrage of unexpected severity. This so broke up the formation that it wandered into Swiss air space and received further ground fire from that side of Lake Constance. Deprived of an escort due to an error in timing, in poor formation and out of the bomber column, the 14th Wing was assailed by an estimated 75 FW190s and Me109s, coming in chiefly from the rear, three or four abreast at a time. These attacks continued for a hundred miles and even when P-38s arrived on the scene, the enemy still made passes at every opportunity.

This mission left a lasting impression on S/Sgt John E. Bode, right waist gunner on the 392nd Group's *Doodle Bug:* "I was scared about this deep penetration to the same target so soon and as it turned out I had good reason to be! Things didn't go right from the start. Just after the French coast a B-24 got into prop-wash and collided with another. I watched both planes all the way down with my binoculars but saw no chutes open. Heard later one man did get out. It was his first mission.) As we neared the target I could see the Alps in the distance but my attention was soon drawn to the biggest mass of flak I was ever to see. To jam the gun-laying radar I had to throw 'chaff' out. The Germans had us bracketed and we were hit in several places. Our bombardier was hit in the face and blinded; he screamed over the interphone. Looking out I was appalled to see five B-24s falling at once over the target—just like fingers on your hand! As the wounded bombardier was being removed from the nose turret I saw a gaggle of about forty fighters flying parallel on our right at 3 o'clock. Looking through my binoculars I recognised them as a mixture of 109s and 190s although our pilot at first suggested they might be our escort arriving. A moment later the air around us was full of white puff balls, I wondered if they were a new type of flak but the pilot yelled 'here they come!' and sure enough outside my waist window an FW190 flashed by from the front, doing a roll between us and the nearest B-24.

"By now I felt it was only a matter of time before they got us as we were already crippled. I tried to swing my point fifty after other Jerries as they streaked by. Our top turret was doing most of the firing and the ball turret gunner was trying to get into the damaged nose turret. A fighter started pumping 20-mm shells at us from behind and though the tail gunner replied, the recently installed link chutes in his turret caused the guns to jam intermittently. Next thing I saw was a B-24 upside down and then to my amazement an Me109 about 100 yards or so below us on my side going in our direction and not much faster. He was probably shooting at a '24 ahead of us and may have assumed our plane abandoned; at any rate he acted as if we didn't exist. I aimed my gun almost straight down, sighted point blank and fired thirty to forty rounds into his wings, engine and cockpit. His glycol sprayed but I'm sure I must have killed the pilot as the plane rolled over and dove straight to the ground, 20,000 ft below. Our fighters finally came to the rescue of what was left of our formation.

Loading magnesium incendiary clusters into a mud bespattered B-24 of 446th BG.—(USAF)

We now had two engines out but though we were losing altitude fast we managed to make a Spitfire field on the English coast. We had one flap shot away, a bad wheel and as the hydraulic lines were cut, no brakes. We went off the end of the runway but our pilot (Lt William E. Meighan) brought the plane to a standstill without further hurt to us." The crew of *Doodle Bug* were comparatively lucky; fourteen 392nd and eight 44th Group Liberators never reached England.

Grey skies predominated throughout the remainder of March, but snatching at every opportunity the Eighth managed to make many heavy visual attacks on important airfields in Occupied Europe and on the 22nd conditions appeared promising enough for another strike on Berlin. Almost 800 heavies were despatched with aircraft factories and associated industries as their objectives. The familiar spread of white "cotton wool" was present by the time the bombers arrived and, though broken in places, it caused loads to be released with radar aid in the vicinity of Friedrichshafen Station. This was the last major mission for the pathfinder aircraft of the 482nd Group. With a recent delivery of H2X-equipped machines a pathfinder squadron had been established in each

Bound for Berlin: 306th BG finds solid cloud concealing Germany. Black burst above 42-31539, O is from a ground launched rocket.—(USAF)

Bombardment Division, these being in the regular combat groups based at Chelveston, Snetterton Heath and Hethel. Procedure was, for the time being, along the lines established by the 482nd with pathfinder B-17s and B-24s distributed to lead groups prior to a mission and flying with them in combat wing lead positions. A command pilot and a senior bombardier from the lead group would usually fly in the aircraft. As more crews and aircraft became avilable it was hoped to expand pathfinder facilities to each wing and eventually to each group. The 482nd was then confined to training radar operators for all US forces in Europe, and operational experiments with new or improved radar devices.

The March 22nd mission was the fifth and last attack of the month on the German capital. Notable was the fact that of the 4,799 tons dropped in these raids, 40% were incendiaries. These bombs were being used on a larger scale now that aimable clusters were available and resulted in better accuracy. Known as the M-17 type, they had been introduced in January; at the end of March the Eighth was receiving another new fire bomb, the M-76, known as the 'Block burner'.

Chapter 15: In the Air, On the Ground

While the bombers had progressed to striking at the heart of Germany, the fighters increased their activities in other ways than direct escort. Early in the new year General Kepner's Headquarters made a number of decisions on operational policy with far reaching effects on air actions in 1944. If air superiority was to be established over enemy-occupied Western Europe and Germany, the Luftwaffe had to be brought to battle and defeated. As the German fighters now usually avoided their American counterparts, except when intercepting a bomber mission, VIII Fighter Command would have to seek out and engage the enemy aircraft wherever they might be. Hitherto the escort had operated at altitudes in the vicinity of the Fortresses and Liberators and were, as a rule, not permitted to range out or go down after hostile aircraft. Now these restrictions were gradually removed; after a group had finished escort duties—fuel supplies permitting—it would be allowed to descend to those levels where enemy aircraft had usually been secure, and even to tree-top height in order to shoot up airfields. In this way the German Air Force would be given little respite; VIII Fighter Command was set on meeting the punch-line of General Arnold's New Year message to the full: " . . . in the air, on the ground".

That the battlefield could be profitably deepened was due in part to engineering advances affecting the Command's predominant weapon, the P-47 Thunderbolt, which had originally been considered outclassed by the best German fighters below 15,000 ft. The turn of the year saw improvements to enhance its performance and allow its use with confidence at lower altitudes. In November the installation of a water injection system on P-47 engines had commenced and the makers were fitting this device to all the new P-47s from D-20-RE models onwards. Water injection into the intake manifold boosted the engine by an additional 200-300 hp with resulting increases in top speed and rate of climb, although limited to short periods to avoid engine overheating. Modification of aircraft with the squadrons was spread over two months, and it was incorporated in aircraft of most of the older groups by the end of December 1943. To obtain the best advantage from the power increase, the fitting of a wide diameter paddle blade propeller was commenced, a squadron at a time, during December. Pilots were unanimous on the advantages of water injection, but not all liked the new propellers which were given to feathering difficulties at first. Together, these additions to the P-47 gave a vastly improved rate of climb and allowed it to outclimb the FW190 at altitudes below 15,000 ft although the German machine still had better initial acceleration. Tests showed that the P-47 was at least capable of holding its own at low altitudes providing reasonably high speeds were maintained. But these modifications did little to improve performance above 30,000 ft because of limitations of the turbo-supercharger.

The VIII Air Service Command also began fitting P-47s with shackles and the necessary plumbing to enable the carriage of a drop tank under each wing to further increase range. 1st Base Air Depot at Burtonwood commenced this work in mid-December but as each fitting required many man-hours it was estimated that a good nine months was needed to effect the installation throughout. However, a combined effort by Eighth and Ninth Air Service Command depots saw the job completed by April 1944, and by February 1944 P-47 Groups were able to take full advantage of this fixture.

With a stronger force at their disposal, VIII Fighter Command was able to introduce improved tactics; during January a modified form of bomber support relay system proved very successful. Instead of flying to a pre-determined rendezvous point and then flying with a part of the bomber stream until relieved by another unit, a group was given a defined area along the bomber route to patrol while the whole bomber stream passed through. The most experienced P-47 groups were assigned to areas where enemy opposition was most likely while the target leg of the bomber route would be given to P-51s and P-38s because of their extra range. This system became common practice on deep penetrations for the rest of the war.

January was the month that the P-51B Mustang proved its merit as a long range escort for the heavies. Their first encounters with the Luftwaffe during December had brought no outstanding results in claims but had shown that even a single group of P-51s was well able to take care of itself even though frequently outnumbered. On January 5th the Mustangs of the 354th came home from target support over Kiel with an 18 for no loss victory. They repeated the performance on the 11th with a score of 15-8-16 for 0, largest contribution to the 28-13-24 claimed that day by the groups under VIII Fighter Command control (ten of the remainder fell to the 56th Group). When the large force of B-17s and B-24s set off to bomb aircraft industry targets in and around Brunswick, the first deepish penetration to the central part of Germany since October and prompting the strongest opposition that month, all 13 operational US fighter groups were scheduled to provide escorts with P-38s and P-51s flying right to the targets. The weather deteriorated and over half the bombers were recalled while still some distance from Brunswick. The rest went on but, unhappily, the P-38s found the forecast 'thin overcast' to be 22,000 ft thick and only one squadron of 14 aircraft was able to meet an aborting wing of bombers. The 354th Group arrived alone over Brunswick and endeavoured to stave off determined enemy attacks on the bombers with its 44 P-51s.

Major James Howard, CO of the 356th Fighter Squadron, separated from his unit, came across a formation of Me110s about to attack a Fortress group. He at once dived on the Zerstörers and in the course of some brilliant manoeuvres broke up their attack single-handed. He claimed six probables and as the action was fought with faltering guns until only one was operative, it is understandable that his claims were indecisive. His effort brought him the only Medal of Honor to go to a fighter pilot engaged in air combat over Europe.

Repetitive gun failures with the P-51B forced curtailment of operations during January 1944. The problem took some time to solve. Guns lined up on the Boxted butts worked perfectly, but once in the air trouble started again. The four .50 guns had an angled seating in the wing and it was eventually discovered that when firing during fast turns or violent manoeuvres the pull on the ammunition connecting links was such that they would buckle and foul the gun. Preventive modification took many weeks to effect during which time the only assured way of avoiding trouble was to fire only when the aircraft was in straight flight—a grave handicap in combat. The guns were eventually reseated.

"Bugs" had been expected in the P-51B, as with any new type hurried into service, but the fact that both airframe and engine were already well tried had led to hopes that the aircraft would not experience difficulties such as beset the early P-47s. The RAF had so far only used the Mustang for low altitude work, and an airframe that was without vices at 10,000 ft proved otherwise at 30,000 ft. As with the Lightning, the Mustang was affected by intense cold at high altitudes. Gun actuating mechanisms failed to operate due to oil congealing; windscreens and windows froze up, sometimes putting pilots in the position of having to scrape away ice in order to see out; troubles with fuel systems and radios were also encountered.

The American-built Rolls-Royce Merlins had their snags; there were frequent coolant leaks causing overheating, and rough running due to faulty sparking plugs. British plugs were found to be more reliable and generally had a longer life. These items took time to rectify and meanwhile the 354th and following Mustang groups flew and fought, often under extreme difficulty. With the knowledge that all was not well, a six to seven hour trip through a hostile sky was not a very encouraging prospect. Nevertheless, there was no lack of enthusiasm by fighter pilots eager to do battle in the Mustang, which was superior to the two main German interceptors in most respects. At altitudes up to 28,000 ft it was 50 mph faster than the FW190A, increasing to 70 mph above that height. It had a similar lead on the Me109G being 30 mph faster at 15,000 ft and increasing to 50 mph by 30,000 ft. The Me109G had better acceleration in the initial stages of a dive but the Mustang could overhaul it if the 109 pilot was foolish enough to prolong the dive: there were no problems in out diving the FW190. In dogfights it could easily out-turn the Messerschmitt and usually had the edge on the Focke-Wulf. The latter had a much better rate of roll though the P-51B was on a par with the Me109G in this respect. Rate of climb was also superior to most models of these German fighters that were met in battle at this time.

The Eighth Air Force was pressing for the re-assignment of the pioneer Mustang group, the 354th, now flying under its operational control, but the Ninth was disinclined to part with its only active and very distinguished fighter unit. To aggravate the situation two more P-51B groups were established in this tactical air force. Eventually, an agreement was reached whereby VIII Fighter Command would exchange one of its new P-47 groups, the 358th, for the Ninth's second P-51 group, the 357th, which was in training at Raydon. In this way the Ninth gained an already active group while the Eighth received a yet untried and partly equipped unit—but nonetheless its first with the coveted Mustangs. The two groups exchanged bases on the last day of January, with their new assignments formally recognised two days later.

When determined and heavy opposition was encountered during support of bomber missions to Frankfurt and Brunswick at the end of January, there was a marked rise in fighter claims. Fighters claimed 45-5-10 for a loss of 14 on the 29th and 45-16-33 for 4 next day. On the first of these two days the Lightning put up its most successful showing so far when the 20th Fighter Group shot down 10 for a loss of 4 (two went down after a collision). One pilot, Captain Lindol Graham, made claims of three destroyed.

Another group in action that day was the 352nd, flying from Bodney. Two of their pilots, Captain George Preddy and 1/Lt William Whisner, having shot down an Me109 apiece were returning across Belgium when the engine of Preddy's P-47 was hit by flak. Forced to bale out of the faltering P-47 over the Channel, Preddy transmitted a 'Mayday' emergency call. After landing in the water he freed himself from his 'chute and inflated the seat dinghy, while Whisner and another member of the flight, 1/Lt Fred A. Youchim, circled their

comrade until an RAF Walrus appeared. The amphibian landed successfully and retrieved Preddy, but the sea proved too rough for take-off and broke off a pontoon float. For over four hours the Walrus was tossed about by the sea while the pilot, Flying Officer E. Wilson, out on the wing to balance up the aircraft, clung to wing struts until an Air Sea Rescue launch arrived and took the crippled Walrus in tow. Wilson, an Australian, discovered that Preddy had flown in the defence of Darwin before coming to England, and that they had acquaintances in common. British ASR had saved the lives of many American fighter pilots but few rescues proved to have such a significant outcome. Preddy was to become one of the great names in the Eighth.

Over 200 enemy fighters rose to battle with the invading bombers of the Eighth on January 30th mission. Extensive cloud and bitter cold caused a quarter of the Lightnings despatched to return early, chiefly as a result of engine failures. Once again the "Wolfpack" enhanced its reputation as the terror of the German twin-engined fighters by "bouncing" a formation of Me410s and Ju88s. In shooting down further single-engined fighters it passed the 200 mark in enemy planes destroyed. The nearest rival in VIII Fighter Command was the 4th which had 106. Nobody argued as to which was the most successful American fighter group in England.

There was no wide gap separating the individual scores of top ranking VIII Fighter Command aces. Captain Walter Beckham of the 353rd had been building up an impressive record. On February 3rd he drew level with the 56th's Walter Mahurin by adding two victories to bring his total to 16, and Mahurin who had previously led by one, added another to come up to the same figure. On the 8th the Metfield pilot bagged an Me109 and FW190 to pass his friendly rival and become leading ace in the Eighth with 18 victories. That same day the Lightning received a boost in prestige. The 20th Group was flying out on normal bomber support when one of the aircraft comprising the 77th Ftr. Sqdn's leading flight developed supercharger trouble. Because of this the flight dropped to 12,000 ft where the P-38 was more able to take

1/Lt James Morris and his crew chief S/Sgt Joe McCarland chat beside *Black Barney* Morris's P-38J.—(IWM)

care of itself. Ranging over the German countryside, one of the flight members, Lt James M. Morris, had on three occasions the good fortune to surprise and destroy enemy aircraft at very low altitude. He also shot up a railway locomotive near Saarburg before heading for home. Separated from the flight he came upon and successfully stalked another enemy fighter in the clouds making his fourth aerial victory of the day. This was believed a record number of victories for a single mission —and it had been achieved in a Lightning. But ill luck still dogged the 20th and 55th. Four days previously, nearly half their P-38s had been forced to "abort" when once again extreme cold caused a spate of engine failures. Losses were often high in such circumstances for the Luftwaffe were quick to exploit the situation if a P-38 was observed to have a feathered propeller. Because the likelihood of these troubles increased with altitude, Lightnings did not of choice operate above 30,000 ft. In consequence Me109 "top cover" which was usually around the 35,000 ft mark had been repeatedly bouncing the P-38s on nearly every mission.

These dive and zoom tactics by enemy interceptors brought the 20th Group one of its blackest days on February 11th, with

Eighth's first P-51 group, the 357th, drew first blood on 20 Feb. 1944 when Cpt Calvert Williams shot down an Me 109.—(Elliott)

8 pilots missing from bomber support to Frankfurt. There were two notable events this day that foreshadowed future trends in VIII Fighter Command operations. Colonel Hurbert Zemke leading two Squadrons of his famous group back from a battle with Me109s caught sight of an enemy airfield near Rheims—later identified as Juvincourt—on which a number of enemy aircraft could be seen. He led the Thunderbolts down to make a single strafing pass, and the enemy aircraft that then burst into flames as a result of his fire became the first credit under the Command's new claims category for aircraft destroyed on the ground. This was not, however, the first occasion a Luftwaffe aircraft on the ground had been blasted by fire from Eighth Air Force fighters. That distinction was probably held by Glenn Duncan and two other 353rd Group pilots who shot up a Do217 north of Amiens on January 21st.

Ground strafing attacks soon played an important part in the American fighter activities, and already small missions were being run specifically to attack ground targets with gunfire, the 78th Group having started the ball rolling on February 6th. Another event on February 11th was the first operation of Mustangs assigned to the Eighth. Lt Col James Howard from the 354th led 41 of the 357th Group's aircraft on a sweep of the Rouen area in support of B-24s bombing the Pas de Calais V-weapon sites. It had time for only one other "wing stretching" mission before being committed on the 20th to the first of the extensive aerial battles that raged in the series of concentrated attacks on German aircraft industry known as

Cpt Maurice McLary shows Col Fred Castle, CO of 94th BG, holes made by two 30 calibre bullets which came within inches of him during a combat near Frankfurt; 29 Jan. 1944. Damage to hydraulics and right engine caused the 20th FG pilot to belly in at Bury St. Edmunds.—(IWM)

'Big Week'. Here Captain Calvert L. Williams made the group's first "kill". In all, 835 fighters were despatched that day and claims made of 61 enemy planes destroyed plus 7 probables, for 11 US fighters missing in action: a 6 to 1 ratio! On the 21st, VIII FC fighters returned with 33 for 5, 61 again on the 22nd, for 11, 27 for 10 on the 24th and 26 for 3 on the 25th. On the 29th over 500 fighters went out to support a raid on Brunswick and for the first time the Luftwaffe did not rise to protect their homeland; although their absence was due more to the solid overcast that day, rather than any reluctance to fight.

Although the enemy had over 1,500 fighters in the West at this time, no more than 200 to 300 were active on any one mission. This was in part due to the saturation of the defences by Allied formations and the problem of deciding which were major attacks and which were feints or small diversionary missions. Sometimes incidents caused American pilots to question enemy morale. On the 21st, Captain J. W. Wilkinson of the 78th Group while diving his P-47 to attack an Me109 was surprised to see the enemy pilot bale out while he was still some 800 yards away. Not a shot had been fired, but it is possible that the Messerschmitt was already in difficulty and thus the pilot's action was prudent.

Major Walter Beckham and the team who looked after *Little Demon*. Crew chief S/Sgt Henry Bush, on Beckham's right, and Sgt Richard Verity, armourer, on his left. Other man is assistant crew chief, Sgt Marvin Eichstaedt. Aircraft insignia was in red and yellow.—(IWM)

The idea of shooting up ground targets—particularly airfields—on the way home from bomber support duties was catching on fast. On the 22nd, Colonel Glenn Duncan leading the returning 353rd Group called his flight to follow him down to blast Ju88s seen on Ostheim airfield, north-east of Bonn. Another formation, led by Major Walter Beckham, peeled off into a steep dive with his flight to follow Duncan's strafing run. Defending gun crews, unable to catch Duncan, were fully alerted by the time Beckham swept over the airfield boundary. A burst beneath the nose of his Thunderbolt *Little Demon* crippled the engine. Pulling up and away from the airfield Beckham called over the R/T to his wingman, Lt George Perpente, "Stay down. Take the boys home, George, I can't make it". Beckham then baled out and was later heard to have been taken prisoner. The Eighth had lost its leading ace.

At first, in contrast to the Luftwaffe fighters often adorned with bright colours on spinners and noses, American fighters had a uniform drab paintwork. To aid recognition, the P-47s were given white fronts to engine cowls, plus white wing and tail bands, and the only form of unit identification was the white unit code letters on the fuselage. But with the spring of

The new paddle-blade propeller backed by a touch of colour; the yellow cowl of *Whack*, Dave Schilling's P-47D. Belly tank is 108 gl. metal type.

1944 came forth splashes of colour on the East Anglian airfields, that distinguished each group to friend and foe alike. As might be expected the splash first appeared at Halesworth, as another inspiration from the VIII Fighter Command pacesetters. The noses of each squadron's Thunderbolts were painted a different colour.

There were two basic reasons for the colourings; firstly, it was considered that FW190 pilots might mistake bright-nosed P-47s for their own kind and in so doing give the Americans a tactical advantage. Secondly, bright colours were more easily discerned than identification letters and aided in quicker reforming when squadrons had become separated. The 56th, given permission to carry out this scheme in January, found it worthwhile, particularly as on a few occasions the Luftwaffe appeared to fall for the trick. The idea soon caught on with other groups and in March VIII Fighter Command stepped in with a standardised system whereby a different nose decoration identified each particular group.

The Luftwaffe came to know the elite of the Eighth's fighters, Hubert Zemke's "Wolfpack", as the red-nosed Thunderbolts. They were still adding to their impressive score. Catching two Staffeln of III/Z.G.26, cruising near Minden preparatory to attacking bombers on the initial 'Big Week' mission, they "bounced" them from the rear and out of the sun; some 18 of the 24 Me110Gs were shot down in a matter of seconds. On this occasion the first use was made of the US metal 150 gallon drop tanks (actual capacity 165 gallons) under the bellies of the P-47s. Next day the 56th claimed another dozen single-engined fighters in a fight over Holland, and on the 22nd a mixed bag of 17 which enabled one of its

squadrons, the 61st commanded by Major James Stewart (not the film star), to become the first US fighter squadron in England to claim 100 victories: this was not far behind the scores of the 4th and 78th Groups at that date. The 56th stood supreme, a highly polished organisation with the ability to vanquish the enemy in nearly every combat. Their record of 250 victories acted as an incentive to other groups in the Command: what the "Wolfpack" could do, they would emulate. It became as much a fetish to beat the 56th as defeat the Luftwaffe to some groups, such was the competitive spirit. None felt so keenly about surpassing this lead in victories as did the 4th Group.

The 4th had condemned the Thunderbolt while the "Wolfpack" proved its worth and deprived the 4th of some of their prestige as the Command's oldest unit. With a determination tinged by jealousy and contempt, the 4th looked round for a means to prove that the heirs of the Eagle Squadrons were still the finest fighter pilots in the ETO. They settled on the Mustang.

Command of the 4th passed to Don Blakeslee on January 1st 1944, when Colonel Chesley Peterson went reluctantly to a desk job in the Ninth Air Force. With 9 victories he was at the time highest scoring pilot produced by the Group. Blakeslee had led a few Mustang missions with the 354th and after assuming command of his own group had taken time off to lead the 357th as well. As far as he was concerned, the Mustang was the aircraft for the 4th and in this there was almost unanimous agreement at Debden where Blakeslee had on occasion displayed an example borrowed from a group he was tutoring. Command was already going ahead with plans to convert P-47 and P-38 groups to this type, and the 355th at Steeple Morden was training to convert early in March. Impatiently the 4th clamoured to be first and Blakeslee pressed General Kepner for priority in obtaining Mustangs. He pointed out that many of his pilots had flown Spitfires and were therefore familiar with the idiosyncrasies of the liquid-cooled Merlin engine. The General found Blakeslee a likeable, if irreverent, character and recognised his qualities of leadership: he is quoted as having been swayed by the promise, "General, I give you my word I'll have them on operations in 24 hours".

A training P-51B was sent to Debden on February 22nd and for the next five days most combat pilots on the base took their turn in flying it, and had averaged about 40 minutes flying time apiece when the first of their operational Mustangs arrived. To enable the 4th to have sufficient aircraft a number scheduled for the 355th were hurriedly transferred, enabling Blakeslee to keep his promise. Within 24 hours he was leading 22 P-51s on a sweep over France. Spirits were high at Debden that night, with much talk of what the 4th and the Mustang would do.

Such was the urgency to increase P-51 escort on extreme range bomber missions that the 4th had little time for more familiarising flights before being sent into the thick of battle. The mission to Frankfurt on March 2nd gave the 4th a chance and two enemy aircraft were shot down for one P-51 lost. Claims were not high that day and the 17 Luftwaffe aircraft claimed fell mostly to the guns of Thunderbolts. One P-47 pilot returned unaware that he had sent down Egon Mayer, Kommodore of J.G.2, who had fought the Eighth Air Force since its earliest days and was known as "The Fortress Specialist". Credited with 103 victories, Mayer was one of the Luftwaffe's best air leaders and had on many occasions during the previous summer and autumn tangled with Zemke's 56th Group.

When on the morrow the first Berlin mission was recalled due to bad weather, Blakeslee had led the 4th spearheading the bombers, but its squadrons had become separated in the clouds over Germany. Nine aircraft of the 336th Ftr. Sqdn. then suddenly found themselves in the midst of 50 to 60 hostile fighters, but managed to escape with the loss of one and

1/Lt Willard Millikan (left) upon his return to Debden, 3 Mar. 1944, tells of 336th FS's involvement with a mass of enemy fighters.—(IWM)

claims of six-two of these victories were the work of Captain Don Gentile the Squadron's top ace. The 354th Group's Mustangs also ranged near Berlin, but it was the Lightnings that made the day's news as Lt Col Jack Jenkins, commander of the 55th Group, noted in his diary that evening: "Intelligence called early this morning. A big mission is on. It was the long-awaited show to Berlin. General Kepner told me that we would go there, and today we did it! I led the Group, flying with the 38th Squadron. We went straight in and were pretty well shot up by flak over Magdeburg, Hanover, etc. We kept calling the bombers but could not contact them. I had a rough right engine and wondered whether I would make it. Many pilots had engine trouble and dropped out. We arrived over Berlin with only about half our Group. We saw a few unidentified aircraft on the way in, but they did not approach us. We circled the edges of Berlin for about 15 minutes, waiting for the B-17s, but could not see them. We came out by Leipzig, dropped our tanks and about that time I had to drop down to a lower altitude with my flight, due to right engine trouble. A member of my element became separated when I did a 360° turn, so Lt Kreft and I came out alone. We had to outrun about 15 Germans. Doing this with one bad engine was not fun. General Doolittle released the story of our trip to the press and I have been swamped by 'phone calls this evening. I learned later that the bombers had actually turned back at Hamburg and we did not get the word. Therefore, we were the only Allied planes to reach Berlin. I got so cold that my crew chief had to help lift me out of my cockpit. It took one hour and 45 minutes to make the trip *to* Berlin". So it was that Jenkins' P-38J *Texas Ranger IV* was the first USAAF combat aircraft to point its nose over Berlin.

First Eighth AF pilot and aircraft over Berlin: Jack Jenkins and *Texas Ranger IV*.—(Jenkins)

A third Lightning group, the 364th stationed at Honington, became operational under rather unhappy circumstances that day. On the last day of February the CO, Lt Col Grambo, had accompanied the 20th Group mission to gain operational experience. Coming back, first one and then the other engine failed and the Lightning crashed near Zwolle, killing Grambo. The novitiate group was plagued with the troubles that still hampered P-38 operation and these, plus a combination of flight conditions, inexperience and the enemy, accounted for 16 of its aircraft failing to return during March. In an effort to lessen the chance of engine failures the P-38 groups during penetration and withdrawal often kept to lower altitudes where temperatures were less severe. If the escort proved routine, engines were periodically cleared; one scheme was for a group leader to call "Buster" over his radio at twenty minute intervals, for pilots to open up to a boosted 3,000 rpm for thirty seconds.

Blakeslee was selected to lead the first US bombers over Berlin. This was the occasion on March 4th when the bombers were recalled, but one box continued alone. Although

Betty A III from the Eighth's third Lightning group, the 364th.—(IWM)

Jenkins, as related, rather stole his thunder the day previous, Blakeslee was still the first to head the bombers over the city. Nearing Berlin, thirty enemy aircraft attacked the bombers and the remnants of the 4th—half the Group's P-51s had turned back with various troubles—went to the aid of the heavies. The 354th and 357th also reached the Berlin area and saw some action, the P-51s accounting for the total claims of 8 destroyed put in by the fighters that day. The raid proved disastrous for the Command who sustained one of their highest losses. No less than 23 "Little Friends" failed to return and others were involved in crashes seeking their bases in the bad flying conditions. The particularly foul weather—cloud reached as high as 29,000 ft in places—had a hand in most of these losses although a well executed surprise attack by Me109s of II/J.G.1 was responsible for the loss of 8 Mustangs. These were all from a fourth P-51 group, the 363rd assigned to the Ninth Air Force, which had been operating under VIII FC control for less than a fortnight.

On the March 6th mission to Berlin, the costliest the Eighth Air Force ever had to face, the Luftwaffe had concentrated fighters along the flight plan route. Even so the 400-odd aircraft known to have been airborne was only half the German fighter force available. Numerous twin-engine fighters including night fighters were thrown into the battle. In all, 803 US fighters were involved in the mission and the 81 enemy planes destroyed for a loss of 11 of their own number was the best record so far. Once again the fighter force over Berlin was spearheaded by the 4th and led by its accomplished leader, Don Blakeslee; the rejuvenated Eagles accounted for at least 15 of the enemy. The biggest score of the day was made by the 357th Group from Leiston, which had been on operations less than a month. Like the 4th it was sent to

Outward bound on 4 Mar. 1944, Lt Albert Fogg's 42-67736 had an engine failure and was then attacked by what was presumed to be an enemy operated P-47. He managed to reach Spanhoe but over-shot on his landing approach. His remaining engine failed and he crashed in an opencast mine. Rescuers had to cut off his shoe to free him from the burning P-38. Fogg was little harmed.—(Bowers)

provide target and withdrawal support and to arrive over Berlin with the first bombers, remaining to the limit of endurance, giving support to successive boxes of bombers as they arrived.

The Mustang was still suffering from mechanical troubles and every group had a large percentage of early returns. Of the 48 P-51Bs that took off from Leiston fifteen had turned back, chiefly through engine coolant troubles but by the time the Group had reached Berlin, two and a quarter hours later, those aborting included the new CO Colonel Don Graham, who had assumed command when Colonel Spicer was shot down on a long-range sweep over France the previous day. On arrival at the rendezvous point they found the 3rd Bomb Division's B-17s under heavy attack by over a hundred single and twin-engined fighters, ranged in Gruppe formations. Major Hayes who was commanding the 364th Ftr. Sqdn., and had taken over leadership, immediately led the Group into the attack, each flight of Mustangs tackling up to 30 enemy aircraft at a time. When the enemy broke away and attempted to reform below the bombers, elements of the Group followed

S/Sgt Tony Cardella refuels Cpt Don Gentile's P-51B. The angled seating of guns can be seen.—(IWM)

them down to engage in combat and try to prevent their re-formating. After 30 minutes in the target area the 357th escorted the last box of B-24s on their leg 39 miles south of Bremen. On the way home Hayes led a flight of five Mustangs down towards an airfield at Ulzen, destroying an Me109 at tree-top height and then strafing the field and damaging five parked aircraft and various installations. This was probably the first airfield strafing carried out by Mustangs of VIII Fighter Command. Incredibly, all the 357th's Mustangs returned safely to Leiston; to veterans who had battled with the Luftwaffe a year or eighteen months before their success seemed almost unbelievable. Yet the evidence was there on film from the gun cameras: 28 enemy aircraft of which 20 were assessed as destroyed.

The Ninth Air Force's 354th Group also had a successful day with a score of 8 for 1. The three Mustang groups had together accounted for 45 of the Luftwaffe fighters shot down during this great battle: there was now no doubting the Mustang's prowess. Many fighter groups saw some action that day and foremost among those flying the Thunderbolt was the 56th. Making its first fully effective use of the wing shackles holding the two 108 gallon paper tanks, enabling them to take the P-47 475 miles and back, both A and B formations—10 minutes apart—flew penetration support.

After passing Dummer Lake the 61st Ftr. Sqdn. flying in 56th "A" Group was engaged in combat, but this was over by the time Colonel Zemke and the other two squadrons arrived on the scene. Zemke caught sight of a lone FW190 flying at 3,000 ft below his position and towards a formation of Fortresses; in his own words: "Since the other battle was over, I launched an attack on the FW. He continued closing on the Combat Wing and even though I used water injection, my rate of closure was not enough to prevent him from closing on the rear of a Fortress and strafing the aircraft badly. He immediately turned left which allowed me to out-cross and tag on his tail. When he filled the 300 yard division in the sight I opened up and immediately saw strikes. This burst was held for more than fifty rounds and until I broke off for fear of a mid-air collision. The 190 was last seen going down in a steep dive, trailing a mile of smoke as he burnt.

"Shortly thereafter an Me109 was identified at some distance to the south and below. I flew in its direction and then found myself able to fire at about 300 yards with 20 degrees deflection. No hits were registered at first, but then several showed up on his right wing and he began diving straight away at an angle of 30 degrees. My diving speed carried me well within good firing range and I opened up to see hits over the entire plane. Fire broke out and he fell into a downward spin.

"After this engagement my flight was told to climb up to 20,000 ft in a circle. A lone Me109 was spotted at the same altitude and some distance away. As we approached him he must have seen us for he went into a steep diving turn toward the deck, as the enemy is so often prone to do when trying to elude us. My reactions were to step up the manifold and rpm and go down into the attack. Very shortly thereafter, this enemy aircraft broke into violent flame and went tumbling into a vicious spin toward the earth. No rounds of ammunition had been expended by my flight and there had been absolutely no one in the vicinity of the E/A to cause him to burn. He was almost totally consumed by flame before striking the ground. This Me109 is claimed by our flight as destroyed and there can be no definite claim made by any of us. Our attack only caused him to break downwards". Such were the mysteries of combat. In all probability this Messerschmitt had already been damaged in a fight prior to Zemke's arrival.

Meanwhile 56th "B" Group was also seeing action, particularly the 63rd Fighter Squadron contribution. Major Gerald Johnson who was leading, reported: "As we passed Bremen we could see the rear boxes of Forts that were ahead of us being attacked so we headed in their direction. By the time we reached there the E/A were dispersed, but I saw an FW190 at about 12,000 ft and started after him. He saw me coming, however, and kept giving me such a great deflection shot that I was unable to get more than a few hits. After chasing him through the clouds for a while another P-47 managed to get dead astern and destroy him''.

Captain Walker Mahurin, leading Red Flight, said: ''At the time of the attack, we were unaware of the actual presence of the E/A. We first noticed them when we began to see the flashes of the 20-mm shells bursting around the first division of bombers . . . by the time we got into the combat vicinity the concentrated attack had been dispersed leaving the E/A flying singly and in twos and threes down on the clouds at 7,000 feet.

''I noticed three of these E/A about 11 o'clock to me down low: after considerable manoeuvring, I was in a position to attack one of these E/A, a single Me109. As I came down on

Mahurin in his P-47D. Faired projection ahead of windscreen is a rear view mirror.—(USAF)

him he saw me, and after one turn to the left, he headed down for the clouds. I found myself closing on his tail. I fired several short bursts, none of which hit him. He finally disappeared into the clouds.

''When I pulled up from this attack, I sighted a single FW190 at about 9 o'clock to my flight, heading down for the deck. This Jerry also saw me. As soon as the element of surprise was gone I knew I would be forced to follow him before he straightened out, before I could make a proper attack. We milled around and around in a turning circle to the left, until suddenly the 190 straightened out and headed for one of the half-mile-in-diameter clouds which covered the area. As he did so, I closed in behind him and started to fire. By this time we were both in the cloud and it turned out to be considerably thinner than either one of us had anticipated. I could still see the Hun, and when I fired I saw many hits on both of his wings, as well as a few on his fuselage. I was close enough to him so that my hits did not converge to a point. I was then forced to break off the attack as the cloud obscured him. This 190 I claim as probably destroyed, because I hit him quite heavily.

''By this time the flight had worked itself down to about

3,000 feet and were darting in and out of the clouds trying to spot more Huns. The Huns were darting in and out of the clouds trying to evade Thunderbolts.

''As we climbed back towards the bombers, I looked over the side of my ship and spotted a Thunderbolt in a turning circle to the left with an FW190 on it's tail. I immediately called on the R/T to tell the '47 to break left, however, I later discovered that it was a ship from the 78th Group and on a different frequency to ours. I led the flight into attack the 190, which was all silver and with a large black ''V'' painted on its side. He saw us coming, because he broke the attack and began to turn left to save his own hide. I throttled back and closed in behind him, but held my fire until he, too, would straighten out.

''In the turn itself I was only just able to stay with him, both of us would stall a bit and then recover. However, when I added water I was able to out-turn him and also able to go around the circle faster than he did. I got within 150 yards of him and stayed there. After we had both gone around the circle several times, he pulled up into a steep climb. I followed and was able to get in a few shots, as I closed on him in the climb. As he fell off, he rolled over in order to pull the old stand-by of the Luftwaffe—the split S. I followed this also, gaining on him in the dive. When he pulled out of the dive he headed straight for the clouds in the same manner as the other Jerry had. I was able to pepper him soundly; seeing many hits on both wings and fuselage. The Jerry appeared to be having difficulty in flying his ship. He made a 180 degree turn to the left, and as I pulled up I saw his canopy fly off and saw him jump over the side''. Time was, when a Thunderbolt pilot would never have attempted to duel with the Luftwaffe's most vaunted fighter in such manoeuvres as those described in the last of Mahurin's encounters.

Many personal scores were raised as a result of the 81 enemy aircraft shot down by the Eighth's fighters during this first great air battle over Berlin. Mahurin's Focke-Wulf brought his score to 17, but 1/Lt Robert Johnson, also of the 56th, had been credited with two victories and equalled Mahurin as leading ace of the Command. The 353rd Group's commander, Colonel Glenn Duncan, was another ace who added two victories on this mission, to make 15. At this date, 56th's Lt Col Francis Gabreski and Major Gerald Johnson had 14 each, Zemke had 11, while Lt Col Dave Schilling and Major Leroy Schreiber (62nd Ftr. Sqdn. CO) had won 10 each. The highest

The man who conducted VIII FC's first strafing with a P-47, Quince Brown, in one of his aircraft named *Okie*. He was to emerge as 78th FG's top scoring ace.—(USAF)

score achieved by a 78th Group pilot so far was still the 9 of Lt Col Eugene Roberts. This brilliant pilot who at one time led the field was never presented with another opportunity to score a victory during his tour, finally being taken off operations after 87 missions. The 78th's current ace was Quince L. Brown with 5; he was the pilot who had first used the Thunderbolt for strafing back in July 1943. All these were men who had earned fame at the controls of a Thunderbolt, but already the Mustang was being used to good effect to promote the personal scores of two 4th Group pilots. One was Captain Duane Beeson of the 334th Ftr. Sqdn. who was renowned for his expert deflection shooting. While the 4th was bemoaning its plight at having been saddled with P-47s, Beeson slowly set about building himself the highest score in the group and now had 14. His closest rival in the 4th was Captain Don Gentile of the 336th Ftr. Sqdn., also one of the original transferees from the Eagle Squadrons. On every mission there was keen rivalry between the 334th and 336th Squadrons to see whose champion would collect the honours.

The rivalry between units and pilots in the matter of shooting down or shooting up enemy aircraft, gave the impression they were engaged in a sport rather than bitter and bloody conflict. Press releases often made it appear so, by making public facts and figures about the fortunes of the groups and the high scoring fighter aces. Security forbade the mention of unit numbers at this time, but identity was established by the names of commanding officers, e.g., 'the Zemke Group' or 'the Blakeslee outfit'. The achievements of one group provided others with an incentive to do better and paid handsome dividends in esprit de corps and establishing an aggressive spirit. Supposedly interested only in team work, VIII Fighter Command nonetheless appreciated that the basis of a unit's morale often stemmed from the successes of individuals.

To encourage ground strafing the Command decided that an enemy aircraft destroyed on an airfield would rate equal to an air victory in unit and personal scores. Thereby a pilot could reach acehood by destroying 5 enemy aircraft whether on the ground or in the air. There was no doubt that ground strafing a heavily defended airfield was far more dangerous than air-to-air combat. Many pilots, perhaps most, declared that once the art of shooting at a stationary target had been learned, success became chiefly a matter of luck. Some pilots refused to count their ground victories equal to those obtained in air combat and went so far as to use different forms of symbol in signifying their victories on personal aircraft. The fact remains that VIII FC pilots needed little encouragement to harrow the Luftwaffe's bases. The combined in-the-air and on-the-ground offensive had a catastrophic effect upon the fortunes of the Luftwaffe, as will be related.

Having made a limited job of bombing their targets on the 6th, the Eighth's bombers returned to the German capital two days later when at last the weather offered an opportunity for visual bombing. Luftwaffe opposition was strong but little was seen of the ZG and NJG units whose twin-engined aircraft had suffered so heavily on the previous raid. Fighter claims against the enemy were high—79. Again, the Mustangs bore the brunt of the fighting over Berlin. The 4th came back with 15 victories; four the work of Don Gentile and two by his sharp-eyed wingman, John Godfrey. Gentile ribbed news reporters with, "There were so many enemy planes up there today that we were choosy about which ones we shot down". The "Wolfpack" did even better and returned to Halesworth with a bag of 27; it also suffered its heaviest loss since its mauling by J.G.2 in June 1943. Between Dummer and Steinhuder Lakes, the Luftwaffe had sprung a trap. Between 20 to 25 of its fighters, leaving contrails, were seen at about 30,000 ft heading for the bombers and the 56th climbed to intercept. Several other Staffeln lurked below the altitude at which contrails formed, and so remained unseen until they commenced a vicious attack upon the 56th. Mahurin shot down

"Top Brass" visited Halesworth on 14 Mar. 1944, to see the new 150 gall. drop tanks. L. to r.: Doolittle, Auton (65 FW CO), Schilling, Spaatz and Zemke.—(USAF)

two enemy aircraft this day to become the first pilot in the Eighth Air Force to have a total of 20 victories. Most of the Group's victories were obtained by waiting in the vicinity of German airfields for the enemy aircraft to return to base. Five of the 56th's P-47s were lost.

Berlin the target for the 9th, when dense cloud veiled most of northern Europe, brought the comment from Blakeslee, "The only land we saw from the time we left our airdrome until we returned to it were the peaks of mountains standing from clouds south of Berlin. The clouds were so thick they formed a four-mile-deep floor over the continent". The Luftwaffe did not put in an appearance. The weather continued to be unsuitable for visual attacks in the Berlin area and the Eighth turned to other targets.

At a critique on this Berlin mission it was considered that the escort flew too close to the bombers to intercept enemy fighters before they attacked. On the Brunswick mission of March 15th, new tactics were introduced. The escort squadrons flew well ahead and out to either side of the bombers. The 56th had not lost the magic touch and claimed 24 of the 35 credited to the escorting fighters. 1/Lt Robert S. Johnson made three kills and with 21 victories replaced Mahurin as the leading American ace in England.

Since the former leading ace, Walter Beckham of 353rd Group went down on a strafing attack the previous month, his superior, Colonel Glenn Duncan, had come to the conclusion that there was a lot to be gained from the establishment of a special squadron, to develop and specialise in the art of ground strafing. He put the idea through to General Kepner who ordered Duncan to go ahead. Four volunteers, one each drawn from the 353rd, 355th, 359th and 361st Groups, assembled on March 18th at Metfield. Officially known as the 353rd "C" Fighter Group and headed by Duncan himself, it was not long in gathering the nickname "Bill's Buzz Boys"—Bill being General Kepner.

The new unit began by practising low flying, with Metfield as a mock target, coming in at hedge-top height and making life hectic for the personnel of the 353rd to say nothing of neighbouring cattle. The squadron experimented around the UK and then, between March 26th and April 12th, flew six successful strafing missions in which ideas were put to the test. The pattern that evolved was first to become thoroughly conversant with the layout, local landmarks, and known flak installations in the area of the selected target. In action, when about 20 miles from the target, one flight would dive down from 15,000 feet gaining speed in excess of 400 mph and levelling out to skim in across the countryside from five miles distant, usually in line abreast. The element of surprise usually achieved by these attacks gave opportunities of shooting up aircraft or vehicles in their path before the enemy was alerted. Ground fire was a serious problem, but providing the P-47s continued to fly low until out of range, the effect could be minimised. It was decided that an airfield should only be attacked by a single pass if losses were to be kept low, and not advisable to attack other defended installations in the vicinity, since these were often alerted by the first attack. During the initial six raids, 14 enemy aircraft and 36 trains were shot up. Three P-47s were lost—one hit a house—but a pilot who baled out over the Channel was saved; 13 P-47s received some sort of damage. On April 12th the special unit was officially disbanded and pilots and aircraft returned to their home stations. Enough effective work had been done and lessons learned for VIII FC to plan strafing operations on a large scale.

In addition to its work in developing ground strafing tactics, the 353rd was still experimenting with the P-47 as a bomb carrying vehicle. The new wing shackles, though primarily intended for carrying drop tanks, could support a 1,000 lb bomb each. To find how the aircraft would fare with these, Colonel Duncan and his deputy Lt Col Rimmerman set off on March 15th to conduct trials much to the discomfort of an unfortunate barge that they came upon in the Zuider Zee. A shallow dive was made and one bomb released from 12,000 ft, then one from 8,000 ft. and two from 1,500 ft. No direct hits were scored but the last two came very near to hitting. The experiments did prove, however, that it was feasible to use the P-47 with externally slung bombs in dive attacks.

The 361st FG caused havoc and these pictures at Chartres on 17 Mar. 1944. As bullets from one P-47 hit a flak tower they also narrowly miss the element leader who turned in front of his wingman. Impressed LeO 45 is getting hits as element leader pulls up after attack. —(USAF)

The deadly duo—Gentile and Godfrey arrive back at Debden after a mission.—(Meehan)

March and April 1944 were decisive months in the struggle for air superiority, few days passed without action by US fighters based in England. While the Luftwaffe showed signs of exhaustion after the battles of "Big Week" and "Berlin" VIII FC, aided by groups of IX FC, went from strength to strength.

When the US bombers struck deep into Germany on March 16th to hit Augsburg and Friedrichshafen, the Luftwaffe decided to meet force with force. Success against the bombers was achieved at high cost for 75 German fighters were claimed by the American fighters. The 4th's Mustangs despatched 13 of these, while the 354th decimated a formation of Me110s near Augsburg. For the rest of March it was the Debden Group that almost daily took the major share of victories. In fact, from the 18th to the end of March 100 claims were made by the 4th. During the same period the 56th was only able to claim ten.

Successes with the Mustang had transformed the 4th. They were now probably the most aggressive group in the Command and were intent on bettering the 56th's score. Just how eager, is shown by the events of March 21st when weather limited operations. Lt Col James Clark, an old Eagle Squadron man and deputy CO of the Group, sought permission from 65th Fighter Wing to run a strafing sweep to the Bordeaux area of France. Being granted, 48 P-51Bs set out under Clark. Of the 41 that attacked, 7 failed to return, mostly victims of ground fire at the enemy aerodromes attacked. Twelve hostile aircraft were hit in the air as they prepared to land or had just taken off, and more were destroyed on the ground. Except for a small escort sent to cover a few B-24s bombing the Pas de Calais, no other US fighters were over the Continent that day.

On the morrow another mission by the heavies to Berlin brought little opposition and those enemy airfields that did put in an appearance kept well away from the escort. The Luftwaffe rose to meet the bombers heading for Brunswick next day and the 4th took the honours with 13 for 0. The Commander of J.G.3, Oberst Wilcke with 162 victories, fell to the guns of a P-51 that day. The 4th followed their success up with a trip to Bordeaux on the 27th where 26 enemy aircraft were claimed and a similar fate befell another 24 on another haul to Brunswick on the 29th. The newly-acquired red paint on the spinners of their Mustangs was a distinctive marking that the Luftwaffe was beginning to know only too well. Their 300th victory was reached on April 1st when Beeson, Hofer and Gentile contributed the three victories of that day. This score also put Gentile one ahead of the 56th's Robert Johnson and thus gave the 4th the highest scoring ace in the business.

Chapter 16: Assembling for Action

On March 23rd, the Eighth's bombers made for Brunswick and aircraft plants in Germany. Through a miscalculation the 3rd Division commenced penetration early and in consequence flew unescorted except for five minutes in the Dummer Lake area on its withdrawal. It suffered for its error which was exploited by the enemy. But evidence of a decline in Luftwaffe prowess was evident when Schweinfurt was visited the following morning. This target name had fearful associations and the mission was embarked upon apprehensively; yet the only report of an enemy fighter attack was a single incident involving a straggling B-17. Of the three Fortresses missing two resulted from mid-air collision.

The incidence of collisions had risen with the increase in aircraft and were becoming an all too common occurrence.

with the sudden influx of new groups these difficulties grew, resulting in a few groups having to fly to areas some distance from their bases before attempting to orbit, to relieve congestion. The Second Division had to extend its area well over the North Sea. Even so, bombers would frequently pick up the wrong formation in the half-light of dawn and the muddle could become so great that missions were abandoned. A succession of coloured flares were fired by lead aircraft as an aid to assembly and in the 2nd Division, in particular, the practice of having a special aircraft for this purpose was widespread. Known as Forming Ships, Circus Leaders or Judas Goats, but mostly as Assembly Ships, these were combat-retired Liberators, at first B-24Ds. All armour and armament was removed to reduce weight and many lights, laid out to form the shape of

Men of the 445th BG gather round as Lt Sam Miller brings 42-110037, IS: B + to a halt. Miller and crew had just completed their 25th mission, first crew at Tibenham to finish a tour of duty.—(USAF)

This danger was soon brought home to the freshman 466th Group. Its maiden mission to Berlin on March 22nd proved a far gentler initiation than that experienced by other groups who had cross-Channel "break-ins". Only the collision of two B-24s en route marred this trip. Out after a German airfield next day, another two 466th bombers collided near Osterburg. Then, on the 27th when the Eighth launched heavy raids on airfields in France, yet another two Attlebridge B-24s hit in cloud while forming up, taking crews to their deaths in fields at Hoe and Cressenhall. Six aircraft went down in five days and all without intervention by the enemy. Pilot error was behind most of these tragic happenings; constant vigilance was necessary, more so in poor visibility, if they were to be avoided. Replacement pilots and those in new units were particularly vulnerable for, imbued with the necessity for tight formations during training in the less demanding aerial environment of continental USA, they were flying too close to their neighbours. A heavily laden bomber, momentarily unbalanced by turbulence, had little room for safe recovery in a close-knit formation. Despite warnings and all attempts to reduce these accidents, collisions remained a feature of Eighth Air Force operations until the last days of the war.

Many collisions occurred during assembly as a result of single aircraft and even formations becoming lost and crossing the paths of others. Assembly always presented problems and

the group identification letters, were installed on either side and in the roof of the fuselage. Further, the whole machine was painted in the most bizarre way with either stripes, checkerboard or polka dot schemes, each group having its own. Some of these aircraft must be good contenders for the most exotic paint job ever carried by a warplane.

It was the procedure, prior to a mission, for the Assembly Ship to be first off the airfield, to fly to the assembly area and commence orbiting with its signs illuminated, while the crew fired a continual succession of flares from the large supply carried. When the formation was complete the Assembly Ship

At 20,000 ft *E-rat-icator* heads for Bordeaux airfield, 27 Mar. 1944. She was destined to be the only original aircraft of 452nd BG to survive the war.—(USAF)

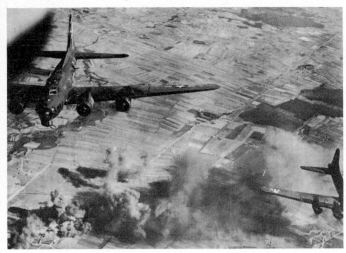

GY: K of 306th BG leaves the buildings of Dijon airfield veiled in smoke; 28 Mar. 1944.—(IWM)

would break away and return to base. Several of these machines expired in flames; there being a high fire risk with the vast number of pyrotechnics carried.

This was one use for tired bombers and others, likewise stripped of weapons, served as ambulances, target tugs and liaison transports. Most Fortress groups had one of the early B-17Es assigned for such duties at this date. Not all the veterans were non-combatant: a few that had flown the pioneer missions had surprisingly survived the flak and fighters for more than a year. The supreme champion was *Knock Out Dropper* which had returned to Molesworth on March 27th having completed its 75th mission, the first Fortress in the Eighth Air Force to reach this figure. This was one of the two remaining B-17Fs that the 303rd Group had brought to England in September 1942. In the course of the 75 missions the aircraft had hauled 150 tons of bombs and amassed 675 hours of combat flying, while none of the many crew members involved had been killed or even wounded. This veteran was by then in a war-weary state and due for retirement in the US. Another bomber flown back was *Bomerang*, the 93rd Group's record breaking B-24D, which took some of the Group's airmen on a War Bond drive tour of industrial cities. Among the men selected, was her crew chief, M/Sgt Charles Chambers, who helped save it from the scrap heap after its first mission and who had nursed her through another 52.

Preparation for Overseas Movement inspector did such a thorough job with 467th BG personnel prior to their leaving the US, as to inspire the nickname of the aircraft that prepared the Group's formations for regular 'overseas movements' from England.—(Gile)

During March the Eighth's bombers had been active on 23 days, involving 11,943 sorties, pushing a monthly bomb tonnage up to well over 20,000. Conditions, however, had allowed less than half to be dropped visually. The cost, 349 heavies missing in action or lost in crashes in England, was equivalent to the complements of between five and six bomber groups. Allied intelligence agencies believed—and there appeared ample evidence from photographs of ruined and gutted factories—that German fighter production had been severely curtailed, and that this, coupled with losses through air combat, had brought insuperable difficulties for the Luftwaffe. At the end of the month General Doolittle reflected the beliefs of his command when he broadcast to the US: *Our immediate goal is the destruction or neutralisation of the German Air Force, the one factor which might have defeated our purpose had it been permitted to develop and expand according to known German plans. In most of our recent operations, the German fighters have shown little inclination to come up and fight, an indication that their losses are now exceeding their replacements and that they are conserving their forces.*

448th BG's Assembly Ship was named *You Cawn't Miss It,* after an oft encountered English saying. In normal olive drab finish she had previously served with 44th BG.—(USAF)

Unknown to the Allies, the German fighter aircraft production although disrupted was still meeting Luftwaffe needs; the vast expansion programme and dispersal of production facilities initiated the previous year having borne fruit. It was in trained manpower that the German fighter arm was experiencing serious shortages; fuel economies at training establishments and rush courses lowered pilot quality. Shortcomings in personnel and of material was the primary reason for the lessening of opposition to the Eighth's raids noted by Doolittle.

Officially, the coming of April marked the end of the Combined Bomber Offensive and the Eighth Air Force, together with the other strategic forces, passed to the overall command of the Supreme Allied Commander; but as yet this did not directly affect the pattern of operations. During the first week of April only the 2nd and 3rd Divisions conducted operations in the unsettled weather. On the last two days of March they had been scheduled for pathfinder missions to Ludwigshafen but conditions proved too bad, and an All Fool's Day encounter with cloud tops at 21,000 ft caused this mission to be abandoned for the third day running. The B-24s did continue, but got badly off course and 38 machines of the 44th and 392nd Groups mistakenly bombed Schaffhausen in Switzerland, an incident of which Nazi propaganda made much. One of ten B-24s missing that day carried the 448th Group Commander, Colonel James Thompson.

For six days thereafter the heavy piled cloud confined Eighth bomber activity to the familiar NOBALL targets on the French coast. Not until the 8th did 1st Division return to the fight after having been stood down for five days and held down by weather for four. From all divisions, 644 heavies were launched at air depots and aircraft targets in Western Germany, notably

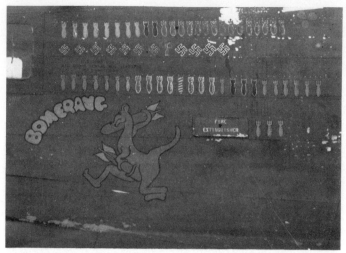

Record of the most distinguished B-24 in the Eighth. Victory symbols are for 11 German and one Italian fighter. 53 bomb symbols for missions: first 8 yellow bombs for operations from UK, 2 black bombs for Tunisian based operations, 15 outline bombs for Lybia, 7 yellow for England again, 8 for further Lybian missions—with a striped bomb for the low level Ploesti raid, a single yellow for the UK again, black for more Tunisian missions and the rest for UK operations. Green Shamrock leaf under cockpit is for visit to Northern Ireland modification base.—(USAF)

Brunswick where the Liberators were met by fierce fighter attacks. The Brunswick area had become notorious for the frequency and calibre of air opposition which was seen to be, by debators at the evening recreational establishments on bomber bases, the handiwork of one elite Nazi unit—"The Battling Bastards of Brunswick"—who were looked upon with the same awe as that reserved for the "Yellow-nosed Goering Squadron". Whichever Luftwaffe unit this was, they invariably cost the bombers dear, as on this occasion when the still green 466th Group lost six B-24s.

For 2/Lt Claude V. Meconis, co-pilot of the *Snark*, this was his second mission. That night he recorded his feelings in his diary: "They don't come any harder than the one we flew today to Brunswick. The Jerries threw everything they had at us, fighters and flak. It was a big 'maximum effort' raid our operations had long predicted. Well, it came today, on Holy Saturday. Personally, I'll remember it as Unholy Saturday! At the outset, things were in the usual mess. We took off an hour later than expected, through a ground haze that wasn't quite thick enough to be fog. The delay was caused by armament, who didn't have enough time to load up the bombs. The field order came through at 4 a.m. and we were originally scheduled out at 8.30 am. Though we had CAVU all the way up to altitude our assembly was 'poor' (they have a better word for it at

413th BS provided Pathfinder aircraft for 3rd Division during the spring of 1944. It suffered a high rate of attrition. One new B-17G collided with another Fortress at Rattlesden on 6 Apr. 1944. Wrecked H2X radome hangs in the mud.—(USAF)

briefing) and we didn't have anything near so good formation when we crossed the Channel and saw the Zuider Zee below us. About then prop wash from other wings began bothering us, causing planes to cavort all over the sky, just missing each other and putting our hearts in our throats more than once. Our formation was all over. We were simply asking for trouble —and we sure got it later.

"We were quite a way into Germany before I spotted enemy fighters. Evidently our P-47 escort had seen several rising to meet us. They tangled in a dogfight thousands of feet below; then I saw one plane, followed by another, dive away in a half roll, down—down, and then disappear in a gob of oily smoke and flame as it crashed to earth. First plane I'd ever seen shot down. I could feel the presence of opposition coming at us.

"We arrived at the wing IP fairly well in what might, by a stretch of imagination, pass for a formation. As we began turning I got a good look at what a thousand (*sic*) planes look like all over the sky. Also saw the city of Hanover on our right covered by a smoke screen. We had just completed our turn when the boys began calling off 'one . . . two . . . three . . . B-24s going down'. I saw them go down from a group far off on our right, two of them blazing balls of fire and the third sickeningly flopping and spinning down. I couldn't believe my eyes—that last one looked just like a Nazi fighter going down, except that it fell too slowly. We knew fighters were attacking us but didn't see any close until later.

"We were almost over the target when real trouble hit. What looked like a P-47 escort high on our left changed devilishly into a pack of Me109s, who peeled off, about three or four to a queue, and came through our loose formation like lightning, machine guns and 20 mm cannon firing like hell. What a sight—to see those noses pointed right at our plane, and a second later that same nose screaming by almost close enough to touch! Enough to make a believer out of anyone.

"They continued to make passes at us, coming head-on and then following up from 4 o'clock on the rear. I tried to keep the boys informed on interphone, but I'm afraid they were too busy half the time, and I sounded too excited the other half. Miller (bombardier) let go with the nose guns at first, and I could see his tracer cone crackling at the 109. Damn Jerry was nervy, kept right on coming, his nose cannon spitting shells. I heard a loud bang on our left. Miller's guns jammed after that first burst, so he never got another shot.

"Number 1 supercharger conked out. Calderalo (tail gunner) saw more B-24s going down, some of them stragglers. We were having our share of hard luck trying to keep near the ship ahead of us, despite terrific prop wash from the group ahead. I was plenty worried, couldn't help ducking when a fighter made his pass at us. Wished I had a gun to shoot back—not much fun just sitting there ducking by instinct. I wondered what in hell had happened to our escort. Evidently the Jerries had lured them below, where the boys reported many dogfights in progress.

"Brunswick on our left had a solid ball of flak smoke, two thousand feet in diameter, over it. It didn't look as if a plane could go through it. We only hit the light stuff and white rocket flak bursts to the north of the town. Our target was an aircraft plant housed in a hangar on a field north of Brunswick, but we dropped our bombs all over Germany, some of them on another field. We didn't see the results because we were too busy. Only glad to be rid of the heavy load.

"Rooney, our radioman, must have been hit just before our radio was shot out. I turned to attract his attention and saw Shorty (engineer gunner) working on him. From the cockpit I couldn't tell where he'd been hit, but could see his pained face. Hoped he hadn't been hit in the stomach. I told Dike to carry on alone and, after fighting to loosen my shoes which were tangled in the seat, got out of the cockpit to help Shorty, who was picking away at Rooney's pants with a jacknife. I took the knife, slashed Rooney's shorts open, gave Shorty the first

Might of the Eighth, outward bound. Beyond 42-99982, RR: H + and YO: G of 389th BG, a whole combat wing of B-17s can be seen.

Beyond this brand new 'silver' 91st BG Fortress more than a hundred B-17s and B-24s can be seen joining the bomber stream. B-17s of 381st BG in foreground.—(USAF)

Crew of the *Snark*. Back row (l. to r.): Dike, pilot; Meconis, co-pilot; Brooks, navigator; Miller, bombardier; Thompson, engineer. Front row: Rooney, radio op.; Calderalo, tail gunner; Bertie, waist gunner; Beavers, ball gunner; and Smith, waist gunner.—(Meconis)

aid kit, told him to sprinkle sulfanilamide powder on the wound and, at Rooney's request, went back to the cockpit.

"So there we were—no radio, no interphone, no nose guns, little gas, wounded radio operator, constant fighter attacks, and difficulty staying in formation. Plenty to keep us worried. The 109s followed us back to Holland, pecking at our rear all the time. Before our interphone went out Cal reported they killed a straggler.

"When we reached the Channel and the Jerry fighters turned back, Shorty reported that the ball turret was down and that Beavers and Smith, our gunners, had been wounded by fragments of a 20 mm shell that burst in the waist after severing the interphone system and turret hydraulic lines. The news gave us worries anew—just after we had begun relaxing. The turret ball had to be raised before landing. Miller went back to help, and returned later to report the turret up again. We lost altitude quickly over the Channel after breaking away from our formation. Just trying to conserve gas with low power settings. England sure looked good when its coast slid under us.

"Plain and simple—everyone agreed it had been a rough day. Beavers, Caderalo, and Bertie got a fighter apiece; Miller damaged one. All I got was grey hair and a 'slight' increase in blood pressure."

On this occasion the Fortresses had a comparatively easy time although for one returning crew the ball turret produced problems. The B-24 ball retracted; that on the B-17 did not and therefore when a wheels up landing had to be made the turret had to be severed to make touch-down safer and less damaging to the aircraft. This was the situation facing 2/Lt Leslie Bond when the undercarriage of *Carolina Queen* refused to lower upon arriving over Ridgewell. Unfortunately, it was discovered that the special tools needed for jettisoning the turret were not on board. When Bond notified the control

tower of his plight, the air executive, Lt Col Conway Hall, decided to try an aerial transfer operation. Taking off in a liaison aircraft, he flew over the orbiting Fortress for 15 minutes while an attempt was made with a hundred foot rope to lower the tools in a soil ballasted bag into the open radio room hatch of the bomber. The slipstream proved too great, but Hall believed that with more ballast and a longer rope there was still a good chance of success. Having landed and made the necessary changes he took off again, this time in a Fortress so that relative speeds could be more easily matched. After half an hour his crew hit their target and Sgt W. R. Jones, *Carolina Queen's* radio operator, was ready with a knife to cut the rope and secure the bag. After jettisoning the turret over the sea, Bond brought his bomber in for a belly landing with minimum damage.

Carolina Queen was one of the new aircraft left in bare natural metal finish that were fast becoming a common sight in England. The familiar olive drab and neutral grey camouflage finish had been dispensed with primarily because its weight and drag took several mph from performance. Authorities in the US considered the value of camouflage colours extremely doubtful and their omission also made production economies. Initially these views were certainly not shared by crews who had to fly the naked bombers. The first "silver" bombers had arrived in February, but due to aircrew apprehension that they were bound to attract the attention of enemy fighters many groups did not despatch them on missions until a whole flight or more was available. By April replacements arriving at B-17 bases were almost exclusively in bare metal finish.

On several occasions the Eighth had reached out along the north of the Nazi empire to strike aircraft factories near the Baltic coast. Some, such as Marienburg, had been hit with much success. Others had been damaged, but one, the FW190

Carolina Queen bellies in at Ridgewell: 8 Apr. 1944.—(USAF)

component factory at Poznan just inside the Polish border was, so far, unscathed having been befriended by clouds on the four occasions when the 1,800 mile round trip had been undertaken. On April 9th a visual bombing of Poznan, Marienburg and other important aircraft plants in the area appeared worth a try and 542 heavies left England with the proviso that, if thwarted, Rostock with its good radar image should be sought. Third Division wings which had previously been concerned were again briefed for the elusive objective, but once again it appeared that it was to elude its seekers with a canopy of cloud. Layer upon layer confronted the Fortresses after crossing the Danish coast and one complete combat wing and some boxes from the leading 45th Wing abandoned the operation. The leading 96th Group, with a composite box of 388th and 452nd Group aircraft, continued onwards and were somewhat surprised to find it possible to discern their primary objective clearly. In spite of a flak barrage, damaging 13 of the 33 aircraft attacking, aiming was good with 28% of bombs striking within 1,000 ft of the aiming point and 71% within 2,000 ft, destroying many buildings used for fuselage assembly. When 900 miles from home, the formation received radio orders to join the 1st Division force which had been attacking Marienburg, as it could afford it some protection. Before making contact the 45th Wing ran the gauntlet of enemy fighters vectored to their small unescorted formation but came through with the loss of only two B-17s. For the 96th Group, which a few days earlier had entertained Spaatz, Doolittle and Le May at Snetterton Heath to celebrate the attainment of 100 missions, this attack on Poznan was possibly their most successful operation.

Flak damaged *Piccadilly Pete* of 448th BG was brought to rest on her tail skid when her pilots sought the sanctuary of Bulltofta airfield in Sweden; 9 Apr. 1944.

Liberators of 467th Group commenced operations on April 10th, as part of the 730 strong fleet seeking aviation targets in France and the Low Countries; on the morrow, they added their numbers to swell the bomber force to record proportions when the Eighth Air Force again strove to annihilate centres of aircraft production in Eastern Germany. Over 900 B-17s and B-24s, sent to six plants concerned with Focke-Wulf and Junkers aircraft assembly, were given six P-51 and four P-38 fighter groups as escort; but with the bomber force so divided the escort was hardly adequate. And this was one of the occasions when the Luftwaffe intervened with considerable skill. There was little weather improvements over that of the previous mission to this area and some bombing had to be accomplished by radar. The 45th and 13th Wings, again briefed for Poznan, found it had regained its cloud shield; so the American ordnance was deflected to Rostock. In the absence of Mustangs, these wings were assailed by rocket-firing Me410s and Ju88s, followed by line abreast frontal passes by FW190s. Vicious and ordered, this assault accounted for most of the 25 bombers missing from these two wings and, as if in retribution for its success two days before, the 96th Group was punished to the tune of ten.

Cottbus and Sorau held targets for 88 1st Division B-17s with 131 tons of high explosive and incendiaries which destroyed half the production facilities at the Sorau Focke-Wulf plant. Elsewhere, other formations of this Division were not so fortunate in finding visual conditions at primaries. The 40th Wing was also unfortunate in that when it turned unescorted for Stettin, it was caught by Zestörers of Z.G.26 which proceeded to disperse and despatch the formation with rockets and heavy cannon.

Bertie Lee, piloted by 1/Lt Edward Michael, one of the 305th Group Fortresses, riddled with cannon shells from a frontal pass, was sent spinning earthwards out of control. Fighters following it down, closed in for the kill. A cannon shell exploding against a starboard window wounded both pilot and co-pilot. Instruments were wrecked and vision was impaired by a film of hydraulic oil forming on the windshield. After losing 3,000 feet the pilots managed to pull the bomber out of its dive only to find that part of the incendiary bomb load had taken fire. The emergency release lever failed to jettison the bombs and as the aircraft appeared doomed, Michael commanded the crew to bale out. The top turret gunner then appeared in the cockpit with terrible head wounds and holding one of his eyes which had been shot out of its socket in his hand. In spite of his own wounds, Michael aided the injured gunner to the nose hatch and helped him jump. Seven men left the bomber but the wounded bombardier, Lt Leiber, found that his parachute had been badly damaged by shell fragments. Seeing this, Michael decided to try a crash landing and the co-pilot, 2/Lt Westberg, elected to remain on board to assist. While the bombardier managed to free the burning incendiaries, Michael flew the Fortress in violent evasive manoeuvres whenever an enemy fighter attempted to attack, and after 45 minutes managed to gain the sanctuary of a cloud bank to escape his tormentors.

At reduced altitude the aircraft was an inviting target for flak, so after emerging from cloud *Bertie Lee* was taken down to a few hundred feet above the French countryside where it would also be possible to make an emergency landing if the situation deteriorated. But the aircraft flew on and there seemed a good chance of getting it home across the Channel. All this time Michael had been bleeding profusely from the right thigh and now began losing consciousness through exhaustion. Westburg took over and brought the aircraft to England, found an RAF airfield and circled it while the bombardier tried to revive the pilot so that he could be consulted about the landing —both undercarriage and flaps were inoperative, the bomb bay doors were jammed fully open, there was no air speed indicator and the ball turret was jammed with guns pointing downwards. A successful crash-landing under such circum-syances was doubtful but there was no alternative. Michael insisted he had enough strength to make the landing himself and skilfully brought the bomber down on its belly despite the danger from crumpling bomb doors and protruding turret guns. This feat brought him the second Medal of Honor awarded to a member of the 305th.

Bertie Lee never flew again but had returned, whereas 52 B-17s, 12 B-24s and 16 fighters had not. The total loss equalled the record loss of the Berlin epic of March 6th. The Germans claimed 129, 105 as bombers. Bomber gunners were allowed 73-24-33 and the fighters 51 in combat against approximately 200 enemy fighters involved.

There was no respite after this long mission of nearly eleven hours for within a few hours the bombers were once again flying to aircraft targets, this time in Central Germany. This venture, however, was short lived, as weather conditions caused the mission to be abandoned, but not before some Liberators had been intercepted near the French/German border.

On April 13th the offensive was switched to Southern Germany. The 3rd Division had to pass through heavy and accurate anti-aircraft fire to bomb the Messerschmitt plant at Augsburg so that although it succeeded in its task, several bombers went down and a high proportion of the others were damaged; ten limped into Switzerland. Sixty B-24s managed to destroy storage and repair buildings at Dornier's Oberpfaffen-hofen factory, while others went for the important air base at Lechfeld. The First Division went to Schweinfurt where the 41st Wing was given a sample of the mass frontal assault which the Luftwaffe was perfecting. The Wing leader, Colonel Maurice Preston, CO of the 379th Group who had been combat flying since the previous May, considered this the most severe fighter attack he had ever witnessed. The enemy approached at Geschwader strength and concentrated on the high group, the 384th, shooting down eight Fortresses.

After this week of intensive activity against the German Air Force and the industry that sustained it, unsuitable weather enforced a lull. A pause was sorely needed at the bomber bases. Engineering staff were hard put to keep up with the repairs necessitated by the tremendous amount of battle damage accumulated over the past few days. Aircrew were in need of rest, particularly pilots and navigators. Flying forma-tion in a B-17 or B-24 was hard work, both physically and mentally; the concentration required of a lead navigator on a seven or eight hour mission was exhausting to the extent that many of these men spent the greater part of their off duty time in "the sack". Some who completed their 30 missions in a short period of time never went far, when at base, beyond the confines of their barracks.

Chapter 17: Flak Fortissimo

Early on April 18th the base operations teletape machines, producing the Field Orders from Divisional HQ, began to chatter again—primary objectives aero-engine and electrical plants in the Berlin area. With one exception, the 745 bombers heading for "Big B" did not lure the Luftwaffe to battle. The exception was a tribute to the enemy controller's up-to-the-minute knowledge of the position and strength of formations as a mission progressed inland, and his ability to exploit any weaknesses that occurred. Near the IP, the 3rd Division found its way barred by a high bank of cloud with tops at 30,000 feet. The leading combat wing, the 4th "A", elected to fly through this front but the second and subsequent wings decided it was too great an obstacle and turned for targets of opportunity. The fighter escort was confused but eventually turned with the trailing wings. On emerging from the cloud the lead wing groups—two 94th and one 385th Group boxes—were well separated, alone and on the wrong heading. Almost immediately, at 13.00 hrs in the Havel area, north-west of Berlin, the third box came face to face with a substantial force of FW190s led by Major Friedrich Müller, an ace claiming 130 victories.

In a half hour battle the fighters of J.G.3 claimed 31 B-17s destroyed (three by Müller) and reported that nine escaped into the clouds. Further, the German press announced that this number of wrecks, plus those of two US fighters, had been found in the area. Total German claims of heavy bombers shot down were 43, but actual US losses were only 19. The most J.G.3 could have been responsible for were the eight Fortresses of 94th Group and two pathfinders missing—a third of the German claims. Claims by Luftwaffe fighter units were invariably inflated during the winter of 1943-1944 while those made by ground defences were often near to the truth. There is little doubt that the German fighter pilots believed their claims and while errors in assessing were inevitable, the Luftwaffe's methods appear to have been reasonably sound. One suspects that other agencies with an eye to morale and propaganda were responsible for promoting claims.

Having pursued its campaign against aircraft targets with much success on the 19th the Eighth was forced on the 22nd to turn its attention to a lower priority target, west German marshalling yards, notably Hamm, scene of their first venture into the Ruhr early the previous year. The despatch of this

When Lt Furnace reached Attlebridge on 19 Apr. 1944 after flak had 'shot out' two engines and all hydraulic pressure was lost, there was nothing for it but to make a wheels-up landing on the grass in 90° crosswind conditions. Unfortunately the B-24, after touchdown, continued to slide along, broadside on, until its back broke. The crew emerged unhurt but the flak gunner's intentions towards *Shack Rat* were achieved.—USAF)

force was delayed due to doubtful weather conditions, so that when the go-ahead was finally given the return to base was scheduled as darkness fell. The Luftwaffe had not seriously attempted attacks on the heavies over England or on their bases, although the odd incident had occurred in East Anglia. Single enemy intruders had bombed or strafed landing fields when runway lights were illuminated, but had usually achieved little result. Occasionally intruder sorties had more serious effects; indeed the early hours of April 12th saw a Ju88 down a pathfinder B-17 landing at Framlingham prior to the morning's mission.

On the 22nd, knowing that the heavies must land at their bases after light had faded, the Luftwaffe put up about fifteen Me410s to follow the Liberators of 2nd Division back to England. Shortly after 21.30 hrs the blows fell as the bombers made landfall along the Suffolk coast and as many entered the traffic patterns for landing. The first bursts of fire and flaming aircraft brought confusion to the bomber crews suddenly aware that the enemy was in their midst. Aircraft flew in all directions with some gunners firing wildly at any shape that appeared to be bearing down on them. Over Beccles a B-24 formation dropped flares, only to illuminate beneath them a Fortress group making haste to the west. Five bases were either bombed or strafed, those of the 20th Wing near the Waveney valley came in for most attention; five Liberators went down in this area alone in a short space of time. At Rackheath the newest group in the Division had a hectic homecoming; in the confusion two of its aircraft were brought down and another under repair on the ground was bombed, killing one man. Near Norwich anti-aircraft guns inadvertently brought down another B-24. Altogether nine B-24s were shot down or destroyed in crash-landings and two more bombed and shot up; another nine were damaged in the air; 38 men were killed and 23 wounded or injured. In reply, air gunners of the 448th Group had destroyed an Me410. The experience of this evening made mission planners ever mindful of the risks involved in bringing the bombers back after dark, and though night landings would occur again, the Germans never exploited the situation to the same degree against day bombers or with so much success.

Germany's aircraft industry and airfields in the Munich area had the attention of some 750 heavies on April 24th and the escort took a heavy toll of the large numbers of interceptors encountered. At Friedrichshafen the Germans repeated their successful screening of the town by sending a score of boats some five miles out on Lake Constance to discharge heavy smoke. The black smoke generated by bursting shells 25,000 ft above also greeted the 3rd Division Fortresses. Part of the 1st Division, headed for Oberpfaffenhofen, ran into an estimated 200 fighters and suffered grievously due to the enemy again bringing his forces to bear where the heavies flew without escort—and this formation was without for over an hour. The brunt fell on 41st "B" Wing, led and largely composed of 384th Group Fortresses: from the deadly head on passes and flak over the target this wing lost fifteen machines and for the second time in the month the 384th was sorely hurt, losing seven aircraft and having 19 crewmen wounded in the battered remnants regaining England. Aircraft of the 40th Wing in the same force also took heavy losses. Thirteen bombers of the overall losses were in Switzerland.

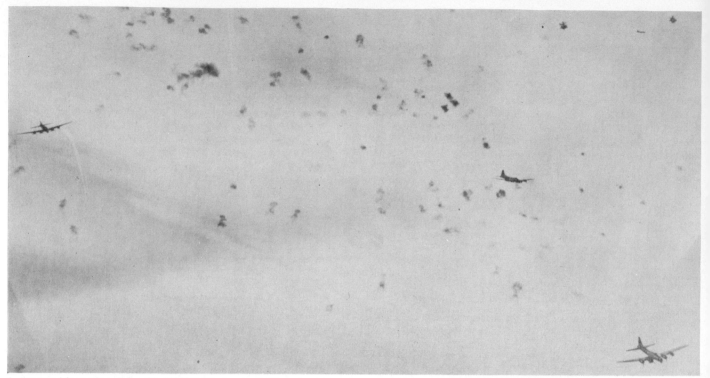

A dispersed formation of the 4th CBW B-17s received this welcome near Handorf airfield on 8 Apr. 1944. There are over 130 bursts in the picture, filling an area approximately half a mile square, with thousands of lethal steel splinters.—(IWM)

One of the hazards of bombing in formation was the danger of bombs striking other aircraft. Theoretically each bomber had its own "slot" in the formation to prevent this occurring, but aeroplanes moved out of their assigned positions, particularly in the heat of battle. 1/Lt Gordon Clubb of the 92nd Group thinking the flak over Oberpfaffenhofen too accurate, put his bomber in the way of two 500 lb GP bombs in the course of taking violent evasive action. One hit and knocked off most of one side of the tailplane and the other, hitting the wing root fairing near the dinghy stowage, glanced off and buried itself in No 3 engine. For sixty nerve-racking minutes the crew watched as their pilot tried to dislodge the bomb by jiggling the aircraft, a task made more difficult by the damage. Finally the bomb did fall out and after the machine made an emergency landing at Bradwell Bay the fuse was found still embedded in the engine.

When ten combat wings of heavies went to Brunswick on the 26th the Luftwaffe was absent in spite of reasonably fair weather. Even the flak gunners' aim was poor and for all the bombers to return safely from this notorious target was a notable event.

With lengthening hours of daylight the groups were able to undertake two separate missions for the first time on the 27th. The opening raids against transportation targets, a prerequisite to the cross-Channel invasion, were flown this day by 190 B-24s against rail yards at Blainville and Chalons-sur-Marne. Airfields and NOBALL sites were targets for other formations and for groups operating the following day when the growing numbers of anti-aircraft guns in these areas claimed twelve bombers. Colonel Robert H. Kelly, the "Bloody Hundredth's" CO of nine days, went down in one Fortress when two direct hits severed its rear fuselage and part of a wing.

If, in selecting Berlin as the target for the mission of April 29th the Eighth Air Force hoped to flush the Focke-Wulfs and Messerschmitts, they were certainly successful. Not since the early March missions had the enemy responded in such strength to a threat against his capital; on this morning he did so with a vengeance, taking his toll of bombers past the sixty mark for the second time in April. These losses were due principally from a dispersed bomber stream making the tight escort

schedule impossible, despite the direct route taken. Over 700 bombers flew above the overcast that extended all the way to Berlin, where they deposited 1,402 tons through the clouds. The 3rd Division, leading the mission, had trouble assembling and on penetration was so badly strung out that effective escort could not be maintained: one of its combat wings was fifteen minutes early and another 25 minutes late. Repeating the blunder of the previous Berlin mission, 4th "A" wing formation wandered over 40 miles south of the main force as a result of faulty navigation and paid the price. Near Magdeburg Focke-Wulfs struck and in 20 minutes shot down or fatally crippled 17 Fortresses. In the van, 385th Group (navigation was the responsibility of a pathfinder B-17 assigned to it from another group) lost seven in this attack, a bitter way to celebrate its hundredth mission. The rest of the formation were 447th Group B-17s of which eleven failed to return (one ditched and the crew was saved) to make the mission the most costly one of the war for the Rattlesden group.

The rest of 3rd Division's B-17s and all those of 1st Division had good fighter escort at hand for the whole mission and were unmolested by the Jagdverbände. The trailing 2nd Division was flying behind schedule and after leaving Celle had only a single group of P-51s to guard it. By the time the B-24s had bombed all planned escort had had to withdraw and, thirty minutes late, the bombers were on their own until met by P-47s near Dummer Lake. This lapse did not go unnoticed and near Hanover a hundred German fighters dealt so viciously with the Liberators that 25 failed to return.

One 44th Group Liberator was put down in the sea 40 miles north-east of Cromer by 1/Lt Richard Hruby. Ditching a B-24 was recommended only as a last resort as the flimsy bomb bay doors usually gave way on impact resulting in the aircraft being flooded in a few seconds or breaking in two. From the very rare partially successful B-24 ditchings in the North Sea only a few men had escaped. Hruby was lucky; somehow he managed to bring his Liberator to rest in one piece and the entire crew survived. While this was encouraging, chances of survival in a B-24 ditching were only about one to every ten in a B-17.

An estimated 300 enemy fighters operated against this Berlin mission and among units claiming victories was IV/J.G.3

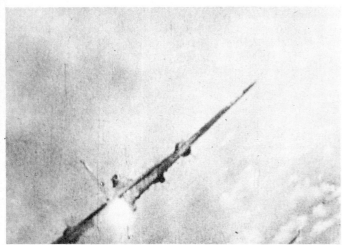

The Sturmgruppe scored a major success against 447th BG on 29 Apr. 1944. These pictures, taken from the gun camera film in Uff. Maximowitz's FW 190A-7, show cannon shells exploding along the fuselage and against the tail gunner's position of a floundering B-17. The first objective in an attack from the rear was to put the tail guns out of action. The last picture shows smoke coming from an engine as Maximowitz passes his victim.

formed at the beginning of the month, the Sturmgruppe led by Hptm. Wilhelm Moritz. This successful unit, specially trained and equipped to "storm" USAAF bomber boxes, developed from the experimental Sturmstaffel. The technique evolved, consisted of attacking head on at Gruppe strength (30 air-

craft) to take the maximum advantage of the initial surprise and saturate defensive fire from the bombers. Each pilot would pick out a suitable target and press his attack to very close quarters before breaking away. The FW190As used were heavily armed with four 20 mm cannon and had extra armour plate to give better protection to engine components and the pilot. The method was basically one of hit and run, but it required much skill and the results were impressive. Had such tactics been met a year previous the Eighth's campaign might quickly have come to grief. As it was, the Sturmgruppe could now only do its work properly when Allied escort fighters were absent. The extra weight of armour and armament reduced the performances of these Focke-Wulfs and it was the practice of other Gruppen in the Geschwader to act as an escort force to shield the Sturmgruppe from fighters.

To bomber airmen a change of month was but incidental; for them the passage of time was marked by the number of missions each still had to fly to complete an operational tour. For record purposes the end of a month is a demarkation point for assessment, and so far as April 1944 went it was a month of sustained aerial conflict that has no equal in the annals of the Eighth Air Force. It saw the highest claims against enemy fighters: 1223-142-763, and the highest expenditure in men and machines: 512 aircraft missing in action with another 65 written off as Category E (wrecked beyond repair). Of those lost, 361 were heavy bombers.

A disturbing fact, causing much concern was that 131 of these aircraft losses fell victims to flak—or to which flak was a contributory cause; whereas only eight were known to have been lost to flak in January, but the following month 54 instances had been recorded. Bomber credit sorties totalled 10,552 in March when 68 heavies were claimed by flak; yet in April, when bomber sorties increased by less than a thousand, the German guns were able to double their successes. In March Doolittle had asked his Division commanders to study the problem of adjusting formations to avoid flak damage as far as possible without prejudicing bombing patterns. The very nature of the tactics in flying large close formations meant that every shell exploding in the vicinity had a high probability of causing damage or destruction. Trials were carried out with the currently favoured 12-plane squadron box and it was found that the position of each aircraft could be staggered in such a way as to limit the amount of damage which any one shell could achieve. Measures were also taken to improve and add armour on the bombers. Some B-17s were experimentally fitted with extra protective steel sheets around engine components, but due to the weight factor it was not generally adopted. Apparently a characteristic of exploding shells was that fragments were blasted up and outwards, and with this knowledge some men took (unofficially) pieces of armour plate to sit or stand on.

The increased effectiveness of flak was largely due to improved gunlaying radar the Germans had developed. This was being countered to a degree by stepping up jamming techniques. Carpet, an electronic set to create noise disturbance, had been used with some success since the autumn of 1943, while Window and Chaff, code names for the metallic paper strips cast out from bombers during target approach, were also designed to saturate radar screens. More sophisticated apparatus had been developed by the British for what was known as RCM (Radio Counter Measures). USAAF interest in this new field of warfare led to a special RCM unit, given provisional status as the 803rd Bombardment Squadron (P), being formed for the Eighth Air Force. In January selected aircrew had been sent to Sculthorpe, Norfolk, to operate a few Fortresses which were being fitted with Carpet, Mandrel and other devices.

Hitler, it is reported, was convinced that only flak could eventually defeat the day bomber. His views were certainly enforced during 1944 when 30% of all artillery weapons manufactured were of the flak type, mostly the highly effective

Famous people got in on the naming business. On 23 Apr. 1944, Vivien Leigh, Laurence Olivier (extreme rt.) and other stage personalities went to Ridgewell to see Mary Churchill christen *Stage Door Canteen*. A bottle of coke on the nose guns did the job whereas General Eisenhower used a bottle of Mississippi river water at the Bassingbourn ceremony launching *General Ike*. Col Leber (with moustache) of the 381st BG appears to have been in on both occasions.

—(USAF)

457th BG Fortresses take evasive action from flak.—(USAF)

88 mm. Moreover, a million men and women were engaged in manning or maintaining anti-aircraft guns and, by the end of May, half of these were in Germany proper. Since the fall of 1943 it had been evident to the Allies that the Germans were making strenuous efforts to improve both quality and quantity of their anti-aircraft weapons. While places like Berlin had already built up considerable flak defences against the visits of the RAF, new installations were observed with increasing regularity, chiefly around important strategic targets and the V-weapon coastal belt. During the Eighth's first winter missions, the intense flak encountered over St Nazaire became something of a criterion for intensity; now it was invalidated; the huge concentrations over Berlin were unparalleled.

Although losses for April were the heaviest of the war, because of the very large number of bombers operating these only represented 3·6% of total credit sorties. By comparison, during the costly month of October 1943 losses ran to 9·2% of all sorties. In view of the scale of operations in April, individual unit losses could be expected to be far less severe than those of the autumn month, but this was not always the case. The 379th Group at Kimbolton had been particularly lucky for it was the only group that had not lost an aircraft. What was even more extraordinary was that the 384th Group, part of the same wing and whose B-17s had often flown alongside those of the 379th during the month, had sustained the highest loss any 1st Division group was to suffer during the war—20 missing. Apart from having no losses, the 379th had achieved an operational "grand slam" by bombing with greater accuracy, hauling the greatest tonnage, having more bombers over targets, and a lower "abortion" rate than any other group in the Eighth. In the 3rd Division, which fairly consistently suffered more severely than the 1st, three groups, the 94th, 96th and 447th, had lost 21 Fortresses each, a figure only surpassed by the 100th Group the previous month.

Sgt De Sales Glover was grounded after flying six missions in B-24s—including the 6 Mar. 1944 attack on Berlin. It was discovered that he was only 16! He had managed to enlist in Oct. 1942 by falsifying his age when he was, in fact, only 14.—(USAF)

Chapter 18: May Day to D-Day

May Day brought the Eighth's bombers their first major involvement in the pre-invasion plan to disrupt the rail network in France and Belgium when 328 B-17s and B-24s were sent to six marshalling yards. (The initial raids had been undertaken by 190 Liberators four days previous.) The decision to bomb railway centres in Occupied Europe had been a controversial issue among Allied planners: some opponents of the scheme considered interdiction with fighters and light bombers a far better means to the same end, while others feared that any such campaign would cause heavy loss of life among workers in France and the Low Countries and so lose the Allies goodwill. Also, USSTAF was loth to see the Eighth Air Force directed to this campaign, when there were more promising strategic objectives. It was finally resolved that the Eighth, while continuing to pursue its offensive to neutralise the German Air Force, would share in attacking rail targets with the Ninth Air Force and RAF Bomber Command.

During the first week of May, bad weather over the Continent restricted B-17s and B-24s to visiting the Pas de Calais NOBALL targets. Whereas in the first raids on these targets, all attacks were made visually, radar bombing G-H had come into increasing use. In any case, efficient visual sighting on these small targets was extremely difficult due to the problems of identification by bombardiers at from six to ten miles, using the Norden sight. To obtain a more concentrated bombing pattern, the size of formations were specially reduced on these occasions to six aircraft and squadrons bombed on their leader. Early missions had mostly been made at medium altitude of 12,000 ft, but the rapid build up of flak around some installations had caused bombing to be done from 20,000 ft. Even so, the intensity and accuracy of fire was often on a par with that encountered over some of the important German industrial targets. What had earlier been considered milk runs had by May become viewed with nearly as much apprehension by the participants as a major mission deep into the Reich. Here again, the diversion of heavy bombers from POINTBLANK objectives was also warmly contested by USSTAF generals who considered the task more justifed to fighter-bomber operations—which appeared to have a higher degree of success with their strikes. Nevertheless, once committed to this campaign, the Eighth used it as a breaking ground for the inexperienced, assigning them to fly accompanied by a competent leader. It is a recorded fact that Fortresses achieved better bombing at NOBALL targets than Liberators, accomplishing a comparable amount of damage with half the bomb tonnage.

A large V-weapon site at Sottevast was the first target given to the 398th Group, the last Fortress unit to join the Eighth. On its opening gambit the unit experienced the frustration all too familiar to their earlier compatriots who had brought the Boeing bomber to England. Take-off was late and assembly far from successful with ten bombers joining other formations in the combat wing, and an overcast at the target causing the 398th's distinctive "all silver" fleet to return to Nuthampstead without bombing. On the afternoon of the following day, two more recent arrivals from the States acquitted themselves little better when making their combat debut over Liege's rail yards. These were the 486th and 487th Groups, forming a new 3rd Division wing in south Suffolk. Both were equipped with B-24H/J Liberators and, together with another three groups

so equipped, made this Division a composite B-17/B-24 unit.

As far as the Eighth's commanders were concerned, it was undesirable to operate two different types with varying performance in the one bomber column. The reasons for this mixed assignment stemmed from earlier plans when large-scale Liberator production was underway with the intention of forming more B-24 than B-17 units. Planned distribution to the different theatres of war being altered several times, the Eighth Air Force found itself with more B-24 groups than were required for the 2nd Division and not enough B-17 groups to bring 3rd Division to a strength comparable with that of the other two. For the most part, 3rd Division would prefer to operate its Liberators as a separate target force.

May 7th brought another milestone; for the first time the significant figure of 1,000 bombers despatched was reached when the main force flew over a sea of unbroken cloud to Berlin and two other targets in Central Germany. There was little opposition only nine enemy aircraft being sighted but for Fortresses visiting the German capital again next day, the enemy had limited success when attempting to exploit a particular situation. The 45th Wing lost the main force and joined the B-24s that had been sent to Brunswick. Devoid of escort the Wing's progress towards Brunswick did not go unnoticed and in the Nienburg area it was suddenly subjected to a mass frontal attack by FW190s, pressed so closely that one fighter collided with a bomber and both went down. Another Fortress was destroyed by a parachute bomb dropped into the formation by a fighter. The deviation from the allotted path cost the Wing dear, some thirteen Fortresses in this single action. Strangely, the German radio that day claimed the formation had been escorted by "flak cruisers . . . Boeing 40s with 30 super heavy machine guns and two cannon . . . met in countless air battles".

Apparently the ghost of the YB-40 (and a formidable one at that for no true YB-40 sported such an arsenal) still haunted Luftwaffe pilots, influencing their battle reports nine months after the type had been withdrawn from combat.

Some Liberator formations were also strongly opposed on the 8th. The 453rd Group's *Valkyrie* was so badly damaged that it had to be abandoned by the crew over England. The Liberator crashed into a thicket at Long Stratton and from the crumpled

Liberators join 3rd Division. *Chief Wapello* taxies past the tower at Lavenham. Note crewman in hatch forward of turret.—(USAF)

On 8 May 1944 96th BG should have gone to Berlin but followed the B-24s to Brunswick. Fighter attacks killed a gunner and shattered much of the tail section of *Reluctant Dragon*. Out of control in a dive, it took 2/Lt Jerry Musser (rt.) 10,000 ft to effect recovery. Six men jumped out but 2/Lt John Flemynk, bombardier (lt.), and T/Sgt Leon Sweet, engineer gunner, stayed with Musser. *Reluctant Dragon* returned to Snetterton Heath, nine other 96th B-17s did not.—(USAF)

fuselage the uninjured ball turret gunner emerged unaware that the bale out order had been given and that he was alone!

The unexpected happened with almost every mission. Over the Pas de Calais on May 8th the 379th Group's *Patches* was one of a force of B-17s that encountered a particularly nasty barrage. Flak severed one of her propellers which flew back embedding itself in the top of the port wing where it remained throughout the rest of the flight. When outward bound 94th Group gunners test-fired their weapons over the Channel next day, one B-17 was hit by their ill-directed fire and had to crash-land on the French coast. Yet another bombing accident occurred when a 100 lb GP bomb from a B-17 taking evasive action over Laon struck a lower machine. Falling on the tail of the 100th Group Fortress 42-107011 it lodged in the tail gunner's compartment between the ammunition box and fuselage skin, trapping and fatally wounding the gunner. Pilot 1/Lt Burdette Williams managed to keep control and flew the bomber back to Thorpe Abbots for a safe landing. Throughout the return the crew had expected the bomb to explode at any moment. Fortunately the arming vanes were still intact and there was no danger while the bomb remained wedged.

On this fine day, May 9th, 772 heavy bombers went to airfields and transportation targets. The Eighth had frequently given its attention to bombing German fighter fields in occupied Europe as part of its campaign for air supremacy. Rendering untenable about 100 enemy airfields within 350 miles of the Normandy coast was part of the pre-invasion plan.

According with the pre-invasion programme, 973 heavies sought marshalling yards in the fine weather of May 11th. Second Division Liberators bombing four yards in north-eastern France were joined for the first time by the 492nd Group from North Pickenham. Some of this bombing was good but the 96th Wing's groups, attacking the Epinal yards, made bad approaches dropping some of their loads into the town. It was later reported that 300 prisoners of war had been killed by a salvo that fell in their camp. The 70 aircraft from 3rd Division's two B-24 groups on their fourth mission never attacked their target at Troyes. The 487th Group trespassed into a flak area near Chateaudun, where their reception claimed the leader and his deputy, crippled a third B-24 and caused such confusion for the rest of the force that the raid was abandoned. Colonel Beirne Lay Jr, the leader, was one of Eaker's original seven officers, who held a staff appointment until he had been given command of a new B-24 group. He

had also flown with the 100th Group on the Regensburg shuttle mission and his graphic account of this epic became famous. Lay parachuted safely from the B-24 and then evaded capture.

A run of luck was brought to an end this day when a B-17 of Chelveston's 365th Bomb Sqdn. for reason unknown failed to return. The Squadron had set a record of 56 missions without loss since December 22nd 1943.

Oil targets had attracted the attention of USAAF commanders for some time, but the production and processing centres were considered too numerous and dispersed for successful attack by the limited forces available in the early stages of the Combined Bomber Offensive against Germany. Now that the Luftwaffe was in decline and Allied air supremacy undoubted, planners at USSTAF looked for other strategic objectives and, if effectively attacked, none appeared to offer better opportunity of bringing chaos to the German war economy than oil installations. In spite of the conquest of the rich Balkan fields, over three-quarters of Germany's current oil product consumption was met from synthetic manufacturing plants, most of which had been grouped near the source of their raw material, coal. The strategic air forces were now, however, at the call of the Supreme Allied Commander, General Eisenhower, and his priorities at this time were those objectives that would more directly assist the forthcoming cross-Channel landings. Also, many British and American leaders did not consider this an opportune time to commence another strategic campaign. Nevertheless, although not officially acknowledged as such, USSTAF was able to initiate an offensive against oil under the pretext of meeting the first priority of the Supreme Commanders directive to the strategic forces—the neutralisation of the enemy's air force. For in so much as USSTAF had come to believe a successful campaign against oil was well within the capability of their forces, and could be a major factor in hastening the demise of the Third Reich, they also believed oil targets would be warmly defended by the Luftwaffe.

So both Eighth and Fifteenth Air Forces began attacks on oil targets. For the Eighth these missions were limited by the various invasion plan commitments and Doolittle looked for fine days when a maximum effort could be launched with the expectation of good visual bombing. The first targets, synthetic plants, had been scheduled for attack on April 21st but the raid was abandoned in the early stages of assembly. Not until May 12th did a favourable situation develop to open the campaign from the UK. Over 900 bombers were detailed and 886 were actually despatched over the Essex coast for plants in the Leipzig area; although the two leading combat wings attacked an FW190 repair depot at Zwickau in the same area which, apart from its own importance, served to mislead the enemy as to the chief objectives.

Hell's Angels Out of Chute 13 and her companions in 401st BG on the bomb run. 27 mission symbols grew to over 100 by the end of hostilities.
—(Rust)

500 pounders go into a B-17 bomb bay. Bombs were shackled one above the other in columns.—(IWM)

Soon after the leading bombers of the 3rd Division had turned north-east after a south-easterly thrust across Belgium, they were met by an estimated 200 enemy interceptors. Spaatz was correct in his speculation that the Luftwaffe would rise to meet strikes against oil plants, although at this point the enemy could not have known the bombers ultimate destination. From 12.25 hrs, for 35 minutes, the two composite 4th Wing formations heading for Zwickau experienced determined opposition. Mass saturation tactics were pressed so close that at least one fighter rammed a B-17. From this ordeal the 4th Wing emerged in some disorder. Colonel Vandevanter flying with his 385th Group in the lead, ordered the formation to reduce speed so that others could reform; this undoubtedly added to the good bombing later achieved—the 385th managed to place 97% of their bombs within 2,000 ft of the aiming point. Four times the 4th Wing was attacked on this mission, losing 11 Fortresses, 7 from the 447th Group.

The 3rd Division's 45th and 13th Wings attacked the Brux oil plant leaving it burning and inoperative, while Liberators of 2nd Division achieved similar results at Zeitz and Bohlen; great damage too, was inflicted at Merseburg and Lutzendorf by the 1st Division. Bombing had taken place at 18,000 ft to achieve maximum accuracy and in the good visibility this had achieved results although losses were severe. Me410 Zestörers attacked 45th Wing B-17s on return, boldly pressing their attacks right into the bomber formations to an unusual degree for twin-engined fighters. In all, 46 aircraft were missing, mostly from the leading 3rd Division.

Doolittle sent the 1st Division to Poland next day, the 13th, in the hope of hitting other oil targets but the good weather, that allowed the 2nd Division to do an excellent job at the Tutow FW190 assembly plant and the 3rd to devastate Osnabruck rail yards by visual sightings, did not extend to regions further east and the force had to seek targets of opportunity.

For the best part of a week, weather brought the bomber crews the most wearying of activities—scrubbed missions. Not until the 19th was pressure again applied on Germany with visits to the two ''Bs'' that had so often in the past brought a challenge from the Luftwaffe, Berlin and Brunswick. True to reputation, determined air opposition was encountered although primarily by the 331 B-24s attacking Brunswick in the early afternoon. Here two enemy formations at Geschwader strength operated, one engaging the escort while the other hit the bombers with some success. The luckless 14th Wing caught the brunt of their attention resulting in eight B-24s going down from 492nd Group, the newest operational unit of the Eighth.

May 20th had all the makings of a fine spring day. But the sun had not risen high enough to dispel the early morning ground mists as bombers prepared to take-off for invasion plan targets in occupied countries. At Podington the first of thirty-six 92nd Group Fortresses bound for Orly airport, with six 1,000 lb bombs apiece, began rolling down the main runway at 06.55 hrs. Approximately 25 minutes later the nineteenth B-17 failed to become airborne and ran into the woods beyond the airfield boundary. The twentieth aircraft in line, already started on its run, stopped halfway down the runway, the crew having either heard a radio command to cease take-off or seen red warning flares fired by Flying Control. Whatever the

Squawkin Hawk, first 100th BG Fortress to survive 50 missions, was one of several veteran B-17Fs sent back to the USA in the spring of 1944 for use in training units. Group personnel were permitted to autograph the aircraft before she left Thorpe Abbots. In distance is Pulham St. Mary hangar which was originally built to house airships in the 1914-18 war.—(USAF)

100th BG's Frank Valash does it again. It is said he 'used up' seven B-17s, all nicknamed *Hang the Expense*. This is number six, a precious H2X model on loan from 96th BG. Wheel marks extending back to the haze shrouded Thorpe Abbots runway, and the main wheel torn off by a country roadside ditch, tells what happened to this one on 19 May 1944.—(USAF)

reason, the pilot then turned the B-17 round and started to taxi back up the misty runway. The pilots of the twenty-first aircraft, apparently neither having heard any radio command nor seen the warning flares, opening the throttles wide, thundered on into the haze. From the resultant head-on collision, five men escaped before the first bombs in the flaming wrecks detonated. This tragic accident cost 21 lives and seriously injured four. The runway was so badly blasted it took three days and nights to repair. At other bases five more heavies were destroyed in take-off crashes in poor visibility. On this occasion the morning mists were far more of a hazard than the enemy, for only two heavies failed to return.

During the remainder of May the heavy bomber effort was chiefly against invasion area rail centres and airfields, although on the 25th the heavies started a systematic pounding of coastal batteries along the French channel coast. Frequently over a thousand B-17s and B-24s were despatched and where visual attacks were made much havoc was wrought. Airfield after airfield was pitted with craters and buildings blasted, with little interference from the Luftwaffe. Enemy retaliation was mild in comparison. Before dawn on May 22nd an intruding Ju88 dropped seven small bombs on the 385th Group's Gt Ashfield base. One bomb hitting a hangar, set fire to *Powerful Katrinka*; making the only occasion on record when the Luftwaffe had destroyed a B-17 on its English base.

The weather over much of France and Germany on May 22nd was unfavourable for operations, so the Eighth made one of its increasingly rare northern missions to naval installations,

While some personnel take a look at a German bomb crater, others brush lumps of earth from a nearby 385th BG Fortress; 23 May 1944.—(USAF)

taking the North Sea route to Kiel. Two days later, while B-24s made many visual bombings of French airfields, both Fortress divisions rose high over scattered cloud for another visit to "Big B". This was an occasion when, despite poor visibility, the Luftwaffe was present in strength. Contrails thickened from the leading bomber formations and hung in the path of those following so that the escort did not see the enemy, elements of J.G.1 and J.G.3, in time to intercept them. Three Gruppen of J.G.3 attacked just after the target in their usual mass head-on manner. Losses ran to 33 B-17s; five to the heavy flak over Berlin and eighteen known to have gone down through fighter action. It was the usual story of one or two groups taking severe punishment. The low box of 1st Wing, mostly 381st Group aircraft becoming separated from the others due to weather and contrails, had eight of its number shot down. Few groups flew missions for long without experiencing "a rough one", yet it was very much a case of a dog with a bad name, that the loss of nine Fortresses from Thorpe Abbots this same day had men shaking their heads and chiding the luck of the "Bloody Hundredth."

Those not in the know must have been mystified by the instructions for a small formation of 390th and 401st Group

3rd Division B-24s followed in the wake of B-17s when the Eighth went after oil targets on 28 May 1944. The Lützkendorf plant was belching black smoke by the time 486th BG arrived. B-24H (42-52693) in picture is from the Zodiac Squadron (834 BS).—(IWM)

B-17s and 389th Group B-24s to use radar to drop bombs on Channel coastal defences on May 25th, for it was a very fine day, ideal for visual sighting. The reason was a need to know if pathfinder techniques could succeed should cloud cover the French coast when the great day of invasion arrived. This initial test left much to be desired but subsequent bombings, and improvements in apparatus and techniques, gave more satisfactory results.

The second opportunity to strike at Germany's oil industry came on May 28th when Doolittle despatched a record force of 1,282 heavies; 610 1st Division Fortresses, 255 from the 3rd Division with 106 B-24s tacked on behind (a third B-24 group for this Division, the 34th, had become operational five days before) and 311 Liberators of the 2nd Division. Briefed for seven primary targets, including three damaged in the previous raid, the ruse of sending the leading combat wings to attack other highly important targets in the area of the oil installations was repeated and with equal success. For a while the first wings of both Fortress Divisions were hit hard by some of the 300 fighters the enemy had airborne and waiting near Magdeburg, the other thirteen combat wings involved in the mission had no losses from enemy aircraft.

The Luftwaffe concentrated its forces and having saturated the fighter escort, followed with a mass attack on the 94th

Wing heading the 1st Division. The assault was aimed chiefly at the low group, the 401st, which had six B-17s shot down while another was later forced to ditch in the Channel. These seven missing in action constituted the Deenethorpe group's highest loss of the war for a single mission; the Group being at other times comparatively fortunate. While one enemy force had taken 12 bombers out of 1st Division's leading wing, others carried out similar moves against the early 3rd Division formations, principally 13th Wing and the 390th Group. Once again the bombing was generally good and huge palls of smoke gave crews first-hand evidence that inflammable products had been ignited.

Fair weather again prevailing on the 29th, 224 B-24s were sent to hit the synthetic oil plant at Pölitz, to the north-east of Berlin. Only one sharp encounter with enemy interceptors was experienced by the Liberators, such was the quality of the escort. Elsewhere B-17s went about their task of pounding the long suffering aircraft industry with little but flak to contend with. At Sorau and Poznan they completed work commenced early in April: 58 Fortresses placed 88 tons of HE and 42 of IC on the Focke-Wulf factory at Poznan halting production until August. At Sorau 50% of the production facilities and about 80 Focke-Wulf 190s were destroyed. At a third Focke-Wulf factory, Cottbus, 48 Fortresses dropped their loads on the assembly shops and flight test facilities wrecking buildings and hindering production for two or three weeks. In all, a very satisfactory day for the five combat wings of 1st Division.

During the first few days of June 1944 the Eighth's total effort was against tactical targets in a "softening up" of areas in Northern France pending the cross-Channel landings. On most of these days the heavies continued to operate at near maximum strength, their numbers swelled still further by yet two more new Liberator groups. The 3rd Division's 490th Group flew its initial mission from Eye on May 30th, as did the 2nd Division's 489th Group from Halesworth, and a rather inauspicious debut it was for both. Over the North Sea the 490th, finding heavy cloud building up ahead, commenced a 360° turn to climb above but in the process became enveloped in it. The formation ceased to exist as such and with aircraft dispersed far and wide the "Mission Abandoned" command was given. One pilot, not hearing the order, continued, to find after emerging from cloud that his aircraft was alone. After orbiting for a while he unloaded his bombs on an airfield near Rotterdam, returning safely to Eye some two hours overdue. The 489th bound for Oldenburg, crossed the Dutch coast ten miles south of its briefed checkpoint and ran into an accurate flak barrage. A navigator was killed by a shell splinter a few minutes after he took off his helmet because it was uncomfortable. One aircraft had to ditch in the North Sea on return through a fuel shortage.

The 491st, the last Liberator group to join the 2nd Division, took off from its Metfield base on the afternoon of June 2nd to join the 489th Group in the first full 95th Wing raid (there were only two groups assigned to this Wing). It proved to be a very amateur and painful performance all round and stemmed primarily from the leader's deviation from the briefed route, carefully chosen to avoid the large anti-aircraft gun concentrations in the French coastal belt. The outcome of their more direct route at far too low an altitude was recorded by 1/Lt Chester Weeks, bombardier on *Betty and Jim*, a Liberator flying No 3 position in the high element of the 489th's lead squadron. "My second mission and we flew over all the worst flak spots in Northern France at 16,000 ft, because our lead didn't want to climb for fear of leaving stragglers. We got hit at the coast by the first burst of flak but no serious damage. Intermittent flak all the way to the IP, getting several light hits on us. One of our group hit over Chartres and aborted with both Nos 1 and 2 engines feathered. They called for escort and turned home with four P-51s, but never made it. We made a run on the primary but a decision was taken not to bomb due

to bad visibility, although a few ships bombed anyway. At this point we got a flak hit in our hydraulic lines and couldn't close the bomb doors so left them open as we proceeded to the secondary. Crossed Paris and began secondary run on Creil airfield. Another flak hit tore through left side of ship, breaking pilot's rudder control cable, more hydraulic lines and an accumulator and tore his boot, bruising his foot and numbing his leg to the knee. We thought the hydraulic fluid was blood but the skin wasn't broken. He couldn't use his foot, however, and the co-pilot had to fly the rest of the mission by himself. Flak—apparently an unexploded shell tore through the nose, making a gash two feet long and six inches wide, knocking the navigator down. A later burst sent fragments through the left nose window, tearing his map and putting a small hole in the back of his flak vest but he was still unhurt. Watched another of our group spin in near Paris and explode. Two more went down; one began dropping back and then blew up. The other caught a burst in No 3 engine, which exploded breaking off the wing. This ship turned on its back and went down burning.

"We turned towards the coast near Rouen getting hits in tail turret and surfaces. From Rouen to the coast constantly hit, picking up holes in fuselage and flaps. Crossed coast at Dieppe where very accurate flak got in farewell hits on lead's No 2 engine, another ship in our squadron's No 2, and on the front of my nose turret and bombardiers window. One ship in trouble got as far as London but the crew had to bale out, the ship making a tremendous explosion when it hit. Another ship crash-landed on a fighter field killing one gunner. In the mix-up

Foam covered 453rd BG B-24 *Goldern Gaboon* was crash-landed at Old Buckenham by 1/Lt Wilbur Earl after a mission to Oldenburg 30 May 1944. Four days later 2/Lt Lester Baer brought *Zeus* in on one main wheel. This time firecrew were able to smother the flames.— (USAF & IWM)

of night landing four crews put down at Metfield by mistake. We cranked flaps and wheels down by hand and circled the field until all others had landed for which consideration all the field lights were turned off and we had to circle about ten minutes until they went back on. Everybody shooting red flares, indicating wounded aboard. We landed indicating 145 mph with full flaps, while the crew ran to tail to brake with tail skid. Had enough brake to stop on runway but rolled on through parking space into field. Engineering officer amazed that we got the plane back. Says by rights the nose turret should have fallen off. Trim tabs also shot off somewhere along the line. Didn't hit either target although we accidentally made a big hit on an ammunition dump."

Of 77 B-24s put up by the two groups, the 489th lost four and had three wrecked in crashes, the 491st lost one, and 58 of the remainder had some form of repairable flak damage. The briefed route over *Festung Europa* was rarely straight but always narrow. Those who failed to keep it invariably shed much of their protection.

On the eve of D-Day when the heavies were pounding coastal defences between the Cherbourg peninsula and the Pas de Calais, the 489th Group was bracketed by flak again.

Not so lucky. Men of the *Lucky Buck* in typical crew pose before their aircraft. Flying another B-24 they went down on 491st BG's first mission. All bailed out but 2/Lt Malcolm Blue (3rd lt. back row) was killed when his 'chute did not open properly and the ball turret gunner, Pvt LeMay (not in this group) was dead when he reached the ground, hit by machine gun fire. Some weeks later *Lucky Buck* was lost with another crew.—(Blue)

The lead aircraft took a burst near the right side of the cockpit, killing the co-pilot and practically severing the right foot of the air commander, Lt Col Leon R. Vance, who was standing on the flight platform behind the pilot's seats. Despite this injury Vance ordered the bomber to be kept on its bomb run for fortifications near Wimereaux. The ailing Liberator, hit in three engines, managed to reach the English coast where Vance ordered the crew to bale out. Told there was an injured man in the rear, who could not jump, Vance remained alone in the wreckage of the cockpit and by some miraculous effort succeeded in the difficult task of ditching a B-24. An explosion as the aircraft settled beneath the waves, blew him clear severing his mutilated foot. Clinging to a piece of wreckage he managed to inflate his life jacket and began to search for the wounded man he believed aboard. Failing to find anyone he began swimming and was picked up 50 minutes later by a rescue craft. Vance survived this extraordinary episode. By the irony of fate, his air evacuation C-54 to the US in late July disappeared without trace on the Iceland-Newfoundland leg. Leon Vance's unquestionable courage, skill and self-sacrifice brought him the only Medal of Honor to go to a Liberator crewman engaged on operations from the UK.

Leon Vance (with bandaged leg) visits the Halesworth Officers' Club after his discharge from hospital. Col Napier, 489th BG CO sits on his left.—(Duffy)

The chances of being rescued from the sea were now considerably greater for Eighth Air Force combatants. In April 43% of crews ditching had been saved, as against 28% in the previous April. The Eighth had formed its own Air Sea Rescue organisation and in May, a squadron of Thunderbolts carrying rescue apparatus became operational in a search and rescue capacity.

Flak had not claimed as many bombers in May as in April although the Germans were still busy expanding their anti-aircraft network. Points where bomber streams could enter continental airspace without coming into effective range of the numerous coastal flak sites became fewer as the weeks passed. Flak at vital targets could not be avoided for to achieve accurate bombing the bombers had to pass over the target. Skilful manipulation of a formation in evasive action could and did help to lessen effects of ground fire but had its limitations. Approximately 25% of bombers could now expect to be hit by flak during their combat life and one would be lost for every 13 damaged. A great deal of effort was expended in developing effective countermeasures. To attack targets from outside the flak area, USAAF agencies had experimented with devices to give bombs a longer trajectory. One such development was a glider bomb, comprising a wooden wing and empennage strapped to a normal 2,000 lb HE bomb. Production versions, after promising tests were shipped to the UK in the autumn of 1943.

The Eighth's commanders were, for various reasons rather dubious of the value of a glider bomb and as flak was not then

Two 2,000 lb glide bombs released by 384th BG B-17F JD: L fall towards Cologne, some twenty miles distant.—(USAF)

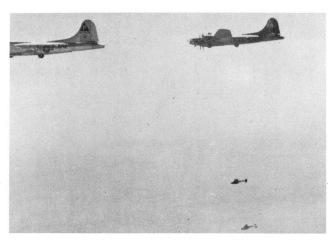

of major concern, these weapons were set aside. With the growing incidence of flak in the spring of 1944, interest revived and plans were made to give the gliding bomb a battle trial. Accordingly, the three 41st Wing groups with their B-17s fitted with wing racks, were assigned the task, and while the main force sought Hitler's oil on May 28th, 59 aircraft of 41st Wing visited Eifeltor/Cologne marshalling yard, a large target considered ideal for the experiment. Each Fortress carried two of the 12 ft span bombs, which incorporated a simple automatic pilot acting on movable ailerons and rudders to compensate for any induced roll after release. Aimed release was made of 109 bombs but, as had been anticipated by Eighth ordnance experts, their accuracy was insufficient for attacking even such a large target. Some did glide into the yards, but others exploded miles away. It was recommended that no more such bombs be ordered.

The Azon bomb was another "stand-off" weapon under development, although this had no real flak evasion advantage it had the means for steering a missile after release. It comprised a normal 1,000 lb bomb with special radio tail attachment and moveable fins. Plans for 100 Azon bombs to be shipped to the UK during February 1944 for use against special targets on the French coast, notably V-1 sites, were discarded as larger targets were thought more suitable for early trials. The first bombs were then diverted to the Fifteenth Air Force in Italy.

Interest revived, however, and in early May Spaatz requested ten specially modified B-24s for Azon bomb use. These arrived some days later and were assigned to the 458th Group at Horsham St Faith. On the 31st the first experimental mission was despatched. Four of the five Azon B-24s sent, aimed for the Beaumont-sur-Oise bridge and then, as targets of opportunity, bridges at Melun and Meulan. Heavily escorted and flying in line at only 10,000 ft the bombers were without success as none of the 14 bombs released hit a bridge although some were close.

Technical developments, both offensive and defensive, were constantly in hand, even so the bombardment equipment and techniques employed by the Eighth remained basically unchanged and there appeared little prospect that radical changes would occur during the immediate future. The Fortress and Liberator continued as the chief vehicles for the day bombing campaign and the latest models of these bombers were now arriving in substantial numbers. By early June there were 2,500 heavies on hand in operational units and sufficient replacements to make up losses speedily. In April 50 B-17Fs were withdrawn from first line squadrons and returned to the US for training purposes. Others were to follow, not that there were many to withdraw for although the entire Fortress force was composed of B-17F models until September 1943 some 75% of these had been shot down or wrecked during the following six months. Few groups that had arrived in England the previous summer with forty B-17s apiece now had more than half a dozen of the originals left. By June the average life of a heavy bomber in the Eighth was 145 days with a combat group, inclusive of time spent on the ground.

On the morning of Tuesday, June 6th, 1944, Liberators took off for the first operation flown from Debach airfield in east Suffolk; they were from the 493rd Group, last of the 40 combat bomb groups assigned to the Eighth Air Force. Two years had passed since the combat build up began, but its culmination in the last group becoming operational was eclipsed by the momentous happenings of this day, the launching of the cross-Channel invasion—a feat of arms that the advocates of strategic bombing had hoped would be unnecessary.

Chapter 19: Fighters Crescendo

The fighter element of the Eighth Air Force, built up to support the bombers by escort work were, in the months directly preceding the invasion of the Continent, aspiring to comprise a strike force of their own.

On April 5th, when a completely overcast sky caused most of the Fortresses and Liberators to remain on the ground, 456 US fighters went on a mass straffing mission to France and Germany. Only 3 of the 11 groups participating were able to attack their assigned targets because of ground haze and cloud, but the resultant devastation was almost totally the work of two Mustang Groups. The 4th and 355th Group, given targets in the Berlin and Munich areas respectively, found improved weather conditions. The 4th descending on five air-fields near Berlin, claimed 43 aircraft on the ground and two in the air; Don Gentile alone left 5 Ju88s wrecked at one base. The 355th, recently converted from P-47s, dealt with six air-fields resulting in claims of 43 destroyed and 81 damaged, plus 8 in the air, most being obtained at Oberpfaffenhofen.

Most striking of the new group identification markings were the checkerboard designs on P-47s. Wearing 78th FG's black and white *War Eagle* served at Duxford for a year before being 'bellied in' 15 Dec. 1944.—(USAF)

Ground fire brought down four 4th and three 355th Mustangs; one of the former, Major Duane Beeson, a leading ace in *Boise Bee*, was able to gain sufficient height to balc out, becoming a prisoner. A few days previously the 56th had suffered the loss of two top ranking aces: Gerald Johnson's P-47 was also a victim of ground fire and crash-landed, while Walker Mahurin, master of a score of aerial battles, was shot down by the rear gunner of a Do217 bomber.

Having destroyed 88 enemy aircraft on the ground, three days later VIII FC fighters took the same number in the air. Indeed, on April 8th, it can be said the battle between the German Air Force and the US fighters reached its zenith. Including 40 ground victories the total for the mission was 128 —approximately the complement of a whole Jagdgeschwader. The Luftwaffe could not sustain such grievous losses without serious strain on its resources; yet this was not an isolated occasion, it was now losing heavily nearly every day. When 644 bombers went to Brunswick and various targets connected with aviation in North-West Germany, a force of 712 fighters went with them. The German fighters were again drawn into combat with the 4th Group's Mustangs, this time shortly after rendezvousing with a box of B-24s. Engaged with a determined and larger force of Me109s, they achieved a 31 for 4 win, a VIII FC record score for a single mission. The date marked the anniversary of the first combat sorties of the other old stagers of VIII FC, the 56th and 78th Groups, making the occasion particularly memorable for 1/Lt Charles M. Peale who had been one of the Duxford pilots on that first mission. For a year he had flown his Thunderbolt without once being able to claim an enemy plane destroyed. Then, on this his 99th combat sortie, he shot down one of the three claimed by the 78th. Peale had flown most of his early missions as a wing man; there were many such men who never once had an opportunity to fire at an enemy during their tour of combat.

April 8th also proved a memorable day for the Lightning equipped 20th Fighter Group, scheduled to escort B-17s to Oldenburg. However, the 20th's base at Kings Cliffe, several miles north-west of the general area of VIII FC bases, remained shrouded in fog until noon. Command of the Group had recently been vested in Lt Col Harold Rau, who had the rare distinction of having once been a private in the organisation he now led. Disappointed that his men had been denied this "crack at the enemy", and eager to boost morale, Rau sought permission from Wing for his Group to carry out an independent fighter sweep. The 4th Group had been allowed to do this with Mustangs—so why not Lightnings? The P-38 had always given a good account of itself at low altitudes.

The go-ahead was given to the 20th and airfields in the Salzwedel area, 80 miles west of Berlin, were selected as strafing targets. This was the first time P-38s were despatched alone to such targets deep in Germany. The 48 P-38s scheduled took off at 14.02 hrs and 112 minutes later arrived near Salzwedel where the three squadrons separated as planned. Led by Rau, the 79th Fighter Squadron attacked an airfield just north of the town and in four passes wrote off 13 aircraft, mostly bombers. As ground fire had become intense, the Squadron then moved off to strafe an army barracks that one section had found and, after giving this a good going over, two locomotives were shot up. Shortly afterwards seven Me109s bounced the Lightnings and shot one down. Rau climbed and came down on an Me109 that was preparing to attack another 79th machine. Unfortunately the Colonel's burst of fire caused the Messerschmitt to crash into the P-38 ahead and both went down in flames. Other P-38s destroyed two more Me109s during the course of this action.

Meanwhile, the 77th Squadron had gone for an airfield south-east of the town, destroying two enemy aircraft caught in the air and eight on the ground as well as damaging 21. The 55th Squadron did not locate an airfield, but went on a strafing spree leaving havoc in its wake. Both these squadrons lost a Lightning. When the Group returned to England and totted up the record, it was found that all but 2 of the 42 P-38s reaching the target area had fired their guns—21,475 rounds of ·50 and 3,850 20 mm shells had been expended on targets which included 18 locomotives, 50 rail wagons, 16 flak towers, various factory buildings, hangars and oil storage dumps.

Low altitude work of this nature suited the Lightning far better than escorting bombers at 25,000 feet and above. Their "bugs" were slowly being ironed out but the major problem, engine failure, was not easily overcome. One immediate, though rather unsatisfactory, solution for operation at low temperatures at high altitude was the blocking off of oil cooling radiators to raise the temperature of the engine oil and improve lubrication. The trouble with turbo-superchargers through

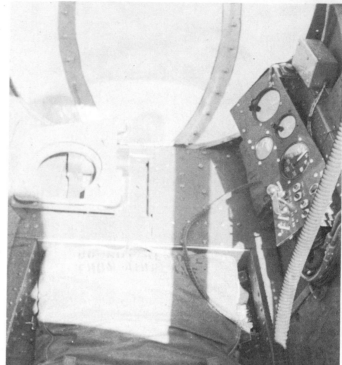

42-68184, the Bovingdon Droop Snoot unloads on its first experimental mission.—(Hough)

Col Hough prepares to climb into the cockpit of the Droop Snoot, while Col Don Ostrander enters the nose through the top hatch. Picture taken prior to a combat mission on D-Day.—(Hough)

Interior of Droop Snoot nose. Stand for bomb sight forward of bombardier's couch. Instruments and control panel on right. Note shadow of entrance hatch.—(Hough)

Col Harold Rau's *Gentle Annie* displays a white Droop Snoot decoy nose band.—(USAF)

exhaust condensation, was remedied by a water trap devised by members of the 55th Group and enlarged duct scoops, to convey warm air from engines to the cockpit, helped eliminate the pilots' problems of intense cold and frosted windscreens.

During the winter months hush-hush work had been in progress at Lockheed's Speke depot on an aircraft known as the "Droop Snoot". This was really an extensively modified P-38J, and principally the handiwork of Colonels Cass Hough and Don Ostrander (an armament and ordnance expert). Current activities in bombing and strafing by the fighters had led to the installation of a cabin for a bombardier and bomb sight in the nose of a Lightning, to enable it to be used as sighting aircraft for mass formation bombing by fighters. This type of bombing had first been tried out by the 56th Group's P-47s in November, when a B-24 was used but found to have many disadvantages. The Lightning conversion offered a more versatile aircraft for this purpose and better suited to operations involving fighters. Additionally, it would prove difficult for the enemy to detect the nature of the attack until bombs began to fall, and a formation able to bomb at twice the speed of heavy bombers should prove less vulnerable over heavily defended targets.

To make the conversion, ATS arranged for Lockheeds to strip the gun and ammunition compartments and fit a plexiglass nose through which a Norden bomb sight could be operated. As such aircraft were unarmed and liable to be singled out for attack once their purpose and weaknesses were known, an ingenious camouflage was devised. Each P-38 group was ordered to paint a white band around the forward section of their aircraft's noses, and to remove the paint forward of this, polishing the exposed metal. By this means it was hoped that it would be difficult to tell the plexiglass-nosed and unarmed models from the lethal variety.

The first operational use of the Droop Snoot by VIII FC units was made by the 55th Group on April 10th 1944. St Dizier airfield in France, the target selected, was to be bombed from 20,000 feet by two of the group's squadrons dropping on the Droop Snoot's signal; each of these aircraft was fitted with one drop tank and a 1,000 lb bomb. The third squadron of the group acted as escort. As St Dizier was found to be obscured by cloud, Colonel Jenkins selected Coulommiers airfield. The 28 bombs dropped appeared to be well aimed and after bombing, the Colonel led a squadron down to strafe the field. At lower altitude the Colonel was hindered by a foggy wind-screen—another common affliction with the P-38 when dived —and his run was spoiled. When a second pass was made, the alerted gunners of the field brought down the leader and his wingman. Jenkins managed to belly-land and get out safely.

The 20th Group by now had also been provided with a Droop Snoot and went to attack Florennes airfield. This group also found its primary target obscured by cloud, but was unable to find an alternative target and set course for home, dropping their 1,000 pounders in the Channel. During the afternoon a second Droop Snoot mission was run by the 20th, this time to Gutersloh in Germany. Here, unhindered by cloud, the 27 aircraft attacking placed 2 x 500 lb and 25 x 1,000 lb bombs in a good concentration among airfield buildings. All in all, the employment of the P-38 as a medium high altitude fighter bomber showed considerable promise and operational experiments to determine the best procedures for Droop Snoot attacks continued.

The day following the first operational use of the Droop Snoot, none other than General Dwight Eisenhower went for a flight in this two-place version of the Lightning. It occurred during the General's visit to Debden, where he had gone to see something of the fighter force that was gradually gaining air superiority over the western area of Europe. He took the occasion to present Blakeslee, Gentile and Robert Johnson (who had flown over from Halesworth) with DSCs. The 4th Group was in high spirits that day for its combined totals of air and ground victories now stood at 405½ and surpassed that of the 56th Group. Its impressive score continued to rise rapidly during the following weeks of April for it was predominately the longer-ranged Mustangs that saw most of the action and made big claims on VIII Fighter Command missions. Even while Eisenhower inspected examples of American fighter equipment drawn up at Debden for his inspection, the Mustangs of 357th Group from Leiston were fighting the Luftwaffe on an escort to Sorau, from which they returned with 25 of the 51 victories fighters claimed.

The "Bills's Buzz Boys" strafing venture prompted the tacticians at VIII Fighter Command to draw up an ambitious plan for large scale strafing assaults on Luftwaffe airfields. The plan called for each fighter group to be assigned specific areas in Germany where it alone would be responsible for attacking airfields during such a mission. This served two main purposes first, it allowed pilots of a group an opportunity to become familiar with the defences and targets in an area, putting them in a better position to formulate methods of attack. It also helped to prevent overlapping when the effect of a group arriving over an airfield which had previously been alerted by an attack by another group could be disastrous. In the plan, Germany was divided into northern and southern sections each subdivided into fairly rectangular areas of several hundred square miles, size depending on the number of airfields within the boundaries. Each group was assigned one or more of these

areas in both northern ("A") and southern ("B") sections, and on receipt of the code word JACKPOT A or JACKPOT B in a Field Order was to despatch its aircraft to strafe airfield(s) in the appropriate areas.

The first full scale mission of this kind was on April 15th when the 616 fighters involved left 40 aircraft destroyed and 29 damaged on airfields in France and the Low Countries, while taking another 18 in the air. It proved a costly venture for 32 pilots failed to return, seven in P-38s of Honington's 364th Group. With heavy cloud extending to 24,000 ft weather was extremely bad and was held responsible for half the missing aircraft.

Interspersed with JACKPOT strafing, Droop Snoot attacks continued. The Lightnings of the 55th Group went out on April 20th but all feasible targets were cloud covered and the English Channel was again used as a dump. Three days later the Group was luckier and deposited 93 x 500 lb bombs on what was thought to be Laon/Athies airfield but which turned out to be nearby Laon/Couvron! The 20th was also out but its attack on a Focke-Wulf repair plant at Tours brought inconclusive results.

The Luftwaffe continued to be harried in the air. On the 22nd, the 4th inflicted a resounding defeat on a formation of Me109s that attempted to "bounce" its Mustangs. Blakeslee shot down two, John Godfrey three and another 4th Group ace, Willard Millikan, 4 of the 17 claimed by the Debden men. Two days later the 357th came home with another 22 victories from a mission where VIII FC fighters claimed a total of 66 air and 58 ground victories. The four operational Mustang groups accounted for nearly three-quarters of the enemy aircraft destroyed by the Command during April. With 348 air and 155 ground victories the 4th had passed the 500 destroyed mark by the end of April; a month in which it had destroyed 222. The 355th from Steeple Morden had a total of 153, while the newly operational 352nd at Bodney claimed 140. Mustang losses were also high. The four groups lost 67 aircraft— almost equivalent to the strength of one entire group—whereas the six Thunderbolt groups lost but 42 of their numbers. This reflects not only the extensive action seen by the Mustang but the fact that it could not sustain battle damage and return home safely to the same degree as its Republic companion. The Merlin's coolant system was particularly vulnerable and many pilots had to bale out when a punctured coolant caused the engine to overheat and seize up.

A dozen Droop Snoot bombing missions were despatched during the last week of April but many were frustrated by cloud. The 55th made its most successful attack so far on the 27th when it came down to 17,000 ft to drop on Roye/Amy airfield. On the same date the 20th Group went to Peronne but was turned away by cloud and selected Albert/Meaulte instead. While the P-38s were in the process of running up on the target, P-47s of the 56th Group approached the formation causing some aircraft to jettison their bombs under the misapprehension that they were FW190s. Chateaudun was a Droop Snoot target for the 55th next day, when 49 x 1,000 lb bombs were dropped from 18,000 ft. After this the Group acted as top cover for the 56th Group which made a dive bombing attack (its first) on the same airfield. The 20th went again to the Tours target on the 28th and 30th. On the latter occasion one bomb from a P-38 struck without exploding and glanced off the port engine cowling of a lower and following aircraft. Some of the 20th's aircraft went down and tried "skip" bombing from 500 feet. Most of these raids were against enemy airfields and on some occasions, when distances from base were not too great, two 1,000 lb bombs were carried, a load comparable to that of the A-20 Havoc light bomber.

A new Mustang equipped fighter group, the 339th at Fowlmere, became operational on the last day of the month and two more P-47 groups were scheduled to convert in May which would make the Mustang the dominant type in the

Don Gentile came down a little too low while buzzing Debden on 13 Apr. 1944. Somehow *Shangri-La* appeared 'on the books' as missing in action!—(USAF)

Command. Fate, meanwhile, had dealt a cruel blow to the man primarily responsible for hastening the procurement of the Merlin-engined Mustang. Lt Col Tommy Hitchcock was killed piloting a Mustang on April 18th when it broke up in the air near Salisbury.

During April, as forces assembled for the invasion, the Ninth Air Force had moved its five fighter groups from the Colchester area to landing strips in Kent. The 55th Group thereupon moved into Wormingford, the 56th to Boxted and the 353rd to Raydon, as their former bases were required for bomber units.

A sharp decline in enemy air activity was apparent in May but the Luftwaffe still rose to give battle when some vital target appeared to be the object of a bomber mission. Attacks on Berlin and Brunswick brought intense action on May 8th when it was estimated 200 Me109s and FW190s were air-airborne, mainly in the Hanover area. The honours of the day went to the up and coming blue-nosed Mustang group from Bodney, the 352nd, which was given the job of taking the bombers over Brunswick. The three squadrons had to fly through solid overcast on their climb towards enemy territory, emerging over Holland where they contacted the last elements of the bomber stream at 20,000 feet, and after flying over successive boxes, overtook the leading group near Neinburg, Germany. The Luftwaffe had positioned a large formation of Me109s and FW190s ahead and above the advancing bomber stream and these eventually came down in successive waves of two or three Staffeln to make frontal passes. Two squadrons of the 352nd moved to intercept but the Mustang pilots could not deflect the attack. After firing the Luftwaffe aircraft plunged through the formations and continued to descend. There was a time when orders kept the American fighters from following the enemy down, but the German interceptors were no longer given the opportunity of reforming at lower altitude for another attack. Colonel Joe Mason, leading the Group that day, ordered the 328th and 487th Squadrons to go down after the enemy and for an hour the Mustangs of these squadrons

1/Lt Carl Luksic holds up his hand to signify his credits on 8 May 1944. In less than a month's combat he had 8 air and 7 ground victories.—(IWM)

attacked and harassed any Focke-Wulfs and Messerschmitts seen. Claims of 27-2-7 resulted for only one 352nd Group Mustang being lost. The German fighters, generally, did not display any organised resistance. 1/Lt C. J. Luksic of the 487th shot down 3 Me109s and 2 FW190s to make a new "first" for a VIII FC pilot; 5 on a mission. Lt Col John C. Meyer of the 487th and 1/Lt John Thornell of the 328th got three apiece and Colonel Mason also had a victory.

The exploits of the Group that had led the way in beating the Luftwaffe had been somewhat overshadowed by the phenomenal successes of Mustang organisations. On this day two of the six victories claimed by the 56th Group pilots gave Major Robert Johnson a total of 27 (a later re-assessment of his combats awarded him a total of 28 destroyed). This was the highest score so far achieved by an American ace fighting the Germans. Johnson had been the Eighth Air Force's leading ace after Mahurin went down and until Gentile of the 4th brought

Cpt Robert Samuel Johnson explains nickname of his 62nd FS P-47D to Brig Gen Jesse Auton, 65 FW CO and Brig Gen Francis Griswold, C of S, VIII FC. Names of Booth Tarkington schoolboy characters also fit pilot and crew chief—Sgt J. C. Penrod.—(USAF)

his score to 23 in April. Gentile returned to the States and Johnson had gone on adding German crosses to the panel on the side of his P-47. Many distinguished aces had disappeared from the scene having completed the 200 hour tour, or gone down over Europe. Beckham, Gerald Johnson, and Beeson were high scorers now in prison camps. Mahurin had escaped capture and returned to England via the French Resistance movement. Those who had been sent back to the States on leave included Godfrey and Schilling. Now Robert Johnson would follow leaving a fellow 56th pilot as leading ace. Lt Col Francis Gabreski had not made the headlines like some of his colourful compatriots yet he had been outwitting and out-gunning Luftwaffe fighters for a year with 20 victories as the impressive result.

"Gabby" Gabreski was of Polish extraction and had flown on detachment with a Polish Spitfire squadron in the RAF when the 56th first came to England. His contact with these fliers led to the 61st Squadron of the Group having a strong Polish atmosphere during 1944 and to the very end of the war. Grounded by the RAF who considered they had done enough flying in one war, many Polish pilots elected to fight in a USAAF Thunderbolt rather than take a desk job. The whole thing was "rather unofficial" for although the half dozen pilots concerned flew for the Americans, they wore RAF uniform and received British rates of pay. As far as Zemke was concerned, all that mattered was that they were good pilots with an insatiable appetite for fighting the enemy. The leading light was a character named Michael Gladych whose exploits read like fiction. On one of the Berlin raids Gladych was being

Glenn Duncan's LH: X *VI* came to grief at 1808 hrs, 27 Apr. 1944, when it suffered engine failure and was crash landed in a field at Red House Farm, Copdock. Two HE bombs were jettisoned seconds before and exploded harmlessly in farm land.—(USAF)

hotly pursued by two FW190s at low altitude and escaped when German flak gunners at Vechta airfield mistakenly fired on the pursuers and not their quarry. The "Mad Pole" was really a very competent pilot and had provided 16 of the 56th's total of enemy aircraft destroyed by the end of the war.

Zemke, the architect of much of the 56th's success had lost none of his flair for tactics. In comparison with earlier days there was now a comparative dearth of enemy fighters in areas within Thunderbolt range. To better the chances of contacting Luftwaffe formations, Zemke conceived the idea of the Group flying to a predetermined point and there splitting into three forces. Two of these would branch out and away on either side of the central and strongest force which flew midway between the others and was in a position to render prompt aid to either should the enemy be met in strength. This tactic, known as the Zemke Fan, first put into practice on May 12th in the Frankfurt area, resulted in 18 claims for a loss of 3. Captain R. Rankin accounted for five Me109s, emulating the recent success of 352nd Group's Lt Luksic. Eighth Air Force heavies made their first major mission against the German oil targets this day and an estimated 300 enemy fighters were airborne and VIII FC saw that 66 did not come back to earth gently. Though the Luftwaffe did give battle on other days the opposition was often weak, the plain facts were that it was an exhausted force no longer controlling the sky over its homeland.

As D-Day drew nearer the German transportation system was brought into the strafing scheme; the same grid plan being used for JACKPOTS (airfield attacks) as CHATTANOOGAS (transportation attacks, principally railways). The first CHATTANOOGA was not run until May 21st but it had devastating results when 552 fighters ranged over Northern Germany. No less than 225 locomotives were attacked, 91 of which were considered destroyed. Stations, rail installations, bridges, barges and a variety of other targets were shot up. Although the mission was primarily launched against transportation it also yielded the largest claims so far against aircraft on the ground; 102 were destroyed and 76 classified as damaged. The 361st Group from Bottisham and newly converted to Mustangs, was credited with 23 locomotives left as wrecked and two damaged. Some of the Lightnings were frustrated by cloud but the 55th Group had plenty of opportunity to indulge in slaughter on the permanent way, a task for which it was soon renowned. In fact, P-38 units achieved much success in this work probably because locomotives and rolling stock were more susceptible to damage from the explosive 20 mm cannon shells. On this occasion the 55th wrecked 23 locomotives and damaged another 15, left 16 trains in flames and shot up four river steamers and fourteen barges among other ground targets. An unsuspecting Hs129 was caught in the air and another six enemy aircraft were left burning on an airfield. The cost was six pilots who did not return to Wormingford.

That a P-38 could not fly with tail damage was generally believed by their pilots—until this day. Lt Peter Dempsey of the 55th, having shot-up two Me109s and a hangar, was hedge-hopping home when a high tension wire suddenly appeared in his path. Being too low and too near to climb over, he attempted to fly under, and snapped a cable which sheared off the upper half of the port fin. Collecting a two-foot length of cable around the other fin which jammed the rudder, Dempsey displayed remarkable skill in bringing the Lightning back to make a safe landing at base, where he was jokingly commended for his novel method of disrupting the enemy's electricity supply!

Another pilot who brought home souvenirs was Lt Wilton Johnson, who helped wreck one of seven locomotives the 353rd Group claimed. He passed over his target just as his bomb exploded and returned to England with pieces of an engine embedded in his Thunderbolt.

The May 21st operation was the climax of pre-invasion strafing attacks by VIII FC. Since these attacks began in February some 1550 aircraft and over 900 locomotives had been destroyed or damaged, not to mention a vast variety of other military and other targets. The enemy, seriously embarrassed by these developments, lost no time in bolstering airfield defences to make these attacks extremely unhealthy for the participants.

Towards the end of May Thunderbolt groups were sent out on medium altitude bombing missions with a Droop Snoot Lightning. The 78th tried to destroy the Criel rail bridge on the 24th without success and six days later the 56th borrowed the 20th's Droop Snoot and 1/Lt Herschel Ezell, an ex-B-17 bombardier who worked the Norden, to see if they could do better. Anti-aircraft fire proved too heavy at Criel, so the formation flew to a similar bridge at Chantilly. Coming down to 12,000 feet to drop, the P-47s bombs took out three spans of the bridge. Thereafter, Droop Snooting activities subsided as the P-38s were allotted a vital task for the forthcoming invasion.

The Luftwaffe could not retreat, for there were now few

A 356th FG P-47 pulls up after aiming a bomb at this rail bridge at Hasselt, Belgium 22 May 1944. The bomb, seen exploding in right hand corner of picture, fell wide. Other P-47s succeeded in hitting track and left side of bridge.—(USAF)

When 359th FG's George Doersch was strafing an airfield near Rheims, his P-51B's propeller hit the ground. He managed to keep the Mustang airborne and flew back to Manston.—(Bowers)

Squadron CO of 436 FS was killed on a local flight when his P-38J 9B: A, crashed near Rattlesden on 26 May 1944, the day his group was to fly its first operation.—(USAF)

places to which the long arm of VIII Fighter Command could not reach. Targets for the bombers on May 13th had been mainly near the Baltic coast, beyond Berlin, yet well within the range capabilities of the 384 escorting Mustangs. The British-made 108 gallon "paper" drop tank had become the standard fitment on P-51s for long missions and using these the 355th Group flew a record trip of 1,480 miles from Steeple Morden to Politz and back. The Leiston based 357th flew a 1,470 mile round trip to Poznan in Poland while the 359th from East Wretham, flying its newly acquired green-nosed Mustangs, met the bombers near Dramburg some 645 miles from its base. For single-engine fighters these were fantastic distances which few Allied planners would have thought possible a year before.

Apart from the engineering problems, no combat pilot had been expected to fly in the limited confines of a fighter cockpit for six or seven hours, much of it on oxygen. Yet it was now being done with as little fuss as if for a half-hour sweep of the Pas de Calais. Such missions were not restricted to the most experienced: the freshman 339th from Fowlmere covered

1,420 miles when it flew with the bombers to East Germany on May 29th. The Lightnings also ranged far afield this day with the veteran 55th Group going as far as Vordingbord in Denmark for a 1,040 mile round journey. Towards the end of May over 1,000 American fighters were despatched. The highest figure was reached on the last day of the month when 1,204 sortied, of which 596 were Ninth Air Force machines. The VIII FC had now received its full complement, the last group—the P-38 equipped 479th—having become operational on May 26th giving the Command 4 P-38, 4 P-47 and 7 P-51 groups. Effective aircraft strength (those in fully serviceable condition) stood at 885 while the Luftwaffe had approximately 1,500 single-engine day fighters within the Eighth's area of operations—although their effective strength was much lower. The Ninth Air Force had an effective strength of around 1,000 fighters at this time and the RAF about 1,900. With an overwhelming fleet of 3,000 Allied fighters to contend with, the Luftwaffe could not hope to regain air superiority, particularly on its current showing. That Eighth Air Force was primarily responsible for its predicament, there can be no doubt.

The demise of the Luftwaffe Jagdverbände can be attributed to a number of factors. Many mistakes were made by the German air leaders; the most damning was failure to appreciate the threat of the long-range fighter and lack of determined effort to counter it until too late. Little was done about the first efforts of the American fighters in the spring and summer of 1943 thus allowing pilots to gain experience and become proficient in the unwieldy P-47s. Even when the dangers that lay ahead must have been obvious to the enemy, the Luftwaffe failed to make an effective challenge. Instead, it chose to concentrate on the bombers and finally found itself in a position where it was frequently prevented from reaching them. Both the Me109G and FW190A were good fighters but the average German fighter pilot was not equal to his American counterpart in the matter of training. During the winter of 1943-1944 the German fighter pilot received an average of only $27\frac{1}{2}$ hours flight training prior to an operational posting compared with the American's 120. The German day fighter pilot was particularly weak on instrument flying and in bad weather had much difficulty in combat operations. While inadequate training made new German pilots no match there were still some of the old hands around who could and did put up a valiant fight and claimed many American fighters in their long string of victories.

In vanquishing the enemy in the sky one technical development was paramount; the expendable long-range fuel tank. Without it fighters would never have been able to reach to the heart of the Reich. If any one thing could be said to have made Allied air supremacy possible, then it was the drop-tank.

The Jagdverbände had suffered a crippling defeat but was far from finished. German aircraft production was rapidly increasing—to a much greater extent than Allied intelligence estimated at the time—and it should also be remembered that nearly half of the German pilots shot down lived to fly again. Nevertheless, air supremacy was now in Allied hands and Eisenhower could, with more than a measure of truth, tell his troops on the eve of D-Day—"Don't worry about the 'planes overhead. They will be ours".

Chapter 20: Cloak and Dagger, Rockets and Jets

By June 1944 the English were well accustomed to their dawn slumbers being disturbed by the sound of aircraft engines. In East Anglia the early morning chorus of Cyclones and Twin-Wasps had grown in volume over past months until few places were free from the reverberating throb when ten million horse power sought the thinner air. The inhabitants of Norwich were awoken unusually early on June 6th: it was just over an hour past midnight, yet the familiar roar of engines being run up was coming from the American Liberator airfields that ringed the city. The thought that something big was afoot passed through many a mind; the long anticipated cross-Channel invasion. In the hours that followed, long before the first news bulletins, suspicion had become conviction in the presence of tumultuous activity.

Major Earle Aber (lt.) piloted the first Leaflet Squadron B-17 to set out on invasion night to drop warning leaflets on the French. Here he talks with two members of his crew, Sgt Benito Cipollini and Sgt John Kolton, as they gather their kit after leaving their aircraft at Chelveston.
—(IWM)

Aircrews at Bungay were surprised to be alerted for a briefing held at 23.30 hrs on the evening of June 5th; then astonished and excited to learn that their group, the 446th, was to lead the Eighth Air Force heavies on a pre-landing bombardment of the Normandy coast. Briefings of various units followed during the next few hours to ensure the many special considerations for this mission were well understood. Second Division Field Order No 328 was probably the longest and most detailed ever tele-taped to a B-24 base. It called for the 20th, 2nd and 14th Wings to provide 114 aircraft each and the 96th Wing to provide 108. The new 95th Wing, limited in experience, was not scheduled for this first take-off which would be in darkness. Of paramount importance were the directives aimed at ensuring no short bombing occurred as the first assault troops would be from 400 yards to a mile off-shore during the attack. The aircraft would go over their targets (check points and coastal defences) chiefly in waves of three six-plane flights in line abreast. An H2X pathfinder Liberator would fly in every third flight in case weather prevented visual bombing. No second runs were to be made. Strict flight procedures held that any aircraft returning over the Channel along the defined bomber penetration corridors would be fired on regardless; any

aborts had to be made before leaving England. There were also strict instructions on the use of distress flares and gunners were not allowed to fire at other aircraft unless actually attacked.

Because of the congested air space over England that night and difficulties of assembling such a large force in darkness, searchlight beacons had been set up to mark the limits of the assembly areas allotted to the three bombardment divisions. The 2nd Division would take off and fly north-east to a specially designated area stretching from the Mersey to the Humber estuaries. One of the 3rd Division's Wings was also to assemble in this area. Heights had to be carefully observed to avoid colliding with other forces assembling at lower altitudes and RAF bombers returning from their operations.

In bright moonlight the first Eighth Air Force heavies were airborne shortly before 2 am but over the next few hours heavy cloud began to form and hamper those units taking off later in the night. In company with a 389th Group H2X pathfinder, the 446th's leadship *Red Ass*, carrying Colonel Jacob Brogger, led the 2nd Division Liberators over the target area at 05.55 hrs and within twenty minutes the last of this force had bombed. Overcast conditions necessitated the use of radar for this attack and that of the other two divisions which arrived on the scene some forty-five minutes later, to pound the centre and eastern sectors of the designated beach-head.

Before all the first mission bombers had returned to base another force had set out with the object of bombing villages that gave access to roads leading to the beach-head. Leaflets had previously been dropped to warn the French inhabitants. There was only one pathfinder aircraft available for this force of 296 B-24s and 84 B-17s, and as conditions were still not much improved only 37 of the 3rd Division Liberators were fortunate enough to find clear patches through which they could drop. Early in the afternoon 73 B-24s of the 2nd Division flew to blast enemy positions in and around Caen using PFF techniques. One six-plane formation did not bomb due to failure of the leader's G-H equipment. Finally, late in the afternoon, 736 B-17s and B-24s took off to attack mainly transportation targets in the beach-head area. Cloud became exceptionally heavy resulting in many aircraft attaching them-

D-Day: 486th BG B-24s pass over a few of the ships gathered off the Normandy beach-head near Caen.—(USAF)

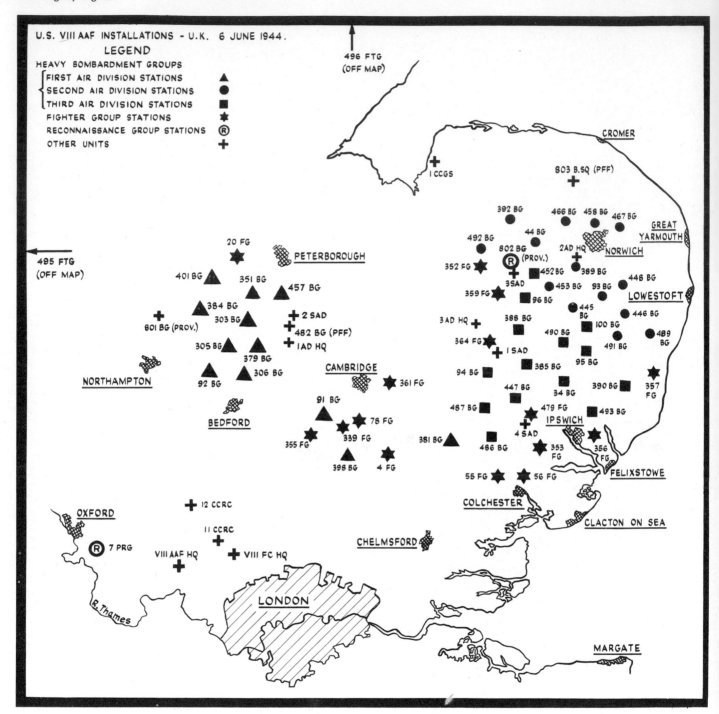

Unit	Location	Equipment	Unit	Location	Equipment
VIII AAF HQ	HIGH WYCOMBE		96 BG	SNETTERTON HEATH	B-17
VIII FC HQ	BUSHEY HALL		100 BG	THORPE ABBOTTS	B-17
1AD HQ	BRAMPTON GRANGE		303 BG	MOLESWORTH	B-17
2AD HQ	KETTERINGHAM HALL		305 BG	CHELVESTON	B-17
3AD HQ	ELVEDEN HALL		306 BG	THURLEIGH	B-17
4 FG	DEBDEN	P-51	339 FG	FOWLMERE	P-51
7 PRG	MOUNT FARM	F-5	351 BG	POLEBROOK	B-17
20 FG	KINGS CLIFFE	P-38	352 FG	BODNEY	P-47
34 BG	MENDLESHAM	B-24	353 FG	RAYDON	P-47
44 BG	SHIPDHAM	B-24	355 FG	STEEPLE MORDEN	P-51
55 FG	WORMINGFORD	P-38	356 FG	MARTLESHAM HEATH	P-47
56 FG	BOXTED	P-47	357 FG	LEISTON	P-51
78 FG	DUXFORD	P-47	359 FG	EAST WRETHAM	P-47
91 BG	BASSINGBOURN	B-17	361 FG	BOTTISHAM	P-47
92 BG	PODINGTON	B-17	364 FG	HONINGTON	P-38
93 BG	HARDWICK	B-24	379 BG	KIMBOLTON	B-17
94 BG	BURY ST EDMUNDS	B-17	381 BG	RIDGEWELL	B-17
95 BG	HORHAM	B-17	384 BG	GRAFTON UNDERWOOD	B-17

selves to the wrong formations in the murky conditions, and two units were so scattered they elected to abandon the raid prior to leaving England. On the far side of the Channel some cloud gaps allowed visual attack while formations not so fortunate again resorted to H2X.

A total of 2,362 heavy bomber sorties were flown by the three divisions on June 6th. A solitary 487th Group B-24 was the only Eighth heavy lost to enemy action—this on the first raid of the day. The perils of formation flying in ragged skies were brought home early to the 493rd Group on its ineffectual maiden mission when two B-24s collided and went down. To all intents and purposes the Luftwaffe failed to make any challenge to the day's operations; for the gunners in the bombers, at least, the occasion was something of an anti-climax.

Massive retaliation by the Luftwaffe was anticipated by the Eighth's airmen flying the two 500-bomber tactical missions launched the following day, but the Luftwaffe was still absent. The 487th Group again contributed the only loss in action when a B-24 was hit by flak. A 381st Fortress had to ditch in the Channel, but the crew were saved. The last mission brought the bombers back to their bases at dusk and as Liberators of the 34th Group began peeling off to land at Mendlesham "all hell broke out on the radio and intercom", to use the words of Captain Robert M. Simpson, pilot in a squadron lead aircraft. A few intruding Me410s shot down four Liberators in a matter of minutes; one crashed into an equipment store on the airfield, destroying heated suits, parachutes, oxygen masks, etc. To survive, individual bombers doused navigational lights and headed westwards. No further B-24s were shot down, but two 490th Group machines were wrecked in a runway collision while seeking refuge at Feltwell. Night fighters accounted for one of the intruders. This fright alerted air gunners once more to realise that crossing in over the English coast did not necessarily signify safety. The general standard of aircraft recognition among gunners still left much to be desired, as was illustrated some days later when a black RAF Beaufighter imprudently stole up on a Liberator flying near Colchester. The tail gunner was convinced the machine he despatched was an intruder.

Tactical missions in support of the ground forces were the orders for a week following D-Day, the heavies flying in strength whenever weather permitted. Targets were principally bridges, rail and road junctions, and airfields, with attacks at group or wing strength. During this period it was the Liberators that were involved in the most notable incidents.

The new groups were still having their trials with formating and assembly and there were also technical difficulties, notably

Not a double winged Liberator but the result of a runway collision between two 490th BG machines. No. 2 propeller of *Madame Shoo Shoo,* completely severed the tail and rear end of *Flying Ginny* when landing too close behind after dark at Feltwell on 7 Jun. 1944.—(USAF)

with bomb clusters in the B-24 racks. Cluster attachments allowed a greater number of small bombs to be carried but the attachments and the bomb bay gear were not good partners. On June 7th several clusters failed to release and eight fell through the bomb doors as 491st Group aircraft returned over England. Similar trouble was experienced by the 489th three days later when the Group attempted to bomb Conches. Many clusters of two or three 100 lb bombs jammed in the shackles. Some clusters were not held all that tightly and by the time the Group arrived over Halesworth eleven Liberators had their bomb doors torn off and flapping by dislodged clusters falling through. Again some bombs fell on the English countryside; indeed, similar incidents occurred with some frequency throughout June as Liberators sought their bases. Bombs went astray for other reasons, also on the 7th two squadrons of the 93rd Group unloaded their bays 40 miles north-east of their assigned targets, at Alencon, due to a field tele-tape error which gave incorrect data for setting up the G-H equipment.

It was a Liberator formation that experienced the first—if meagre—fighter interception on heavies since the invasion began. Twelve Me109s shot down a 446th Group aircraft in a surprise encounter near Jersey on the 8th. The air gunners claimed two of the enemy. Another 446th machine fell to Me109s near Rennes on the 12th: a brief engagement that also resulted in the Group's last fighter "destroyed" credit of the war.

The Luftwaffe's effort was an insignificant menace compared to the coastal flak which usually claimed two or three

Unit	Location	Equipment	Unit	Location	Equipment
385 BG	GREAT ASHFIELD	B-17	486 BG	SUDBURY	B-24
388 BG	KNETTISHALL	B-17	487 BG	LAVENHAM	B-24
389 BG	HETHEL	B-24	489 BG	HALESWORTH	B-24
390 BG	FRAMLINGHAM	B-17	490 BG	EYE	B-24
392 BG	WENDLING	B-24	491 BG	METFIELD	B-24
398 BG	NUTHAMPSTEAD	B-17	492 BG	NORTH PICKENHAM	B-24
401 BG	DEENETHORPE	B-17	493 BG	DEBACH	B-24
445 BG	TIBENHAM	B-24	495 FTG	ATCHAM	P-47
446 BG	BUNGAY	B-24	496 FTG	GOXHILL	P-38 & P-51
447 BG	RATTLESDEN	B-17	801 BG	HARRINGTON	B-24
448 BG	SEETHING	B-24	802 BG	WATTON	B-24 & MOS.
452 BG	DEOPHAM GREEN	B-17	803 B.SQ.	OULTON	B-17
453 BG	OLD BUCKENHAM	B-24	11 CCRC	BOVINGDON	B-17
457 BG	GLATTON	B-17	12 CCRC	CHEDDINGTON	B-24
458 BG	HORSHAM ST FAITH	B-24	1 CCGS	SNETTISHAM	
466 BG	ATTLEBRIDGE	B-24	1 SAD	TROSTON	
467 BG	RACKHEATH	B-24	2 SAD	ABBOTS RIPTON	
479 BG	WATTISHAM	P-38	3 SAD	NEATON	
482 BG	ALCONBURY	B-17	4 SAD	HITCHAM	

The first four-engine bomber to land on a beach-head airstrip, awaits repair in a French field.—(USAF)

bombers on each of these days. A 467th Group B-24 crippled by flak on the 12th became the first four-engined aircraft to make use of an Allied airstrip freshly carved from the Normandy countryside. With two engines out and two damaged, pilot 1/Lt Charles W. Grace could not attempt the Channel crossing. After eight crew members had parachuted he and the co-pilot successfully put the B-24 down on the short strip.

Another aspect of Liberator activity at this time was the efforts of the 458th Group's special unit charged with testing the Azon radio-controlled bombs. This new weapon was highly secret and the small formations, at most 15 aircraft, were well cosseted by fighters. Flak, however, was the real danger as to deliver its three 1,000 lb missiles each aircraft had to circle the target three times. Perfect weather conditions were a pre-requisite to the Azon technique, so that the controller in the B-24 could keep the smoke marker attached to the bomb in sight and radio the necessary control adjustments. The attacks were aimed at bridges which were highly suitable targets for the technique, but only on five occasions were conditions favourable and even then the attacks were unfruitful. On June 19th, Doolittle voiced his disappointment of the device and further missions were postponed.

Theoretically the B-24 was a better bomber than the B-17, being superior in speed, range and bomb load. In practice, it was not so well suited to the invironment of daylight operations as the Fortress, due to a number of factors that made the margin between control and loss of same much narrower than with the Boeing. Among measures to improve stability was the removal of ball turrets which began in June 1944. The benefits derived in high altitude flight were now considered to far outweight the defensive value of the turret. However, the record of the Liberators during the early months of 1944 had brought Doolittle and many of his staff to consider the Fortress the better vehicle for their purposes. The mixture of B-17s and

44-40066, an Azon B-24J of 458th BG. Rearmost of three aerial posts can be seen under tail turret.—(USAF)

B-24s in the 3rd Division had already presented problems and it was planned to convert the five Liberator groups to Fortresses at any early opportunity.

Expanding the B-17 force began in mid-June when the fourth squadron of the 305th Group was reformed. This Group had been operating with only three squadrons since the previous October when its 422nd Bomb Sqdn. had been transferred to night leaflet dropping operations. On June 19th the 858th Bomb Sqdn. belonging to 492nd Group was taken off operations and transferred to Cheddington to become the new night leaflet squadron; in truth, this was little more than a changing of designations as the operational personnel and aircraft complement remained substantially that of the 422nd, although the CO of the old 858th and a number of ground men did move to Cheddington and conversion from B-17s to B-24s followed. The aircrews and B-24s of the original 858th were divided amongst the three remaining squadrons at North Pickenham. On the very day this move was carried out (June 20th) the Luftwaffe was to take—in effect—another squadron from the 492nd Group.

Battle damage resulted in this brand new 34th BG aircraft being written off at Manston, 14 Jun. 1944.—(USAF)

Support for the ground forces in the crucial stages of strengthening the hard won bridgehead held precedence throughout June and July for the Eighth's heavies but at not infrequent opportunities Doolittle and Spaatz were able to return the B-17s and B-24s to strategic targets, principally oil. Indifferent weather brought indifferent results when part of the Eighth visited refineries at Misburg, Hamburg, Bremen and Hanover on June 15th and 18th. With fair conditions on the 20th a record force of 1,402 heavies plus 718 escort fighters set out for twelve such installations and other targets. Third Division B-17s and B-24s had primaries in the Magdeburg and Hanover areas: 1st Division B-17s at Hamburg, while the 2nd Division B-24s made the deepest penetration to Pölitz and Ostermoor.

Anticipating the probable target area of the B-24s, the Germans marshalled a large twin-engined Zerstörer force at a point where Mustangs would be less likely to appear. As the Liberators turned in from the Baltic over the Greifswalder Bodden they were assailed by Me110s and Me410s, firing rockets into the rear and flanks. The 14th Wing, in the van of Division, were singled out for particular attention and the trailing low group, the 492nd, suffered most. When a count was taken back at North Pickenham it appeared that fourteen of the Group's Liberators had been shot down. All told, 34 were missing from 2nd Division; but the picture was not as grim as first feared. Bulltofta airfield near the southernmost point of neutral Sweden had gathered many ailing US bombers during the past months, but the Swedes were somewhat startled when no less than 16 Liberators arrived on this fine June afternoon.

In all, 19 B-24s and a B-17 put down in Sweden that day, five from the battered 492nd Group. Relieved that the 2nd

Completion of 40 missions seemed a good occasion for the men who flew and serviced *Ol' Gappy* to get together for a photograph (12 Jun. 1944). S/Sgt Joe Sligoski and the ground team would send this 379th BG Fortress on 157 missions by the end of the war: believed a record unequalled by any other Eighth AF bomber.—(USAF)

Division had not suffered as severely as first feared, Eighth Air Force was nonetheless perturbed that such a large number of bombers should seek sanctuary in Sweden, particularly as it was reported many were undamaged. Sweden offered an easy escape from combat and although the explanations for seeking the sanctuary of this neutral country were said to be valid, an uneasy doubt remained. Despite its mauling the 2nd Division was able to cause extensive damage to the synthetic oil plant at Pölitz. Two Third Division wings did likewise at Megdeburg's Rothensee plant and experienced the only other German interceptors to evade the escort, when single-engined fighters attacked the 45th Wing from the rear, and shot down three bombers. Intense flak was met at all these vital oil targets and at V1 sites in France attacked by other forces, accounting for 22 bombers of the 49 lost this day and over 400 damaged to some degree.

The "new" B-24 groups visiting the Pas de Calais had a very rough passage through accurate flak. A lead 489th Group machine, the only MIA loss of the evening raid, was believed to have come to grief through following a "spoof" VHF message to make a 5° course correction. It brought the Liberator and those following within range of several batteries.

Such trips to NOBALL targets were certainly not milk runs and the 489th could hardly forecast a safe return for Prince Bernhard of the Netherlands who stole a flight in the co-pilot's seat of Lt Rumler's aircraft the following day. His mother-in-law, Queen Wilhelmina, had forbidden him to fly combat operations, but there were few of the ominous black puffs at 21,000 ft to threaten the royal presence and the Queen would not hear of the escapade.

The major mission of June 21st reached epic proportions, being so far the largest Eighth Air Force attack on Berlin and its environs. This mission had been planned as a combined RAF/USAAF strike at the German capital, with the British element as some measure of retaliation for the V1 attacks then being mounted on London. RAF participation fell through because of insufficient fighter escort being available to take care of the slower and less heavily armed British bombers. The Eighth Air Force eventually launched 1,311 heavies with 1,190 fighters (including five groups from the Ninth Air Force); the bombers used the North Sea skirting route to confuse the German defences and minimise the time over hostile territory. The bomber stream was spearheaded by two combat wings of 3rd Division, B-17s of the 1st Division were next in line, then the Liberators of the 2nd Division with a larger 3rd Division Fortress formation bringing up the rear. It was anticipated that

in the excellent weather conditions prevailing the Luftwaffe would make some effort to intercept, despite the almost one-to-one escort to bomber ratio. This materialised in the form of Me410s at Geschwader strength coming in on the tails of 1st Wing's Fortresses near Berlin. But by far the heaviest fighter opposition was directed from nose and tail at B-24s which for the second day running took heavy losses. A score of the 44 total heavies missing were from this force, with the 389th Group suffering most. A suspected enemy decoy Liberator, seen near Berlin by the escort, was carrying markings of this group; possibly it was a machine captured on an earlier mission. The Berlin flak barrage again proved a formidable obstacle and claimed many victims. Some 2,000 tons of bombs were delivered at a number of targets in the vicinity, with what was termed "excellent" results.

Highlighting the day's activities was the leading B-17 force which, having bombed, swung eastwards to fly on and land at Soviet bases. Shuttle missions had always held some appeal for planners in the AAF although the first and famous shuttle to North Africa via Regensburg in August 1943 had brought

Another famous Fort and her ground crew: l. to r. Sgt William Hemmila, Cpl Howard McKinney, M/Sgt Magnuson (chief) and Sgt Herbert Westendorf. *Fancy Nancy IV* started operations 3 Feb. 1944 and flew 134 by the end of the war.—(Magnuson)

Flight Jacket of crewmember records his missions and escapes from earlier *Fancy Nancy's*.—(Magnuson)

Taxiway collisions could be nasty. This one, between 43-37€86 and 44-6010 occurred at Thorpe Abbots on 21 Jun. 1944. Machines had been pulled apart when this picture was taken.—(USAF).

many difficulties in maintenance and aircraft repair on arrival, making further missions impracticable. Attention then shifted to Russia, where there seemed several attractive advantages. Apart from political motives aimed at winning Russian confidence, the chief benefit was greater ability to strike at industries the Germans were re-establishing in Eastern Europe to escape aerial attack. Also, to contest Russian-based missions the enemy would also have to stretch further his defences. There were, nevertheless, many obstacles, not least the Russians' suspicions with their restrictions on the numbers of US personnel required to provide technical services at the bases. By the end of May 1944 three bases were available to the Eastern Command of USSTAF. These were Poltava, Mirgorod and Piryatin, all east of Kiev. The first Russian shuttle was successfully executed by Fifteenth Air Force B-17s on June 2nd; Eighth Air Force involvement with the cross-Channel invasion had precluded its participation until later.

Six 3rd Division groups were prepared for the Eighth's first venture to Russia, and five of these had also flown the African shuttle. With the usual secrecy, selected crews were given special indoctrination on Russian base facilities, being told how to conduct themselves and given language cards. After a few abortive alerts the mission was finally briefed for the 21st, when special escape packs were issued. This was also officially the Division's first operation under its new commander, Major General Earle Partridge; the talented Le May (who had flown the African shuttle) being transferred to the Pacific to prove the B-29 force.

Each of the 163 B-17s despatched was fitted with a bomb-bay tank to increase endurance, and most carried a ground crew technician. In three combat wing formations, the first headed by 388th Group with the task force commander, Colonel Archie Old, the assembly led the way for the bombers into Germany. Their target, a synthetic oil plant some fifty miles south of Berlin, was reached without encountering any aerial opposition, and was accurately bombed. At this point the bombers were met by four squadrons of Mustangs ready to accompany them to Russia which proved able to effectively deal with the meagre opposition encountered on the long haul. The journey from England had seen the Fortresses airborne for nearly twelve hours when the 45th Wing prepared to put down on Poltava and the 13th Wing at Mirgorod. Unsuspected by the Americans, the Luftwaffe had a high altitude shadowing aircraft following the B-17 formations over the eastern battle lines into Soviet territory, far enough to establish the bases for which they were making. The Russian night air defences were of a different calibre to those in England for the Luftwaffe mounted a night raid, something it had never attempted against the Eighth's home bases.

Five hours after the Americans had arrived some 60 He111 and Ju88 bombers illuminated Poltava with flares and proceeded to drop over 100 tons of assorted ordnance before flying off without hurt to themselves. Ammunition dumps were hit and 450,000 gallons of fuel was ignited. Twenty-five Russians were killed, chiefly in brave efforts to fight the fires, but miraculously only one US serviceman. The morning brought a fantastic sight—44 of the 72 Fortresses on the field were burnt out or blasted wrecks and another 26 had damage. Fifteen other US and Russian aircraft were also smashed. The 13th Wing at Mirgorod and the fighters at Piryatin had not been molested but in anticipation of another visit from the Luftwaffe the following night the B-17s were moved to Zaporozhe, 150 miles to the south. A wise move, for Mirgorod was indeed the recipient of a great many bombs which struck fuel and ammunition supplies and caused much havoc.

The brilliantly executed and timed attack on Poltava brought the Germans a better return than all their costly efforts to contest the Americans over the Reich a few hours before. All told, within 24 hours the Eighth had lost 88 bombers and 22 fighters plus several aircraft condemned as salvage. In terms of aircraft probably the most costly 24 hours in its history, but not in their personnel.

Throughout the remainder of June, British based B-17s and B-24s were despatched at every opportunity with more than a thousand sorties recorded on many days, in fact, it was to be their busiest month of the war. On the 24th the 1st Division made an unsuccessful attempt to hit an oil refinery on H2X

Oxygen bottles lie in the burnt out hulk of a 452nd BG Fortress at Poltava.

A direct flak hit ignited the fuel tanks of 493rd BG's *Little Warrior* in an instant. Fourteen aircraft of the group were bombing a target of opportunity, Quakenbrück; 29 Jun. 1944.—(USAF)

The first *Jamaica Ginger* was lost at Poltava. Lt Frank Prendergast and crew were given this 'silver' B-17G on which they bestowed the same name. Picture was taken soon after she was received at Knettishall and before the nickname was painted on.

images at Bremen, while on the 29th a major raid to oil and aircraft production installations in the Leipzig area was also disappointing. Fortunately the Luftwaffe offered little counter action on this last occasion, as bomber formations lagged and wandered so that the escort could not have offered adequate protection for the 200 mile long column that resulted at one stage.

For the most part operations continued to be of a predominately tactical nature, with French airfields and communications in the fore. During this period, however, the 3rd Division was presented with another unusual task, the dropping of supplies to French partisans. The first of these special operations was flown on June 25th and another three would be undertaken during the next three months, all of which proved to be comparatively easy and most successful.

The Maquis strongholds lay in the sparsely populated southeastern area of France, away from the known anti-aircraft defences so that the B-17s could safely descend to altitudes as low as 2,000 feet prior to releasing parachute containers. For June 25th five dropping zones were arranged and visual and radio contact was established on arrival so that formation leaders knew that the Maquis, and not the Germans, would receive the supplies—mostly small arms, bazookas and ammunition. A formation of Fortresses attacked a Toulouse airfield as a ruse to hide the purpose and destination of other units.

In muggy weather 180 B-17s left the English coast and as the mission progressed, so the sky cleared. Two B-17s aborted, two were lost en route, one to flak and the other to a sneak attack by a single enemy fighter. This left 176 aircraft to drop 2,077 containers; as contact could not be established with partisans at Cantel the formation assigned this zone took its loads to another locality. From some bombers "very special passengers" parachuted; OSS men charged with instructing

the Maquis on use and maintenance of the weapons delivered. This mission was to supplement the work of the US element engaged in regular delivery of supplies and agents to underground agencies in western Europe, the 801st Group (P) at Harrington, known as the "Carpetbaggers" from the code word given to these secret operations.

This provisional 801st Group was created from two squadrons of a disbanded anti-submarine group; personnel and some B-24Ds had moved to Alconbury in November 1943 to form the nucleus of these so-called Bomb Sqdns. numbered the 36th and 406th. Equipped and trained at Alconbury, they moved to Watton in February and to Harrington early in April when they were assigned to the 801st Group, a specially established HQ under Lt Col Clifford Heflin. Harrington was near Tempsford, the RAF base engaged in similar activities from where the US units derived their initial know-how. In fact, the first operation was flown from Tempsford on the night of January 4th/5th, 1944.

While this work was highly secret, the aircraft of the 801st stood out significantly from their fellows and were the cause of much curiosity wherever they put down, for normal camouflage was replaced by an overall coat of gloss black. Nose, waist guns and ball turret were removed, the opening left by the turret being utilised as an exit for parachutists. Waist windows were blacked out and tear-drop perspex blisters were added to both cockpit side windows to allow pilots better visibility in searching for landmarks and signals. Internally, navigator and bombardier had separate compartments to afford them more room. Special equipment was installed, a two-way radio for direct contact with a ground operator, and ultimately Rebecca, a directional air-ground device that received radar impulses from a ground set and aided the navigator in bringing the aircraft over the dropping point. A demand for services had increased as the invasion came nearer and on May 27th two further squadrons were assigned, the 788th and 850th from the 467th and 490th Groups, both hitherto normal daylight units.

Operating individually in darkness, the "Carpetbaggers" had undertaken 792 sorties during their first six months of which 465 had resulted in successful delivery to French patriots. They had delivered 115 special agents and cargo comprising 5,439 arms containers, 2,707 other packages, several thousand leaflets and 17 pigeon hampers. The work was not without risk, as it was often necessary to orbit a given location until satisfactory signals were received from the ground: time enough for a night fighter to make contact. Twelve aircraft had so far been lost, the cause was not always established.

During July 1944, Eighth Air Force bombers were out on 27 days. The tactical needs of Allied armies in Normandy still held

With undercarriage lowered to restrict speed, 94th BG B-17s drop supply canisters to French partisans at Vercors; 14 Jul. 1944.—(IWM)

492nd BG's *Boulder Buff* under Swedish guard after arrival at Bulltofta, 6 Jul. 1944.—(Olausson)

first claim, but a number of missions into Germany, notably against oil targets, were flown. With 2,000 aircraft and crews available in 40 groups, and half VIII FC now equipped with long range Mustangs, the ventures into hostile air space were usually on a grand scale. Instead of the one or two targets per day of the previous summer, it was now not unusual for a dozen to be briefed. The contrast in scope is best illustrated by totals of bombers despatched in June 1943 and 1944—2,154 and 28,791 respectively. Even with such numbers the Eighth did not move with impunity from the Luftwaffe which continued to extract a toll whenever the opportunity allowed; although these incidents were but small wounds to the giant.

Yes, it can be hot in England. A mechanic works in the shade of *Mizpah* at Ridgewell, Independence Day 1944.—(USAF)

The first notable occasion in July was on the 7th when 756 Forts and 373 Liberators returned to the area of operations of June 29th; on this occasion Böhlen, Merseburg and Lutzendorf, synthetic oil plants and aircraft factories at Leipzig. The executioners were Wilhelm Moritz's Sturmgruppe of J.G.3 who were responsible for the greater part of the 23 Liberators cut down in this action. Their claims of 30 for the Gruppe and 54 for the whole Geschwader were optimistic, as only 37 heavies failed to return from all operations that day. This was the third occasion that 492nd Group had suffered severely at the hands of fighters in barely two months of operations and it now had the unenviable record of sustaining the highest loss rate of all Eighth groups. Yet most of the Liberator groups that became operational around the same time as the 492nd, had yet to see an enemy fighter. The superstitious averred that the jinx that had started with the "Eightballs" and passed to the second Group to join the Wing, the 392nd, had now settled on the 492nd. The 14th Combat Wing, in which it served certainly had more than its share of disastrous missions, yet its bombing record was good and sometimes outstanding; it was headed by Leon Johnson one of the most able commanders in the Eighth.

Strangely, the Group with the bloodiest record in the Eighth Air Force was not the 492nd, the "Eightballs", the "Bloody Hundredth" or any of the jinx groups that were so often linked with ill fortune in airmen's conversation. This was the 96th at Snetterton Heath, which suffered persistently. During 1944 up to D-Day it had lost a hundred B-17s in the course of as many missions probably a greater loss rate than any other USAAF bomber group in the Second World War. Two days before the 492nd's disaster at Bernburg, the remnants of the 96th had returned with the rest of the 3rd Division shuttlers from the Soviet Union, having struck an oil plant in Poland and gone on to Italy, from there flown a mission to Rumania with the Fifteenth Air Force, and finally bombed a rail yard while winging over France on their way home. The remnants of the 96th amounted to only three B-17s—17 of the 21 reaching the Soviet Union had been destroyed at Poltava.

To the unit concerned, assaults such as that experienced by 492nd Group on July 7th assumed large proportions. While the improving strength and quality of fighter escort had lessened the opportunities for the Luftwaffe, there was nearly always some unguarded point which the enemy exploited. The ability of the Eighth Air Force to sustain its Fortress and Liberator fleet as viable purveyors of ordnance was now almost wholly dependent upon fighter escort. Furthermore, it was plain that had the Luftwaffe developed the techniques and tactics it now employed a year previously, the unescorted bomber doctrine would have faltered long before it did. As previously mentioned, many bomber crews completed their 30 or 35 missions (the length of a tour had been extended after D-Day) without ever seeing an enemy fighter; a year before, a mission without sight of Messerschmitts or Focke-Wulfs was unusual. In the weeks following the Allied invasion most Jagdgruppen committed to the defence of the Reich were despatched to France in support of the Wehrmacht, leaving behind some ten Gruppen chiefly those of J.G.300 and J.G.301 originally formed for night fighting, plus a few battle-weary oddments. The most successful IV/J.G.3 was, however, retained and frequently clashed with the Eighth, the basis of its success being by hitting hard, fast, and in strength. This Gruppen had now largely forsaken head-on attacks for those directed at the rear.

An idea of an airman's experience of these tactics is given in the words of Lt Marion Havelaar, bombardier in the 91st Group Fortress *The Peacemaker*, flying to attack an airfield at Leipzig on July 20th:—

"It happened as the lead formation began to space out for the bomb run. Our squadron, the 401st, was in the low position, the most vulnerable if fighters were going to attack. I had been

Bombardier Lt Marion Havelaar squints in the glare of the bare metal as he surveys the damage to *The Peacemaker*. Havelaar wears a standard electrically heated suit (gloves hang by electric flex), Mae West lifesaver, and harness for chest pack parachute.—(USAF)
Bombardier and ball turret gunner of *The Peacemaker* carry out a holes count. They soon gave up.—(USAF)

checking over the bombsight getting all the data set up when I suddenly noticed a line of small white puffs ahead of us. At the same moment as my mind registered 'self-destroying cannon shells', one of the crew yelled 'fighters!' Almost immediately I caught sight of the grey shapes of Focke-Wulfs flashing past and S-ing away down. The next moment our formation leader, afire from one wing tip to the other, slid across our nose. An FW190 appeared not more than 200 feet from the left of my window, firing at a bomber ahead. By this time I had reached the nose guns and swung them after him as he dived away. In the turmoil there was no chance to see whether my fire claimed him. Then it was all over: where a few moments before there had been smoke, flame, Forts and FWs, now there was just sky. I suddenly realised *The Peacemaker* must be damaged and had slipped away back from the rest of the formation. The navigator told me we were probably in bad shape and went up to the pilots. It seemed like a year before he came back and said we were losing altitude and had got to get rid of anything we could spare. We started throwing out all odds and ends of loose equipment. As we could not converse he pointed to the 20 lb bombsight: I shook my head. Later he went back to the pilots returning to point at the bombsight again. I gently pulled the pin, picked it up and carried it over to the hatch. We dropped it out carefully trying not to damage it in the process! Ridiculous perhaps, but long training in the care of this valuable piece of equipment still had its effect in spite of the emergency." *The Peacemaker* made it back to Bassingbourn; eight others did not.

Another threat to the day bombers loomed large. For months the cameras of RAF reconnaissance aircraft had been following the introduction of the German jet fighters. There was now evidence that they were being brought into the battle. Tell-tale marks, left by jet exhaust scorch, were well in evidence at Leipheim, Lechfeld and Swabisch-Hall airfields during May and June. By the end of June thirty airfields had been identified as having the special buildings associated with the servicing of these aircraft. Early in July intense activity had been noticed at Rechlin.

The mission by the 91st Group on July 20th was a strike on an airfield suspected of harbouring jet activity and, as with a number of missions during the month, an attempt to further delay their operational employment apart from stifling any resurgence of Jagdverbände strength. Then, on July 28th, returning bomber crews reported sighting strange tail-less aircraft above them leaving exhaust trails. The Me163 rocket fighters were abroad: the jet menace was a reality.

While the Eighth reacted to this new threat, another receded. After mid-July the twin-engined Me410 Zerstörers were noticeably absent, in fact Z.G.26 and Z.G.76 were being disbanded. While they had achieved many notable successes against the heavies during the spring and early summer they had suffered repeatedly at the hands of the US fighters. With the steady increase in Mustang units there was no longer a safe area of the Nazi empire where Zerstörers could be employed without undue risk. The bombing of factories and depots had also brought maintenance and replacement problems and, with the improvement in single-engined fighter production, the decision was taken to withdraw them from combat.

The Eighth looked to its fighter units to maintain their supremacy and protect the bombers. There could be no newer and faster bombers to replace the Fortresses and Liberators in this war: they would have to finish the job with the tools in hand. The Force looked, as it constantly did, for improved methods of application both to reduce losses and to better bombing, and in July a notable development yielded encouraging results. Like many good ideas it arose largely through the endeavours of one persistent individual.

Colonel Budd Peaslee had come to the ETO as Commander of the 384th Group, leading it through its early, gruelling missions during the summer of 1943. During a later Wing posting he had flown as Task Force Commander on a number of major operations, including the costly October Schweinfurt

1st Wing bombs Lechfeld, 19 Jul. 1944. This airfield was the scene of development work on the Me 262 jet. Aircraft can be seen dispersed over a wide area, but jets were kept in covered emplacements so as to hide them from Allied photographic reconnaissance.—(USAF)

mission. On more than one occasion he was foiled by the unpredictable European weather, and faced the difficult decision of whether or not to abandon a mission involving several hundred bombers. Weather reconnaissance had always been a prerequisite of any mission and, apart from the constant RAF sorties flown into hostile skies with this object, the Eighth Air Force had stepped up its own participation. In spite of frequent weather reports, it often transpired that conditions would deteriorate while a mission was in progress leading to complications and sometimes failure or abandonment. One such instance was the Knaben raid in November 1943, where Peaslee had to manoeuvre his B-17 wing around the area to bomb through a cloud break; here his idea germinated. Peaslee advocated weather scouting aircraft preceding the bombers by a few minutes to transmit on-the-spot reports of weather encountered en route and in the target area to the Force Commander. In this way a weather front might be avoided by

changing course or altitude, or seemingly impenetrable cloud formations found to be capable of safe penetration. Such scout aircraft could also give warning of enemy aircraft, keep an eye on the bomber stream for wandering formations and similar relevant information.

Peaslee interested Doolittle in his idea and in May 1944 started experiments to evolve the best methods. He started with the Mosquito used by the weather squadron at Watton, but in spite of its speed the aircraft appeared too vulnerable to loiter in the target area, particularly as its function would soon become obvious to the enemy. He then endeavoured to persuade the leading elements of the normal fighter escort to undertake this work, but it proved impracticable principally because the average fighter pilot did not have the necessary knowledge of bomber problems to evaluate situations. Peaslee's next step was to recruit experienced bomber pilots who had completed a tour, send them to Goxhill for a fighter

Birmingham Blitzkrieg, a B-17E that flew to Rouen on the Eighth's first mission, served out her last days as 'hack' with 379th BG. Painted with white stripes she acted on tow-target and assembly duties.—(USAF)

During the major missions of July, the Eighth Air Force almost attained some of the ideals of strategic bombing that its sponsors had hoped for earlier. The cumulative effect of the mounting attack on oil installations was such that production was estimated to have been reduced by half during this month alone. The effort was apportioned among synthetic plants, crude oil refineries and storage depots, trans-shipment points and even inactive refineries. Coupled with the efforts of the Fifteenth Air Force, the oil situation became even more critical for the German war machine. Again aircraft targets were featured. The complexes making Ju88 and Me410 components suffered particularly severely and whenever intelligence pointed to jet aircraft construction or activity, the bombers were also soon upon the scene; Friedrichshafen/Löwenthal and Manzell works, believed engaged on final production and experimentation, the Junkers factory at Dessau and Leipzig/Taucha engaged on engine and airframe assembly, the Leipham Me262 works, and four other installations all suspected of some connection with jet aircraft.

Calls for tactical support were also answered and on a number of occasions the heavies flew at reduced altitude over France to drop bombs on bridges and check-points, and on the 14th at much lower altitude to make another very successful delivery to the Maquis. The most notable tactical missions of the month were saturation bombing attacks as softeners for an attempt by Allied armies to break out of the Normandy beach-head. The first of these fell to the Liberators of 2nd Division in support of the British attack at Caen, where the Germans had their strongest positions. The 571 B-24s unloaded 1,425·4 tons of HE and fragmentation bombs 300 yards in front of the British troops. Six squadrons failed to bomb as they could not identify ground markers and feared hitting friendly personnel. On July 24th a massive force of 1,586 was sent to give similar treatment to German positions facing American troops near St Lo. The first comers of 2nd Division found 10/10th cloud and returned without bombing. Third Division arrived next but only 35 aircraft of the 388th Group were able to attack and then only after three runs looking for a gap in the clouds. The last arrivals found the cloud broken and 317 dropped, others attempted a second run but received a recall signal.

There were two incidents that turned this largely abortive mission into one of disaster. The bombardier in a Second Division B-24 accidentally hit the release switch when startled by a packet of chaff (radar jamming strips) striking the nose turret. Unhappily the bombs released fell on Chippelle landing strip, killing four and wounding fourteen 404th Group personnel, plus the destruction of two P-47s. In another bomber a lead bombardier had trouble with a sticking release mechanism and, in his efforts to free it, inadvertently salvoed part of the bomb load. As a result of 12 other aircraft following this lead, forward US troops had casualties of 16 killed and 60 wounded.

Mushroom cloud over Suffolk. 19.30 hrs, 15 Jul. 1944. The Metfield bomb dump blows up.—(Blue)

conversion course, and eventually to Honington where he had established his base equipped with P-51D Mustangs. By using normal fighters they would arouse less attention from the Luftwaffe and, being armed, were able to defend themselves. However, as the main object was to scout, the wing man in a two-plane element would be a regular fighter pilot. The aircraft of the 1st Scouting Force, as it came to be known, were maintained by the 385th Ftr. Sqn. which also provided the wingmen.

Forty-two year old Peaslee led his scouts on their first operation when over a thousand heavies made for Munich and other targets in the southern part of the Reich on July 16th. Five days later they proved their worth conclusively during a major mission to the same area. Preceding the 1st Division, heading for Schweinfurt and other targets in the vicinity, the Scouting Force ran into high cloud towering to 28,000 feet across the bombers run in. Skirting the front they found a clear route and transmitted this information to the 1st Division leaders on the special fighter-bomber frequency which, unfortunately, could not be heard by the following divisions.

In consequence, the 1st Division bombers avoided the clouds whereas formations of the 2nd Division ploughed into the overcast and most emerged in disarray. Some B-24s, completely lost, ended up in Switzerland. A few collided, and the bombing was largely abortive with most formations finding targets of opportunity. First Division losses amounted to three; 2nd Division lost 23, most—if indirectly—to penetrating the cloud front. After this the 2nd and 3rd Divisions lost little time in forming their own scouting forces.

Weather scouts found good visibility for the heavies on the long mission of July 18th; *The finest example of precision bombing I have ever seen* is how General Spaatz viewed the results at Peenemünde and Zinnowitz. Heavily and accurately bombed, the targets were experimental and testing establishments for V-weapon development. On the following three days, thousand-bomber forces were launched at oil and aircraft plants, and the bearing industry in Germany with Regensburg and Schweinfurt revisited.

Moment of release as 492nd BG's *That's All Brother* catches the signal over Saarbrucken; 16 Jul. 1944. Note bombs from higher aircraft falling 'in train'.—(USAF)

The heavies were called out again the following day to attempt a saturation attack. This time even stricter precautions were taken to avoid short bombing, but once again it occurred with even greater loss of life. The first error happened when a lead bombardier failed to synchronise his bomb sight before making a visual release, with the result that twelve B-24s dropped 470 x 100 lb bombs in US lines. A few minutes later another lead bombardier failed to identify his target properly, mistaking gun flashes for red artillery smoke markers. Eleven B-24s added 352 x 260 lb fragmentation bombs on the same area where the previous short bombing occurred. The third incident involved a command pilot who, under the impression bombing was by wings and not groups, ordered bombs released when he saw the lead group drop and while his bombardier was still sighting for range. In all, 102 army personnel were killed (including a Lieutenant-General) and 380 wounded.

With the high rate of operations attained during the summer of 1944—there were 28,776 heavy bomber sorties in July, second only to the 28,791 flown in June—the pace began to tell on both ground and aircrews alike. Fatigue was evident, particularly during periods when missions were flown on several consecutive days. Some airmen took only a couple of months to fly their tour of between 30 and 35 missions, and when not flying combat or training missions were to be found in "the sack". And this despite a ratio of nearly two crews to each bomber reached in July. In practice, however, this was rarely the case on a station. Also repeated flak damage on top of normal aircraft maintenance made life hectic for ground servicing personnel who were equally as weary as the fliers.

Constant operations made veterans of the groups that had arrived earlier in the year while some pioneer outfits had now passed their 200 mission mark. The first was "Hell's Angels" the 303rd Group on July 11th, followed two days later by the "Travelling Circus" (93rd Group) and shortly thereafter by the

467th BG's *Witchcraft* (after 59 missions) with her crew chief at Rackheath, Sgt Joe Ramirez.

other old stagers. The 467th Group Liberators flew their 100th mission on August 15th to Vechta having been operational only 140 days. A B-24H of this group, *Witchcraft*, had averaged one mission every two days having completed its 70th trip at this time without once having had to turn back.

Many B-24s and B-17s had run up impressive records in August. A fifty mission bomber was not uncommon while a few B-17s were nearing the 100 mark. First centenarian was probably an unnamed machine in the 384th Group crewed by M/Sgt Louis G. Hopps which had only one turn-back for mechanical reasons. Publicity however, was now almost exclusively given to record breakers having no turn-backs for mechanical reasons, as an incentive for good maintenance.

Chapter 21: Fighter Shield: Neptune and Frantic

Fighters of the Eighth Air Force were entrusted with diverse tasks for the invasion of Europe and on the days that followed. In the dark hours before dawn on June 4th 1944 there was feverish activity at Honington, Wormingford, Kings Cliffe and Wattisham. The previous evening ground crews had been issued with brushes and cans of paint with orders to apply alternating white and black stripes around the wings and tail booms of the P-38 Lightnings. The paint consignment had been labelled "For the cake walk". No explanation was given, but none was needed; every man believed this was for the long expected "Invasion". As each paint job was completed the work was covered to conceal it from passers-by on the roads running close to airfield boundaries. Base security was also tightened and visitors were neither allowed in nor out.

Because of their unique configuration, the P-38s were the first Allied aircraft to be adorned with what came to be commonly known as "Invasion stripes". They, and the P-38 groups of the Ninth Air Force, had been selected to fly shipping cover for the Allied convoys sailing to and from France as, however poor the standard of aircraft recognition of ship's gunners, they could hardly mistake the Lightnings. Low cloud and unfavourable winds put off the sailing of the first convoys for 24 hours and not until the afternoon of June 5th were the covers removed and aircraft readied for take-off. A rota-system ensured that two P-38 squadrons would be on Channel patrol at any time between dawn and dusk. The honour of the first patrol went to the 77th and 79th Ftr. Sqdns. flying from Kingscliffe, who took off for the Solent at 16.51 hrs.

Under plan NEPTUNE the P-38s were to provide a constant air umbrella for the 4,483 Allied ships in the Channel; Ninth Air Force P-47s and P-51s were to fly high cover over the beachhead, and the RAF fighters close support. The Eighth's P-51s and P-47s, then having the zebra-like markings applied, were assigned high altitudes—above 8000 feet—to provide high cover for bombers and troop carriers and to prevent enemy aircraft approaching the assault area. Nine groups were allotted patrol areas fanning out from Dungeness, across Dieppe and Rouen through Avranches and Jersey to Torquay, with the P-47s in the east and P-51s in the west. Two other

P-51 groups, the experienced 4th and 355th, had patrol areas outside this arc north-west and west of Paris during the first phase. Second phase operations consisted of strafing and bombing attacks against rail and road transport, fuel and ammunition dumps, troop concentrations and airfields. On receipt of special code words, the Poker terms STUD, ROYAL FLUSH and FULL HOUSE, the VIII FC groups would undertake various types of mission ranging from dive and skip bombing to escort for transports.

Fighter pilots expected an all-out effort by the Luftwaffe to oppose the landings and that vast air battles would ensue. They gathered excited and alert at the first briefings that night. At 03.00 hrs June 6th, the first P-51s units were taking off to commence patrols. Light rain at many places restricted visibility in the darkness. At Bodney, one Mustang taking off on a wrong heading crashed into the control tower killing the pilot; the burning wreckage providing a warning beacon for following aircraft. The unfamiliar task of formating in darkness was nevertheless accomplished and despite the adverse weather conditions and the many hundreds of other aircraft airborne, the fighter formations were marshalled and despatched much according to plan.

Surprisingly, Luftwaffe reaction to the landing was extremely limited and the relays of P-47s and P-51s, patrolling their respective areas, returned with reports of no opposition. The VIII FC put up 1,873 sorties between dawn and dusk in 73 patrols and 34 fighter-bomber missions; it was only later in the day that clashes were reported. The 355th Group caught a Ju88 formation trying to sneak up the Channel and claimed 15 shot down, while the 4th, 352nd and 56th Groups were embroiled with a few Focke-Wulfs and Messerschmitts. Total claims by VIII FC groups for the day amounted to 26 in the air, the same figure as Command fighters missing. J.G.26 had a minor success when it caught the elite 4th Group unawares and brought down four of its P-51s that were busy strafing.

The following day's operations were in similar vein—patrols, dive bombing, strafing and still comparatively little interference from the Luftwaffe. The 56th and 353rd Groups given the task of destroying parts of four main rail routes north-west

A pair of 359th FG P-51s found an ammunition train near Le Mans on D-Day. Good shooting by 1/Lt Oliphint produced this spectacular result.—(USAF)

of Paris by bombing, ran into several Staffeln of enemy fighters claiming 12 and 11 respectively; this constituted the majority of VIII FC air claims for the day (total Allied claims were 58). Losses were again heavy for the Eighth's fighters—27, mostly from ground fire although one 56th Thunderbolt was destroyed by the explosion of its own bombs on a marshalling yard. For the Lightning groups excitement had given way to routine as they droned over the Channel without interruption—save the occasional discharge of anti-aircraft weapons from ships whose gunners evidently did not consider even the P-38s unique form as friendly.

On the 8th 130 enemy aircraft were sighted during the day, mostly Me109s and FW190s in twos and threes, and the Eighth's fighters took the largest share of the claims, 31 of the 46 destroyed by all Allied forces. For the third day running the 56th and 353rd P-47 groups had the lion's share, the 56th catching seven enemy aircraft taking off from Illiers while the Raydon-based group scored five. Again the VIII FC loss was high, running to 24 MIA, albeit a small fraction of the 1,469 sorties. Targets for bombing and strafing included 25 marshalling yards, 13 bridges, 10 trains, 6 road convoys, 3 airfields, 2 groups of barges, a troop concentration, two radio towers, a transformer station, and a coastal battery. In nine attacks on rail tracks pilots claimed 27 locos destroyed and 116 rail wagons, with 13 locos and 232 rail waggons damaged. On the road they shot up 303 trucks, 17 other vehicles and two tanks.

By the late afternoon cloud interfered with air activity and on the following day it was so low and piled that the only mission VIII FC ran was a 16-plane escort for reconnaissance aircraft by 357th Group, while only 28 Lightnings managed the shipping patrols. On June 10th, however, when VIII FC groups were able to fly 1,525 sorties, their highest since D-Day, they found aerial opposition had stiffened.

At the time of the Allied landings in Normandy there were only some 80 operational Luftwaffe fighters in France with the "old faithfuls" J.G.2 and J.G.26. These depleted units could have little effect against the combined RAF and USAAF air fleets. Offensive action by bomber and anti-shipping units too, was limited and mostly carried out at night. The bulk of the Jagdverbände was in the Reich where some 1,000 fighters endeavoured to counter the daylight strategic missions of the Eighth and Fifteenth Air Forces. In truth, they had been forced within the borders of Germany by the overwhelming air superiority of the Allied fighter formations. With news of the landings, the German High Command had quickly decided to commit most Jagdgruppen in the Reich to action on the new Front, and by June 10th ten had arrived at bases ringing the Normandy area. Though the enhanced German fighter force was still numerically far inferior to the Allies it could, and did, assert its presence with telling effect on several occasions.

The Luftwaffe also started daylight fighter bomber operations against the Allied troop positions. The 352nd Group's 328th Ftr. Sqdn. encountered forty bomb-laden Me109s at 300 feet making for the beach-head. Led by Captain John Thornell the Mustangs intercepted the German aircraft causing them to jettison their loads and make off, but not before Thornell had added his 17th and 18th victory. More often it was the Allied fighter bombers that were bounced, particularly when low cloud favoured such tactics.

A Gruppe of Me109s and FW190s caught the 78th Group as it was attempting to bomb a marshalling yard on the 10th, shooting down five of the P-47s, although an equal toll was exacted by the 78th. The group lost four other aircraft this day, plus two in a cloud collision south of London. This by no means subdued the aggressive tendencies of the Group's pilots, for next day a radio monitor at the 66th Wing was surprised to hear the 78th's leader call, "Hello Oilskin, Hello Oilskin. I'm orbiting over Dieppe. I am at 15,000 ft and flying east—and that goes for you German bastards too, just in case you're listening in. Come on up!" This was a flagrant breach of radio silence, but

in the circumstances one to which authority turned a deaf ear.

Ground fire was also increasing in intensity as Wehrmacht reinforcements were brought up. Also on the 10th Mustangs of 359th Group escorting four F-5s photographing a marshalling yard just outside Antwerp, were briefed to cross the coast at Breskins at 1,500 ft and then come down to tree-top height and make for a canal check point. Intense anti-aircraft fire made detours necessary and the PRU aircraft lost their way. It was twenty minutes before the target was finally located by which time gun positions were fully alerted and put up such a heavy concentration of fire that the F-5s had to veer away on every attempted run. Captain Wayne Bolefahr, leading a section of the escort, apparently decided that with such heavy fire the reconnaissance aircraft would be unable to take satisfactory photographs, for on the next run he deliberately took his Mustang up to 100 feet and flew straight towards the main gun position. He successfully drew fire so that the F-5s had their chance to take the required pictures, but his Mustang hit several times, crashed into trees and Bolefahr perished in the wreckage.

Morale at Lightning stations soared when it was announced that the patrols flown on June 11th would be their last, and that the task of keeping an eye on Channel shipping would thereafter pass to RAF and Ninth Air Force fighters. The same day the Lightnings were sent on Droop Snoot fighter-bomber missions in the course of which they saw their first action since D-Day; the 55th Group engaged a Staffel of FW190s in the Tours area with a three for two result in the P-38s favour.

Sightings of enemy aircraft amounted to only 25 on the 11th, but the largest numbers since D-Day, over 200, reported on the 12th, reflected the influx of units transferred from Germany. The 352nd Group chased a Staffel of 109s that attacked B-24s near Rennes, shooting down three without loss. The 359th Group encountered eight Focke-Wulfs over Paris and claimed one, also without loss. But the 353rd Group, which had run into more airborne opposition than any of the other VIII FC units during the post D-Day period, was less fortunate. On a fighter-bomber mission the Group's P-47s were attacked by a Gruppe of Me109s whose pilots were reported as "experienced and aggressive". The 353rd fought off the enemy but eight of their P-47s were missing on return to Raydon.

There had always been a good deal of co-operation between the 56th and 353rd, even though their groups came under different Wings. They were originally neighbours at Halesworth and Metfield and when moved south they were again adjacent at Boxted and Raydon. The 353rd made another mission later in the day on June 11th, to attack Dreux/Evreux airfield (then occupied by II/J.G.3) from which the "experienced and aggressive" Me109s were believed to have come. This time it was planned that the 353rd would proceed to the neighbourhood of the target alone where, as the only Allied formation in the area, it was hoped the enemy would consider it weak

Ralph Hofer puts *Salem Representative* down on the first airstrip built on the Normandy beach-head: 13 Jun. 1944. Rifle fire had punctured an oil line.—(USAF)

A 20 mm shell hit the windscreen of Lt Col Wilson's P-38J, 42-104307, over France on 13 Jun. 1944. The 55th FS commander escaped with slight face cuts, first man in the squadron to be wounded in action during six months of combat. P-38's 'wheel' control column and the firing button are prominent in this picture.—(USAF)

enough to attack. The 56th Group was sent off to cover the 353rd, timed to arrive thirty minutes later and be in radio contact. The ruse worked, and the 353rd ran into 20 Me109s which made off towards Paris where another 40 joined them in a battle. The morning's action was avenged with claims of 9 Me109s and 3 damaged. When the 56th arrived they engaged a dozen Me109s that had just taken off, and a similar number of Messerschmitts joined in but the combat was in the "Wolfpack's" favour with five victories for no loss, although one P-47 was badly damaged and had to be bellied in by its pilot on a beach-head airstrip.

Despite the occasional reverses, the P-47 and P-51 groups could more than hold their own in these low altitude dog fights. Again on the 13th when the total VIII FC claims amounted to six destroyed, the 361st's Mustangs took four Me109s and elsewhere the 78th's Thunderbolts two, both without loss to themselves, although the enemy had initiated the action. Even if the American claims proved to be incorrectly assessed—and there were occasions when destroyed claims were made but no German aircraft were lost—they were never far from fact. The superiority of the VIII FC was, as related earlier, the cumulative effect of better aircraft, better trained pilots and better tactics. The Luftwaffe, well aware that they were outnumbered ten to one, wisely conserved their forces and joined battle only when favourable terms were presented. When they were brought to battle, the P-51 could outpace both Me109G and FW190A at low altitudes, and out-turn the 109 and hold its own with the 190. Further, a new Mustang model, the P-51D, began reaching groups early in June with improved visibility and heavier armament, by use of a full-view "teardrop" cockpit canopy and re-positioned machine guns allowing an extra ·50 in each wing. The Thunderbolt P-47D-25 series onwards, also introduced a bubble canopy and these too reached groups in late May and early June. With the water-injection, paddle-blade propellers, 160 octane fuel, and other minor refinements introduced during the previous six months even the hefty Thunderbolt could perform well at lower altitudes. It could not compete in acceleration with the enemy fighters but could out-turn them, although a weakness was the fall-off of power during a turn. Its chief advantage still lay in its exceedingly heavy firepower and not infrequently an FW190 or Me109 exploded on receipt of a single short burst.

The two or four heavy calibre cannon of the German fighters were well suited to bomber destruction but for fighter-fighter combat their slower rate of fire and poorer muzzle velocity was less effective than the "buzz saw" destruction of a battery of

six or eight ·50s. A one-second burst from a P-47 released over 100 rounds; from a P-51 80, and FW190 sixty and an Me109G thirty.

American fighter pilots were now receiving another piece of equipment that gave them an advantage over their German counterpart, the "G-suit". Aerial manoeuvres at speed were often limited by the amount of G-force a pilot could tolerate, that is the forces exerted on the body due to sudden changes in direction at speed, causing blood to drain from the brain to the lower part of the body, dimming vision and causing a "blackout". Experiments had been conducted both in the US and UK to perfect a suit which would at the appropriate moments put pressure on the blood vessels in the lower body and restrict the flow of blood. The British suit (the Frank) used water and the American (the Berger) air. Comparative tests conducted by the Eighth Air Force Central Medical Establishment found both effective, but as the Frank suit could be more easily procured this was the first supplied for operational testing. The 4th Group used the Frank suit during March and April 1944 but found it uncomfortable due to weight and heat and pilots preferred to fly without it. Attention then turned to the Berger suit with which most Ninth Air Force P-47 units were equipped by D-Day, and these were issued to the 339th Group at Fowlmere in the first week of June. British accelerometers and the necessary adapting parts were installed in the Group's Mustangs and test flights proved very satisfactory with pilots stating they could make much tighter turns than hitherto. The 4th Group also received the suit in June and found it equally advantageous.

While the Ninth Air Force and RAF 2nd Tactical Air Force were the primary tactical air arms supporting the Allied ground forces, VIII FC flew in a ground attack role on more than half its missions during the second week of the invasion. Fourteen such missions were flown on June 16th alone, when there was no interference from the Luftwaffe. The principal objective was the French railway system that was being used to bring

The G-Suit was inflated by the exhaust of the P-51s vacuum system. In this demonstration at Fowlmere, Cpt Charles Nethaway provided the puff and Lt Donald Johnson was the wearer. Pressure was applied to upper and lower legs and the abdomen.—(USAF)

reinforcements from the Reich. The 352nd and 357th Groups were briefed to look for troop trains scheduled to pass between Poitiers and Angouleme. Drop tanks were needed but the only type available at Leiston were 108 gallon "paper" tanks with a capacity far in excess of that needed. Lt. Col Tom Hayes, Group Executive of the 357th, decided to fill the tanks and use the surplus as an expedient to engulf a target in flames, a trick he had learned while flying P-39s in the Pacific. At St Pierre marshalling yard the 357th located a suspected ammunition train in a siding. Hayes led his squadron and another over the yard, dropping their wing tanks—which by then contained approximately 75 gallons each—among the waggons. The Mustangs then came back and strafed the tanks and waggons which resulted in enormous explosions and left four large fires blazing. Later the other squadron of the group (363rd) which had been giving top cover went down to shoot up the Poitiers yard leaving some 30 waggons blazing. Elsewhere P-47s of the 356th Group found some 75 freight box waggons and strafed them heavily, while P-38s of the 55th Group hit two locomotives, derailing one, but some deadly ground fire claimed from them three-quarters of the VIII FC loss of four fighters for the day.

The two oldest P-38 groups were now undertaking Droop Snoot led bombing missions against selected targets or "glide bombing"—the name given to a shallow approach technique where bombs were unloaded at low level. The Lightning groups also tried releasing their partly filled drop tanks on targets they intended to strafe but found that more often than not the tanks would tumble and land nowhere near the required spot. To stabilise the tanks, the 55th Group experimented with fitting 2,000 lb bomb tail fins to their 150 gallon tanks. Using a Droop Snoot they conducted trials over the Bradwell Bay range, and found a finned tank released at 210 IAS at 5,000 ft could be satisfactorily aimed. Not until July 14th was the development tried operationally when the Group's Droop Snoot, plus another P-38 as escort, flew to Foret de Boulogne and dropped two fin tanks plus a 200 lb incendiary against a suspected V-1 warhead dump. A fire was started, although the outcome was not spectacular.

The diverse tactical activities of VIII FC groups during the immediate post-invasion period were additional to their role of shepherding the heavy bombers. While B-17s and B-24s were bombing in direct support of the Allied landings, the Eighth's fighters were on hand as escorts before descending to seek targets to strafe. The forays into Germany returned as the heavies resumed their strategic offensive on favourable days later in June. The first large scale raid on Germany since D-Day was on the 20th when the Germans made skilful use of their remaining fighter force in the Reich to intercept the bombers. Many fighter formations, seeing nothing of the Luftwaffe, went down to strafe. While shooting up airfields another distinguished pilot was lost; he was Major James Goodson, probably the most accomplished ground strafer in the Command with 15 aircraft victories (plus an equal number in air combat). While making a second pass over Neubrandenburg airfield, a cannon shell punctured his Mustang's coolant system and he was forced to belly the Mustang into a field. 1/Lt Charles Shilke, his wingman, then made three strafing passes at Goodson's beautiful new P-51D, one of the first delivered to 4th Group, which he had used only a few days. The dejected Goodson sat on a fence post and watched while the Mustang burnt.

To improve visibility some 'razor back' P-47s were fitted with locally made 'bubble' canopies. This example was sported by 356th FG's *Zombie*.—(USAF)

Many of the 4th's distinguished pilots had now either been shot down or returned to the US. The tremendous days of March and April had given way to a comparatively quiet period of air combat for the Group. Yet as the most experienced Mustang Group in the Eighth, the 4th could be sure it would be likely to receive any difficult assignment that arose, and when Eighth Air Force decided to run its first "shuttle" mission to Russia, the 4th was the obvious choice to accompany the bombers all the way.

To supply the required numbers for escort, a fourth squadron of P-51s, the 352nd Group's 486th Ftr. Sqdn. now joined the 4th at Debden prior to the mission. Seventy Mustangs took off at 07.28 hrs on June 21st with Don Blakeslee in the fore. Six of the aircraft were reserves, three to return to England if unwanted on the first stage of the outward flight. The route lay across the North Sea, entering the enemy coast north of Overflakke Island. A complete overcast was encountered so the Mustangs had to fly above it at 20,000 ft although briefed for 15,000 ft at which level oxygen would not have been necessary. Enemy aircraft were not to be engaged prior to rendezvous with the bombers at Leszno, Poland, as jettisoning drop tanks would mean the Mustangs would have insufficient fuel to enable them to continue to Russia. Protection of the bombers, 144 B-17s of 3rd Division bound for an oil plant near Berlin, was to be left to other escort groups. Rendezvous with the Fortresses was on schedule at 11.13 hrs and the drop tanks were released. It looked as if there would be no interference from the Luftwaffe but at 12.40 hrs over twenty "Black-nosed and yellow wing-tipped" FW190s intercepted near Siedlce, Poland, the Mustangs claiming six against the loss of one of their number and a B-17. At 13.50 the Russian front lines were crossed and the Mustangs left the Fortresses—which they had escorted for 580 miles—to make for their destination, Piryatin airfield where they arrived at 14.50, exactly on time, after nearly 7½ hours in the air and covering 1,470 miles; a creditable bit of navigation. In addition to the P-51 lost in the brief fight near Warsaw, Lt Ralph Hofer was missing, but word later came through that the irrepressible Hofer had put down on an airfield near Kiev after getting lost.

A skeleton force of Mustang ground crew had travelled in the B-17s acting as waist gunners, the bombers also carried

4th FG ace, Cpt Howard Hively gives the thumbs up before starting the engine of QP: J for the flight to Russia.—(IWM)

special maintenance tools and empty 108 gallon drop tanks in the rear fuselage as these were not available at the Russian bases. While the pilots enjoyed potent Russian hospitality, the Mustangs were readied for action and on June 26th the 55 available took off to escort the B-17s to Italy, bombing Droho-bycz on the way. Rendezvous with the heavies was made at Lvov, Poland, at 19.07 hrs but the flight proved uneventful and the four P-51 squadrons left their charges at the Yugoslav coast to make for Lucera airfield near Foggia, landing after a five-hour flight. Two P-51s were left in Russia damaged beyond repair. Other pilots whose Mustangs were unservice-able at the time, flew to Italy over the next few days—including Hofer who this time ended up on Malta! On July 2nd the 4th and 352nd Mustangs flew in support of Fifteenth Air Force bombers over the Balkans. Near Budapest the 4th ran into a large number of Me109s, believed to have been J.G.52, a distinguished unit. The "Eagles" did not have it all their own way, six failing to return and two other pilots were badly wounded in the combat; one of those missing was Ralph Hofer. This time he failed to turn up and some weeks later it was learned that he died in the wreck of his Mustang at a spot in Yugoslavia some 300 miles south of the area of combat. Evidence suggests he was wounded and his aircraft damaged in the fight. It is also known that some of the ace pilots of J.G.52 saw action against P-51s this day. Hofer, probably the most colourful character to emerge as a top scoring fighter ace, is the only high scoring Eighth Air Force ace known to have fallen in combat with Luftwaffe fighter aircraft.

The Eighth's B-17s made a mission into the Balkans while in Italy and the Mustangs flew as escort before the whole force flew back across France to England on July 5th. Of the 67 P-51s sent to Russia, seven from 4th Group were missing in action, two were left in Russia and six in Italy, their pilots being flown to the UK by transports.

During the absence of the four Mustang squadrons, VIII FC pilots continued to display their incredible versatility in engaging in zero altitude bombing missions one day, and dog-fights six miles high the next. A successful escort on June 29th received high praise from General Kepner. The bombers went to targets set several hundred miles apart in Central Germany and although the Luftwaffe apparently put up most of its single and twin-engined fighter force still available for daylight defence they were singularly unsuccessful in attacking the bombers, due to a combination of their own poor guidance and superb VIII FC escort. Several Staffeln of Me109s and 410s launched an attack on the heading B-17 wing near Leipzig, but their effort was quickly broken up and the attackers, especially the vulnerable Me410s, were dispersed by the 357th Group's Mustangs with claims of 21 destroyed. The

Back at Debden, a weary looking Don Blakeslee tells General Kepner about the trip to Russia and Italy; 5 Jul. 1944.—(IWM)

Resplendent with red, white and blue cowling and black and white invasion stripes an Air Sea Rescue Squadron Thunderbolt sets out for the Channel. 5F: A was one of the few machines to carry the dinghy pack under the fuselage and smoke markers under the wings.

361st Group also broke up a formation of Me109s and after-wards strafed an airfield near Oschersleben where a four-plane flight, led by Lt Col Webb, netted at least 16 aircraft destroyed and many damaged in eight passes over the poorly defended field.

The job of the P-47 Air Sea Rescue squadron was to save, not to take life. Its war-weary Thunderbolts were, however, armed with four ·50 machine-guns for defence if attacked. On June 30th, Lt Tucker had cause to use the armament of his Thunderbolt for a purpose which is recorded as a first for the Eighth Air Force. While flying over the Channel, he spotted a V1 flying bomb on course for England. Although the missile had the advantage of speed Tucker was able to approach close enough to fire and good sighting on his part destroyed the Doodlebug. Flying bomb catching was chiefly in the realm of RAF fighters; American fighters rarely having an opportunity to intercept. The Air Sea Rescue Squadron lived at Boxted, with Zemke's "Wolfpack" whose near 500 aerial victories made the former organisation's solitary, if unique, victory seem in-significant.

Despite the vast numbers of Allied aircraft operating over France, the 56th still managed to find combat. On a dive bombing mission on July 4th the Group was dropping on Conches airfield when about a score of Me109s were seen. The Thunderbolts thereupon gave chase and in dog fights, ranging from 10,000 ft down to the deck, twenty Me109s were shot down and 12 claimed as damaged, all without loss. It seemed incredible, but camera film gave proof. This took the 56th to 508 aerial victories, the first group in VIII FC to pass the 500th mark—and with a substantial lead over its nearest competitor, the 4th. The Group could now boast 38 pilots who had reached ace status. 1/Lt George Bostwick of the 62nd Ftr. Sqdn. who had flown 65 missions prior to this one without ever firing his guns at an enemy aircraft, on this day returned to Boxted with camera gun film that saw him credited with 3 Me109s.

The 56th had another claim to fame next day, when VIII FC sent 139 Mustangs and 89 Thunderbolts to support the shuttle B-17s returning from Italy and bombing Beziers in the south of France en route. The 56th "mixed it up" with Me109s and near Evreux Lt Col "Gabby" Gabreski scored his 28th con-firmed victory, the highest individual score achieved by any USAAF pilot in Europe.

In terms of enemy aircraft destroyed, the P-38 Lightnings service with the Eighth Air Force was still not auspicious; it was already planned to convert all four groups to the P-51 that summer. Since the introduction of the P-38H in December 1943 there had been a constant technical battle to effect improvements; much had been achieved "in the field" and the J-25-LO models, reaching squadrons late in June, had elec-trically operated dive flaps under the wings to counter the dangerous nose down pitching movement which occurred if

California Cutie never had to turn back through engine failure in 370 hrs flying. Her first set of engines went 161 hrs. This was something of a record at a time when engine failure was a constant hazard to P-38 operations. T/Sgt Thomas Dickerson was the man who maintained this 20th FG Lightning and 1/Lt Richard Loehnert flew her on most occasions. Escort, top cover and sweeps are represented by symbols.—(USAF)

the P-38 was dived at excessive speed. Hydraulic boost ailerons were also fitted to this model to give a higher degree of manoeuvrability through easing pilot effort on the stick—an early application of powered controls. Pilots acquired a greater confidence in the Lightning to compete with German fighters and this had been borne out on more than one occasion.

Perhaps the most fruitful mission ever undertaken by Eighth Air Force Lightnings was that of July 7th 1944 when major missions to oil and aircraft targets in the Reich evoked more Luftwaffe opposition than at any time since May, even though 500 single-engined fighters in 17 Gruppen had been diverted

Cpt Fred Chistensen and the men who kept *Miss Fire* flying. From the left: S/Sgt Carl Conner, crew chief, Christensen, Pfc Tom Myers, and Cpl Urbain Hymel.—(USAF)

to France. The forces remaining in Germany took a heavy toll of the Liberators in the first task force making for Halle and Bernburg. In so doing, they suffered heavily themselves with VIII FC groups making claims of 77-1-23 in the air, a figure on a par with the great battles of March. Nearly one third of these victories were the work of two P-38 groups defending B-24s assailed by Me410s and FW190s with a top cover of Me109s. The 20th Group moving in to break up the attack, claimed 7 for the loss of one—Captain James Morris, the Group's leading ace with 7½ air victories and 3½ by strafing, who was shot down by fire from the barbette guns of an Me410 he was attacking. He parachuted to captivity. Captain Orville Goodman of the 55th Group, took his squadron down onto a formation and claimed 8 FW190s and 3 Me109s without loss while Major John D. Landers, leading a flight of four P-38s from the same Group's 38th Ftr. Sqdn. then engaged a score of Me410s and in a twenty minute chase shot down three and damaged four. Total claims of 18 destroyed for no loss brought the 55th Group one of its most successful actions.

Distinguished visitors around the operational planning table at 352nd FG Hq. US Secretary for War, Stimson's tour of some Eighth AF installations took him to Bodney on 17 Jul. 1944. Kepner and Spaatz stand either side of Stimson. Behind Doolittle—leaning on table—is Col Joe Mason, 352nd FG's CO.—(Mason)

The greater part of the remaining claims were made by Mustang units, but the ubiquitous Thunderbolts of the 56th had a share. Captain Fred Christensen and his wingman were returning from an escort to Leipzig, when they spotted a group of Ju52s in the traffic pattern at Gardelegen airfield. Christensen immediately joined the pattern himself and quickly shot down six of the transports. German propaganda later referred to an attack on transport aircraft, presumably this one, saying they were piloted by women. There was, however, no truth whatsoever in this statement.

Led by its commander, Colonel Glenn Duncan, the 353rd Group went down to strafe an airfield on the way home and the defence took yet another top ace. Duncan bellied his P-47 in, walked away evading capture, and joined up with the Dutch underground before returning to England.

The 355th Group amassed a high total of aircraft claims through ground strafing during July. In four missions its total in this category was 118 destroyed and 130 damaged which, with 14 aircraft it had shot down on the 7th, put its grand total past the 400 mark—approximately half in the air. At the time Lt Col Kinnard led the Group's strafers with 12½. The 352nd Group also passed the 400 mark by the end of the month—nearly 300 being aerial victories. The VIII FC score of 21 Me410s and Me109s on July 18th was all the 352nd Group's work.

Ground fire during strafing attacks continued to be the chief

UN: C, loaded with a 150 gl. drop-tank and two 250 lb HE bombs pulls up off the east-west Boxted runway, for fighter-bomber work in France. This aircraft was a presentation machine, 'bought' with bonds and inscribed *Spirit of Crawford County, Missouri.*—(USAF)

reason for fighters failing to return. In June 38 fighters were known lost to enemy aircraft and 66 to ground fire; in July, 18 and 26 respectively—reflecting the small number of ground attack missions—but in August it became 14 and 76. Accident took a large toll too, in fact 37, the largest of the 109 missing in action in July, but the fate of 28 was unknown. Collisions, always a hazard in formation flying, caused many of the accidents, as did, of course, severe weather. On July 21st, for example, a whole flight of 352nd Group Mustangs disappeared into thunder cloud over the North Sea and were never seen again.

"Gabby" Gabreski, the highest scoring ace in the VIII FC, was lost through accident on July 20th when the 56th strafed He111s and Me110s on Bassinheim airfield east of Coblenz. On his second pass across the field, Gabreski went too low to avoid tracer fire and his Thunderbolt's propeller hit a small hillock on the far side of the field. As the aircraft would not lift Gabreski had to belly it in about half a mile away, and having seen him run into a wood his squadron then shot up and set fire to his immaculate P-47 coded HV-A. Gabreski eluded capture for five days. When caught he was brought before a Luftwaffe interrogator who greeted him—"Hello Gabby, we've been waiting for you for a long time."

The Lightning groups were now converting to Mustangs. In air combat the best record had been that of the 20th Group which had claims of 89 victories with the Lightning. Its losses, however, were 87 P-38s. For the 55th and 364th, their losses were slightly higher than their claims, but in all cases malfunctioning and accidents played a larger part in these losses than the enemy.

By mid-July the pilots of the 55th and 20th Groups had obtained sufficient experience flying in war-weary P-51Bs and had received enough new P-51Ds to fly their first operations in the Mustang, on the 19th and 20th respectively. The practice was for a gradual change-over by squadrons and for a few missions the group formations were made up of both P-38s and P-51s. By the last week in the month the 364th Group at Honington was also in the process of converting, flying its last P-38 sorties on the 29th.

Only the youngest group in the Command continued to fly the Lightning although it too was destined to go over to the Mustang in September, in the interim it did some excellent work with the Lockheeds.

Chapter 22: The Sky was never Still

Early in August many changes in organisation occurred. On the Command side Major General Hodges had been transferred from the 2nd Division and Major General Kepner was moved to this command from VIII FC (which would later lose its fighter wings to the jurisdiction of the three divisions). There were other changes at Headquarters involving senior commanders, with Brigadier General Orvil A. Anderson being made Deputy Commander of Operations.

The move to build up the B-17 force in preference to using the B-24 began to take effect. The 92nd Wing's two stations at Sudbury and Lavenham were inoperative during the last two weeks of July while converting to B-17s and on August 1st both the 486th and 487th Groups were ready with the Fortress. At first there was resentment at the change, established loyalties being not easily revoked, but soon aircrew were generally enthusiastic about their new charges. Pilots were aware of the easier handling of the Fortress, particularly in high altitude formations; navigators and bombardiers found the nose compartment more spacious for their work, and the whole crew considered the heating system superior. The former Liberators of the 486th and 487th Groups went to depots for overhaul, and were stored for use as replacements in the 2nd Division. This also applied to aircraft of the three other 3rd Division groups which made the change between the end of August and mid-September.

The various special operational units that had been necessary prior to the invasion had resulted in the Eighth having outgrown its authorised establishment. The situation was now regularised and the authorities looked at the two provisional groups and the one provisional squadron—the 801st Group who were engaged in "Carpetbagger" duties at Harrington, the 802nd Reconnaissance Group at Watton, and the 803rd Bomb Sqdn. on radio counter measures.

First mission for some of 486th and 487th BG's new B-17Gs was Berlin on 6 Aug. 1944. Flak barrage brackets formation in distance.—(Rust)

On the 802nd with its B-24 and two Mosquito squadrons the designation 25th BG (Recon) was bestowed; the original 25th Group, a Stateside unit, having been disbanded. The 801st comprised the 36th, 406th, 788th and 850th Bomb Sqdns. all equipped with B-24s. The latter two squadrons rejoined their original groups, the 467th at Rackheath and the 490th at Eye. The 36th Bomb Sqdn. now became the revised designation of the original 803rd Bomb Sqdn. (P) which moved at the same time from Oulton, Norfolk, to Cheddington, Hertfordshire, to continue its specialist RCM work, having recently converted to B-24s. The 406th's designation passed to the 858th Bomb Sqdn. stationed at Cheddington which conducted leaflet sorties. The "Carpetbagger" group at Harrington and its four squadrons were then redesignated with the group number and squadron designations of the 492nd Group which, on August 7th, ceased operations at North Pickenham. All this, in fact, was principally a shifting of unit designations. Physically the Harrington units were little affected, similarly the RCM and Leaflet squadrons.

Of the original 492nd Group personnel, most went to other 2nd Division stations, the 859th Bomb Sqdn. took aircraft and low mission crews from the whole group to Rackheath to become the re-established 788th Bomb Sqdn., while a few personnel followed their unit designations to the new 492nd at Harrington. All these changes amounted to the loss in unit strength of one combat squadron although increased crew and aircraft availability in heavy bombardment squadrons nullified the effect.

Although the 492nd Group still lived on it was a different entity to the original, whose brief three-month history was extraordinarily violent. On four occasions it had been set upon by Luftwaffe elements with heavy loss, so that many crews were convinced the group was being deliberately singled out. The same revenge story of a disabled bomber lowering its wheels to surrender, enemy fighters moving in to shepherd it down when gunners opened up on them, was told of the 492nd, as it had been told of others before. Another theory held, was that as most 492nd aircraft were in natural metal finish they were especially conspicuous while others thought that the Group flew in poor formation rendering themselves more vulnerable. While no other B-24 group in the Eighth had such a high loss rate over such a short period of time, none of these reasons could be taken seriously.

German records reveal nothing to substantiate the notions that units were singled out. Action by Luftwaffe pilots was largely governed by their controllers vectoring them to the weakest part of the bomber stream—which the unfortunate 492nd had occupied on a number of occasions. Certainly the group had more than its share of ill fortune; enough to influence the 491st Group, from the 95th Wing, which was moved from Metfield to North Pickenham to fill the gap in 14th Wing, to insist on retaining their green tail markings rather than don the black diagonal bar on silver sign that was 492nd's. The decision to break up the 492nd in the tidying up programme, outlined above, was probably partly due to its unhappy history, but the fact that one of its squadrons was already involved in the special operations business no doubt put the Group on the short list. With the movement of the 491st Group to the 14th Wing, the 489th Group joined the 20th Wing as a fourth group and the 95th Wing became inoperative. There were, however,

44-10534, 3Q: B banks over 852nd BS hardstands and revetment area at 491st BG's new base at North Pickenham.—(Blue)

other very special units which hid beneath the cover of a code name or behind the number of a normal Bombardment Group.

The spectacle of an aeroplane crashing to earth and erupting with flame and an explosion was unfortunately by no means a rare sight in East Anglia during 1944. However, when on the sunny afternoon of August 4th a Fortress plunged into a wood at Sudbourne Park, Suffolk, the explosion was on an unprecedented scale. Though muffled by innumerable oaks, the sound deafened three roadmen a considerable distance away. People arriving at the scene found a crater some 100 feet across and the trunks of fully grown oaks completely severed for two hundred feet around it. Of the Fortress that had been, only shreds of metal could be found, the largest recognisable parts being cylinder blocks. The heat of the explosion had fused the metal to an extraordinary degree. Small wonder, for this was no ordinary B-17 with a 4,000 lb bomb load, but one packed with 20,000 lbs of explosive and, as such, was probably the most lethal missile ever to descend on Britain. This machine and three others, similarly packed, were the opening salvo of an experiment in guided weapons—PROJECT APHRODITE.

The German flying bomb campaign triggered off Allied retaliation with guided weapons. At this time huge concrete structures being prepared in the Pas de Calais area, were identified with V-weapon delivery but because of their size were little harmed by the usual Allied bombs. The idea of filling war-weary bombers with a maximum amount of explosive, installing radio control equipment and guiding the "bomb" from a "mother" aircraft onto a target, appealed to both Doolittle and Spaatz. Project A or Aphrodite was initiated on June 23rd and conducted by the 3rd Division, which in turn picked the 388th Group at Knettishall to staff and provide base facilities, as the nearest unit to Fersfield, the airfield specially selected in a sparsely populated area of Norfolk.

As the 388th Group had also to maintain its regular operations, one of its squadrons, the 562nd, provided most of the base and maintenance personnel while special technicians were brought in from the OES (Operational Engineering Section, previously ATS) to deal with the radio control problems. War-weary B-17s, stripped of all unnecessary equipment, armament and armour, had special radio equipment installed. Control "mother" aircraft were usually B-34s (ex-RAF Venturas), while another B-17 was sent to navigate and observe, and fighter escort would also be on hand; also a P-38 was necessary to act as executioner if plans went awry in the air. The Aphrodite drones were to be flown off Fersfield manually by two pilots who, after attaining altitude and putting the machine on course, would set the fuses and descend by parachute near the English coast. The control aircraft would

then guide the bomber to its target and to enable the controller to keep the drone under observation, parts of the upper surfaces were painted white. Initial experiments met tragedy, for some of the aircrew struck radio antennas when they parachuted.

The first drones were despatched from Fersfield on August 4th; one each to V-site at Mimoyecques, Siracourt, Watten and Wizernes, but those reaching the vicinity of their targets achieved little damage. Two days later, two more Aphrodite B-17s were despatched to Watten again with little success. On August 12th, the US Navy also participating in the project, made a contribution, a PB4Y Liberator piloted by Lt Kennedy (brother of the future President) was sent to Heligoland. At 15,000 ft over the Blyth estuary, as the crew were apparently preparing to jump, the machine disappeared in two consecutive explosions. Nothing was left but a pall of smoke in the bright afternoon sunshine and nothing larger than the engine parts were ever found. The explosion which had obliterated men and machine also caused blast damage over an area of some five to six miles in diameter. In all 150 damage reports to property were received.

Naturally, British authorities were apprehensive lest other Aphrodites should fail in this fashion. The effect of one plunging into a town was a frightening prospect. The inhabitants of this part of east Suffolk were literally more shaken by American activities than by those of the enemy. This second blast was only fifteen miles from the Sudbourne Park crash, and a few weeks before that the 491st Group's bomb dump at Metfield exploded. No more missions of this type were run for a month while equipment was re-evaluated and modified in the light of the first seven attempts, by which time the sites were in British hands and other targets had to be sought. Fersfield also housed a parallel venture with the GB-4 television-directed bomb under

The Careful Virgin lived up to her name and by the spring of 1944 was one of two original B-17Fs still with the 91st BG. Unlike many other veterans she was not retired to training grounds in the USA. She became an Aphrodite bomber, was stripped of all bombing equipment, had her top deck remodelled, and was painted white on upper surfaces (the peculiar swathed effect is due to hasty work with a spray gun). On 4 Aug. 1944 she went to destruction with 20,000 lbs of Torpex.— (USAF & Air Museum)

Cut down decking and open cockpit allowed quick exit from an Aphrodite. This machine is believed to have been *Gremlin Gus* of 388th BG.—(USAF Museum)

the code name "Batty". Involving highly sophisticated equipment, this venture was also fraught with technical difficulties.

The Luftwaffe would launch similar explosive laden bombers against England in the months ahead, but Germany's principal effort in guided weapons was the V1 flying bomb and V2 rocket. Eighth Air Force, in company with the Ninth Air Force and RAF, had been pounding the launching sites in the Pas de Calais for a year. For the Eighth's part, its heavies flew their last mission of the CROSSBOW campaign on August 30th a year and three days since their opening strike at the curious structures at Watten. It was on Christmas Eve 1943 that the first true NOBALL mission (launching sites) was flown and between then and August 30th, 16,272 heavies had been despatched on 69 days at a cost of 63 B-17s and B-24s. There had been some disagreement among Allied Commanders on

Eighth AF sent bombers to the V-weapons research establishment at Peenemünde, near Stettin on 25 Aug. 1944. Photo shows concentration of bursts on installations for fuelling V-2 rockets. B-17G is SC: M of 401st BG.—(USAF)

the value of using heavy bombers to attack the small V1 "ski-sites". Doolittle, for one, felt that attacks on the sources of production and supply would have a greater effect on restricting firings. A later assessment found that despite a regular destruction of sites, the preparation of new ones outpaced the rate of destruction. So as not to interfere with the strategic campaign, the Eighth Air Force had endeavoured to visit NOBALL targets when unsuitable weather prevailed over Germany and the difficulty of operating B-17s and B-24s in the same force, had often resulted in the 3rd Division's five Liberator groups being employed on V-site missions while the rest of the heavies went to Germany. The last flying bomb launched from a ground site against England was on September 1st. The British advance up the Channel coast had overrun most sites and thereafter V1s reaching England were principally air launched.

Eighth Air Force operations continued at a prodiguous rate and on a vast scale; in the area of the East Anglian bases it seemed the sky was never still. For the most part bomber activities during August followed the pattern of the previous month. Sources of oil, centres of the German aircraft industry and attacks against ordnance and armoured vehicle stores and factories were the major targets in order of priority. The formula was the same: bomb, photograph, and if the target had not been satisfactorily blasted, bomb again. The bombers did their best work in good visibility and many days that summer had been blessed with such conditions, and the Eighth was quick to bring its power to bear with telling effect. Eleven primary objectives, chiefly aircraft manufacturing plants in Central Germany, were squarely hit by a thousand heavies on August 5th. Within twenty-four hours an equally strong force, in equally fine conditions, did exceptionally heavy damage at ten major targets, taking in oil refineries at Hamburg and Harburg, a torpedo factory at Kiel, a diesel works and aircraft engine plant in Berlin; also the Focke-Wulf factory at Rahmel in Poland, where 76 B-17s of the 95th and 390th Groups unloaded, and flew on to complete their second flight to Russia. The shuttle force, smaller than on the disastrous previous occasion in June, flew a mission next day to the Trzebinia synthetic oil refinery and returned to their Mirgorod base. They took off for Italy on the 8th, bombing two Rumanian airfields en route, and on the 12th attacked Toulouse/Francaal airfield while making for England, all without operational loss.

During the Allied armies spectacular advance across France, the Eighth's bombers were required on a number of occasions to attack bridges and transport centres to hinder the German retreat and prevent reinforcement arriving. So rapid was the advance that it also became increasingly difficult to get supplies to the leading elements. The various C-47 troop carrier and transport organisations were overtaxed and to supplement their efforts in meeting urgent appeals for help, B-24s of the special 492nd Group and some 200 of the 2nd Division were temporarily diverted to a transport role. The 20th Wing groups were taken off bombing operations on August 28th and the following day commenced hauling food and medical supplies from staging bases in England down to Orleans/Bricy, about 70 miles south of Paris. On their final day, September 9th, a 489th Group aircraft was missing, believed to have wandered over an enemy-held sector of the front. On the 12th, the 96th Wing took over and on the 17th the 2nd Wing made its sole contribution to this activity. Thereafter, food and medical supplies were not so critical but Allied armour was hindered by lack of petrol. Commencing on the 20th the 96th Wing spent eleven days fuel trucking, flying 2,117,310 gallons into France. A constant stream of fuel tanker vehicles plied between the home bases of Horsham St Faith, Rackheath and Attlebridge and petrol depots, to provide 80 octane fuel flown to Chartres, St Dizier and Florennes. At first this had to be laboriously conveyed in 5-gallon jerrycans, being loaded into the B-24s through the waist windows from which the gun mounts had been removed. Later pumping apparatus was available at some of the French delivery stations so the petrol could be carried in bomb bay tanks and fighter drop tanks stacked in the fuselage. Each aircraft had a crew of five on these sorties, the two pilots, navigator, engineer and radio-operator. No more than two passengers were allowed. This ruling had to be strictly applied as apart from the opportunity of a brief visit to France, the wine, liqueurs and German souvenirs brought back from the first missions made this an exceptionally popular duty. It was not without its risks for on the final day's operations the 466th Group's *Jamaica* was hit by ground fire and lost with all hands, and a 492nd Group B-24 crashed on take-off at Lyneham on September 13th with its volatile load, and all aboard perished. In all, 2,248 trucking trips were flown by the Eighth's B-24s during this emergency to take 9,880 tons of all requirements to forward areas.

While this had been going on the remaining 2nd Division groups had continued to fly bombing missions, but on one occasion also carried out delivery of supplies in an environment far from safe. In mid-September the Allies launched their

Out House Mouse comes home to Bassingbourn.—(USAF)

In Aug. 1944 1st Division B-17s appeared with coloured group and wing markings on their tails. A dark blue diagonal band graced Glatton based aircraft.—(Blakebrough)

plan to secure a foothold over the Rhine, by dropping British forces at Arnhem and two US airborne divisions at Eindhoven and Nijmegen. Additional supplies for these armies were air dropped the following day and the 14th and 20th Wing were selected to supplement the troop carrier forces. After low level practice missions on previous days, trucks brought supplies to the bases during the night of September 17th and bomb racks and the waist area of each B-24 was loaded with 20 containers of about 200 lbs each. A trained dropmaster from a special Ninth TCC unit flew in each B-24 to direct the pushing out of bundles through the ball turret opening and rear hatch.

Plans were made on the lines of the Ninth's troop carrier units, to fly at 1,500 ft to the IP, descend to 300 ft for dropping, then make a climbing turn to 1,500 ft or higher for the return flight. Twenty-eight squadrons of nine aircraft, each in Vee formation, would fly in trail at thirty second intervals. Speed planned was an indicated 165 mph, reduced to 150 for dropping.

Early in the afternoon 252 B-24s were airborne on the dropping mission, but not before last minute panic over the discovery of a staff error, causing the individual crew briefing documents and maps for the 14th Wing to be sent to the 20th Wing, and vice versa. In consequence, pilots and navigators had to familiarise themselves with the correct details en route. Some minutes out from Orfordness, the leading elements of the 20th Wing were forced to make a 360° turn to the left to avoid running into C-47s of a troop carrier unit. This caused some

confusion among following groups and in the sea haze existing the 448th Group lost sight of the others completely, and proceeded on its own. Five Liberators of the 93rd Group, after losing their way, eventually went home. At the IP, the 20th Wing turned into its dropping zone but was further confused as the radio location beacon was not operating and smoke and recognition markers were difficult to see. The 448th dropped five miles short by mistaking the wrong area and part of 489th had to make three runs.

The 14th Wing reached the IP in great disorder, many formations having overrun each other and been forced to lower altitudes. Nevertheless, all but one of its aircraft found its way to the two dropping zones assigned although the bundles were badly scattered with only 20% recovered as against 80% of those put down by the 20th Wing. The fighter support provided included two P-47 groups assigned to suppress ground fire, even so, this was murderous and seven B-24s were shot down, one crash landing at Brussels and four more at Watton and Woodbridge. In addition 70 were damaged and some 30 men wounded.

Six hundred miles further east on the same afternoon, Fortresses of the 3rd Division were also dropping supplies. The groups from this Division had experience of flying to remote areas to deliver arms to the French Resistance movement. Now, in September 1944, it was to be to Poland. The advancing Russian armies, poised at the gates of Warsaw, seemingly waited while the Germans dealt with its inhabitants who had risen in open revolt believing their liberation imminent.

"The Eightballs" deliver supplies to 1st Allied Airborne Army in Holland; 17 Sept. 1944.—(USAF)

The plight of the resistance forces in Warsaw was known to the Western Allies through wireless contact with their Government in exile in London. Pleas to the Russians were apparently ignored and the Poles position became critical. The 13th Combat Bomb Wing, the "Fireball" outfit with experience of two shuttle missions to Russia, was given the job of supplying the Poles with arms and ammunition. The first attempt on the 15th was abortive due to bad cloud conditions encountered over the Continent. On the 18th the same Wing set out again, led by Colonel Karl Truesdell of the 95th Group, the formation descended to between 13,000 and 18,000 ft to unload 1,284 containers amid accurate, if limited, flak. Although 64 P-51s of the 355th FG were on hand, they were unable to prevent an estimated 20 enemy fighters from attacking the low group (the 390th) on the target run. One Fortress exploded while the pilot of another, *Bugs Bunny*, was killed in the attacks. One B-17 had to land at Brest Litovsk but the rest continued into Russia to bases at Poltava and Mirgorod. The following day the Wing took off with 250 kg Russian bombs and attacked a rail centre at Szolnok in Hungary on their way to Italy. From Foggia to England there were no targets to attack as most of France beneath their flight path had been liberated. This was the last shuttle mission by the Eighth to Russian bases.

By the fall of 1944, the bombing of refineries and synthetic plants in the Reich, coupled with the Rumanian capitulation and loss of the Ploesti fields, had critically reduced German oil supplies. Only the construction of new plants, carefully hidden from Allied reconnaissance, could sustain this stricken industry that had proved so vulnerable to air attack. The speed of repairs of bombed plants, indicative of their importance, surprised Allied intelligence, and meant that targets written off as destroyed had to be revisited.

Around these vital oil installations, inevitably, grew some of the strongest concentrations of anti-aircraft weapons in the Reich. Hundreds of guns defended the Hamburg and Leipzig area complexes. Flak was claiming an ever increasing toll of heavy bombers; 131 were known lost by this means in August alone, whereas only 39 had succumbed to fighter action. Unable to match the Allies in the air, the Germans had turned their attention to improving flak defences both quantitatively and qualitatively the previous winter and to some extent paralleling the build-up of the US and British bomber forces. Organisation and technique played an important part in the improved effectiveness of flak, that became apparent to the Allies during the summer of 1944. To meet the large, tight formations employed by the USAAF, 88 mm guns were eventually sited in groups of 12, 16, 18 or 24 (known as Grossbatteries) so that, firing in salvos, the concentrated pattern of bursts would have a shot-gun effect. The more powerful 105 mm and 128 mm guns were also usually grouped in twelves or fours respectively. The main advantages lay in centralized control of fire power and the availability of several sets of prediction equipment to speed the tracking of individual bomber formations. Earlier 88 mm guns had an effective ceiling of only 26,000 ft enabling bombers to lessen the risk of being hit by operating at higher altitude. Newer versions could fire shells to over 30,000 ft thus thwarting this evasion. Apart from actually bringing down aircraft, the Germans believed bombing was 25% to 33% less effective if the formations faced flak.

The Eighth's countermeasures were chiefly to jam the gun-laying radar at the flak sites. Carpet was gradually installed in most bombers except H2X leaders and Chaff was released by bombers prior to entering a known flak area so as to saturate the radar screen. For many months it had been evident that lead formations suffered higher losses from flak, by their lack of a chaff screen that following formations received. A screening force was a measure to meet this, a small formation ahead of the main force charged solely with Chaff discharge. Both the rate and volume of discharge of Chaff was important and success hinged on creating an image that equalled that made

398th BG B-17s, contrails in dark relief against the white cloud bank, ride through flak. Photograph was taken from the open bomb bay of a 91st BG aircraft in a high group.—(USAF)

by a bomber formation. Experiments to ensure an accurate distribution to the end were tried out using modified fighter drop tanks which broke open on release, scattering the strips, but this and other schemes were only partially successful. In November 1944, Mosquitos equipped with an electric dispensing mechanism in their bomb bays were found to provide the best solution and three such aircraft from the 25th Group were thereafter regularly employed on this task. Chaff saturation over a wide area was important as the Grossbatteries were often linked by a "Zug 44" Central Conversion Mechanism. This equipment enabled a battery suffering jamming of its radar to instantly draw data from a set functioning in an adjacent area.

Both sides continued to evolve countermeasures to meet the constant developments in radar; this battle of skills was not decisive for either side, although the British were perhaps the most advanced in this field. A fear most bomber crews held was the possible introduction of an unjammable homing missile, while during the summer and early fall of 1944 a prevalent rumour was that the Germans were using the H2X transmissions from pathfinder aircraft in predicting anti-aircraft fire: a rumour that had to be officially squashed as untrue. The foundation for this belief lay in the seemingly large number of lead aircraft hit, due no doubt to their inadequate Chaff cover. Protective measures were improved; better personal body armour for crewmen was introduced and towards the end of 1944 the substitution of flak curtains for much fuselage armour plate—flak curtains were made up of small overlapping special steel plates on the same lines as flak jackets.

There were also experiments with formations to limit the number of aircraft in the vicinity of one salvo of bursts, and brief changes of altitude in flak areas to make prediction difficult. But for the most part, flak was unavoidable if it surrounded a target. For aircrew flak held considerable horror, much more than any brush with the Luftwaffe. "The sight of those ugly black bursts leaves you with a numb helpless feeling. All you can do is try and concentrate on your job and pray that in all that steel flying around there isn't a piece with your number on it." These sentiments of Lt Gordon Courtenay, a 398th Group bombardier, were echoed by every airman in the Eighth.

Courtenay had flown one of his first missions to Merseberg on July 29th. Looking ahead he saw what he took to be a pall of black smoke rising from the burning target. Realisation that what he was looking at was smoke from several thousand shell bursts aimed at preceding groups, was a most uncomfortable shock.

Merseburg was synonymous with flak to crews late in 1944; it was what Schweinfurt had been to their predecessors in the autumn of 1943, for it became the most heavily defended place in Hitler's crumbling empire, with more guns than Berlin. There were over a thousand flak guns defending the Leipzig area oil plants by late November and Merseburg had 506 of these in 39 sites at its peak. This underlined the importance of the large IG Farbenindustrie plant at Leuna three miles south of the town, which produced an estimated 10% of Reich oil, half the ammonia, plus other chemical by-products. The Eighth ran a score of missions to Merseburg and it became, in the eyes of the combatants at least, the No 1 target.

The mark of Merseburg flak is graphically illustrated in this entry from a diary kept by 2/Lt William Duane, 388th Group navigator on the September 28th raid. "Up early for an 03.30 briefing. Take-off at 07.10. Again I'm navigator and not minding it too much. With this being our 13th mission I anticipated a hot one but didn't say much to the rest of the crew, I guess they were sweating it out enough themselves.

"... After plenty of flying we reached the IP. The bomb run was about 13 minutes long. About $2\frac{1}{2}$ minutes before 'bombs away' we got intense and very accurate flak. About a minute later, at 12.00, King (engineer) was hit in both legs. He fell down into the passageway, crawled forward and I plugged in his oxygen mask ... I took off my flak suit, grabbed a knife, and cut open five layers of clothes. After noticing the extent of the bleeding I applied a tourniquet. All this took place in some very intense and tracking flak—and me without my helmet! I applied a gauze dressing and tried to get blankets and morphine. Interphone shot out so I started back to the flight deck to inform the pilot. The co-pilot was cranking closed the bomb doors so I got on his interphone. I got down in the hatchway on an oxygen bottle and stayed there relaying messages back and forth between the nose and the pilot. Finally came the blanket and the first-aid kits. King had a piece of flak go through the meaty part of his upper left leg and puncture his right leg. Bleeding was not arterial so it stopped soon. I was pretty cramped in the passage way where I was for more than an hour —until 13.30. In the meantime I had given King some morphine, but it was a hell of a job as it froze up and we had to experiment several times jabbing King's leg before I had finally discovered just how it worked. Hoff (bombardier) was giving most of the actual first aid while I wrapped King's legs in blankets and tried to keep them warm as he was complaining about them being numb with cold.

Shimmering in the morning sunlight, a 388th BG Fortress heads out across the English coast; 08.30 hrs, 5 Sept. 1944, destination Stuttgart.
—(Duane)

2/Lt William Duane, bombardier, wearing a flak helmet designed to take earphones.—(Duane)

"... We fired a couple of red flares over the home field. Upon landing we got King into an ambulance OK and then taxied back to the hardstand. I was really tired after this mission so I took a good stiff drink to make me forget what was the worst flak I had ever seen. At first we had nine crews missing, but that narrowed down to six by midnight. Some of the boys had landed in Belgium. . . . Three ships went down over the target after a collision. I hope that we won't see anything like this again.'

Duane's hope was not fulfilled. Five days later flak fatally wounded his co-pilot and he had the bitter experience of watching the man die as he administered first-aid.

The whole nature of the war fought by the bomber men heightened the individual's concern with flak. Knowledge that the safety and comfort of an English base must be forsaken thirty-odd times for the chilling fear of flying into flak was a strain on the most stable character. Those men who became "Flak Happy" were sent to a "Flak Home" to rest and recoup before completing their tour. Some of the concern was reflected in the nicknames that decorated their bombers viz *Flak Eater, Flak Wolf, Flak Dodger, Flak Magnet, Ole Flak Sack, Mrs Aldaflak* and so on.

The Luftwaffe made sporadic appearances throughout the late summer. Typical instances occurred on August 15th when two dozen FW190s of II/J.G.300 sallied out of cloud near Trier to shoot down nine Fortresses from the veteran 303rd Group which was low box in a formation sent to Wiesbaden. The "Hells Angels" Group claimed 4-0-2. Gunners of 466th Group Liberators flying high right, near Meppel, did better, claiming 9-1-2 from a Staffel of 109s that took four Liberators down with fused cannon shells.

The following day a score of FW190s from IV/J.G.3 assailed the 91st Group on its way to Halle; six B-17s and a like number of the enemy fell during the four-minute action. *Outhouse Mouse* also went briefly out of control when hit. After recovering some 2,000 feet below, about two miles away from the formation, Sgt Robert Loomis, who had taken over the tail guns from a wounded gunner, was surprised to see a tailless, swept-wing craft approaching astern at great speed. He immediately alerted the pilot, 1/Lt Walker Mullins, who started evasive action, skidding *Outhouse Mouse* to and fro and succeeding in foiling the aim of the pilot in the attacking fighter then recognised as jet-propelled. Having overshot the Fortress, the Me163 was promptly shot down by a Mustang.

Me163s had also attacked the high right group of a 1st Division wing near Bohlen. Two passes were reported, both starting from above and with power off, by four fighters coming within 200 yards to fire, before breaking away. These were

Out House Mouse salvoes a mixed load over unbroken cloud. She was to survive the war with 139 missions.—(USAF)

the first occasions that the mysterious rocket-powered fighters had attacked a US bomber formation, although their presence had been reported for some weeks. J.G.400, the unit formed to operate these fast interceptors with limited duration, flew its first operation this day involving 5 sorties. Thereafter Me163s were encountered fairly frequently, though never in numbers large enough to make them a serious threat.

Luftwaffe reaction remained sparse until September 11th, when it put up its strongest opposition to the heavies since May 28th, flying an estimated 400 sorties to meet a major Eighth Air Force mission to oil targets. A whole Geschwader evading the escort, concentrated on a lagging low group as it passed Annaberg. In five minutes 11 B-17s went down and another managed to struggle to a crashlanding in France, all from the 100th Group. Had it not been for the arrival of Mustangs, the number would probably have been greater. The 92nd Group also suffered with 8 missing and 4 others so badly battered they had to seek sanctuary on the Continent. Not much was said outside Podington of the 92nd's reverse, but news of another misfortune for the 100th Group soon spread abroad; and so the legend perpetuated.

The Eighth returned to oil targets next day and was again met by a sizeable force of Luftwaffe fighters that managed to shoot down 23 heavies despite loosing heavily to the US escort. The 493rd Group, low box of a combat wing headed for Magdeburg, was viciously attacked by a Group of Me109s which came in singly from both nose and tail. It was the first

aerial opposition this youngest of Eighth Air Force groups had encountered, and it cost them seven of the B-17s to which they had only recently converted.

When for the third successive day the Eighth flew to oil and other targets in Germany, the Luftwaffe again made efforts to intercept. This time they were down to between 100 and 150 sorties and the majority were kept at bay by the escort. Then once again there was a period when little air opposition was experienced by the bombers, although weather conditions and the direction of effort to tactical targets played some part in this lull.

The success of the Sturmgruppe tactics, perfected by Moritz with IV/J.G.3, encouraged General Galland to propose the formation of like units in each Jagdgeschwader. In August 1944 J.G.4 had been reorganised along these lines and Gruppe II equipped with the "heavy fighter". This was the FW190A-8, specially modified to give the pilot extra protection against defensive fire when attacking the rear of a bomber formation. A 60 mm sheet of armoured glass was placed inside the cockpit canopy to protect the head; and to shield legs and body against lateral fire, armour plates were fixed on either side of the front cockpit extending down to the wing roots. However accurate a bomber gunner's aim, the Sturm pilot was well protected from ·50 bullets; only serious hits on some vital part of his aircraft could deflect his own aim; and in any case a rear gunner faced a very small target in a FW190 approaching from dead astern. The full armament of the FW190 used by II/J.G.4 was two 13 mm and two 20 mm guns plus wing-mounted 30 mm cannon. The tactics employed by J.G.4 were modelled on those of J.G.3 although the new Sturm organisation made almost all its interceptions from the rear when it was a "company front" (line abreast saturation formation) occasion.

In August, IV/J.G.3 had been caught over its airfield by Mustangs and 15 of its pilots were killed in the unwieldy Focke-Wulfs. Rendered temporarily inactive, II/J.G.4 replaced it as the Luftwaffe's star performer.

The 445th Group at Tibenham had a remarkably high reputation. Its bombing record was good and during the three months following D-Day it led all Eighth B-24 groups in accuracy ratings. The 445th had flown some rough missions, notably that to Gotha in February 1944 since when it had fared relatively well. But on September 27th the 445th Bomb Group and II/J.G.4 came together in a violent action, resulting in the highest loss of a single group on a single mission.

The 2nd Division had sent 315 B-24s over solid undercast to the Henschel engine and vehicle plants at Kassel with 37 aircraft of the 445th Group leading in the second combat

I/J.G.400 Me 163Bs took off to meet 1st Division approaching Merseburg on 24 Aug. 1944. Fw Schubert climbed towards the 92nd BG formation and scored hits on the port wing of a 'Silver' Fortress before overshooting it. He then approached the 457th BG and fired a burst into the No. 4 engine of 42-97571 'H', piloted by Lt Pugh. This B-17G failed to return. Fw (Sgt) Schubert was later killed when the Me163B he was preparing to fly blew up.

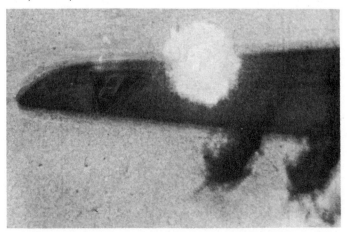

Oil targets for 2nd Division lay in the Hamburg-Hanover area. Recipient of repeated visits was Misburg, here seen blazing as 489th BG's *The Sharon D* and her sisters go home on 12 Sept. 1944. Refineries at Hamburg were attacked on 6 Oct. 1944, although target for 489th BG was an aircraft factory in that city. Lead and deputy lead have H2X radomes extended. Only one smoke marker bomb from S4: V- has ignited. 95th Wing green and white tail markings have given place to 20th Wing's yellow.—(USAF)

wing, navigating by Gee. At the IP, the Group apparently took a wrong heading and edged away from the bomber column; their divergence went unnoticed by friends but not by the enemy. The Group then made a PFF attack believing Kassel to be below, whereas the bombs actually fell just outside Göttingen some 20 miles away. Turning away, and still unaware of their error, the 445th simulated the withdrawal plan, which placed them well behind and to the east of the rest of the 2nd Division force. Ten minutes after bombing, while a few miles from Eisenach, three line-abreast waves of FW190s came in from 6 o'clock, closing at 150 mph, and split-S'ing downwards after firing. They were quickly followed by two Me109 Gruppen of J.G.4 who finished off the cripples in the now widely dis-

persed formation. Within three minutes the attack was over. Fire from the estimated ninety enemy fighters had sent down 25 Liberators and damaged most of the remainder, before P-51s of the 361st Group arrived in answer to a plea for help. Survivors described the scene as fantastic, a sky full of blazing aircraft, parachutes, smoke and the debris of battle. Of the badly damaged Liberators, two managed to make the special "lame duck" runway at Manston, two others bellied in at French bases, and a fifth succumbed near Tibenham. In addition to the 236 men missing, one dead and 13 injured were taken from the damaged B-24s that struggled to safety.

The efficiency of the German raid reporting system and the skill of their fighter controllers had been seen on many occasions, but none had yielded such a spectacular result.

The 445th was able to find ten serviceable B-24s to fly to Kassel next day, all returning safely. The Luftwaffe was abroad again and managed to break through the American escort to shoot down eleven Fortresses of the 303rd Group making for Magdeburg. Despite such success, of the 49 heavies missing this day, half were sent down by flak and possibly another ten. There were nearly always bombers lost to unknown causes, machines that mysteriously dropped out of formation without giving any sign of why they were stricken. Others just disappeared and no one saw their going.

The next notable interception came on October 6th and again amounted to a saturation attack by a Gruppe. Third Division went to Berlin and at the IP (near Nauen) was forced to fly about 1,000 feet below very high cloud. Above this cloud lurked two or three Gruppen of J.G.4 and J.G.300 who were vectored down at the right moment to surprise the high group of the last combat wing—just as the high squadron was somewhat separated from the rest of the formation while turning for the target. Eleven aircraft, principally of the 549th Bomb Sqdn., this time, were destroyed. P-51s quickly arrived to avenge the loss but by then the 385th Group had suffered its heaviest loss of the war.

Another 4th Wing group caught the full force of the few Luftwaffe sorties flown when 1,422 heavies went to oil and engineering plants next day. Near Leipzig IV/J.G.3 came down out of the clouds en masse to engage an old adversary, the 94th Group. Aircrew reported that the German pilots seemed inexperienced, but this hardly qualifies the outcome, for in eight minutes the Wing lost a dozen Fortresses.

During all these saturation attacks of the late summer and autumn the German fighters suffered themselves. Air gunners took their toll while the escort often shot down as many, or more FW190s and Me109s as B-17s and B-24s lost. For the rest of October the Luftwaffe was strangely absent from the

Probably the first B-17 to complete 100 missions over hostile territory was *Pistol Packin Mama* of the Night Leaflet Squadron at Cheddington. (The majority were not bombing missions.) Note black undersides.

On 15 Oct. 1944 a shell burst against 91st BG's *Little Miss Mischief* with this result. Miraculously ball gunner Sgt Ed. Abdo survived without serious injury. 1/Lt Paul McDowell and crew survey the damage. One gun barrel is bent up to the side of the fuselage. Statistics later showed that there were fewer casualties in ball turrets than with any other crew position in a B-17 or B-24.—(USAF)

scene. To Doolittle and his staff the creditable performance of comparatively small numbers of German fighters at this time held alarming prospects of what could happen if the Germans were to contest a mission with a substantial force—a loss of a hundred heavies was conceivable if the escort was overwhelmed. Indeed, Goering was conserving his forces and fuel for such an enterprise when he ambitiously hoped to net 1,000 bombers. His plan, however, was not upheld by his superior, who preferred to use the Luftwaffe in direct support of the land armies. Nevertheless, what had been conserved was unleashed on November 2nd in the biggest Luftwaffe reaction to an Eighth Air Force mission since September 11th. Fortunately most of the sorties flown (an estimated 400) were successfully intercepted by Mustangs.

It was said that Goering informed the Jagdverbände that unless 500 heavies were brought down on the next American raid, they would be sent to the trenches. The story does not embrace the Reichsmarshall's reaction on learning that perhaps only 26 of the 40 destroyed fell to fighters. As it was, a quarter of this total was another triumph for J.G.4 and the "company front" technique; the plot was only too familiar. A bomber formation wandering out of line, the German fighter controller vectoring a Geschwader in when the escort was absent. This time a Sturmgruppe and escorting Me109s put down nine 457th Group B-17s and twelve from the 91st Group. The chief objective for this 1,000 bomber raid was Merseburg/Leuna and it was the notorious flak that brought about the most notable human drama of this mission. Fortress L-Love of the 447th Group sustained damage from three near shell bursts with shrapnel hitting the navigator, Lt Robert Femoyer, in the back and side of his body. In spite of extreme pain and loss of blood, Femoyer refused a morphine injection in order to keep his mental faculties clear to navigate the return route. Too weak to get back to his seat, he asked to be propped up so that he could see his charts and instruments. Crew members did what they could to make him comfortable while he insisted on directing the navigation of the Fortress and negotiating a safe passage around flak areas. Not until the North Sea was reached did Femoyer permit the injection of a sedative. He died shortly after being removed from the aircraft and was posthumously awarded the Medal of Honour early the following year.

Two further posthumous Medals of Honor were awarded a week later to two 452nd Group pilots. The Group formation flew into a flak area while making for a secondary target, with a fatal outcome for at least three B-17s. One, *Lady Janet* piloted by 1/Lt Donald Gott and 2/Lt William Metzger, received several hits damaging three engines beyond control: No 1 caught fire and its propeller windmilled, No 2 smoked badly and lost power while No 4 afire, had flames reaching back as far as the tail. The interphone and electrical systems were inoperative, while flares ignited on the flight deck and the resulting fire was fed by leaking hydraulic fluid from damaged lines. The engineer was wounded in the leg and a shell fragment

Over Cologne, 15 Oct. 1944, an AA shell went through the chin turret of 398th BG's 43-38172 and exploded in the nose. Despite the failure of cockpit instruments and oxygen system and the sub-zero gale rushing in, 1/Lt Lawrence De Lancey brought the B-17 back to Nuthampstead. Lack of damage to lower part of nose illustrates tendency of blast to carry fragments upwards. Bombardier was killed.—(USAF)

severed the radio operator's arm below the elbow. Bill Metzger went back and applied a tourniquet to stop the haemorrhage but through loss of blood and extreme pain the man lapsed into unconsciousness. Meanwhile, Gott had decided to jettison the bombs and attempt to regain Allied territory, a few miles away.

When over friendly territory, Metzger went to the rear again and indicated to the remaining crew members—two had apparently already gone—that they should jump. One gunner's parachute had been damaged, so Metzger unhesitatingly gave him his. He had told Gott that the radio operator was in no state to parachute and they would have to try and crash-land.

With only one engine functioning normally and the others on fire, Gott found an open field. As he banked into a final landing approach at approximately 100 feet, the fire reached a fuel tank and the bomber exploded, struck the ground and exploded again, her three occupants perishing.

On 7 Nov. 1944, Lt Murray and crew could pose with pride before their B-17G, *Leading Lady*. First 305th BG aircraft to complete 100 missions.—(USAF)

Lady Janet and the 452nd Group had been part of the force sent out on November 9th to blast forts at Metz and Thionville preparatory to a ground offensive. Cloud interfered and poor conditions at bases was instrumental in destroying eight bombers and three fighters in take-off and landing accidents. On November 16th the heavies were called out to attack gun positions east of Aachen as a prelude to another Allied push. To avert the risk of short bombing a number of special measures were taken: red smoke shells were fired every 500 yards along the north-south front line and fused to burst at 18,000 feet. Fifteen silver barrage balloons were spaced 300 yards apart along the line and at a height of 2,000 feet—and in case there was good visibility, fluorescent red and orange cloth markers were laid on the ground. The most reliable device, however, was the adaption of the SCS-51, a radio aid normally used for instrument landings at USAAF bases. The ground transmitters were placed along the troop-line and when passing directly overhead an aircraft's receiver gave an immediate indication on a dial. With 8/10ths cloud, it was this radio technique that proved its worth. The one bomb that fell in Allied territory (without causing harm) had hung up in the bay of an aircraft turning back after bombing. The very low ceiling and still hazy conditions at East Anglian bases caused most returning groups to be diverted to the west and north of England, where some were unable to return home for three days.

By November 20th the murk had cleared sufficiently for the Fortresses to fly to Merseburg for the thirteenth time, and as the results left much to be desired they returned again on the 25th—and on the 30th. On this last mission of November the flak was the most formidable yet, with first reports of 56 heavies lost, but eventually fixed at 29 when the others were located at continental bases. Most of these losses were sus-

At 23,000 ft above the undercast 20th Wing B-24s prepare to bomb enemy positions in the Metz area 9 Nov. 1944. 93rd BG lead plane has special equipment to pick up signals from ground forces. Circle marking on 446th BG's FL: V signifies a PFF aircraft.—(USAF)

tained by the 3rd Division due to an unfortunate sequence of events. The bomber column was led by the 1st Division briefed to attack the Zeitz synthetic plant, while Merseburg, twenty miles to the north, was to be bombed by the 3rd Division. Both divisions planned to follow the same route, separating for their respective runs at Osnabruck. However, the 1st Division overshot this point and the 3rd Division followed. By the time the error was appreciated, the 3rd Division wings were some five to fifteen miles to the south of their correct course and a similar distance beyond their turning point. This brought them into range of the ninety guns defending Zeitz and on the

Lt Loye Lauraine was pilot of a flak stricken 487th BG B-17 returning from Merseburg. He made radio contact with the Lavenham control tower. Control: "See if you can head the Fort out to sea." Lauraine: "It's all I can do to keep it going. We tried to tie the control cables together to save the plane, but it's no go." Control: "Use your own discretion." Lauraine: "We will try and turn around and head out to sea. We have no bombs." Control: "Keep in touch with us." Moments later, Lauraine: "We are ready to bail out. If we don't make it, good luck to you." Control: "I won't need the luck—good luck to you." Lauraine held the Fortress steady long enough for the rest of the crew to jump, but when he tried to leave the aircraft went out of control and dived into the ground from 9,000 ft.

The bomb bay camera of another 487th BG Fortress caught this stricken victim of Merseburg flak as it falls away in flames: 30 Nov. 1944.—(USAF)

wrong approach to Merseburg, plus facing a strong wind which slowed their speed. The defences at Merseburg covered an elongated area so that both the Leuna and Buna plants were protected. Bomb runs were therefore planned to cross these defences at the narrowest points. The 3rd Division now found itself attacking on the longest axis and for periods of up to 18 minutes each group was subjected to a concentration that was probably without parallel. Some 80% of the Division's Fortresses were damaged in what was to be its last visit to this, the most dreaded of targets.

Oil targets in the Leipzig area were for long the prerogative of the Fortresses. The 2nd Division Liberators were kept mainly to oil targets in North-West Germany, with the Hamburg/Harburg and Misburg plants predominating. During an attempt to destroy the last operative plant at Misburg on November 26th, the Luftwaffe was again able to pull off a successful mass assault on the two groups of B-24s that bombed. The 491st Group had just turned at the IP when a Gruppe of FW190s came down out of clouds. With the low squadron having bombed short (due to accidental tripping of the toggle switch in the lead aircraft) and then pulling out from the other squadrons to avoid flak ahead, the German fighters could not have picked a more opportune moment. Successive waves went through the Liberators with deadly effect. All told, twenty B-24s went down in this affray; 15 from the 491st and the remainder from the other group involved, the 445th.

The price the heavies paid in denying the Germans oil was higher than at any of the other priority targets on the Eighth's list. But it did not deter the Eighth Air Force from continuing to press this campaign. By the end of November over half of the 87 major crude and synthetic oil plants were considered either temporarily or indefinitely inactive—the remainder being the smaller and less productive sites. Early the same month, Allied strategists had produced a plan for an all-out campaign against the German transportation system in the west. This was second only to oil in priority status, and a great many missions were directed against such targets during the final weeks of 1944.

The Eighth's bombers were out on eighteen days in both October and November, a reduction in effort reflecting the deterioration in weather. The last three months of 1944 were, in fact, far worse for cloud and fog than the two previous winters. About 80% of all bombing in October had been by radar and a similar percentage held for operations to the end of the year. Radar techniques had improved greatly during the year. H2X remained the most promising method and enough trained operators and equipment had been received by August for a programme of setting up a pathfinder unit in each bomb group to be commenced. Some groups favoured radar aircraft and crews in each squadron whereas others assigned all to one specific squadron. By the end of November, when the last pathfinder squadron was formed in the 3rd Division, all Fortress groups had at least two H2X aircraft on strength. H2X operators had originally decided on the moment to release bombs from information derived from their instruments. This, however, left much to be desired and a system had been developed whereby the radar operator passed the information

Red flares, fired when a bomber had wounded aboard, gave it landing priority and an ambulance at the end of the runway to meet it took the casualty to base hospital as quickly as possible. This 487th radio man collected flak in an arm.—(Lerner)

to the bombardier, so that this could be set up on the bomb sight with a better chance of avoiding an ill-timed release.

A further refinement of the G-H blind bombing technique was introduced in November when the 3rd Division B-17s employed it during some attacks in Western Germany. This was Micro-H, combining G-H and H2X methods. Beacons on the Continent at Namur and Verdun transmitted signals which could be picked up by a bomber's H2X equipment and used to set a straight course to the objective. Because the beacons were limited in range, use of Micro-H was confined to the Ruhr and western areas of Germany, where 3rd Division came to rely heavily upon it to bring a formation to a cloud-concealed location. The success of radar missions varied widely and Eighth Air Force analysts considered that at least half these missions were failures during the fall and early winter of 1944. That there was as yet no substitute for the accuracy of the Norden sight and an experienced bombardier, had been demonstrated time and again when visibility was good. Even so moves were always afoot to strengthen the bombardier's aim, and many of the new developments were originally contrived by men at combat stations. An altitude drum lock, to make the Norden more fool-proof, originally contrived by Sgt Sigmund Kramer of the 384th Group, became a standard fitting on all Norden's in the Eighth. Sgt Waclaw M. Osinski of the 401st Group constructed an all-electric mechanism to salvo bombs automatically when the hair lines of the sight aligned on target. This eliminated possible delay in fumbling with hand levers and the device was ordered to be installed in all lead B-17s in the 1st Division.

A senior bombardier at the 388th Group, Captain Charles M. Zetlek, evolved a successful method of "grid bombing" to beat the smoke screens that so often foiled sighting at the oil targets. (The grid was on transparent material which laid over a map enabled calculations of distance to be made between check points that could be seen on the ground and those that were obscured.) The 44th Group was experimenting with radio release of a whole squadron's bombs by the lead aircraft bombardier.

Another aid to better visual bombing was the use of smoke markers. These were originally used for blind attacks but since the spring of 1944 had also been employed in visual attacks, where their employment gave a clear signal for the rest of a formation to drop and also marked the target for following formations. Unfortunately, the liquid smoke trail had corrosive effects and aircraft that flew through it suffered discolouration of plexiglass parts. In some cases the chlorsulfonic acid responsible ruined complete nose pieces. This problem was not overcome until July when a delayed fuse Skymarker bomb was brought into use.

In the first three weeks of December the B-17 and B-24 bombardiers had little opportunity to make visual sightings on any target. Exceptions were December 12th and 16th when some formations were able to see the marshalling yards and rail centres they were attacking. It was on the first of these occasions that the hazards of operational flying even without

All that was left of 493rd BG's *Devil's Own* after it exploded on Debach.—(IWM)·

attention from the enemy were brought home to the crew of the 493rd's Fortress *Devil's Own*. Outward bound for the rail centre at Darmstadt, an exhaust stack "blew" on the port outboard engine as the aircraft was gaining altitude over the sea. Forced to turn back, the Fortress was on her way home when the offending engine suddenly burst into flames. The pilots dived the bomber, but the fire continued to take hold. Now at low altitude, *Devil's Own* headed for the home base at Debach where, faced with the imminent failure of the left wing, the pilot, Lt John E. DeWitt, had no option but to bring her straight in narrowly missing a parked B-17 and an army truck before belly landing beside the runway. As the machine ground to a halt, the blazing wing folded back enveloping the fuselage in flames. The crew ran and within two minutes of DeWitt scrambling out of the right cockpit window, the whole bomb load went up. The 30 ft high doors on a nearby hangar were lifted off their rollers and slammed to the ground by blast from the explosion.

The war which many had thought would be over by Christmas now looked like enduring for many months. The Allied advance had succumbed to the grip of winter. Then on December 16th von Rundstedt launched his surprise offensive in the Ardennes, the last Nazi gamble, aimed at cutting the Allied front in two and reaching the Channel. The Germans had also chosen a period of bad weather when they knew the Allied air support would be minimised. While von Rundstedt moved, the airfields in England and France were mostly shrouded in fog. The few formations that were able to assemble on the 18th and 19th were diverted to airfields in Cornwall, Wales or the north on return, where some "socked in" for a week. As the men of the heavy bomb groups knew only too well, clouds were the enemy's greatest asset in shielding him from attack from the sky.

Chapter 23: Jet Menace

It was a 479th pilot, Captain Arthur Jeffrey who, on July 29th, had the first Allied combat with a German jet fighter. The Group was returning from escort to Merseburg, with the flight led by Jeffrey keeping an eye on a straggling 100th Group Fortress at 11,000 ft. At 11.45 hrs, near Wesermünde, an Me163 was seen making towards the Fortress from the rear but pulled away under it without attacking. Jeffrey, with his wingman, dived after the jet but as he closed the enemy aircraft started climbing. Jeffrey fired at 1,000 yds but the enemy aircraft continued to climb and weave for 5,000 ft emitting short spurts of smoke from its exhaust. It then made a left turn allowing Jeffrey to engage again, turning inside it and getting in a deflection shot from about 300 yards and seeing hits. The jet then went into a near vertical dive, Jeffrey following. When last seen the Me163 was still pulling away in a dive and entered the overcast at 3,000 ft. Jeffrey's P-38 was indicating 500 mph when he pulled out of his dive, blacking out in the effort. The Me163 was awarded to Jeffrey as "destroyed" after examination of the camera film but the jet apparently escaped as there was no mention of one being lost this day in German records.

The first sightings by VIII FC of the Luftwaffe's new jets had occurred the previous day. It involved 359th Group P-51s escorting 45th Wing B-17s near Merseburg. The Group's CO, Colonel Avelin Tacon, reported—"The bombers were heading south after bombing, and we were flying parallel to them about 1,000 yds to the east, 25,000 ft. Someone called in, 'Contrails high at 6 o'clock'. I looked back and saw two contrails at about 32,000 ft about five miles away. I immediately called them to the flight as jet-propelled aircraft. There is no mistaking their contrail—it was white and very dense, as dense as a cumulus cloud and with the same appearance, except that it was elongated. The two contrails I saw were about three-fourths of a mile long, making a 180 degree turn back toward the bandits.

"It has since turned out in interrogation that there were five Me163s—one flight of two, which I saw with jets on, and

New adversary: Me 163 liquid-rocket-powered fighter pulls away from Cpt Jeffrey's Lightning.—(USAF)

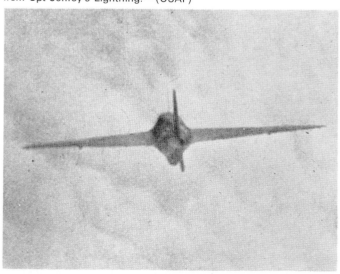

another flight of three without jets. The two I saw made a diving turn to the left, in good close formation, and started a 6 o'clock pass at the bombers. As soon as they turned they cut off their jets.

"We started a head-on overhead pass at them, getting between them and the rear of the bombers. When they were still about 3,000 yards from the bombers they saw us and made a slight turn to the left into us and away from the bombers. Their bank was about 80 degrees in this turn but they only changed course about 20 degrees. They did not attack the bombers. Their rate of roll appeared to be excellent, but the radius of turn was very large. I estimate, conservatively, that they were doing between 500 and 600 mph. Although I had seen them start their dive and watched them throughout their attack, I had no time to get my sights anywhere near them.

"Both ships, still in close formation and without jet propulsion, passed about 100 ft under us. I split-S'd to try and follow them. As soon as they had passed under us one of them continued on in a 45 degree dive and the other pulled up into the sun, which was about 50 or 60 degrees above the horizon. I glanced quickly up into the sun but could not see this one. When I looked back at the one which was continuing the dive, approximately a second later, he was about five miles away and down to perhaps 10,000 ft.

"Although I did not see it, the leader of my second flight reports that the plane that pulled up into the sun used his jet in short bursts. The flight leader described it as looking as if he were blowing smoke rings. This ship disappeared and we don't know where he went.

"The aircraft is a beautiful thing in the air. It was camouflaged a rusty brown, similar to some FW190s, and was highly polished. It looked as though it had been waxed.

"Although these two pilots appeared very experienced, they were not aggressive, and apparently were just up for a trial spin."

Colonel Tacon was right in his assumption, the Me163s were up on trial flights, the unit concerned, I/J.G.400, was not yet ready for combat operations. Nevertheless, these aircraft were armed and apparently ready to strike if opportunity allowed, as the report of a B-17 radio operator on a mission to Magdeburg a week later indicates. "Within two minutes after turning at the initial point I saw puffing vapour trails at about 35,000 ft and about 9 o'clock to our course. They flew in the direction of our formation, then turned left to attack three P-51s which were flying approx 3,000 ft above and to the left of our formation. The jets dived onto the P-51s which were at about 8 o'clock to our formation at the time. The 163s were in trail as they swooped down on the P-51s. The attacks were pressed almost to point-blank range, then the enemy aircraft zoom-climbed into the clear sky above. I saw each of the three P-51s catch fire and dive earthward." Three 352nd Group P-51s were missing.

The appearance of the German jets was not unexpected. As related Allied intelligence had been aware of their existence and development for several months. But the prospect of having to deal with opponents capable of speeds up to 150 mph faster than Mustangs caused some concern. Bomber strikes had been mounted against factories suspected of manufacturing the jets, and against airfields harbouring them, but it was realised that in time substantial numbers would be met in was hidden in another siding and blasted wreckage of the carriages caused heavy casualties to the troops taking cover nearby. Little was ever found of the Mustang and pilot who caused this explosion.

While anything that moved on the permanent way—other than hospital trains—was fair game, more discretion had to be used in strafing road transport, particularly near villages and towns where French civilian life could be endangered. The risk of VIII FC fighters accidentally attacking friendly troops was not great in view of missions being conducted far ahead of the battle front. There was however the isolated occasion when things went wrong. Perhaps the most extraordinary occurred on August 15th when two 356th Group Thunderbolts strafed a Ninth Air Force headquarters near Laval, more than 200 miles from their briefed area of operations! American anti-aircraft gunners brought down one of the offending P-47s, killing the pilot.

For ground attack two 500 lb bombs were the most common load for a P-47 or P-51 (the actual weight of individual bombs varied considerably), the exact load being determined by range and target considerations. Fragmentation bombs were carried in clusters and P-47s occasionally hauled 250 lb GP bombs in clusters of three on each wing rack. A new weapon was added to the inventory during August, the air-to-ground 5 inch rocket, already in use with some Ninth Air Force Thunderbolt Groups. Lt Col David Schilling of the 56th first tried the rockets against rolling stock at Braine-le-Compte on

Local Frenchmen in the 10 ft deep, 30 ft wide crater that resulted from the flying bomb train explosion at Remy. Pieces of rolling stock were scattered far and wide.—(USAF)

combat. That this threat did not materialise earlier was due chiefly to mechanical problems with such advanced aircraft, and vacillating attitude of the German High Command, which included using many Me262 jets in a ground attack role.

Following the US forces offensive at St Lo on July 25th, and the subsequent rapid advance of the Allied armies across Northern France, VIII FC fighters were called upon to play a substantial part in the programme of transport interdiction. Close support of the ground armies was the responsibility of the Ninth and Second Tactical Air Force fighter-bombers, the Eighth's missions generally involved the extensive French railway system which they continually harried with devastating effect. Life for the train drivers of occupied France became fraught with danger; hundreds of gun camera films bore witness to steam shrouded locomotives and exploding ammunition wagons. Such was the havoc wrought that rolling stock, locomotives and train crews had to be imported from Germany. In any case, the French crews naturally had little heart for their work.

The results of interdiction were at times spectacular. During the evening of August 2nd 364th Group, spotting a locomotive in a siding at Remy, went down to strafe it. Only then did the pilots see that there was a complete train with a dozen or more box wagons cleverly camouflaged with green vegetation. The Mustangs made three length-ways passes, but their fire had little effect. A flight of four then came in at right angles, three fired and passed over the train, but as the fourth fired it was enveloped in a tremendous explosion. So great was the blast that some pilots of a squadron of 364th, flying top cover over 1,000 ft above, called out that they had been hit by flak. The three P-51s that had led the last pass were hurled upside down as they pulled away at less than 50 ft, but their pilots managed to effect a recovery. Haystacks, and buildings several fields away, were observed on fire and roofs were torn off houses in a village a mile distant. The train evidently contained warheads for flying bombs. Where each wagon had stood was a crater 10 feet deep and 30 feet wide. A German troop train

4.5″ rocket tube clusters fixed on a 351st FS P-47D at Raydon, Aug. 1944. Blunt nosed drop tank was 150 gl. type from different manufacturer.—(Rust)

Experimental 20 mm cannon pack on the wing pylon of Col Fred Gray's P-47D. 150 gl. fuel tank is installed on the fuselage shackles.—(USAF)

Unusual still from VIII FC gun camera film shows pilot of an Me 109G a moment after bailing out and before opening his 'chute.—(USAF)

August 17th, and was not over-pleased with the weapon. Colonel Fred Gray, the 78th Group's CO tried them next day but found difficulty in aiming and hit none of his targets. Other trials were carried out but the rockets were not popular. The three-tube clusters under each wing were unwieldly, besides which pilots felt they could do better work with gun fire and bombs. The 78th also tried out 20 mm cannon packs slung on the wing racks of its P-47s but vibration among other difficulties led to them being discarded.

MEW (Microwave-Early-Warning) control was introduced in VIII FC during August. This mobile radar with an operating range of 25 miles, could obtain both direction and altitude of enemy aircraft for transmission direct to the airborne fighter units under its control. Invaluable for monitoring air activity in advance of the battle lines, MEW facilitated many successful interceptions and gave warning of impending "bounces" to aircraft engaged in bombing and strafing. The 353rd Group's P-47s were under MEW control on August 2nd when Lt Col Ben Rimmerman shot down the only enemy aircraft seen by Eighth Air Force fighters that day—an Me109.

When the bombers went on their second shuttle mission to Russia, the 357th Group were chosen to go all the way with the bombers. The 64 Mustangs, plus eight spares, led by the group commander, Colonel Donald Graham, were airborne at 09.30 hrs and reached its destination in Russia at 17.00 hrs after a rendezvous with B-17s bombing Rahmel, where some brief skirmishes with enemy aircraft took place. Next day the 357th took the B-17s to Cracow airfield and returned to Russia to prepare for shepherding them to Italy on the 8th. Support for C-47s evacuating wounded from Yugoslavia was undertaken on the 10th and on the 12th the B-17s were brought back to England after bombing Toulouse airfield. All without loss to the bombers or themselves.

To ensure that the 357th Group would not have to do battle before rendezvous with the bombers on the shuttle, the 55th Group had been sent in its recently acquired P-51Ds to watch over the B-17s on the pre-target leg. Their leader, Major John Landers, had engine trouble after take-off; radioing for another P-51 to be readied, he landed, took off again, caught up with the Group and resumed his leadership. The journey from Wormingford to Gdynia and back was 1,595 miles, a seven hour flight and a record round trip for any fighter group flying from England.

Two notable VIII FC aces were involved in incidents that day. Major John Godfrey of Gentile/Godfrey team fame, recently returned to the 4th Group after home leave, having destroyed an Me410 in the air, was leading his squadron to strafe a German airfield when flak caused a coolant leak. Jettisoning the Mustang's hood, Godfrey prepared to bale out but Captain Fred Glover, another 4th Group ace, advised him to pump neat fuel into the engine with the priming pump, thus lowering the engine temperature. By pumping the primer all the way to the first airfield (Beccles) seen on the English coast Godfrey survived. Major George Preddy, leading the 352nd Group, was about to rendeavous with the bombers south-east of Hamburg, when he spotted 30 plus Me109s similarly intent. In his haste to join combat, both he and his wingman became separated from the rest of the fighters. He reported "These Me's were flying in a tight formation at about 28,000 ft and though they saw me coming they did not take evasive action, since they figured that their top cover—which I never saw—would take care of me.

"I went right in for the pack and shot down five, starting with the tail end Charlie. Only one of the five managed to parachute out. The rest of them went down in flames.

"After splitting them up I got on the tail of the sixth and chased him down to 5,000 ft. This was the best part of the mission for me. The first five never had a chance—not one of them fired a shot at me—but the sixth gave me a real dog fight."

The extraordinary behaviour of the German fighters had enabled Preddy to take five of their number with comparative ease, but there was more to it than that. George Preddy was a tenacious combatant and excellent marksman with a penchant for numerous and quick "kills" in a fight. On July 18th he had claimed four enemy fighters in combat, and on two previous occasions a triple and double. Like John Godfrey and Duane Beeson, Preddy was a resolute and dedicated fighter.

The spectacle of several enemy fighters continuing blindly to follow their leader when attacked was to astonish other American pilots in the months ahead. This was an outcome of the critical pilot shortage and the inadequate training. The majority of replacement pilots from the Luftwaffe training schools went to the Jagdgruppen operating in defence of the Reich, with an average of only 30 hours flying. They were expected to gain competence in operational units where a few experienced pilots had the difficult task of leading them against adversaries who had averaged five times their number of hours in training alone.

On August 8th the 4th Group was given the task of providing escort for RAF Beaufighters on a shipping reconnaissance to

John Godfrey with small wound on forehead where he was nicked by flak, and bandaged hand chaffed raw through pumping the fuel primer for $2\frac{1}{2}$ hours. On right is Fred Glover.—(USAF)

George Preddy poses with his *Cripes A'Mighty 3rd* the day following his spectacular combat.—(Mason)

Norway. Encountering no aerial opposition, the 4th attempted to strafe an airfield near the coast, a largely abortive effort due to difficult terrain and well directed ground fire that cost them dear—3 pilots. An escort for 200 RAF heavies, Lancasters and Halifaxes, attacking V1 sites, was provided by 339th Group Mustangs and 78th and 353rd Group Thunderbolts on August 15th and proved "uneventful".

Next day escort duties for some VIII FC fighters was far from uneventful. The 359th Group, which had sighted the Me163s in July, was escorting three B-17 boxes at 27,000 ft south-east of Leipzig when the thick rocket trails of Me163s were seen heading towards the rear of the bombers. Lt Col John Murphy considered his flight too far away to intervene, but noticing a straggling B-17 he guessed, correctly as it proved, that the enemy would make for this; he made in its direction, followed by his wingman, 1/Lt Cyril Jones. The Me163, however, overshot the Fortress and decreased speed, the pilot apparently not seeing the approaching Mustangs until after they had opened fire. Jones, in a favourable position to fire, saw strikes on the enemy aircraft and claimed it as destroyed, but through blacking out while recovering from his dive, he did not see it fall. Colonel Murphy meanwhile, had seen another Me163 5,000 ft below him and dived down. The 163, beginning to turn, was easily out-turned by Murphy whose fire caused an explosion. This aircraft, as German records confirmed, was shot down. Two other 359th pilots engaged two more Me163s with inconclusive results.

From these early encounters with the rocket fighter, VIII FC gained valuable information on its manoeuvrability, performance and tactics. Combat reports suggested that the 163 was at a disadvantage in a turning fight. Its erratic flight caused by the brief bursts of power followed by free flight with the rocket off, had allowed the US fighters to close. It was known the reason for this was the limited endurance of the fighter and the efforts of the German pilots to eke out the fuel. The US pilots did not know that like so many aircraft hurriedly pressed into service, the Me163 had more than its share of difficulties, some of which had troubled the I/J.G.400 pilots on this occasion, their first organised operation against the US heavies.

Cyril Jones enjoyed a meteoric success in his brief span as a fighter pilot. In 16 missions he shot down six enemy aircraft, and damaged one and had strafing claims of five destroyed and one damaged. His first victory came on his first mission. He was lost on his sixteenth, presumed killed. His was a group where aces were few: for example, Captain John McNeill, a flight leader in the 359th, flew a complete tour and extension, yet never had the opportunity to engage.

The hard pressed conventional fighter defence force in the Reich, though having some successes against the US heavies,

again suffered heavily at the hands of the P-51s on August 16th. Frequently it was the Me109 top cover that suffered, yet this was specifically put up to do battle with the US escort! A typical example occurred south of Hanover when the 355th Group sailed into a score of 109s and destroyed 12 for the loss of one. The remarkable audacity of some pilots is illustrated by an incident involving the 355th Group on August 18th. Some 20 miles west of Soissons the engine of Captain Bert Marshall's P-51D was hit and he was forced to belly the aircraft into a large hay field. There was no written command about landing and taking-off behind enemy lines, simply because no one considered such a stipulation necessary—not that this would have been any deterrent to 2/Lt Royce Priest, who lowered his undercarriage and landed near Marshall. A German lorry appeared at one end of the field but this was promptly strafed by other P-51s that were circling the spot. The cockpit of a Mustang was not as confined as that of many fighters of the time, but it was barely large enough for two. Priest discarded his parachute and dinghy pack to make room. Marshall climbed in and sat in the seat and Priest sat on his lap, pulled the canopy shut, gave his engine maximum power, and cleared the far boundary. Back at Steeple Morden, Priest was jokingly accused of "bucking for promotion", to which Priest retorted that if that was the case he would stand a better chance by leaving Marshall where he'd crashed, thus creating a command vacancy in the squadron.

While not in such spectacular circumstances, the commanders of the 355th's other two squadrons had recently been rescued. Major John Elder (357th) was pulled out of the Channel by French fishermen and a few days later Major Larry Sluga was also fished from "the drink" by a British naval vessel.

On the same day that Marshall and Priest flew home together from France, Colonel Hubert Zemke was working some of his old magic with a new command—the 479th Group. The former CO, Lt Col Kyle Riddle, had gone down while strafing on August 10th; he had escaped from his blazing P-38 and evaded capture, but the Group was still without a commander. The Group was due to convert to the P-51, and General Kepner offered the command to the 56th's Group Executive, Dave Schilling, but he preferred to stay with the 56th and P-47s. On hearing this, Zemke 'phoned Kepner and said that he would like the command, and was promptly given it. Zemke owed no allegiance to a particular fighter type; he was more dedicated to the art of air fighting and the continual challenge it provided. When the P-51B first appeared Zemke had been quick to appreciate its potential but he was on a bond tour of the US when priorities for conversion were established for VIII FC groups. The 56th could have stood fourth in line, but the other officers did not wish to forsake the Thunderbolt: Zemke would have done so because he believed the 56th could do better work with the Mustang.

The prospect of leading the youngest group in the command appealed to Zemke and the news was not disagreeable to the 479th either. Zemke flew a P-38 at first. He went with the 479th to Nancy/Essey airfield on the 18th to escort B-24s. After the Liberators had departed he led two flights down to strafe an area untouched by the bombs, and found a great many He111s and little flak. Calling the 434th and the remainder of the 435th Squadron down, he conducted a shooting party wrecking practically every aircraft on the airfield. The P-38 pilots returned to Wattisham to register claims in excess of 100. Due to the confused nature of the action there was some duplication and after experts had looked at the combat films a revised figure of 43 destroyed and 28 damaged was awarded the Group. Zemke was asked to distribute individual awards fairly amongst those concerned. It is notable that the Colonel took none for himself.

Strafing continued to take its toll. Two VIII FC Group commanders, additional to Zemke's predecessor, were lost

Luftwaffe aircraft burn on Nancy/Essey after the attack by the 479th FG shot up 72.—(USAF)

during August. Colonel Thomas Christian was killed on the 12th in the crash of his P-51D *Lou IV*, missing with three other 361st Group Mustangs. Lt Col Cy Wilson, 20th Group, "caught it" over Esjberg airfield, baled out off the coast and was rescued by Danish fishermen. Flak was also thought to have claimed the 4th's Major John Godfrey as he was shooting up Ju52s on August 24th. He escaped from the crashed Mustang and was eventually taken prisoner; examination of another pilot's combat film suggests that he might have been accidentally shot down by his own wingman through evasive action he was taking to avoid ground fire. The liquid-cooled Merlin, fine engine that it was, could not withstand the batterings many a P-47 Double Wasp had sustained and continued to function. A Mustang pilot flew in dread of that sudden rise in temperature indicating a punctured cooling system and the imminent seizure or disintegration of the engine.

A new Luftwaffe jet aircraft making its bow, was observed on the evening of August 29th when eight P-47s of 78th Group were flying top cover for other aircraft of the Group engaged in ground attacks at Termonde near Brussels. Their leader, Major Joe Myers, who had flown a first tour with the 55th Group P-38s the previous winter, and now commanded the 82nd Ftr. Sqdn., caught sight of an aircraft which he at first mistook for a B-26 Marauder. The P-47s were at 11,000 ft and the strange aircraft was flying low, and extremely fast, on a southerly heading. Myers realising that a B-26 could not travel at that speed, dived his Thunderbolt to investigate. In the 45° dive the P-47 registered 450 IAS and gradually overhauled the unidentified craft which Myers recognised to be a German twin-jet. The enemy pilot saw the approaching Thunderbolts before they were in range and started evasive action of flat turns. Myers, gaining on the jet, was about to open fire when it crash-landed in a field. The pilot fled, but was killed in the strafing run made by following Thunderbolts to destroy the wreck. Myers and a member of his flight, Lt Manford Croy, were credited with the destruction of this aircraft, the first example of an Me262 met and destroyed in an engagement with Eighth fighters, although really a case of scuttling!

By early September the battle line had moved out of most of France into the Low Countries and was poised towards Germany itself. In consequence on tactical missions the Eighth's fighters roamed further afield for targets to bomb and strafe. On the first day of the month the four Thunderbolt groups were sent to blast anything that moved on rail or road between Brussels and Antwerp. The 138 aircraft involved were credited with 94 locomotives destroyed and twenty damaged, 537 items of rolling stock either destroyed or damaged, and the same fate for 382 road vehicles including 15 tanks. While there was little the enemy could do to protect his road and rail system other than move at night, it was surprising that many

of his airfields were still poorly defended and often with aircraft parked in exposed positions inviting strafing. Indeed, claims for aircraft destroyed on the ground reached a new peak in September as the Eighth's fighters struck at airfields in the Reich. More than a third of the month's total was taken on one day, 143 destroyed and 90 damaged on the 5th, and the greater proportion of this was the work of two groups, Zemke's old and Zemke's new, in two missions to the Hanau and Gissen areas. At these airfields the 56th Group netted sixty for the cost of four pilots MIA and three wrecked aircraft left in France, the pilots safe; while the 479th Group had 52 for one pilot missing and one force-landing in France. The liberation of most of France was a life-line for many fighter pilots who a month or so previous would have fallen into enemy hands.

On the same day the 55th Group's Mustangs on an escort to the Stuttgart area ran into a flock of primary trainers and shot down, or caused to crash, seventeen. The only other engagement during this escort was with three Me109s, two of which were claimed. There were some red faces when it was learned that the Swiss had complained that one of their machines had been shot down (the other was badly damaged). The P-51s had evidently strayed over the Swiss border. Happily, the Swiss pilot parachuted safely.

Temporarily depleted after D-Day when many Gruppen were sent to France, Luftflotte Reich had gradually rebuilt its strength, despite the not infrequent maulings some units received in combat with US escort fighters. The fact remained that since the last great battle of May the Jagdverbände had only attempted one major organised challenge to the American day raids into the Reich, raids that during August brought more telling damage to the German war economy than ever before. Why September 11th should have been chosen by the Luftwaffe to re-assert itself over their Homeland is not known, but that day a bigger effort was made to deal with the American intruders than on any occasion since May 28th. The targets for the heavies had been chiefly the precious oil plants, with 75 B-17s of 96th and 452nd Groups bombing Chemnitz before making the third shuttle to Russia. All-the-way escort this time was provided by the 20th Group; four sixteen-plane squadron formations plus spares. While no enemy formations were encountered en route a weather front with high cloud barred the way to Russia. Colonel Rau scouted ahead and advised that there were gaps between the layers through which they could pass. The front was successfully negotiated and the Mustangs flew on to Piryatin, save two that became separated in cloud; one put down at another airfield and later rejoined, while the other, piloted by Lt Harold Horst, remained unable to locate Piryatin. Trying to land on a field he had discovered, Horst was disconcerted to find that every time he approached, a Russian fighter attempted to get on his tail with obvious hostile intent. After the third attempt, Horst decided to seek a landing elsewhere to the west. All he could see was forest and farms and when finally his fuel was expended, he crash-landed without being hurt in a clearing after 9 hours 20 minutes flying! Returning, the 20th took the B-17s to Discsgyor in Hungary on the way to Italy. They returned to Kings Cliffe on the 17th without having had any contact with the enemy.

The other P-51 units flying escort on September 11th saw plenty of action. For once it appeared the Germans had conformed to a plan of attack, putting up substantial numbers of fighters along the penetration route at the Rhine and a second concentration in the general target area near Leipzig. The escort for the two B-17 divisions headed here fought most of the battles. Led by Major Edgar B. Gravette, part of the 339th, came to the aid of the 100th Group's B-17s that were under attack and in the course of dispersing the German fighters shot down fifteen. In numerous battles ranging from above 25,000 ft to "zero", Lt Col John L. McGinn and Captain William Forehand led formations of the 55th and 359th Groups respectively to make claims of 28 and 26 shot down. Individuals such as Henry Brown of the 355th, John Meyer of the 352nd, Ray Wetmore of the 359th added victories to their records this day, in the unprecedented total of 116 destroyed in the air. The Luftwaffe had destroyed perhaps 15 Mustangs in combat and caused several others damaged to make emergency landings in France. One Mustang shot down was reported to have been the victim of an Me262 jet.

On the two following days the Jagdverbände rose again, with sorties reported as between 125 and 150 on both occasions. Combat with the Eighth's fighters resulted in seven to one in the Americans' favour. While German pilots were unaware of this ratio, most experienced hands must by this date have appreciated the hopelessness of combat under the prevailing conditions and with the aircraft available. Many veteran pilots were shot down two or three times in the course of a year.

The bold move to outflank the Siegfried Line and gain a foothold on the northern bank of the Dutch Rhine, launched by the Allied armies on September 17th, brought the four Thunderbolt groups their most difficult and deadly missions of the war, during the week that followed.

The landings did not go well from the start, there was stronger opposition on the ground to the airborne troops than expected and substantial anti-aircraft defences. The Thunderbolt with its heavy firepower, and reputation for absorbing punishment was the obvious choice for ground attack in such circumstances, and the 56th, 78th, 353rd and 356th Groups were handed the job of "flak-busting", neutralising of gun emplacements in the drop-zones to lessen the risk to the lumbering transports and supply-dropping bombers. This was an unenviable job which usually entailed being fired at before it was possible to locate the gun positions. The howls and

Not all the losses in the big September fighter battles were on one side. This 4th FG Mustang bellied in with a coolant leak somewhere in Germany, 12 Sept. 1944.—(Holmes)

derisive remarks at briefing when the mission was announced was typical of fighter pilot banter, but every pilot was well aware of the dangers to be faced. Two hundred P-47s were sent out as "flak bait" on the 17th, flying over the transports' route to Nijmegen and Arnhem at 2,000 ft to 2,500 ft, and as soon as guns opened up on them an element would peel off and attack with 260 lb fragmentation bombs and then strafe. By their efforts, they managed to suppress all but one or two unlocated guns by the time the C-47s arrived. On the following day B-24s were sent in to drop supplies to the airborne forces and the P-47s of the 56th and 78th received a much hotter reception when they arrived before the bombers to deal with anti-aircraft emplacements. The weather was atrocious with an overcast down to 500 ft in places, and haze that seriously limited horizontal visibility. While German gunners could see the Thunderbolts, the pilots had great difficulty in locating the gun positions. The 56th Group, which operated in the Arnhem

A P-51D flown by Lt Urban Drew of 361st FG (not his personal aircraft). Parts of upper surfaces have been painted olive drab.—(USAF)

area, sent out 39 P-47s and sixteen were either shot down or crash-landed through damage. Eight of the pilots came down in Allied controlled territory and eventually returned to base. Nearly every Thunderbolt that returned to Boxted had some damage. It was the Group's blackest day.

The Luftwaffe was flying both bomber and fighter sorties against Allied operations, although the extremely low cloud and mist must have similarly hindered their pilots. On the 18th several Staffeln of 109s and 190s fell foul of the 357th Group's Mustangs and a low altitude battle resulted in 26 for 2 in the Mustangs favour. The 359th could only claim a two-each draw after it fought 35 FW190s 15 miles north-east of Arnhem, but the important point was that no hostile aircraft approached the supply aircraft that day. The Luftwaffe was equally active on the two following days, but a deterioration in the weather kept many Eighth Air Force groups on the ground. Very low cloud permitted only the 56th and 353rd Groups to operate over the battle area on the 21st when enemy fighters made a strong and successful effort to intercept transports and gliders, troop carriers and supply aircraft, coming into Holland. The better part of 35 RAF and US transport aircraft lost this day were shot down by the Luftwaffe. The two P-47 groups were kept busy. The 353rd under MEW guidance caught several enemy fighters attacking C-47s near Nijmegen and claimed six of the enemy. The 56th, led by Dave Schilling, were flying north-east of Nijmegen at 3,500 ft when they spotted about twenty FW190s below them. In the surprise attack and dog fight that ensued the "Wolfpack" shot down fifteen for three, Schilling taking three himself. If the Jagdverbände often got the worst of it in these encounters, their activities were nevertheless sufficient to have some bearing on the outcome of the overall battle. Some stiff fights took place over Arnhem on Saturday, September 23rd, with the 353rd playing a leading role. The 78th Group P-47s neutralised many flak positions in the drop area for an RAF re-supply mission that day, probably saving disastrous losses. However the German land forces being too strong, the British forces were withdrawn. In this ill-starred venture, VIII FC groups had played a major part but suffered 73 fighters missing, 45 of them Thunderbolts.

The 479th had received its first Mustangs early in September and from the 13th was flying a Mustang squadron with the P-38s. At least the P-38 Lightning finished its days in VIII FC with a certain amount of glory. Zemke took the 479th on a MEW control sweep east to the Münster/Haltern area on September 26th and was vectored towards a formation of enemy aircraft apparently setting out to interfere with supply dropping to the First Allied Airborne Army. Engaging, 29 Me109s were claimed by the 31 Lightnings and 12 Mustangs involved. Commander of the 434th Ftr. Sqdn., Lt Col Herren, claimed three by his P-38 and Zemke bagged two for his first P-51 victories. The last known combat of VIII FC P-38 occurred two days later when Zemke was leading his Group near Halberstadt. Due to a shortage of P-51s, P-38s remained part of the 479th force for a few missions in early October, the last being on the 9th.

The exit of the Lightning as a fighter coincided with the last mission of the fifteen fighter groups under the operational control of VIII FC. As from October 10th the three fighter wings came completely under the jurisdiction of the three Bombardment Divisions having been assigned from VIII FC on September 15th. Three training organisations, the 495th and 496th Fighter Groups, and the 1st Combat Crew Gunnery School at Snettisham, which had recently been transferred to VIII FC, remained under its control, although these too were also transferred, one to the three divisions late in November. The 65th, 66th and 67th Wings, now under the 2nd, 3rd and 1st Divisions respectively, were a further step to making the divisions an air force within an air force. The chief advantage was a simplified chain of command and easier planning of fighter support for bomber operations, each fighter wing supporting its respective Division. In practce, fighter groups often supported bombers from other Divisions. The VIII FC had conducted operational planning for all three fighter wings when fighters were on escort and bomber support duties, co-operating with the three divisions. The new move gave each division planning responsibility for its own fighter wing, although as under VIII FC individual wings were still allowed operational planning of those missions which involved only their own aircraft.

Although the new command structure administratively linked the bomber and fighter units closer together, groups remained very much clans unto themselves. The worlds of the fighter pilot and the bomber crews were as different as the aircraft they flew, despite the fact that their operations were essentially complementary.

Throughout October comparatively few enemy sightings were made on any of the escort missions and only occasionally was there any action. Total destroyed claims by the Eighth's fighters ran to only 72, the lowest figure for a year and a somewhat sudden drop considering September yielded 469 in this category. There were fairly regular reports of German jets but most evaded combat apart from the odd attempt by Me163s to pick off stragglers. Occasionally attacks were made on the Me262 fighter-bombers operating along the northern sector of the ground front but these usually escaped by their superior speed. Over Rheine airfield on October 6th the 353rd Group's Lt Mueller spotted an "Me262 and an He280" preparing to land. He put his P-47 into a dive towards the Me262 which made ineffectual shallow turns to evade. Closing range, Mueller saw two strange parachutes appear before a burst of fire from

his guns caused fragments to fly off the jet. The "He280" was pursuing the P-47 at this juncture, so Meuller broke off his attack. The 262 crashed, the second of this type to fall.

Next day as many as 25 jets were reported on a mission to eastern Germany. Three 364th Group pilots, Lts Elmer Taylor, Everett Farrell and Willard Erkamp, trapped an Me163 which fell under their combined fire. Major R. E. Conner of the 78th Group surprised and destroyed an Me262, while Lt Urban Drew of the 361st Group, finding himself in an advantageous position to attack two Me262s taking off from Achmer, shot down both. What advantage the Me262 had in speed, it apparently lacked in manoeuvrability. Its speed, however, was such that the US fighters only stood a chance of coming within firing range during a dive or by some error on the part of the enemy pilot. Whether or not the Mustangs and Thunderbolts would still be able to protect the lumbering B-17s and B-24s from them, was causing some concern. Early combats had given valuable information on tactics to employ against the jets and these were further developed through experiments with the RAF's first squadron of Meteor jets.

Five Meteor Is went to Debden on October 10th so that their pilots could discuss anti-jet evasion measures with Eighth Air Force pilots. Two days later 140 B-24s with P-47 and P-51 escort flew from Peterborough to Colchester, where Meteors made mock attacks on them. A critique was later held at Debden. Similar practices were staged on following days and in early November.

On the final Eighth Air Force mission of October, 264 P-51s and 179 P-47s were sent to escort heavies into Germany where fine weather and good visibility was forecast, but over the North Sea unpredicted heavy cloud appeared and spread. Colonel Zemke, on what was probably his last flight before being transferred to a desk job at Wing HQ, was leading the 479th Mustangs when, somewhere near Celle, they became engulfed and scattered like leaves by the elements. Three, including a squadron CO and the Colonel, did not return to base. Zemke's Mustang was thrown onto its back by rough air and went into a power dive during which a wing came off, forcing the Colonel to bale out. His place was taken by Lt Col Riddle, who had been shot down in August and evaded capture to return to the 479th as Zemke's deputy. It was Zemke's joke when he returned from a prison camp—which he ran with the same zest as he ran his fighter commands—that Riddle had sawn half-way through his Mustang to regain leadership of the Group. There was another outcome from the loss of this most distinguished pilot.

Don Blakeslee, having returned from the US and hoping to get a flying command, was grounded. A fighter pilot's tour was 300 hours combat flying. No one knew how many hours Blakeslee had logged but around a thousand was a conservative estimate; his own records were doctored to confuse the authorities. So Zemke and Blakeslee, the two great fighter leaders, were out of the air; very few of the old famous names remained. The young fighter pilots who now filled the ranks, however, were equally as proficient and eager as their predecessors; this they were soon to show.

In the Mustang the Eighth's fighter pilots had a superb machine of exceptional all-round performance; good firepower and excellent endurance. The G-suit allowed pilots to turn quickly with confidence—the Luftwaffe did not provide its own combat pilots with similar equipment. Now, in the late summer of 1944, another item of equipment was added to give the Mustang pilots yet another advantage over their opponents —the K-14 Gyroscopic Gunsight, known familiarly as the "No Miss Um". Like many other items of equipment used by the Eighth, it originated with the British. Specifications of this gun sight were given to USAAF in June 1944 and production was arranged in the US.

The new instrument, at first unwelcomed because of its size and apparent complication, became a magic box to fighter

Col Graham's *Bodacious* is run up on its Leiston dispersal point. One of the few examples of a shadow shaded P-51. Tanks are 108 gl. metal type.—(Elliott)

pilots in combat. It allowed successful shooting at twice the previous maximum range, but its principal value was in allowing a deflection shot, even from right-angles to as likely find its mark as one from dead astern. Deflection shooting with the old N-9 sight had largely been a matter of guesswork and skill.

Some of the first examples from the US were sent for the 357th Group to test. It was found that these were intended for P-51B/C models, already out of production and constituting but a quarter of the 357th's strength. Colonel Donald Graham asked the service group at Leiston to try to instal the sight in his P-51D *Bodacious*, and the job was handed to S/Sgt Idalo E. Augugliaro. To place the sight so as not to impede the pilot called for considerable ingenuity and skill. "Oggie" Augugliaro removed the old sight and dispensed with the anti-glare shield, rarely used in combat because of the time taken to get it into position. He then cut away part of the panelling projecting over the instrument panel—a continuation of the forward fuselage cowling—and strengthened the area with braces. The K-14 was then carefully fixed in the resulting recess. Graham used his sight in combat in September and was so impressed that he asked the service group to similarly modify other P-51Ds.

The K-14 was originally developed for bomber turrets and it was the Eighth's engineers at Bovingdon who had arranged for its production in the US as a standard fighter sight. Eventually, a factory installation was available for the P-51D but this was considered inferior to that devised by 357th's mechanics. Other Eighth AF groups saw the 357th modification, borrowed the plans and fitted out their aircraft. Eighth Air Force Modification Center finally took up the work and from March 1945 onwards all Eighth Mustangs had the K-14 installed in the fashion originating at Leiston.

The USAAF did not take up the gyro gunsight with enthusiasm. Many pilots were convinced that the existing N-9 was adequate and there was a general dislike of complicated instruments for fear of malfunctioning. RAF and FAA pilots who had experience of the K-14 were seconded to fighter groups and flew P-51B/Cs to "sell the sight". The sight was sold, however, well and truly in November 1944.

In November operational training units were established in each combat fighter group. Fighter pilots fresh from training grounds in the US then by-passed the 495th and 496th Groups which had given theatre training for the past year, and went straight to the group with which they would eventually enter combat. There were some misgivings amongst fighter group commanders that this was an unnecessary burden for an operational station. The value of the scheme soon made itself

plain, however, in that the trainees quickly became imbued with the spirit of the group and were eager to take part in combat flights. Moreover, in obtaining the necessary final polish to their art they became versed in the operational peculiarities pertaining to their particular group, and were as up to date on the latest procedures and tactics as the operational pilots themselves. This, in fact, was the idea behind the scheme, a smooth transition for the newcomer. The veteran pilots who ran the "Clobber Colleges" as the OTU's were called, were usually men who had recently completed operational tours. Some of the Eighth's most distinguished aces acted as OTU mentors for their group. The 495th and 496th FTGs now continued to provide conversion and refresher courses for the Eighth as well as handling new pilots destined for the Ninth Air Force.

The small number of enemy aircraft encountered during the October missions into the Reich led to much speculation as to the status of the Luftwaffe as a threat to further operations. On the one hand Allied intelligence knew that during the late summer months production of single-engined fighters had been increasing and on the other it estimated a critical fuel shortage which kept these machines on the ground. There had not been a significant challenge to a major Eighth Air Force raid for nearly two months and this led, not unnaturally, to the conjecture that the Germans were building their strength for an operation on some scale. That this proved to be the case was clear by the evening of November 2nd when in terms of numbers destroyed the Eighth's fighters had their most successful day so far.

Five forces of heavies were sent into Germany with the two main portions, 683 B-17s, making for the notorious Merseburg oil plants. Despite the somewhat erratic course planned, there can have been little doubt in Luftwaffe defence circles of the eventual area for which the heavies were heading, and as the leading 3rd Division with its escort of over 400 P-51s and thirty Ninth Air Force P-38s reached the IP around noon, many sightings of enemy fighter formations were called.

The 55th Group spotted three Gruppen of between 75 to 100 Me109s and FW190s making towards the bombers; by splitting his force the Group leader, Major Eugene Ryan, intercepted each and effectively dispersed them while shooting down nineteen for one P-51 missing. One of the largest Me163 formations so far encountered, about 15 aircraft, avoided other Mustangs and about nine got through to make single, unsuccessful passes at the bombers.

Some 200 Mustangs of the 20th, 352nd, 359th and 364th

Col Joe Mason, distinguished fighter leader who did much to put the 352nd FG on its road to fame. He poses with the ground crew of his personal P-51D (nickname in white).—(Mason)

Groups were escorting a similar number of 1st Division B-17s, who encountered the strongest opposition, about twenty minutes later. At 12.21 hrs Major George Preddy, leading his new command, the 328th Ftr. Sqdn. now, called Colonel Joe Mason the 352nd Group leader: "Hello Topsy, this is Ditto Black Leader. Fifty plus bandits headed for the big friends". Within minutes other large formations of German fighters had been spotted and the 352nd divided forces to do battle. During a fifteen minute engagement the 328th Squadron made claims of 28 destroyed, a new high for a squadron on one mission, with Preddy getting an Me109 to become leading active Eighth ace with $24\frac{1}{2}$ air and 5 strafing victories claimed. The 352nd altogether ran up a score of 38; a record for a single action. Captain Donald Bryan, leading the 328th's Yellow Flight, became involved in fifteen separate combats in as many minutes and came out with five victories.

Another pilot who distinguished himself this day was the 359th Group's Captain Ray Wetmore. His leadership in tackling another formation of Me109s and destroying two himself led to the award of a DSC. The largest formation encountered during the Merseburg battle was a force estimated variously at 150, 200 and 250, which attacked two groups of B-17s which had gone off-course to the north of the planned route and were trailing the main stream on withdrawal. The 20th Group, assigned to guard the left flank of the 1st Division, became embroiled with these fighters, claiming 28. Three fell to the leader Lt Col Robert Montgomery, and another triple to 1/Lt Ernest Fiebelkorn who at 21 was probably the largest fighter pilot in the Eighth, being 6 ft 4 ins tall, weighed 225 lbs—and insisted that he had to exhale every time he got in or out of his Mustang! Finishing his tour late in November his nine aerial victories were the highest individual score for a 20th pilot.

The 134-3-25 claims were the second highest ever made by the Eighth's fighters, and these were all concentrated into the battles that raged during forty minutes around Merseburg. Four hundred German fighters were estimated to have been involved, although German records indicate only some 300 aircraft of ten Gruppen in action. In any case, the battle proved once again a disaster for the Jagdverbände, for not only did they arrive too late to intercept before the bombing, but only 26

B-17s and possibly 8 of the P-51s missing were due to their efforts.

While this undoubted victory for the Eighth's fighters further established their overwhelming superiority it gave rise to some concern at higher command levels. There could now be little doubt about the flow of new aircraft to the Luftwaffe—particularly as on this occasion Allied monitoring services learned that Luftwaffe units in the north and eastern areas of the Reich had been held down by poor visibility at bases and

1/Lt Ernest Fiebelkorn, 'giant of a man' who became 20th FG's top air ace.—(USAF Museum)

were not involved in the Merseburg battle. In fact, German production of the Me109 and FW190 single-engine fighters had trebled since the Spring of 1944 with a peak figure of 3,000 being produced in September, and this despite the dispersal programme which entailed shifting production from 27 to 729 plants with the resultant complexity of transportation and final integration for assembly.

The resurgent Luftwaffe, quantitatively and technically, caused Doolittle to voice his concern that saturation of the escort might result in the Luftwaffe bringing down 100 bombers on a single mission. He felt it was essential to increase the escort fighter/bomber ratio from one to two, to the ideal of two to one, and conveyed these opinions to Spaatz in the hope that Washington might be prevailed upon to act.

As it was, the effective strength of the Eighth's fighter arm had increased since D-Day by 150 more aircraft, although no new groups had been added. Indeed, during November the 15 groups each averaged 86 first line fighters ready for operations and 135 assigned was to be the peak figure. It had become regular practice for all groups to operate two separate forces when required on the same mission, an A and B group of three twelve-plane squadrons each, instead of the usual three sixteen-plane squadrons of a single group operation.

Doolittle's concern was not misplaced, for the Luftwaffe's fighter arm had the potential strength to assail the US bomber fleets as never before. Such was the plan on which Goering and his commanders had been working: aiming to put up 2,000 fighters, and bring down 1,000 bombers. It appeared that the November 2nd interception was an abortive, mishandled attempt to attain this goal with only part of the force available being airborne.

For the Americans perhaps the most worrying aspect of the strengthened Luftwaffe was the menace of the new jet aircraft, the Me163 and Me262, now frequently observed. US jet aircraft would not be available for at least nine months and though the RAF already had one Meteor squadron, the production schedule for this excellent British jet was deplorably unhurried in the light of the potentially critical situation that was developing.

Eighth Air Force had no alternative but to hold its air superiority with existing equipment and set about devising tactics to employ against the jets. The Me163, the small rocket-powered machine first encountered in July was a particularly difficult adversary. Enough information was forthcoming from intelligence agencies and actual combat encounters for a reasonably accurate estimation of its performance to be made. Due to its extremely brief duration—some eight minutes powered flight—it could only be profitably employed as a target interceptor, and this was confirmed by its regular appearance in the Leipzig areas. The basic plan of bomber interception by the Me163 was a climb to a few thousand feet above the bombers, then a power-off descent to a position where an attack could be made on the rear or low elements of a formation, or preferably a straggler. The 163 would then use its motor to pull away to position itself for another attack, or dive down to its base. Because of its limitations it was usually met in single passes, drawing heavy defensive fire from bombers—for which reason they often made for stragglers. Its incredible speed—nearly 600 mph—allowed it to climb or dive away from the US fighters with ease, but it was noticed that in approaching a bomber it would reduce speed in order not to close too rapidly and overshoot.

US pilots did not then know its imperfections and limitations—all its fuel could be consumed in a single climb to 30,000 ft, making it imperative to operate only on days of good visibility when bombers could be spotted without time-wasting search.

Signs were that the turbo-jet Me262 was being produced in quantity and though first appearing as a fighter-bomber, during September, there was now evidence of its increasing use as an interceptor. In level flight it appeared 75-100 mph faster than the Mustang and could easily pull away from the US fighter in a climb. Nevertheless its manoeuvrability appeared inferior to both the P-47 and P-51, and it had shown on several occasions a marked inability to make sudden changes of direction when attacked and was also averse to steep dives. The jet engines seemed particularly vulnerable, bursting into flames with but a few hits by ·50 bullets. The fact that the Me262s were encountered in specific areas, plus Allied knowledge of the limitations of jet engines, pointed to limited duration. But the truth was that the Me262 had a fairly respectable endurance varying up to ninety minutes, with the maximum figure obtained at high altitude on restricted throttle settings. With its speed and armament of four 30 mm cannon, it was a formidable opponent. Most of the early Me262s shot down that had not been caught at some disadvantage, were overhauled by building up speed in a dive. Eighth Air Force tacticians took measures to ensure that escort fighters had the necessary altitude advantage in areas where jet interception was most likely.

The first true Me262 fighter unit, the Kommando Nowotny (after its commander and leader Major Walter Nowotny, a distinguished ace reported to have 258 victories) was formed in September 1944 and established at Achmer near Osnabrück. Thirty aircraft were assigned to this unit which Nowotny developed.

While the great air battle was being fought out at Merseburg, a flight of Me262s made their first use of air-to-air rockets on B-24s flying near Minden. Their missiles went wide and the jets made off hotly, but vainly, pursued by Thunderbolts of the 56th. Two days later Kommando Nowotny made attempts to attack a US fighter escort, picking on isolated elements in the Zuider Zee to Hanover area; a 359th P-51 and a 356th P-47 missing may have been their victims.

On November 6th four P-51 groups escorting B-24s in the Minden area had several scattered combats with Me262s a 361st and a 357th Group pilot being credited with destroying one each, while the sole P-51 lost is not thought to have fallen to the jets. The report of Captain Charles "Chuck" Yeager of the 357th (in later years famous as the first man to exceed the speed of sound in level flight) gives an idea of the difficulty of engaging the Me262. "I was leading Cement White Flight when north of Osnabruck we spotted three Me262s going 180

New shape in the gunsight. This Me 262 suffered engine trouble on 8 Nov. 1944, allowing 357th FG's James Kenney to close. The German pilot, Lt Schall parachuted.—(IWM)

Charles Yeager, fighter pilot at Leiston; later the first man to exceed the speed of sound in level flight.—(Olmstead)

degrees to us at about 2 o'clock low. We were at 10,000 ft. I and my flight turned to the right and headed the last man off. I got a hit or two on him before he pulled away. They were flying a loose V-formation and they did not take any evasive action, but seemed to depend on their superior speed. They pulled out of range in the haze.

"We were flying along in overcast which was very thin and the edge of it was over to the right, altitude about 5,000 ft. I went under it and flew along for a minute or two and I met them head-on again only they were now flying at about 2,000 ft. I split-s'd on the leader and they all separated. I fired a high deflection burst from above on the leader, got behind him and was pulling 75 ins hg and indicating 430 mph. I fired two or three bursts and got hits on the fuselage and wings from 300 yards, then he pulled away and went into the haze where I lost him.

"In this engagement I lost the rest of the flight and found myself alone. I climbed to 8,000 ft and headed north. I found a large airfield with black runways about 6,000 ft long, and started flying around it. I got a few bursts of flak, but it was very inaccurate. I spotted a lone 262 approaching the field from the south at 500 ft. He was going very slowly (around 200 mph). I split-s'd on it and was doing about 500 mph at 500 feet. Flak started coming up very thick and accurate. I fired a short burst from about 400 yards and got hits on the wings. I had to break off at 300 yards because the flak was getting too close. I broke straight up, looked back, and saw the enemy jet aircraft crash-land about 400 yards short of the field in a wooded area. A wing flew off outside the right jet, but the plane did not burn."

The Kommando Nowotny stepped up its activity on the 8th, took at least one P-51 in combat, but lost two Me262s including their leader who perished. In fact the Eighth fighter pilots had claimed 2-0-1. Shortly after this the unit was withdrawn from combat and sent to Lechfeld to recuperate. During its six weeks of operations 22 Allied aircraft were claimed destroyed and 4 probably destroyed while 26 Me262s were lost by all causes. Insufficient training was the chief factor in this rather poor showing with the Luftwaffe's most promising fighter, as pilots had only 10 hours on the type prior to operations. By committing this small force the Allies probably benefited more than the Luftwaffe in measuring its capabilities and planning counter measures at an early stage of its introduction. Certainly the confidence of

the US fighter pilots was not shaken for here were enemy pilots, in superior aircraft, fleeing from P-51s and P-47s. Eighth Air Force fighter pilots hunted jets, if anything, more vigorously than 109s and 190s.

The last known contact between Kommando Nowotny and the Eighth occurred on November 11th, when a single Me262 disappeared as quickly as it had arrived after attempting to attack four radio-relay Mustangs patrolling over Holland. These aircraft were a regular feature of long distance missions, their purpose being to relay the out-of-range radio messages of fighter pilots in distant combat areas, to fighter wing control rooms in the UK.

After this encounter, little was seen of the Me262 in combat for several weeks, but to ensure life was made difficult for their promoters, a long range fighter sweep by 355 P-51s and 47 P-47s on November 18th took in the Lechfeld development centre where the 4th and 353rd Groups picked off 14 more of these aircraft of the 20 visible on the field.

Probably disheartened by the losses at Merseburg at the beginning of the month, the German high command abandoned its plan for a vast Luftwaffe operation against a major USAAF day raid. Here internal politics played a part and by the end of the month many units that had been rebuilding their numbers at central German bases were returned to tactical duties, leaving only those of J.G.300 and 301, in the main, to meet the Eighth Air Force in battle. Before this occurred, however, the Jagdverbände was sent up in three large scale operations

The 357th FG had some odd trophies and mascots. Film actresses underwear decorated the pilot's room—obtained by request and autographed by the donors. Major England displays a slip from Faye Emerson. Lt Schmanski kept a pet duck.—(USAF & Elliott)

Jack Daniell, the 339th FG pilot who became an ace in his first combat.—(USAF)

as if by some forlorn hope they could reverse their fortunes.

The first of the three came on another mission to Merseburg on the 21st, the bomber stream following much the same route to the target as taken on the 2nd, but this time with over 700 B-17s and 650 escorting Mustangs. To the west of the target lay a large cloud front beyond which the German defence controller probably did not expect the US force to pass. In consequence the Luftwaffe fighters were late in arriving in the target area and the several hundred put up became embroiled with Mustangs in the clouds. Some were caught assembling and one unit of FW190s, encountered by elements of the 352nd and 359th Groups, did not drop their belly tanks when attacked. Markings suggested that this Gruppe was a tactical fighter unit, a possibility borne out by the inexperience exhibited. In the chase through rain clouds Captains William Whisner and Claude Crenshaw of the 352nd and 359th respectively both made claims of 5 FW190s each plus others damaged! The score for the day read 73 enemy aircraft destroyed for two P-51s lost in combat. Crenshaw entered the revealing note on his combat report: "The success of my encounter is attributable to the presence of Jerries as well as the superlative working of my K-14 gunsight and G-suit. The G-suit enabled me to make all the violent manoeuvres necessary to protect myself and still be an efficient fighting force. The sight allowed me to fire short bursts with astonishing accuracy. I missed on only two bursts, one while firing at 90 degrees deflection and the other while rolling with the enemy aircraft".

The next challenge came on November 26th again when the oil installations were the destination of the bombers but in a different locality, the Hanover area. An estimated 400 German fighters were in the air and though managing to bring down several bombers they were again decimated by the fighter escort, this time to the tune of 110. Again the inexperience of some Luftwaffe pilots was evident, with Lt Jack Daniel shooting down five FW190s, during his first combat, of the 29 claimed by his group, the 339th. The 355th Group claimed 27, and the 361st Group 19 under

Captain John Duncan's leadership. The 356th Group, guided by Lt Col Baccus, brought down 23 without loss, despite widespread gun jamming in its recently acquired P-51s. For this group such a victory was a much needed fillip, as in thirteen months combat it had rarely met the enemy and then seldom with the advantage, and this in spite of now being part of the 67th Wing whose groups had been seeing most of the recent air action.

The following day, November 27th, the Allies estimated 750 fighter sorties were flown against the Eighth Air Force missions to central and south-east Germany, a record number and never surpassed. Although Allied estimates were usually on the high side they were nonetheless indicative of the Luftwaffe effort, which was certainly on a vast scale and all the more disastrous in that several Gruppen were apparently vectored towards bombers that materialsed as Mustangs: the 357th and 353rd Groups which had been directed to meet the threat. Led by Major Joe Broadhead the 357th Group, which had a knack of being in the right place at the right time when enemy fighters were afield, attacked one of the novice formations that stupidly clung together while Mustangs shot them down. Of the 30 claimed destroyed by the Leiston Group, Captain Leonard Carson took 5, Yeager and England four apiece, and Clarence Anderson three. Major Wilbert Juntilla took the 353rd Group into another large assemble and 'bagged' 21 when once again the Germans continued to hold formation. Juntilla narrowly missed being shot down by a P-51 from another group. The latter's pilot was heard to say over the radio: "Did I get that guy?" To which a 353rd pilot was quick to retort: "I hope not. He's my Squadron CO!" Another Mustang, with a "red nose" was shot down by one of its own kind in this battle. The pilot baled out. Mistaken identity incidents were not infrequent, and common to both sides.

Separated from the rest of his group in a fight, the 359th Group's Ray Wetmore later caught sight of a whole Geschwader and while he tried in vain to call others to the scene, he and his wingman followed the German fighters for hundreds of miles. As no more Mustangs appeared Wetmore and wingman proceeded to bounce the formation themselves. Two against 120!

Altogether, for the loss of 11 P-51s, 98 enemy fighters were claimed destroyed. Whatever fears the Eighth Air Force commanders had of a resurgent Luftwaffe fighter force were largely settled by the outcome of the four major air battles in November.

The winter of 1944-1945 produced the worst weather in Western Europe for many years. Radio and radar aids were still very much in their infancy, and aircraft were often grounded due to heavy cloud, fog or blizzard conditions. In war, the situation often justified the risk on many days when "even the birds were walking". So when the B-17s and B-24s were sent out the escort went too, although conditions that troubled bombers with a crew of nine were much more hazardous to a pilot who had to navigate himself in a single-seat fighter. The dangers facing the fighter pilot on long escorts into Germany during the winter months were probably much less from the enemy than from the elements and malfunction. In December 1944 alone, of 87 fighters missing, sixty were lost to unknown causes and eight to accident. Of the sixty many were later known to be due to reasons other than enemy action. Engine failure was a not infrequent cause of loss, but vertigo in cloud or an oxygen fault could get a pilot into a fatal spin. There was also the possibility of radio trouble thus becoming lost above an overcast. Severe icing or storm conditions could quickly claim the unwary pilot. Men just 'failed to return' and in many instances no trace of them or their aircraft was ever found. The primary cause might be sloppy maintenace, or pilot error, but more often than not it was the result of an unfortunate chain of circumstances if

Donald Bochkay, one of 357th FG's leading aces puts his Mustang down on Leiston, 10 Dec. 1944.

one 'got it'. Unfortunate in the extreme for some. Lt Robert Pigg of the 479th Group who had engine trouble over Belgium on December 12th, was forced to bale out of his Mustang. Floating down through cloud he was struck and fatally injured by a passing B-26 Marauder.

On occasions, in 'soup' conditions, fighter aircraft had to be abandoned over friendly territory as it was impossible to find a landing field. When the 56th Group returned from a strafing and support mission on December 4th the cloud extended from almost ground level to several thousand feet in altitude and nine of its aircraft were either abandoned in the air, or 'bellied' into France.

For the 56th Group, with P-47s, it looked as though the big battles were past. The Mustang groups with their extra endurance reached those distant areas of the Reich where the Luftwaffe usually chose to do battle. During November the 'Wolfpack' pilots had watched enviously as the P-51 groups ran up high scores. Some range advantage had accrued from the liberation of France and Belgium, but this applied to all fighters operating from England. A slow climb at minimum power settings could be made in gaining the necessary altitude to enter enemy airspace, now often a hundred or more

Replenishment activity especially for the cameraman around Mike Gldych's P-47D—which sports 32 victory symbols.—(USAF)

miles further away from the fighter bases, and thus effecting a considerable saving in fuel and extending duration. Previously, high power settings had to be used in order to reach the required 25 to 27,000 ft level at the enemy coast. Even so the Thunderbolts appetite for fuel kept it in check. In October, Maintenance and Technical Services had designed a 200 gallon drop tank to help matters, and the first became available to operational units in mid-November. These were basically a widened version of the 165 gallon 'flat tank' and had a true capacity of around 215 gallons.

On December 17th the Germans launched their Ardennes offensive and backed it with a great number of conventional fighters. For the first few days activity was restricted by appalling flying weather but on the 23rd the sun occasionally broke through permitting the Eighth Air Force to play a part. The 56th, sent on a patrol sweep ahead of the heavies under MEW control, were in a good position for action, as they would be vectored onto any enemy aircraft spotted by the MEW Controller. Fifty-six P-47s led by Colonel Schilling left Boxted that morning to take up a patrol area west of Bonn. Almost immediately, they were vectored towards a large group of enemy aircraft but could not make contact; twice more they were guided to other German aircraft but frustratingly were unable to reach them. MEW then advised of 'bigger game' near Bonn and soon the 56th pilots saw two formations of FW190s orbiting high over Euskirchen airfield. While the 61st and 63rd squadrons attacked one formation, Schilling led the 62nd towards the rear of the other, closing his own formation to simulate another German Staffel. The ruse worked; the P-47s approached close enough to attack before being recognised. The ensuing action lasting 45 minutes, ranged from 28,000 ft to 'the deck' with opponents who proved experienced and skilful. When stock was taken back at Boxted, 37 Me109s and FW190s had been destroyed for the loss of four P-47s, one of which managed to reach Belgium before the pilot baled out. It was a record for the 56th and probably the most successful action ever fought with the Thunderbolt. Their opponents were a Gruppe of J.G.27 whose losses included Heinz Bartels, an ace with 94 victories. Some of their aircraft had been FW190Ds with longer noses housing liquid cooled engines.

The same day MEW control was also successful in vectoring the 479th Group to a 'gaggle' of FW190s where the Mustangs took 12 for 1, with one of the Group's top aces, Major Jeffrey, bagging 3. But while the Eighth Air Force continued to attack, the situation on land had suddenly changed and the Allied forces were faced with a critical situation—The Battle of the Bulge.

Chapter 24: Focus Cats

The pre-knowledge of the German jet aircraft was but one facet of air intelligence culled from photo reconnaissance. The RAF had established its doctrine for reconnaissance through the experience of the first two years of war, and influenced the USAAF in its approach to this vital mission. Basically reconnaissance fell into two distinct roles, strategic and tactical; the former involved photographic intelligence, a constant watch on enemy territory from altitude, the latter was both visual and photographic, up-to-the moment reports in the vicinity of a battle front, and usually conducted at very low altitude. Strategic photographic reconnaissance was the chief requirement of Eight Air Force, although prior to the establishment of Ninth Air Force in England, it also fostered an embryo tactical mission.

Membury had become the home of Eighth Air Force reconnaissance in September 1942 when the 67th Observation and the 3rd Photographic Group arrived from the US. On paper these two groups were assigned four squadrons each, but in fact Membury received a few hundred partly trained men and a half dozen camera-equipped B-17s. The only other reconnaissance aircraft in the Eighth at this date were 13 F-4s (P-38F Lightnings with camera equipment in place of nose weapons). Nine of these were assigned to the 5th Photo Squadron which had arrived in England in June 1942 and was eventually assigned to the 3rd Photo Group. Preparations for the North African invasion in November 1942 led to a hasty build-up of reconnaissance units and by the end of the year only the depleted 67th Group remained, with the remnants of the 3rd Photo Group, for which no aircraft were available.

The 67th then received nine Spitfire Vs for each of four squadrons and eventually obtained a few Piper L-4 Cubs and Douglas Havocs to swell its numbers. The reconnaissance mission however, faded into the background as the services of men and aircraft were required to support units in other commands through the early months of 1943. The Spitfire squadrons were used as training units for other Spitfire organisations, pilots were detached to fly target-towing Havocs on gunnery training, and the L-4s provided liaison transport at various operational stations. Aircraft types at Membury during this period included Masters, Oxfords, and such oddities as ex-RAF Turbinlite Havocs.

Eventually tactical reconnaissance training came to the fore again, the Spitfires engaging in observation, photography and the correction of artillery fire during British and Canadian troop manoeuvres. The term Observation was dropped from the Group's designation in June, and replaced by Reconnaissance.

Officially the 67th did not become operational until after transferring to the Ninth Air Force in December 1943, but its aircraft and men were in action long before that time. In the summer of 1943 most pilots flew on detached service with the RAF, many taking part in cross-Channel sweeps. From one of these Captain John R. Walker failed to return on July 14th and other Spitfire pilots were missing at later dates. A-20 crews also flew with the RAF. After a raid on Schiphol with No. 107 Squadron RAF on 30th July, the aircraft flown by Lt McQuvie suddenly broke formation and spun into the sea.

A provisional unit, the 2911th Bombardment Squadron (L) (P) was formed in the 67th to fly A-20Bs fitted with cameras, but capable of carrying bombs. These aircraft flew combat sorties from Exeter on 18th and 19th August and again in September. Prior to this some crews had flown operationally with RAF Boston Squadrons.

Piper L-4s and Spitfire Vs made up the flying complement of 67th Observation Group early in 1943. The Spitfires were chiefly those left behind by 31st and 52nd FGs when they departed for North Africa. BN635 still wears 309th FS markings.—(USAF)

Spitfire XI returns to Mount Farm. Ground crew men remove film and take pilot's report on aircraft.—(USAF)

By February 1943 the 13th Photographic Squadron, originally a component of the 3rd Photo Group had sufficient F-4s and F-5As (photo version of P-38G) to embark upon its business, high altitude reconnaissance. On the 16th it moved into Mount Farm, Oxfordshire, a satellite airfield of Benson, home of the RAF's Photo Reconnaissance Unit. The 13th was under the command of Major James G. Hall, a World War I pilot who, at 45, was something of an "oldie" in this young man's war. Guided by RAF Benson, the squadron flew simulated missions practicing photography over the UK. Two or three cameras were carried in the nose of each Lightning and the set-up was usually about 400 lbs lighter than the fighter version, giving a slight increase in speed—about 400 mph at 25,000 ft, the optimum level for F-5 operations. Above this altitude trouble was experienced with the Lightning's engines in European climatic conditions, as has been related.

Speed, altitude, and an erratic flight course were the essentials for avoiding interception by enemy fighters. The Germans were well aware of the purpose of the single aircraft sorties and appreciated the difficulties in intercepting them. It was necessary for Me109s to have a height advantage and overhaul the photo aircraft in a dive, but this situation was difficult to achieve as their opponents flight courses were planned to conceal the objective of the reconnaissance—the best method of avoiding the defences. Thus the passage of a photo aircraft over occupied Europe and Germany in 1943 was something akin to that of a drunken bee.

The first operation had been on March 28th when Major Hall set off to conduct mapping photography of the French coast. From then on the squadron flew regular missions over the Cherbourg peninsula and northern France. Its first losses came in April, another in May and four in June—two mysteriously disappeared while off St Nazaire on June 29th. With seven lost and no replacement the F-5 complement shrunk to eleven. Mostly it appeared that the missing F-5s had suffered engine trouble and fallen easy prey to the Luftwaffe. Early in July the 7th Photographic Group was established at Mount Farm as an headquarters and Hall, promoted to Lt Col, was placed in command. Two more squadrons were assigned to the station but for a period operations were conducted solely by the 13th Photo Squadron.

By August, with sufficient experience in hand, the 7th Photo Group's F-5s were set to photograph targets bombed by the Eighth's heavies, a period marked by four months without an aircraft missing in action. But there were still troubles with the Lightnings and on August 19th for example,

a pilot had to bale out over the English coast while outward bound when his aircraft broke up.

Sometimes the images brought back revealed some startling finds. When Major James Wright, newly in command of the 13th Photo Squadron, had completed his assignment to the Huls area of Germany, he followed normal procedure and turned on the cameras to use up unexposed film. On some of these exposures a large, new synthetic rubber plant was discovered.

As the F-5 had some shortcomings which tended to make it more vulnerable to interception on deep penetrations, it was decided to add a squadron of Spitfire XIs as used by RAF Benson. Another unit shed by the 3rd Photo Group, the 14th Photo Squadron, was put into training and became operational with the type late in 1943.

Since operations began in April, the Lightnings had averaged around fifty sorties a month throughout 1943. It was not until December when a third F-5 squadron (the 27th) was added to the Group and aircraft strength increased, that operations were extended. Despite the winter weather, 111 sorties were flown in January and 161 in February of 1944. Following the heavies attack on Berlin, March 6th, Major Walter L. Weitner, flew the first Spitfire photo mission to the German capital. In April, 304 sorties were flown by the four squadrons and on April 11th Lt Robert Dixon took his Spitfire over Brandenburg, Weisswarte and Stendal on the 1,000th sortie by the Group's squadrons.

While the Spitfires continued to fly the majority of target photography sorties, the Lightnings returned to photographic mapping during early 1944, to survey coastal areas for the cross-Channel invasion. To mask the zones of interest, the F-5s covered an area extending from Blankenberge to Dunkerque and from Le Touquet to St Vaast de la Hague. The 7th Photo Group pilots were trained for high altitude flight, but to meet the requirements of photographic intelligence immediately prior to D-Day they had to descend to extremely low altitudes. Beginning on May 31st the F-5s flew a great many sorties along the French coast to obtain detailed

Dusk had fallen when 24-year-old Walter Weitner returned from photographing the damage to Berlin on 6 Mar. 1944.—(IWM)

Mosquito XVI of 802 RG(P) in Jun. 1944. Tail marking identifies squadron.—(Havelaar)

photographs of assault obstacles and defences at the proposed landing sites. Sometimes this work was carried out at 15 feet.

In the spring of 1944 another reconnaissance group was formed in the Eighth Air Force. It grew out of the need for special units to engage in weather reporting around the British Isles and over hostile territory, particularly in advance of a bomber mission. The 18th Weather Squadron, purely concerned with meteorological work, had a detachment at every combat base to advise on weather situations and to supply its headquarters with data on local conditions. Weather flights had been undertaken for the squadron by various stations since September 1943. To establish a flying organisation specifically charged with gathering weather information, the 802nd Reconnaissance Group (Provisional) was brought into being at Watton, in April 1944. The three component units, designated Bombardment Squadrons, were the 652nd with B-24s to engage in long range weather flights around the British Isles (extending sometimes as far as the Azores), the 653rd with Mosquito XVIs for similar duties over enemy territory, and the 654th, also with Mosquito XVIs, for photographic reconnaissance where a two-place aircraft could better supplement the work of the F-5s and Spitfires of 7th Photo Group. Duties were later expanded to include scout work, night photography and Chaff dispensing—in fact a variety of jobs where a fast multi-seat aircraft could be used with advantage. In August the 802nd was given the authorised designation 25th Bomb Group (Recon), but was otherwise unaltered.

In the late summer of 1944 there was an alarming upward trend in losses—twelve in September. Unarmed F-5s, Spitfires and Mosquitos were easy targets for new German jets. Lt Robert Hillborn, flying over Stuttgart on September 5th,

The two aircraft types used by 7th PG were snapped by a higher flying photo aircraft.—(USAF)

had his Spitfire PL182, hit by cannon shells and saw an Me262 climb swiftly past. The Merlin seized up and caught fire, forcing Hillborn to take to his parachute; probably he was the first victim of an Me262 attack. It became necessary to send a flight of P-51s to protect reconnaissance aircraft flying into Germany, and these did not always prevent the jets from occasionally bringing down a photo aircraft. The danger did not always lie with the enemy; bounces by P-51s on 25th Group Mosquitos led to these aircraft being given bright scarlet tail surfaces as identifying markings.

At the end of January 1945 the 7th Photo Group obtained its own P-51s and started providing escort for its photo aircraft. The squadron was at this time based on the Continent at Daon Couvron, France, to help relieve pressure on Ninth Air Force Photo Units.

Late in 1944 this Mosquito at Watton, looked after by T/Sgt S. L. Housman, had completed 50 weather reconnaissance missions without mechanical turnback. Symbols are comic mosquito in clouds.—(IWM)

It was Spitfire XIs of the 14th Photo Squadron that flew most of the deep penetrations and kept watch on the important oil plants in Germany, so that Eighth Air Force was kept aware of repair activity and could decide if and when a target needed to be bombed again. Such reconnaissances were the most likely to be intercepted and the danger was not restricted to jets. On February 14th, Captain Robert Dixon took off in Spitfire PL868 for Merseburg, with three 3rd Division Mustangs escorting. On arrival it was found that Merseburg was obscured by cloud so Dixon took his Spitfire down, from 26,000 ft to about 12,000 ft before he was in the clear. Making photo runs over the Leuna works at that altitude, he was an easy target for the infamous Merseburg flak. On his fourth run the Spitfire was hit and caught fire. Dixon radioed the escort to keep clear of the area, gave them a windage correction for the homeward flight, and then described the oil plant, concluding: "Listen to this carefully. There are ten chimneys down there. Only one is smoking. This plant is almost inoperative. I'm going to bale out. Get for home at once". Successful photographic reconnaissance later backed up this description. Dixon spent the last few months of the war in a prison camp.

A few weeks after this incident 1/Lt Jack H. Roberts also of the 14th Photo Squadron flew the Group's 4,000th sortie. By the end of hostilities the 7th Photo Group's reconnaissance aircraft had flown over 4,247 credit sorties with 53 aircraft missing in action, one loss for every 80 sorties. The 25th Group had flown over 3,000 sorties and lost 16 aircraft, but a large proportion of its sorties were not in hostile airspace. The photographic reconnaissance pilots of Eighth Air Force, known as "Focus Cats", received little limelight: their task was frequently dangerous and the intelligence they gathered invaluable to the direction of the Eighth's offensive missions.

Chapter 25: Eventful Yuletide

The Field Orders that came chattering out of the bomber station teletype machines in the small hours of Christmas Eve 1944 listed an unusual requirement. A total effort, with every serviceable B-17 and B-24 participating. The vast overcast shrouding Western Europe for a week had begun to lift on December 23rd allowing the Eighth's heavy bombers to play some part in the critical situation that had developed since von Rundstedt launched his offensive in the Ardennes. Their aid was of limited scope, as the damp vapours had only partly cleared, but the signs were there and weather men predicted clear skies for the 24th. Eighth Air Force moved to bring about the maximum bombardment of airfields from which the Luftwaffe might operate in support of the Wehrmacht, and places through which supplies and reinforcements would pass to the front.

The Field Order detail was amply met; most groups put up every bomber that could fly a mission. The outcome was the largest single operation ever mounted by the Eighth Air Force, 2,034 bombers sent into the cold blue of a frosty English morning. Additionally, 500 RAF heavies and Ninth Air Force bombers also out made this the largest single air strike of the Second World War.

With most Eighth Air Force groups flying a fourth squadron, individual group totals ran to record numbers too, many launching fifty to sixty aircraft. The fourteen 3rd Division groups flew more than their average operational strength on this strike by impressing 1st Division Fortresses diverted to some of their bases after previous raids. The 66 home force and 5 lodgers taking off from Knettishall that morning are believed to represent the largest number of heavies ever despatched on a single mission by one group. To put up such a high total meant in many cases flying machines classified War Weary, i.e. bombers that either through amassing a great number of flying hours or due to battle damage causing strain on a major component, were restricted to local flying. Even some of the 2nd Division's gaudy Assembly Ships went along, hastily armed with machine guns in the waist windows. A 92nd Group B-17 crashed on take-off at Podington, only

In the late afternoon murk of 23 Dec. 1944 two B-17s collided over Thurleigh with this result. There were no survivors.—(USAF)

three men getting out before it exploded, and a similar disaster befell a Fortress at Glatton.

The vast column of bombers led by the 3rd Division, with the following 1st Division, was to attack eleven airfields east of the Rhine. The 2nd Division B-24s briefed for 14 communication centres west of the Rhine, brought up the rear, some elements leaving England as the first B-17s moved over Germany. The planned route lay from Clacton to Ostend, then across Belgium to a point north-east of the Luxembourg border where a turn into Germany was made in the region of the battle lines.

Electing to make the trip and lead this force was Brigadier General Fred Castle, Commander of the 4th Wing, and a veteran of 29 missions. Riding in a 487th Group B-17 from Lavenham that morning he found the weather much as predicted, but ground haze so restricted visibility that the take-off of fighters assigned to escort the forward bomber boxes was delayed, although it was expected that they would overhaul the bombers before crossing into hostile territory. The Luftwaffe, however, made an unprecedented move in bringing a fighter Gruppe over the Allied lines in the Liége area to meet the head of the bomber column. Before Mustangs arrived on the scene, four 487th B-17s were shot down and five so badly battered that they were abandoned after making emergency landings in Belgium. One victim was that carrying General Castle. Engine trouble had caused the Fortress to abandon its position in the formation at the time of the first surprise pass by Me109s. While trying to join the rear box the Fortress was hit again, the navigator wounded and the engines set on fire. Castle took control and though the bomber was still under attack he would not jettison the bombs for fear of killing Allied troops or civilians below, nor would he take evasive action as it would endanger the crew while they parachuted. A further burst of cannon fire severed the burning wing and sent the Fortress spinning down from which there was no escape for the General. Six of his crew lived.

General Castle was posthumously awarded the Medal of Honor, this incident being the last for which such an award was made to a member of the Eighth. A colourful personality, one of Eaker's "original seven" who left the safety of a desk job to take over a demoralised B-17 group in the summer of 1943, Castle was the highest ranking officer in the Eighth to be awarded the Medal of Honor.

In general the mission fulfilled its purpose in neutralising forward enemy airfields and obstructing and destroying highways and rail tracks. The Luftwaffe interception was insufficient even to scatter the lead units and other aerial opposition encountered was limited. Visual sighting in good visibility put much of the 4,300 tons where planned, even if haze did confuse bombardiers at some targets. This same haze, raised by the winter sunshine, was fast concealing the airfields in the east midlands when the first formations regained the English coast, and by the time 1st Division Fortresses had arrived the area west of Cambridge was completely submerged beneath white mists. Practically the whole of the "triangle" force had to be quickly diverted to Fortress fields in Suffolk where in a few cases the refugees from the gathering mists came to outnumber the resident aircraft. The only 1st Division base still visible was that farthest east, Ridgewell, here the 381st Group was joined for

Eighth Air Force launches its biggest mission of the war: 24 Dec. 1944, with the Assembly Ship lined up on the Horsham St. Faith's runway ready to roll, some 50 458th BG Liberators wait to follow.—(USAF)

Christmas by the crews of the 351st and 398th Groups plus a few wanderers from other units, making 79 visiting B-17s for a total of around 150 all jammed on the same airfield.

Similar numbers received at Bury St Edmunds were later expanded by a squadron of RAF Lancasters. All this put exceptional strain on base facilities, to say nothing of the task that faced ordnance and maintenance personnel when they received orders to re-fuel and re-arm the visitors in addition to their own charges for a further mission. Arrangements for

The Eighth was well nourished. Bassingbourn cooks prepare pancakes for combat crews.—(USAF)

enjoying Christmas fare went by the board. At Bury St Edmunds a 92nd Group B-17 losing power while pulling away from the runway for a second approach, crashed and in the ensuing fire seven of the men perished and one of two survivors died later. Elsewhere a crash landing, while not harming the crew, marked the end of the remarkable career of the 303rd Group Fortress *The Floose* which had started operations from Molesworth in May 1944 and completed 100 missions without an early return through mechanical or crew failure in the space of just over six months. On returning the crew found the landing gear jammed and were forced to put *The Floose* down for a wheels-up landing.

Hampered by ground mist and frost, and with the majority of 1st Division aircraft at other bases, only a moderate force of 2nd and 3rd Division bombers flew to the general area of the previous day's operations on Christmas Day. The Luftwaffe was on the scene but quick action by the escort saw only a few elements slip through to the bombers. This was near St Vith where the 389th and 467th Groups fought a short if costly battle. Returning 467th crews reported three of their formation lost in this engagement. It was therefore with some incredulity that the Group Headquarters later received the news that one of their missing bombers was reposing in a Welsh marsh, little harmed, but with no trace of the crew. This extraordinary incident had started when an engine was set on fire by cannon shells. The pilot apparently decided the wing would soon burn through and used the bale out alarm bell, which was not received by any of the men in the nose and rear sections of the Liberator. Some minutes later the navigator noticed to his horror that there were no feet at the controls above his head. He alerted the bombardier who climbed to the flight deck and found no sign of its four occupants. The engine fire had subsided and the aircraft was in a gentle turn by this time, so the bombardier, who had some knowledge of pilotage, set the bomber on a course for Allied territory. With the auto-pilot engaged, the men baled out over France but the bomber continued on across the Channel, traversing southern England until the fuel ran out. It then made a perfect belly landing in marshy ground.

The bomber effort on Boxing Day was even smaller than at Christmas—some 150 sorties. Winter now had most of Western Europe in an unusually icy grip. Freezing fog clung to the East

Insignia of *The Floose*.—(USAF)

Anglian countryside. Even at mid-day the sun was unable to diminish its persistence. Thin films of ice formed on everything, coating the surfaces of aircraft and building up inside stilled engines. Such severe conditions had never been experienced at Eighth Air Force bases during either of the previous winters and during this spell the number of take-off accidents rose alarmingly. At 08.40 hrs on the morning of December 27th, a 390th Group Fortress rose from the east-west runway at its base, gained fifty feet and then started to drop away following the fall of the countryside to its limit before plunging into a roadside bank in the centre of Parham village. The crew perished but despite the explosion of fuel and some of the bomb load, the local inhabitants were uninjured, although every house in the vicinity was blast damaged. Icing was the suspected cause of this, and many other crashes that pushed the accident rate to its highest point, often claiming more victims than the enemy. Many crashes occurred during take-off in poor visibility and adverse conditions, such as on the 29th when the 467th Group attempted an instruments take-off in ground fog. Visibility was so bad that pilots had difficulty in seeing the sides of the Rackheath runway. Two B-24s crashed at the end of the runway killing fifteen and injuring four of their crewmen. Two other B-24s were damaged on take-off, one later crashing at Attlebridge and the crew of the other baled out after heading the bomber out to sea.

To aid the Ninth Air Force in combating any interference to its fighter bombers from the Luftwaffe during the crisis, two of the Eighth's fighter Groups were placed one each under the control of the IX and XIX Tactical Air Commands. It was further decided to move their air echelons to the Continent. C-47s collected about a hundred essential ground men from Bodney and Little Walden and 150 Mustangs and pilots from the 352nd and 361st Groups flew to Y-29 Asch, and A-64 St Dizier in Belgium. The few Mustangs and pilots left with the groups at their English bases were airborne on Christmas Eve in a maximum effort call to all Eighth Air Force units to support tactical bombing or airfields and communication centres in the rear of the German thrust. Considerable opposition was encountered, and again on Christmas Day when the Eighth tragically lost one of its greatest fighter pilots.

In a fight near Bonn, George Preddy of the 352nd Group, the highest scoring active fighter ace in the Eighth, destroyed his 26th and 27th enemy aircraft but while crossing US positions near Liége he was shot down and killed by "friendly flak". Another Mustang flying in the vicinity was also hit but its pilot Lt James Bouchier of the 479th Group was more lucky and baled out.

The Luftwaffe continued to employ the greater part of its fighter force in the west tactically in support of the offensive and when the Eighth's fighters encountered them during this

period it was usually in the vicinity of the battle front. The MEW controlled fighter sweeps were the most fruitful operations in this respect and the most sought after by the groups. On December 27th those fighters escorting a comparatively medium sized bomber mission to the Rhineland in fine weather met no opposition while the 364th Group, assigned to sweep ahead of the bombers, encountered several Gruppen-sized formations of Focke-Wulfs. Under Lt Col John Lowell, group executive, the three squadrons each had successful encounters running up the total Eighth Air Force claims of the day, $29\frac{1}{2}$ (the $\frac{1}{2}$ was shared with Ninth AF P-51s Mustangs), with Captain Ernest Bankey bringing off an "ace in a day" performance with $5\frac{1}{2}$ victories. The 364th Group, having led a rather inauspicious career with P-38s, had its most successful period of air fighting during the turn of the year with P-51s. On the last day of 1944 several formations of FW190s offered opposition to a B-17 raid on the Hamburg oil refineries and the 364th made nearly half the day's claims with Major S. Wicker himself shooting down four. This same day Captain Julius Maxwell of the 78th Group brought about a fitting climax to the Group's use of the Thunderbolt. He spotted a lone FW190, apparently blissfully unaware that there were any Allied aircraft within miles of him, and by the time the German found out it was too late. This victory made the Group's total 400 and the last it would achieve with the P-47. After a final small P-47 mission two days later its conversion to the Mustang was complete, leaving the 56th as the sole Thunderbolt group in the Eighth. Like the 56th, the 78th had been one of the three original P-47 groups of VIII FC, and the change was very unpopular at first, particularly as the transition was made during weeks of bad weather which aggravated the difficulties of getting to know the quirks of the more sensitive steed.

The proud 56th wanted nothing of the Mustang. It had been the first in the USAAF with the P-47, it had proved its worth and shown the way for the Eighth's other fighter groups, and would not lose faith. But the P-47D was hindered by range limitations in the escort fighter role and the new FW190D appeared to outmatch the Thunderbolt by its turn of speed and climb. The makers had given the P-47 a new wing with greater internal fuel capacity and a more powerful engine but this model, the P-47N, would not be available until the spring (a few examples arrived in the last few days of the war but never reached the 56th). The engine for the new P-47, the R-2800-57, was available and Republic fitted this to the P-47D airframe as an interim model, the P-47M. Production ran to the 130 and these were sent to England for the 56th, which received its first on January 3rd, 1945. The new engine gave the P-47M a top speed in level flight as high as 473 mph, a considerable advance over the 433 mph maximum of the latest P-47Ds. There were also many other performance advantages, particularly in rate of climb which enabled the M to reach 30,000 ft nearly 5 minutes faster than the D. While the new Thunderbolt did nothing with the range problem—in fact it proved hungrier than the D—it did give the 56th a fighter which kept abreast of improvements by the enemy.

During the last days of December the Eighth's bombers had been able to raise their numbers to well over the thousand sortie mark on three occasions when seeking Rhineland communication targets. The persistent ground fog which enveloped much of the Continent as well, could have been responsible for the little aerial opposition to these raids, although at the time the Luftwaffe was preparing its forces in the west for a monumental strafing attack on Allied airfields in France and Belgium. Nevertheless, on the last day of the year a Gruppe of FW190s made contact with a box of B-17s to produce an incident of some significance. On this day, Eighth Air Force had chosen to return the 3rd Division to strategic bombing of oil installations and a jet aircraft factory while 1st and 2nd Divisions continued to disrupt German communications. The oil targets were at Hamburg where the flak defences were

Freezing mists encrusted the natural scene with glistening ice particles. Pretty but perilous for those who had to fly. Here an attempt is being made to clean the rear gunner's window on OR: W, 44-8431 at Bassingbourn.—(USAF)

expected to take a toll. Of the 3rd Division bombers lost, ten fell to flak and fourteen to fighters. Half the Divisional loss was borne by one unit: the 100th Group. Most casualties were in the fighter action but two occurred when a Fortress, out of control from a direct flak hit, fell onto another. A second collision at 19,000 ft had an extraordinary outcome. Either 43-38457 went into an uncontrolled climb after being hit

Bomber man in fighter cockpit. Lt Col Allison Brooks led 401st BG on some of its roughest missions during his tour as a bomber pilot. Later he joined 1st Scouting Force and as its commander flew many sorties during the critical period at Christmas 1944. Tinted goggles were worn to prevent sun glare and protect the eyes from fire or flash burn if the aircraft was hit.—(USAF)

or its pilots were trying to fill a position from which another B-17 had fallen. In any case it struck the underside of 42-31981 piloted by Lt Glenn Rojohn and the two aircraft became locked together. While four men parachuted from the nose and tail of the lower Fortress and seven from the other, Rojohn and 2/Lt W. Leek, his co-pilot, cut the engines of their machine and found to their surprise that they still had some control through the power from three engines still functioning on the lower Fortress. Turning the pick-a-back towards the German coast, the two pilots decided to try to crash-land as the aircraft would undoubtedly go out of control the moment they left their seats to bale out. After some agonising moments Rojohn and Leek managed to bring off a successful crash-landing in a German field without injury to themselves. Not until the impact did their Fortress slide off the lower one.

This was the sixth time that the 100th Group had suffered high losses on a single mission, and as time would show, the last. Other individual groups had also taken severe punishment on occasions but the 100th invariably suffered in circumstances which drew particular attention to their plight. The pattern was set at Regensburg and Münster in 1943, and when fifteen B-17s of the "Bloody Hundredth" failed to return from the first full Berlin raid, the bitter epithet stuck. By the closing months of 1944 the 100th was no less fortunate than many of the other bomb groups whose rank and file still considered it "the jinx group"—even members of the 91st and 96th whose losses exceeded those of the 100th.

New Year's Day was marked by the surprising Operation *Bodenplatte*, the Luftwaffe's mass strike against Allied airfields in Belgium and northern France which, while causing considerable destruction at some bases, cost the Luftwaffe at least 91 aircraft, with 63 prisoners and 33 bodies being recovered in Allied territory. The 352nd Group, then operating with IX TAC, became involved in this with a further demonstration of Mustang prowess. At 09.10 hrs, Lt Col John Meyer was preparing to get the 12 aircraft of the 487th Ftr Sqn airborne on a patrol when an estimated 50 enemy single-engined fighters appeared over the airfield at Asch. The Mustangs immediately took off while the enemy aircraft were distracted by P-47s flying in the vicinity. During the course of the next 45 minutes the 487th shot down 13 FW190s and 10 Me109s, while US anti-aircraft fire badly damaged one Mustang. Eleven of the twelve pilots scored, with Captains Sanford Moats and William Whisner claiming four each (Whisner had taken 5 in one action during a November battle). Lt Col Meyer, the deputy CO of the 352nd, brought down his 23rd and 24th confirmed victories and continued to hold the leadership of Eighth Air Force aces since Preddy's death. In the afternoon another mission saw him complete his tour. A few days later, prior to another assignment, he was badly injured in a motor accident in Belgium. For its action on January 1st 1945, the 487th received a Distinguished Unit Citation, the only fighter squadron in the Eighth to be so honoured. Spaatz, Doolittle and Generals Quesada and Vandenberg of the Ninth paid the 352nd Group a surprise visit when Meyer and Whisner received bars to their DSCs—for Meyer, his second, a unique honour for an Eighth Air Force fighter pilot.

Chapter 26: Clarion

The opening days of 1945 saw the German offensive in the Ardennes turned while the Allied air forces continued to concentrate their effort in support of land forces. For the Eighth Air Force this meant delivery of bombs to rail yards, bridges and transport bottle-necks, a continuation of the programme of assault upon the German lines of communication begun in earnest in November and stepped up through necessity during the "Battle of the Bulge". Only occasionally did the heavies turn to oil and other targets, in fact, during January, some three-quarters of the missions were directed at tactical targets.

Snow covering some heavy bomber bases added further discomfort to ground crews and brought more hazards to the aircrews. Two Liberators attempting take-off in a snow storm ay North Pickenham on the morning of the 5th crashed, and a similar fate befell a Fortress at Mendlesham. The falling wreckage of a bomber resulting from a collision during assembly, fell on the Thorpe Abbots bomb dump, setting off bombs and ammunition. Heavy snow clouds also brought problems over the Continent.

The frozen hulk of 42-50793, one of 491st BGs B-24s that crashed during the disastrous attempt to fly the mission of 5 Jan. 1945.—(Blue)

Damaged by flak while bombing rail yards at Hanau, the 452nd Group's *Panting Stork II* was forced to descend through a cloud break to force-land on a deserted airfield near a French town. Soldiers from a nearby US Army unit suggested the airmen stay with their bomber until transport could be arranged for them, as German paratroops were suspected of being in the area. They supplied the crew with three rifles and rations for the night. When the men awoke they found it snowing heavily and a blizzard continued for most of the day. The crew stayed in the Fortress, as snow showers continued and there was no human habitation in sight. Not until the sixth day with the weather improving and rations running low, did some of the crew set off to establish contact with the outside world.

Another bomber having to make an emergency landing on the Continent on January 5th was *Ronnie*, a B-24H of the 446th Group, on its 105th mission—at the time probably a record for any Eighth Air Force Liberator. This veteran was an original aircraft of the Group, named by her first crew in memory of S/Sgt Ronald Gannon, a waist gunner who contracted a form of paralysis and died while the Group was training in the US. At first *Ronnie* had seemed a technician's nightmare, for on the first four missions it had turned back early with mechanical difficulties. Then it was transferred to the

704th Bomb Sqdn where it was put in the care of M/Sgt Michael P. Zyne's team who sent it on a first successful mission exactly a year to the day from her 105th. Now, two months would elapse before it could be returned to the Group fit for operations.

The pride of the 467th Group at Rackheath was *Witchcraft*. This B-24H had flown on the Group's first operation in April 1944 and, in the care of M/Sgt Jose Ramirez, continued to complete operations with near mechanical perfection. One of her pilots, Lt John Oder, said of Ramirez, "Joe was totally devoted to this aircraft. She was kept immaculate. To him a minor oil leak was a major disaster". Ramirez's attention was no doubt instrumental in this aircraft becoming the first B-24 in the Eighth to fly 100 missions without an abort, on the January 14th mission to Hallendorf's steel works. During its time, some 300 flak holes had been made in "The Witch" but none of her crewmen were ever injured.

The ground crew's lot in winter was always hard. Servicing aircraft on the exposed expanse of an airfield, often in snow, slush, wind and rain was miserable work. The general high standard of maintenance says much for the quality of these men. The US Army was turning its eyes to the ground complement at air stations at this time. A scheme to transfer unskilled men to the infantry and replace them with soldiers no longer fit for combat was initiated. It was not popular for those eligible for transfer. Suddenly no one was heard bitching about the English weather, the discomforts of a Nissen hut, or with their present work. Station administration officers were not happy about the scheme for it produced many problems with training replacements.

On January 14th a force of over 600 heavies engaged in the Eighth's first large scale strategic mission since the Ardennes emergency. With a bright clear day promised the operational planners turned to their first priority, oil, sending part of the 2nd and all the 3rd Division to refineries and storage sites in North-West Germany. A strong force of Mustangs cossetted the bombers, anticipating that the combination of a fine day and an oil target would bring the Luftwaffe to battle. The Mustangs, however, managed to deflect the majority of enemy fighters before they reached the bombers.

North-west of Berlin the escort for the head of the 3rd Division column surprised a whole Geschwader preparing for a "company front" assault. About a score of FW190s, with a few Me262s and Me109s covering them, managed to get to the 95th Group, making single head-on passes which brought them no successes. Fortress gunners claimed five of the enemy and those of the 100th Group claimed eight in a similar fruitless attack by the same, or a similar, enemy force a little later. The third group of the Fortress wing, the 390th, was not so fortunate. Its low squadron, comprised of only eight aircraft, was lagging due to supercharger trouble in their leading aircraft. When the Luftwaffe appeared on the scene, this unit was flying some 2000 ft below and behind the rest of the group, presenting the obvious choice of target. The German fighters showed signs of inexperience, for they attacked mostly in pairs from the rear, without any apparent co-ordination and often opening fire at maximum range; it took them the best part of half an hour to despatch the eight B-17s and one other from the main formation. The 390th gunners claimed a score and were allowed 14. For the Group it was their unluckiest day, the

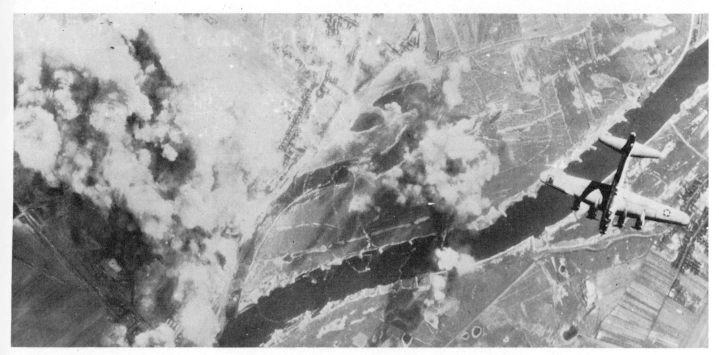

A 390th BG Fortress that survived the fighter attack turns from the burning oil storage at Derben; 14 Jan. 1945.—(USAF)

highest losses on a single mission and, incidentally, the last sustained assault by a Luftwaffe formation on a single Eighth AF heavy bomber unit.

Luck had a prominent place in the thoughts and conversation of many combat crewmen as if it was an invisible commodity, with which an individual was either loaded or lacked. Many believed luck could be fostered by the possession of some object or by a ritual; for some fatalism held precedence over religious beliefs. Many were superstitiously inclined, particularly about their personal equipment and the aircraft in which they flew. Most were religious men, but could not equate the teachings of Christ with the job in hand. Revealing, is the excerpt from a letter to his parents written by S/Sgt Albert E. Wyant, tail gunner on *Satan's Sister,* a 452nd Group B-17, describing his preparations for a mission. "My flying dress consists of one pair of ODs, my electric heated suit, my winter flying suit and then my heavy flying suit. Then I put on three pairs of socks and the red pair for luck, then my heated flying shoes and heavy flying boots. After this comes my flying helmet, sun goggles, earphones, throat mike, oxygen mask, scarf, Mae West (which is nothing more than a life preserver). Then comes my parachute harness, silk gloves and my heated gloves. When this is done I check to see if I have my dog

A shell burst against the left fin of this 392nd BG machine. Pilots were able to make a successful landing at Wendling.—(Barnes)

tags, horseshoe, baby shoe, flower and the Bible. Then I take my 'chute and head for the ship . . .' Luck, however, was exceedingly fickle. Nineteen-year-old Wyant had seen and survived some murderous flak barrages in his 22 missions. On his 23rd to Augsburg, where the official summary later classified the flak as "very meager", a shell fragment tore into his turret and took his life. Not one of the 640 heavies out that day was lost to enemy action.

Luck stayed with Lt Charles Boisclair and his crew the following day. The 466th Group bombed Dresden but their Liberator was one of the formation that never reached that far. On the target approach both port engines suddenly stopped, apparently starved of fuel, and had to be feathered. Jettisoning the bombs, Boisclair turned for home while a flight of Mustangs arrived in answer to his emergency call to keep an eye on the ailing bomber striving to regain Allied territory. Throughout the 350 mile flight across the Reich, the B-24 gradually lost altitude and was down to 1,500 feet when it finally reached the battle front, indicated by a fusillade. A shell tore off part of the tail surfaces and another exploded against the bomb bay before the Liberator was brought down for a crash-landing which resulted in a complete wreck. Boisclair and all his crew extricated themselves uninjured to learn that the open space they picked was only re-taken from the Germans five minutes previously.

Sergeants Fred Walsh and Louis Conser had a narrow escape from the wreckage of two 390th Group B-17s that collided over Hertfordshire during assembly. Walsh, in his top turret, saw the other Fortress dropping down on them. He lost consciousness momentarily after the impact. "When I came to I was lying at the base of my turret. The whole cockpit was ablaze, I could see the skipper and co-pilot slumped in their seats, their bodies burned almost black. I thought of getting out, but discovered that my 'chute was gone. It was a terrible realization—almost as if I were doomed to die. I glanced at the escape door leading into the bomb bay and found myself looking into the sky. The plane had been blown in half by the explosion and the wind was whistling through the opening.

"Then I saw my parachute dangling in space, held only by part of the harness which had caught on a jagged edge of metal a few feet from me. I was almost afraid to reach for it, for fear it might slip out of my grasp. Finally I grabbed it, and

A direct flak hit on No. 3 engine of 43-38633 ignited a main fuel tank over Cologne on 29 Jan. 1945. 2/Lt Newton Kerr dived the B-17 in an attempt to extinguish the flames. He then ordered the crew to bail out and was himself preparing to leave when the fire subsided. Although left alone he decided to stay and fly the aircraft back to England. An A/S/R P-47 led him to Woodbridge. This picture shows the gaping hole burnt in the wing and the elevator damage caused by the 40 ft flames.

slipped it on. The whole cockpit was flaming as I stepped out of the escape door. My 'chute opened when I was only a few feet from the ground above the tree tops, and I landed on the ground with a rough jolt, too stunned and too exhausted to move. People from a nearby English town gathered around and helped me up.''

In the severed tail section of the other B-17, Louis Conser attempted to reach his parachute. ''Every time I stood up, the tail section would lurch and throw me to the floor again. Then the force of gravity would nail me there. I must have died five times before I finally crawled to where my parachute hung.'' Conser was about to jump when he remembered the ball turret gunner, and opened the turret escape door. The gunner was semi-conscious and Conser helped him out, only to discover that the ball-turret gunner had no parachute and with little time to spare they did the only thing possible, jumped together. ''I only remember the hard jerk as the chute opened. A second later I realised the other gunner was gone. He didn't have a chance.'' Two other men besides Walsh and Conser survived; fourteen others perished.

To assist the Russian offensive attacks were planned on Berlin, Leipzig, Dresden and other places in the east where disruption to communication centres might hamper retreat and reinforcement. With dismal weather prevailing it was not until February 3rd that an opportunity arose to implement such a mission. Berlin, which had not had a visit in strength from the Eighth Air Force for two months, was selected, the large Tempelhof marshalling yard being the primary objective for 1,003 B-17s of the 1st and 3rd Divisions, while the 2nd Division visited oil targets in the Magdeburg area. The Luftwaffe did not contest the Fortresses or their escort and bombing was visual in good conditions, with the 2,265 tons of bombs making this so far the American's heaviest concentration on the centre of the Reich capital. Photo reconnaissance brought evidence of severe damage to rail facilities and other targets picked out by bombardiers when smoke obscured the primary, plus 1½ square miles of devastation in the southern half of the Mitte area. The German press and radio reported between 20,000 and 25,000 civilian casualties in the ''terror raid'', and while enemy propaganda made much of such figures, on this occasion neutral sources reported exceptionally heavy loss of life. USAAF leaders were still sensitive about bombing urban areas, and therefore particularly concerned in this instance when visual attacks on specific installations should have kept casualties to a minimum. In fact, since its earliest missions, the Eighth Air Force bombers had been killing civilians through the inevitable spillage of bombs around targets. The aircrews were no less sensitive than their commanders, but not so sanctimonious on the subject: it was all part of the ''dirty game of war''. The mental despair of the toggler on the 388th Group's *Supermouse* is captured in the brevity of his combat diary. ''Berlin, Saturday. Barrage flak, weakening as each group went over. No damage to ship. Visual! 5 x 1000 pounders. Shacked women and children!'' His observation on the flak belittles the intensity and accuracy of the most fearful concentration the Eighth had ever experienced over the capital. One or two bombers were taken out of nearly every formation, 21 going down over the city and another six managing to make the Russian line before crash landing. Ninety-three of the returning aircraft suffered major battle damage. The 379th Group's *Birmingham Jewel* went down over Berlin on her 128th mission; a total unsurpassed by any other Eighth B-17 at that date.

Rose of York, the 306th Group Fortress christened by Princess Elizabeth (now H.M. Queen Elizabeth), was lost. Last seen leaving the Continent with two engines out and losing height it was presumed that the North Sea claimed another aircrew. Also on board for this, her 63rd mission, was Guy Byan a BBC correspondent.

Crippled bombers turning eastward was a new twist to operations prompted by the proximity of Russian troops, then only some twenty miles from the German capital. One pilot who veered his blazing bomber this way was Major Robert Rosenthal, in the leadship of the 100th Group and 3rd Division. Rosenthal had piloted *Rosie's Riveters*, the only 100th Group B-17 to return from the disastrous Münster mission in October 1943. On two later occasions he had only just been able to get a disabled bomber to safety and now, on his 52nd mission, he was again in a precarious position. Ten of his crew jumped, Rosenthal followed later and word reached Thorpe Abbots in due course that Rosenthal was safe in Moscow. The 100th were elated for they regarded Rosenthal as something of a symbol, an extra special "unkillable" man who had survived all their bloody history.

Stardust of the 384th Group also turned towards the Russian lines after one engine caught fire and a second seized due to hits in oil lines. The fire abated, but as the bomber was losing altitude, Lt George Ruckman ordered the crew to jettison every movable object. Just when it seemed that a forced landing would be inevitable, an airfield at Torun on the Vistula was spotted and *Stardust* was put down for a normal landing on the badly repaired runway, coming to a halt with a burst tyre.

The crew were warmly received by a group of Russians who informed them the Germans had only vacated the airfield that morning and were ten miles away. In the circumstances, the crew thought it wise to destroy the Carpet, Gee and IFF sets, the Russians raising no objections. The B-17 was then towed off the runway because Russian fighters were expected in, and the crew were given quarters in deserted German barracks off the airfield. The following day two English speaking Russian officers arrived to interrogate the crew for transmission to the US authorities; they were told that a transport aircraft would collect them as soon as possible. After three more days, with no sign of the transport, the men received permission to go back to *Stardust* which had been under guard, and look at the damage incurred over Berlin.

The damage did not seem too bad and the crew decided amongst themselves that they could repair it sufficiently to use three engines, at the same time agreeing it would be politic to tell the Russians that they were doing it to pass the time. Their early efforts met with misfortune, for in trying to start No 3 engine it caught fire. That same day, February 8th, another Fortress crew arrived at Torun, their machine having crash-landed some sixty miles away at Plock after the Berlin mission, and from them the 384th crew learned of possible materials they could salvage. In any case, the Russians would not allow *Stardust* to take off with only three engines, so Ruckman then asked if they could borrow a vehicle to drive to Plock and obtain an engine and a tyre from the other Fortress. When eventually countenanced, a Russian officer accompanied the four Americans on this journey and solved the problem of lifting the required engine into the lorry by impressing 18 Polish civilians to sling it between two telegraph poles. Using tools and other items from wrecked German equipment on the airfield, *Stardust* was fully shod and powered by February 24th and the next day Ruckman was allowed to take her up for a test flight. She was pronounced fit for the journey back to England but first the necessary clearance had to be obtained from Moscow. This took three weeks before *Stardust* carrying her crew, plus that of the other Fortress, and a P-51 pilot who had joined the party, set course for Foggia in Italy, en route to Grafton Underwood.

Cloud masked the British Isles and much of the Continent on most days for two weeks following the Berlin raid. There seemed a chance to attack oil and other targets in Central Germany on February 6th but the weather men were wrong and above the overcast most bombers had to seek targets of opportunity. This day 22 heavies were written off as Category E through battle damage, forced landings and crashes. Unusual was the Eighth's bomber operations next day—a solitary B-17 attacked! Weather scouts encountered a high front over the Continent and some 300 1st Division B-17s bound for Germany were recalled while over the North Sea—all save one, that is, separated from its formation and failing to receive the recall signal. Continuing alone, it unloaded its three tons of bombs on Essen and returned to base untroubled by the enemy's defences.

For the most part bombing continued to be "blind" using the comprehensive selection of aids available. Despite more thorough training schedules and improved techniques, Eighth Air Force bombing accuracy during PFF attacks was not much improved. Calculations on photographic evidence of radar bombings during the early part of the winter found an average circular error of 2 miles. Practice radar bombing missions were flown at every opportunity in an effort to improve matters. British towns and cities were the "targets" and "bombing" took the form of a photograph of the radar scope image at the moment of "release". For the airmen not directly concerned with bombing these flights were tedious and unpopular. Some men claimed to have flown as many practice missions as real ones. Well aware of the inconsistent results from PFF bombings the aircrew jibe for this form of attack was "Women and children day treatment". Despite the poor showing of PFF attacks as against visual, there were several occasions when "blind" missions brought considerable success. Above all, these techniques enabled the Eighth to despatch its bombers in weather conditions which two years previously would have caused them to be grounded.

Even more advanced equipment was available. Early in November the 482nd Group, operating the training and experimental station at Alconbury, had received two B-24Ls fitted with an improved H2X designated the APS-15A. Tests having proved satisfactory, sets for operational use were made available in December. The 482nd Group had also been experimenting with a completely new type of blind bombing radar called Eagle (AN/APQ-7), employing an oscillating scanner which swept in azimuth through 60°, instead of rotating as in the H2X. This was contained in a 16 ft span aerofoil housing, attached by short pylons just aft of the B-24s nose wheel doors, giving the appearance of a miniature wing. Although Eagle offered a sharper image than H2X, through use of a much higher frequency, it was beset with troubles, not least of which was the breakage through landing shocks due to its proximity to the nose wheel. Later the 482nd had a B-17 with Eagle where the aerofoil containing the scanner was also fixed under the nose pylons. Despite efforts to iron out the technical trouble Eagle was only employed operationally on a few experimental missions.

It was almost inevitable that new equipment, hurried into service, would develop snags. Even the venerable Fortress, a ten-year-old design, was still producing problems for MTS (ex ATS and OES). A spate of top turret fires on long service aircraft was traced to fracture of an oxygen pipe and electrical wiring running through the bearing post on which the turret revolved. A temporary but effective solution was to fill the centre cavity of the turret post with concrete to firmly anchor

Carpet-blinker RCM antenna in their perspex covers show up clearly behind the nose wheel doors of 392nd BG B-24M *Hazee*. Her crew had a pre-take-off ritual of touching a prominent bolt head that secured the co-pilot's armour-plate panel.—(Barnes)

all wiring and the oxygen line. If breakage still occurred it would be outside the fire hazard area. An epidemic of generator failures also plagued Fortress units for several weeks and this was eventually traced to a mechanical fault which was cured by the Bovingdon experts. These and such similar troubles often arose through component changes in production.

Although the current production Fortress model was still the B-17G, those reaching the Eighth embodied progressive modifications and improvements. The Liberator, on the other hand, was then appearing in two new models, B-24L and M; both were attempts to lighten and improve weight distribution by installing a lighter tail turret. On the B-24L, first appearing in England in the autumn of 1944, the turret was hand-operated and weighed some 300 lbs less than the power turret on the B-24J. This was not entirely satisfactory and a model with a lighter power turret, introduced on the line in October 1944, was subsequently designated the B-24M which formed the bulk of new aircraft reaching the groups in 1945.

With both the Fortress and Liberator there were some long standing problems for which a practical solution was only now in sight. The danger of wing fires—that had caused the loss of many heavies—could, it was discovered, be reduced be air vents in the wingtips. This stemmed from Fifteenth Air Force experiments with Fortresses, while the Eighth had tried a more complicated system involving the injection of inert gasses into wing tanks to exclude oxygen and prevent the accumulation of the petrol/air mixture that might explode on being hit.

Many B-24 take-off crashes were found to have one common factor; loss of power on an outboard engine soon after becoming airborne. This was finally traced to difficulty in rotating a trimming control quickly enough to prevent loss of directional control. A modification was in hand, but like so many changes, its need had not become apparent until after much loss of life. Another hazard facing a B-24 pilot was in abandoning a badly damaged machine. Time and again, crew members would successfully parachute down, but as soon as the pilot left the controls to follow, he would be trapped by vicious spinning. Attempts to devise a control lock had been without success. The recommended way for pilots to vacate a Liberator with damaged flight surfaces was to jump from the flight deck, through the open bomb bay, immediately upon relinquishing the controls. 1/Lt Albert Novik was one man who had cause to do this twice, the first time (on January 16th) successfully, the second occasion, exactly one month later, went awry.

The 392nd Group was part of a force of nearly a thousand raiding oil and rail targets that day, their particular objective being Salzbergen oil refinery. During manoeuvres for a PFF bombing, a B-24 released six 500 lb bombs above Novik's *P-Peter*, shearing off the port tailplane. The Liberator sank 500 ft while the pilots strove to correct the violent nose heavy attitude. Novik was a strong man and although keeping control required considerable effort, he was able to follow the Group formation back over the clouds to Norfolk. Here, unfortunately, the cloud base reached to the ground, closing in airfields and the 392nd, in company with other formations, was advised to re-cross the Channel and land in France. Novik, in his ailing Liberator, elected to try to find a cloud break and an airfield in some other part of England. For two hours *P-Peter*, a veteran of 70 missions without a turn back, flew above the clouds while the crew searched in vain. There appeared no alternative but to abandon it, so the aircraft was flown towards the Wash while the crew parachuted.

The co-pilot held the controls while Novik left his seat, donned his parachute and standing behind his seat took over the controls again while the co-pilot left the aircraft. It was a situation where the auto-pilot would not be effective. Having given the co-pilot time to clear the aircraft, Novik prepared to jump himself, with the intention of taking his hands from the

The crippled P-Peter (42-95031) follows the 392nd BG home over 'solid' undercast.—(USAF)

controls and jumping through the bomb bay as he had done before. The instant he released the control column, the aircraft heeled over and dived, forcing Novik up against the cockpit roof. Then he became aware of flames in the cabin, as an engine trailed fire. His prospect of being incinerated only diminished when some portion of the aircraft, breaking off, caused a change of direction, allowing him to pull himself to the bomb bay and tumble out. Only just in time for, after falling some 7000 ft and seconds after Novik's escape, the Liberator exploded. His troubles were not over yet, as only a small amount of parachute emerged after the ripe cord was pulled. He pulled again violently with both hands, and the parachute blossomed out at less than 700 ft from the ground. Pieces of blazing wreckage were tumbling past, the main portion striking the ground directly beneath him. For a few moments he envisaged his canopy catching fire on landing and engulfing him in flames. His struggles to make the parachute change direction were successful in that the canopy fouled a tree. A cut hand, singed face and hair was the only hurt Novik suffered in this terrifying experience. It is said he complained more of his aching fingers from the strain of flying the half-tail Liberator for four and a half hours.

Centrifugal force had taken many a bomber crew to their deaths, pinned inside the fuselage as the bomber spun in its death dive. Returning crews often reported a bomber going down in a spin "but nobody baled out". The horror of such circumstances has been described by the lucky, like Novik who escaped its clutches. The crew of the 385th Group's Fortress *Satan's Mate* also knew this feeling for several unpleasant seconds when returning from Germany on February 19th. The formation had passed into cloud and due to its persistence the machine was set to climb out of it. In so doing, the slipstream of another unseen aircraft up-ended the climbing Fortress which fell away backwards into a power dive while the crew were transfixed on the roof until the pilot could extricate it from a 380 mph dive. All Lt James Fleisher's rather unnerved crew had to show for this experience were a few bruises. As for the aircraft, it had 74 broken rivets in a strained tailplane and was held in some reverence at Great Ashfield as "the Fort that looped".

As in the previous February, when clearing skies had enabled USSTAF to launch the offensive against the German air industry known as "Big Week", the foul weather of early February 1945 gave way to fine during much of the last ten days of the month. This time the Allied air leaders took the opportunity to launch Operation CLARION, an all-out assault on German communications over a wide area, embracing many smaller centres hitherto untouched. The extensive and heavy attack aimed to cause further devastation to a crumbling system and might bring wheeled communications to a standstill. Both Allied strategic and tactical forces were involved, the Eighth being assigned targets in north and central Germany.

With a clear day forecast, the mission was briefed for February 22nd. To achieve a high degree of accuracy, and to spare German civilian life, the bombing altitudes were to be from near the 10,000 ft mark, less than half the normal. Because of the small nature of many targets selected, bombing was mostly at group strength. There were some misgivings among US commanders as to the outcome, by losses that might result from such unusually low altitudes and such a dispersed force, particularly as weather conditions would also favour both flak and fighter defences. Fortunately these fears were not realised for although 1,411 heavies were abroad, the enemy apparently did not appreciate the dispersed nature of the operation until it was too late to direct substantial numbers of fighters. The only bomber known lost to Luftwaffe air activity was a straggling B-17 picked off by an Me262. The route skirted heavy flak areas and although 85 bombers returned with damage only 4 were lost. The 1st Division was briefed for 8 targets in the north, 2nd Division for 9 in the central area and 3rd Division 8 targets in the southern part, one being in Czechoslovakia. The 3rd Division ran into cloud extending from 6,000 to 20,000 ft and all but two of the groups climbed above it. Because of this only elements of the 95th, 385th and 493rd Groups were able to bomb a primary target (Bamburg). Some groups turned back and others sought targets of opportunity.

With little opposition and good results, the Eighth returned next day to attack targets which had escaped. Only two of the 1,193 heavies failed to return, one ditched and the crew of the other baled out over friendly territory. Flak caused minor damage to 48 and major to 8 bombers.

For the next eight days through February into March the Eight Air Force sent out forces of over a thousand bombers, a figure by now almost a matter of form. Targets were generally connected with transportation but when opportunity allowed, oil, aircraft and armament objectives were attacked. On all these operations losses were extremely light, there were signs that anti-aircraft fire was being restricted, as indeed was the case. Even when the bombers went to Berlin on the 26th the guns brought down only five. A shortage of ammunition forcing the enemy to introduce conservation measures, coupled with improvement in jamming techniques led to the lower losses. The Eighth's heavies were enabled to strike back at their tormentors on March 2nd when B-17s were sent to targets in the synthetic oil complex around Leipzig. Bohlen was assigned to part of the 1st Division, but due to a 100 mph north-westerly wind and the inadvisability of routing the force through the Merseburg flak area to the north-west, an in-to-wind approach route to the target seemed unavoidable. To reduce the effectiveness of some 90 heavy guns including a formidable 28 gun Grossbatterie in the path of the bombers, it was planned to have the lead group of B-17s attack this main battery.

For the 305th Group at Chelveston, March 2nd was its 300th operation and, as was customary on such "milestone" occasions, the Group was given the head of the Eighth Air Force column, and also the task of attacking the Bohlen battery. Loaded with 260 lb fragmentation bombs, 36 B-17s set out from Chelveston and found excellent visibility for their task. The bombing was highly accurate and probably contributed to the low loss of three sustained by the 1st Division force attacking this target. Two of these were 305th bombers,

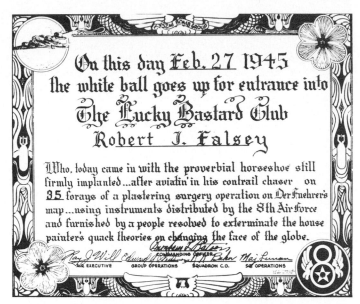

On this day Feb. 27 1945 the white ball goes up for entrance into **The Lucky Bastard Club** Robert J. Falsey

Who, today came in with the proverbial horseshoe still firmly implanted...after aviatin' in his contrail chaser on **35** forays of a plastering surgery operation on Der Fuehrer's map...using instruments distributed by the 8th Air Force and furnished by a people resolved to exterminate the house painter's quack theories on changing the face of the globe.

Bomber crewmen who completed a tour of operations automatically qualified for membership of the Lucky Bastard Club. The 452nd BG had its own design variation of the certificate for this highly unofficial—if elite—body.—(Falsey)

however, and one carrying the command crew. Cloud prevented many formations sighting on their primaries, in fact 255 of the 450 strong force that set out unloaded over Chemnitz.

2/Lt Charles "Hotrock" Carpenter, pilot of a Fortress that developed mechanical trouble soon after take off, returned to Ridgewell and transferred his crew to another serviced and bombed-up Fortress. Being only five minutes behind the group formation, there seemed a good chance of regaining their position in the formation. They saw a "great mass of planes" heading east but drawing nearer, Carpenter was dismayed to discover he was following Lancasters. With little chance of locating a US formation, he elected to continue with the Lancasters. Bringing up the rear of the RAF formation the Fortress followed to Cologne, bombed and returned with them. Later the Fortress was named *RAFAAF* to commemorate this event. Both *RAFAAF* and Carpenter were to have eventful careers; a fortnight later Carpenter crash-landed a Fortress at Woodbridge after it was attacked by fighters and damaged by flak and a few days later *RAFAAF* was hit by flak over Münster and came home on two engines, and in April it was involved in a collision and flew back with a complete stabiliser gone.

The Luftwaffe was in evidence on March 2nd and one formation made a spirited attack on the head of the 3rd Division which had been forced to forsake Ruhrland oil for a pathfinder run on Dresden. The following day the largest number of jet fighters so far encountered made hit and run attacks on the bombers, bringing down three. The Luftwaffe was also active over England that night, when after an absence of nine months about 30 Me410s descended on East Anglia and proceeded to strafe and bomb American bomber bases in Norfolk and Suffolk, although nowhere did they cause any serious damage. They returned the following night and again their activity was hardly fruitful.

Weather started deteriorating again on March 4th and the ground was hidden from the heavies' view by the familiar white cloud carpet. For most formations it was a question of targets of opportunity, which unfortunately resulted in one squadron of Liberators dropping bombs on Basle and another on Zürich, both in Switzerland; towns they mistook for Freiburg, a German target some 25 and 45 miles away respectively. This incident, following a similar lapse by the Fifteenth AF the previous month, necessitated General Spaatz making a secret visit to Switzerland to give explanations and make apologies.

During March the Eighth's heavies operated on 26 days and put up a total of 30,358 sorties to eclipse the previous record set in June 1944 (28,791) and unloading the largest tonnage of bombs in any month of their war. Operations on such a scale, averaging over 1,100 heavies plus the work of RAF Bomber Command and the Fifteenth Air Force, caused tremendous devastation within the shrinking borders of the Reich. Certainly it was the sustained bombardment of the whole target system, rather than any specific attack or series of attacks that ground the German war economy to a halt and assisted the Allied land armies. Frequently a target would have to be bombed again and again over a period of months due to the efficiency of German repair work, or only partial destruction in previous attacks. The effect of the effort was now evident by fuel and ammunition shortages that restricted both air and ground defences. Despite periods of inclement weather as winter receded, visual bombing accuracy showed improvement. Even at this late date Eighth Air Force endeavoured to improve formations with an eye to achieving better control and a more concentrated bomb pattern. With the March 3rd mission, 3rd Division's 4th Wing groups employed a four squadron 9-plane formation instead of the usual three squadron 12-plane one. The fourth squadron was placed centrally behind the other squadrons so that the group had a diamond shape in plan view. The position of aircraft in each squadron also gave a diamond arrangement. Towards the end of the month 1st Division groups were experimenting with a similar formation. The general concensus of opinion was that the new formations were easier to maintain and control and resulted in more concentrated bomb patterns. But with all its expertise, there were targets that Eighth Air Force had difficulty in destroying. The Bielefeld viaduct, an important rail link with the Ruhr was a good example. For several months the B-24s of 2nd Division had attempted to breach it without success. The RAF finally wrecked the viaduct on March 14th with 22,000 lb Grand Slam.

Eighth Air Force was aware of the limitations of its bombs and on this same day was conducting a second experimental attack with a promising weapon against the reinforced concrete E-boat pens at Ijmuiden. These and U-boat shelters were impervious to the 2,000 pounders, the largest bombs for B-17s and B-24s. So it was with some interest that Eighth Air Force became involved in development trials of a weapon designed to penetrate massive concrete structures—the Disney project. This was basically a large bomb with rocket motors in its tail. Dropped in the conventional manner, at 5,000 ft above ground level the rocket motors would start so that on impact the missile was travelling at 2,400 ft a second and could pierce

Flak severed a propeller from *General Ike's* No. 3 on her 65th mission with this result. No one was hurt.—(IWM)

above
1st Sea Lord, Sir Andrew Cunningham, visits Bovingdon to see the Disney rocket bomb. L. to r.: Col Cass Hough, 1st Sea Lord, Cpt Terrell RN, Col Al Key and Col Ben Kelsey of Maintenance and Technical Services.—(Hough)

below
Cass Hough shows 1st Sea Lord the tail cone covering rockets in rear of Disney bomb.—(Hough)

20 ft of concrete before exploding. The length of the bomb meant that it was not possible to carry it internally in any bombers then available in the UK and only the B-17 had the racks and necessary strength to haul it externally. Maintenance and Technical Services at Bovingdon co-operated with the bomb's inventor, Captain Edward Terrell, a Royal Navy officer, and by January 1945 sufficient bombs were forthcoming and trials satisfactorily completed for the device to be employed operationally. The 92nd Group at Podington had a trial run on the massive concrete structure captured at Watten in France and was then all set to attack E-boat pens at Ijmuiden where normal ordnance showed little effect. U-boat shelters in Norway were other attractive targets, but as each rocket bomb grossed 4,500 lbs the B-17s range would be too restricted for that distance.

opposite
14 Mar. 1945. 92nd BG attacks Ijmuiden E-boat pens with Disney bombs. Pictures show: (1) bombs at moment of release from 20,000 ft; a few seconds later (2) three pairs of bombs from B-17 element are nearly lost from sight (3) rockets on only four bombs ignite at 5,000 ft and (4) score hits on seaward edge of shelter.—(Hough)

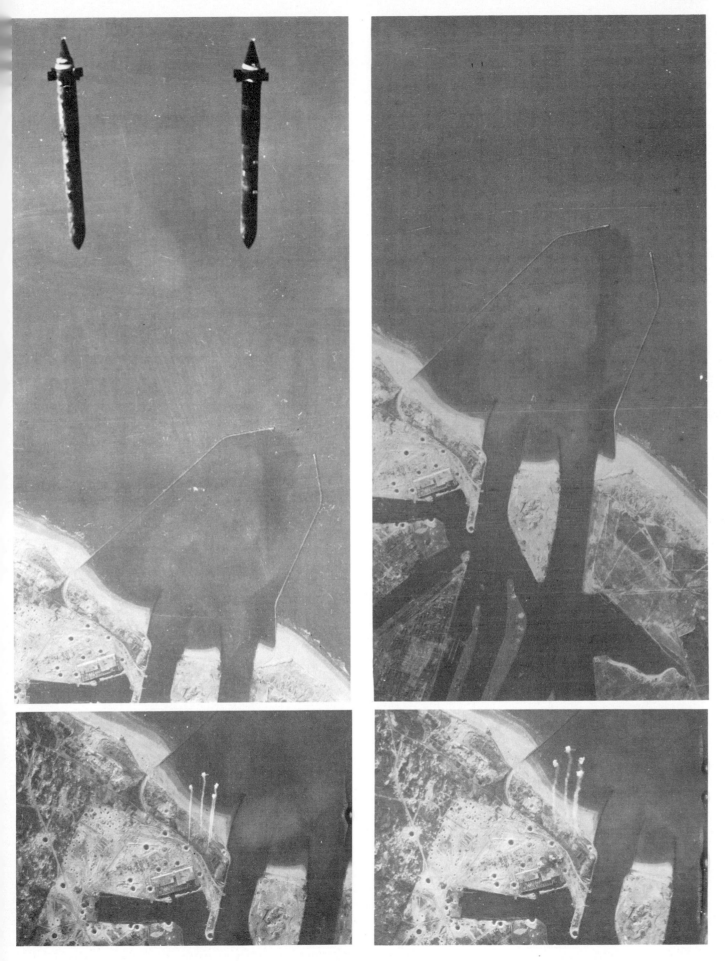

In hazy visibility, incendiaries go down on Berlin from 93rd BG Liberators; 18 Mar. 1945. Gunner can be seen silhouetted in waist window of YM: J. Bumps just forward of bomb bays are RCM antenna covers.—(USAF)

The first mission involved nine B-17s, each with two of the strange shaped missiles nestling under each wing. The 92nd's commander, Colonel James Wilson, and Cass Hough went along to watch the results when the Group unloaded from 20,000 ft. Photo reconnaissance later showed that only one bomb had hit but the damage seemed encouraging. The second mission with these weapons also showed promise. Further missions were hindered by unfavourable weather and Allied advances made further attacks unnecessary.

Luftwaffe opposition was now comparatively meagre; fuel and other shortages, plus the attrition of experienced pilots, had brought it to a mere shadow of its former self. Furthermore the Jagdverbände were now completely overwhelmed by the weight of Allied air attacks. However, by the end of February, jet activity showed a marked increase as the Me262 Jagdgeschwader (J.G.7) entered the conflict. During March almost the entire high altitude interception of the US heavies was by Me262s, and from March 18th onwards these attacks were at Gruppe or Staffel strength and showed some degree of co-ordination. On this date the Eighth mounted its heaviest assault of the war on Berlin, 1,327 bombers of the three Divisions, to aid the Russian armies advancing in that direction. The jets took full advantage of the hazy day with contrails at altitude persisting and merged. Concentrating first on the rearmost groups of 1st Division as they neared Berlin, between ten and twenty Me262s approached unseen in the contrails before climbing to press their attacks in which two B-17s were shot down.

A similar number intercepted the 3rd Division. Here, uncannily, they picked on 13th Wing, and the 100th Group, the second box in line. Near Salzwedel, some 20 minutes from the target, four Me262s came out of clouds and attacked the 100th's low squadron which was badly strung out and in poor formation. Coming in from 75 yards to point-blank range before firing, the enemy pilots could hardly miss and left three B-17s

in a sorry state. One dived away on fire and crashed behind the Russian lines. The port wing of the lead machine was also in flames and the crew parachuted. Soon three Me262s returned for a second pass in which they shot the complete tail section off another B-17 and further damaged an aircraft hit in the first attack. This machine fell behind and was later attacked again, went out of control, and the seven men still alive abandoned it. Bomber calls for fighter help went largely unheeded as there was difficulty in making contact, beside which those fighters that did respond were hampered by the poor visibility.

The action was not all one-sided for although the escort made no destroyed claims, the bomber gunners were allowed eight. Two of these were fact, for of the 37 Me262s sent up by J.G.7, two were lost. The jets claimed 12 bombers, the Eighth's actual loss to their attacks being eight B-17s. Berlin's flak remained formidable and took the remainder of the 24 bombers missing and caused 16 badly damaged B-17s and B-24s to seek forced landings behind the Russian lines.

Possibly of greater value than its speed, was the Me262s substantial armament, heavier than that of any other standard single-seat fighter in the Luftwaffe. The four 30-mm nose cannon were sufficient to bring down a heavy bomber if a burst was well-placed.

The following day the jet fighters concentrated on the 3rd Division as they flew north of Chemnitz, approaching through cloud tops when the escort was some miles away. This time three 45th Wing B-17s were brought down by a 12-plane formation; the escort arrived before other jets could join combat. The Me262s appeared next day over Hamburg to meet the 1st Division but only succeeded in dropping two 303rd Fortresses while the Group gunners claimed 5 of the attackers from their defensive fire. J.G.7 was more successful on the 21st, when once again able to make use of high cirrus cloud to hide their approach. The first attacks came as the B-17s were in the vicinity of Wittenberg-Torgau some 20 minutes from the target, a motor works at Plauen. The 96th Group, flying third in the column, experienced repeated attacks against its low squadron for five minutes, as a result of which the three Me262s involved managed to shoot down the lead Fortress. A stronger force of Me262s spent nearly ten minutes battling with the 490th Group, last in the column, pressing their attacks to as close as five yards before breaking away. Three B-17s went down, one reported as a result of a collision with a jet that had been disabled by defensive fire. The 100th Group was also attacked at a later stage in the mission and a B-17 lost by this Group was presumed a victim of these fighters. The German jets appeared in like numbers during most of the other March missions but their efforts rarely claimed more than a single bomber. Nevertheless, more than 24 B-17s were known to have fallen to jet fighter interceptions during March. Yet it was but a slender percentage of the vast air fleets, and still amounted to a figure below that of collision and accident loss for the same period.

Perhaps the most extraordinary and gruesome outcome of a collision occurred in cloud on March 17th when a 490th Group B-17, apparently caught in propeller wash, veered upwards striking the nose and engines of another before falling away cloven in two. Miraculously, the higher Fortress survived despite a badly mangled wing and smashed engines. Lt Robert Tannenberg managed to maintain control and sought an emergency field in Belgium. The nose section had been severely crumpled in the collision but both the men in it survived shaken but uninjured and evacuated to the radio room. On landing the crew examined the damage and were horrified to discover the mangled torso of the radio-operator from the other bomber lodged in the nose wreckage.

On several occasions the Eighth's bombers were despatched to bomb airfields connected with jet activity as a means of neutralising the menace. The programme of airfield bombardment initiated on March 21st, however, was aimed at making all airfields untenable from which the Luftwaffe could harass the Allied offensive scheduled to be launched across the Rhine in a few days time. In four days of excellent weather the heavies pulverised 34 airfields many of which were thereafter abandoned by the Germans.

Maj Gen William Kepner joins 389th BG fliers in a cup of coffee after a mission.—(USAF)

Chapter 27: The Hunters

Since the battle for supremacy in German airspace was won by VIII FC in the spring of 1944, the Jagdverbände had made six major attempts to stage a comeback on the Eighth Air Force strategic bombing missions; once in July, once in September, and on four occasions in November. On each, despite the increasing scale of effort, it had taken a progressively heavier beating from the Mustang escort, and only the few formations that had reached the bombers were able to inflict any punishment, which though serious, was a relatively poor showing. The approximate seven to one loss ratio the Luftwaffe suffered in combat with the Eighth Air Force fighters seemed irreversable. Most of these major battles had been primarily in defence of Germany's vital oil supplies and this again was the objective that the Jagdverbänd rose to defend on January 14th 1945, although the course of the bomber column could have led the enemy to suspect Berlin as the destination. Possibly 350 defensive sorties were flown, this figure being augmented by a number of fighters usually employed on tactical operations.

The 3rd Division B-17s penetrated Schleswig-Holstein and then turned south-east towards Berlin the leading groups having a target at Derben to the west of the city while following groups made for targets in the Magdeburg area and Stendal further west. The 357th Group had Mustangs ahead of the bombers, and twenty miles north-west of Brandenburg, in excellent visibility, they caught sight of a large assemble of enemy fighters approaching. The 357th leader, Colonel Dregne, immediately took the Mustangs in a climb towards the enemy who had a Gruppe of FW190s at 28,000 ft and three of Me109s some 4,000 ft higher, about 130 aircraft all told. The German formation was J.G.300 preparing for a company front assault on the bombers.

Dregne led the 364th Squadron towards the FW190s and successfully caused them to dive away to lower altitudes without attacking. He then despatched the 363rd Squadron to follow the fleeing 190s down to stop them reassembling for

another attack. The 109 top cover had by this time belatedly decided to come to the aid of the Focke-Wulfs and it was the third 357th squadron, the 362nd, that moved to engage these. A thirty-minute conflict ensued in which many of the German pilots showed no lack of fight and proved to be particularly good in evasive tactics. Even so, the result followed the familiar pattern, on this occasion the group of Mustangs claimed 56 enemy fighters destroyed for the loss of three of their own. This figure was a new high for a single group in one battle, the previous record having been 352nd Group's 38 on November 2nd. The Luftwaffe had a two-to-one advantage numerically and yet eighteen 109/190s had been destroyed for every 357th P-51 lost! While the 357th was routing the company-front assembly, other formations of Luftwaffe fighters were

January 1945 was unusually cold for England. Snow and frost made the ground crews' work highly unpleasant. These three were readying a 343rd FS Mustang at Wormingford for an escort mission on 18 Jan. 1945.—(USAF)

able to attack the bombers but these too were caught near Ludwigslust and engaged, chiefly by the 20th Group's Mustangs which unaided attained another twenty victories. All told, of the 331 Mustangs supporting the 3rd Division bombers, eight were lost for $89\frac{1}{2}$-0-14 claims in the air, from perhaps 200 German fighters. Elsewhere Eighth Air Force fighters encountered opposition, even the Thunderbolts got into a successful dogfight during which Captain Felix Williamson claimed five enemy machines and the 56th a total of 19. The total air claims for January 14th ran to 161 destroyed, a figure higher than anything previous and one which was to be unsurpassed. The cost was 13 Mustangs and 3 Thunderbolts. The Luftwaffe would never again challenge an Eighth Air Force raid in strength. The crushing defeat on top of a series of defeats must have at last brought home to some Luftwaffe commanders the hopelessness of even attempting interceptions in the face of such superiority.

The majority of missions in which the Eighth's fighters took part in January were, like December, handicapped by the

CO in congratulatory pose with Cpt Richard Peterson on latter's completion of his tour. Peterson's P-51s were named *Hurry Home Honey,* the phrase with which his girl friend finished her letters.—(Elliott)

adverse weather conditions. The accident rate increased during this period of snow, ice and vast cloud formations taxing the skills of even the most accomplished pilots. Those returning from a mission on January 16th were mainly diverted to Continental bases. For the 356th Group this was a costly matter, two P-51s crashed on the snow-packed runways when landing. Two days later, when the Group returned to Martlesham Heath, one Mustang was wrecked attempting take-off, and another disappeared into the overcast cloaking the Channel and was never heard of nor seen again. A third reached the vicinity of the home base only to go out of control and spin into a Suffolk field. The damp days of winter made the life of mechanics difficult enough, the periods of severe frost and snow made the job of repair to an engine or airframe in the bleak exposed expanse of an airfield sheer misery. Yet a remarkably high standard of maintenance was achieved. Probably the best sustained record of any P-51 group at the time was that of the 20th at Kingscliffe which had more of its assigned strength ready to fly than any other of the fourteen P-51 groups.

In January, a new model of the Mustang was reaching the squadrons. The P-51K, however, had only one major change, the substitution of an Aeroproducts propeller for the Hamilton type on the P-51D. Performance was, if anything, slightly inferior, and pilots generally thought the new propeller slower acting than the Hamilton type. The P-51K arose out of production matters and not from an attempt to better the P-51D,

Gun camera film from 55th FG P-51 flown by 1/Lt Bernard Howes recorded this Me 109/Ju 88 pick-a-back shortly before it crashed into the snow covered terrain below. German pilot had just bailed out from the flaming cockpit of the Me 109 and can be seen below the tail of the Ju 88.—(USAF)

above
Gear down, 350th FG's *Fran 2nd* comes home to Raydon: Feb. 1945.—(USAF)

below
Mustangs fly home after escorting bombers to Lutzhendorf: 9 Feb. 1945. *Jersey Jerk* was personal aircraft of Major Don Strait, 361st FS CO and 356th FG's highest scoring air ace (13½).—(USAF)

which continued in production. The P-51Ds in service at this time were far superior to the first examples received the previous June. Some 25 'in the field' modifications were responsible for enhancing early D models still in service.

Apart from the mission of January 14th, the Eighth's fighters had only sporadic encounters with the Luftwaffe and terminated many escort missions by going down to strafe. The Germans were apparently more guarded against these activities, as their airfields did not yield the rich pickings of the autumn. The German railways system continued to receive a goodly amount of attention; the 55th Group's Mustang pilots had a bent for following the permanent way and leaving many a locomotive enveloped in the steam of its punctured boiler. It was not unusual for fighter pilots to practice the art of loco-busting by speeding up the English railway tracks at extremely low altitude. On one occasion an over zealous 479th Group pilot collided with a passenger locomotive at Haughley in Suffolk. There was little left of the Mustang and the loco was extensively damaged, its crew receiving injuries.

The leading light in the 55th's strafing activities was its Executive Officer, Lt Col Elywen Righetti, "Eager El" to his men, through his insatiable appetite for action. While shadowing two locomotives south-east of Hamburg on February 3rd, Righetti and three other 55th pilots had an unusual encounter. The flight of Mustangs was positioned to strafe when Righetti caught sight of three large aircraft flying towards him, at almost 800 ft, on a north-westerly heading. Leading the flight towards the rear of the three aircraft, which Righetti at first took to be He111s carrying V1s, he saw on attacking that they were composites—Me109s each with a Ju88 (at first thought FW190/He111 combinations below. The first pair attacked crashed and burned after a Mustang had almost shot off the bomber's tail assembly. The Mustangs then attacked another of the "pick-a-backs" and on Righetti firing a burst the Me109 released the Ju88 and tried unsuccessfully to escape. Meanwhile the second P-51 element had tackled the third composite which also came apart prior to being shot down. Another flight of three composites was then seen about a mile away, but observing the Mustangs the fighters released the lower components and made off, although the Mustangs managed to catch one.

The purpose of these composites was not clear at the time (the lower aircraft was to be filled with high explosive and guided to a target, aimed by the fighter aircraft—these examples were on a training flight) nor was it known whether

Flak wasn't the only hazard when ground strafing. Cpt Robert Maloney of 38th FS was shooting at a train north of Ulm on 17 Feb. 1945 when his wing tip hit a telegraph pole. Maloney kept control of CG: Z and brought her back to Wormingford.—(IWM)

the bombers or fighters were manned; so the 55th pilots pondered on whether to claim one or two aircraft shot down for each composite. The 55th went back to harrowing the German rail system with a vengeance in February and on the 19th and 20th alone attacked 170 locomotives in probably the most successful action of this nature ever carried out by a fighter group. The indications are that these fighter strafing attacks on the German railway system caused as much loss to rolling stock and locomotives as the infinitely more expensive bombing attacks on railyards.

The German transportation system had long been a major prioroty for the Allied Air Forces and on February 22nd the Eighth's fighters added their contribution to CLARION, the extensive operation involving 6,000 Allied aircraft to bring the maximum chaos to rail, road and canal traffic in a short period of time. The heavies had lost only 7 this day but the fighters took punishment from small arms fire losing 13 with 17 more badly damaged. One loss was not to be the enemy, however; while strafing Halberstadt airfield a 479th Mustang was hit in

Debris from an exploding enemy aircraft shattered the canopy of Major Merle Gilbertson's Mustang and injured his face. Gilbertson was leading 79th FS in strafing Esperstedt airfield where they 'bagged' 34: 9 Feb. 1945.—(IWM)

the coolant system by fire from a 4th Group Mustang making a run on the airfield from another direction. The 479th Mustang bellied in.

On this day a squadron of 479th Mustangs had an engagement with a Staffel of Me262s, the first occasion when the jet fighters had been encountered in strength and willing to engage in combat; as it happened both sides were numerically similar, and for the Americans it revealed how formidable an antagonist the Me262 could be if employed with skill. The combat report made on the 435th Ftr Sqdn's encounter with sixteen Me262s while flying at 12,000 ft near Berlin, read "The bounce was directed at Red Flight as squadron was making shallow turn to left from an easterly direction. Bounce came from 3 o'clock position at our level by four Me262s looking like P-51s with belly tanks. Our Red flight broke into jets but they crossed in front of our flight up and away. A second flight of four Me262s then made a bounce from the rear, 6 o'clock high. Our flight turned into this second Me262 flight and the Me262s broke climbing up and away. At this time the first flight of Me262s came back on us again from above and to the rear. We broke into this flight and this kept up for three or four breaks, neither outselves or Jerry being able to get set or close in for a shot. Each time we would break they would

Some 30,000 ft above Europe a flight of 435th FS yellow-tailed Mustangs hug their range-giving 108 gl. paper tanks. 479th FG generally removed the tail serials on its Mustangs.—(Preston)

climb straight ahead outdistancing us. Within the Jerry flight the No. 4 man, while turning would fall behind and slightly above, so that it was necessary to take on this No. 4 man or he would slice in on our tail if our flight would take on the rest of the Jerry flight.

"White Flight encountered four Me262s in the same area. They came in on pass from above. High and to the side, two ships on each side. Our White flight would turn into jets and they would climb up and away. To follow would have left our flight open to a bounce from the remaining two jets.

"The Jerry pilots were aggressive and experienced. They were not caught in a turn, and if caught in such a position would roll out and climb up and away. It was impossible to catch or climb with them. Broke off engagement at 12.10 hours. Fighting took place from 12,000 ft up to 26,000 ft. A P-51 cannot climb with the jet particularly if the jet has an initial altitude advantage. However, P-51 can out-turn a jet. Red flight out-turned jets just after being bounced without dropping tanks. The jet is faster on straight and level run. Their rate of roll is excellent, but turning radius is poor. Their job seemed to be to force us to drop tanks so that we would have to leave. After we had used up all but a minimum of gas for the return trip jets did not press an attack as we left. Apparent

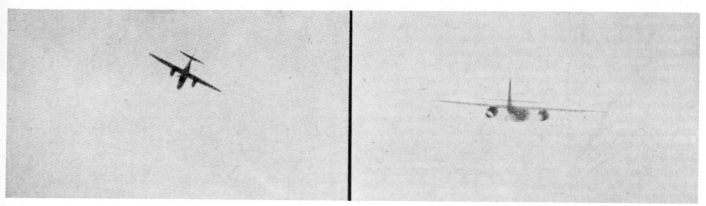

The AR 234 abandoned by its pilot when intercepted by 356th FG Mustangs.

that they were vectored to us. Flights found that expenditure of gas while attempting to close was very heavy, as it is necessary to use full power all the time. Jets flew excellent formation and never allowed themselves to be caught in a bad position."

After only sporadic encounters during December and January, jet activity had increased markedly during February, due to the emergence of the first Me262 Geschwader, J.G.7.

With three Gruppen at Brandenburg/Briest, Neumünster and Parchim, the formation was better trained and had more competent pilots than the hurriedly committed Kommando Nowotny. Eighth Air Force, and indeed most Allied air agencies, viewed these increasing sorties with some concern, despite the not infrequent destruction of Me262s in air combat. But there was no escaping the fact that the P-51s could only obtain such kills if in an advantageous position such as catching the jets during a landing approach or directly after take-off when speed would be restricted, and for this reason the Eighth's pilots kept an eye on airfields associated with jet activity. Probably the most profitable occasion occurred on February 25th, when the 55th Group, in the vicinity of Giebelstadt airfield, saw several Me262s taking off. Catching them unawares, six were shot down and one pilot, Captain Donald Cummings, later caught another attempting to land at Leipheim. A 364th Group squadron flying south-west of Steinhuder Lake that same day, saw four or five jets in the circuit for an airfield and Lts Murphy and White managed to obtain sufficient strikes to bring down one. This proved to be an Arado Ar234 another twin-jet coming into service for reconnaissance and bomber work, and probably the first occasion that an Eighth Air Force fighter had brought down an example, although the type had been known and seen on airfields for some months.

The Ar234 first became prominent as a jet bomber in the series of raids made by the Luftwaffe in an attempt to destroy the Ludendorff bridge at Remagen which had been captured intact by the Allies and gave them a bridghead over the Rhine. On March 14th, Captain D. S. Bryan of the 352nd Group dived on one making a run for the bridge and brought it down in a field where the aircraft was blown up by its own bomb load. The 352nd, together with the 361st, were still based on the Continent although their temporary assignment to the Ninth Air Force had terminated at the end of January and they were from February 1st under the control of VIII FC which had been given a new lease of life as an Eighth Air Force headquarters on the Continent. Both groups were now stationed at Chievres and while continuing to provide support for tactical operations when requested, escort missions with the Eighth's heavies predominated.

Three other Ar234s fell on March 14th. One was evidently due to a case of funk. The 356th Group was sweeping the Bielefeld area when they spotted and gave chase to an Arado jet which climbed away from them to 19,000 ft. However, the pilot apparently thought the Mustangs had given up the chase and was surprised a few moments later to find this was not the case when his antagonists suddenly appeared again. As one Mustang got within range and the pilot was about to fire, the pilot of the Ar234 suddenly baled out. The jet continued to fly in a gentle curve while the Mustangs flew alongside to take photographs. After ten minutes the jet was still unwilling to leave its element so Captain Robert Barnhart shot it down. The two other Ar234s were picked off by Thunderbolts of the 56th Group, while another pilot of the Group, Lt John Keeler, shot down an Me262.

The 56th at this date was in dire trouble with its P-47Ms, which had been flown on operations since mid-January. Initially the pilots were well pleased with the new Thunderbolt which was faster than the Mustang; this enthusiasm was soon tempered by a spate of troubles. Engines began to run rough and examinations showed burnt pistons. Far more serious was a complete cut-out during high altitude flight. Four pilots were killed on local flights in P-47Ms. Lt George Bradley, a former Liberator pilot taking a tour on fighters, was more fortunate on February 9th when his engine failed while flying near the 56th's base. By the time he had attempted to restart the engine there was little option but to try a belly landing. He picked out a large field at Dedham, but two small oaks on the boundary stood in the way. Bradley pointed the nose of the Thunderbolt between them and walked away from the wingless remains that came to rest 300 yards further on!

By mid-March the situation was such that consideration was given to converting the 56th Group to P-51s and training Mustangs arrived at Boxted so that pilots could familiarise themselves with the type. Happily for those who were aghast

P-47Ms of 62nd FS display their green and grey shadow shading against a background of farmsteads at Boxted. Leading edges remained bare metal.—(Rust)

at the thought of the 56th being separated from the P-47, the troubles were solved. Faulty ignition leads and poor correlation of power settings varying at altitudes were the cause of the failures, while insufficient "pickling" before shipping the engines to the UK had allowed corrosion to foul some parts. An engine change for every P-47M on the field—75—saved the day and by the end of the month the threatening shape of the P-51 disappeared from Boxted. Typical of its individuality the 56th gave the P-47Ms special paint schemes, each squadron adopting its own distinctive livery under the guise of camouflage.

Since the 56th had topped the 800 mark in enemy aircraft destroyed late in December, its rivalry with the 4th Group had heightened. The question being posed around fighter bases early in 1945 was who would be the first to reach 1,000 destroyed—the "Wolfpack" or the "Eagles"? The policing of the Reich skies had become something of a contest between two teams with points awarded for the destruction of enemy aircraft! In this bloody war, the confidence of the US fighter pilots in dealing with their adversaries had led to a match between two groups—with others hoping to overhaul them.

The missions into the Reich had become hunts for enemy aircraft. For the 4th and 56th it was rapidly becoming an obsession.

There was a dearth of enemy aircraft and the 4th and 56th were but two groups among fifteen all imbued with the hunting spirit. When over a thousand bombers and their escort flew near Berlin on March 15th, one solitary claim resulted from the day's operations. This was an Me163, one of two circling in the Wittenberg area that the sharp-eyed Captain Ray Wetmore spotted and successfully shot down. Wetmore was then the highest scoring active ace in the Eighth and this was his 22nd and last victory. In Wetmore's case it was more than being in the right place at the right time. Only one other pilot in the 359th Group, Major George Doersch, ran up an aerial score

Vultee Vengeances, originally built for the RAF, were converted for drogue-towing duties and as A-35Bs turned over to Tow Target Flights in the latter half of 1944. 41-31311, D pictured at Halesworth on 22 Feb. 1945, suffered undercarriage failure while parked on a hardstand.—(Forward)

into double figures (10½) and only nine other pilots achieved "acehood" (5 or more destroyed) during the whole of the Group's operational career. Wetmore's last victory was also the last of four Me163s known to have fallen to Eighth AF fighters. Because of its tremendous speed and acceleration it was the most difficult to catch.

The 359th Group was in the news again on March 18th. After escorting a heavy raid on Berlin, many Mustang pilots, skirted the east of the city, saw Soviet aircraft. Captain Ralph Cox saw two unidentified aircraft heading east and gave chase. The Mustangs caught up with the strangers near Zackerick airfield on the Oder and found they were Soviet Yak-9s. Cox then saw four FW190s strafing this Soviet occupied field and shot one down while the rest fled. Then more Yaks appeared and a waggling of wings took place, as stories about Soviet shortcomings in aircraft recognition made this a somewhat cautious meeting. In fact, elsewhere near Berlin, the 353rd Group was fired on by some La-5s and one Mustang that bellied in behind Soviet lines was suspected to have been hit during this encounter.

The audacity of the US fighter pilot was well known. But when Major Pierce McKennon of the 4th Group had to belly land his Mustang in a field after his engine was hit by flak while strafing Prenzlau airfield, nobody expected an attempt to rescue him. While Lt Priest's landing in a German field to pick up Captain Marshall the previous August had been a great feat, the authorities did not approve of escapades which could easily result in the unnecessary loss of another aircraft and pilot. This did not deter Lt George Green who lowered his undercarriage and put down in a field alongside McKennon to successfully repeat another incredible snatch on the Marshall-Priest pattern. Squeezed in the Mustang cockpit the two pilots flew all the way back to Debden.

March 18th however was a fruitful day for the Me262s of J.G.7, which were able to use the cloud and hazy conditions to advantage in coming to grips with the bombers while the Mustangs could only claim one damaged. Me262s were much in evidence the following day but less successful in interfering with the bomber mission. The 78th Group was sweeping ahead of the 1st Division bombers, when in the vicinity of Hesepe three Me262s attempted to bounce a P-51 squadron which immediately turned into them without dropping tanks. It was suspected that these swift passes by Me262s during the early stages of penetration were deliberate attempts to cause Mustangs to release tanks and thus limit their range. Therefore the Mustangs clung to their precious tanks and turned into such attacks whenever possible, with the usual result that the Me262s would soon make off, as on this occasion. Shortly after the departure of the jets the 78th came upon Me109 Gruppen in the process of forming up for a tactical operation.

The female form graced many a Nissen hut wall. The engineering section of 63rd FS had a goodly collection. "Do Not Hump" meant "Hands Off": even so the more interesting samples were likely to be removed to some other premises.—(USAF)

There were five formations at Staffel strength between 7,000 and 14,000 ft, the topmost group in cirrus cloud presumably acting as top cover. The sweep progressed no further as 78th Group engaged in its first large aerial battle since converting to the Mustang. The 48 P-51s were involved with about an equal number of Messerschmitts whose pilots were not averse to combat. The result was 32-1-13 for the loss of five P-51s. During the engagement four 78th pilots were also able to pounce on two Ar234s and bring them down. The Arados were reported next day as being used in an interceptor role to launch rockets, but it is possible that in some cases there was misidentification between the 262 and 234. For the 78th which had lost some 30 pilots, mostly while strafing, since conversion to the Mustang the battle of March 19th was a much needed fillip for sagging morale. The Group followed this victory up with some remarkable successes against the jets. On the 21st 78th pilots claimed six Me262s that attacked 3rd Division bombers, and the following day another three. Its claim of 13 jets in air combat was the largest share by a single group of the 43 destroyed by Eighth Air Force fighters during March.

The competition between the 4th and 56th Groups moved in favour of the former on March 22nd when 150 Mustangs were given the unusual task of taking care of Fifteenth Air Force B-17s bombing Ruhrland oil refinery. The 4th which formed part of the escort came upon FW190 fighter-bombers taking off for operations against the Soviets from an airfield near Berlin. Eleven were shot down, and with wingman 2/Lt Richard Moore, following his leader's manoeuvres closely, Lt Col Sydney Woods, claimed five of these. Such feats owed much to the efficiency of the two-man element that allowed the leader to select the opponents and attack, knowing his wingman would follow to keep a watchful eye for any enemy that might slip in from the rear. The loyalty of US wingmen to their leaders impressed German fighter pilots. Undoubtedly, overall team training was another facet of US fighter pilot superiority.

The 4th had now regained the lead, in air and ground totals for aircraft destroyed, from the 56th. The totals at the end of March stood at 867 and 865½ respectively although these fluctuated with re-assessment of combat films and information from pilots delayed on the Continent.

Chapter 28: The Cow is Killed

The airborne assault and crossing of the Rhine on March 24th involved the Eighth Air Force in 1,747 heavy bomber sorties and a protective fighter screen in advance of the crossing points. While the Fortresses pounded airfields in the Ruhr area the Liberators of 2nd Division were to deliver supplies to the airborne forces on the east side of the Rhine. The news that they were to carry out this low level task was met with little enthusiasm by those who remembered the similar mission to Holland in September 1944. Anticipation that it was to be a hot trip was justified for the 240 Liberators met murderous small arms and light cannon fire which probably accounted for the 14 missing, although it was reported that one B-24 had flown into a pylon. Each aircraft carried $2\frac{1}{2}$ tons of supplies

Tyre smoke streams back from the point of impact as *Shady Sadie* settles back on Bungay after dropping supplies on 24 Mar. 1945.

The 24-year-old CO of 78th FG, Lt Col John Landers, settles into the cockpit of *Big Beautiful Doll*, prior to leading the Group in an area sweep east of the Rhine crossing. Landers, who flew with 49th FG in the Pacific, and 55th and 357th in the UK, before joining the 78th, had total credits of $8\frac{1}{2}$ and 20 ground victories by the end of hostilities. —(USAF)

Parachuted supplies go down on marshland east of the Rhine from 41-28943, H6: L of 453rd BG.—(USAF)

for the ground troops in 20 or so bundles (a dozen were situated in the bomb bay, 5 or 6 around the ball turret aperture and 3 at the emergency escape hatch in the tail). Even so the Liberators would be tail heavy, and ammunition was concentrated forward. The accuracy of drop in the Wesel area was extremely high, only part of 448th Group erring due to an accidental release by one aircraft west of the river with the other four aircraft in the flight following suit. Two squadrons of the 389th Group had to make a second run to enable their loads to be dropped in the right area. Despite damage to 104 B-24s that returned (one machine was wrecked in an overshoot landing) the 2nd Division groups were still able to fly a bombing mission later that day.

Several Eighth fighter groups flew three missions this day. This was another occasion when very strong reaction in the air was anticipated but never materialised. Most of the Luftwaffe aircraft that did appear ran into 3rd Division Mustangs on patrol. The 353rd attacked two Gruppen of tactical fighters headed for the front and brought off its biggest bag of the war. Lt Col Wayne Blickenstaff and Major Robert Elder both claimed 5 apiece of the 29 credited to the Group. Five P-51s were lost in this fight.

Jet aircraft continued to constitute the German air defence against the US strategic forces and despite the sweeping Allied advances into Germany itself and the inevitable disruption of services and supplies their effort continued to be formidable if not particularly successful. The US fighters bettered their March average of one jet destroyed claim for every 6 to 7 combats to more than one in four in the weeks to come.

With the Allied armies advancing on both west and eastern fronts, the shrinking confines of the Reich offered few remaining strategic objects for the Eighth. An unusual period of fine weather and the calls for tactical strikes still provided work for the heavies with few breaks after April 3rd for nearly three weeks.

The accelerated campaign during the early months of 1945 had brought many bomber group milestones; the 93rd Group had completed its 380th mission by the end of March, 331 of these from England. The 303rd led the field in this respect with 349 missions; the other three pioneer groups, the 91st, 305th and 306th were not far behind. Many Fortresses and Liberators had flown 100 missions; there were now close on a hundred such veterans. Champion of the lot was the 379th Group B-17 *Ol' Gappy* with more than 140 to its credit but it had been forced to abort a mission through mechanical

Sgt Davis touches up the 120th mission symbol on *Nine-O-Nine* B-17 that would achieve the best maintenance record of all. Eight trips to Berlin are signified by the letter B on symbol.—(IWM)

failure and was not looked on in the same kindly light as *Nine-o-Nine* of the 91st Group which had over 125 without once having failed to complete a mission. *Witchcraft* still led the Liberators in this category.

Whereas a hundred mission bomber was no longer a rarity there was still one century milestone that had not been attained—until early April 1945. That day the 390th Group

Back from his 100th mission with the Eighth, M/Sgt Hewitt Dunn is carried in triumph by his friends: Framlingham, 5 Apr. 1945.—(IWM)

was part of a 450 strong force despatched to targets in the Leipzig area. An uneventful mission for the group and all aircraft returned to Framlingham without loss or damage. There was a reception party at the hardstand of *The Great McGinty* as this 569th Bomb Sqdn's Fortress came taxying to a standstill. They were there to greet 24-year-old M/Sgt Hewitt T. Dunn, the toggler who had just completed his hundredth mission with the Eighth Air Force. There were a few men who had flown many missions in other theatres and made their hundredth sortie in a later tour with the Eighth, but no other American reached this figure through operations solely in Europe. For most men one tour was more than enough! Some had flown two tours and reached the 50 and 60 mission mark. Hewitt "Buck" Dunn had come to the 390th Group in December 1943 and commenced combat flying in January when the chances of survival were less than half what they had become by April the following year. By April 1944 he had completed his first tour of 30 and applied for another which lasted into the late summer of 1944. When he asked to fly a third tour, rather than return to the US, fellow airmen questioned his sanity, "A man just didn't have that much luck". Dunn had flown missions to almost every danger spot on the Eighth's target list, with nine visits to Berlin (including the first successful one). His early missions were as tail gunner (26 times) and top turret gunner (2) and the balance as bombardier/nose gunner. Of his hundredth sortie Dunn said: "I was a little nervous at briefing when I learned Leipzig was the target, but it turned out to be just another mission—a

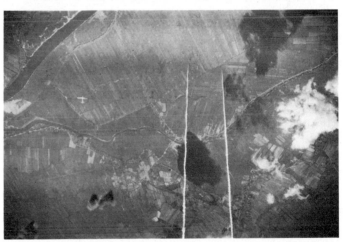

Marker bombs streak towards a target at Bremen, 30 Mar. 1945 as 1st Wing B-17s attack. Dark bursts from flak (lower left) contrast with clouds and their shadows (right). Flak caused major damage to 68 B-17s at this target and brought down one, a 381st BG machine which can be seen heading down but apparently under control.—(USAF)

milk run". He was credited with the destruction of an FW190 over Leipzig eleven months before. Hewitt Dunn went on to fly four more missions with the 390th. His record of 104 combat sorties is unique in the annals of personnel of the Eighth Air Force.

By the first week in April many Luftwaffe Jagdgeschwadern were no longer an entity, but the Luftwaffe was not yet a spent force and while it had fuel and aircraft the Jagdverbände continued to fight. Its target in these final days was frequently the Eighth Air Force bomber fleets.

After a two-day lull dictated by heavy cloud, the jets were airborne to attempt an interception of B-17s over Kiel. They were more successful on April 4th and managed to make their first contacts of consequence with the Liberators. The 448th Group lost three of its bombers while another 20th Wing group lost its commander in unusual circumstances. All heavy bomber groups had a retired fighter aircraft—usually a P-47— for formation monitoring purposes. This aircraft was airborne

Spaatz and Doolittle look in at the interrogation of the 303rd BG lead crew after 31 Mar. 1945 attack on Halle marshalling yard. Mission leader, Maj Harold Nye, sits with back to camera on the right of interrogator, Cpt Charles McQuaid, On Nye's right is navigator Lt Michael McCarty and on Spaatz's right is Lt Francis Downey, bombardier. Speaking is Cpt Harold Stouse, the man who piloted *The Duchess* on 18 Mar. 1943.—(IWM)

at assembly with an experienced pilot whose job it was to keep an eye on the marshalling bombers and advise on the state of the formation. On some shallow penetrations the monitor aircraft would accompany the bombers to their target. Colonel Troy Crawford of the 446th Group was viewing his group's formation from a Mosquito loaned by the 25th Group when Me262s attacked on April 4th. Unfortunately for him an excited gunner in one of his own B-24s thought the Mosquito was an Me262 and promptly despatched it. The Colonel escaped to spend two weeks as a POW.

Three or four Me262s managed to shoot down a single B-17 from the leading 1st Division on the 5th—a day when the heavies assembled over France on beacons located near Paris. On the 6th the jets were absent from what remained of German airspace. They were back with a vengeance on the 7th, and so were the conventional fighter aircraft.

A thousand plus force of heavies, with a delivery list that took in airfields, oil storage and explosive factories, was forging into North-West Germany when the escort encountered a score of Me262s and, for the first time for many weeks, a

Me262s reached Liberators of 20th Wing as they made for jet airfield targets on 4 Apr. 1945. Three 448th BG aircraft were lost. This one was torn completely in half.—(USAF)

force of Me109s and FW190s numbering well over a hundred. Contact was made in Dümmer and Steinhuder Lake areas, the interception points that were once almost routine regions for Luftwaffe attacks on the US bombers. Although the escorting Mustangs dealt very effectively with most of the enemy, about 50 fighters, including a dozen jets, managed to reach the leading bombers and attacks were made on several units over a period of 45 minutes. The 45th Wing, heading for Kalten-kirchen airfield came under a series of attacks from near Steinhuder Lake. The 452nd Group bore most of these, two of its aircraft and one from the 388th Group being rammed by FW190s. In the 93rd Wing, a 385th Group B-17 was rammed and one from the 490th was shot down by an Me109 and another badly damaged in an attempted ramming which proved fatal for the 109 but not the Fortress. Jets penetrated the 13th Wing making two passes at the 100th Group and one at the 390th, taking a B-17 out on each occasion. The B-17 gunners made claims of 26 destroyed and 10 probables or damaged against the enemy fighters, while Liberator gunners claimed 15 and 6 respectively.

At the head of the 2nd Division, bound for the Duneburg explosive plant an attacking Me109 crashed into the nose of the lead B-24 of the 389th Group. The B-24, its nose sheared completely off, crashed into the starboard wing of the deputy lead plane. Both these PFF Liberators went down, taking the Group Commander, Lt Col Harboth, to his death. Another enemy fighter flew into the starboard fin and rudder of a 467th Group B-24, but the crew managed to bring this half-tailed bomber back over friendly territory before baling out. The bomber gunners made their biggest claims against the Luftwaffe for many months, 26 destroyed, ten probables and damaged by the B-17s, and 14 destroyed and six damaged by the B-24s.

On 4 Apr. 1945 the 364th FG dispersed two flights of Me 262s that attacked B-24s near Hamburg. Major George Ceullers chased one as it flew south in a shallow dive and 182 miles later shot it down near Leipzig. The chase began at 29,000 ft and the jet was down to 400 ft when Ceullers got within range. The Mustang's engine was somewhat hot.—(USAF)

At first these battle collisions were considered the outcome of enemy fighters pressing their attacks too closely and going out of control when disabled by defensive gunfire. Further information revealed that the oft rumoured "Ramstaffel" was at last reality.

Not until March 1945 did Goering ask for volunteers for "special and dangerous" operations, the exact nature not being divulged. Volunteers numbering some 300 were assembled at Stendal for training and about half of these were formed into a Geschwader known as Sonderkommando Elbe. The training is said to have been 90% political, to ensure the volunteers had sufficient fervour not to waver in their patriotic suicide. The pilots were instructed to open fire at extreme range and continue firing until in a position to ram the bomber, preferably in the fuselage just aft of the wing. Only then were they—if possible—to bale out.

The Defence of the Reich force of single-engine conventional fighters had not challenged an Eighth Air Force mission since March 2nd and intelligence sources were beginning to assume that these had been committed in some last ditch activity against the Russians as ground attack and

With two engines set on fire by flak, 43-39163, S of 835th BS falls away from the 486th BG formation bombing Parchim airfield, 7 Apr. 1945. Position of ball turret guns suggests gunner had been signalled to vacate his position and collect his parachute in the fuselage.—(Rust)

Wee Willie dies; 8 Apr. 1945; last 91st BG B-17 to go down. More bombers were MIA from Bassingbourn than any other station. *Wee Willie* was the oldest operational aircraft in the 91st and had more than 120 missions to her credit. A direct flak hit took off the wing but some of the crew escaped including pilot 1/Lt Robert Fuller.—(USAF)

support aircraft. The remnants of the J.G.300 and 301 and some odd units were to be employed in one further organised attempt to bring down a fair number of the B-17s and B-24s that invaded what remained of the Reich. With J.G.7's Me262s their chief purpose on this day appears to have been to afford cover for the Me109s of Sonderkommando Elbe which were to ram as many bombers as possible: an operation which the Luftwaffe appears to have considered more a politically motivated stunt for propaganda, purposes rather than a serious military operation.

On April 7th the path of the bombers was marked by VHF beacons, on which the pilots of Sonderkommando Elbe homed, to bring them into contact with the US formations. A VHF commentary was also broadcast, interspersed with a woman's exhortations designed to keep the suicide pilots from faltering in their task. "Deutschland über Alles" and "Remember our dead wives and children buried beneath the ruins of our towns" were two examples said to have been heard.

Probably the majority of the 59 piston-engined fighters shot down by the escort were from the "suicide" unit judging by frenzied actions of the pilots and lack of recognised evasive tactics. It was estimated that three-quarters of the enemy effort this day fell before the guns of Eighth Air Force bombers and fighters. As Sonderkommando Elbe put up 120 aircraft and only 8 instances of ramming are known with 15 machines returning to base, this estimate appears near the truth. Not one of the three American fighters missing was lost in combat.

An estimated eight of 18 bombers missing after this battle were brought down through ramming on Sonderkommando Elbe's only operation against the Eighth.

On the following three days the Eighth Air Force heavies dropped a goodly proportion of their loads on airfields known or thought to be the bases of jets and other active elements of the Jagdverbände. These targets lay in an area west of Berlin on April 10th, and the thirteen hundred heavies involved met with a most determined attempt by Me262s to deplete their ranks. A force estimated at fifty strong was airborne although their ranks were broken up by the escort and those making

contact with the bombers attacked singly or in pairs. Several Me262s got through to the 1st Division Fortresses while the bombers were in the vicinity of their targets at Oranienburg. Tactics followed the pattern of previous interceptions by jets, a single pass from the rear by one or two aircraft, mostly directed at stragglers or outer elements. In this way they brought down five Fortresses The 3rd Division also lost five to similar tactics; and again following the pattern of recent jet encounters, the attacks were directed at groups all along the line with no attempt to concentrate on a particular formation. The Me262s had things far from their own way, and while the gunners' claims of 15 may have been unrealistic, a score of the jets were shot down by the Eighth Air Force that day.

Although the Mustangs and Thunderbolts had been unable to prevent many attacks on the bombers they were waiting for the jets as they returned to their bases short of fuel. The tactic of 'capping' the airfield suspected of harbouring jets paid off handsomely and the majority of the twenty Me262s claimed as destroyed were caught in this way. Albeit, this was the jets' most successful day against the Eighth Air Force heavies.

Combats with Me262s, important as they were, were somewhat overshadowed by the high strafing claims made by several groups at German airfields this day. The 56th, having

Old 457th BG B-17s were equipped with airborne lifeboats and assigned to 5th ERS at Halesworth.—(Forward)

taken two jets, descended to strike airfields and a seaplane base to make claims of 45 destroyed and boost its total past the 900 mark. The 78th Group made claims of 52-0-43 and its new commander, Lt Col John Landers, alone left eight burning. The 339th left 105 wrecked German aircraft in its wake, with Lt Col Thury adding four to his impressive total to make 18½ personal strafing victories. Totalling 284, the claims of April 10th surpassed the previous great strafing success of 177 on September 5th. Assessment of ground claims as either destroyed or damaged rested on combat film evidence of whether an aircraft was left burning or exploded; filling it full of holes only rated damage but the assessment was often a matter of opinion and credits given at group level might later be amended when wing or division intelligence agencies saw the evidence. There was also little doubt that most of the aircraft damaged now were no longer of any use to the Luftwaffe. But in the deteriorating situation there was always the possibility that some desperate suicide mission might be undertaken or that aircraft would be used to escape to a neutral country. And despite the danger of airfield flak defences, there was no stopping the fifteen groups that were seemingly only happy when hunting the now very weary enemy. Strafing and the oft illustrated danger of mistaking friendly troops for those of the enemy led to a ban on this activity when the Eighth flew out next day, in view of the rapidly advancing British, Canadian and US forces. This was too much for the pilots of 339th

For most of the war it was RAF A/S/R who rescued US fliers. 5th ERS obtained OA-10As in 1945 and occasionally saved RAF men. This one being lifted from the waist of 44-33913 was in a Wellington that ditched.—(IWM)

Group who could not resist pointing their P-51's red and white chequered noses at an airfield stocked with cross-marked aircraft and shooting up the field with 118 destroyed claims, topping the record for a single group set the day before. Nevertheless, it is said that higher command was somewhat displeased by this disregard of the ban.

Thirteen hundred B-17s and B-24s of the Eighth had ranged over Germany in perfect weather on April 11th, bombing marshalling yards, airfields and an oil storage and ordnance depot at Regensburg, a mission which proved to be the last large scale operation under the strategic flag. A relatively small scale raid against marshalling yards followed on the 13th and then for three consecutive days the Eighth's power was turned to the German batteries that still held out on the French coast in the Royan area to deny the Allies the use of Bordeaux as a port.

French ground forces had been unable to dislodge the German troops and now that air forces could be spared the decision was taken to attack the major strongpoints and gun batteries in this area as a prelude to a further ground offensive. The weather was ideal, the targets were isolated spots in Allied territory, and the anti-aircraft guns were few and unlikely to reach the heavies. About the best 'milk run' the bomber crews had ever been offered and yet for the 389th

RAFAAF, the 381st BG Fortress whose exploits are mentioned in a previous chapter, lost her complete right stabiliser in a collision on 11 Apr. 1945. Picture was taken soon after she landed at Ridgewell. Pilot 2/Lt Turner Brashear.—(USAF)

Group it brought tragedy. A 3rd Division B-17 group was making a second run on the target as the 389th formation passed below. Fragmentation bombs dropped by the B-17s struck five B-24s, two going down immediately, two of the others managed to be kept in the air and later crash-landed at French airfields, while the fifth struggled back to the UK.

At Pointe de Grave the 467th Group made Eighth Air Force history that day. Twenty-four of its Liberators arrived to deal with a coastal battery and when the three squadrons had released, all their 2,000 lb bombs fell within 1,000 ft of the MPI, half within 500 ft—a feat never achieved by any other Eighth Air Force group on any occasion. A feat that many people would never have believed possible, the 'pickle barrel' ideal come true. No doubt the meagre flak and good visibility all played their part, but the 467th had gradually established a reputation for consistently good bombing. From November until the end of the war it led the 2nd Division by bombs within the 1,000 ft circle of MPI.

Returning to the same area the following day, the 2nd and 3rd Divisions carried incendiaries and for the first time, Napalm. A jellied petrol, Napalm was a particularly powerful form of fire bomb. The 1st Division carried 1,000 and 2,000 GP bombs, and the three groups of its 41st Wing acted as a 'circling fire brigade' with orders to bomb any gun emplacement or position that showed signs of activity after the main force had bombed. As they were to circle at 15,000 ft four Mosquitos were on hand to put down a screen of Chaff to thwart possible radar-directed flak.

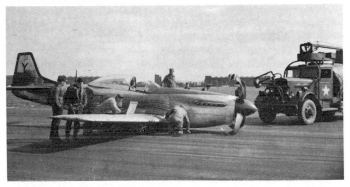

Pilot of this 1st Scout Force P-51D failed to lower the undercarriage when he approached the Bassingbourn runway on 12 Apr. 1945. After the forceful reminder, it is said he was so livid that he refused to vacate cockpit.—(Havelaar)

In spite of the strafing embargo still applying 56th Group swept towards Eggebeck airfield near Kiel in North Germany and finding it full of German aircraft proceeded to 'work it over'! With negligible anti-aircraft fire the Thunderbolts came home with claims of 95 destroyed and Lt Randal Murphy set a new one-man, one-place strafing record of ten left blazing. April 13th was the second anniversary of the Group's initial operation and it could now claim to be the first Eighth Air Force group to have destroyed 1,000 enemy aircraft. All the 4th Group could do was pick off a few seaplanes at Denmark as part of the day's record strafing total of 266 German aircraft. This figure was soon dwarfed by the fantastic total of 752 on April 16th when attention was shifted to south-eastern Germany and Czechoslovakian airfields. The 353rd Group had 110 credits mostly obtained at Pocking. The 339th also had a large number with Captain Robert Ammon topping Murphy's individual record of the 13th by claiming 11 destroyed. But the most accomplished act was by the 78th Group's Mustangs at an airfield in the Prague-Pilsen area where 125 were destroyed and 86 damaged in the face of fierce ground fire for an unsurpassed record. The 4th Group also had a field day, and with approximately 100 credits passed the 1,000 destroyed mark. But the cost of this unprecedented laying

First use of Napalm bombs by the Eighth. Two about to be loaded into the bay of 452nd BG's *E-rat-icator*, veteran of over 100 missions. Drop-tank type containers were filled with jellied petroleum by chemical companies on stations.—(IWM)

waste of remaining German airfields took a heavy toll, 34 Mustangs and a Thunderbolt. The leader of the 4th, Lt Col Woods, went down but escaped. Thury, the 339th's strafing ace, had his aircraft badly hit but managed to fly to safety. The following day the Mustangs went back to the same terrain and found another 200 to wreck but again with heavy cost. On this day the man who had emerged as the greatest strafer of them all, the 55th's commander Elwyn Righetti, was lost. His Mustang was hit while he made a pass over an airfield and he crash-landed it. Members of his group last saw him get out of his aircraft where he was surrounded by a crowd of civilians. He was never heard of again and it is believed that he was lynched by a hostile mob. Righetti had 27 enemy aircraft credits from strafing and numerous locomotives. Under his leadership the 55th had become the most prolific "railroad busters" in the Eighth, and by this date had destroyed some 600 locomotives since the beginning of the year. On the same

Lt Col Joe Thury does a cockpit check with his crew chief.—(USAF)

day the 352nd Group left 68 burning wrecks on Plattling airfield. The Group, like the 361st, had returned to its English base from Belgium a few days previously.

On the evening of April 16th General Spaatz informed Doolittle that they must now consider the strategic air war closed and that future targets for the heavy bombers would be purely tactical. Much of the effort had been predominantly tactical since the Allies set foot on the European mainland in June 1944, and the interpretation of what were tactical and what were strategical targets was often obscure. In layman's terms tactical bombing was likened to kicking over the bucket of milk every day, strategic bombing was trying to kill the cow: the cow was now dead. For the airmen in the B-17s and B-24s this was by the way.

The heavies had experienced a lull until April 17th when a solitary B-17 fell to about two dozen Me262s attacking the Fortress. *The Towering Titan* of 305th Group, had the unfortunate distinction of being the last 1st Division B-17 lost to fighter action.

'Eager El' Righetti, the greatest strafer of them all.—(Jenkins)

With Germany nearly cut in half and opposition dwindling in the north, operations were now predominantly in the southern area. The final engagement between the jets an the Eighth Air Force heavies took place on April 19th when the 3rd Division was despatched to bomb marshalling yards in the south-eastern extremities of the Reich. As the 490th Group was making a 270° turn over Prague prior to its run on Aussig, an Me262 made a head-on pass out of cloud, shooting down a B-17 in the lead squadron. Shortly afterwards two Me262s suddenly appeared from the clouds and climbing swiftly through the low and high squadrons of the 490th, sent three more B-17s down out of control. This spectacular success was followed shortly afterwards by the destruction of both jets by Mustangs. Another Me262 made a fast pass from 8 o'clock on the 447th Group's high squadron claiming B-17 42-31188, piloted by 1/Lt Robert Glazner. All but one of his crew was liberated a few days later. These six B-17s were the last heavies lost to Luftwaffe fighters.

Again the policy of sending fighters ahead to catch the jets taking off from likely airfields paid off. Lt Col Jack Hayes, formerly a bomber pilot, led a part of the 357th Group towards Prague/Ruzyne airfield and began orbiting to the south using the sun for concealment in the perfect visibility. He did not have to wait long for soon pairs of Me262s took off. Hayes then brought the Mustangs down to 15,000 ft but still taking care to keep up sun. When some 16 jets were airborne the 357th went into action and managed to shoot down four and damage three before the jets used their superior speed to pull away. During this action other Me262s continued to take off

'Category E', a P-47D converted for two-seat flight, at Boxted in Oct. 1944 was used operationally in Apr. 1945 with airborne search radar. —(USAF)

from the airfield and avoid combat. Another squadron of the 357th later chased two Me262s that had attacked the bombers and shot these down. In all cases the P-51s had used their altitude advantage to gain sufficient speed to close.

On the same day the Eighth's Mustangs had their last tussle with FW190s although it was a rather one-sided affair. A flight of 364th Group were flying near Lübben when much to pilots' astonishment a twin-engined aircraft, identified as a Do217, dived through their formation. This was promptly followed and shot down. While re-forming, the same Mustangs then ran into four FW190s at 5,000 ft and despatched all four. A sweep over Czechoslovakia produced what would be the Eighth's last known encounter with the Luftwaffe's piston-engined fighters. The 355th Group encountered a dozen Me109s over Letnany airfield and claimed seven destroyed and four damaged for no loss. Nothing was seen of enemy aircraft on the 21st and with a ban on strafing the Mustangs and Thunderbolts returned without firing their guns. It was the 25th before the heavies, and then only part of the 1st and 2nd Divisions, were called out again.

Czech workers were warned by radio that Pilsen *might* be the target for Fortresses. It was, and 307 set off for the Skoda

Due to an accelerated training programme in the US, replacement crews reaching the Eighth towards the end of hostilities tended to be younger than their predecessors. The youngest heavy bomber crew in the ETO was that of 2/Lt Joe Novicki (21) of 34th BG at Mendlesham. From l. to r. back row: Corporals Guinn (20), Corrigan (19), Alvord (20), Tremblay (19), and Ford (19), all gunners. Front row: Corp Pittman (20) radio operator, Novicki, 2/Lt Olsen (20) co-pilot and F/O Fournier (20), navigator.

Armament plant and a nearby airfield, while 282 Liberators flew to attack rail centres at Salzburg, Bad Reichenhall, Hallstein and Traunstein. In perfect visibility all hit their primary objectives, the 1st Division making several runs to ensure good results, but the flak guns, alerted by the broadcast, took six B-17s. At 11.16 hrs the last formation had reached the climax of its run as 27-year-old bombardier 1/Lt Earl Fisher pulled the switch to release the bombs in *Swamp Angel*. As they fell in company with those of the rest of the formation, they marked the last of the 696,450 tons the Eighth Air Force had dropped in anger. For, although not realised at the time, this was the last mission the Eighth's bombers would fly. By coincidence (or did someone suspect there would be no further call for the heavies?) Fisher's formation was the 384th Group from Grafton Underwood. From Grafton, 966 days before, twelve B-17s had set out on the Eighth's very first heavy bomber mission.

On this occasion the usual escort had been given other tasks. Some of the Mustangs escorted Lancasters uneventfully to Berchtesgaden while others shepherded B-17s and had a look over Prague/Ruzyne again for jets. A few Me262s were sighted but only one was attacked and damaged. The 479th

Tucked in close, five miles above Germany, the 390th BG goes to war. BI: N with radome extended is *This Is It!* CC: A is *Yardbird* and CC: M *The Great McGinty.*—(IWM)

Group's Mustangs escorted a combat wing of B-24s to Traunstein near Salzburg. South-east of the target Lt Hilton Thompson caught sight of an aircraft below him travelling east at an estimated 300 mph. Thompson quickly recognised it as an Ar234, gave his Mustang full power and came up behind the jet from below so that his intended victim would be less likely to notice his approach and pull away. A long burst set fire to the unsuspecting Arado and it went down near Reichenhall, the last known Luftwaffe aircraft to fall to the guns of the Eighth Air Force. For Thompson it was his second victory over a jet, one of perhaps half a dozen men in the Eighth with this distinction. Colonel Riddle the 479th's CO saw a twin-engined aircraft east of Salzburg and with his wingman flew towards it. Before he could identify the machine it suddenly went into a diving turn while a top turret opened fire. Assuming the aircraft hostile, Riddle immediately got onto its tail and fired, hitting the port engine; then as he overshot he saw to his horror that the machine had a red star marking. The Soviet aircraft departed eastward with a smoking engine but probably got safely home. Riddle and his wingman also departed the area smartly as they were attracting a considerable amount of flak.

The following day the Soviet and American armies met at the Elbe and Germany was cut in half. The airspace in the remaining pockets of resistance was congested by the tactical air forces. There remained nothing for the fifteen US fighter groups in England to hunt.

Chapter 29: Diminuendo

The final days of April 1945 held suspense for Eighth Air Force airmen: would they, or would they not, be called upon to undertake further missions to the few remaining strongholds of the crumbling Nazi empire. With each day the prospect seemed more unlikely. Then, on the last day of the month, a field operation order went out to 3rd Division: but it demanded the services of Fortresses as agents of goodwill, not as purveyors of destruction.

Wehrmacht divisions in Western Holland had been isolated by the Canadian and British advances into the North German plain. Flooding of the countryside and disrupted communications aggravated a situation whereby the Dutch population were reduced to starvation level. The Allies arranged with the Germans, through neutral sources, for food supplies to be dropped from the air and US participation was handed to 3rd Division. Special routes and dropping points were designated, outside of which the Germans would not guarantee the supply aircraft undisputed passage.

The first day of May saw 396 B-17s set course over the Suffolk coast, coming down to 500 feet upon reaching Holland and unloading over 700 tons of '10 in 1' rations at two airfields and a race track at The Hague, and an open space near Rotterdam. There was some apprehension that the German gunners might not keep the agreement, but all went well. Over the next six days, with the exclusion of May 4th, supply missions of similar strength were run. For aircrew this was a most satisfying task—"The pleasantest missions we ever flew". People waving their appreciation from the fields and streets, "Thank you boys" and similar messages spelled out in fields with white linen, were in marked contrast to the kind of reception B-17s had received over the same country during past months.

These flights were not considered combat sorties and the only credits given were to the crews of 15 385th Group B-17s who apparently wandered into a flak area. Ground staff took the opportunity to have their first view of the Continent and went along to push out ration boxes. Yet even these mercy missions took their toll. That old hazard collision claimed two B-17s during assembly and the blazing remains fell at Bocking in Essex. On the final "Chow Hound" mission, the 95th Group's B-17 44-8640 had an engine on fire. As it threatened to engulf the whole aircraft the pilot ditched in the North Sea but in so doing hit a swell, the bomber breaking up and sinking almost immediately. Air Sea Rescue pulled two men out of the water; only one survived.

To give ground personnel an opportunity of seeing something of the destruction they had helped to promote over the past 2½ years, a programme of observation flights over the Ruhr valley was commenced with the cessation of hostilities on May 7th. Known as "trolley runs", some 10,000 men enjoyed these sight-seeing tours, including those from fighter stations who were transported in B-17s and B-24s of their respective divisions. The ruins of factories, bridges and marshalling yards evoked amazement amongst men who had led a hectic but safe war at English airfields. To quote Sgt James Caskey, a 44th Group operations clerk, "I didn't realise Germany was so all beat to hell".

While these trips were running other B-17 units were engaged in the so-called "Revival" missions, the transportation of Allied prisoners of war and displaced persons from Austria to France. Each B-17, with a five man crew, had up to forty passengers crammed in on each flight, twenty of them often travelling on timber platforms stretched across the bomb bay. There were no complaints—the 8,000 US and 1,500 British POWs flown out by May 14th were only too pleased to find such a quick means of leaving their former domicile.

For the fighter groups the first days of peace provided few duties outside a stepped up training programme. The expectation of seeing action in the Pacific theatre of war led to study and lectures on Japanese equipment and tactics. The Mustang groups were assigned a P-47 for pilots to fly, as the new long-range P-47N was scheduled for extensive use in the war with Japan.

Even though hostilities had ceased, the combat claims of the fighter groups were still being evaluated in the light of information provided by returning prisoners-of-war and first hand examination of the destruction to German aircraft on enemy airfields that had been strafed. The 4th Group which had 1,002 enemy aircraft destroyed both in the air and on the ground as against the 56th's 1,005½ was delighted to learn that in fact, it had been credited with a greater number of victories than its old rival. At first this was a matter of 1,011 against 1,003½, but by the time the final figures were issued by VIII FC in September 1945 the 4th's score had been boosted to 1,052½ and the 56th's reduced to 985½. In second place came the 355th Group with 868, 502½ of these were ground strafing claims, highest for any group in this category and sixty more than its nearest rival the 339th. The 56th Group

Dutch collect up food parcels as a 385th BG Fort unloads some more.
—(Zwanenburg)

Group and 175 for 355th, units well known for their ground strafing prowess.

Many other facts and figures were established at this time. Among individual pilots the highest scoring aces were the 56th's Francis Gabreski with 31 and Robert S. Johnson with 28 in air combat. Highest scoring Mustang pilots were George Preddy ($25\frac{1}{2}$), John Meyer (24) and Ray Wetmore ($22\frac{1}{2}$). With the P-38 alone, Robin Olds and James Morris had nine. Highest scoring strafing ace was Elwyn Righetti of the 55th (27) and Joe Thury of 339th Group runner-up with $25\frac{1}{2}$. These figures were revised in later years (see reference section).

In claims of enemy fighters destroyed by bomber men, always a thorny problem, Donald Crossley (94th) with 12 and Michael Arooth (379th) with 9, led gunner aces. Largest group claims were those of the 91st (420 destroyed), which also had more bombers missing in action (197) than any other group. Highest claims for a B-24 group were those of the 44th (330) and its 153 missing in action was the top Liberator figure. The 93rd Group with 396 missions led the bomber organisations in this respect, while 303rd had flown 364. Whereas the 93rd's total included 41 missions from North African bases the 303rd's were all flown from the UK.

But the most striking record of bomber work was that of the 379th Group at Kimbolton and the 467th at Rackheath. The 379th put more bombs on targets, its 26,459 tons being far in excess of that achieved by other groups, including those that were operational long before the 379th arrived in the UK. Much of this record was due to the inspiring leadership of Colonel Maurice Preston, the original CO and his headquarters team who were continually promoting ideas towards better bombing. The best record of bombing accuracy was probably that of the 467th Group Liberators which had achieved the 100% strike in April 1945. Its bombing was consistently better than the average of the other B-24 groups. Here, the dedication of the CO, Colonel Albert Shower, had much to do with this excellent record. Shower also had the unique distinction of being the only CO to bring a group to the UK, remain in command and return home with it. His group was chosen to

'Trolly' missions gave ground personnel an opportunity to see some of the destruction in Germany wrought by the heavies they maintained. The 487th BG took in Paris on the way. Here 44-8312 sweeps by the Eiffel Tower; 9 May 1945.—(Lerner)

had by far and away the highest credit for aircraft destroyed in air combat, $674\frac{1}{2}$. Second came the 357th Group with $609\frac{1}{2}$ then the 4th with $583\frac{1}{2}$. The 357th's Mustangs had the highest rate of destruction during the final twelve months of the war. The lowest total of $276\frac{1}{2}$, was that of 356th Group at Martlesham Heath. Though seeing 18 months of action it had rarely had an opportunity to do battle with the Luftwaffe. The highest operational losses, 241, were those of the 4th Group, nearly double that of the 56th and reflecting the vulnerability of the P-51. The next heaviest loss was the 181 for 55th

The men on *Patriotic Patty* and other 446th BG Liberators take a look at the bomb scarred surface at a former Luftwaffe airfield, now occupied by a Ninth AF P-47 group.—(USAF)

Flying for flying's sake. Mustangs of 361st FG cavort in the summer sunshine high above their home base. *Daisy Mae III* has yellow nose markings swept back to code letters.—(Morris)

lead the victory flypast on May 13th over the Eighth's headquarters at High Wycombe. Despite the decided Command preference for B-17s from the spring of 1944 onwards, the B-24s led the two B-17 divisions in bombing accuracy average for the last four months of the war. The performance of individual groups, however, was influenced to a large degree by how they fared with German fighters and flak; the best records were those of units who had a comparatively untroubled passage—although all had their bad times.

The Fort v. Lib controversy is a battle of words and wits that continues down the years, promoted by the men who entrusted their lives to the one or the other. In May 1945 the exchange was razor sharp as the following letters, appearing in the US forces daily newspaper, shows:—

> *To the B-Bag   May 15, 1945*
> *We would like to know why there are never any pictures of B-24s in "The Stars and Stripes". Every time you use a picture of a heavy, its always a B-17. We'll admit we did pull such milk runs as Big B, Kiel, Magdeburg, Gotha, etc, and have never, as yet, dropped food to Dutch civilians, but don't you think we deserve one picture occasionally?   Some 389th BG Boys.*

(The B-17 advocates could not let this pass).

US occupation troops found this P-47D used by the Luftwaffe experimental unit in a hangar near Göttingen. Nearby a 353rd FG Mustang was stripped down.—(USAF)

> *To the B-Bag: May 26, 1945*
> *Memo to "Some 389th BG Boys": We don't begrudge your wish for publicity, but—since when have targets like Big B, Kiel, Magdeburg and Gotha compared to targets like Schweinfurt, Merseburg, Politz and Munich? When you can number these as part of your accomplishments, then start crying for publicity. And speaking of crying, isn't it a bit too late now? We'll see you in the South Pacific, if your banana boat can get there in time.   Publicity-mad Fort Bombardiers, 351st BG.*

With peace, the chief subject of all USAAF bases in the UK was "redeployment": where and when men and units would be moved. Coupled to this was the individual's desire to return to the USA. USSTAF plans were gradually made public; three Mustang and nine Fortress groups would become part of the occupation forces in Germany or be retained in Europe for other duties. The remainder of Eighth Air Force were to return to the US where selected units would go into training for service in the Pacific. The bomb groups had priority, the B-17s and B-24s would be flown back across the Atlantic and ground echelons would follow by sea.

The men who helped put the bottles on 447th BG's *Milk Wagon*. Her final total of 129 trips without once turning back through mechanical trouble was a record for 3rd Division. T/Sgt Robert Orlosky was her crew chief.—(Via Rust)

The movement of this great force began in the third week of May and on the 19th the first B-24 was on its way. At 11.42 hrs three days later, Lt Gordon Kretchmar brought the 389th Group's HP-V into Bradley Field, Connecticut. During the next seven weeks 2,118 heavies arrived from Britain at this and other airfields in the US bringing over 41,500 men, an average of 16 men per aircraft, a few key ground men flying in each. While some flights left via Prestwick, more than 90% of the bombers were staged through Valley, in Anglesey, which by this homeward bound association became known as "Happy Valley". From this Welsh airfield on July 9th 1/Lt Gean Williams piloted the last B-24 to leave. The movement was marred by two accidents one, on June 19th, was when a 446th Group B-24 with 15 aboard disappeared between Valley and the Azores.

The units remaining in Europe were those of the 92nd, 94th, 96th, 100th, 303rd, 305th, 306th, 379th and 384th Bomb Groups and the 55th, 355th and 357th Fighter Groups. During the second week in June the 92nd and 384th moved to Istres in Southern France and the 303rd and 379th to Casablanca, where all were to engage in the transportation of US troops on the first stage of their journey home—"The Green Project". The services of the 303rd and 379th however, were apparently not required by the North African Division of Air Transport Command and both groups were inactivated on July 25th, the first former combat units of the Eighth to go.

The veterans go home. Posing beneath the nose of *Jamaica Ginger* shortly before saying goodbye to Knettishall. This B-17G's 137 missions was a record for 388th BG.—(Duane)

Ole Miss Destry, with four leaf clover emblem for luck, was once inspected by the King and Queen. Luck held and she completed 138 trips with the 305th BG. Note chin turret guns wrapped for trans-Atlantic flight.—(USAF)

The 305th Group moved to St Trond, Belgium late in July and the three Mustang Groups took up their occupational stations in Bavaria during the same month.

On July 16th the Eight Air Force was re-established on Okinawa in the Pacific as another USAAF bomber organisation in the war with Japan. While the commander and some personnel were drawn from its former forces, for the most part the new Eighth had little to connect it with its former self. Two B-29 Superfortress groups, the 333rd and 346th were ready for action early in August 1945, but hostilities ceased before they operated. At this time some of the former Liberator groups of the UK days were in training with B-29s in the US and would have eventually gone out to Okinawa. Foremost were those that had been part of the 20th Wing, the 489th Group which had gone home in December 1944, was already equipped, and the 93rd and 448th were also receiving new aircraft.

High Wycombe, formerly HQ of the Eighth Air Force, now housed VIII Fighter Command; appropriately, as by this time the groups remaining in England were predominantly fighter. Pressure on shipping caused them to languish in England throughout the summer and into the autumn of 1945, although personnel changes were frequent as long service men were shipped home and others transferred to other units. Aircraft in exotic colours soon appeared in the East Anglian sky, chiefly two-seat adaptions of the Mustang painted overall yellow, red, blue or whatever the owners fancied. Most fighter groups acquired a B-17 for a transportation 'hack' while the four remaining B-17s groups procured P-47s or P-51s. The 56th, true to form, had to go one better and an He111H and FW190A were 'acquired' on the Continent and decked out in the Group's colours at Boxted. These were happy times when flying was enjoyed for flying's sake under the guise of training, and men found time to see Britain in the pleasant summer days.

Accidents marred some occasions, particularly so when they involved men who had survived long periods of combat duty. Two such personalities killed during this period were Lt Hilton Thompson who destroyed the last enemy aircraft claimed by the Eighth and Colonel Ben Rimmerman, a 353rd ace, who had been given command of the 55th Group at the end of the

Glory Bee, 98 missions with 44th BG, taxies out at Valley to commence the flight to Iceland, first leg of the journey home.—(IWM)

On 1 Aug. 1945 Eighth AF stations were opened to the British public. Visitors to Duxford admire the distinctively marked P-51D *Contrary Mary* of 78th FG's CO. Trim to checkerboard was red.—(USAF)

war. Thompson spun into the Channel and Rimmerman crashed during a night training flight.

It was October before the fighter group personnel left their bases and sailed for home, the remaining P-51s and P-47s having been delivered to depots for shipment, destruction or storage on the Continent.

With but a few groups under its command the VIII FC moved to Honington in October, the area of its remaining flying units. After November 21st, when the 7th Reconnaissance Group left Hitcham (Wattisham depot) for their port of embarkation, only the 94th, 100th, 96th and 306th Bomb Groups remained. The B-17s of these units had taken part in a number of activities mostly photography and "Nickeling" missions—the dropping of propaganda leaflets over Germany and former occupied countries, chiefly directed at displaced persons. By December these groups were a shadow of their former selves, the 94th, 96th and 100th's B-17s flew back to the US, and on the 12th the remaining personnel at all three stations left to embark on the *Lake Champlain.* At the same time the 306th moved to Germany. When its last elements left Thurleigh on December 15th, the Group had spent three and a quarter years in England and had the longest combat career of any. On arrival in New York the other three B-17 groups were inactivated, the fate of all but

a few of the Eighth's former units. Within twelve months, even the occupational groups had gone the same way. In fact, only one group, the famous 93rd Bomb Group, escaped inactivation and soldiered on in the post-war USAF.

By February 1946 VIII Fighter Command at Honington remained the last of the 122 stations occupied by the Eighth Air Force in England and the time had come to leave even that. A fitting ceremony was arranged for February 26th. Brigadier General Emil Kiel, VIII FC Commander, and Air Marshal Sir James Robb, AOC and RAF Fighter Command, were present at a parade to mark the handing back of the station. An RAF band rendered 'The Star Spangled Banner' on the rain-swept parade ground while the US flag was brought down. Then the RAF Ensign was hoisted in its place and the Press took photographs of Air Marshal Robb receiving the keys of the station from General Kiel. It was further intended that General Kiel should take off in the last remaining Fortress but a low overcast and rain caused this mission to be scrubbed, typical of so many occasions in the past. Nevertheless appropriate pictures were taken of the 'last B-17', 44-83273, taxying out. March had come before the VIII FC personnel were finally gone from Honington, a gradual departure spread over several weeks. In the best tradition, they faded away.

Chapter 30: Conclusions

This book set out to tell something of the history of the Eighth Air Force in terms of the men, units and equipment directly involved in operations. The higher strategy affecting the Eighth's place in the overall Allied offensive against the European Axis has been but superficially touched upon, being well documented in US official works and the biographies of those in command. Nevertheless, the story of the combat elements is, indeed, the overall saga of the Eighth Air Force, revealing much that allows a number of general observations to be made.

Strategic Bombardment and the daylight high-altitude precision bomber.

The Eighth Air Force was looked upon by USAAF commanders as their prime instrument to test their doctrine of strategic bombardment. The supreme hope was that such a campaign could render massive devastation to the war industry of a highly industrialised nation, like Germany, so that it would be unable to supply and support its armed forces; in effect, bombing into submission. In the event the combined strength of all Allied strategic forces proved unable to achieve this against Germany. What strategic bombing could achieve was evinced in the spring of 1945, but that it was decisive with the weapons and delivery systems of the Hitler war, must always remain speculative.

At the end of hostilities the US Strategic Bombing Survey was produced by a large team of specialists with the object of evaluating the work of the strategic bomber: a formidable task in view of the complexity of the subject. Some of the general conclusions published were not universally accepted, but the Survey did underline its finding that air power's overall part in achieving victory in Europe was decisive.

The Eighth Air Force delivered 75% of its bombs after the Allies invaded the Continent, and it was the cumulative effect of sustained bombardment on such target systems as oil and transportation with its direct and indirect strain on German war economy, that brought the B-17s and B-24s their greatest contribution to victory.

The effect of the US heavies from the fall of 1942 until the spring of 1944, although often spectacular, was never serious enough to have profound effect. Germany's powers of recuperation were far greater than appreciated, and the small bombs carried by the B-17s and B-24s might destroy a factory building but not the precious machine tools within. Attacks against aircraft factories, even the intensive period in early 1944, saw only a temporary decline in production. On the other hand, it has been estimated that the dispersal programme instigated by the Germans in 1943 to escape the bombing possibly cost them more lost production than through actual damage to installations. In assessing the part played by the Eighth and other Allied strategic bombing forces, the considerable tying down of personnel and material in defence, both active and passive must not be overlooked. Such manpower and material might have been channelled into extra panzer divisions and so turned the scales in a land campaign.

The chief obstacle to daylight precision bombing was the inconstant weather. Cloud continually hampered and foiled attacks. Tight formations and the performance of the lead bombardier was imperative to accurate bombing, and while precision was difficult, when visibility was hampered by weather conditions, error was inevitable and sometimes frequent. The likelihood was even greater when a formation was under attack, as was illustrated on many occasions. The B-17 and B-24, the vehicles available, were far from ideal for the task in which employed, yet in the circumstances they were utilised with undeniable zeal and often with remarkable effect.

The long range fighter

Probably the greatest single contribution of the Eighth Air Force to victory in Europe was the star part its fighters played in attaining combat superiority in continental air space. Originally furnished for bomber protection, the US fighters came to be a potent offensive weapon. Fighter and bomber operations were complementary, the bombers becoming important as bait to draw the Luftwaffe to battle, apart from their primary function.

The development of the long range fighter rested chiefly on technical and operational endeavours within the Eighth Air Force. The rapid production of a good, reliable drop-tank plus the undeterred policy of despatching single-seat, single engined fighters on, sometimes, seven hour flights in appalling weather, reaped astonishing success. By 1944 the total strength of Allied fighters was vastly superior to the Luftwaffe's, but it was predominantly the fighters of VIII Fighter Command that were able to carry the fight into Germany and achieve the air supremacy that was essential to any invasion of the Continent.

German defences

The record of the Luftwaffe against the Eighth Air Force is an inconsistent one. Like the British, the Germans were cautious in the use of bombers by day through experience in the Battle of Britain and other campaigns. When the first B-17 formations appeared over the French coast in the fall of 1942, the Luftwaffe did not foresee their activity developing into a serious threat despite difficulties in interception. Not until the B-17s struck into Germany in 1943 were fighter reinforcements forthcoming and spirited efforts made to evolve means of breaking up the US formations. The Luftwaffe was usually too preoccupied with the bombers to deal with the escort that eventually transpired, even when the P-47s appeared with drop tanks over the very borders of the Reich. The Luftwaffe's first incredible error was not to undertake determined and regular interception of the US escort in order to force them to jettison their tanks and thus restrict their range. Instead the German fighters continued to pursue the same policy with dire consequences for themselves until, with P-51s giving near continuous escort, they found themselves the hunted and not the hunters.

A second extraordinary omission on the part of the Luftwaffe was not to press a campaign against the Eighth's bases or against bomber formations during assembly or prior to landing, in spite of success on the rare occasions when this was tried. British air defence was good but the congested East Anglian sky was ideal for intrusion with minimum risk.

While anti-aircraft guns gradually came to take a heavy toll from the US formations, the most successful means of bringing down bombers was undoubtedly the Luftwaffe's Company Front technique, evolved early in 1944 and practised with deadly effect throughout that year by the Sturmgruppen. The heavily armed and armoured FW190s attacking as a body reduced the effectiveness of counter fire through saturation.

Although the Luftwaffe fighter force was rebuilt after June 1944 it suffered acute shortage of trained pilots and later its activities were curtailed through low fuel stocks. Its aircraft and armament of this period too were on most counts less suited to fighter-fighter combat than those of the Americans. The appearance of jet aircraft, while giving the Allied air leaders concern, did not alter the picture. The Me262s performance was high, but not such an advance over the P-51s that—with artifice—the US pilots could not engage it. The Me163 did have a vastly superior performance and was rarely caught. Its appearance was limited due to development problems, chiefly its own explosive nature.

During wartime it was policy to denigrate the prowess of enemy personnel—a practice which was not confined to one side. The German fighter pilots encountered during the earlier battles with the Eighth were usually skilful and formidable opponents. In the last year of the war they were at a disadvantage in training, equipment and numbers, but despite the hopelessness of their cause and the lack of any clearly defined defensive policy on the part of the Luftwaffe administration and the Nazi hierarchy, they continued the fight with much courage.

The Character of the Eighth Air Force

In carrying out its mission the Eighth was aided by its location in the UK. Far enough removed from the Pentagon and government administration in the USA, it was able to enjoy a great degree of autonomy; it flourished in an environment where many of its requirements could be met locally.

Despite a certain natural impetuosity and a highly developed national pride, its officers readily acknowledged that in many instances throughout its operational existence—particularly during the early days—lack of know-how and sometimes inferior equipment necessitated the Eighth leaning heavily upon the battle-hardened expertise of the RAF and facilities of the UK. Having survived and surmounted the initial troubles, however, it pressed forward with characteristic élan on its elected course. In this the American superiority complex played its part. Untempered by ideas of caution, the men of the Eighth Air Force pursued their concept of strategic bombardment with dogmatic faith. It was this fervour to get things done, to surmount all technical and operational obstacles, that took the Eighth further along the road it chose than ever the British or Germans would have deemed possible. Procrastination and the negative were scorned, and even bloody experiences did not deter the overwhelming intention to succeed. This spirit percolated from the top to the bottom; each isolated combat group set in the English countryside proclaimed itself "the best damn group in the AAF", and in a sense, it probably was. For each was more of an enduring entity than any collection of military flying units have ever been.

The Eighth Air Force was not without its share of human failures, tactical blunders and mistaken policies. These shortcomings were, nevertheless, far outweighed by the development, to a unique degree, of such admirable characteristics as a remarkable esprit de corps, dogged bravery and supreme determination to succeed. It was, indeed, these attributes which have so rightly conferred upon the Eighth the honour of becoming one of the most famous military organisations in history.

Unit reference Histories

Explanatory Notes

Group Designation
Bombardment Groups were popularly termed Bomb Groups. The bracketed suffix for Heavy, Medium or Light was also omitted in general references. Provisional designations stemmed from Eighth Air Force for groups formed in the UK and not officially constituted.

Assignment Eighth Air Force
Assignment usually dated from the arrival of a group on British soil. In the case of bomber and troop-carrier groups, where ground and air echelons travelled separately, assignment dated from either the arrival of the commanding officer (who would fly in) or the arrival of Group Headquarters party (by sea) dependent on which was first. On July 16th, 1945, the Eighth Air Force was transferred, less personnel and equipment, to Okinawa in the Pacific. Units still remaining in the UK were then assigned to VIII Fighter Command. In fact, this was a re-designation of the High Wycombe headquarters.

Wing & Command Assignments
Assignment could be on either an administrative or operational control basis. Occasionally one organisation would have both. The Combat Bomb Wing had operational control of groups assigned to it, whereas administrative control was usually vested in Command or Division. There were instances where a group was assigned to one Air Force but under operational control of another. See page 295 for abbreviations.

Component Squadrons
For space economy, full title given for last squadron only. Squadrons activated with a group usually remained as components of that group throughout hostilities. The exceptions were chiefly in special organisations and reconnaissance groups.

Combat Aircraft
The main aircraft types assigned to a group for combat operations. The production blocks given are the lowest from which the bulk of original equipment was drawn. Even so, there were often a few examples from earlier blocks. For example, the 386th BG had one B-26B-10 (the CO's a/c) when it reached the UK; all other B models being from block 15. Aircraft from earlier blocks were also often assigned at later dates, being machines overhauled at depots and returned to combat. Groups occasionally had a lone example of another aircraft type for use on special operations; e.g., 56th FG employed a P-38J Droop Snoot for a few weeks. Where a group converted from one type to another, where possible the dates of last and first operational use of each type are given.

Stations
These are the official Air Ministry names. In most instances the name is that of the parish in which the airfield was situated, but it often happened that the complete station took in parts of two or three villages and in such cases the name of the station was usually that of the most important place. Another factor was the avoidance of similar sounding names that might lead to confusion. The locations of stations are listed in the Station index. Official USAAF date of a new group taking up station is that for the arrival of Headquarters staff. New bomber groups from USA were sometimes preceded by a small advance party, then air and ground echelons would arrive, usually on different dates, often weeks apart. The dates of arrival given here are usually specified. A date for commencement of group residence is that of the first main body of air or ground echelon to arrive. Where there is no specification then the date is the official date, i.e., arrival of group Hq. party with ground echelon. A double date indicates movement taking some days with no precise date of establishment.

Group Commanding Officers
Ranks given are the highest attained while in command of a group. A high proportion of commanders who were with a group for several months were promoted from Lt Colonel to full Colonel. Most bomb group commanders flew home with the air echelon after VE-day. Their command of the group ceased upon arrival at Valley or Prestwick, and the movement came under the jurisdiction of Air Transport Command.

The ground echelon, remaining in the UK, had another officer designated as commander by Eighth Air Force, but it appears that in many instances he was not officially recorded as group CO.

Operational Statistics
Several sets of figures exist for each group as a result of assessments at group and various command levels. Here the totals for missions, bomb tonnage, sorties, enemy aircraft claims, etc., are derived from the final statistical summaries of 1st, 2nd and 3rd Divisions in order to obtain a common basis for comparison. Fighter group claims of enemy aircraft destroyed come from VIII FC's final assessment (Sep. 45). 1st Division records do not give a comparative table of Other Operational Losses. See glossary for further explanation of terms.

Major Awards
Only the highest decorations for units and personnel, the Distinguished Unit Citation and the Medal of Honor, are dealt with under this heading. See further under Awards section.

Claims to Fame
Many of these entries are not truly a matter of fame but rather notable facts about units. All groups could find something to claim as a special achievement.

Early History
Units of the USAAF were first *Constituted*—in simple language, a designation for a unit was put on the books. *Activation* was to bring a unit into physical existence by assigning personnel and equipment. However, because of shortages and the overloading of training facilities, many wartime activations were initially of a token nature with perhaps one officer and one enlisted man assigned. Sometimes it was purely a 'paper' activation, the order to activate was made but personnel were not assigned for some weeks. Many Eighth Air Force groups began life in this way and were often transferred 'less personnel and equipment' to another base before the first batches of men arrived to make it a physical entity. The original cadres frequently came from old established groups which performed an amoeba act. Bomber training was in three phases; the first with emphasis on individual skills, the second was concerned with team training, and the final phase with advanced training simulating combat operations. The actual curriculum for each group varied due to a number of factors. To accelerate training of bomber units, a School of Applied Tactics was established at Orlando, Fla. and commencing with the 390th BG on 1 Mar. 43, the key men of all new groups underwent a month's intensive course there during the period of first phase training. Movement overseas for the ground echelon, i.e., those personnel who served in an administrative and support capacity, was usually on a familiar pattern. A train journey to one of the transit camps in the New York area—Camp Kilmer or Camp Shanks—where they would await a ship to convey them to the UK. The two Cunard Queens carried the majority of Eighth Air Force personnel from New York to the Clyde estuary in Scotland. Some travelled on smaller vessels from Boston to Liverpool. The air echelon would receive its combat aircraft at the end of, or during final phase training, and move to an overseas processing station before making the flight to England. The northern ferry route was the shortest but only used during summer months. Those groups crossing during winter and spring flew by the southern route. A crew did not know their destination until opening sealed orders on the first leg of the journey. In 1942 and 1943 the movement of many air echelons was delayed by having to await new aircraft from the factories. Both air and ground echelons of fighter groups travelled together, with few exceptions. Where a group was to fly an aircraft type which its pilots had not handled during training, the pilots were sent to OTUs on arrival in the UK, and often some high experience pilots from other units transferred to the new group.

Subsequent History
Movement of bomber aircraft back to the US was chiefly through Valley, Wales. From there they were despatched either south to the Azores or north to Iceland depending on weather conditions but in both cases the ultimate point of arrival in US was Bradley Field, Conn. A points system allowed long serving men priority of return and to

enable this a great many transfers between units took place in the UK. Fighter groups, which were the last to be shipped, were a shadow of their former selves by the time their turn came, as most of the long-serving personnel had already departed. Aircraft with low hours were also transferred, going to units scheduled for service with occupational air forces. Once it had departed the UK a group ceased to exist as an organised formation. Its assignment to a station on arrival in the US was a paper transaction and only a few men were returned after leave to be present at its inactivation. Those units that were perpetuated as B-29 organisations were entirely new with fresh personnel.

The Groups

1st Fighter Group

Assigned Eighth AF: 10 Jun. 42.
Wing & Command Assignments

| VIII FC: | 10 Jun. 42. |
| VIII FC, 6 FW: | 16 Aug.-13 Sep. 42. |

Component Squadrons
27th, 71st, & 94th Fighter Squadron.
Combat Aircraft
P-38F.
Stations

GOXHILL	10 Jun. 42-24 Aug. 42 Hq. & 71FS (air ech. in 6 Jul. 42 and 25-28 Jul. 42).
KIRTON IN LINDSEY	10 Jun. 42-24 Aug. 42 94FS: (air ech. in 25-28 Jul. 42).
IBSLEY	24 Aug. 42-14 Nov. 42 Hq. 71 & 94FS (Gnd. ech. out 21 Oct. 42).
HIGH ERCALL	27 Aug. 42-15 Sep. 42 27FS.
COLERNE	15 Sep. 42-6 Nov. 42 27FS (To Chivenor for staging).

Group COs

| Major John O. Zahn: | 1 May 42-9 Jul. 42. |
| Lt Col John N. Stone: | 9 Jul. 42-7 Dec. 42. |

First Mission 2 Sep. 42. **Last Mission** 25 Oct. 42. **Total sorties** 237.
E/a claims None. **A/c MIA** 1.
*(First air defence sorties flown by 94FS 29 Aug. 42).
Early History
Organised 5 May 1918 at Toul, France. Principal US Army fighter organisation between wars. Based Selfridge Fd, Mich, 1922-1941. Moved San Diego NAS, Cal, 9 Dec. 41 and received early P-38s. Los Angeles MAP, Cal, 1 Feb. 42 and fully equipped P-38F prior to commencement of overseas movement in May 42. Ground echelon sailed on *Queen Elizabeth* from New York 3 Jun. 42, arriving Gourock 9 Jun. 42. Air echelon flew a/c to UK via northern ferry route. First P-38s left Dow Fd, Me, 27 Jun. 42. Air echelon 27FS remained in Iceland and did not rejoin Group until late Aug. 42. 27FS flew ocean patrols 6 Jul.-25 Aug. 42. Lt Elza K. Shahan shared in destruction FW200 14 Aug. 42. 27FS ground echelon to Goxhill, while Air echelon in Iceland. No combats on UK ops.
Subsequent History
Assigned 12 AF, XII FC, 14 Sep. 42 but continued to operate under VIII FC. First contingent of ground echelon left Ibsley 21 Oct. 42 and sailed on *SS Orbita* from Gourock 26 Oct. 42. Two other parties left bases 23 and 26 Oct. 42 the first sailing on *HMS Mooltan* from Bristol, and the second on *Empress of Canada* from Gourock. These ships in convoy to North Africa. Air echelon flew to Africa from Portreath 14-16 Nov. 42. Two a/c lost en route, one in Portugal. Group fought in North Africa with 12AF and later in Italy with 15AF on bomber escort. Established as air defence organisation in the USA in post-war years. From 1955 at Selfridge AFB, Mich as interceptor wing. Flew F-106 during nineteen sixties.

3rd Photographic Group

Assigned Eighth AF: 5 Sep. 42-16 Oct. 42.
Wing & Command Assignments

| VIII GASC: | 8 Sep. 42. |
| VIII ASC: | c. 18 Sep. 42. |

Component Squadrons
5th, 12th 13th & 14th Photographic Squadron & 15th Photographic Mapping Squadron.
13 & 14 PS detached from Group at Membury and not equipped until later (see 7 PG).
5 PS originally arrived UK as separate unit. Assigned 3rd PG Oct. 42.
Combat Aircraft
F-4 Lightning, 5PS.
F-5 Lightning, 12PS.
B-17F Fortress, 15PMS.
Stations

| MEMBURY | 8 Sep. 42-26 Oct. 42. |
| STEEPLE MORDEN | 26 Oct. 42-22 Nov. 42. |

Group COs

| Lt Col Furman H. Limeburner: | 13 Aug. 42-30 Sep. 42. |
| Lt Col Elliott Roosevelt: | 30 Sep. 42-3 Jun. 43. |

No operations from the UK
Early History
Activated 20 Jun. 42 at Colorado Spring, Col. where it remained until 13 Aug. 42. Trained under 2nd AF and then attached AAF Hq. Ground echelon sailed New York 31 Aug. 42 and arrived Greenock 5 Sep. 42.
Subsequent History
Assigned to 12AF and sent to North Africa. Ground echelon at Liverpool 22 Nov. 42 until sailing on 27 Nov. 42. Arrived Gibraltar 4 Dec. 42 and left for North Africa 12 Dec. 42. Air echelon flew to staging areas 5 Nov. 42 and first a/c arrived in Africa 9 Nov. 42. 15 PMS B-17s did not leave UK until after mid Nov. 42. Group later moved to Italy and was inactivated there on 12 Sep. 45.

4th Fighter Group "The Eagles"

Assigned Eighth AF: 12 Sep. 42.
Wing & Command Assignments

VIII FC:	12 Sep. 42.
VIII FC, 4 ADW:	30 Jun. 43.
VIII FC, 65 FW:	7 Aug. 43.
2 BD, 65 FW:	15 Sep. 44.
2 AD, 65 FW:	1 Jan. 45.

Component Squadrons
334th, 335th & 336th Fighter Squadron.
Combat Aircraft
Spitfire V: Sep. 42-1 April 43.
P-47C in combat from 10 Mar. 43-Feb. 44. P-47D, Jun. 43-Feb. 44.
P-51 B in combat from 25 Feb. 44. P-51D from Jun. 44. P-51K from Dec. 44.
Stations

| DEBDEN | 29 Sep. 42-20-27 Jul. 45. |
| STEEPLE MORDEN | 20-27 Jul. 45-4 Nov. 45. |

(336FS at satellite GREAT SAMPFORD 23 Sep. 42-30 Oct. 42).
Group COs

Col Edward W. Anderson:	27 Sep. 42-20 Aug. 43.
Col Chesley C. Peterson:	20 Aug. 43-c. 23 Dec. 43.
Col Donald J. M. Blakeslee:	1 Jan. 44-c. 1 Nov. 44.
Lt Col Claiborne H. Kinnard Jr:	1 Nov. 44-6 Dec. 44.
Lt Col Harry J. Dayhuff:	7 Dec. 44-21 Feb. 45.
Col Everett W. Stewart:	21 Feb. 45-Sep. 45.
Lt Col William E. Becker:	Sep. 45-Nov. 45.

(Kinnard acting CO c. 1 Sep. 44-c. 1 Nov. 44 while Blakeslee on leave).
First Mission: 2 Oct. 42. **Last Mission:** 25 Apr. 45.
A/c MIA 241. **E/a Claims** 583½ air; 469 ground.
Major Awards
Distinguished Unit Citation: 5 Mar.-24 Apr. 44; destroying 189 e/a air and 134 ground.
Claims to Fame
Formed from the RAF Eagle Squadrons.
Oldest fighter group in 8AF.
Combined totals air and ground claims of e/a highest for USAAF.
First to engage e/a over Berlin and Paris.
First 8AF fighter group to penetrate German air space-28 Jul. 43.
Early History
Activated 12 Sep. 42 at Bushey Hall, Herts, England. Official ceremony transferring RAF squadrons 71, 121 & 133 (Eagle Squadrons) to 4 FG 29 Sep. 42. They became 334, 335 and 336FS respectively. Ground echelon formed from that of 50FS, ex 14 FG, Atcham, RAF

personnel trained USAAF ground echelon in servicing Spitfires. Flying control still vested in RAF FC.

Subsequent History

Returned to USA in Nov. 45. Moved to Steeple Morden end Jul. 45 as RAF required Debden. Group gradually run down and a/c flown to depots for disposal. Sailed on *Queen Mary* from Southampton 4 Nov. 45, arriving New York 9 Nov. 45. Group inactivated at Camp Kilmer, NJ 10 Nov. 45.

Activated again in Sep. 46 as P-80 jet fighter group. Converted F-86 in 1949 and operated in Korean War 1950-1954 destroying 506 Migs in air combat. Returned to USA and later became first wing to operate F-105. Some squadrons detached to fly in Vietnam War.

7th Photographic Group (R)

Assigned Eighth AF: 7 Jul. 43.

Wing & Command Assignment

325 PW(R):   9 Aug. 44.

Component Squadrons

13th, 14th, 22nd & 27th Photographic Squadron.
(27PS based on continent Jan.-Mar. 45).

Combat Aircraft

F-4A (from Mar. 43); F-5A (from Jun. 43); F-5B (from Dec. 43); F-5C (from Mar. 44); F-5E (from May 44).
Spitfire IX (from Oct. 43); P-51 D & K (from Jan. 45).

Stations

MOUNT FARM	7 Jul. 43-22 Mar. 45.
CHALGROVE	22 Mar. 45-25 Oct. 45.
HITCHAM	25 Oct. 45-21 Nov. 45.

Group COs

Col James G. Hall:	7 Jul. 43-14 Sep. 43.
Col Homer L. Saunders:	14 Sep. 43-31 Dec. 43.
Col Paul T. Cullen:	1 Jan. 44-17 Feb. 44.
Lt Col George A. Lawson:	17 Feb. 44-7 May 44.
Lt Col Norris E. Hartwell:	7 May 44-9 Aug. 44.
Lt Col Clarence A. Shoop:	9 Aug. 44-25 Oct. 44.
Col George W. Humbrecht:	25 Oct. 44-18 Jun. 45.
Maj Hubert M. Childress:	19 Jun. 45-Sep. 45.

First Operation: 28 Mar. 43 (13PS). **Last Operation:** late Apr. 45.
Total Credit Sorties: 4,247. **A/c MIA** 58 (5 P-51).

Major Awards

Distinguished Unit Citation: 31 May-30 Jun. 44: photo sorties in support of Normandy invasion.

History

Activated 1 May 43 at Peterson Fd, Colo. 28, 29 & 30PS assigned but transferred when Group transferred less personnel and equipment to 8AF, 7 Jul. 43. 13, 14 & 22PS assigned as of this date but only 13PS operational having moved to Mount Farm Feb. 43. 13 & 14PS originally arrived in UK with 3PG Sep. 42 but were left behind when this group moved North Africa due to shortages of personnel and a/c. 14PS trained Spitfire V during late summer 1943 and equipped Spitfire XI. 27PS officially assigned 21 Dec. 44. By summer 1944 14PS had strength of 14 Spitfires and the other three squadrons 16 F 5 apiece. 27PS was detached to operate with 9AF. Moved 9–18 Nov. 44 to Daon Couvron, Fr. Moved Denain Prouvy late Jan. 45. To Chalgrove 18 Apr. 45. P-51s were assigned to 7PG in Jan. 45 to escort F-5s. Made claims of 0-1-1 during 880 credit sorties. Group took over three million intelligence photos during the course of 4,251 sorties that were effective.

Subsequent History

Many personnel transferred post VE-day. A/c to depots for disposal Aug./Sep. 45. Remaining personnel moved Hitcham air depot adjacent Wattisham late Oct. 45 and inactivated there 21 Oct. 45.

14th Fighter Group

Assigned Eighth AF: 18 Aug. 42-14 Sep. 42.

Wing & Command Assignments

VIII FC, 6 FW: Aug. 42-14 Sep. 42.

Component Squadrons

48th & 49th Fighter Squadrons.
(50FS also assigned but only air echelon reached UK).

Combat Aircraft

P-38F.

Stations

ATCHAM	18 Aug. 42-6 Nov. 42 (Air ech. in 28 Jul.-early Aug. 42). (Gnd. ech. out 30 Oct. 42).

(Part 48FS at Ford 11 Oct. 42-26 Oct. 42, and part 49FS at Tangmere same dates).

CO

Col Thayer S. Olds: 18 Apr. 41-28 Jan. 43.

First Mission: 2 Oct. 42. **Last Mission:** 21 Oct. 42.

No combat or losses

Early History

Activated 15 Jan. 41 at Hamilton Fd, Cal. Moved March Fd, Cal, early Jun. 41 and back to Hamilton Fd, 7 Feb. 42 to equip with P-38s. Ground echelon departed 16 Jul. 42 on first stage of movement to UK. Sailed *USS West Point* early Aug. 42 and arrived Liverpool 17 Aug. 42. Air echelon departed to Bradley Fd. Conn, 1 Jul. 42. Flew P-38s to UK via northern ferry route, with first a/c leaving Presque Isle 22 Jul. 42. 50FS remained in Iceland and did not rejoin Group. (Ground echelon at Atcham and later transferred to 4FG). Flew sweeps and practise missions under RAF guidance from Ford and Tangmere.

Subsequent History

Assigned 12AF, XII FC on 14 Sep. 42 but continued to operate under VIII FC. Ground echelon left Atcham 30 Oct. 42 and sailed *USS Brazil* and *USS Uruguay* from Liverpool. Arrived Oran 10 Nov. 42. Air echelon departed for Portreath 6 Nov. 42 and flew to North Africa 10-14 Nov. 42. Fought with 12AF in North Africa and later with 15AF in Italy on bomber escort duties.

A unit of Air Defence Command in post-war years. In 1966 designation given to special operations wing in Vietnam.

20th Fighter Group

Assigned Eighth AF: 25 Aug. 43.

Wing & Command Assignments

VIII FC:	25 Aug. 43.
VIII FC, 67 FW:	6 Oct. 43.
1 BD, 67 FW:	15 Sep. 44.
1 AD, 67 FW:	1 Jan. 45.

Component Squadrons

55th, 77th, & 79th Fighter Squadron.

Combat Aircraft

Aug. 43-11 Dec. 43.
P-38H, P-38J in combat from 28 Dec. 43 to 21 Jul. 44.
P-51C-10-NT; P-51D (from blocks 5) in combat from 20 Jul. 44.
P-51K from Dec. 44.

Station

KINGS CLIFFE   26 Aug. 43-11 Oct. 45.

Group COs

Col Barton M. Russell:	c. 20 Aug. 43-2 Mar. 44.
Lt Col Mark E. Hubbard:	2 Mar. 44-18 Mar. 44 MIA.
Lt Col Harold J. Rau:	20 Mar. 44-25 Jun. 44.
Lt Col Cy Wilson:	25 Jun. 44-27 Aug. 44 MIA-POW.
Col Harold J. Rau:	27 Aug. 44-18 Dec. 44.
Col Robert P. Montgomery:	18 Dec. 44-3 Oct. 45.

(Maj Hubert E. Johnson Jr acting CO 19-20 Mar. 44, and Maj Jack C. Price 3-11 Oct. 45).

First Mission: 28 Dec. 43.* **Last Mission:** 25 Apr. 45. **Total Missions:** 312. **A/c MIA:** 132. **E/a Claims:** 212 Air: 237 Ground.

Major Awards

Distinguished Unit Citation: 8 Apr. 44, sweep over Germany.

Claims to Fame

Oldest USAAF group to be assigned 8AF for extended period of time. Best P-51 maintenance record of any 8AF group for latter months of war.

Early History

Activated 15 Nov. 30 at Mather Fd, Cal, as 20th Pursuit Gp. Moved Barkersdale Fd, La. late 1932 and based there until late 1939. Equipped successively with P-12, P-26 and P-36. Moved California in Nov. 39 and equipped P-39 and later P-40. Moved NC in 1942 and to Paine Fd, Wash, later that year. Provided nucleus for new groups during period 1940-42. Established at March Fd, Cal. in Jan. 43 and equipped with P-38s. First scheduled for service with 8AF in Jan. 42 but not ordered overseas until Aug. 43. Air and ground echelons departed March 11-Aug. 43 and sailed on *Queen Elizabeth* 20 Aug. 43, arriving in Clyde 25 Aug. 43.

Subsequent History

Group gradually run down, many personnel transferred and a/c flown to depots for disposal. Remainder in UK until Oct. 45. Sailed in *Queen Mary* from Southampton 11 Oct. 45, arriving New York 16 Oct. 45. Moved to Camp Kilmer, NJ, where Group inactivated 18 Oct. 45. Activated again in Jul. 46 with P-51 and later F-84. Moved to Wethersfield, UK in 1952 later converting F-100.

*First Group operation. Individual sqdns flew as fourth sqdn to 55FG on 3, 7, 10 & 11 Nov. 43 (79FS), 25, 26, 29, 30 Nov. 43 (77FS) and 5 and 11 Dec. 43 (55FS).

25th Bombardment Group (R)

Established Eighth AF: 22 Apr. 44 as 802nd Reconnaissance Group (P), and activated as 25th Bombardment Group (Recon.) on 9 Aug. 44.

Wing & Command Assignment
325 PW(R): 9 Aug. 44.

Component Squadrons
652nd Bombardment Squadron (H), 653rd Bombardment Squadron (L) and 654th Bombardment Squadron (SP).

Combat Aircraft
B-24D, B-24H (Apr.-Nov. 44) and B-17G (from Nov. 44, 652 BS only).
Mosquito XVI (from Apr. 44), 653 and 654BS, B-26G, 654BS (few).

Station
WATTON 22 Apr. 44-23 Jul. 45.

Group COs
Lt Col Joseph A. Stenglein: unkn.-23 Sep. 44.
Col Leon W. Gray: 23 Sep. 44-14 Apr. 45.
Lt Col John R. Hoover: 14 Apr. 45-19 Jun. 45.
Maj Ernest H. Patterson: 19 Jun. 45-Jul. 45.

First Operation: 22 Apr. 44. **Total Credit Sorties:** 3,370 (1,493 by 652BS).

A/c MIA: 15 (652BS 2).

Major Awards
None.

History

Prior to 28 Mar. 44 weather flights for 8AF carried out from a number of heavy bomber stations for 18th Weather Squadron. This squadron had no flying unit but detachments of personnel on many bomber stations. Aircraft and non-specialist crew members were provided by the bomber stations. From Sep. 43 to end Mar. 44, 231 weather sorties flown by B-17 and B-24 a/c. These flights were to obtain meteorological data over Atlantic and waters adjacent and weather information necessary in planning combat missions. 8WRS(H)(P) (later 652BS) took over 28 Mar. 44. Two other squadrons were established at the same date for special reconnaissance operations in enemy air space. Equipped with Mosquitos, WRS(L)(P) engaged chiefly in weather flights over the continent. Later weather scouting missions in advance of bomber formations and visual coverage of target strikes. WRS(Sp)(P) flew photo recon. sorties by day and night. Later duties included 'chaff' screening flights for bomber missions. Nucleus for both Mosquito squadrons came from ex-P-38 pilots of 50FS who were transferred Iceland from Feb. 44. Redeployed USA Jul./Aug. 45. Group established Drew Fd, Fla, and inactivated 8 Sep. 45.

31st Fighter Group

Assigned Eighth AF: Jun. 42-14 Sep. 42.

Wing & Command Assignments
VIII FC: 10 Jun. 42.
VIII FC, 6 FW: 18 Aug. 42.

Component Squadrons
307th, 308th and 309th Fighter Squadron.

Combat Aircraft
Spitfire V.

Stations
ATCHAM 11 Jun. 42-1 Aug. 42. Hq. 307 & 308FS.
HIGH ERCALL 11 Jun. 42-4 Aug. 42. 309FS.
WESTHAMPNETT 1 Aug. 42-21 Oct. 42 (309FS in 4 Aug., 308FS in 24 Aug. 42).
MERSTON 24 Aug. 42-unkn. 307FS.
(307 and 309FS at Warmwell 19-27 Jul. 42; 307FS at Biggin Hill 1 Aug. 42-24 Aug. 42; 308FS at Kenley 1 Aug. 42-24 Aug. 42).

Group CO
Col John R. Hawkins: 1 Jul. 42-4 Dec. 42.

First Mission: 29 Aug. 42.* **Last Mission:** 9 Oct. 42. **Total Sorties:** 1,286.
*(First sorties with RAF 26 Jul. 42. First squadron operation 5 Aug. 42).

A/c MIA: 5. **E/a Claims:** 2-1-6 air.

Claims to Fame
First group to commence operations with 8AF.

Early History

Activated 1 Feb. 40 at Selfridge Fd, Mich. Trained with early P-39s. Moved Baer Fd, Ind, 6 Dec. 41 and to New Orleans AB, La, in Feb. 42. Scheduled to fly P-39s to UK via north Atlantic ferry route but project cancelled. Ground echelon sailed on *Queen Elizabeth* 4 Jun. 42 arriving Clyde 10 Jun. 42. Pilots followed later in month. Commenced flying training at Atcham 26 Jun. 42.

Subsequent History

Assigned 12AF, XII FC 14 Sep. 42 but continued to operate under VIII FC. Off operational status 10 Oct. 42. Spitfires shipped to Gibraltar. Personnel sailed from Clyde for Gibraltar 26 Oct. 42.
Fought with 12AF in North Africa and Italy. In May 44 converted P-51s and flew escort for 15AF. Inactivated Nov. 45.
Activated again in 1946. Operated F-51s in Germany and in 1947 returned to USA. Equipped with F-84 1948. A TAC unit for many years. Flying F-100s, operated in Vietnam War.

34th Bombardment Group (H)

Assigned Eighth AF: Apr. 44.

Wing & Command Assignments
3 BD, 93 CBW: Apr. 44.
3 AD, 93 CBW: 1 Jan. 45.

Component Squadrons
4th, 7th, 18th and 391st Bombardment Squadron (H).

Combat Aircraft
B-24H (from blocks 15-CF and FO) and B-24J in combat to 24 Aug. 44.
B-17G (from blocks 50-VE, 85-BO) in combat from 17 Sep. 44.

Station
MENDELSHAM 18 Apr. 45-c. 2 Aug. 44 (Gnd. ech. in c. 26 Apr. 44).

COs
Col Ernest J. Wackwitz Jr: c 5 Jan. 44-Sep. 44.
Col William E. Creer: Sep. 44-29 May 45.
Lt Col Eugene B. LeBailly: 29 May 45-Aug. 45.

First Mission: 23 May 44. **Last Mission:** 20 Apr. 45. **Total Missions:** 170* (62 B-24). **Total Credit Sorties:** 5,713. **Total Bomb Tonnage:** 13,424.6 tons (131.6 tons leaflets, etc.).

A/c MIA: 34. **Other Op. Losses:** 39. **E/a Claims:** 8-4-12.

Major Awards
None.

Claims to Fame
Did not lose a single bomber to enemy fighter action over enemy territory. Only losses to e/a over its own base.
Oldest USAAF bomb group to serve with 8AF.

Early History

Activated 15 Jan. 41 at Langley Fd, Va. 391BS originally designated 1RS. Group equipped with B-17s and on completion of training moved Westover Fd, Mass. Took part in anti-submarine patrols on eastern seaboard flying from Pendleton Fd, Ore. from end Jan. 42 to mid-May 42. Moved Davis-Monthan Fd, Ariz. and on 4 Jul. 42 to Geiger Fd, Wash, where it became a replacement training unit. Prior to this many cadres drawn from 34BG to build new bomb groups destined for 8AF. On 15 Dec. 42 moved to Blyth Fd, Cal, where it formed part of 358 CCTS but reverted to an operational role 5 Jan. 44 to train in B-24s for overseas duty. Air echelon began overseas movement 31 Mar. 44, taking southern ferry route, Florida, Trinidad, Brazil, West Africa, Marrakesh to Valley. Ground echelon to port of embarkation c. 1 Apr. 44.

Subsequent History

Redeployed US Jun./Jul. 45. First of air echelon departed 19 Jun. 45. Ground echelon sailed *Queen Elizabeth* from Southampton 6 Aug. 45. Personnel 30 days R & R. Group established Sioux Falls AAFd, SD, and inactivated there 28 Aug. 45.

*(6 food missions May 45, 446 tons).

44th Bombardment Group (H)
"The Flying Eightballs'

Assigned Eighth AF: Sep. 42.
Wing & Command Assignments
VIII BC, 2 BW: Sep. 42.
VIII BC, 2 BW, 201 PCBW: 25 Mar. 43.
VIII BC, 2 BW, 202 PCBW: 2 Sep. 43.
VIII BC, 2 BD, 14 CBW: 13 Sep. 43.
2 BD, 14 CBW: 8 Jan. 44.
2 AD, 14 CBW: 1 Jan. 45.
Component Squadrons
66th, 67th, 68th and 506th Bombardment Squadron (H).
(506BS not assigned until Mar. 43).
Combat Aircraft
B-24D (from blocks 1); B-24E (few); B-24H, B-24J, B-24L, B-24M and B-24M Eagle.
Stations
CHEDDINGTON   11 Sep. 42-9 Oct. 42 (66BS Air ech. in 10 Oct. 42).
SHIPDHAM   10 Oct. 42-15 Jun. 45.
(Temporary stations in North Africa: Benina Main, Libya; 28 Jun. 43-25 Aug. 43 and Ounda No. 1, Tunis; 19 Sep. 43-4 Oct. 43).
Group COs
Col Frank H. Robinson: 1 Apr. 42-4 Jan. 43.
Col Leon W. Johnson: 4 Jan. 43-2 Sep. 43.
Lt Col James T. Posey: 3 Sep. 43-3 Dec. 43.
Col Frederick R. Dent: 4 Dec. 43-29 Mar. 44.
Col John H. Gibson: 29 Mar. 44-15 Aug. 44.
Col Eugene H. Snavely: 15 Aug. 44-9 Apr. 45.
Col Vernon C. Smith: 13 Apr. 45-1 Jun. 45.
First Mission: 7 Nov. 42. **Last Mission**: 25 Apr. 45. **Total Missions**: 343 (18 from NA). **Total Credit Sorties**: 8,009. **Total Bomb Tonnage**: 18,980 tons.
A/c MIA: 153. **Other Op. Losses**: 39. **E/a Claims**: 330-74-69.
Major Awards
Two Distinguished Unit Citations: 14 May 43; Kiel (66, 67 & 506BS)
                  1 Aug. 43; Ploesti.
Medal of Honor: Col Leon W. Johnson; 1 Aug. 43.
Claims to Fame
First USAAF group to be equipped with B-24 Liberators.
Operated from England for longer period than any other B-24 group.
Sustained highest MIA loss of 8AF B-24 groups.
Claimed more enemy fighters than any other 8AF B-24 group.
First group in 8AF to be awarded a DUC (for 14 May 43).
Early History
Activated 15 Jan. 41 at McDill Fd, Fla. Received first B-24 B-24C later that year. Moved Barksdale Fd, La, 16 Feb. 42 and acted as training unit for 98th, 93rd and 90th BGs. During same period took part in anti-submarine patrols over Gulf of Mexico and credited with destruction of one U-boat. On 26 Jul. 42 moved Will Rogers Fd, Okla, and prepared for overseas movement. Ground echelon left by train for Fort Dix AAB, N.J., 28 Aug. 42, arrived 1 Sep. 42 and sailed *Queen Mary* 4 Sep. 42. Arrived Clyde 11 Sep. 42. Air echelon left Will Rogers Fd, 30 Aug. 42 for Grenier Fd, NH, and remained there until first a/c left for UK late Sep. 42. 404BS originally part of Group but reassigned while in US.
Subsequent History
Redeployed USA May/Jun. 45. First a/c left UK 22 May 45. Ground echelon sailed on *Queen Mary* 15 Jun. 45, arriving New York 20 Jun. 45. Personnel 30 days R & R with some assembling Sioux Falls AAFd, SD, Jul. 45. Group selected for reforming as B-29 unit, and in late Jul. 45 established at Great Bend AAFd, Kan. for training. Aircraft and personnel transferred to another unit, and Group inactivated 12 Jul. 46. Activated again 1951 as B-29 wing in SAC, later B-47s. Finally re-established 1963 as Minuteman missile wing Ellsworth AFB, SD.

52nd Fighter Group

Assigned Eighth AF: 13 Jul. 42-14 Sep. 42.
Wing & Command Assignments
VIII FC, 6 FW: 18 Aug. 42.
Component Squadrons
2nd, 4th and 5th Fighter Squadron.
Combat Aircraft
Spitfire V.
Stations
EGLINTON   13 Jul. 42-c. 25 Aug. 42 (5FS remained until 13 Sep. 42).
GOXHILL   c. 26 Aug. 42-c. 21 Oct. 42 (Main air echelons 2 & 4FS in 13 Sep. 42).
(2FS at Biggin Hill 25 Aug.-13 Sep. 42; 4FS at Kenley 25 Aug.-13 Sep. 42). (Maydown also used from 7 Aug. 42-Sep. 42 as satellite for Eglington).
Group CO
Lt Col Dixon M. Allison: 27 Feb. 42-1 Mar. 43.
Early History
Activated 15 Jan. 41 at Selfridge Fd, Mich. Trained with P-40 and P-39 a/c. Completely equipped with P-39s early 1942 and moved Florence AB, SC, 18 Feb. 42 and Wilmington NC, 27 Apr. 42. Scheduled to move to UK flying its a/c via northern ferry route and moved to Grenier Fd, NH, mid-Jun. 42 to prepare, but project cancelled. Air echelon sailed for UK end Jul. 42. Ground echelon early Aug.
2 and 4FS flew sorties up to squadron strength between 27 Aug. 42 and 11 Sep. 42 in conjunction RAF Fighter Command. Total 83 sorties including 12 on defensive patrols. No combat or losses. 5FS did not take part in ops from UK.
Subsequent History
Assigned 12AF, XII FC 14 Sep. 42. Spitfires shipped to Gibraltar. Personnel sailed in convoy 26 Oct. 42. Fought with 12AF in North Africa and Italy. Converted to P-51s in Apr. 44 and flew escort for 15AF. Inactivated Nov. 45. Activated again, in Germany, 46. Transferred USA 47 and established as all weather fighter group with P-61 and later F-82s. Active in air defence role for twenty years, chiefly at Suffolk County, AFB, NY.

55th Fighter Group

Assigned Eighth AF: 16 Sep. 43.
Wing & Command Assignments
VIII FC: 16 Sep. 43.
VIII FC, 66 FW: 5 Oct. 43.
3 BD, 66 FW: 15 Sep. 44.
3 AD, 66 FW: 1 Jan. 45.
Component Squadrons
38th, 338th and 343rd Fighter Squadron.
(See also 3rd Scouting Force).
Combat Aircraft
P-38H; 20 Sep. 43-end Dec. 43; P-38J; mid Dec. 43-21 Jul. 44. P-51D (from blocks 5) in combat from 19 Jul. 44; P-51K, from Dec. 44.
Stations
NUTHAMPSTEAD   16 Sep. 43-16 Apr. 44.
WORMINGFORD   16 Apr. 44-21 Jul. 45.
Group COs
Lt Col Frank B. James: 15 May 43-3 Feb. 44.
Col Jack S. Jenkins: 6 Feb. 44-10 Apr. 44, POW.
Col George T. Crowell: 10 Apr. 44-22 Feb. 45.
Lt Col Elwyn C. Righetti: 22 Feb. 45-17 Apr. 45, MIA.
Col Ben Rimerman: 22 Apr. 45-20 May 45, KAS.
Lt Col Jack W. Hayes Jr: 21 May 45-Unkn.
First Mission: 15 Oct. 43. **Last Mission**: 21 Apr. 45.
A/c MIA: 181. **E/a Claims**: 316½ air; 268½ ground.
Major Awards
Two Distinguished Unit Citations: 3-13 Sep. 44, destruction 106 e/a
                  on mission.
                  19 Feb. 45, ground strafing achievements.
Claims to Fame
First P-38 group in combat with 8AF.
First 8AF a/c over Berlin—3 Mar. 44.
Destroyed more locomotives by strafing than any other Group.
Lt Col Righetti was 'King' of 8AF strafers.
Early History
Activated 15 Jan. 41 at Hamilton Fd, Cal. Equipped with P-43s and moved Portland Fd, Ore, 21 May 41 and operated from there until Feb. 42. Moved Paine Fd, Wash, 10 Feb. 42 and re-equipped with P-38s before moving McChord Fd, Wash, 22 Jul. 42 where it remained for over a year. Originally activated with 37, 38 and 54FS but 54FS transferred to Pacific theatre 11 Sep. 42 and replaced by 338FS, and 37FS transferred to 14FG in North Africa 15 Mar. 43, 343FS having been assigned to take its place the previous month. Group left McChord for Camp Kilmer, NJ, 23 Aug. 43 and sailed on *Orion* 5 Sep. 43,

arriving UK 14 Sep. 43. 50FS, ex-Iceland, absorbed into Group 11 Feb. 44.

Subsequent History

Selected for duty with occupational air forces in Germany. Some personnel transferred other units for return to US. Group moved Giebelstad, Bavaria, in Jul. 45, move completed 21 Jul. 45. Seriously undermanned until Jul. 46 when equipped with P-80 jets. Inactivated 20 Aug. 46, in fact, re-numbered as 31FG.

Activated as a strategic reconnaissance group with RB-17 and RB-29 a/c in 1947. Inactivated late 1949 but activated again a year later for same role. Flew RB-50 and later RB-47. In 1966 converted to RC-135.

56th Fighter Group

Assigned Eighth AF: 12 Jan. 43.
Wing & Command Assignments

VIII FC:	12 Jan. 43.
VIII FC, 4 ADW:	30 Jun. 43.
VIII FC, 65 FW:	7 Aug. 43.
2 BD, 65 FW:	15 Sep. 44.
2 AD, 65 FW:	1 Jan. 45.

Component Squadrons

61st, 62nd and 63rd Fighter Squadron.

Combat Aircraft

P-47C-2 and 5, Feb. 43-Apr. 43; P-47D (blocks 1 to 30), Jun. 43-Mar. 45; P-47M, Jan. 45-Sep. 45.

Stations

KINGS CLIFFE	13 Jan. 43-5 Apr. 43.
HORSHAM ST FAITHS	5 Apr. 43-8 Jul. 43.
HALESWORTH	8 Jul. 43-18 Apr. 44.
BOXTED	18 Apr. 44-9 Sep. 45.
LITTLE WALDEN	9 Sep. 45-10 Oct. 45.

Group COs

Col Hubert A. Zemke:	1 Sep. 42-30 Oct. 43.
Col Robert B. Landry:	30 Oct. 43-11 Jan. 44.
Col Hubert A. Zemke:	19 Jan. 44-12 Aug. 44.
Col David C. Schilling:	12 Aug. 44-27 Jan. 45.
Lt Col Lucian A. Dade Jr:	27 Jan. 45-Aug. 45.
Lt Col Donald D. Renwick:	Aug. 45-Oct. 45.
(Lt Col Schilling acting CO	11 Jan. 44-18 Jan. 44).

First Mission: 13 Apr. 43. **Last Mission:** 21 Apr. 45. **Total Missions:** 447.

A/c MIA: 128. **E/a Claims:** 674½ air, 311 ground.

Major Awards

Two Distinguished Unit Citations: 20 Feb. 44-9 Mar. 44; destroying 98 e/a.

18 Sep. 44; Holland, in support airborne forces.

Claims to Fame

Destroyed more e/a in air combat than any other 8AF fighter group.
Had more fighter aces than any other USAAF group.
Top scoring fighter aces, Francis Gabreski and Robert Johnson flew with 56th.
First USAAF group to fly the P-47.
Only 8AF group to fly P-47 throughout hostilities.

Early History

Activated 15 Jan. 41 at Savannah, AAB, Ga. Expansion of Group began after move to Charlotte AAB, NC in May 41 when equipped with small number of P-39 and P-40 a/c. Intensified training at Charleston MAP, SC, in Dec. 41 and from Jan. to Jun. 42 at airfields in New York area (Hq. Mitchel Fd, NY) where air defence patrols also flown. Selected to train with new P-47B receiving first example Jun. 42. Moved Bridgeport MAP, Conn. c. 7 Jul. 42 and continued testing and training with early P-47s. Alerted for overseas movement Dec. 42 and sailed on *Queen Elizabeth* 6 Jan. 43 arriving Gourock 11 Jan. 43.

Subsequent History

A/c to depots Sep. 45; remaining personnel to Little Walden. Returned USA Oct. 45, sailing on *Queen Mary* 11 Oct. 45, and arriving New York 16 Oct. 45. Group established Camp Kilmer, NJ, and inactivated there 18 Oct. 45.

Activated again May 46 at Selfridge Fd, Mich. Flew P-47 and P-51 a/c until 1947 then F-80s. Moved O'Hare IAP, Ill. Aug. 55 and equipped F-86D, 62FIS with F-101 remained until 1969. Designation given to special operations wing in Thailand 1967.

60th Troop Carrier Group

Assigned Eighth AF: 12 Jun. 42-14 Sep. 42.
Wing & Command Assignments

VIII GASC:	Aug. 42.
VIII GASC, 51 TCW:	1 Sep. 42.

Component Squadrons

10th, 11th, 12th and 28th Troop Carrier Squadron.

Combat Aircraft

C-47.

Stations

CHELVESTON	12 Jun. 42-7 Aug. 42 (Air ech. 7 Jul. 42-28 Jul. 42).
ALDERMASTON	7 Aug. 42-Oct. 42.

Group CO

Lt Col A. J. Kerwin Malone:	15 Apr. 42-11 Oct. 42.

History

Activated 1 Dec. 40 at Olmsted Fd, Pa. Moved Westover Fd, Mass. May 41 and remained there until movement to UK Jun. 42. Flew northern ferry route. 53 a/c on hand on 28 Jul. 42. Trained with paratroopers for North African landings. Dropped entire 2 Bt. 503 Para. Inf. Regiment on 16 Sep. 42. Assigned 12AF 14 Sep. 42. First mission carrying paratroopers to North Africa 7 Nov. 42, flying from St. Eval and Predannack. Served in Mediterranean theatre during remainder of war. Inactivated Trinidad Jul. 45. Activated again in 1946 and served in Europe until 1960 flying C-47 (1946), C-82 (49) and C-119 (53). Established as MAC transport wing in mid-nineteen sixties.

62nd Troop Carrier Group

Assigned Eighth AF: 6 Sep. 42-14 Sep. 42.
Wing & Command Assignments

VIII GASC, 51 TCW:	6 Sep. 42.

Component Squadrons

4th, 7th, 8th and 51st Troop Carrier Squadron.

Combat Aircraft

C-47 and C-53.

Station

KEEVIL	7 Sep. 42-25 Nov. 42 (Air ech. in 26 Oct. 42).

Group CO

Col Samuel J. Davis:	1 Jul. 42-26 Mar. 43.

History

Activated 11 Dec. 40 at McClellan Fd, Cal. Moved UK Aug.-Sep. 42. Ground echelon left Florence Fd, SC, 14 Sep. 42 and sailed on the *Queen Elizabeth* 30 Aug. 42, disembarking Greenock 6 Sep. 42. First a/c left Presque Isle, Me. 22 Sep. 42 and last on 7 Oct. 42. Air echelon flew paratroopers to North Africa 11-18 Nov. 42. Ground echelon sailed on *Samaria* 27 Nov. 42. MAC transport wing in nineteen-sixties.

64th Troop Carrier Group

Assigned Eighth AF: 18 Aug. 42.
Wing & Command Assignments

VIII GASC, 51 TCW:	1 Sep. 42.

Component Squadrons

16th, 17th, 18th, 35th Troop Carrier Squadron.

Combat Aircraft

C-47.

Station

RAMSBURY	18 Aug. 42-11 Dec. 42 (Ground ech. in 21 Aug. 42. Air ech. out 30 Oct. 42).

Group CO

Col Tracey K. Dorsett

History

Activated 4 Dec. 40 at Duncan Fd, Tex. Commenced overseas movement from Westover Fd, Mass. in Jul. 42. Air echelon flying by northern ferry route and arriving UK from 18 Aug. 42. Ground echelon arrived in UK 20 Aug. 42. Transferred 12AF 14 Sep. 42 and air echelon flew to Gibraltar with paratroops 9 Nov. 42. Served in Mediterranean theatre for remainder of war. Inactivated Trinidad Jun. 45.

Activated again as troop carrier group in TAC 1952 with C-82 and later C-119.

67th Reconnaissance Group

Assigned Eighth AF: 5 Sep. 42-13 Nov. 43.
Wing and Command Assignments
VIII GASC:	5 Sep. 42.
VIII ASC:	18 Sep. 42.
VIII ASC, 1 FD (P):	c. Jun. 43.

Component Squadrons
12th, 107th, 109th and 153rd Reconnaissance Squadron.
Combat Aircraft
Spitfire VB; L-4 and A-20B.
Station
MEMBURY	6 Sept. 42-12 Dec. 43 (last unit in 6 Oct. 42).

Group CO
Col Frederick R. Anderson:	4 May 42-6 Dec. 43.

No group operations while assigned 8AF. A number of sorties with RAF from Jul. 43 to Oct. 43 flying Spitfires and Bostons. At least one Boston crew and two Spitfire pilots MIA.
Early History
Activated 1 Sep. 41 at Esler Fd, La. as 67th Observation Group. 113 OS originally assigned but replaced by 12 OS in Feb. 42. While training flew anti-submarine patrols from a number of east coast bases. Used a variety of a/c including A-20, B-25, L-1, O-47, O-52, P-40 and P-43 while in the USA. Sailed on *Queen Elizabeth* for UK 31 Aug. 42 arriving 5 Sep. 42. As Group had no aircraft RAF supplied Spitfire Vs and Masters. During its early months in UK the Group became a support organisation for other 8AF groups. Furnished old Havoc and Bostons for target towing duties at bomber bases. Provided Spitfires and pilots on detachment to fighter CCRC at Atcham and when L-4 became available these were detached for liaison duties at various stations. Squadrons had mixed a/c complements. Group and squadrons redesignated as Reconnaissance 29 Jun. 43. In summer 1943 153RS crews began operating with RAF flying Bostons. On 1 Oct. 43 this squadron inactivated and Bostons and a few A-20Bs came under 2911BS(L) Provisional. Group's a/c operated with RAF on sweeps from a number of south coast bases but never at Group or squadron strength.
Subsequent History
Assigned 9AF on 13 Nov. 43 and re-equipped with P-51A and P-51B. Some squadrons later transferred to other 9AF groups. Flew tactical recon. and photo recon. missions from Dec. 43. Moved France Jul. 44. Returned to USA late 45 and inactivated Mar. 46.
Activated again in 1947 and in 1951 moved to far east. Took part in Korean War, and thereafter based in Japan until inactivated. Activated as tactical recon. wing in USA in 1965 and equipped RF-4C.

78th Fighter Group

Assigned Eighth AF: 29 Nov. 42.
Wing & Command Assignments
VIII FC:	29 Nov. 42.
VIII FC, 4 ADW:	30 Jun. 43.
VIII FC, 65 FW:	7 Aug. 43.
VIII FC, 66 FW:	18 Aug. 43.
3 BD, 66 FW:	15 Sep. 44.
3 AD, 66 FW:	1 Jan. 45.

Component Squadrons
82nd, 83rd and 84th Fighter Squadron.
Combat Aircraft
P-38G, Dec. 42-Feb. 43.
P-47C, from late Jan. 43; P-47D from Jun. 43-Jan. 45.
P-51D (from block 20) and P-51K, in combat from 29 Dec. 44.
Stations
GOXHILL	1 Dec. 42-3 Apr. 43.
DUXFORD	3 Apr. 43-10 Oct. 45.

Group COs
Col Arman Peterson:	May 42-1 Jul. 43, KIA.
Lt Col Melvin F. McNickle:	12 Jul. 43-30 Jul. 43, POW.
Col James J. Stone:	31 Jul. 43-22 May 44.
	(Acting 1-12 Jul. 43).
Col Frederic C. Gray:	22 May 43-1 Feb. 45.
Lt Col Olin E. Gilbert:	1 Feb. 45-21 Feb. 45.
Col John D. Landers:	22 Feb. 45-1 Jul. 45.
Lt Col Roy B. Caviness:	1 Jul. 45-c. Oct. 45.

First Mission: 13 Apr. 43. **Last Mission::** **Total Missions:** 450.
A/c MIA: 167. **E/a Claims:** 338½ air; 358½ ground.
Major Awards
Distinguished Unit Citations: 16-23 Sep. 44, Holland, Action in support airborne forces.
16 Apr. 45. Ground strafing, Czechoslovakia.
Claims to Fame
Produced first 8AF ace—Cpt Charles London.
First 'triple kill' on one mission by VIII FC pilot—Maj Eugene Roberts, 30 Jul. 43.
Only 8AF group to fly all three main US fighter types, P-38, P-47 and P-51.
First strafing attack by P-47 pilot—Lt Q. L. Brown 30 Jul. 43.
Brought down first Me262 jet claimed by 8AF—28 Aug. 44.
Held record for highest claims of e/a while strafing—135 destroyed 16 Apr. 45.
Early History
Activated 9 Feb. 42 at Baer Fd, Ind. Expansion and training at Hamilton Fd, Cal. in May 42 as one of the first groups selected to fly the P-38. High level of experience in this type on departing Hamilton in Nov. 42. Sailed from New York on *Queen Elizabeth* 24 Nov. 42.
Subsequent History
Remained in UK until Oct. 45. Many personnel transferred after VE-day. A/c to depots for disposal Sep. 45. Sailed from Southampton on *Queen Mary* 11 Oct. 45 and arrived New York 16 Nov. 45. Inactivated at Camp Kilmer, NJ, 18 Oct. 45. Activated again 20 Aug. 46 at Straubing, Germany, by a re-numbering of 368 FG, an occupation force P-47 group (9AF, WW 2). By Jun. 47 Group run down and transferred 'less personnel and equipment' to Mitchel Fd, NY. Remained unmanned until Nov. 48 when rebuilt as F-84 unit at Hamilton AFB, Cal. Association with Hamilton continues and as 78FW is part of ADC with operating F-106.

82nd Fighter Group

Assigned Eighth AF: Sep. 42-Dec. 42.
Wing & Command Assignment
VIII FC:	Sep. 42-Oct. 42.

Component Squadrons
95th, 96th & 97th Fighter Squadron.
Combat Aircraft
P-38G.
Stations
EGLINGTON	5 Oct. 42-3 Jan. 43 (Air ech. in 16 Nov. 42. Out 16-29 Dec. 42).
MAYDOWN	6 Oct. 42-c. 16 Dec. 42 (97FS only).

Group CO
Lt Col William E. Covington Jr.
History
Activated 9 Feb. 42 at Harding Fd, La. Commenced overseas movement 16 Sep. 42 arriving in UK early Oct. 42. Trained in Northern Ireland with P-38s and moved to North Africa to join 12AF in Dec. 42. Later assigned 15AF in Italy to fly bomber escort. Established as fighter interceptor wing in ADC during nineteen-fifties.

91st Bombardment Group (H)
"The Ragged Irregulars"

Assigned Eighth AF: Sep. 42.
Wing & Command Assignments
VIII BC, 1 BW:	Sep. 42.
VIII BC, 1 BW, 101 PCBW:	Feb. 43.
VIII BC, 1 BD, 1 CBW:	13 Sep. 43.
1 BD, 1 CBW:	8 Jan. 44.
1 AD, 1 CBW:	1 Jan. 45.

Component Squadrons
322nd, 323rd, 324th and 401st Bombardment Squadron (H).
Combat Aircraft
B-17F (from blocks 10-BO); B-17G.
Stations
KIMBOLTON	12 Sep. 42-13 Oct. 42 (Air ech. arrived 10 Oct. 42 to 17 Oct. 42).
BASSINGBOURN	14 Oct. 42-23 Jun. 45.

Group COs

Col Stanley T. Wray:	15 May 42-1 May 43.
Lt Col William M. Reid:	1 May 43-23 May 43.
Lt Col Baskin R. Lawrence:	23 May 43-25 Jun. 43.
Lt Col Clemens L. Wurzbach:	25 Jun. 43-12 Dec. 43.
Col Claude E. Putnam:	12 Dec. 43-16 May 44.
Col Henry W. Terry:	17 May 44-30 May 45.
Lt Col Donald E. Sheeler:	30 May 45-Jun. 45
	(also acting 15 Nov. 44-30 Dec. 44).

First Mission: 7 Nov. 42. **Last Mission:** 25 Apr. 45. **Total Missions:** 340.
Total Credit Sorties: 9,591. **Total Bomb Tonnage:** 22,142.3 tons.
A/c MIA: 197. **E/a Claims:** 420-127-238.

Major Awards

Two Distinguished Unit Citations: 11 Jan. 44-Oschersleben (to 1st Division).
4 Mar. 43; Hamm.

Claims to Fame

Highest total claims of e/a destroyed of all 8AF bomb groups—420.
Highest loss of all 8AF bomb groups—197 MIA.
First group to attack a target in the Ruhr—4 Mar. 43; Hamm.
Led the famous Schweinfurt mission of 17 Aug. 43.
First 8AF bomb group to complete 100 Missions—5 Jan. 44.
Selected to test first flak suits—Mar. 43.
B-17G "Nine-O-Nine" completed 140 missions without a turn back for mechanical reasons—an 8AF record.

Early History

Activated 15 Apr. 42 at Harding Fd, La. Nucleus commander 1/Lt Edward R. Eckert. Expansion began with first phase training at McDill Fd, Fla. 16 May 42 to 22/25 Jun. 42. Second and third phase training Walla Walla AB, Wash, under 2AF between 26 Jun. 42 and 24 Aug. 42. Ground echelon by train Fort Dix, NJ, and boarded *Queen Mary* 2/5 Sep. 42. Arrived Gourock 11 Sep. 42. Air echelon left Walla Walla 24 Aug. 42 for Gowen Fd, Idaho, where first new B-17s assigned. Air echelon then moved Dow Fd, Me. but not until early Oct. 42 were enough new B-17s available to complete Group's complement. First squadron flew north Atlantic route late Sep. 42.

Subsequent History

Redeployed USA May/Jun. 45. First a/c left 27 May 45. Ground echelon sailed on *Queen Elizabeth* 24 Jun. 45. Disembarked for Camp Kilmer, NJ, 29 Jun. 45. On 2 Jul. 45 Group established at Drew Fd, Fla. Scheduled for Pacific service but never fully manned. Inactivated 7 Nov. 45. Activated again in SAC 1947 as a Strategic Reconnaissance Group, using RB-17 and RB-29. In Jul. 1950 equipped RB-45 and later RB-47. Inactivated in the late 1950's but given further lease of life as a B-52 wing and flew sorties in Vietnam war. In 1968 designation given to Minutemen missile wing at Minot AFB.

92nd Bombardment Group (H)
"Fame's Favoured Few"

Assigned Eighth AF: Aug. 42.
Wing & Command Assignments

VIII BC, 1 BW:	Aug. 42.
VIII BC, 102 PCBW:	May 43.
VIII BC, 1 BD, 40 CBW:	13 Sep. 43.
1 BD, 40 CBW:	8 Jan. 44.
1 AD, 40 CBW:	1 Jan. 45.

Component Squadrons
325th, 326th, 327th and 407th Bombardment Squadron (H).
Combat Aircraft
B-17F (block 1 BO) (Aug. 42); B-17E (Aug. 42-Apr. 43); B-17F (from blocks 55-BO, 15-DL, 25-VE); YB-40 (May 43-Jul. 43); B-17G.
Stations

BOVINGDON	18/28 Aug. 42-4/11 Jan. 43.
ALCONBURY	4/11 Jan. 43-11/15 Sep. 43.
PODINGTON	11/15 Sep. 43-20 May/9 Jul. 45.

Group COs

Lt Col James S. Sutton:	27 Mar. 42-1 May 43.
Lt Col Baskin R. Lawrence:	2 May 43-23 May 43.
Lt Col William M. Reid:	23 May 43-27 Sep. 44
	(WIA 26 Aug. 44).
Lt Col James W. Wilson:	27 Sep. 44-4 Aug. 45.

First Mission: 6 Sep. 43 (4 missions 1942, did not resume ops. until 14 May 43). **Last Mission:** 25 Apr. 45. **Total Missions:** 308.
Total Credit Sorties: 8,633. **Total Bomb Tonnage:** 20,829.4 tons.
A/c MIA: 154. **E/a Claims:** 207-42-89.

Major Awards

Distinguished Unit Citation: 11 Jan. 44 (All 1st BD group).
Medal of Honor: F/O John C. Morgan, 26 Jul. 43: Hanover.

Claims to Fame

Oldest Group in 8AF.
First bomb group to make non-stop Atlantic flight to UK (Aug. 42).
Group's 327BS only unit in USAAF to be equipped with YB-40 for combat.
Flew the secret Disney rocket-bomb experimental missions early in 1945.
Acted as VIII BC Combat Crew Replacement Centre Aug. 42-May 43.
Led 8AF on last mission of war.

Early History

Activated 1 Mar. 42 at Barkesdale Fd, La. Assembled at McDill Fd, Fla. 16 Mar. 42-18 May 42. Trained Sarasota AB, Fla. May-Jul. 42. Air echelon left 19 Jun. 42 for Westover AB, Mass. and moved to Dow AB, Maine on 29 Jun. 42. Between 12/15 Aug. 42 squadrons took off for Newfoundland, then flew direct to Prestwick. Ground echelon left for staging area on 18 Jul. 42 and arrived Fort Dix 20 Jul. 42, sailing *USS West Point* 6 Aug. 42 and docking Liverpool 18 Aug. 42. On same day first a/c (326BS) arrived Bovingdon: last (407BS) on 28 Aug. 42.

Subsequent History

Assigned to Green Project (movement of US troops from Marseilles staging area at Casablanca). Moved to Istres, France, between May and early July 1945, first personnel arriving 3 Jun. 45. 327BS detached to Port Lyautey, French Morocco. Between 15 Jun. 45 and 9 Sep. 45 moved 19,935 troops while 5,672 Frenchmen returned France. Displaced Greeks Munich to Athens. Run down during winter 1945/46 and on 28 Feb. 46 absorbed into 306 BG. Reactivated Fort Worth, Tex. 4 Aug. 46 as B-29 unit (redesignation of 448 BG). Flew missions in Korean War. Converted B-36 1951. As 92 BW became B-52 unit.

93rd Bombardment Group (H)
"The Travelling Circus"

Assigned Eighth AF: 6 Sep. 42.
Wing & Command Assignments

VIII BC, 1 BW:	6 Sep. 42.
VIII BC, 2 BW:	6 Dec. 42.
VIII BC, 2 BW, 201 PCBW:	25 Mar. 43.
VIII BC, 2 BD, 20 CBW:	13 Sep. 43.
2 BD, 20 CBW:	8 Jan. 44.
2 AD, 20 CBW:	1 Jan. 45.

Component Squadrons
328th, 329th, 330th and 409th Bombardment Squadrons (H).
Combat Aircraft
B-24D (from blocks 1); B-24E (few); B-24H, B-24J, B-24L and B-24M.
Stations

ALCONBURY	6 Sep. 42-6 Dec. 42 (Ground ech. in same day as first a/c).
HARDWICK	6 Dec. 42-12 Jun. 45.

(Temporary bases Air echelon in North Africa; Tarfaroui, Algeria, 7 Dec. 42-15 Dec. 42. Gambut Main (LG 139), Lybia 16 Dec. 42-23/25 Feb. 42. Benghazi, No. 7 Lybia, 27 Jun. 43-24 Aug. 43. Oudna No. 2 Tunis, 17 Sep. 43-2 Oct. 43). (329BS based Hardwick 27 Nov. 42-3/10 Dec. 42; Bungay 3 Dec. 42-c. 12 Mar. 43. 330BS based Holmsley South 25 Oct. 42-28 Nov. 42. 409BS based St. Eval 25 Oct. 42-26 Nov. 42).
Group COs

Col Edward J. Timberlake Jr:	26 Mar. 42-17 May 43.
Lt Col Addison E. Baker:	17 May 42-1 Aug. 43. KIA
Col Leland G. Fiegel:	9 Aug. 43-27 Sep. 44.
Lt Col Harvey P. Barnard Jr:	27 Sep. 44-27 Nov. 44.
Col William R. Robertson Jr:	5 Dec. 44-6 Apr. 45.
Lt Col Therman D. Brown:	6 April 45-Jun. 45.

(Lt Col George S. Brown acting 2 Aug. 43-9 Aug. 43. Lt Col Gibson E. Sisco acting 27 Nov. 44-5 Dec. 44).
First Mission: 9 Oct. 42. **Last Mission:** 25 Apr. 45. **Total Missions:** 396 (49 from NA).
Total Credit Sorties: 8,169. **Total Bomb Tonnage:** 19,004 tons.
A/c MIA: 100. **Other Op. Losses:** 40. **E/a Claims:** 93-41-44.

Major Awards

Two Distinguished Unit Citations: 17 Dec. 42-20 Feb. 43: Operations, North Africa.
1 Aug. 43: Ploesti.

Medal of Honour: Lt Col Addison E. Baker: 1 Aug. 43.
Maj John L. Jerstad: 1 Aug. 43 (Assigned 201 PCBW).

Claims to Fame
Oldest B-24 group in 8AF.
Flew more missions than any other 8AF bomb group.
Most travelled group assigned to 8AF.
"Bomerang" was first 8AF B-24 to fly 50 missions.

Early History
Activated 1 Mar. 42 at Barkesdale AAB, La. First phase training at this base. Moved Ft. Myres, Fla. 15 May 42 and continued training while flying anti-sub patrols over Gulf of Mexico. Claimed destruction of 3 U-boats. Left Ft. Myres from 2 Aug. 42 for Ft. Dix, arriving 15 Aug. 42, ground echelon embarking on *Queen Elizabeth* 31 Aug. 42. Disembarked 5 Sep. 42 at Greenock, Scotland. Air echelon moved Grenier Fd, NH. from Ft. Dix and received new B-24D. Made first formation crossings of Atlantic early Sep. 42.

Subsequent History
Redeployed USA May/Jun. 45. First a/c left UK 24 May 45. Ground echelon sailed *Queen Mary* 15 Jun. 45 arriving New York 20 Jun. 45. Personnel to Camp Shanks 20 Jun. 45 then 30 days R & R. Group re-established as B-29 unit in Jul. 45. Converted B-50 1949. Later B-47 and in 1955 with B-52 as 93BW. Only wartime organisation in USAF that has not been inactivated since original formation.

94th Bombardment Group (H)

Assigned Eighth AF: Apr. 43.
Wing & Command Assignments
VIII BC, 4 BW, 401 PCBW: 11 May 43.
VIII BC, 3 BD, 4 CBW: 13 Sep. 43.
3 BD, 4 CBW: 8 Jan. 44.
3 AD, 4 CBW: 1 Jan. 45.
(4 CBW incorporated with 92 CBW in 4 BW(P) from 22 Nov. 44 to 16 Feb. 45).
Component Squadrons
331st, 332nd, 333rd and 410th Bombardment Squadron (H).
Combat Aircraft
B-17F (from blocks 60-BO, 20-DL, 30-VE) and B-17G.
Stations

BASSINGBOURN	Mid Apr. 43-27 May 43.
EARLS COLNE	12 May 43-12/13 Jun. 43 (Air ech. in 27 May 43).
BURY ST EDMUNDS	13 Jun. 43-12 Dec. 45.

Group COs

Col John G. Moore:	15 Jun. 42-22 Jun. 43.
Col Frederick W. Castle:	22 Jun. 43-16 Apr. 44.
Col Charles B. Dougher:	17 Apr. 44-7 Mar. 45.
Col Nicholas T. Perkins:	16 Mar. 45-c. 3 Jun. 45.
Lt Col Ernest B. Maxwell:	3 Jun. 45-late 45.

First Mission: 13 May 43. **Last Mission:** 21 Apr. 45. **Total Missions** 324.
Total Credit Sorties: 8,884. **Total Bomb Tonnage:** 18,924.6 tons (226.2 tons supplies, etc.).
A/c MIA: 153. **Other Op. Losses:** 27. **E/a Claims:** 342-92-154.
Major Awards
Two Distinguished Unit Citations: 17 Aug. 43 (all 4 BW groups: Regensburg).
11 Jan. 44: Brunswick.

Activated 15 Jun. 42 at McDill Fd, Fla. Nucleus established Pendleton Fd, Ore. 29 Jun. 42 and engaged in initial training. Detailed training at Davis-Monthan Fd, Ariz. between 28 Aug. 42 and 31 Oct. 42, and at Biggs Fd, Tex. between 1 Nov. 42 and 2 Jan. 43. Final phase training at Pueblo, Col. Jan. 43 to end Mar. 43. Air echelon began overseas movement c. 1 Apr. 43. Ground echelon left for Camp Kilmer, NJ. 17 Apr. 43 and sailed on *Queen Elizabeth* 5 May 43, arriving Greenock 11 May 43.
Subsequent History
Scheduled for occupational air forces in Germany but plans changed in Sep. 45. Remained in UK during latter part of 1945 flying 'Nickle' Project missions—dropping leaflets over former occupied countries and to displaced persons in Germany. Assigned 1 AD, 8 Aug. 45. In Nov./Dec. 45 a/c flown back to US or transferred other units, and squadrons inactivated. Remaining personnel left Bury St. Edmunds c. 11 Dec. 45 and sailed on *Lake Champlain* 12 Dec. 45, arriving New York 20 Dec. 45. Group inactivated Camp Kilmer 21 Dec. 45.

Allotted to the USAF Reserve and established first as a light bomb group in 1949, and then as a troop carrier organisation with C-119.

95th Bombardment Group (H)

Assigned Eighth AF: April 43.
Wing & Command Assignments
VIII BC, 4 BW, 401 PCBW: 12 May 43.
VIII BC, 4 BW, 402 PCBW: 6 Jun. 43.
VIII BC, 3 BD, 13 CBW: 13 Sep. 43.
3 BD, 13 CBW: 8 Jan. 44.
3 AD, 13 CBW: 1 Jan. 45.
Component Squadrons
334th, 335th, 336th and 412nd Bombardment Squadron (H).
Combat Aircraft
B-17F (from blocks 20-DL, 30-VE, 65-BO); B-17G.
Stations

ALCONBURY	c. 15 April 43-early Jun. 43 (Air ech. only).
FRAMLINGHAM	12 May 43-15 Jun. 43 (Air ech. in prior 11 Jun. 43).
HORHAM	15 Jun. 43-3 Aug. 45.

Group COs

Col Alfred A. Kessler:	23 Oct. 42-22 Jun. 43.
Col John K. Gerhart:	22 Jun. 43-28 Apr. 44.
Col Chester P. Gilger:	29 Apr. 44-9 May 44.
Col Karl Truesdell Jr:	10 May 44-14 Dec. 44.
Col Jack E. Shuck:	15 Dec. 43-27 Apr. 45.
Lt Col Robert H. Stuart:	28 Apr. 45-Jun. 45.

First Mission: 13 May 43. **Last Mission:** 20 Apr. 45. **Total Missions:** 320.*
Total Credit Sorties: 8,903. **Total Bomb Tonnage:** 19,769.2 tons (211.1 tons supplies, etc.).
A/c MIA: 157. **Other Op. Losses:** 39. **E/a Claims:** 425-117-231.

Major Awards
Three Distinguished Unit Citations: 17 Aug. 43: Regensburg (All 4 BW Groups).
10 Oct. 43: Munster.
4 Mar. 44: Berlin.

Claims to Fame
Only 8AF group awarded three DUCs (see above).
First USAAF group to bomb Berlin (4 Mar. 44).
Last a/c lost by 8AF on a mission went down in sea 7 May 45.
First 8AF General KIA lost while flying with this group (13 Jun. 43).

Early History
Activated 15 Jun. 42 at Barkesdale Fd, La. Formation did not commence until late Aug. 42 at Geiger Fd, Wash. Moved Ephrata, Wash. 31 Oct. 43 and back to Geiger Fd, 24 Nov. 43. Final training at Rapid City AAB, SD from 14 Dec. 42 to 11 Mar. 43. Air echelon moved Kearney Fd, Neb. for final processing prior overseas movement. Took southern route via Florida, Trinidad, Brazil, Dakar and Marrakesh to UK, arriving early Apr. 43. Ground echelon arrived Camp Kilmer, 21 Apr. 43 and sailed on *Queen Elizabeth* 5 May 43, arriving Greenock 11 May 43.

Subsequent History
Redeployed USA Jun.-Aug. 45. A/c departed 19 Jun. 45 and arrived Bradley Fd, Conn. 21 Jun. 45 and 26 Jun. 45. Ground echelon sailed on *Queen Elizabeth* from Greenock 5 Aug. 45, arriving 11 Aug. 45. Group established at Sioux Falls AAFd, SD and inactivated there 28 Aug. 45. Activated in nineteen-fifties as heavy bomb group with B-36s. Later converted to B-52. Inactivated in 1967.

*(6 food missions May 45, 456.5 tons).

96th Bombardment Group (H)

Assigned Eighth AF: April 43.
Wing & Command Assignments
VIII BC, 4 BW, 401 PCBW: 12 May 43.
VIII BC, 4 BW, 403 PCBW: c. 23 Jun. 43.
VIII BC, 3 BD, 45 CBW: 13 Sep. 43.
3 BD, 45 CBW: 8 Jan. 44.
3 AD, 45 CBW: 1 Jan. 44.
Component Squadrons
337th, 338th, 339th and 413th Bombardment Squadron (H).
Combat Aircraft
B-17F (from blocks 70-BO, 45-DL, 30-VE); B-17G.

Stations

GRAFTON UNDERWOOD 16 Apr. 43-27 May 43 (Air ech. only).
ANDREWS FIELD   13 May 43-11 Jun. 43 (Air ech. in 27-
                     29 May 43).
SNETTERTON HEATH   12 Jun. 43-c. 11 Dec. 45.

Group COs

Col Archie J. Old Jr: 6 Aug. 42-6 Sep. 43.
Col James L. Travis: 6 Sep. 43-Jun. 44.
Col Robert W. Warren: Jun. 44-27 May 45.
Lt Col Robert J. Nolan: 27 May 45-late 45.

First Mission: 14 May 43. **Last Mission:** 21 Apr. 45. **Total
Missions:** 321.*

Total Credit Sorties: 8,924. **Total Bomb Tonnage:** 19,277.3 tons
(131.6 tons supplies, etc.).

A/c MIA: 189. **Other Op. Losses:** 50. **E/a Claims:** 354½-100-222.

Major Awards

Two Distinguished Unit Citations: 17 Aug. 43: Regensburg (All 4
                                  BW groups).
                                  9 Apr. 44: Poznan.

Claims to Fame

Second highest MIA losses in 8AF, and highest in 3 BD.
Highest loss rate sustained by any 8AF group (first five months
1944).
Led first Shuttle mission Regensburg—Africa, 17 Aug. 43.

Early History

Activated 15 Jul. 42 at Salt Lake City AAB, Utah. Formed at Gowen
Fd, Idaho, where Group established 6 Aug. 42. Moved Walla Walla
AAB, Wash. 14 Aug. 42 and to Rapid City AAB, SD, 30 Sep. 42.
Acted as operational training unit at Pocatello AAB, Idaho, where
Group moved 30 Oct. 42. Reverted to training for combat when moved
to Pyote AAB, Tex. 3 Jan. 43. Air echelon began overseas movement
4 Apr. 43, taking northern ferry route via Presque Isle, Newfoundland,
Iceland to Prestwick. Ground echelon left Pyote 16 Apr. 43 for Camp
Kilmer, NJ. and sailed on *Queen Elizabeth* 5 May 43, arriving Greenock
11 May 43.

Subsequent History

Scheduled for occupational duties in Germany but plans revised in
Sep. 45. During latter part 1945 flew training and transporation flights
over Europe. Assigned 1 AD, 12 Aug. 45 but reassigned 3 AD 28 Sep.
45. A/c flown back to US or transferred continental units Nov. 45.
Squadrons inactivated and remaining personnel left Snetterton early
Dec. 45, sailing on *Lake Champlain* 12 Dec. 45. Arrived New York
20 Dec. 45 and Group inactivated at Camp Kilmer, NJ. 21 Dec. 45.
Activated as a B-47 wing in nineteen-fifties. Later as a B-52 wing at
Dyess AFB, Tex.

*(5 food missions May 45, 366.1 tons).

97th Bombardment Group (H)

Assigned Eighth AF: 20 May 42.
Wing & Command Assignments
VIII BC: 20 May 42.
VIII BC, 1 BW: Aug. 42.

Component Squadrons

340th, 341st, 342nd and 414th Bombardment Squadron (H).

Combat Aircraft

B-17E: 17 Aug. 42-29 Aug. 42.
B17-F (from blocks 1) in combat from 5 Sep. 42.

Stations

POLEBROOK   13 Jun. 42-25 Nov. 42 (Hq. 340 and 341 BS
                     only until 8 Sep. 42) (Air ech. in 6-27
                     Jul. 42).
GRAFTON UNDERWOOD   6 Jul. 42-8 Sep. 42 (342 and 414BS
                     to Polebrook 8 Sep. 42).

Group COs

Col Cornelius W. Cousland: 3 Feb. 43-c. 29 Jul. 42.
Col Frank A. Armstrong Jr: 31 Jul 42-27 Sep. 42.
Col Joseph H. Atkinson: 27 Sep. 42-5 Jan. 43.
(Col Frank H. Walsh acting CO 29 Jul. 42-31 Jul. 42).

First Mission: 17 Aug. 42. **Last Mission:** 21 Oct. 42. **Total
Missions:** 14.

Total Credit Sorties: 247. **Total Bomb Tonnage:** 395.1 tons.

A/c MIA: 4. **E/a Claims:** 16-3-9.

Major Awards

None.

Claims to Fame

Flew 8AF's first heavy bomber mission from UK—17 Aug. 42.

Early History

Activated 3 Feb. 42 at MacDill Fd, Fla. formed and trained there until
end Mar. 42. Moved Sarasota AAB, Fla. for intensive training. Commenced overseas movement 15 May 42, with air echelon 340 and
341BSs flying to Dow Fd, Me. and those of 342 and 414BSs to Grenier
Fd. NH. Elements detached to Pacific coast bases 2-11 Jun. 42. First
B-17s left for UK 23 Jun. 42, flying by northern ferry route, Goose Bay,
Greenland, to Prestwick. First B-17 arrived UK 1 Jul. 42. Ground
echelon sailed on *Queen Elizabeth* 4 Jun. 42 arriving Clyde 10 Jun. 42.

Subsequent History

Assigned 12AF, XII BC, 14 Sep. 42, but continued to operate under
VIII BC. Main part air echelon left Polebrook 18-20 Nov. 42 for Hurn,
prior to flying direct to North Africa. Ground echelon sailed in convoy
late Nov. 42. Operated in Mediterranean theatre with 12AF for a year,
then established in Italy as part 15AF. Flew first shuttle mission to
Russia from Italy. Attacked targets chiefly in southern Germany and
Balkans.
Established as B-29 group in USA, 1946. Served as SAC wing for
over twenty years flying B-47s, and later B-52s.

100th Bombardment Group (H)
"The Bloody Hundredth"

Assigned Eighth AF: Jun. 43.
Wing & Command Assignments
VIII BC, 4 BW, 402 PCBW: 6 Jun. 43.
VIII BC, 3 BD, 13 CBW: 13 Sep. 43.
3 BD, 13 CBW: 8 Jan. 44.
3 AD, 13 CBW: 1 Jan. 45.

Component Squadrons

349th, 350th, 351st and 418th Bombardment Squadron (H).

Combat Aircraft

B-17F (from blocks 80-BO, 40-DL); B-17G.

Stations

PODINGTON   2 Jun. 43-8 Jun. 43 (Ground ech. in 3 Jun.
                    43).
THORPE ABBOTS   9 Jun. 43-c. 11 Dec. 45.

Group COs

Col Howard M. Turner: c. 28 Apr. 43-Jun. 43.
Col Harold Q. Huglin: Jun. 43-c. 1 Jul. 43.
Col Neil B. Harding: 2 Jul. 43-28 Mar. 44.
Col Robert H. Kelly: 19 Apr. 44-28 Apr. 44, MIA.
Col Thomas S. Jeffrey: 9 May 44-1 Feb. 45.
Col Frederick J. Sutterlin: 2 Feb. 45-23 Jun. 45.
Lt Col John B. Wallace: 23 Jun. 45-late 45.
(Lt Col John M. Bennett Jr acting CO 28 Mar. 44-18 Apr. 44 and
28 Apr. 44-9 May 44).

First Mission: 25 Jun. 43. **Last Mission:** 20 Apr. 45. **Total
Missions:** 306.*

Total Credit Sorties: 8,630. **Total Bomb Tonnage:** 19,257.1 tons
(137.8 tons supplies, etc.).

A/c MIA: 177. **Other Op. Losses:** 52. **E/a Claims:** 261-101-139.

Major Awards

Two Distinguished Unit Citations: 17 Aug. 43: Regensburg (All 4
                                  BW groups).
                                  4/6/8 Mar. 44: Berlin.

Claims to Fame

Spectacular heavy loss at intervals throughout period of combat.

Early History

Activated 1 Jun. 42 at Orlando AB, Fla. Originally scheduled to be
B-24 group. Formation did not commence until late Oct. 42 at Gowan
Fd, Idaho, thereafter Group was transferred to Walla Walla AAB,
Wash. c. 1 Nov. 42 and received first B-17s for training. Moved to
Wendover Fd, Utah, 30 Nov. 42 and to Sioux City AAB, Iowa, 28
Dec. 42. At end Jan. 43 moved again, to Kearney AAFd, Neb. Ground
echelon left Kearney for port of embarkation 2 May 43 and sailed on
Queen Elizabeth 27 May 43, arriving Greenock 3 Jun. 43. Air echelon
left Kearney 1 May 43 for advanced training and processing at Wend-
over Fd, Utah, before taking northern ferry route to UK c. 21 May 43.

Subsequent History

Scheduled for occupational duties in Germany, but plans revised
Sep. 45. Assigned to 1AD, 12 Aug. 45 but reassigned 3 AD 28 Sep. 45.
A/c flown to US or transferred continental units Oct.-Dec. 45, and
squadrons inactivated. Remaining personnel sailed *Lake Champlain*
12 Dec. 45 and arrived 20 Dec. 45 New York. Group inactivated at
Camp Kilmer, NJ. 21 Dec. 45.

Activated as B-47 wing in nineteen-fifties. Designation later given to a strategic recon. wing with U-2 at Davis Monthan AFB, Ariz.
*(6 food missions May 45, 435.1 tons).

301st Bombardment Group (H)

Assigned Eighth AF: 9 Aug. 42.
Wing & Command Assignments
VIII BC:	9 Aug. 42.
VIII BC, 1 BW:	Aug. 42.

Component Squadrons
32nd, 352nd, 353rd and 419th Bombardment Squadron (H).
Combat Aircraft
B-17F (from blocks 1).
Stations
CHELVESTON	9 Aug. 42-8 Dec. 42 (Air ech. in 9-26 Aug. out 23 Aug. 42).
	(Ground ech. in 18 Aug. 42).
PODINGTON	18 Aug. 42-2 Sep. 42 (352BS Gnd. ech. Satellite field).

Group CO
Col Ronald R. Walker:	3 Feb. 42-29 Mar. 43.

First Mission: 5 Sep. 42. **Last Mission:** 8 Nov. 42. **Total Missions:** 8.
Total Credit Sorties: 104. **Total Bomb Tonnage:** 185.8.
A/c MIA: 1. **E/a Claims:** 3-5-1.
Major Awards
None.
Early History
Activated 3 Feb. 42 at Geiger Fd, Wash. Equipped with B-17s and moved Alamogordo AAB, NM, 27 May 42. Air echelon went to Muroc and did not reach Alamogordo until mid-Jun. 42. Ground echelon moved Richmond, Va. at this date and on 19 Jul. 42 left for Fort Dix, NJ. at the start of overseas movement. Air echelon to Brainard Fd, Conn. 23-30 Jun. 42 and then moved Westover Fd, Mass. First a/c departed for UK on 23 Jul. 42 flying northern ferry route. Last left Westover 3 Aug. 42.
Subsequent History
Assigned 12AF, XII BC 14 Sep. 42 but continued to operate under VIII BC. A/c left for south-west coast bases 20-23 Nov. 42 and flew direct to North Africa. Ground echelon left Chelveston 8 Dec. 42 and sailed in convoy from Liverpool. Group operated with 12AF in Mediterranean theatre and later with 15AF from Italy. Flew strategic bombing missions over southern Germany and the Balkans. Established as B-29 group in USA 1946. Later as B-47 wing and when this type withdrawn became KC-135 tanker wing.

303rd Bombardment Group (H)
"Hell's Angels"

Assigned Eighth AF: 10 Sep. 42.
Wing & Command Assignments
VIII BC, 1 BW:	10 Sep. 42.
VIII BC, 1 BW, 102 PCBW:	Feb. 43.
VIII BC, 1 BW, 103 PCBW:	May 43.
VIII BC, 1 BD, 41 CBW:	13 Sep. 43.
1 BD, 40 CBW:	8 Jan. 44.
1 AD, 40 CBW:	1 Jan. 45.

Component Squadrons
358th, 359th, 360th and 427th Bombardment Squadron (H).
Combat Aircraft
B-17F (from blocks 25-BO); B-17G.
Station
MOLESWORTH	12 Sep. 42-11 Jun. 45 (Air ech. in 21-27 Oct. 42).

Group COs
Col James H. Wallace:	13 Jul. 42-12 Feb. 43.
Col Charles E. Marion:	13 Feb. 43-19 Jul. 43.
Col Kermit D. Stevens:	19 Jul. 43-1 Sep. 44.
Col William S. Raper:	29 Oct. 44-19 Apr. 45.
Lt Col William C. Sipes:	19 Apr. 45-11 Jun. 45.

(Lt Col Lewis E. Lyle and Lt Col Richard H. Cole, acting COs 1 Sep. 44-29 Oct. 44).
First Mission: 17 Nov. 42. **Last Mission:** 25 Apr. 45. **Total Missions:** 364.
Total Credit Sorties: 10,721. **Total Bomb Tonnage:** 24,918.1 tons (176.3 tons leaflets).

A/c MIA: 165. **E/a Claims:** 379-92-174.
Major Awards
Distinguished Unit Citation for 11 Jan. 44 (All 1 BD groups).
Medal of Honor: Lt Jack W. Mathis, 18 Mar. 43.
T/Sgt Forrest L. Vosler, 20 Dec. 43.
Claims to Fame
"Hell's Angels" first B-17 in 8AF to complete 25 missions (Jun. 43).
"Knock Out Dropper" first B-17 in 8AF to complete 50 and 75 missions.
First 8AF bomb group to complete 300 missions from UK.
Flew more missions than any other 8AF B-17 group.
Only one other group delivered a greater bomb tonnage.
Early History
Activated 3 Feb. 42 at Pendleton Fd, Oregon. Assembled at Gowan Fd, Idaho, 11 Feb. 42 where it trained until 12 Jun. 42. Advanced training at Alamogordo Fd, NM. until 7 Aug, 42, when Group moved to Biggs Fd, Texas, to be readied for overseas duty. Ground echelon moved fort Dix, NJ. on 24 Aug. 42. Sailed on *Queen Mary* 5 Sep. 42, arriving Greenock 10 Sep. 42. Air echelon flew to Kellogg Fd, Mich. then Dow Fd, Maine to start its flight to the UK.
Subsequent History
Scheduled to transport US troops from Europe to North Africa. Moved Casablanca end May 45 to join North African Division, Air Transport Command. Group's participation not required and Group inactivated 25 Jul. 45 at Casablanca. A/c flown back to US.
Activated in 1951 as SAC B-29 unit and later as 303rd BW flew B-47 until inactivated in early nineteen-sixties.

305th Bombardment Group (H)
"Can Do"

Assigned Eighth AF: Sep. 42.
Wing & Command Assignments
VIII BC, 1 BW:	Sep. 42.
VIII BC, 1 BW, 102 PCBW:	Feb. 43.
VIII BC, 1 BD, 40 CBW:	13 Sep. 43.
1 BD, 40 CBW:	8 Jan. 44.
1 AD, 40 CBW:	1 Jan. 45.

Component Squadrons
364th, 365th 366th and 422nd Bombardment Squadrons (H).
Combat Aircraft
B-17F (from blocks 25-BO); B-17G.
Stations
GRAFTON UNDERWOOD	12 Sep. 42-11 Dec. 42 (Air ech. in by 27 Oct. 42).
CHELVESTON	6-11 Dec. 42-20-25 Jul. 45.

Group COs
Col Curtis E. LeMay:	4 Jun. 42-15 May 43.
Lt Col Donald K. Fargo:	18 May 43-late Oct. 43.
Col Ernest H. Lawson:	Nov. 43-18 Jun. 44, KIA.
Col Anthony Q. Mustoe:	22 Jun. 44-22 Oct. 44.
Col Henry G. MacDonald:	23 Oct. 44-22 Apr. 46.

First Mission: 17 Nov. 42. **Last Mission:** 25 Apr. 45. **Total Missions:** 337.
Total Credit Sorties: 9,231. **Total Bomb Tonnage:** 223,62.5 tons (73 tons leaflets).
A/x MIA: 154. **E/a Claims:** 332-97-185.
*(422BS dropped 68 tons bombs in 8 night missions during Sep./Oct. 43).
Major Awards
Two Distinguished Unit Citations: 11 Jan. 44 (All 1 BD groups).
4 Apr. 43: Paris.
Two Medals of Honour: 1/Lt William R. Lawley Jr: 20 Feb. 44.
1/Lt Edward S. Michael: 11 Apr. 44.
Claims to Fame
Under Col LeMay the Group pioneered many formation and bombing procedures that became SOP in 8AF.
422BS undertook first night attacks by 8AF.
Suffered heaviest loss of 14 Oct. 43 Schweinfurt mission, and for this reason given Nazi flag found flying in that city when captured by US troops.
Early History
Activated 1 Mar. 42 at Salt Lake City AB, Utah. Training at this base and from 11 Jun. 42, at Geiger Fd, Wash. Intensive training at Muroc Lake AB, Cal. from 29 Jun. to 20 Aug. 42. Ground echelon by train to Fort Dix, NJ. Sailed on *Queen Mary* 5 Sep. 42 and disembarked Greenock on 12 Sep. 42. Air echelon assembled at Syracuse, NY. and

spent six weeks in advanced flight training. Received new B-17F and left for UK Oct. 42, via Presque Isle, and Gander to Prestwick.

Subsequent History

Between 20-27 Jul. 45 Group moved St. Trond, Belgium, where it conducted photo-mapping flights (Project "Casey Jones") over Europe and North Africa. On 15 Dec. 45 moved to Lechfeld, Germany (which it had bombed 18 Mar. 44) to continue photographic work. Gradually run down during 1946, with inactivation of 364BS on 1 Jul. 46. 423BS of 306BG attached to Group after this date but by end of Oct. 46 Group had ceased all operations. Officially inactivated 25 Dec. 46. On the Continent came under 9AF and on 15 Nov. 45 under USAFE.

Activated in 1951 as SAC B-29 unit and as 305BW converted to B-47s in 1953. Later became one of USAF's two B-58 units.

306th Bombardment Group (H)

Assigned Eighth AF: Sep. 42.

Wing & Command Assignments

VIII BC, 1 BW:	Sep. 42.
VIII BC, 1 BW, 101 PCBW:	Feb. 43.
VIII BC, 1 BW, 102 PCBW:	Jun. 43.
VIII BC, 1 BD, 40 CBW:	13 Sep. 43.
1 BD, 40 CBW:	8 Jan. 44.
1 AD, 40 CBW:	1 Jan. 45.

Component Squadrons

367th, 368th, 369th and 423rd Bombatdment Squadron (H).

Combat Aircraft

B-17F (from blocks 10-BO); B-17G.

Station

THURLEIGH	7 Sep. 42-1-15 Dec. 45 (Air ech. arrived 8-13 Sep. 42).

Group COs

Col Charles B. Overacker:	16 Mar. 42-3 Jan. 43.
Col Frank A. Armstrong Jr:	4 Jan. 43-17 Feb. 43.
Col Claude E. Putnam:	17 Feb. 43-20 Jun. 43.
Col George L. Robinson:	20 Jun. 43-23 Sep. 44.
Col James S. Sutton:	23 Sep. 44-16 Apr. 45.
Col Hudson H. Upham:	16 Apr. 45-May 46.

First Mission: 9 Oct. 42. **Last Mission:** 19 Apr. 45. **Total Missions:** 342.

Total Credit Sorties: 9,614. **Total Bomb Tonnage:** 22,574.6 tons (248.9 tons leaflets).

A/c MIA: 171. **E/a Claims:** 332-97-185.

Major Awards

Two Distinguished Unit Citations:	11 Jan. 44 (All 1 BD group).
	22 Feb. 44: Bernburg.

Medal of Honor: Sgt. Maynard H. Smith: 1 May 43.

Claims to Fame

Oldest operational bomb group in 8AF.

Stationed in England, and at one base, longer than any other group.

First man in VIII BC to complete a tour (T/Sgt M. Roscovich: 5 Apr. 43).

367BS had heaviest losses in VIII BC between Oct. 42 and Aug. 43.

369BS flew for over six months in 1943 without loss.

Princess Elizabeth 'named' "Rose of York" at Thurleigh.

Early History

Activated 1 Mar. 42 at Salt Lake City AB, Utah. Personnel moved Wendover AB, Utah, 6 Apr. 42 and began flying training. Left Wendover 1 Aug. 42 to begin movement to UK. Ground echelon first moved Richmond AAB, Va. remained a week, leaving for Fort Dix, NJ. 13 Aug. 42. Sailed *Queen Elizabeth* 30 Aug. 42 arriving 5 Sep. 42 at Greenock, Scotland. Air echelon flew from Wendover to Westover Fd, Mass. 2 Aug. 42. Departed for UK, 1 Sep. 42 via Gander-Prestwick ferry route.

Subsequent History

Selected for duty with occupational air forces in Germany. Engaged in "Casey Jones" mapping photography project. Moved Giebelstadt, Germany, 1 Dec. 45 and on 28 Feb. 46 to Istres, France, where it absorbed remnants of 92 and 384BGs. In Aug. 46, re-established in Germany at Furstenfeldbruck and in Sep. 46 located at Lechfeld. Inactivated 25 Dec. 46, although the group had virtually ceased to exist as flying unit in the late summer of that year.

Activated again as SAC B-29 group 1948, and in 1952 became USAF's first B-47 jet bomber wing. When B-47 withdrawn designation given to B-52 wing, which flew sorties in Vietnam war.

315th Troop Carrier Group

Assigned Eighth AF: 1 Dec. 42-16 Oct. 43.

Wing & Command Assignment

VIII ASC:	1 Dec. 42.

Component Squadrons

34th and 43rd Troop Carrier Squadron.

Combat Aircraft

C-47-DL and C-53.

Station

ALDERMASTON	1 Dec. 42-6 Nov. 43 (Air ech. in 12 Dec. 42).

Group CO

Lt Col Howard B. Lyon:	27 Sep. 42-9 Jan. 45.

History

Activated 14 Feb. 42 at Olmsted Fd, Pa. Two other squadrons assigned but transferred in 1942. Trained Bowman Fd, Ky. and Florence Fd, SC. Sailed on *Queen Elizabeth* 24 Nov. 42 arriving Clyde 30 Nov. 42. Air echelon departed Florence from 11 Oct. 42 and flew to Presque Isle, via Kellogg Fd, and Battle Creek AAB. Commenced flight to UK via northern ferry route but on reaching Bluie West 1, Greenland, weather conditions were so bad that a month elapsed before a/c could continue journey. Left 8 Dec. 42 for Iceland, and arrived UK 12 Dec. 42. While principal mission was the conveyance of airborne troops the two squadrons were employed chiefly as a transport organisation around the UK during Group's assignment to 8AF. Attrition and pressure on troop carrier groups in North African theatre during spring of 1943 saw a detachment of 315TCG despatched to Blida, Algeria in May 43 to carry out routine transport duties for 12AF. This was Dt 'A' consisting of 200 personnel and 16 aircraft. Six a/c remaining in UK continued transport duties until Group assigned to 9AF in Oct. 43. Two new squadrons assigned and Group returned to troop carrier mission. Moved France Apr. 45. Inactivated Trinidad Jul. 45.

Activated during Korean war and served on airlift duties in the far east flying C-46. Later involved in Vietnam war flying C-123s and redesignated as special operations wing.

322nd Bombardment Group (M)

Assigned Eighth AF: 12 Dec. 42-16 Oct. 43.

Wing & Command Assignments

VIII BC, 3 BW:	Dec. 42.
VIII ASC, 3 BW:	12 Jun. 43.

Component Squadrons

449th, 450th, 451st and 452nd Bombardment Squadrons (M).

Combat Aircraft

B-26B (from blocks 4) 450 and 452BS: (from blocks 10 and 15, 449 and 451BS).

B-26C (from blocks 5).

Stations

BURY ST EDMUNDS	1 Dec. 42-12 Jun. 43 (Air ech. in from 7 Mar. 43).
RATTLESDEN	Dec. 42-Apr. 43 (451 and 452BS Gnd. ech. only).
ANDREWS FIELD	12 Jun. 43-19 Sep. 44.

Group COs

Lt Col Robert M. Stillman:	17 Mar. 43-17 May 43, WIA-POW.
Lt Col Glenn C. Nye:	19 May 43-31 Jul. 44.

(Lt Col Nye also acting CO c. Mar 43-20 Apr. 43 prior Stillman's arrival. Lt Col Cecil C. McFarland acting CO 17 May 43-19 May 43).

First Mission: 14 May 43. **Last Mission:** 8 Oct. 43. **Total Missions:** 34.

A/c MIA: 12. **E/a Claims:** 6 destroyed.

Major Awards

Distinguished Unit Citation:	14 May 43-24 Jul. 44: Operations during this period.

Claims to Fame

Flew first B-26 mission from UK—14 May 43.

Flew the disastrous low-level mission of 17 May 43.

Early History

Activated 19 Jun. 42 at MacDill Fd, Fla. Trained there with B-26 a/c. Moved Drane Fd, Fla. late Sep. 42. Ground echelon at port of embarkation 23 Nov. 42 and sailed *Queen Elizabeth* 24 Nov. 42 arriving Greenock 30 Nov. 42. Air echelon moved to UK via southern ferry route as new a/c available, first squadron (450BS) departing final processing base, Morrison Fd, on 6 Feb. 42, and arriving Bury St. Edmunds 7-9 Mar. 43. 452BS departed Mar. 43, 45:BS in Apr. 43 and 449BS in Apr. 43, with last a/c arriving Bury St. Edmunds 29 May 43. Col Robert R. Selway was CO 21 Oct. 42-22 Feb. 43 followed by Lt Col John F. Batjer to 17 Mar. 43 but both men remained with air echelon in US. B-26B-2 and -3 used by 450 and 452BS for training in UK.

Subsequent History

Assigned 9AF, IX BC 16 Oct. 43. Moved France Sep. 44 and to Germany after cessation of hostilities. Returned USA Dec. 45 and inactivated. Activated again as TAC fighter unit in 1954 first with F86 and later F-100 but only in existence for a few years.

323rd Bombardment Group (M)

Assigned Eighth AF: 12 May 43-16 Oct. 43.
Wing & Command Assignments
VIII BC, 3 BW: May 43.
VIII ASC, 3 BW: 15 Jun. 43.
Component Squadrons
453rd, 454th, 455th and 456th Bombardment Squadron (M).
Combat Aircraft
B-26B (from block 20) and B-26C (majority original a/c) (from blocks 6).
Stations
HORHAM   21 May 43-14 Jun. 43 (first air ech. in 27-31 May 43).
EARLS COLNE   14 Jun. 43-11-27 Jul. 44 (last air ech. in 25 Jun. 43).
Group CO
Col Herbert B. Thatcher: 14 Aug. 42-c. 13 Nov. 43.
First Mission: 16 Jul. 43. **Last Mission:** 9 Oct. 43. **Total Missions:** 33.
A/c MIA: 3. **E/a Claims:** 3 destroyed.
Major Awards
None.
Claims to Fame
Flew first 8AF medium level bombing missions with B-26.
Early History
Activated 4 Aug. 42 at Columbia AAB, SC. First phase training commenced MacDill Fd, Fla. 21 Aug. 42. Trained with B-26s a/c. Moved Myrtle Beach Fd, SC. 1-3 Nov. 42. First of air echelon departed for Baer Fd, Ind. in mid-Feb. 43 where new B-26C assigned as available. 453, 454 and 455BS moved to Hunter Fd, Ga. in preparation for flight to UK via southern ferry route. Left early May 43. 456BS by northern ferry route, Jun. 43. Ground echelon left Myrtle Beach 25 Apr. 43 and sailed on *Queen Elizabeth* on 5 May 43, arriving Gourock 11 May 43.
Subsequent History
Assigned 9AF, IX BC, 16 Oct. 43. Moved Beaulieu Jul. 44 and to France late Aug. 44. Flew tactical missions in support Allied ground forces. Inactivated USA Dec. 45. Short period of life as F-100 tactical fighter wing in late nineteen-fifties.

339th Fighter Group

Assigned Eighth AF: 4 April 44.
Wing & Command Assignments
VIII FC, 66 FW: 4 Apr. 44.
3 BD, 66 FW: 15 Sep. 44.
3 AD, 66 FW: 1 Jan. 45.
Component Squadrons
503rd, 504th and 505th Fighter Squadron.
Combat Aircraft
P-51B (from blocks 10-NA), P-51C (from block 1-NT), P-51D and P-51K.
Station
FOWLMERE   5 Apr. 44-c. 10 Oct. 45.
Group COs
Col John B. Henry Jr: 17 Aug. 43-13 Apr. 45.
Lt Col William C. Clark: 14 Apr. 45-unkn.
(Lt Col Harold W. Scruggs acting 1 Oct. 44-24 Dec. 44, and Lt Col Carl T. Goldenberg acting 24-28 Dec. 44).

First Mission: 30 Apr. 44. **Last Mission:** 21 Apr. 45. **Total Missions:** 264.
A/c MIA: 97. **E/a Claims:** $239\frac{1}{2}$ air; $440\frac{1}{2}$ ground.
Major Awards
Distinguished Unit Citation: 10-11 Sep. 44: destruction 58 e/a on escort missions.
Claims to Fame
Highest claims of air and ground e/a victories in one year.
Tested the Berger G-suit for 8AF.
Only group to claim over a hundred ground strafing victories on two occasions—105 on 4 Apr. 45 and 118 on 11 Apr. 45.
Early History
Activated as 339BG at Hunter Fd, Ga. on 10 Aug. 42, with 482, 483, 484 and 485BSs. Established Drew Fd, Fla. in Feb. 43 and commenced training with A-24 and A-25 dive-bombers. With abandonment of dive-bomber role Group moved Walterboro AAFd, SC. 4 Jul. 43 and re-equipped P-39. Re-designated as FBG on 15 Aug. 43 and sqdns. renumbered. Moved Rice Fd, Cal. on 16 Sep. 43 and continued training. Commenced overseas movement 9 Mar. 44, arriving Camp Shanks, NY. 14 Mar. 44 and sailing on *Stirling Castle*, 22 Mar. 44 arriving Liverpool 4 Apr. 44. First P-51s arrived 12 Apr. 45—many pilots no P-51 experience.
Subsequent History
Returned to USA Oct. 45. A/c to depots for disposal in Aug./Sep. 45. Many personnel transferred. Remainder sailed on *Queen Mary*, 11 Oct. 45, arriving New York 16 Oct. 45. Group established at Camp Kilmer, NJ. and inactivated there 18 Oct. 45.
In 1946 redesignated 107FG and allotted to New York ANG. Later in tactical fighter role with F-100C.

350th Fighter Group

Assigned Eighth AF: 1 Oct. 42.
Wing & Command Assignment
VIII FC: 1 Oct. 42-Dec. 42.
Component Squadrons
345th, 346th and 347th Fighter Squadron.
Combat Aircraft
P-400 Airacobra and Spitfire V.
Stations
BUSHEY HALL   1 Oct. 42-c. 15 Oct. 42.
DUXFORD   c. 15 Oct. 42-Jan. 43.
SNAILWELL   16 Oct. 42-8 Dec. 42 347FS only (satellite).
(347FS to Kings Cliffe Dec. 42. 346FS to Coltishall late Nov. 42-3 Jun. 43).
Group CO
Lt Col Richard P. Klacko: 14 Oct. 42-23 Feb. 43.
History
Activated 1 Oct. 42 at Bushey Hall as tactical fighter organisation to employ Airacobras in ground attack. Destined from outset for 12AF. Hq. 345 and 346FS established Duxford and 347FS at satellite base Snailwell. Squadrons later moved to other stations for training. Flew a/c to North Africa in Jan. 43 and commenced operations with 12AF. Redesignated 112 FG in 1946 and allotted to Pa ANG.

351st Bombardment Group (H)

Assigned Eighth AF: April 43.
Wing & Command Assignments
VIII BC, 1 BW, 101 PCBW: May 43.
VIII BC, 1 BD, 1 CBW: 13 Sep. 43.
VIII BC, 1 BD, 92 CBW: 1 Nov. 43.
VIII BC, 1 BD, 94 CBW: 15 Dec. 43.
1 BD, 94 CBW: 8 Jan. 44.
1 AD, 94 CWB: 1 Jan. 45.
Component Squadrons
508th, 509th, 510th and 511th Bombardment Squadron (H).
Combat Aircraft
B-17F (from blocks 75-BO, 25-DL and VE); B-17G.
Station
POLEBROOK   15 April 43-23 Jun. 45 (Air ech. from 15 April 43. Ground ech. in c. 12 May 43).

Group COs

Col William A. Hatcher Jr: Nov. 42-Dec. 43, MIA.
Col Eugene A. Romig: 1 Jan. 44-Oct. 44.
Col Robert W. Burns: Oct. 44-30 Mar. 45.
Col Merlin I. Carter: 30 Mar. 45-Jun. 45.

First Mission: 14 May 43. **Last Mission:** 25 Apr. 45. **Total Missions:** 311.

Total Credit Sorties: 8,600. **Total Bomb Tonnage:** 20,357 (43 tons leaflets).

A/c MIA: 124. **E/a Claims:** 303-49-177.

Major Awards

Two Distinguished Unit Citations: 9 Oct. 43: Anklam.
                               11 Jan. 44 (All 1st BD groups).

Claims to Fame

509BS made 54 consecutive missions Jun. 43-Jan. 44 without loss.
"Ball Boys" squadron (511BS) was part of Group.
Clark Gable flew missions with this group.

Early History

Activated 1 Oct. 42 at Salt Lake City AB, Utah. Established at Geiger Fd, Wash. in Nov. 42 where Group was assembled for initial training. Second phase training at Biggs Fd, Tex. between Dec. 42 and Mar. 43. Pueblo AAB. Col. for preparation for overseas movement. Ground echelon left Pueblo for New York c. 12 Apr. 43. Air echelon began movement c. 1 Apr. 43.

Subsequent History

Redeployed USA May/Jun. 45. First a/c left 21 May 45. Ground echelon sailed for US on 25 Jun. 45 aboard *Queen Elizabeth*. Docked 30 Jun. 43. Personnel 30 days R & R. Assembled Sioux Falls AAFd, SD. Jul. 45 but Group inactivated 28 Aug. 45. Activated as a Minuteman missile wing in 1963 and established at Whiteman AFB, Mo.

352nd Fighter Group

Assigned Eighth AF: 6 Jul. 43.
Wing & Command Assignments

VIII FC: 6 Jul. 43.
VIII FC, 67 FW: 6 Oct. 43.
1 BD, 67 FW: 15 Sep. 44.
 9 AF, IX TAC: 23 Dec. 44 (Temp. assignment air ech. for op. control).
VIII FC: 1 Feb. 45.
1 AD, 67 FW: 13 Apr. 45.

Component Squadrons

328th, 486th and 487th Fighter Squadron.

Combat Aircraft

P-47D (blocks 5 to 16), c. 13 Jul. 43-20 Apr. 44.
P-51B (from blocks 5) in combat from 8 Apr. 44, P-51C, P-51D and P-51K.

Stations

BODNEY   *8 Jul. 43-7 Feb. 45 (Air ech. left 23 Dec. 44).
ASCHE   23 Dec. 44-27 Jan. 45 (Air ech. only).
CHIEVRES   27 Jan. 45-13 Apr. 45 (Gnd. ech. in c. 9 Feb. 45).
BODNEY   13 Apr. 45-3 Nov. 45.

*(Some personnel quartered temporarily at Watton due to insufficient accommodation at Bodney).

Group COs

Col Joseph L. Mason: 18 May 43-15 Nov. 44.
Col James D. Mayden: 16 Nov. 44-Sep. 45.
Lt Col William T. Halton: Sep. 45-Nov. 45.
Col Mayden acting CO 24 Jul. 44-c. 1 Sep. 44).

First Mission: 9 Sep. 43. **Last Mission:** 3 May 45. **Total Missions:** 420.

A/c MIA: 118. **E/a Claims:** 519½ air; 287 ground.

Major Awards

Two Distinguished Unit Citations: 8 May 44: Brunswick escort.
                          1 Jan. 45, 487FS only: destruction 23 e/a.

Claims to Fame

George Preddy, highest scoring Mustang ace in 8AF.
487FS only 8AF squadron to be independently awarded a DUC.
Destroyed 38 e/a in 2 Nov. 44 battle, second highest record for single day's kill.

Early History

Activated 1 Oct. 43 at Mitchel Fd, NY. Actual formation at Bradley Fd, Conn. in Oct. 42, with 486 and 487FS being redesignations of 21 and 34FS (famous for early SEA actions). Early training at Westover Fd, Mass. and Trumbull Fd, Conn. On 9 Mar. 43 moved to Farmingdale AAFd, NY. and commenced training on P-47 a/c. Moved Westover Fd, 24 May 43, and. operated there until 16 Jun. 43 when overseas movement began with move to Camp Kilmer, NJ. Sailed on *Queen Elizabeth* 1 Jul. 43 and arrived Clyde 6 Jul. 43.

Subsequent History

Many personnel transferred for early return to US after VE-day. A/c to depots Aug. 45. Remaining personnel returned USA Nov. 45, sailing *Queen Mary* 4 Nov. 45 and arriving New York 9 Nov. 45. Group established Camp Kilmer, NJ. and inactivated 10 Nov. 45.

Redesignated 113FG and allotted to DC ANG in 1946, and activated as air defence organisation. Equipped various fighter a/c. Later as 113TFW flying F-100 a/c.

353rd Fighter Group

Assigned Eighth AF: 7 Jun. 43.
Wing & Command Assignments

VIII FC: 7 Jun. 43.
VIII FC, 66 FW: 18 Aug. 43.
3 BD, 66 FW: 15 Sep. 43.
3 AD, 66 FW: 1 Jan. 45.

Component Squadrons

350th, 351st and 352nd Fighter Squadron.

Combat Aircraft

P-47D (from blocks 1), Jul. 43-10 Nov. 44.
P-51D (from blocks 10) in combat from 2 Oct. 44; P-51K, Dec. 44.

Stations

GOXHILL   7 Jun. 43-3 Aug. 43.
METFIELD   3 Aug. 43-12 Apr. 44.
RAYDON   12 Apr. 44-10 Oct. 45.

Group COs

Lt Col Joseph A. Morris: 15 Oct. 42-16 Aug. 43, MIA.
Lt Col Loren G. McCollom: 18 Aug. 43-25 Nov. 43, POW.
Col Glenn E. Duncan: 25 Nov. 43-7 Jul. 44, MIA-
                                      evaded.
Col Ben Rimerman: 7 Jul. 44-21 Apr. 45.
Col Glenn E. Duncan: 22 Apr. 45-9 Sep. 45.
Lt Col William B. Bailey: 9 Sep. 45-24 Sep. 45.
Lt Col Robert A. Elder: 24 Sep. 45-Oct. 45.

First Mission: 12 Aug. 43.* **Last Mission:** 25 Apr. 45. **Total Missions:** 447.

A/c MISA: 137. **E/a Claims:** 330½ air; 414 ground.

Major Awards

Distinguished Unit Citation: 17-23 Sep. 44: support of airborne landings in Holland.

Claims to Fame

Pioneered the P-47 dive-bombing and ground attack technique adopted by both 8 and 9AFs.
Walter Beckham was leading 8AF ace at time of his loss.

Early History

Activated 1 Oct. 42 at Mitchel Fd, NY. Nucleus established Richmond AAB, Va. shortly thereafter transferring to Baltimore MAP, Md. late in Oct. 42. Trained with P-40s until Feb. 43 when a few P-47s assigned. Continued training with P-47s until alerted for overseas movement May 43. Sailed on *Queen Mary* 1 Jun. 43 arriving Clyde 6 Jun. 43.

Subsequent History

Many personnel transferred after VE-day. A/c to depots Aug./Sep. 45. Group returned USA Oct. 45, sailing on *Queen Mary* from Southampton 11 Oct. 45 and arriving New York 16 Oct. 45. Group established at Camp Kilmer and inactivated there 18 Oct. 45.

Redesignated 116FG and allotted to Ga ANG in May 46. Operated F-80 and later F-84 a/c. Took part in Korean war from Jul. 51 to Jul. 52, then redesignated as regular USAF wing. 116FG re-established in Ga ANG, later redesignated as transport organisation flying C-97 and then C-124.

*First official group mission. On 9 Aug. 43 353FG provided 16 a/c to fly as fourth sqdn. with 56th FG.

355th Fighter Group

Assigned Eighth AF: 6 Jul. 43.
Wing & Command Assignments

VIII FC:	6 Jul. 43.
VIII FC, 65 FW:	Aug. 43.
2 BD, 65 FW:	15 Sep. 44.
2 AD, 65 FW:	1 Jan. 45.

Component Squadrons
354th, 357th and 358th Fighter Squadron.
Combat Aircraft
P-47D (blocks 5 to 16), Jul. 43-c. 13 Mar. 44.
    P-51B (from blocks 1) in combat from 9 Mar. 44; P-51D and P-51K.
Station
STEEPLE MORDEN   8 Jul. 43-3 Jul. 45.
Group COs

Col William J. Cummings Jr:	12 Nov. 42-4 Nov. 44.
Lt Col Everett W. Stewart:	4 Nov. 44-21 Feb. 45.
Lt Col Claiborne H. Kinnard Jr:	21 Feb. 45-7 Jun. 45.
Lt Col William D. Gilchrist:	7 Jun. 45-Oct. 45.

First Mission: 14 Sep. 43. **Last Mission:** 25 Apr. 45.
A/c MIA: 175. **E/a Claims:** $365\frac{1}{2}$ air; $502\frac{1}{2}$ ground.
Major Awards
Distinguished Unit Citation: 5 Apr. 44, attack on German airfield.
Claims to Fame
Destroyed more e/a by ground strafing than any other 8AF group.
Early History
Activated 12 Nov. 42 at Orlando AB, Fla. and trained there until Feb. 43. Moved Richmond AAB, Va. 17 Feb. 43, and to Philadelphia MAP, Pa. on 4 Mar. 43. Trained with P-47s until commencing overseas movement mid-Jun. 43. Sailed on *Queen Elizabeth* 1 Jul. 43, arriving in Clyde 6 Jul. 43.
Subsequent History
Selected for assignment to occupational air forces in Germany and moved to Gablingen (R-77) in early Jul. 45. Group gradually run down and 358FS absorbed by 56TRS in Dec. 45. Moved Schweinfurt in Apr. 46 but remnants transferred other groups during summer 46. Group transferred less personnel and equipment to Mitchel Fd, NY. as of 1 Aug. 46 and inactivated 20 Nov. 46.
    Activated again in 1955 as F-86 wing in ADC. Later assigned TAC and became second wing equipped F-105. Took part in Vietnam war flying F-105s from Thailand.

356th Fighter Group

Assigned Eighth AF: 25 Aug. 43.
Wing & Command Assignments

VIII FC, 65 FW:	26 Aug. 43.
VIII FC, 67 FW:	8 Aug. 44.
1 BD, 67 FW:	15 Sep. 44.
1 AD, 67 FW:	1 Jan. 45.

Component Squadrons
359th, 360th and 361st Fighter Squadrons.
Combat Aircraft
P-47D (blocks 5 to 28) Sep. 43-late Nov. 44.
P-51D (from blocks 15) in combat from c. 20 Nov. 44; P-51K from Dec. 44.
Stations

GOXHILL	27 Aug. 43-5 Oct. 43.
MARTLESHAM HEATH	5 Oct. 43-c. 2 Nov. 45 (Most air ech. in 9 Oct. 43).

Group COs

Lt Col Harold J. Rau:	9 Feb. 43-28 Nov. 43.
Col Einar A. Malstrom:	28 Nov. 43-23 Apr. 44, POW.
Lt Col Philip E. Tukey Jr:	24 Apr. 44-3 Nov. 44.
Lt Col Donald A. Baccus:	3 Nov. 44-10 Jan. 45.
Col Philip E. Tukey Jr:	11 Jan. 45-Oct. 45.

First Mission: 15 Oct. 43. **Last Mission:** 7 May 45. **Total Missions:** 413.
A/c MIA: 122. **E/a Claims:** 201 air; $75\frac{1}{2}$ ground.

Major Awards
Distinguished Unit Citation: 17, 18 and 23 Sep. 44: support airborne forces, Holland.
Claims to Fame
The 'hard luck' fighter group. Despite excellent leadership had highest ratio of losses to enemy a/c claims of all 8AF fighter groups.
Early History
Activated 12 Dec. 42 at Westover Fd, Mass. and trained there until 12 Mar. 43. Moved Groton Fd, Conn. and trained in P-47s. Further moved to Mitchel Fd, NY. 30 May 43, and Grenier Fd, NH. 4 Jul. 43. Ground echelon commenced overseas movement 15 Aug. 43 and journeyed to Camp Miles Standish, Mass. Sailed on *Queen Elizabeth* 20 Aug. 43 arriving Clyde 25 Aug. 43. Apparently some P-47s for Group flown to UK by northern ferry route. Group pilots reached UK by different ship and after Ground echelon.
Subsequent History
A/c to depots Aug./Sep. 45. Many personnel transferred after VE-day. Remainder sailed *Queen Mary* from Southampton, 4 Nov. 45, arriving New York 9 Nov. 45. Group established Camp Kilmer, NJ. and inactivated there 10 Nov. 45.
    Redesignated 118FG in 1946 and allotted to Tenn ANG. Role changed to tactical reconnaissance in 1951. In later years redesignated as air transport wing, first with C-97 and then C-124.

357th Fighter Group

Assigned Eighth AF: 31 Jan. 44.
Wing & Command Assignments

VIII FC, 66 FW:	31 Jan. 44.
3 BD, 66 FW:	15 Sep. 44.
3 AD, 66 FW:	1 Jan. 45.

Component Squadrons
362nd, 363rd and 364th Fighter Squadron.
Combat Aircraft
P-51B (from block 1); P-51C; P-51D; P-51K.
Stations

RAYDON	30 Nov. 43-31 Jan. 44.
LEISTON	31 Jan. 44-8 Jul. 45.

Group COs

Lt Col Edward S. Chickering:	7 Jul. 43-17 Feb. 44.
Col Henry R. Spicer:	17 Feb. 44-5 Mar. 44, POW.
Col Donald W. Graham:	7 Mar. 44-10 Oct. 44.
Lt Col John D. Landers:	11 Oct. 44-2 Dec. 44.
Col Irwin H. Dregne:	2 Dec. 44-21 Jul. 45.

First Mission: 11 Feb. 44. **Last Mission:** 25 Apr. 45. **Total Missions:** 313.
A/c MIA: 128. **E/a Claims:** $609\frac{1}{2}$ air; $106\frac{1}{2}$ ground.
Major Awards
Two Distinguished Unit Citations: 6 Mar. and 29 Jun. 44: for defence of bombers on missions to Berlin and Leipzig.
    14 Jan. 45: action on Derben mission.
Claims to Fame
First P-51 group in 8AF.
    Faster rate of air victories than with any other 8AF group during final year of war.
    Highest e/a air claims for single mission—14 Jan. 45—56.
Early History
Activated 1 Dec. 42 at Hamilton Fd, Cal. Moved Tonopah AAFd, Nev. 4 Mar. 43 and equipped P-39s. Moved Santa Rosa AAFd, Cal. 3 Jun. 43, and Orville AAFd, Cal. 18 Aug. 43 and Casper AAFd, Wyo. 7 Oct. 43. On 9 Nov. 43 commenced overseas movement by leaving Casper from Camp Shanks, NY. Sailed on *Queen Elizabeth* 23 Nov. 43, arriving Clyde 29 Nov. 43. Assigned to 9AF, IXFC, 30 Nov. 43 and based Raydon. Trained with a few P-51Bs. In Jan. 44 8AF exchanged 358FG for 357FG Hq. and 362FS moved 31 Jan. 44, 363 and 364FS moved 1 Feb. 44.
Subsequent History
Selected for service with occupational forces in Germany. Moved Neubiberg (R-85) early Jul. 45. Suffered shortages aircraft and personnel during following year. Inactivated at Neubiberg 20 Aug. 46, in fact, a redesignation of group as 33FG.
    Redesignated 121FG and allotted to Ohio ANG in 46. Since 52 as tactical fighter wing. Equipment for many years F-84F.

358th Fighter Group

Assigned Eighth AF: 20 Oct. 43.
Wing & Command Assignments
VIII FC: 21 Oct. 43.
VIII FC, 66 FW: Nov. 43-31 Jan. 44.
Component Squadrons
365th, 366th and 367th Fighter Squadrons.
Combat Aircraft
P-47D (blocks 5 and 10).
Stations
GOXHILL   21 Oct. 43-29 Nov. 43.
LEISTON   29 Nov. 43-1 Feb. 44 (367FS moved in 31
                 Jan. 44).
Group CO
Lt Col Cecil L. Wells: 1 Jan. 43-13 Sep. 44, KIA.
First Mission: 20 Dec. 43. **Last Mission with Eighth AF:** 30 Jan.
44. **Total Missions:** 17.
A/c MIA: 4. **E/a Claims:** 1-5-6 air.
Major Awards
None.
Early History
Activated 1 Jan. 43 at Richmond AAB, Va. Moved Baltimore MAP,
Md. 28 Apr. 43 and to Camp Springs AAFd, Md. a month later, then
Philadelphia MAP, Pa. on 16 Jun. 43. Trained with P-47s and moved
back to Richmond AAB in Aug. 43. Sailed on *SS Monterey* 8 Oct. 43.
arriving Liverpool 20 Oct. 43. Some elements possibly on another ship
in convoy.
Subsequent History
Transferred Ninth AF 1 Feb. 44, in exchange for 357FG. Changed
bases with 357FG at Raydon. Later moved to south coast airstrip
and after D-Day to France. Inactivated 7 Nov. 45. Redesignated
122FG of Ind ANG in 1946.

359th Fighter Group

Assigned Eighth AF: 19 Oct. 43.
Wing & Command Assignments
VIII FC, 66 FW: 20 Oct. 43.
VIII FC, 67 FW: c. Nov. 43.
1 BD, 67 FW: 15 Sep. 44.
1 AD, 67 FW: 1 Jan. 45.
Component Squadrons
368th, 369th and 370th Fighter Squadron.
Combat Aircraft
P-47D (from blocks 5 to 21), Nov. 43-early May 44.
P-51B (from block 5); P-51C (from block 5) in combat from 5 May
44; P-51D and P-51K.
Station
EAST WRETHAM   19 Oct. 43-c. 2 Nov. 45.
Group COs
Col Avelin P. Tacon Jr: Jan. 43-11 Nov. 44.
Col John P. Randolph: 12 Nov. 44-7 Apr. 45.
Lt Col Donald A. Baccus: 8 Apr. 45-Sep 45.
Lt Col Daniel D. McKee: c 16 Sep. 45-Nov. 45.
First Mission: 13 Dec. 43. **Last Mission:** 20 Apr. 45. **Total
Missions:** 346.
A/c MIA: 106. **E/a Claims:** 253 air; 98 ground.
Major Awards
Distinguished Unit Citation: 11 Sep. 44: Merseburg, defence of
                 bombers.
Claims to Fame
Ray Wetmore, leading 8AF air ace during 1945 flew with 359th.
Early History
Activated 15 Jan. 43 at Westover Fd, Mass. Trained at air bases in
north eastern states with P-47 a/c: Grenier Fd, NH. from 7 Apr. 43:
Farmingdale AAB, NY. 11 Jul. 43 and back to Westover Fd, 23 Aug. 43.
Commenced overseas movement 2 Oct. 43; Camp Kilmer, NJ. then
sailing *USAT Argentina* 8 Oct. 43. (369FS personnel sailed on
Thurston and 370FS on *Sloterdyjk* in same convoy). Group arrived
Liverpool 19 Oct. 43 (369 and 370FS disembarked in Clyde).
Subsequent History
Remained in UK until Nov. 45. Many personnel transferred and a/c
to depots Sep. 45. Remaining personnel sailed *Queen Mary* 4 Nov. 45,

arriving New York 9 Nov. 45. Group established at Camp Kilmer, NJ.
and inactivated there 10 Nov. 45.
Redesignated 123FG and allotted to Ky ANG in 46. Ordered active
service in Oct. 50 and based Manston UK, early 52. Re-established
as ANG organisation Jul. 52. In later years assigned tactical reconnaissance role flying RB-57 and RF-84F. Later RF-101.

361st Fighter Group

Assigned Eighth AF: 30 Nov. 43.
Wing & Command Assignments
VIII FC: 30 Nov. 43.
VIII FC, 66 FW: 12 Dec. 43.
VIII FC, 67 FW: 11 Mar. 44.
VIII FC, 65 FW: 8 Aug. 44.
2 BD, 65 FW: 15 Sep. 44.
9 AF, XIX TAC: 24 Dec. 44 (Temporary assignment air
                         echelon op. control).
VIII FC: 1 Feb. 45.
2 AD, 65 FW: 10 April 45.
Component Squadrons
374th, 375th and 376th Fighter Squadron.
Combat Aircraft
P-47D (blocks 10 to 21), Dec. 43-15 May 44.
P-51B (from block 10); P-51C (from block 5) from 12 May 44;
P-51D and P-51K.
Stations
BOTTISHAM   30 Nov. 43-26 Sep. 44.
LITTLE WALDEN   26 Sep. 44-c. 4 Feb. 45.
ST. DIZIER   25 Dec. 44-15 Feb. 45 (Air ech. only).
CHIEVRES   15 Feb. 45-9 Apr. 45 (Gnd. ech. in early
                   Feb. 45).
LITTLE WALDEN   9 April 45-3 Nov. 45.
Group COs
Col Thomas J. J. Christian Jr: 10 Feb. 43-12 Aug. 44, KIA.
Col Ronald F. Fallows: 14 Aug. 44-30 Aug. 44.
Lt Col Roy B. Caviness: 31 Aug. 44-20 Sep. 44.
Lt Col Joseph J. Kruzel: 20 Sep. 44-2 Nov. 44.
Lt Col Roy B. Caviness: 3 Nov. 44-2 Dec. 44.
Col Junius W. Dennison Jr: 3 Dec. 44-15 Apr. 45.
Lt Col Roy B. Caviness: 15 Apr. 45-29 Jun. 45.
Col John D. Landers: 29 Jun. 45-unkn.
(Lt Col Caviness, group executive, as interim CO Aug. and Nov. 44).
First Mission: 21 Jan. 44. **Last Mission:** 20 Apr. 45. **Total
Missions:** 441.
A/c MIA: 81. **E/a Claims:** 226 air; 105 ground.
Major Awards
None.
Claims to Fame
Last P-47 group to join 8AF.
Early History
Activated 10 Feb. 43 at Richmond AAB, Va. Trained at air bases in
eastern USA during spring and summer 43; Langley Fd, Va. from
26 May 43; Millville AAFd, NJ. 20 Jul. 44; Camp Springs AAFd, Md.
28 Aug. 43; returning Richmond AAB, 20 Sep. 43. Equipped with
P-47s. Moved Camp Shanks, NY. 12 Nov. 43 to prepare for overseas
duty. Sailed on *Queen Elizabeth*, 23 Nov. 43 and arrived Clyde 29 Nov.
43.
Subsequent History
Remained in UK until Nov. 45. Many personnel transferred and a/c
to depots Sep./Oct. 45. Remaining personnel sailed on *Queen Mary*
from Southampton 4 Nov. 45, arriving New York 9 Nov. 45. Group
established Camp Kilmer, NJ. and inactivated there 10 Nov. 45.
Redesignated 127FG and allotted to Mich ANG in 46. Changed to
tactical reconnaissance role in later years, flying RF-84F as 127TFW.

364th Fighter Group

Assigned Eighth AF: 10 Feb. 44.
Wing & Command Assignments
VIII FC, 67 FW: Feb. 44.
1 BD, 67 FW: 15 Sep. 44.
1 AD, 67 FW: 1 Jan. 45.
Component Squadrons
383rd, 384th and 385th Fighter Squadron.

Combat Aircraft
P-38J (blocks 5 to 25), Feb. 44-29 Jul. 44.
P-51D (from blocks 5), 28 Jul. 44-Oct. 45.
Station
HONINGTON   10 Feb. 44-3 Nov. 45.
Group COs
Lt Col Frederick C. Grambo: 12 Jun. 43-29 Feb. 44, KIA.
Col Roy W. Osborn: 29 Feb. 44-9 Sep. 44.
Lt Col Joseph B. McManus: c. 9 Sep. 44-c. 23 Oct. 44.
Lt Col John W. Lowell: 23 Oct. 44-2 Nov. 44 (Acting)
Col Roy W. Osborn: 2 Nov. 44-3 Jan. 45.
Lt Col Eugene P. Roberts: 3 Jan. 45-Nov. 45.
First Mission: 3 Mar. 44. **Last Mission:** 25 Apr. 45. **Total Missions:** 342.
A/c MIA: 134. **E/a Claims:** 256½ air; 193 ground.
Major Awards
Distinguished Unit Citation: 27 Dec. 44: Frankfurt, defence of bombers.
Early History
Activated 1 Jun. 43 at Glendale GCAT, Cal. Trained with P-38s at bases in California area during later part of 43; Van Nuys AAB, from 12 Aug. 43; Ontario AAFd, 11 Oct. 43 and Santa Maria AAFd, 7 Dec. 43 until departure for port of embarkation on 11 Jan. 44.
Subsequent Histoty
Many personnel transferred after VE-day. A/c to depots Sep. 45. Remaining personnel sailed on *Queen Mary* from Southampton 4 Nov. 45, arriving New York 9 Nov. 45. Group established at Camp Kilmer, NJ. and inactivated there 10 Nov. 45.
Redesignated 131FG and allotted Mo ANG in 46. Role changed a number of times. During late nineteen-sixties as tactical fighter wing with F-100C.

379th Bombardment Group (H)

Assigned Eighth AF: April 43.
Wing & Command Assignments
VIII BC, 1 BW, 103 PCBW: May 43.
VIII BC, 1 BD, 41 CBW: 13 Sep. 43.
1 BD, 41 CBW: 8 Jan. 44.
1 AD, 41 CBW: 1 Jan. 45.
Component Squadrons
524th, 525th, 526th and 527th Bombardment Squadron (H).
Combat Aircraft
B-17F (from blocks 70-BO, 25 DL and VE); B-17G.
Stations
KIMBOLTON   20 May 43-12 Jun. 45 (Air ech. Bovingdon
                   24 Apr. 43-21 May 43).
Group COs
Col Maurice A. Preston. 26 Nov. 42-10 Oct. 44.
Col Lewis E. Lyle: 11 Oct. 44-5 May 45.
Lt Col Lloyd C. Mason: 6 May 45-22 May 45.
Lt Col Horace E. Frink: 23 May 45-25 Jun. 45.
First Mission: 29 May 43. **Last Mission:** 25 Apr. 45. **Total Missions:** 330.
Total Credit Sorties: 10,492. **Total Bomb Tonnage:** 26,459.6 tons (43 tons leaflets).
A/c MIA: 141. **E/a Claims:** 249-57-135.
Major Awards
Two Distinguished Unit Citations: 28 May 43-31 Jul. 44: operations for this period. 11 Jan. 44: (all 1 BD groups).

Claims to Fame
Flew more sorties than any other bomb group in 8AF.
Dropped a greater bomb tonnage than any other group.
Lower abortive rate than any other group in action from 1943.
Pioneered the 12-plane formation that became SOP during 1944.
"Ol Gappy", a B-17G flew 157 missions, probably more than any other in 8AF.

Early History
Activated 26 Nov. 42 at Gowen Fd, Idaho. Group assembled at Wendover Fd, Utah, 2 Dec. 42, training there until 2 Mar. 43. Sioux City AAB, Iowa, from 3 Feb. 43. On 9 Apr. 43 ground echelon moved for final processing at Camp Douglas, Wis. then to Camp Shanks, NY. Sailed in *Aquitania* 10 May 43, arriving Clyde 18 May 43. Air echelon left Sioux City, 9 Apr. 43 for Bangor. Me. via Kearney, Neb. and Selfridge, Mich. Commenced overseas movement 15 Apr. 43 by north Atlantic ferry route.

Subsequent History
Scheduled to transport US troops from Europe to Casablanca. Moved Casablanca early Jun. with last a/c leaving Kimbolton 11 Jun. 45. Services apparently not required. A/c flown back to US and Group inactivated Casablanca on 25 Jul. 45.
Activated as SAC wing and assigned first B-52H a/c in 1962.

381st Bombardment Group (H)

Assigned Eighth AF: May 43.
Wing & Command Assignments
VIII BC, 1 BW, 101 PCBW: Jun. 43.
VIII BC, 1 BD, 1 CBW: 13 Sep. 43.
1 BD, 1 CBW: 8 Jan. 44.
1 AD, 1 CBW: 1 Jan. 45.
Component Squadrons
532nd, 533rd, 534th and 535th Bombardment Squadron (H).
Combat Aircraft
B-17F (from blocks 75-BO, 25DL and VE); B-17G.
Station
RIDGEWELL   31 Jun. 43-24 Jun. 45 (Air ech. Bovingdon
                   late May 43).
Group COs
Col Joseph J. Nazzaro: c. 5 Jan. 43-c. 9 Jan. 44.
Col Harry P. Leber Jr: c. 9 Jan. 44-6 Feb. 45.
Lt Col Conway S. Hall: 6 Feb. 45-Jun. 45.
First Mission: 22 Jun. 43. **Last Mission:** 25 Apr. 45. **Total Missions:** 296.
Total Credit Sorties: 9,035. **Total Bomb Tonnage:** 22,159.5 tons (24 tons leaflets).
A/c MIA: 131. **E/a Claims:** 223-40-162.
Major Awards
Two Distinguished Unit Citations: 8 Oct. 43: Bremen.
                                  11 Jan. 43 (all 1 BD groups).
Claims to Fame
Highest losses of all groups on first Schweinfurt mission (17 Aug. 43).
Early History
Activated 3 Nov. 42 at Gowen Fd, Idaho. Training did not commence until unit established at Pyote AAB, Tex. on 5 Jan. 43. Final training at Pueblo, Col. 16 Apr. 43-8 May 43. Ground echelon moved to Camp Kilmer, NJ. arriving 12 May 43 and embarked on *Queen Elizabeth* 27 May 43. Arrived Greenock 2 Jun. 43. Air echelon flew to Salina, Kan. early May 43 and started movement to UK 15 May 43, via Selfridge Fd, Bangor, Gander to Prestwick.
Subsequent History
Redeployed USA May/Jun. 45. Majority a/c left UK 24 May 45. Ground echelon sailed *Queen Elizabeth* 24 Jun. 45, arriving New York 29 Jun. 45. Group established Camp Kilmer and after thirty days R & R some personnel assembled Sioux Falls AAFd, SD. where Group eventually inactivated 28 Aug. 45.

384th Bombardment Group (H)

Assigned Eighth AF: May 43.
Wing & Command Assignments
VIII BC, 1 BW, 103 PCBW: Jun. 43.
VIII BC, 1 BD, 41 CBW: 13 Sep. 43.
1 BD, 41 CBW: 8 Jan. 44.
1 AD, 41 CBW: 1 Jan. 45.
Component Squadrons
544th, 545th, 546th and 547th Bombardment Squadron (H).
Combat Aircraft
B-17F (from blocks 80-BO, 30DL and VE); B-17G.
Station
GRAFTON UNDERWOOD: 25 May 43-c. 16 Jun. 45 (Gnd. ech.
                  arrived 3 Jun. 43).
Group COs
Col Budd J. Peaslee: 18 Dec. 42-6 Sep. 43.
Col Julius K. Lacey: 6 Sep. 43-23 Nov. 43.
Col Dale R. Smith: 23 Nov. 43-24 Oct. 44.
Lt Col Theodore R. Milton: 24 Oct. 44-16 Jun. 45.
Lt Col Robert W. Fish: 17 Jun. 45-18 Oct. 45.
First Mission: 22 Jun. 43. **Last Mission:** 25 Apr. 45. **Total Missions:** 314.

Total Credit Sorties: 9,348. **Total Bomb Tonnage:** 22,415.4 tons (16.2 tons leaflets).
A/c MIA: 159. **E/a Claims:** 165-34-116.
Major Awards
Two Distinguished Unit Citations: 11 Jan. 44 (all 1 BD groups).
24 Apr. 44: Oberpfafenhofen.
Claims to Fame
Dropped last 8AF bombs of war (25 April 45).
Early History
Activated 1 Dec. 42 at Gowen Fd, Idaho. Began training at Wendover, Utah, 2 Jan. 43-1 Apr. 43. Moved Sioux City AAB, Iowa for final training, with ground echelon leaving for Camp Kilmer on 9 May 43. Sailed on *Queen Elizabeth* 27 May 43 and arrived Greenock 2 Jun. 43. Air echelon left Sioux City for Kearney, Neb. on 3 May 43 and later in month began movement to the UK via Bangor, and then part via Goose Bay and part by Gander. One B-17 ditched in Atlantic but crew saved. First B-17s into Grafton Underwood on 25 May 43.
Subsequent History
Scheduled for occupational air forces and moved Istres, France in Jun. 45 to participate in Green Project—moving US troops to staging areas. Also moved displaced persons and Greek military personnel. Run down by 1946 and remaining a/c and personnel absorbed into 306th BG. Inactivated at Istres on 28 Feb. 46.
Short period of life as SAC B-47 wing in nineteen-fifties.

385th Bombardment Group (H)
"Van's Valiants"

Assigned Eighth AF: Jun. 43.
Wing & Command Assignments
VIII BC, 4 BW, 401 PCBW: Jun. 43.
VIII BC, 3 BD, 4 CBW: 13 Sep. 43.
3 BD, 4 CBW: 8 Jan. 44.
3 AD, 4 CBW: 1 Jan. 45.
3 AD, 93 CBW: 17 Feb. 45.
(4 CBW incorporated with 92 CBW in 4 BW(P) from c. 18 Nov. 44 to 16 Feb. 45).
Component Squadrons
548th, 549th, 550th and 551st Bombardment Squadron (H).
Combat Aircraft
B-17F (from blocks 85-BO, 45-DL, 30-VE); B-17G.
Station
GREAT ASHFIELD 26 Jun. 43-4 Aug. 45 (Gnd. ech. in 2 and 8/9 Jul. 43).
Group COs
Col Elliott Vandevanter: 3 Feb. 43-23 Aug. 44.
Col George Y. Jumper: 24 Aug. 44-28 May 45.
Col William H. Hanson: 2 Jun. 45-Jul. 45.
(Lt Col H. T. Witherspoon acting CO May/Jun. 45).
First Mission: 17 Jul. 43. **Last Mission:** 20 Apr. 45. **Total Missions:** 296.*
Total Credit Sorties: 8,264. **Total Bomb Tonnage:** 18,494.0 tons (184.9 tons supplies, etc.).
A/c MIA: 129. **Other Op. Losses:** 40. **E/a Claims:** 287-80-95.
Major Awards
Two Distinguished Unit Citations: 17 Aug. 43: Regensburg (all 4 BW groups).
12 May 44: Zwickau.
Claims to Fame
Led famous attack on Marienburg factory—9 Oct. 43.
Last group to be shot at—May 45: Holland.
Early History
Activated 1 Dec. 42 at Davis-Monthan Fd, Ariz. Not formed until Feb. 43 at Geiger Fd, Wash. Trained at this base for two months and then moved Great Falls AAD, Mont. 11 Apr. 43. Completed training end May 43 with air echelon moving to Kearney Fd, Neb. prior to overseas movement by northern ferry route. Two a/c lost en route. Ground echelon left Great Falls, 8 Jun. 43. 548BS sailed on *Queen Mary* 23 Jun. 43 and other sqdns. on *Queen Elizabeth* 1 Jul. 43.
Subsequent History
Redeployed USA in Jun. and Aug. 45. Air echelon left between 19 Jun. 45 and 29 Jun. 45. Ground echelon left 4/5 Aug. 45 and sailed on *Queen Elizabeth* from Greenock 5 Aug. 45. Arrived New York 11 Aug. 45. Personnel 30 days R & R. Group established at Sioux Falls, AAFd, SD. and inactivated 28 Aug. 45.

Brief existence as headquarters for missile and tanker squadrons at Offutt AFB but inactivated 1966.
*(6 food missions May 45, 458.2 tons. One mission combat credit as a/c fired on).

386th Bombardment Group (M)

Assigned Eighth AF: 4 Jun. 43-15 Oct. 43.
Wing & Command Assignments
VIII BC, 3 BW: 4 Jun. 43.
VIII ASC, 3 BW: 15 Jun. 43.
Component Squadrons
552nd, 553rd, 554th and 555th Bombardment Squadron (M).
Combat Aircraft
B-26B (majority original a/c) (from block 15); B-26C (from block 15).
Stations
SNETTERTON HEATH 3 Jun. -43-10 Jun. 43.
BOXTED 10 Jun. 43-24 Sep. 43.
GREAT DUNMOW 24 Sep. 43-2 Oct. 44.
Group CO
Col Lester J. Maitland: 1 Dec. 42-18 Nov. 43.
First Mission: 30 Jul. 43. **Last Mission:** 8 Oct. 43. **Total Missions:** 30.
A/c MIA: 6. **E/a Claims:** 9 destroyed.
Major Awards
Distinguished Unit Citation: 30 Jul. 43-30 Jul. 44: ops. during this period.
Claims to Fame
Developed formation release procedure for B-26.
Early History
Activated 1 Dec. 42 at MacDill Fd, Fla. and trained there under 3rd AF and at Lake Charles AB, La. (9 Feb. 43-8 May 43). Ground echelon sailed *Queen Elizabeth* 27 May 43 and disembarked Gourock 2 Jun. 43. Air echelon flew via south and northern ferry routes.
Subsequent History
Transferred 9AF, IX BC, 16 Oct. 43. Moved Beaumont-Sur-Oise, France in Oct. 44 and to St. Trond, Belgium, Apr. 45. Returned to the US in Jul. 45 and inactivated 7 Nov. 45. Converted to A-26 shortly before end of hostilities. Activated again in TAC Apr. 56 as an F-100 fighter bomber wing but redesignated at a later date.

387th Bombardment Group (M)

Assigned Eighth AF: 25 Jun. 43-16 Oct. 43.
Wing & Command Assignment
VIII ASC, 3 BW: 25 Jun. 43.
Component Squadrons
556th, 557th, 558th and 559th Bombardment Squadron (M).
Combat Aircraft
B-26B (majority original a/c) (from block 15) and B-26C (from block 15).
Station
CHIPPING ONGAR 21 Jun. 43-18 Jul. 44 (Air ech. in 21-25 Jun. 43).
(Gnd. ech. in 30 Jun. 43).
Group CO
Col Carl R. Storrie: c. 19 Jan. 43-8 Nov. 43.
First Mission: 15 Aug. 43. **Last Mission:** 9 Oct. 43. **Total Missions:** 29.
A/c MIA: 2. **E/a Claims:** 2 destroyed.
Major Awards
None.
Early History
Activated 1 Dec. 42 at MacDill Fd, Fla. Formed and trained with B-26s at this base. Moved Drane Fd, Fla. 12 Apr. 43 and to Godman Fd, Ky. in early May 43. Ground echelon left for port of embarkation 10 Jun. 43 and sailed on *Queen Mary* 23 Jun. 43 arriving Clyde 29 Jun. 43. Air echelon flew via northern ferry route to UK early Jun. 43.
Subsequent History
Assigned to 9AF, IX BC, 16 Oct. 43. Moved Stony Cross in Jul. 44 and to France in late Aug. 44. Flew tactical bombing missions in support of Allied land forces. Inactivated USA Nov. 45.

388th Bombardment Group (H)

Assigned Eighth AF: Jun. 43.
Wing & Command Assignments
VIII BC, 4 BW, 403 PCBW: Jun. 43.
VIII BC, 3 BD, 45 CBW: 15 Sep. 43.
3 BD, 45 CBW: 8 Jan. 44.
3 AD, 45 CBW: 1 Jan. 45.
Component Squadrons
560th, 561st, 562nd and 563rd Bombardment Group (H).
Combat Aircraft
B-17F (from blocks 90-BO, 45-DL, 35-VF); B-17G.
B-17 and B-24 Aphrodite; B-34 Ventura control.
Station
KNETTISHALL   23 Jun. 43-c. 5 Aug. 45 (Ground ech. in 8 Jul. 43).
Aphrodite and Batty Projects at Fersfield, 12 Jul. 44-1 Jan. 45).
Group COs
Col William B. David: 1 Feb. 43-6 Oct. 44.
Col Chester C. Cox: 7 Oct. 43-Aug. 45.
First Mission: 17 Jul. 43. **Last Mission:** Apr. 45. **Total Missions:** 306* (plus 19 Aphrodite and 6 Batty).
Total Credit Sorties: 8,051. **Total Bomb Tonnage:** 18,162.4 tons (264.7 tons supplies, etc.).
A/c MIA: 142. **Other Op. Losses:** 37. **E/a Claims:** 222½-80-116.
Major Awards
Two Distinguished Unit Citations: 17 Aug. 43: Regensburg (all 4 BW groups).
26 Jun. 43, Hanover; 12 May 44, Brux and 21 Jun. 44, Russia.

Claims to Fame
Conducted APHRODITE radio-controlled bomber project "guided missiles".
Early History
Activated 24 Dec. 42 at Gowen Fd, Idaho. Nucleus from Gowen moved Wendover Fd, Utah, early Feb. 43 where formation proper began. Final training at Sioux City AAFd, SD. early May 43 to 1 Jun. 43. Air echelon began overseas movement taking northern route via Newfoundland or Greenland, Iceland to Prestwick. Ground echelon left Sioux City 12 Jun. 43 for Camp Kilmer, NJ. and sailed on *Queen Elizabeth* 1 Jul. 43, arriving Clyde 7 Jul. 43.
Subsequent History
Redeployed USA Jun./Aug. 45. A/c left Knettishall between 9 Jun. 45-5 Jul. 45. Ground echelon sailed on *Queen Elizabeth* from Greenock 5 Aug. 45, arriving New York 11 Aug. 45. Personnel 30 days R & R. Group established at Sioux Falls AAFd, SD. and inactivated there 28 Aug. 45.
Activated as a fighter-bomber group in 1953 and equipped with F-86. Later existences as F-100 wing in France and F-106 wing in USA Established Thailand in 1965 as F-105 wing and conducted operations over North Vietnam.
*(5 food missions May 45, 378.4 tons).

389th Bombardment Group (H)
"The Sky Scorpions"

Assigned Eighth AF: 11 Jun. 43.
Wing & Command Assignments
VIII BC, 2 BW, 201 PCBW: 11 Jun. 43.
VIII BC, 2 BD, 2 CBW: 13 Sep. 43.
2 BD, 2 CBW: 8 Jan. 44.
2 AD, 2 CBW: 1 Jan. 45.
Component Squadrons
564th, 565th, 566th and 567th Bombardment Squadron (H).
Combat Aircraft
B-24D (from blocks 15-CF, 75-CO); B-24E (few); B-24H, B-24J, B-24L and B-24M.
Station
HETHEL   11 Jun. 43-30 May 45 (Ground ech. arrived 8/10 Jul. 43: Air ech. 11/25 Jun. 43).
(Temporary bases in North Africa: Benghazi No. 10, Lybia; 3 Jul. 43-25 Aug. 43. Massicault, Tunisia, 19 Sep. 43-3 Oct. 43).

Group COs
Col Jack W. Wood: 16 May 43-29 Dec. 43.
Col Milton W. Arnold: 30 Dec. 43-29 Mar. 44.
Col Robert B. Miller: 29 Mar. 44-17 Aug. 44.
Col Ramsey D. Potts Jr: 17 Aug. 44-4 Dec. 44.
Col John B. Herboth Jr: 4 Dec. 44-7 Apr. 45, MIA.
Lt Col Jack G. Merrell: 14 Apr. 45-Jun. 45.
(Lt Col Chester Morneau acting 9 Apr. 45-13 Apr. 45).
First Mission: 9 Jul. 43 (first from UK 7 Sep. 43). **Last Mission:** 25 Apr. 45. **Total Missions:** 321 (14 from NA).
Total Credit Sorties: 7,579. **Total Bomb Tonnage:** 17,548 tons.
A/c MIA: 116. **Other Op. Losses:** 37. **E/a Claims:** 209-31-45.
Major Awards
Distinguished Unit Citation: 1 Aug. 43: Ploesti.
Medal of Honor: 2/Lt Lloyd H. Hughes: 1 Aug. 43.
Claims to Fame
One of three 8AF B-24 groups that took part in famous Ploesti mission.
At one period provided PFF a/c for all 2 BD groups.
564BS was judged on efficiency, 'best squadron in ETO in 1945'
Early History
Activated 24 Dec. 42 at Davis-Monthan AAB, Ariz. Physical formation began at Biggs Fd, Tex. on 1 Feb. 43 under Lt Col David B. Lancaster. Between 17-20 Apr. 43 moved Lowery Fd, Col. for final training. Ground echelon to Camp Kilmer, NJ. arriving 11 Jun. 43 and embarking on *Queen Elizabeth* 30 Jun. 43, sailing next day and arriving Gourock 6 Jul. 43. Air echelon began overseas movement 13 Jun. 43 via Dow Fd, Me., Goose Bay, Gander, Meeks Fd, Iceland to Prestwick.
Subsequent History
Redeployed USA in May/Jun. 45. First a/c left UK 20 May 45. Ground echelon sailed from Bristol on *USS Cristobal* 30 May 45 and arrived New York 8 Jun. 45. Personnel to Camp Kilmer and from there 30 days R & R. Group established at Charleston AAF, SC. 12 Jun. 45 for transport duties but apparently not fully manned. Inactivated 13 Sep. 45 at that base.
Activated as Atlas missile wing in 1960 at Warren AFB, Wyo. and inactivated six years later.

390th Bombardment Group (H)

Assigned Eighth AF: Jul. 43.
Wing & Command Assignments
VIII BC, 4 BW, 402 PCBW: Jul. 43.
VIII BC, 3 BD, 13 CBW: 13 Sep. 43.
3 BD, 13 CBW: 8 Jan. 44.
3 AD, 13 CBW: 1 Jan. 45.
Component Squadrons
568th, 569th, 570th and 571st Bombardment Squadron (H).
Combat Aircraft
B-17F (from blocks 95-BO, 45-DL, 35 VE); B-17G.
Station
FRAMLINGHAM   14 Jul. 43-4 Aug. 45 (Air ech. in 14-28 Jul. 43).
(Gnd. ech. in 28 Jul. 43).
Group COs
Col Edgar M. Wittan   26 Jan. 43-15 May 44.
Col Frederick W. Ott: 15 May 44-6 Sep. 44.
Col Joseph A. Moller: 6 Sep. 44-21 May 45.
Lt Col George W. Von Arb: 23 May 45-26 Jun. 45.
First Mission: 12 Aug. 43. **Last Mission:** 20 Apr. 45. **Total Missions:** 300.*
Total Credit Sorties: 8,725. **Total Bomb Tonnage:** 19,059.2 tons (295.3 tons supplies, etc.).
A/c MIA: 144. **Other Op. Losses:** 32. **E/a Claims:** 342-74-97.
Major Awards
Two Distinguished Unit Citations: 17 Aug. 43: Regensburg (all 4 BW groups).
14 Oct. 43: Schweinfurt.
Claims to Fame
Highest claims of e/a destroyed by bomb group on one mission—10 Oct. 43.
Only man to fly 100 missions with 8AF, Hewitt Dunn did so with 390BG.
Early History
Activated 26 Jan. 43 at Geiger Fd, Wash. Formation did not begin until late Feb. 43. Training at Geiger until 6 Jun. 43 when Group moved Great Falls AAB, Mont. for final preparations. Air echelon began

overseas movement 4 Jul. 43 taking northern ferry route via Iceland to Prestwick, where first a/c arrived 13 Jul. 43. Ground echelon left for Camp Shanks, NY. 4 Jul. 43 and sailed on *USS James Parker*, 17 Jul. 43, arriving Liverpool, 27 Jul. 43.

Subsequent History

Redeployed USA Jun./Aug. 45. A/c left Framlingham 25 and 26 Jun. 45. Ground echelon sailed Greenock on *Queen Elizabeth* 5 Aug. 45 arriving New York, 11 Aug. 45. Personnel 30 days R & R. Group established Sioux Falls AAFd, SD. and inactivated there 28 Aug. 45.

Activated as Titan missile wing in 1962 with headquarters at Davis-Monthan AFB, Ariz.

*(6 food missions May 45, 436.4 tons).

392nd Bombardment Group (H)

Assigned Eighth AF: Jul. 43.
Wing & Command Assignments
VIII BC, 2 BW:	Jul. 43.
VIII BC, 2 BW, 202 CBW: 2 Sep. 43.	
VIII BC, 2 BD, 14 CBW: 13 Sep. 43.	
2 BD, 14 CBW:	8 Jan. 44.
2 AD, 14 CBW:	1 Jan. 45.

Component Squadrons
576th, 577th, 578th and 579th Bombardment Squadron (H).
Combat Aircraft
B-24H (from blocks 1-FO); B-24J; B-24L and B-24M.
Station
WENDLING	1 Aug. 43-15 Jun. 45 (Air ech. in from 15 Aug. 43).

Group COs
Col Irvine A. Rendle:	26 Jan. 43-21 Jun. 44.
Col Lorin L. Johnson:	21 Jun. 44-27 May 45.
Lt Col Lawrence G. Gilbert:	27 May 45-Jun. 45.

First Mission: 9 Sep. 43. **Last Mission:** 25 Apr. 45. **Total Missions:** 285.
Total Credit Sorties: 7,060. **Total Bomb Tonnage:** 17,452 tons.
A/c MIA: 127. **Other Op. Losses:** 57. **E/a Claims:** 144-45-49.
Major Awards
Distinguished Unit Citation: 24 Feb. 44: Gotha.
Claims to Fame
Despite heavy losses its bombing efficiency better than average for 2BD groups during first 9 months ops.
First B-24H group in 8AF.
Early History
Activated 26 Jan. 43 at Davis-Monthan AAF, Ariz. and trained there until end Feb. 43. Moved Biggs Fd, Tex. 1 Mar. 43, and to Alamogordo AAB, NM. on 18 Apr. 43. On 18 Jul. 43 ground echelon left for port of embarkation. Sailed New York 25 Jul. 43; arrived UK 30 Jul. 43.
Subsequent History
Redeployed USA in May/Jun. 45. First a/c left UK 29 May 45. Ground echelon sailed on *Queen Mary* 15 Jun. 45 and arrived New York 20 Jun. 45. Personnel 30 days R & R. Group established Charleston AAFd, SC. late Jun. 45 for air transport duties but apparently not fully manned. Inactivated Charleston 13 Sep. 45. In nineteen-fifties squadrons of this Group activated as missile experimental and training units in SAC.

398th Bombardment Group (H)

Assigned Eighth AF: April 44.
Wing & Command Assignments
1 BD, 1 CBW:	22 Apr. 44.
1 AD, 1 CBW:	1 Jan. 45.

Component Squadrons
600th, 601st, 602nd and 603rd Bombardment Squadron (H).
Combat Aircraft
B-17G (from blocks 45-BO).
Station
NUTHAMPSTEAD	22 Apr. 44-22 Jun. 45.

Group COs
Col Frank P. Hunter:	1 Mar. 43-23 Jan. 45, MIA.
Lt Col Lewis P. Ensign:	29 Jan. 45-18 Apr. 45.
Lt Col Arthur F. Briggs:	18 Apr. 45-Jun. 45.

First Mission: 6 May 44. **Last Mission:** 25 Apr. 45. **Total Missions:** 195.

Total Credit Sorties: 6,419. **Totam Bomb Tonnage:** 15,781.2 (no leaflets).
A/c MIA: 58. **E/a Claims:** 5-2-11.
Major Awards
None.
Early History
Activated 1 Mar. 43 at Ephrata AAB, Wash. Group assembled at Blyth AAFd, Cal. and then moved to Geiger Fd, Wash. on 20 Apr. 43 to complete training. On 20 Jun. 43 moved Rapid City AAB, SD. to take up Replacement Training Unit duties. Trained 326 B-17 crews from Aug. to Dec. 43 but at beginning of New Year reverted to training for combat. Ground echelon began movement overseas on 4 Apr. 43. Camp Myles Standish, Mass. 7-12 Apr. 43. Personnel embarked on *USS Wakefield*. Sailed Boston 13 Apr. and arrived Liverpool 21 Apr. 44.
Subsequent History
Redeployed USA in May/Jun. 45. A/c left 21-27 May 45. Ground echelon to Greenock 22 Jun. 45 and sailed on *Queen Elizabeth* arriving New York 29 Jun. 45. After 30 days R & R some personnel assembled at Drew Fd, Fla. where Group inactivated 1 Sep. 45.

401st Bombardment Group (H)

Assigned Eighth AF: Nov. 43.
Wing & Command Assignments
VIII BC, 1 BD, 92 CBW: 1 Nov. 43.	
VIII BC, 1 BD, 94 CBW: 15 Dec. 43.	
1 BD, 94 CBW:	8 Jan. 44.
1 AD, 94 CBW:	1 Jan. 45.

Component Squadrons
612th, 613th, 614th and 615th Bombardment Squadron (H).
Combat Aircraft
B-17G (from block 1).
Station
DEENETHORPE	3 Nov. 43-20 Jun. 45 (Air ech. at Polebrook and Bassingbourn from late Oct. 43. In Deenethorpe 19 Nov. 43).

Group COs
Col Harold W. Bowman:	Jun. 43-5 Dec. 44.
Col William T. Seawell:	5 Dec. 44-Jun. 45.

First Mission: 26 Nov. 43. **Last Mission:** Apr. 45. **Total Missions:** 255.
Total Credit Sorties: 7,430. **Total Bomb Tonnage:** 17,778.1 tons (17.7 tons leaflets).
A/c MIA: 95. **E/a Claims:** 75-28-92.
Major Awards
Two Distinguished Unit Citations: 11 Jan. 44 (all 1 BD groups).
20 Feb. 44: Leipzig.
Claims to Fame
Second best rating in bombing accuracy for Eighth AF.
Early History
Activated 1 Apr. 43 at Ephrata AAB, Wash. Moved Geiger Fd, Wash. 28 May 43, and to Great Falls AAB, Mont. in Jul. 43. Completed final training and ground echelon began movement overseas on 19 Oct. 43. After staging at Camp Shanks, NY. embarked on *Queen Mary*, sailing 27 Oct. Arrived Greenock 2 Nov. 43 and disembarked following day. Air echelon left Great Falls 18 Oct. 43 for final inspections at Scott Fd, then via Goose Bay, Meeks Fd, Iceland, to Prestwick.
Subsequent History
Redeployed USA in Jun. 45. Air echelon flew via North Atlantic ferry route a/c departing Deenethorpe 30 May-4 Jun. 45. Ground echelon by train to Gourock on 20 Jun. 45, sailing *Queen Elizabeth* 25 Jun. 45, arriving 30 Jun. 45. Personnel 30 days R & R, some reassembling at Sioux Falls AAFd, SD. where Group inactivated 28 Aug. 45. Reformed as fighter-bomber wing in 1954. For many years based England AFB, La. then assigned USAFE and based Spain.

445th Bombardment Group (H)

Assigned Eighth AF: Nov. 43.
Wing & Command Assignments
VIII BC, 2 BD, 2 CBW: 4 Nov. 43.	
2 BD, 2 CBW:	8 Jan. 44.
2 AD, 2 CBW:	1 Jan. 45.

Component Squadrons
700th, 701st, 702nd and 703rd Bombardment Squadron (H).
Combat Aircraft
B-24H (from blocks 1-FO); B-24J, B-24L and B-24M.
Station
TIBENHAM   4 Nov. 43-28 May 45 (Air ech. in 17 Nov.-
                    21 Dec. 43).

Group COs
Col Robert H. Terrill: 1 Apr. 43-24 Jul. 44.
Col William W. Jones: 25 Jul. 44-12 Sep. 45.
First Mission: 13 Dec. 44. **Last Mission:** 25 Apr. 45. **Total
Missions:** 282.
Total Credit Sorties: 7,145. **Total Bomb Tonnage:** 16,732.
A/c MIA: 108. **Other Op. Losses:** 25. **E/a Claims:** 89-31-37.
Major Awards
Distinguished Unit Citation: 24 Feb. 44: Gotha.
Claims to Fame
Highest Group loss on a single mission: 27 Sep. 44—30.
Above 2BD average in bombing accuracy record for last six months
of war.
Early History
Activated 1 Apr. 43 at Gowen Fd, Idaho, where initial training
undertaken. Established at Wendover AAB, Utah, from 8 Jun. 43.
Moved to Sioux City AB, Iowa, 5-7 Jul. 43 to complete training.
On 20 Oct. 43 ground echelon moved Camp Shanks, NY. and embarked
on *Queen Mary*, 26 Oct. 43, sailing next day. Arrived Clyde 2 Nov. 43.
Air echelon departed Sioux City late Oct. 43 and flew to UK via
southern route, Florida, Puerto Rico, Brazil, West Africa.
Subsequent History
Redeployed USA May/Jun. 45. First a/c left Tibenham 17 May 45
and departed UK 20 May 45. Ground echelon left 28 May 45; 703BS
sailing on *USAT Argentine* from Southampton and other sqdns. on
USAT Cristobal at Bristol. Both ships arrived New York, 8 Jun. 45.
Personnel 30 days R & R. Group established Fort Dix, NJ. and
inactivated there 12 Sep. 45.
Allotted to USAF reserve forces, activated in 1952 as fighter
bomber group, later, as troop carrier wing with C-123. Converted
C-124 and served under MAC.

446th Bombardment Group (H)
"Bungay Buckeroos"

Assigned Eighth AF: Nov. 43.
Wing & Command Assignments
VIII BC, 2 BD, 20 CBW: 4 Nov. 43.
2 BD, 20 CBW: 8 Jan. 44.
2 AD, 20 CBW: 1 Jan. 45.
Component Squadrons
704th, 705th, 706th and 707th Bombardment Squadron (H).
Combat Aircraft
B-24H (from blocks 1-CF and FO); B-24J, B-24L and B-24M.
Station
BUNGAY   4 Nov. 43-5 Jul. 45 (Air ech. arrived late
                    Nov. 43).
Group COs
Col Jacob J. Brogger: 27 Sep. 43-22 Sep. 44
                                (WIA 18 Sep. 44).
Col Troy W. Crawford: 23 Sep. 44-4 Apr. 45, POW.
Lt Col William A. Schmidt: 4 Apr. 45-Unkn.
First Mission: 16 Dec. 43. **Last Mission:** 25 Apr. 45. **Total
Missions:** 273.
Total Credit Sorties: 7,259. **Total Bomb Tonnage:** 16,819.
A/c MIA: 58. **Other Op. Losses:** 28. **E/a Claims:** 34-11-8.
Major Awards
None.
Claims to Fame
Led 8AF and 2BD on first heavy bomber mission of D-Day.
"Ronnie" believed to be first 8AF B-24 to fly 100 missions.
706BS flew 62 consecutive missions and 707BS 68 without loss.
Early History
Activated 1 Apr. 43 at Davis-Monthan Fd, Ariz. Initial assembly at
this base. Moved Alamagordo, NM. on 6 Jun. 43 but immediately
moved again to Lowery AAB, Col. where training completed. Ground
echelon left 18/19 Oct. 43 for Camp Shanks, NY. and embarked on
Queen Mary 25 Oct. 43. Sailed 27 Oct. 43 arriving Clyde 2 Nov. 43.
Air echelon left Lowery AAB, 20/26 Oct. 43 for Lincoln AAB, Neb.
Then to UK via southern route; Florida, Puerto Rico, Brazil, Dakar,
Marrakesh. One a/c missing on Puerto Rico leg, and one shot down by
e/a when off course over France.

Subsequent History
Redeployed USA Jun./Jul. 45. A/c departed mid-Jun. 45. One lost
in UK Azores leg. Ground echelon sailed Greenock on *Queen Mary*,
6 Jul. 45 and arrived New York 11 Jul. 45. Camp Kilmer and 30 days
R & R for personnel. Some assembled Sioux Falls AAFd, SD. where
group inactivated 28 Aug. 45.

447th Bombardment Group (H)

Assigned Eighth AF: Nov. 43.
Wing & Command Assignments
VIII BC, 3 BD, 4 CBW: Nov. 43.
3 BD, 4 CBW: 8 Jan. 44.
3 AD, 4 CBW: 1 Jan. 45.
(22 Nov. 44-16 Feb. 45 4CBW had operational and administrative
control of groups and was termed 4BW(P).
Component Squadrons
708th, 709th, 710th and 711th Bombardment Squadron (H).
Combat Aircraft
B-17G (from blocks 5).
Station
RATTLESDEN   30 Nov. 43-2 Aug. 45 (Air ech. in mid-Nov.
                     43).

Group COs
Col Hunter Harris Jr: 23 May 43-c. 24 Sep. 44.
Col William J. Wrigglesworth: 25 Sep. 44-31 Mar. 45.
Lt Col Louis G. Thorup: 31 Mar. 45-30 Jun. 45.
Lt Col Wilfred Beaver: 1 Jul. 45-Aug. 45.
First Mission: 24 Dec. 43. **Last Mission:** 21 Apr. 45. **Total
Missions:** 257.
Total Credit Sorties: 7,605. **Total Bomb Tonnage:** 17,102.9 tons
(394.9 tons supplies, etc.).
A/c MIA: 97. **Other Op. Losses:** 43. **E/a Claims:** 86-41-66.
Major Awards
Medal of Honor: 2/Lt Robert E. Femoyer: 2 Nov. 44.
Claims to Fame
"Milk Wagon" set record for 3AD B-17 with 129 missions and no
turn-backs.
Early History
Activated 1 May 43 at Ephrata AAB, Wash. After initial training
moved to Rapid City AAB, SD. 13 Jun. 43, and on 31 Jul. 43 to
Harvard AAB. Neb. Completed training at this base with ground
echelon leaving for port of embarkation 11 Nov. 43. Sailed on *Queen
Elizabeth* 23 Nov. 43 and arrived Clyde 29 Nov. 43. Air echelon
moved overseas via southern ferry route in early Nov. 43.
Subsequent History
Redeployed USA Jun./Aug. 45. Air echelon left Rattlesden 29/30
Jun. 45. Ground echelon sailed part on *USAT Joseph T. Robinson* and
part on *USAT Benjamin R. Milam* from Liverpool on 1 and 3 Aug. 45
respectively. Ships arrived Boston 12 and 15 Aug. 45. Personnel 30
days R & R. Group established Drew Fd. Fla. in Aug. 45 but apparently
not manned and inactivated 7 Nov. 45.

448th Bombardment Group (H)

Assigned Eighth AF: Nov. 43.
Wing & Command Assignments
VIII BC, 2 BD, 20 CBW: 30 Nov. 43.
2 BD, 20 CBW: 8 Jan. 44.
2 AD, 20 CBW: 1 Jan. 45.
Component Squadrons
712th, 713th, 714th and 715th Bombardment Squadron (H).
Combat Aircraft
B-24H (from blocks 5-CF, 10-FO); B-24J, B-24L & B-24M.
Station
SEETHING   30 Nov. 43-6 Jul. 45 (Air ech. in c. 7 Dec.-
                    22 Dec. 43).
Group COs
Col James M. Thompson: 1 May 43-1 Apr. 44, MIA.
Col Gerry L. Mason: 3 Apr. 44-13 Nov. 44.
Col Charles B. Westover: 14 Nov. 44-c. 27 May 45.
Lt Col Lester F. Miller: 27 May 45-Jul. 45.
First Mission: 22 Dec. 43. **Last Mission:** 25 Apr. 45. **Total

Missions: 262.
Total Credit Sorties: 6,774. **Total Bomb Tonnage**: 15,272 tons.
A/c MIA: 101. **Other Op. Losses**: 34. **E/a Claims**: 44-19-30.
Major Awards
None.
Claims to Fame
Joe McConnell, top air ace of Korean War was a navigator with Group from Jan. 45.
Early History
Activated 1 May 43 at Gowen Fd, Idaho. Initial training at this base, followed by move to Wendover Fd, Utah, 4 Jul. 43, for second phase training. Sioux City AAB, Iowa, for final training, 16 Sep. 43 to early Nov. 43. Ground echelon to Camp Shanks, NY. later sailing on *Queen Elizabeth* 23 Nov. 43. Arrived Clyde 29 Nov. 43. Air echelon left Sioux City 3 Nov. 43 for Herrington Fd, Kan. After final processing left for UK via Puerto Rico, Trinidad, Belem, Dakar and Marrakesh. Three a/c lost en route.
Subsequent History
Redeployed USA in Jun./Jul. 45. A/c left UK mid Jun. 45. Ground echelon sailed on *Queen Mary* from Greenock 6 Jul. 45 arriving New York 11 Jul. 45. Personnel 30 days R & R. Group established Sioux Falls, SD. Selected to train as B-29 unit. On 6 May 46 715BS was re-assigned to 509BG and survived in that organisation until 1965. 448BG inactivated 4 Aug. 46, in fact, both Group Hq. and squadrons redesignated as 92BG and its units.

452nd Bombardment Group (H)

Assigned Eighth AF: Jan. 44.
Wing & Command Assignments
3 BD, 45 CBW: Jan. 44.
3 AD, 45 CBW: 1 Jan. 45.
Component Squadrons
728th, 729th, 730th and 731st Bombardment Squadron (H).
Combat Aircraft
B-17G (from block 10).
Station
DEOPHAM GREEN   3 Jan. 44-5 Aug. 45 (Gnd. ech. in 9 Jan. 44).
Group COs

Lt Col Herbert O. Wangeman:	1 Jun. 43-7 Feb. 44.
Lt Col Robert B. Satterwhite:	8 Feb. 44-27 Feb. 44.
Lt Col Marvin F. Stalder:	28 Feb. 44-29 Mar. 44.
Col Thetus C. Odom:	30 Mar. 44-c. 24 Jul. 44.
Col Archibald Y. Smith:	c. 24 Jul. 44-c. 1 Aug. 44.
Col William D. Eckert:	c. 1 Aug. 44-12 Sep. 44.
Lt Col Charles W. She.burne:	13 Sep. 44-c. 24 Sep. 44.
Col Burnham L. Batson:	c. 25 Sep. 44-6 Jun. 45.
Col Jack E. Shuck:	6 Jun. 45-Jul. 45.

First Mission: 5 Feb. 44. **Last Mission**: 21 Apr. 45. **Total Missions**: 250.*
Total Credit Sorties: 7,279. **Total Bomb Tonnage**: 16,466.6 tons (150 tons supplies, etc.).
A/c MIA: 110. **Other Op. Losses**: 48. **E/a Claims**: 96½-45-58.
Major Awards
Distinguished Unit Citation: 7 Apr. 45: Kaltenkirchen.
Two Medals of Honor: 1/Lt Donald J. Gott: 9 Nov. 44.
2/Lt William E. Metzger: 9 Nov. 44.
Claims to Fame
More COs than any other Bomb Group during course of hostilities.
Early History
Activated 1 Jun. 43 at Geiger Fd, Wash. Transferred Rapid City AAB, SD. 15 Jun. 43 and trained there until early Oct. 43. Moved Pendleton Fd, Ore. 11 Oct. 43 and to Walla Walla AAFd, Wash. 4 Nov. 43. Ground echelon left for Camp Shanks, NY. on 23 Dec. 43 and sailed on *Queen Elizabeth* 2 Jan. 44, arriving in Clyde,8 Jan. 44. Air echelon began overseas movement early Dec. 43 via southern ferry route, most a/c reaching UK a few days before ground echelon arrived.
Subsequent History
Redeployed USA Jun./Aug. 45. A/c left Deopham Green late Jun. 45. Ground echelon sailed on *Queen Elizabeth* from Greenock 5 Aug. 45, arriving New York 11 Aug. 45. Personnel 30 days R & R Group established Sioux Falls AAFd, SD. and inactivated there 28 Aug. 45.
*(5 food missions May 45, 369.1 tons).

453rd Bombardment Group (H)

Assigned Eighth AF: Dec. 43.
Wing & Command Assignments
VIII BC, 2 BD, 2 CBW: 23 Dec. 44.
2 BD, 2 CBW: 8 Jan. 44.
2 AD, 2 CBW: 1 Jan. 45.
Component Squadrons
732nd, 733rd, 734th and 735th Bombardment Squadron (H).
Combat Aircraft
B-24H (from blocks 1-CF, 5-DT, 10-FO); B-24J, B-24L and B-24M.
Station
OLD BUCKENHAM   22/23 Dec. 43-9 May 45 (Air ech. in early Jan. 44).
Group COs

Col Joseph A. Miller:	29 Jun. 43-18 Mar. 44, MIA.
Col Ramsey D. Potts Jr:	19 Mar. 44-6 Jul. 44.
Col Lawrence M. Thomas:	7 Jul. 44-25 Jan. 45.
Lt Col Edward F. Hubbard:	25 Jan. 45-May 45.

First Mission: 5 Feb. 44. **Last Mission**: 12 Apr. 45. **Total Missions**: 259.
Total Credit Sorties: 6,655. **Total Bomb Tonnage**: 15,804 tons.
A/c MIA: 58. **Other Op. Losses**:   **E/a Claims**: 42-12-19.

Major Awards
None.
Claims to Fame
733rd BS completed 82 consecutive missions without loss—a record.
James Stewart, of film fame, was Group Executive Officer from Mar. 44.
Early History
Activated 1 Jun. 43 at Wendover Fd, Utah. Established at Pocatello AAFd, Idaho, on 29 Jul. 43 and trained there for two months. Moved March Fd, Cal. 30 Sep. 43 to complete training. Ground echelon left March for port of embarkation 2 Dec. 43.
Subsequent History
Removed from operations 12 Apr. 45 to prepare for return to USA and possible deployment in the Pacific theatre. A/c apparently remained in UK. Group personnel left Old Buckenham 9 May 45 for port of embarkation. Established at New Castle AAFd, Del. 25 May 43 as prospective very heavy bomb group but project dropped. From 18 Jun. 45 to 12 Sep. 45 Group located at Fort Dix AAB, NJ. Inactivated 12 Sep. 45.

457th Bombardment Group (H)

Assigned Eighth AF: Jan. 44.
Wing & Command Assignments
1 BD, 94 CBW: 21 Jan. 44.
1 AD, 94 CBW: 1 Jan. 45.
Component Squadrons
748th, 749th, 750th and 751st Bombardment Squadron (H).
Combat Aircraft
B-17G (from blocks 25).
Station
GLATTON   21 Jan. 44-21 Jun. 45 (Air ech. arrived between 21-31 Jan. 44).
Group COs

Col James R. Luper:	4 Jan. 44-7 Oct. 44, POW.
Col Harris E. Rogner:	11 Oct. 44-Aug. 45.

First Mission: 21 Feb. 44. **Last Mission**: 20 Apr. 45. **Total Missions**: 237.
Total Credit Sorties: 7,086. **Total Bomb Tonnage**: 16,915.5 tons (142.6 tons leaflets).
A/c MIA: 83. **E/a Claims**: 33-12-50.
Major Awards
None.
Early History
Activated 1 Jul. 43 at Geiger Fd, Wash. Group assembled at Rapid City, SD. from 9 Jul. 43 and underwent first and second phase training at this base. Training continued at Ephrata AAB, Wash. 23 Oct. 43 to early Dec. 43. Final preparation for overseas service at Wendover Fd, Utah, 4 Dec. 43 to 1 Jan. 44. Col Herbert E. Rice took command

in Jul. 43 and was followed by Lt Col Hugh D. Wallace on 2 Sep. 43.
Subsequent History
Redeployed USA in May/Jun. 45. A/c left Glatton 19-23 May. Ground echelon departed 21 Jun. 45 and sailed on *Queen Elizabeth* from Gourock, 24 Jun. 45, and arrived in New York 29 Jun. 45. After 30 days R & R some personnel assembled Sioux Falls AAFd, SD. in late Jul. 45. Group inactivated at this base 28 Aug. 45.

458th Bombardment Group (H)

Assigned Eighth AF: Jan. 44.
Wing & Command Assignments
2 BD, 96 CBW:	11 Jan. 44.	
2 AD, 96 CBW:	1 Jan. 45.	

Component Squadrons
752nd, 753rd, 754th and 755th Bombardment Squadron (H).
Combat Aircraft
B-24H (from blocks 10-CF and DT, 15-FO); B-24J, B-24L and B-24M.
Station
HORSHAM ST. FAITHS: c. 29 Jan. 44-3 Jul. 45.
Group COs
Col James H. Isbell:	16 Dec. 43-9 Mar. 45.
Col Allen F. Herzberg:	10 Mar. 45-18 Jun. 45.

First Mission: 24 Feb. 44. **Last Mission:** 25 Apr. 45. **Total Missions:** 240.
Total Credit Sorties: 5,759. **Total Bomb Tonnage:** 13,204.
A/c MIA: 47. **Other Op. Losses:** 18. **E/a Claims:** 28-3-14.
Major Awards
None.
Claims to Fame
Carried out operational test of Azon radio-controlled bomb for 8AF.
Early History
Activated 1 Jul. 43 at Wendover Fd, Utah. Assembly began at Gowen Fd, Idaho, on 28 Jul. 43 under command of Lt Col Robert Γ. Hardy. Trained there until early Sep. 43 then moved Kearns Fd, Utah. After four days Hq. moved to Wendover Fd, Utah on 15 Sep. 43. Final move of training period 31 Oct. 43 to Tonopah AAFd, Nev. Ground echelon to port of embarkation 29 Dec. 43. Air echelon flew to UK via southern ferry route, last a/c arriving 18 Feb. 44. G/ech. sailed New York on USS *Florence Nightingale* 18 Jan. 44.

Subsequent History
Redeployed USA in Jun./Jul. 45. A/c left Horsham St. Faiths c. 14 Jun. 45. Ground echelon sailed on *Queen Mary* from Greenock 6 Jul. 45, arriving New York 11 Jul. 45. Personnel on 30 days R & R. Group established Walker AAFd, Kan. 25 Jul. 45, and later March Fd, Cal. to train as B-29 unit but with end of war in Pacific, Group run down and inactivated 17 Oct. 45.

466th Bombardment Group (H)

Assigned Eighth AF: Mar. 44.
Wing & Command Assignments
2 BD, 96 CBW:	7 Mar. 44.	
2 AD, 96 CBW:	1 Jan. 45.	

Component Squadrons
784th, 785th, 786th and 787th Bombardment Squadron (H).
Combat Aircraft
B-24H (from blocks 10-CF, 15-DT and FO); B-24J, B-24L and B-24M.
Station
ATTLEBRIDGE	7 Mar. 44-6 Jul. 45 (Air ech. arrived UK c. 21 Feb. 44).

Group COs
Col Arthur J. Pierce:	17 Dec. 43-1 Aug. 44.
Col Luther J. Fairbanks:	1 Aug. 44-30 Oct. 44.
Col William H. Cleveland:	1 Nov. 44-17 Feb. 45.
Col Elvin S. Ligon:	17 Feb. 45-Jul. 45.

First Mission: 22 Mar. 44. **Last Mission:** 25 Apr. 45. **Total Missions:** 232.
Total Credit Sorties: 5,762. **Total Bomb Tonnage:** 12,914 tons.
A/c MIA: 47. **Other Op. Losses:** 24. **E/a Claims:** 29-3-14.
Major Awards
None.
Claims to Fame
785BS flew 55 consecutive missions (to 25 Jul. 44) without loss.

Early History
Activated 1 Aug. 43 at Alamogordo AAFd, NM. Commenced training for combat at Kearns Fd, Utah end Aug. 43, remaining there until 24 Nov. 43 when base moved back to Alamogordo AAFd, NM. Moved to Topeka AAFd, Kan. early Feb. 44 and after a week's stay began movement to UK. Ground echelon to port of embarkation, air echelon by southern ferry route. G/e sailed New York on *Queen Mary*, 28 Feb. 44.
Subsequent History
Redeployed USA Jun./Jul. 45. A/c left Attlebridge mid-Jun. 45. Ground echelon sailed from Greenock in *Queen Mary* 6 Jul. 45, arriving New York 11 Jul. 45. Personnel 30 days R & R. Group established Sioux Falls AAFd, SD. Selected for B-29 training and established Pueblo AAB, Col. and then Davis-Monthan Fd, Ariz. With termination of hostilities in Pacific, Group run down and inactivated 17 Oct. 45.

467th Bombardment Group (H)
"The Rackheath Aggies"

Assigned Eighth AF: 11 Mar. 44.
Wing & Command Assignments
2 BD, 96 CBW:	11 Mar. 44.	
2 AD, 96 CBW:	1 Jan. 45.	

Component Squadrons
788th, 789th, 790th and 791st Bombardment Squadron (H).
(788BS transferred to 801BG(P) 11 May 45; reformed in 467BG on 12 Aug. 44).
Combat Aircraft
B-24H (from blocks 15-CF, DT and FO); B-24J, B-24L and B-24M.
Station
RACKHEATH	12 Mar. 44-c. 5 Jul. 45 (Air ech. in same day)

Group CO
Col Albert J. Shower:	25 Oct. 43-c. 12 Jun. 45

First Mission: 10 Apr. 44. **Last Mission:** 25 Apr. 45. **Total Missions:** 212.
Total Credit Sorties: 5,538. **Total Bomb Tonnage:** 13,333 tons.
A/c MIA: 29. **Other Op. Losses:** 19. **E/a Claims:** 6-5-2.
Major Awards
None.
Claims to Fame
Set unsurpassed record for bombing accuracy on 15 Apr. 45.
Best overall standing for bombing accuracy in Eighth AF.
Col Shower was only group CO in 8AF to bring a group to UK and remain in command to end of hostilities.
"Witchcraft" held 8AF record for B-24, with 130 missions, no turn-backs.
Early History
Activated 1 Aug. 43 at Wendover Fd, Utah. Assembled at Mountain Home AAFd, Idaho, from 8 Sep. 43 to mid Oct. 43. Temporarily based at Kearns Fd, Utah, before commencing detailed training at Wendover Fd, on 1 Nov. 43 where Group remained for fifteen weeks. On 12 Feb. 44 ground echelon by train to Camp Shanks, NY. Sailed on *USAT Frederick Lykes* 28 Feb. 44 and arrived in the Clyde 10 Mar. 44. Air echelon left Wendover 12 Feb. 44 and flew to UK by south Atlantic ferry route. One B-24 lost with all crew in Atlas mountains.
Subsequent History
Redeployed USA Jun./Jul. 45. Majority a/c left Rackheath 12 Jun. 45. Ground echelon sailed *Queen Mary* from Greenock 6 Jul. 45 and arrived New York 11 Jul. 45. Personnel 30 days R & R. Group selected for training as B-29 unit, first at Alamogordo AAFd, NM. and then Harvard AAFd, Neb. Established at Clovis AAFd, NM. in Dec. 45 and remained there until inactivated 4 Aug. 46. In fact, 467BG and its squadrons were redesigned as 301BG and appropriate squadrons.

479th Fighter Group
"Riddle's Raiders"

Assigned Eighth AF: 14 May 44.
Wing & Command Assignments
VIII FC, 65 FW:	15 May 44.	
2 BD, 65 FW:	15 Sep. 44.	
2 AD, 65 FW:	1 Jan. 45.	

Component Squadrons
434th, 435th and 436th Fighter Squadron.

Combat Aircraft
P-38J (blocks 10-25), May 44 to 27 Sep. 44.
P-51D (from block 10), 13 Sep. 44-Sep. 45.

Station
WATTISHAM 15 May 44-22 Nov. 45.

Group COs

Lt Col Kyle L. Riddle:	25 Dec. 43-10 Aug. 44 MIA-evaded.
Col Hubert A. Zemke:	12 Aug. 44-30 Oct. 44, POW.
Col Kyle L. Riddle:	1 Nov. 44-late 45.

First Mission: 26 May 44. **Last Mission:** 25 Apr. 45. **Total Missions:** 351.

A/c MIA: 69. **E/a Claims:** 155 air; 279 ground.

Major Awards
Distinguished Unit Citation: 18 Aug., 5 and 26 Sep. 44; strafing airfields and air combat, nr. Munster (26 Sep.).

Claims to Fame
Last fighter group to join 8AF.
First combat with 'jet' e/a—Captain Jeffrey, 29 Jul. 44.
Last e/a claimed by 8AF—25 Apr. 45, Lt Hilton Thompson.

Early History
Activated 15 Oct. 43 at Glendale GCAT, Cal. Trained there with P-38s until 6 Feb. 44. Moved Lomita Flight Strip, Cal. and on 7 Mar. 44 to Santa Maria AAFd, Cal. Commenced overseas movement mid-Apr. arriving Camp Kilmer, NJ. 20 Apr. 44. Sailed on *USS Argentina*, 2 May 44 and arrived Clyde 14 May 44.

Subsequent History
Many personnel transferred after VE-day. A/c to depots Sep. 45. Last fighter group to return to US, sailing from UK c. 23 Nov. 44 and arriving New York c. 29 Nov. 45. Group established Camp Kilmer, NJ. and inactivated there 1 Dec. 45.

482nd Bombardment Group (H)

Assigned Eighth AF: 20 Aug. 43.

Wing & Command Assignments

VIII BC, 1 BD:	20 Aug. 43.
1 BD:	8 Jan. 44.
VIII AFCC:	14 Feb. 44.
VIII FC:	1 Oct. 44.
1 AD:	1 Jan. 45.

Component Squadrons
812th, 813th and 814th Bombardment Squadron (H).

Combat Aircraft
812BS: B-17F and G H2X, B-17G Eagle.
813BS: B-17F H2S and Oboe; B-17G H2X.
814BS: B-24H and J H2X, B-24L, APS-15A and B-24M Eagle.

Station
ALCONBURY 20 Aug. 43-24 Jun. 45.

Group COs

Col Baskin R. Lawrence Jr:	20 Aug. 43-1 Dec. 43.
Col Howard Moore:	1 Dec. 43-14 Dec. 44.
Lt Col Clement W. Bird:	15 Dec. 44-21 May 45.

First Mission: 27 Sep. 43. **Last Mission:** 22 Mar. 44.

Total Sorties: with 1 BD (to 11 Feb. 44), 246; with VIII CC approx. 100. **Total Bomb Tonnage:** 496.7 tons.

A/c MIA: 7. **E/a Claims:** (with 1 BD); 14-1-12.

Major Awards
Distinguished Unit Citation: 11 Jan. 44 (all 1 BD groups).

Claims to Fame
Pioneered radar bombing devices for USAAF.
Only bomb group in 8AF raised in UK.

Early and Background History
Activated 20 Aug. 43 at Alconbury. Original personnel specially selected crews from VIII BC plus a few key men who had been involved with 329BS Gee experiments earlier in year. Ground crews from disbanded 479th Anti-Sub. Group. Initial experiments under auspices of 92BG, which also provided personnel. Had three-fold mission: combat operations; to develop technique and test radar devices; train pathfinder crews. As lead aircraft, 482BG B-17s and B-24s usually flew missions from stations of other groups, and some key personnel of host group flying in the PFF a/c. Ceased regular operations late March but continued to undertake special operations, notably D-Day when 18 crews were provided to lead bomb groups.
Transferred Composite Command Feb. 44 when emphasis shifted to training radar operators. Initially RAF instructors, and courses begun 21 Feb. 44. Training and experimentation remained its chief role for the remainder of war. From Aug. 44 to April 45 conducted 202 radar scope and 'nickling' sorties over hostile territory without loss: 45 tons bombs.

Subsequent History
Redeployed USA May/Jun. 45. Air echelon between 27-30 May 45. Ground echelon sailed on *Queen Elizabeth* from Gourock 24 Jun. 45. Group re-established at Victorville AAF, Cal. on 5 Jul. 45 but inactivated there 1 Sep. 45.

486th Bombardment Group (H)

Assigned Eighth AF: Mar. 44.

Wing & Command Assignments

3 BD, 92 CBW:	Mar. 44.
3 BD, 4 BW(P):	22 Nov. 44.
3 AD, 4 BW(P):	1 Jan. 45.
3 AD, 4 CBW:	c. 16 Feb. 45.

Component Squadrons
832nd, 833rd, 834th and 835th Bombardment Squadron (H).

Combat Aircraft
B-24H (from block 15) and B-24J; to 19 Jul. 44.
B-17G (from block 75-BO) in combat from 1 Aug. 44.

Station
SUDBURY Late Mar. 44-c. 25 Aug. 45.

Group COs

Col Glendon P. Overing:	20 Sep. 43-c. 13 Apr. 45.
Col William B. Kieffer:	c. 13 Apr. 45-Jul. 45.

First Mission: 7 May 44. **Last Mission:** 21 Apr. 45. **Total Missions:** 188 (46 with B-24).

Total Credit Sorties: 6,173. **Total Bomb Tonnage:** 14,517 tons (4.6 tons leaflets, etc.).

A/c MIA: 33. **Other Op. Losses:** 24. **E/a Claims:** 8½-1-6.

Major Awards
None.

Claims to Fame
834BS lost no planes or personnel on first 100 missions.

Early History
Activated 20 Sep. 43 at McCook AAFd, Neb. Moved Davis-Monthan Fd, Ariz. 9 Nov. 43, and completed training in early Mar. 44. Air echelon moved overseas early Mar. 44 via southern ferry route.

Subsequent History
Redeployed USA Jul./Aug. 45. A/c left Sudbury first week July. Ground echelon sailed Southampton on *Queen Elizabeth* 25 Aug. 45, arriving New York 31 Aug. 45. Personnel 30 days R & R. Group established Drew Fd, Fla. 3 Spr. 45 and inactivated there 7 Nov. 45.

487th Bombardment Group (H)

Assigned Eighth AF: April 44.

Wing & Command Assignments

3 BD, 92 CBW:	5 Apr. 44.
3 BD, 4 BW(P):	22 Nov. 44.
3 AD, 4 BW(P):	1 Jan. 45.
3 AD, 4 CBW:	c. 16 Feb. 45.

Component Squadrons
836th, 837th, 838th and 839th Bombardment Squadron (H).

Combat Aircraft
B-24H (from block 15) and B-24J to 19 Jul. 44.
B-17G (from block 75-BO) in combat from 1 Aug. 44.

Station
LAVENHAM 4 Apr. 45-24 Aug. 45 (Air ech. in 13-17 Apr. 44).

Group COs

Lt Col Beirne Lay Jr:	28 Feb. 44-11 May 44 MIA-evaded.
Col Robert Taylor III:	12 May 44-27 Dec. 44.
Col William K. Martin:	28 Dec. 44-May 45.
Col Nicholas T. Perkins:	3 Jun. 45-Aug. 45.
(Lt Col Howard C. Todt acting CO May 45-2 Jun. 45).	

First Mission: 7 May 44. **Last Mission:** 21 Apr. 45. **Total Missions:** 185 (46 with B-24).

Total Credit Sorties: 6,021. **Total Bomb Tonnage:** 14,041.4 tons (158.1 tons supplies, etc.).

A/c MIA: 48. **Other Op. Losses:** 37. **E/a Claims:** 22-6-18.

Major Awards
None.

Claims to Fame

Led largest 8AF mission of war—24 Dec. 44.

Led 3AD in bombing accuracy from Jan. 45 to end of war with strikes within 1,000 ft MPI.

Early History

Activated 20 Sep. 43 at Bruning AAFd, Neb. Moved Alamogordo AAFd, NM. 15 Dec. 44 to complete training. Ground echelon left Alamogordo 10 Mar. 44 for Camp Kilmer, NJ. and sailed on *Duchess of Bedford* 23 Mar. 44, arriving Gourock 3 April 44. Air echelon started overseas movement 23 Mar. 44, taking southern ferry route to UK arriving Nuts Corner, Valley and Prestwick early April 45.

Subsequent History

Redeployed USA Jul./Aug. 45. A/c left Lavenham first week Jul. 45. Ground echelon sailed *Queen Elizabeth* 25 Aug. 45 arriving New York 1 Sep. 45. Personnel 30 days R & R. Group established Drew Fd, Fla. 3 Sep. 45, and inactivated there 7 Nov. 45.

489th Bombardment Group (H)

Assigned Eighth AF: Apr. 44-29 Nov. 44.
Wing & Command Assignments

2 BD, 95 CBW: c. 5 May 44.
2 BD, 20 CBW: 14 Aug. 44.

Component Squadrons

844th, 845th, 846th and 847th Bombardment Squadron (H).

Combat Aircraft

B-24H (from block 15-FO) and B-24J.

Station

HALESWORTH   c 1 May 44-c. 29 Nov. 44.

Group CO

Col Ezekiel W. Napier: 20 Oct. 43-c. 29 Nov. 44.

First Mission: 30 May 44. **Last Mission:** 10 Nov. 44. **Total Missions:** 106.

Total Credit Sorties: 2,998. **Total Bomb Tonnage:** 6,951 tons.

A/c MIA: 29. **Other Op. Losses:** 12. **E/a Claims:** 1-0-0.

Major Awards

Medal of Honor: Lt Col Leon R. Vance: 5 Jun. 44.

Claims to Fame

Only Medal of Honor awarded to a B-24 crewman for an action flown from UK.

First 8AF group redeployed USA.

Early History

Activated 1 Oct. 43 at Wendover Fd, Utah. Complete formation and training of Group took place at this base (apart from special detachments). Left Wendover 3 April 44, air echelon flying to UK via southern ferry route. Gnd. ech. sailed Boston on USS *Wakefield* 13 Apr. 44.

Subsequent History

Selected for redeployment to Pacific theatre and became non-operational 14 Nov. 44. Relieved of assignment 29 Nov. 44 and returned USA. A/c and high proportion personnel reassigned to depots or other units in UK. Group established Bradley Fd, Conn. 12 Dec. 44, and was shortly thereafter transferred to Lincoln AFB, Neb. to train as B-29 unit. Equipped with this a/c at Great Bend AAFd, Kan. from Mar. 45. Alerted for movement to 8AF in Pacific late summer of 1945 but with termination of hostilities remained in USA and was inactivated 17 Oct. 45 at March Fd, Cal.

490th Bombardment Group (H)

Assigned Eighth AF: Apr. 44.
Wing & Command Assignments

3 BD, 93 CBW: 7 April 44.
3 AD, 93 CBW: 1 Jan. 45.

Component Squadrons

848th, 849th, 850th and 851st Bombardment Squadron (H).

(850BS transferred 801BG(P) 11 May 44 and reformed in 490BG 12 Aug. 44).

Combat Aircraft

B-24 H (from block 20) and B-24J to 6 Aug. 44.
B-17G (from block 80-BO) in combat from 27 Aug. 44.

Station

EYE   26 Apr. 44-24 Aug. 45 (Air ech. in 28
                 Apr.-1 Jun. 44).

Group COs

Col Lloyd H. Watnee: 30 Dec. 43-25 Jun. 44.
Col Frank P. Bostrom: 26 Jun. 44-c. 9 Jun. 45.
Col Gene H. Tibbets: c. 10 Jun. 45-c. 9 Jul. 45.

First Mission: 31 May 44. **Last Mission:** 20 Apr. 45. **Total Missions:** 158* (40 B-24).

Total Credit Sorties: 5,060. **Total Bomb Tonnage:** 12,407.4 tons (8.9 tons leaflets, etc.).

A/c MIA: 22. **Other Op. Losses:** 32. **E/a Claims:** 4-0-1.

Major Awards

None.

Claims to Fame

Lowest MIA losses of any 8AF bomb group in combat for extended period of time.

Early History

Activated 1 Oct. 43 at Salt Lake City AAB, Utah. Transferred Mountain Home AAFd, Idaho, where Group formed and trained Dec.-April 44. Ground echelon left for Camp Shanks, NY. 11 April 44 and sailed on *Nieu Amsterdam*, 15 April 44 arriving Clyde 25 April 44.

Air echelon commenced overseas movement 12 April 44 taking southern ferry route, via Florida, Trinidad, Brazil, Dakar and Marrakech to UK.

Subsequent History

Redeployed USA Jul./Aug. 45. A/c left Eye 6 and 8 Jul. 45. Ground echelon sailed from Southampton on *Queen Elizabeth* 26 Aug. 45 arriving New York 1 Sep. 45. Personnel 30 days R & R. Group established Drew Fd, Fla. 3 Sep. 45 and inactivated there 7 Nov. 45.

*(5 food missions May 45, dropping 384.4 tons).

491st Bombardment Group (H)
"The Ringmasters"

Assigned Eighth AF: 1 Jan. 44.
Wing & Command Assignments

2 BD, 95 CBW: c. 5 May 44.
2 BD, 14 CBW: 14 Aug. 44.
2 AD, 14 CBW: 1 Jan. 45.

Component Squadrons

852nd, 853rd, 854th and 855th Bombardment Squadron (H).

Combat Aircraft

B-24H (from block 20-FO); B-24J (from block 135-CO); B-24L, and B 24M.

Stations

METFIELD   25 Apr. 44-15 Aug. 44 (Air ech. in 15 May-
                   30 May 44).
NORTH PICKENHAM   15 Aug. 44-4 Jul. 45.

Group COs

Lt Col Carl T. Goldenberg: 12 Feb. 44-26 Jun. 44.
Col Frederick H. Miller: 26 Jun. 44-c. 20 Oct. 44.
Col Allen W. Reed: c. 20 Oct. 44-c. 18 Jun. 45.

First Mission: 2 Jun. 44. **Last Mission:** 25 Apr. 45. **Total Missions:** 187.

Total Credit Sorties: 5,005. **Total Bomb Tonnage:** 12,304 tons.

A/c MIA: 47. **Other Op. Losses:** 23. **E/a Claims:** 9-10-3.

Major Awards

Distinguished Unit Citation: 26 Nov. 44: Misburg.

Claims to Fame

Highest rate of operations of all B-24 groups.

Early History

Activated 1 Oct. 43 at Davis-Monthan Fd, Ariz. Moved Biggs Fd, Tex. 11 Nov. 43. Most of ground echelon transferred to B-29 groups and 8AF required to raise new ground echelon from personnel in UK. Group transferred less personnel and equipment to 2BD Hq. as of 1 Jan. 44. Apparently planned for 14CBW and North Pickenham designated as base in Feb. 44, but in view of advanced state of training of 492BG, 491BG rescheduled for Metfield. Four established groups in 2BD ordered to raise and train an additional squadron ground echelon each; one of the five ground echelons in each group then selected for 491BG. These transferred to Metfield c. 25 April 44. Air echelon continued training in US, moving Pueblo AAB, Col. early Jan. 44. Began movement overseas 21 April 44 via Florida, Trinidad, Brazil, Dakar and Marrakesh. Some key ground personnel (145) ex USA on 11 Apr. 44.

Subsequent History

Redeployed USA Jun./Jil. 45. A/c left 17-19 Jun. 45. Ground echelon sailed on *Queen Mary* 6 Jul. 45 arriving New York 11 Jul. 45. Personnel 30 days R & R. Group established McChord Fd, Wash. but inactivated there 8 Sep. 45.

492nd Bombardment Group (H)

(First organisation)

Assigned Eighth AF: April 44.
Wing & Command Assignment
2 BD, 14 CBW: 18 April 44-12 Aug. 44.
Component Squadrons
856th, 857th, 858th and 859th Bombardment Squadron (H).
(858BS transferred less a/c and aircrew 19 Jun. 44).
Combat Aircraft
B-24H (from block 15-FO) and B-24J (from block 50-CO).
Station
NORTH PICKENHAM 14 Apr. 44-12 Aug. 44 (Air ech. in from 18 Apr. 44).
Group CO
Col Eugene H. Snavely: 26 Jan. 44-12 Aug. 44.
First Mission: 11 May 44. **Last Mission:** 7 Aug. 44. **Total Missions:** 64.
Total Credit Sorties: 1,513. **Total Bomb Tonnage:** 3,757 tons.
A/c MIA: 51. **Other Op. Losses:** 6. **E/a Claims:** 21-0-3.
Major Awards
None.
Claims to Fame
Heavier losses than any other B-24 group for a three month period.
Early History
Activated 1 Oct. 43 at Clovis AAB, NM. Moved Alamogordo AAFd, NM. in Nov. 43 and trained there until end March. Only small part ground echelon (124 men) from US left Alamogordo 11 Apr. 44 and sailed on *Queen Elizabeth* 20 Apr. 44. Main body of ground echelon from four 2BD groups already in UK. These groups had been ordered to raise additional squadron ground echelon each. Air echelon left Alamogordo from 1 Apr. 44, to commence overseas movement by southern ferry route: Florida, Trinidad, Brazil, Dakar and Marrakesh.
Subsequent History
Group withdrawn from combat by order of 5 Aug. 44, for purpose of assuming special operations role conducted by 801st BG(P) at Harrington. This was a move less personnel and equipment and amounted to a redesignation of existing 801BG(P) and its squadrons. 856BS personnel and a/c to 36 and 406BS, 11 Aug. 44. 857BS crews and aircraft to other 2BD units and ground personnel to 490BG to form 850BS, 12 Aug. 44. 859BS crews, a/c and ground personnel to 467BG to form new 788BS. Original 492BG organisation was, in fact, disbanded.

493rd Bombardment Group (H)

"Helton's Hellcats"

Assigned Eighth AF: 1 Jan. 44.
Wing & Command Assignments
3 BD, 93 CBW: Apr. 44.
3 AD, 93 CBW: 1 Jan. 45.
Component Squadrons
860th, 861st, 862nd and 863rd Bombardment Squadron (H).
(862BS established as 3rd Scouting Force 1 Feb. 45: a/c and crews to other squadrons of Group. Ground personnel transferred. Re-established in 493BG May 45).
Combat Aircraft
B-24H (from block 20) and B-24J to 24 Aug. 44.
B-17G (from block 80-BO) in combat from 8 Sep. 44.
Station
DEBACH Apr. 44-6 Aug. 45 (US contingent Gnd. ech. in 27 May 44). (Air ech. arrived mid May 44).
LITTLE WALDEN 1 Mar. 45-1 Apr. 45 (Air ech. only).
Group COs
Col Elbert Helton: 1 Nov. 43-15 Feb. 45.
Col Robert B. Landry: 16 Feb.-May 45.
Lt Col Shepler W. Fritzgerald Jr: 5 Jun. 45-Aug. 45.
First Mission: 6 Jun. 44. **Last Mission:** 20 Apr. 45. **Total Missions:** 158* (47 B-24)
Total Credit Sorties: 4,871. **Total Bomb Tonnage:** 11,733.5 tons (3.8 tons leaflets, etc.).

A/c MIA: 41. **Other Op. Losses:** 31. **E/a Claims:** 11-6-3.
Major Awards
None.
Claims to Fame
Last 8AF group to become operational—6 Jun. 44.
Col Landry only man to command both fighter and bomber group in 8AF.
Early History
Activated 1 Nov. 43 at McCook AAFd, Neb. Owing to confusion in orders original personnel assembled at both McCook and Davis-Monthan AAFd, Ariz. the latter transferring to McCook in mid-Jan. 44. Owing to diversion of personnel to B-29 units Group transferred less air echelon and without personnel and equipment to UK as of 1 Jan. 44. Ground echelon raised with personnel from 3BD groups in UK and moved to Debach Apr. 44. Small ground contingent from US left McCook 2 May 44 and sailed Boston on *USS Brazil*, 12 May 44 arriving Liverpool 26 May 44. Air echelon left McCook c. 1 May 44 for overseas movement, flying northern ferry route to UK.
Subsequent History
Redeployed USA Jul./Aug. 45. A/c left Debach c. 30 Jun. 45. Ground echelon sailed on *Queen Elizabeth* 6 Aug. 45, arriving New York 11 Aug. 45. Personnel 30 days R & R. Group established at Sioux Falls AAFd, SD. 12 Aug. 45 and inactivated there 28 Aug. 45.
· *(6 food missions May 45 dropping 451.2 tons).

495th Fighter Training Group

Established in Eighth AF: 25 Dec. 43.
Wing & Command Assignments
VIII FC: 25 Dec. 43.
VIII AFCC: 14 Feb. 44.
VIII FC: 29 Sep. 44.
1 BD: 28 Nov. 44.
1 AD: 1 Jan. 45.
Component Squadrons
551st and 552nd Fighter Squadron.
Aircraft
P-47C and D.
Stations
ATCHAM 25 Dec. 43-15 Feb. 45.
CHEDDINGTON 15 Feb. 45-Jun. 45.
Group CO
Col Jack W. Hickman: 25 Dec. 43-unkn.
History
Fighter replacement pool established at Atcham late 1942. Originally as 6th Fighter Wing which moved in 27 Aug. 42. During early 1943 pilots newly arrived from USA trained in operational procedures and gunnery. Used Spitfires and pilots of 67 Obs. Gp. in training Spitfire pilots. From May 43 established as two squadron P-47 OTU. From Aug. 43 had a few P-38Hs. On 27 Aug. 43 the organisation re-designated 2906 Observation Training Group (P) and activated as 495 TFG on 25 Dec. 43. From Dec. 43 trained P-47 pilots for both 8AF and 9AF. 1st Gunnery & Tow Target Flight attached to group.

496th Fighter Training Group

Established in Eighth AF: Dec. 43.
Wing & Command Assignments
VIII FC: 25 Dec. 43.
VIII AFCC: 14 Feb. 44.
VIII FC: 29 Sep. 44.
2 BD: 28 Nov. 44.
2 AD: 1 Jan. 45.
Component Squadrons
554th and 555th Fighter Squadron.
Aircraft
P-38 (554 FS).
P-51 (555 FS).
Stations
GOXHILL 25 Dec. 43-15 Feb. 45.
HALESWORTH 15 Feb. 45-c. Jun. 45.
Group CO
Col Harry W. Magee: 25 Dec. 43-c. 1945.

History

Goxhill established as fighter training base in 1942 and served as interim station for newly arrived fighter units where personnel could be instructed in operational procedure etc. peculiar to ETO. In late 1943 became a training establishment for replacement pilots and activated as 496FTG on 25 Dec. 43. 554FS operated P-38s until late 1944, 555FS provided P-51 training. Group served both 8th and 9th AF. 2nd Gunnery & Tow Target Flight attached to group.

Special Operations Group—Carpetbaggers

Established in Eighth AF: 28 Mar. 44 as 801st Bombardment Group (P), and redesignated as 492nd Bombardment Group (H) on 13 Aug. 44.

Wing & Command Assignments
VIII AFCC:	28 Mar. 44.
VIII FC:	1 Oct. 44.
1 AD:	1 Jan. 44.

Component Squadrons
36th and 406th Bombardment Squadron (H) assigned 801 BG(P) 28 Mar. 44.

788th and 850th Bombardment Squadron (H) assigned 801 BG(P) 11 May 44.

These squadrons redesignated as 856th, 858th, 859th and 857th Bombardment Squadron (H) respectively on 13 Aug. 44. 857th BS established as 1st Scouting Force 12 Mar. 45. 859BS on detached service Italy 17 Dec. 44 and permanently assigned 15AF 23 Jan. 45.

Combat Aircraft
B-24D, B-24H, B-24J, C-47; Mosquito XVI and A-26B.

Stations
ALCONBURY	4 Dec. 43-Feb. 44 (36 and 406BS only).
WATTON	Feb. 44-c. 1 April 44 (36 and 406BS only).
HARRINGTON	c. 28 Mar. 44-8 Jul. 45.

Group COs
Col Clifford J. Heflin:	28 Mar. 44-25 Aug. 44.
Lt Col Robert W. Fish:	26 Aug. 44-16 Dec. 44.
Col Hudson H. Upham:	17 Dec. 44-7 Jun. 45.

First Operation: 5 Apr. 44.* **Last Operation:** 26 Apr. 45. **Total Credit Sorties:** 2,809 (less trucking).
*(36 and 406BS commenced ops. 4/5 Jan. 44).
A/c MIA: 26 (24 B-24, 1 A-26, Carpetbagging: 1 B-24 trucking).
Total Tonnage Delivered: 3,889.8.

Awards
Distinguished Unit Citation: 20 Mar.-25 Apr. 45; Germany and German-occupied territory.

History
In Nov. 43 two special units formed to undertake delivery of supplies to resistance forces in occupied territory. Sqdns. of the disbanded 479 Anti-Sub. Group provided the nucleus for the new units; these were assigned to 8AF 11 Nov. 43 and on 4 Dec. 43 the 36BS and 406BS were activated at Alconbury from the ground echelon of 4ASS and the air echelon of 22ASS. Equipped with B-24D on which only tail turret armament retained. Under RAF guidance and first sorties from Tempsford in Jan. 44. Administration by 482BG until 27 Feb. 44 then assigned AFCC. Prior to formation of 801BG(P) the two squadrons flew total 63 credit sorties and delivered 153 tons supplies, etc. Agents carried and parachuted from April 44. 788 and 750BS, ex-2BD groups arrived 11 May 44 with B-24H; total a/c strength raised from approx. 20 to 40 a/c. Operations almost entirely over occupied France and the low countries until Aug. 44. Operated 4 C-47s Jul.-Aug. 44 making landings in occupied territory. Full scale operations ceased after 16/17 Sep. 44. Then engaged in 'trucking' petroleum products to Allied ground forces, approx. 750,000 gls. Only 856BS retained for limited Carpetbagger ops. over Netherlands, Norway and Denmark, and during period Sep. 44-Mar. 45. under direct 8AF Hq. control. 859 BS sent to Italy Dec. 45 and did not return. 857 and 858BS commenced night bombing sorties on limited scale from Dec. 44 but 857 BS a/c and crews absorbed by other units and the designation allotted to 1st Scouting Force at Bassingbourn on 12 Mar. 45. 856BS returned to 492BG control 14 Mar. 45 and on 19 Mar. 45 detachments of both 856 and 858BS to Dijon, France for ops. over Germany. 82 agents parachuted into Germany. These agents had radios and transmitted messages that were picked up by 856BS Mosquitos on recording devices. These ops. conducted under code names Red Stocking (40 sorties) and Skywave (6 sorties). During winter 44-45 21 night bombing missions undertaken by Group B-24s. Redeployed USA Jun./Jul. 45. Established at Kirtland Fd, NM. Aug. 45 for training as very heavy bomb group but project not proceeded with and Group inactivated 17 Oct. 45.

Independent Squadrons

5th Emergency Rescue Squadron

Formed in Eighth AF: early May 44 and designated 65th Fighter Wing Detachment B c. May 44. Redesignated and activated as 5th ERS 26 Jan. 45. Prior to this date generally known as Air Sea Rescue Squadron.

Wing & Command Assignments
VIII FC, 65 FW:	May 44.
2BD, 65 FW:	15 Sep. 44.
2 AD, 65 FW:	1 Jan. 45.

One of the dozen amphibians used by 5th ERS, OA-10A 44-33991, on dispersal at Halesworth.—(Forward)

Combat Aircraft
P-47D, (blocks 5-21) May 44-May 45.
OA-10A, Jan. 45-May 45.
B-17G ABL, c. Mar. 45-May 45.

Stations
BOXTED	c. 1 May 44-16 Jan. 45.
HALESWORTH	16 Jan. 45—unkn.

Squadron COs
Major Robert P. Gerhart:	c. 8 May 44-c. Jan. 45.
Major E. L. Larson:	c. Jan. 45-Unkn.

First Operation: 10 May 44. Flew 3616 sorties, 3520 being effective. (P-47 3481 sorties, B-17 16 sorties, OA-10 119 sorties).
A/c MIA: 3 (1 P-47 & 2 OA-10). **E/a Claims:** 1 V-1.

History
Formed to supplement RAF services. Originally in spotter role and

Known as *The Duchess* during her bombing career with 457th BG, this life-boat equipped Fortress was dubbed *Donna J II* in the 5th ERS.—(Forward)

equipped 25 WW P-47D. First A/S/R configuration comprised two 108 gl. wing tanks, container for two British 'M' type dinghies under belly of P-47, and four smoke marker bombs under each wing, aft u/c stowage. Latter caused drag that affected control of P-47. Revised configuration provided for 150 gl. belly tank, an M-type dinghy pack on each wing rack, and four smoke markers on small rack aft of belly tank. Original 90 personnel on detached service from 16 VIII FC stations. CO Cpt. R. Gerhart from 56FG. A/c war weary P-47D from every P-47 group in Command. Sole P-47 missing (1 Aug. 44) was only metal finish a/c in unit. First 6 OA-10A assigned latter half Jan. 45, total 13 a/c eventually available. B-17G for Airborne Lifeboat work on detachment from 457BG Mar./Apr. 45. First use US aircraft lifeboat 31 Mar. 45 off Denmark. B-17 & OA-10 a/c redeployed USA in May 45. P-47 withdrawn and unit returned to US.

15th Bombardment Squadron (L)

Assigned Eighth AF: May 42-14 Sep. 42.
Wing & Command Assignments
  VIII BC, 1 BW: Aug. 42.
Combat Aircraft
  Boston III (DB-7).
Stations
  GRAFTON UNDERWOOD   12 May 42-9 June 42.
  MOLESWORTH   9 June 42-11 Sep. 42.
  PODINGTON   11 Sep. 42-8 Nov. 42.
COs
  Major J. L. Griffith.
  Major Charles C. Kegelman.
First Mission: 4 July 42. **Last Mission**: 2 Oct. 42.
  Total Missions: 5.
Total Credit Sorties: 48. **Total Bomb Tonnage**: 44.
A/c MIA: none (2 crews with RAF).
History
  Activated 1 Feb. 40 as component of 27BG(L). Separated from parent group and sent to UK April 42 to train as night fighter unit with Turbinlite Havocs. Sailed from Boston 27 April 42 on *Andes* and arrived Liverpool 11 May 42. As Turbinlite technique discontinued by RAF, the Squadron trained for normal bomber operations under guidance of 226 Sqdn., RAF. Several 15BS crews on detachment 226 Sqdn. at Swanton Morley 25 June 42-14 July 42. First operational sortie flown 29 June 42 by Cpt. Kegelman's crew in Boston II AL743 MQ:L. On 4 July 42 six Boston IIIs (AL750 MQ:Z Cpt. Kegelman, AL677 MQ:P 2/Lt Loehrl, AL741 MQ:V 2/Lt Lynn AL746 MQ:M Cpt Odell, AL670 MQ:D Cpt Crabtree, Z2303 MQ:J Lt Howel). On last raid with RAF Bostons MQ:V, H, J, X, Y & D flown. Received own a/c (Boston III) Aug. 42 and commenced ops with 8AF 5 Sep. 42. Assigned 12AF 14 Sep. 42 and flew a/c to North Africa Nov. 42. Squadron later absorbed by 47BG and inactivated.

Radio Counter Measures Squadron

Formed in Eighth AF: 19 Jan. 44 as RCM detachment, designated as 803rd Bombardment Squadron (P) 28 Mar. 44 and re-designated 36th Bombardment Squadron (H) 13 Aug. 44.
Wing & Command Assignments
  VIIIAF CC: 15 Feb. 44.
  VIII FC: 1 Oct. 44.
  1 AD: 1 Jan. 45.
Combat Aircraft:
  B-17F & B-17G   Jan. 44-Sep. 44.
  B-24H & B-24J   June 44-May 45.
  P-51 late 44.
Stations
  SCULTHORPE   19 Jan. 44-c. 16 May 44.
  OULTON   c. 16 May 44-14 Aug. 44.
  CHEDDINGTON   14 Aug. 44-28 Feb. 45.
  ALCONBURY   28 Feb. 45-June 45.
First Operation: 3 June 44. **Total Credit Sorties**: 1152.
  A/c MIA: 2.
History
  Unit resulted from USSTAF's desire to participate in radio counter-measures activities with RAF. Personnel drawn from several stations, originally on detachment, Cpt G. E. Paris in Command, and came under

Snetterton Heath for administration, until 15 Feb. 44 when placed directly under VIII Composite Command. RAF conducted training, supplied and helped instal equipment. First 7 B-17s in 19-21 Jan. 44 for modification. Trained with RAF until mid May when squadron moved Oulton to commence operations. 8 B-17F and 2 B-17G on strength, equipped with Carpet and Mandrel jamming apparatus. First daylight operation 3 June 44. First night operation 5 June 44 in support of D-Day operations. B-24 considered better suited to accommodate equipment and unit received first five a/c in late June. By Aug. 44 had 7 B-24H, 4 B-24J, and 2 B-17 on strength. Moved Cheddington 13-14 Aug. 44 and operated from there, principally on day operations, until early 1945. Moved Alconbury and attached 482BG as a sub-group. Moved USA May/June 45.

Night Leaflet Squadron

Established in Eighth AF: 7 Sep. 43 with 422nd Bombardment Squadron (H). Redesignated as 858th Bombardment Squadron (H) on 24 June 44, and finally as 406th Bombardment Squadron (H) on 11 Aug. 44.
Wing & Command Assignment:
  VIII BC, 1 BD: Oct. 43.
  1 BD: Jan. 44.
  VIII AFCC: c. 14 Feb. 44.
  VIII FC: 1 Oct. 44.
  1 AD: 1 Jan. 45.
Combat Aircraft
  B-17F & B-17G of 422BS, Sep. 43-Aug. 44.
  B-24H & B-24J from July 44; B-24M Apr. 45.
Stations
  CHELVESTON   7 Sep. 43-24 June 44.
  CHEDDINGTON   24 June 44-Mar. 45.
  HARRINGTON   Mar. 45-4 Jul. 45.
First Operation: 7/8 Oct. 43. **Last Operation**: 31 May 45.
  Total Credit Sorties: 2,302. **A/c MIA**: 3. **E/a Claims**: 3-0-1.
  Total Tonnage Leaflets: 3,734·4.
History
  422BS, a regular day bombardment squadron of 305BG, went over to night operations in Sep. 43. After conducting experimental night bombing sorties, the unit commenced leaflet dropping over occupied territory. Unit used B-17Fs and older B-17Gs during winter 43/44. Leaflet bundles originally thrown out of a/c by hand; later in cardboard boxes from bomb-bay. Eventually 422BS armament officer devised leaflet bomb which gave high degree of accuracy. Holding 80,000 leaflets it was a 5 ft by 1½ ft laminated paper cylinder fused to burst at from 1000-2000 ft. Each a/c carried 12 of these bombs as normal load. First regular use from 18/19 April 44. By summer leaflets would be distributed at 20-25 locations by 5 B-17s as a single night's work. Operations extended to Norway in April 44 and to Germany Aug. 44. Original a/c complement 12-14 B-17s. In Aug. 44 operations intensified with up to 8 a/c despatched per night. Complement increased to 24 B-24s—although this not achieved until late in year. Some crews and 7 B-24s transferred from 492 BG in Nov. 44. CO of unit, Col Aber, killed by fragment Allied flak on return from ops over Holland, 4 Mar. 45. Dropped 1,493,760,000 leaflets during its 319 nights operations.
  Involved in OSS activities after VE-day. Moved Wiesbaden (Y-80) on 4 July 45, and flew special missions over Oslo, Paris, etc. Last propaganda flight 23 Oct. 45. Squadron inactivated late 1945.

12th AF Groups at 8th AF Installations

17th Bombardment Group (M)

Component Squadrons
  34th, 37th, 95th & 432nd Bombardment Squadron (M).
Combat Aircraft
  B-26 (none in UK).
Stations
  BASSINGBOURN   c. 4 Oct. 42-c. 13 Oct. 42.
  KIMBOLTON   c. 14 Oct. 42-late Nov. 42.

History

Advance party only to UK. Sailed for UK on *Queen Mary* 27 Sep. 42. Departed Kimbolton in three detachments, one by air. Majority of personnel sailed to North Africa late Nov. 42 on *HMS Derbyshire* from Liverpool. Main party of ground echelon sailed direct USA to North Africa. Air echelon flew a/c by southern ferry route.

47th Bombardment Group (L)

Component Squadrons

84th, 85th, 86th & 97th Bombardment Squadron (L).

Combat Aircraft

A-20B.

Stations

BURY ST. EDMUNDS	19 Sep. 42-4 Oct. 42.
HORHAM	5 Oct. 42-15 Jan. 43.

CO

Lt Col Frederick R. Terrell.

History

Activated 15 Jan. 41 at McChord Fd, Wash. Alerted for overseas movement 16 Aug. 42. Air echelon flew to UK by northern ferry route, losing one a/c and abandoning six a/c en route due to adverse weather. First a/c arrived Bury 25 Sep. 42 and last at Horham 8 Dec. 42. Six A-20s written off in UK crashes, etc. First a/c left for North Africa 15 Nov. 42 and last on 9 Jan. 43. One a/c lost en route Africa. (58 a/c set out from US for UK.) Token ground echelon, 253 men, sailed New York on *Queen Mary* 5 Sep. 42 and arrived Bury 12 Sep. 42. Left Horham for North Africa in three detachments 4 Nov. 42, 23 Nov. 42 and 5 Jan. 43. Main party ground echelon left US and sailed direct North Africa.

68th Observation Group

Component Squadron

16th, 111th, 122nd and 154th Observation Squadron.

Combat Aircraft

P-39D (111 & 154 OS only).

Station

WATTISHAM	4 Oct. 42-1 Dec. 42.

(Air ech. 111 & 154 OS only, & Dts, Hq & Gnd ech. 16 & 122 OS. 111 & 154 OS out 21 Nov. 42, Hq out 23 Nov. 42 and remainder out 1 Dec. 42.)

History

Activated 1 Sep. 41 at Brownwood, Tex. Detachments of Hq, 16 & 122 OS only to UK. Air echelon of these squadrons flying their A-20s to Africa via southern ferry route. 111 & 154 OS attached 8AF for training and received P-39. Flew a/c to North Africa Dec. 42.

81st Fighter Group

Component Squadrons

91st, 92nd & 93rd Fighter Squadron.

Combat Aircraft

P-39D & P-400.

Stations

GOXHILL	8 Oct. 42-c. 15 Nov. 42.	93 FS & Hq. Flt.
ATCHAM	c. 15 Nov. 42-2 Jan. 43.	93 FS & Hq. Flt.
KIRTON IN LINDSEY	8 Oct. 42-23 Dec. 42.	91 FS only.
HIGH ERCALL	8 Oct. 42-12 Dec. 42.	92 FS only.

CO

Lt Col Kenneth S. Wade.

History

Activated 9 Feb. 42 at Morris Fd, NC. Ground echelon sailed direct to North Africa from USA. Air echelon by sea to UK. Equipped Airacobras, each squadron assigned 13 a/c soon after arrival. Trained until 12 Dec. 42 when 92FS left for Predannack and Portreath prior flying direct North Africa. Main body of group a/c left 23 Dec. 43 and last 2 Jan. 43. Five forced down in Portugal en route (including CO). Group later moved India and China. Based in England from 1951 as tactical fighter wing.

310th Bombardment Group (M)

Component Squadrons

379th, 380th, 381st & 428th Bombardment Squadron (M).

Combat Aircraft

B-25.

Stations

HARDWICK	13 Sep. 42-25 Nov. 42.
BUNGAY	29 Oct. 42-Nov. 42 428BS only.

(Some personnel and a/c remained until March 43 and were moved to Hethel 11 Dec. 42).

CO

Lt Col Anthony G. Hunter.

History

Activated 15 Mar. 42 at Tucson Ariz. Ground echelon sailed direct North Africa from USA. Detachment of Air echelon sailed on *Queen Mary* 5 Sep. 42 for UK arriving Hardwick 12 Dec. 42 and left in three detachments for North Africa 5, 11 & 25 Nov. 42. Air echelon flew a/c via northern ferry route to UK but delayed by bad weather. First a/c arrived early Oct. 42 and last in Dec. 42. First a/c flew out to North Africa 11 Nov. 42 and remainder later in month. A few unserviceable a/c did not leave until early 43.

319th Bombardment Group

Component Squadrons

437th, 438th, 439th & 440th Bombardment Squadron (M).

Combat Aircraft

B-26B-2.

Stations

SHIPDHAM	12 Sep. 42-4 Oct. 42	Hq. 439 & 440 BS.
HORSHAM ST FAITHS	Sep. 42-c. 11 Nov. 42.	(437 & 438BS to c. 4 Oct. 42. Hq. 439 & 440BS from 4 Oct. 42.)
ATTLEBRIDGE	c. 4 Oct. 42-Nov. 42.	437 & 438 BS.

(Some personnel and a/c remained at Attlebridge until Mar. 43).

CO

Lt Col Alvord Rutherford

History

Activated 26 June 42 at Barksdale Fd, La. Ground echelon moved UK by sea sailing on *Queen Mary* 5 Sep. 42. Air echelon flew the northern ferry route but lost three a/c and had another three damaged during landings and take-off in bad weather. Most a/c reached Norfolk Oct. Nov. 42. Flew to North Africa mid-Nov. 42 losing two B-26 (including CO) over France. Last B-26s did not leave UK until 10 Mar. 43).

320th Bombardment Group (M)

Component Squadrons

441st, 442nd, 443rd & 444th Bombardment Squadron (M).

Combat Aircraft

B-26 (none in UK).

Stations

HETHEL	12 Nov. 42-c. 21 Nov. 42.	Gnd. ech. only. Hq. & two sqdns.
TIBENHAM	Nov. 42.	Gnd. ech. only. Two sqdns.

History

Activated 23 June 42 at MacDill Fd, Fla. Air echelon was to have flown to UK via northern ferry route but due to losses incurred by 47th and 319th BGs, it was re-routed by south Atlantic to Africa. Ground echelon sailed for UK on *Queen Mary* 5 Sep. 42. Sailed for North Africa 21 Nov. 42. No a/c in UK.

Support Units

This book is primarily concerned with combat elements of the Eighth Air Force. Combat crews comprised approximately one fifth of total personnel, which at peak strength numbered some two hundred thousand officers and men. The majority of non-combat personnel were engaged in support duties at 56 installations situated throughout the UK. Additionally, every combat station had a number of supporting units.

On a combat group station these comprised a Service Squadron with a Headquarters, Ordanance and Quartermaster companies, signals, chemical, weather, finance, postal, fire fighting, military police and other detachments. Total personnel of all support units on such a station averaged about 500. All units were under the command of the station commander—combat group CO—although support units were assigned and administered by headquarters elsewhere.

A Service Squadron provided aircraft maintenance that could not be carried out by ground crews assigned to combat squadrons, viz. engine changes and heavy repair work needing special tackle. There were two Service Squadrons to a Service Group, usually stationed at adjacent airfields with the Group Hq. at one of these stations. A number of organizational changes occurred with support units, the most notable being on 15 April 1945 when all support units on a station were brought under a single administrative headquarters, designated an Air Service Group, and activated on that date. Even so the ASG was still subservient to the combat group, and support personnel continued to consider themselves part of the combat group team, as indeed they were.

The Strategic Air Depots and Air Base Depots dealt with major aircraft overhauls and other requirements necessary to back up local service units. VIII Air Force Service Command handled all Eighth Air Force logistics and paralleled the service units in that although linked to Air Service Command in the USA it was under the Eighth's commander. Even so, in the field of maintenance and supply VIII AFSC enjoyed a good amount of autonomy. With the creation of USSTAF control of much Eighth Air Force logistics was, from March 1944, transferred to that organisation.

VIII AFSC established its own flying units to meet its own particular needs. An air transport and ferrying organisation was created in July 1942 specifically to provide these services between various VIII AFSC bases and other Eighth Air Force airfields. In October 1942 this was designated as Ferry and Transport Service, and from 15 April 1943 as 27th Air Transport Group. Operating first from Hendon, it started with eight pilots and various aircraft borrowed from the RAF—chiefly Oxfords but including an Anson, Argus and Dommine. In 1943 converted B-17s, Hudsons, and a few C-47s became available and operations were expanded. From July 1942 until the end of 1943 4,296.4 tons of cargo and nearly 20,000 passengers were carried. Some 10,500 aircraft were ferried around the UK during this period. The Group had two transport units, the 86th and 87th Air Transport Squadrons. Various ferrying squadrons were attached or assigned. On 7 January 1944 Hq. 27 ATG moved to Heston where it remained until the autumn of that year. In March 1944 the Group came under the jurisdiction of the newly established ASC, USSTAF, and operated on a theatre basis rather than confining its activities solely to the Eighth Air Force.

Awards

In quantitative terms of men and units, the Eighth Air Force was one of the most highly decorated military organisations of the Second World War. A week after the cessation of hostilities the total of awards stood as follows:-

To personnel: *Medal of Honour* 14; *Distinguished Service Cross* 220, plus 6 Oak Leaf Clusters; *Silver Star* 817, plus 47 Oak Leaf Clusters; *Distinguished Flying Cross* 41,497, plus 4,480 Oak Leaf Clusters; *Soldier's Medal* 478, plus 2 Oak Leaf Clusters; *Air Medal* 122,705, plus 319,595 Oak Leaf Clusters; *Purple Heart* 6,845 plus 188 Oak Leaf Clusters; *Bronze Star* 2,972, plus 12 Oak Leaf Clusters; *Distinguished Service Medal* 11, plus 1 Oak Leaf Cluster; and *Legion of Merit* 207, plus 2 Oak Leaf Clusters.

To Units: *Distinguished Unit Citation* 27, and *Meritorious Service Unit Plaque* 19. Further awards were made during the early post-war years.

The *Medal of Honor* (MH), *Distinguished Service Cross* (DSC) and the *Silver Star* (SS) were three decorations for heroism, in order of prominence. The *Distinguished Flying Cross* (DFC) and *Air Medal* (AM) were for extraordinary achievement involving combat. The *Distinguished Service Medal* (DSM) and *Legion of Merit* (LM) were both meritorious service decorations.

In this record only the two top awards to personnel and units are covered. Details of the 17 *Medal of Honor* and 66 *Distinguished Unit Citation* awards can be found under Unit Reference Histories (Part 1) and in the narrative text. Brief particulars of MH recipients follow, order by date of action.

JACK W. MATHIS, 1/Lt, 359th BS, 303rd BG. 18 March 1943
Posthumous
Born 25 Sept. 1921 at San Angelo, Texas. Enlisted in US Army 12 Jun. 1940. Transferred AAF 1941 and began air crew training Jan. 1942. Graduated as bombardier and commissioned 2/Lt in Air Reserve 4 Jul. 1942. Assigned 303rd BG at Salt Lake City, Utah. Moved to UK with Group Sept. 1942. Usually flew with 1/Lt Harold Stouse's crew. Action for which award made (see page 27) occurred while Lt Mathis was serving as squadron bombardier and flying in B-17F, 41-24561, BN: T, *The Duchess*.

MAYNARD H. SMITH, Sgt, 423rd BS, 306th BG. 1 May 1943
Born 19 May 1911 at Caro, Michigan. Son of a circuit judge. Enlisted in USAAF 1942. Sent to UK as replacement gunner in spring 1943. Action for which award was made (see page 30) occurred while Sgt Smith was serving as ball gunner on his first mission, flying in B-17F, 42-29649. Sgt Smith flew four more combat missions before being returned to the US. Nicknamed 'Snuffy'.

JOHN C. MORGAN, Flight Officer, 326th BS, 92nd BG. 26 July 1943 Born 24 Aug. 1924 at Vernon, Texas. Graduated from the New Mexico Military Institute 1931. Attended Schreiner Institute of Texas University 1931-32. Labour overseer in pineapple plantation, Fiji Isles 1934-37, then worked as a salesman in Texas. Joined RCAF Aug. 1941. Underwent flying training in Canada and then sent to the UK as Flt/Sgt, summer 1942. Transferred USAAF 24 Aug. 1943 and trained at Bovingdon on B-17s. Assigned 92nd BG. Action for which award was made (see page 64) occurred while F/O Morgan was acting co-pilot on B-17F, 42-29802, JW: C, *Ruthie II*. In Aug. 1943 assigned 813th BS, 482nd BG. Commissioned 2/Lt Nov. 1943. Became assistant operations officer of 813th BS. Shot down over Berlin 6 Mar. 1944, parachuted, and interned in Stalag Luft 1 for 14 months.

between 1932 and 1940 ran his own service station in Detroit Mich. and worked for a graphite bronze company in Cleveland, Ohio. In Feb 1942 assigned 98th BG at Barkesdale Fd, La. for B-24 pilot training and in Mar. 1942 assigned as CO of embryo 328th BS, 93rd BG at the same station. Moved UK with 93rd BG Sept. 1942. Appointed operations officer 93rd BG in Mar. 1943. CO 93rd BG from May 1943 Action for which award was made (see page 89) occurred while Col Baker was on his 16th mission and acting as co-pilot and group leader on B-24D, 42-40994, *Hell's Wench*. Other awards: SS, DFC, & AM (2 OLC).

LLOYD H. HUGHES, 2/Lt, 564th BS, 389th BG. 1 August 1943.
Posthumous
Born 12 Jul. 1921 at Alexandria, La. Family (imigré Welsh) later moved to Texas. Attended Texas Agricultural and Mechanical College, Sept. 1939-Dec. 1941. Enlisted in AAF 28 Jan. 1942. Accepted for pilot training Mar. 1942. Graduated, commissioned as 2/Lt in Air Reserve, and assigned 389th BG at Biggs Fd. early 1943. Moved to UK with Group Jun. 1943. Action for which award was made (see page 89) occurred while Lt Hughes was serving as pilot on B-24D, 42-40753.

ADDISON E. BAKER, Lt Col, Hq. 93rd BG. 1 August 1943. Posthumous Born 1 Jan. 1907 at Chicago, Illinois. Family later moved New York. Left school 1927 and worked as motor mechanic in Arkon, Ohio. Enlisted in AAC Jan. 1929. Graduated from flying school in 1930 and commissioned 2/Lt in Air Reserve. Assigned inactive status and

JOHN L. JERSTAD, Major, 201st PCBW. 1 August 1943. Posthumous Born 12 Feb. 1918 at Racine, Wis. Graduated with Bachelor of Science degree at Northwestern University, Ill. in 1940. Taught in high school at St. Louis, Missouri. Enlisted as aviation cadet Jul. 1941. Commissioned 2/Lt in Air Reserve 6 Feb. 1942. Assigned 98th BG at

Barkesdale Fd, La, Feb. 1942 and in Mar. 1942 transferred to 328th BS, 93rd BG. Moved UK with Group and flew combat missions. Transferred Hq 93rd BG Mar. 1943, and to 201st PCBW May 1943 as operations officer. Action for which award was made (see page 89) occurred while Major Jerstad was serving as pilot of 93rd BG, B-24D, 42-240994, *Hell's Wench*. Other awards: SS & AM (1 OLC).

1942. Trained as radio operator and gunner at Scott Fd, Ill. Sent to UK as replacement crew member in summer 1943. Assigned 303rd BG and flew several missions. Action for which award was made (see page 102) occurred while Sgt Vosler was acting as radio operator on B-17F, 42-29664, VK: C, *Jersey Bounce Jr*. Temporarily blinded and wounded in face and legs, Vosler was returned to USA early in 1944. Received treatment at Valley Forge Hospital, Phoenixville, Pa, where he recovered his sight in Jul. 1944. Honorably discharged from the USAAF 17 Oct. 1944. Other awards: AM & PH.

LEON W. JOHNSON, Col. Hq. 44th BG. 1 August 1943
Born 13 Sept. 1904 at Columbus, Missouri. Graduated from US Military Academy, West Point, NY, and commissioned 2/Lt in Infantry Jun. 1926. Transferred AAC 1929 and completed pilot training Feb. 1930. Served at various AAC stations in US and Philippines until 1941. Assigned to embryo 8AF as assistant chief of staff for operations, one of 8AF's first four flying officers. Moved UK with Hq staff Jun. 1942. Assumed command of 44th BG Jan. 1943. Action for which award was made (see page 88) occurred while Col Johnson was acting as group leader and co-pilot of B-24D, 41-23817, L, *Suzy Q*. Promoted Brig Gen and in command 14th CBW Sept. 1943–May 1945. Various appointments in post-war USAAF/USAF including command of 3rd AD in UK 1948-50. Other awards: SS, LM, DFC (1 OLC), AM (3 OLC), French Legion of Honor, Croix de Geurre, Belgian Croix de Geurre, and British DFC.

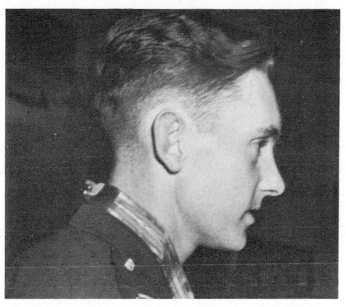

WILLIAM R. LAWLEY, JR., 1/Lt, 364th BS, 305th BG. 20 February 1944
Born 23 Aug. 1920 at Leeds, Alabama. Enlisted in USAAF Apr. 1942. Accepted for flying training Aug. 1942 and commissioned 2/Lt in Air Reserve 22 Apr. 1943. Sent to UK in Nov. 1943 as a replacement crew pilot. Action for which award was made (see page 108) occurred while Lt Lawley was serving as pilot of B-17G, WF:P 42-38109. Returned USA in Sept. 1944 having flown 14 missions (121 hrs). Remained in USAAF/USAF after war.

FORREST L. VOSLER, T/Sgt, 358th BS, 303rd BG. 20 December 1943
Born 29 Jul. 1923 at Lyndonville, NY. Left School 1941 and worked for a year as drill press operator in Livonia, NY. Enlisted USAAF 8 Oct.

WALTER E. TRUEMPER, 2/Lt, 510th BS, 351st BG. 20 February 1944
Posthumous
Born 31 Oct. 1918 at Aurora, Ill. Attended business college for four

years after leaving school, and also work as an accounting clerk. Enlisted in US Army Jun. 1942. Transferred AAF Nov. 1942 and trained as navigator and gunner. Commissioned 2/Lt in Air Reserve 26 Aug. 1943. Sent to UK as replacement crew member Dec. 1943 and assigned 351st BG. Action for which award was made (see page 108) occurred while Lt Truemper was serving as navigator on B-17G, 42-31763, TU: A, *Mizpah*. Other decorations: BS.

replacement air crew. Action for which award was made (see page 133) occurred while Lt Michael was acting as pilot of B-17G, 42-38131, *Bertie Lee*. After hospitalisation in UK he returned to US in May 1944 and served as instructor and ferry pilot. Remained in USAAF/USAF after war. Other decorations: DFC, AM (3 OLC) & PH.

LEON R. VANCE JR., Lt Col, Hq. 489th BG. 5 June 1944
Born 11 Aug. 1916 at Enid, Okla. Attended University of Oklahoma for 2 years before entering US Military Academy, West Point. Commissioned as 2/Lt in Infantry Jun. 1939. Accepted for pilot training summer 1940. On graduation served first as flying instructor and then as squadron CO. In Dec. 1942 appointed director of flying at a basic flying school at Strother Fd, Kansas. In Nov. 1943 appointed deputy CO 489th BG at Wendover, Utah. Helped form Group and went to UK with it Apr. 1944. Action for which award was made (see page 145) occurred while Lt Col Vance was on his second mission and acting as group leader in B-24H, 42-94830. After a period in hospital, Lt Col Vance was to be returned to the USA for further treatment. The C-54 (42-107470) in which he was travelling disappeared on the flight between Iceland and Newfoundland. Other awards: AM (3 OLC) & PH. Lt Col Vance was married.

ARCHIBALD MATHIES, S/Sgt, 510th BS, 351st BG. 20 February 1944
                                                              Posthumous
Born 3 Jun. 1918 in Scotland. Parents emigrated to Pennsylvania. Trained as mechanic on enlisting in USAAF, and later as air gunner. Sent to UK 8 Dec. 1943 as replacement. Assigned 351st BG 19 Jan. 1944. Action for which award was made (see page 108) occurred while Sgt Mathies was on his second mission and serving as engineer/ball turret gunner on B-17G, 42-31763, TU: A, *Mizpah*.

EDWARD S. MICHAEL, 1/Lt, 364th BS, 305th BG. 11 April 1944
Born 2 May 1918 at Chicago, Ill. Enlisted US Army Nov. 1940 as private. Accepted for flying training Jun. 1942 and commissioned 2/Lt in Air Reserve Apr. 1943. Received B-17 training and sent to UK with

ROBERT E. FEMOYER, 2/Lt, 711th BS, 447th BG. 2 November 1944
                                                              Posthumous
Born 31 Oct. 1921 at Huntington, West Virginia. After leaving school he spent three years at Virginia Polytechnic Institute. Enlisted in USAAF

Nov. 1942. Accepted for flying training Jun. 1943, but later transferred to navigator's course. Commissioned as 2/Lt in Air Reserve 10 Jun. 1944. Posted to UK Sept. 1944 and assigned 447th BG. Action for which award was made (see page 180) occurred on Lt Femoyer's seventh mission while he was serving as navigator on B-17G, 42-107052, L. Other awards: AM.

DONALD J. GOTT, 1/Lt, 729th BS, 452nd BG. 9 November 1944
Posthumous
Born 3 Jun. 1923 at Arnett, Okla. On completion of his education at Fargo, Okla, he worked for an aluminium company at Bridgeport, Conn. Enlisted in Air Reserve 21 Sept. 1942. Accepted for pilot training in Nov. 1943. Commissioned 2/Lt in Air Reserve 7 Jan. 1944. Trained with B-17s and sent to the UK with a replacement crew Aug. 1944. Assigned 452nd BG. Action for which award was made (see page 180) occurred while Lt Gott was piloting B-17G, 42-97904, R, *Lady Janet*. Other awards: AM (3 OLC).

WILLIAM E. METZGER JR, 2/Lt, 729th BS, 452nd BG. 9 November 1944
Posthumous
Born 9 Feb. 1922 at Lima, Ohio. Left school 1941 and worked for Lima Electric Motor Company. Enlisted in US Army 5 Oct. 1942. Accepted as aviation cadet Apr. 1943. Graduated 12 Mar. 1944 as pilot and Flight Officer in Air Reserve. Served at a number of bases in US. Commissioned 2/Lt in Air Reserve 24 Aug. 1944. Sent to UK with replacement crew Oct. 1944. Action for which award was made (see page 180) occurred while Lt Metzger was serving as co-pilot on B-17G, 42-97904, R, *Lady Janet*. Metzger was nicknamed 'The Reverend' due to his intention to take holy orders prior to joining USAAF.

FREDERICK W. CASTLE, Brig Gen, Hq. 4th BW. 24 December 1944
Posthumous
Born 14 Oct 1908 at Manila, Philippine Islands. Enlisted in New Jersey National Guard as private 2 Oct. 1924. Accepted by West Point 1 Jul. 1926 and commissioned 2/Lt in US Army Engineers 12 Jun. 1930. Accepted for flying training and rated as fully qualified pilot 22 Dec. 1931. Served with 17th Pursuit Sqdn, Selfridge Fd until resigning the service 17 Feb. 1934. Remained on reserve status. Joined Sperry organisation which manufactured instruments including the Norden bomb sight. Returned to active service 19 Jan. 1942 and selected as one of eight to accompany Maj Gen Eaker to the UK. Arrived 20 Feb. 1942 and between 23 Feb. 1942 and 19 Jun. 1943 was A-4 at VIII BC with responsibility for planning airbase and depot system. Promoted Col, 1 Jan. 1943. Volunteered to command 94th BG Jun. 1943. CO 4th CBW, 14 Apr. 1944. Promoted Brig Gen 20 Nov. 1944. Action for which award was made (see page 201) occurred while Gen Castle was acting as air task force commander and flying in a 487th BG B-17G, 44-8444. Other awards: DSC, LM, SS, DFC (3 OLC), AM (4 OLC), PH, Belgian Croix de Guerre with Palm, French Legion of Honor, Order of Kutuzow, 2nd & 3rd degree (Soviet) & Silver Cross Virtuti Militari, Class V (Polish).

The Fighter Aces

The term 'ace' originated in the First World War for a fighter pilot who had destroyed five or more enemy aircraft in air combat. During the Second World War neither the RAF not USAAF officially recognised ace status and its promotion was due principally to the popular press. The RAF stuck fairly rigidly to this attitude of non-recognition, believing acclaim of the individual acted against teamwork. The USAAF was generally less restrictive in the matter of publicity and in some quarters gave active encouragement to publicising the exploits of individual pilots. This was particularly so in VIII Fighter Command where stimulation of the individual's prowess was not considered detrimental to team spirit or function. Indeed it was deemed a healthy trait in establishing the necessary aggressive outlook of a fighter unit. To this end, VIII Fighter Command let it be known that enemy aircraft destroyed during the strafing of airfields would count equal to air victories in assessing a pilot's score. This policy was not adopted by other USAAFs in Europe. In the following listing of the leading fighter pilots aerial and strafing credits are listed separately, as the true meaning of a fighter ace refers only to aerial victories. This is not to deprecate ground strafing achievements, a far more dangerous activity than air combat as the number of aces lost while strafing indicates.

Name and Home Address. The address is that of the ace's wartime home town and state.

Total of Victories. Original Score refers to the total of air victories credited to a pilot at the end of his tour of combat duty.

Revised Score is that given by USAAF or USAF at a later date on re-evaluation of evidence, chiefly combat film. The exact number of enemy aircraft shot down by any individual pilot will probably always be in doubt. Gun camera film of a combat did not always give a positive answer, however skilled and unprejudiced the assessor. It is known that German fighters which appear destroyed in gun camera sequences did get back to base though badly damaged, and that claims by US pilots are not supported by enemy records in some incidents that can be isolated. Equally, there are instances of air battles where US fighter claims were below the loss figure of the German unit involved. At best the totals for individual aces are an indication of their standing. The true figure may be more or less than that given, although not far from the mark. Generally the claims of US fighter pilots were near to actual losses, the overall picture being one of slight exaggeration.

Fractions arise from two or more pilots firing at one aircraft and registering hits. The highest scoring Mustang pilot, George Preddy, was involved in no less than five shared victories.

Decorations. Abbreviations used are detailed under decorations. Some of these awards were made after the cessation of hostilities.

Victories List. These are given for seven of the nine pilots who were originally credited with over 20 victories.

Personal Aircraft. It was practise for a pilot to be assigned a particular aircraft in which to fly combat. Frequently this machine was out of commission due to mechanical trouble and occasionally battle damage. When this occurred a pilot scheduled for a mission flew the aircraft of a resting pilot. Many aces claimed victories while flying aircraft other than their own. During a tour some pilots 'used up' as many as six aircraft while others had but one. Changes were due to a variety of reasons. Information on all personal aircraft is not forthcoming.

The Eighth Air Force produced 261 recognised fighter aces, details of those originally credited with 15 or more aerial victories being listed here. The total number of victories, is however, not the only yardstick in assessing a fighter pilot's skill. In the early days Eighth Air Force pilots fought enemy pilots of a much higher calibre than those generally encountered late in the war. However, there was often a comparative dearth of Luftwaffe aircraft during the final period of operations and it says much for the ability and sharp eyes of men like Ray Wetmore who claimed 22 victories flying with a group where only one other pilot ran a score into double figures. Possibly the most brilliant fighter pilots of all were some of the Group commanders, Joe Mason, Glenn Duncan, and Don Blakeslee and Hubert Zemke in particular. Their leadership paved the way for the successes of many of the great aces.

FRANCIS S. GABRESKI, Oil City, Pennsylvania
61st Fighter Squadron, 56th Fighter Group. Apr. 1943–Jul. 1944
Original Score 28, *Strafing* 2½ (6½ air victories in Korean War).
Decorations: DSC, SS, DFC, BS, AM, Legion D'Honneur, Croix de Guerre, Polish Croix Des Vaillants.
Born 28 Jan. 1919. Son of Polish immigrants to US. Took a two year university pre-medical course prior to enlisting in USAAC, Jul. 1940. Commissioned as 2/Lt in Air Reserve, Mar. 1941. Posted to Wheeler Field, Hawaii. Serving with 45 FS when Japanese attacked Pearl Harbour. Flew interception sorties but had no victories. Returned to USA Oct. 1942 and assigned 56th Fighter Group as flight leader. Came to UK with Group Jan. 1943 and immediately detached to 315 Squadron, RAF (Polish) at Northolt. Flew 13 operational sorties in Spitfire Vs. Friendships formed with RAF Polish pilots led to subsequent Polish 'lodgers' in 61st Fighter Squadron. Gabreski spoke fluent Polish with US accent. Returned to 56 FG in late Feb. 1943 and led B Flight of 61 FS. Took command of 61 FS 9 Jun. 1943. Rank: Major. Became Group Deputy Flying Executive and Operations Officer on 20 Jan. 1944. Promoted Lt Col. Assumed command of 61 FS again on 13 Apr. 1944. Crash-landed near Bassinheim airfield 20 Jul. 1944 and went into hiding. Captured after five days and imprisoned in Stalag Luft I near Barth. 153 combat missions. Served in USAF as fighter commander until 1967, retiring with rank of full Colonel. Nickname 'Gabby'.

Victories List

1	24 Aug. 43	1 FW 190	Dreux, Fr.
2	3 Sept. 43	1 FW 190	St. Germain, Fr.
3	5 Nov. 43	1 FW 190	S. of Rheine, Gr.

4 & 5	26 Nov. 43	2 Me 110	SE of Oldenburg, Gr.
6 & 7	29 Nov. 43	2 Me 109	NE of Bremen, Gr.
8	11 Dec. 43	1 Me 110	Emden, Gr.
9	29 Jan. 44	1 Me 110	Emden, Gr.
10 & 11	30 Jan. 44	1 Me 410 &	
		1 Me 109	Lingen, Gr.
12 & 13	20 Feb. 44	2 Me 410	Koblenz
14	22 Feb. 44	1 FW 190	Münster-Paderborn area
15 & 16	16 Mar. 44	2 FW 190	Nancy, Fr.
17 & 18	27 Mar. 44	2 Me 109	Nantes, Fr.
19	8 May 44	1 Me 109	Celle, Gr.
20, 21 & 22	22 May 44	3 FW 190	Hopenfofer a/d, Gr.
23 & 24	7 Jun. 44	1 Me 109 &	
		1 FW 190	Dreux, Fr.
25 & 26	12 Jun. 44	2 Me 109	N. of Evreux, Fr.
27	27 Jun. 44	1 Me 109	Connautre a/d, Fr.
28	5 Jul. 44	1 Me 109	Evereux, Fr.

Personal Aircraft: P-47C-2-RE, HV: A (early 1943). P-47D-1-RE, 42-7871, HV: A, (c. Jul. 1943–29 Nov. 1943). P-47D-11-RE, 42-75510, HV: A (c. late Nov. 1943–May 1944). P-47D-22-RE, 42-25864, HV: A (May 1944–early Jun. 1944). P-47D-25-RE, 42-26418, HV: A (Jun. 1944–20 Jul. 1944). Code letters on D-1 & D-11 a/c eventually outlined red. Codes blocked red on D-22, and eventually outlined red on D-25. D-25 at first operated on metal finish; later upper surfaces camouflaged mottled medium grey and medium green. No nicknames on any a/c. Victory symbols Nazi flags on D's 11, 22 & 25. Crew Chief S/Sgt Ralph H. Safford.

Victories List

1	1 Dec. 43	1 Me 109
2	22 Dec. 43	1 Me 410
3	29 Jan. 44	1 FW 190
	22 Apr. 44	½ Ju 88
4 & 5	13 May 44	2 Me 109
6 & 7	30 May 44	2½ Me 109
8	12 Jun. 44	1 Me 109
9	20 Jun. 44	1 FW 190 & ½ Me 410
10	21 Jun. 44	1 Me 109
11, 12 & 13	18 Jul. 44	2 Ju 88 & 1 Me 109
	21 Jul. 44	½ Me 109
14	29 Jul. 44	1 Me 109
15	5 Aug. 44	1 Me 109
16–21	6 Aug. 44	6 Me 109
22	2 Nov. 44	1 Me 109
23	21 Nov. 44	1 FW 190
24 & 25	25 Dec. 44	2 Me 109

Personal Aircraft: 2 P-47D, one nicknamed *Cripes A'Mighty*. P-51B-10-NA, 42-106451, HO: P *Cripes A'Mighty 2nd* (early Apr. 1944–Jul. 1944: lost with another pilot). P-51D-5-NA, 44-13321, HO: P, *Cripes A'Mighty 3rd* (Jul. 1944–Aug. 1944. Flown by other pilots after Preddy's return to US). P-51D-15-NA, 44-14906, PE: P, *Cripes A'Mighty* (Nov. 1944–25 Dec. 1944. Killed in this a/c).

ROBERT S. JOHNSON, Lawton, Oklahoma
61st Fighter Squadron, 56th Fighter Group. (Apr. 1943–May 1944). 62nd Fighter Squadron, 56th Fighter Group (May 1944).
Original Score 27. *Revised Score* 28. No ground strafing credits.
Decorations: DSC, SS, DFC, AM, PH.
Born 1920. Enlisted in USAAC Nov. 1941 and selected for flying training following month. Commissioned Jul. 1942 and assigned to 56th Fighter Group 19 Jul. 1943. Sailed to UK with Group in Jan. 1943. Promoted Cpt Apr. 1944. Promoted Major May 1944 and assigned 62 FS as Operations Officer. Flew 91 combat missions, the last on 8 May 1944. Returned to USA May 1944 but did not see further action. Joined Republic Aviation after war.
Victories List

1	13 Jun. 43	1 FW 190	NW Ypres
2	19 Aug. 43	1 Me 109	NE Koensdretcht
3	8 Oct. 43	1 FW 190	Nr. Lingen
4 & 5	10 Oct. 43	1 FW 190 &	
		1 Me 110	N Münster
6	3 Nov. 43	1 Me 109	N Akeland Island
7	26 Nov. 43	1 Me 110	N Emden
8	22 Dec. 43	1 Me 109	N Almele
9 & 10	31 Dec. 43	2 FW 190	N St. Gilles
11	5 Jan. 44	1 FW 190	N Liege
12	21 Jan. 44	1 FW 190	N Rouen

GEORGE E. PREDDY, Greensboro, North Carolina
487th Fighter Squadron, 352nd Fighter Group. (Jan. 1943–Aug. 1944). 328th Fighter Squadron, 352nd Fighter Group (28 Oct. 1944–25 Dec. 1944).
Original Score 27½ (25 + 5 shared). *Revised Score* 26.83 (25 + 4 shared). *Strafing* 5.
Decorations: DSC, SS (OLC), DFC (8 OLC), AM (7 OLC), PH.
Born 5 Feb. 1919. Flew P-40s with 49th Fighter Group in defence of northern Australia. Engaged in combat with Japanese aircraft damaging one fighter and a bomber. Spent 13 months in SWPA, returning to USA late 1942. Assigned 487th Fighter Squadron Jan. 1943. Rank 1/Lt. Came to UK with 352 Fighter Group in summer 1943. Ditched in Channel 29 Jan. 1944 and rescued. Operations Officer 487th Fighter Squadron 11 Mar. 1944. Promoted Captain. To USA on leave Aug. 1944, returning Oct. 1944. Promoted Major and given command 328th Fighter Squadron Oct. 1944. Killed 25 Dec. 1944 when a/c hit by US AA fire over Belgium front. Flew 143 combat missions totalling 532 operational flying hours while with 352nd Fighter Group. Nicknamed "Ratsy". Crew Chief: S/Sgt Lew Lunn.

13 & 14	30 Jan. 44	1 Me 410 &	
		1 Me 109	E Lingen
15 & 16	20 Feb. 44	2 Me 110	W Hanover
17	6 Mar. 44	1 FW 190	N Dummer Lake
18 & 19	8 Mar. 44	2 Me 109	NE Steinhuder Lake
20, 21 & 22	15 Mar. 44	2 FW 190 &	
		1 Me 109	NE Dummer Lake
23	9 Apr. 44	1 FW 190	NW Kiel
24 & 25	13 Apr. 44	2 FW 190	Kaiserslautern
26 & 27	8 May 44	1 Me 109 &	
		1 FW 190	N Dummer Lake

(Additional victory in revised score an Me 110 'probable' of 26 Nov. 1943).

Personal Aircraft: P-47C-1-RE, *Half Pint* (crash-landed by Lt J. Curtis prior combat ops.). P-47C-2-RE, 41-6235, HV: P, *All Hell* (c. Mar. 1943–26 Jun. 1943). P-47D-5-RE, 42-8461, HV: P, *Lucky* (late Jun. 1943–22 Mar. 1944 lost in sea with 2/Lt D. Stream). P-47D-15-RE, 42-76234, HV: P, *Double Lucky* (name apparently not painted on) (late Mar. 1944–late Apr. 1944). P-47D-21-RA, 42-25512, LM: Q, *Penrod and Sam* (May 1944). LM: Q metal finish a/c with nickname in black. At least 19 and possibly 22 of Johnson's victories claimed in *Lucky*. Gladych, Joe Powers, & Sam Hamilton are credited with another four victories while flying this aircraft. Crew Chief: S/Sgt Ernest D. Gould.

JOHN C. MEYER, Forrest Hills, Long Island
487th Fighter Squadron, 352nd Fighter Group. (Jan. 1943–20 Nov. 1944). Hq. 352nd Fighter Group (20 Nov. 1944–Jan. 1945).
Combat Score 24 (23 + 2 shared). *Strafing* 13 (2 Mig-15 in Korean War).
Decorations: DSC (2 OLC), SS (1 OLC), DFC (5 OLC), AM (14 OLC), PH, Croix de Guerre, Croix de Guerre Belgé.
Born 3 Apr. 1919. Enlisted USAAC Nov. 1939 and commissioned as 2/Lt in Air Reserve Jul. 1940. Served as flying instructor until Jul. 1941 when posted to 33rd Pursuit Sqdn. (P-40s) in Iceland. Flew defensive and convoy patrols. Returned USA Sept. 1942. Assigned 352 Fighter Group at Westover Fd, Mass, Jan. 1943, promoted Major and assumed command 487 Fighter Squadron. Sailed to UK Jul. 1943. Entered combat Sept. 1943. Destroyed first a/c for Group. DSC for action on 8 May 1944, second DSC for action on 21 Nov. 1944. Group Executive of 352 Fighter Group 15 Nov. 1944. Promoted Lt Col late Dec. 1944. Third DSC for leadership of 1 Jan. 1945 action. Involved in vehicle accident in Belgium 9 Jan. 1945 and badly injured. Returned to USA. Continued in USAAF post-war. Commanded 4 FIW 1950–Jun. 1951 in Korean War. Destroyed two Mig-15s in 31 missions. Reached rank USAF Lt General.
Victories List

1	26 Nov. 43	1 Me 109	
2	4 Dec. 43	1 Me 109	

3	22 Dec. 43	1 Me 109	
4	10 Apr. 44	1 Me 109 & ½ FW 190	
5–7	8 May 44	3 Me 109	
8	12 May 44	1 Me 109	
9–12	11 Sept. 44	2 Me 109 & 1 FW 190	
13–15	21 Nov. 44	3 FW 190	
16	27 Nov. 44	1 Me 109	
17 & 18	26 Dec. 44	2½ Me 109	
19 & 20	27 Dec. 44	2 FW 190	
21	31 Dec. 44	1 Ar 234	
22 & 23	1 Jan. 45	2 FW 190	

Personal Aircraft: 2 P-47D, one nicknamed *Lambie*, HO: M. P-51B-5-NA, 42-106471, HO: M, *Petie* (Apr. 1944–Jun. 1944. Lost with another pilot on D-Day). P-51D-10-NA, 44-14151, *Petie 2nd* (c. Aug. 1944–Jan. 1945).

DAVID C. SCHILLING, Detroit, Michigan
62nd Fighter Squadron, 56th Fighter Group. (1941–20 Aug. 1943). Hq. 56th Fighter Group (21 Aug. 1943–27 Jan. 1945).
Combat Score 23. *Revised Score* 22½. *Strafing* 10½.
Decorations: DSC (1 OLC), SS (2 OLC), DFC (8 OLC), AM, British DFC, Croix de Guerre.
Born 15 Dec. 1918 at Leavenworth, Kansas. Graduated with degree in geology Jun. 1939 at Dartmouth College, N.H. Volunteered USAAC and accepted for pilot training late 1939. Commissioned as 2/Lt in Air Reserve, May 1940. Assigned 8 Pursuit Gp. Langley, Va, and later Mitchel Fd, NY. Assigned newly established 56 FG at Charlotte AB, NC. Jun. 1941. Promoted Major and assumed command 62 FS. Group Executive 21 Aug. 1943. Promoted Lt Col Nov. 1943. Acting CO 11 Jan. 1944–19 Jan. 1944 and Group CO 12 Aug. 1944–27 Jan. 1945. Executive Officer 65 FW and later assistant to Director of Intelligence 8AF. Returned USA May 1945. Commanded 56 FG again after war bringing its P-80s to UK on first trans-Atlantic jet flight by USAF, Jul. 1948. Posted to South Ruislip as staff officer in 1956. Killed on 14 Aug. 1956 when his Allard sports car hit a concrete bridge post at Eriswell, Suffolk. 132 combat sorties in 360 operational flying hours.
Victory List

1 & 2	2 Oct. 43	1 Me 109 &	
		1 FW 190	Emden
3	4 Oct. 43	1 Me 110	Düren
4	8 Oct. 43	1 FW 190	Bremen
5	10 Oct. 43	1 FW 190	Münster
6 & 7	26 Nov. 43	2 FW 190	Bremen
	29 Nov. 43	½ FW 190	Bremen
8	11 Jan. 44	1 FW 190	Bremen
9	29 Jan. 44	1 Me 109	W Koblenz
10	8 Mar. 44	1 Me 410	NW Germany
11	29 Mar. 44	1 Me 109	Solingen

12 & 13	9 Apr. 44	2 FW 190	Schleswig area
14	13 Apr. 44	1 Me 109	W Germany
15-17	21 Sept. 44	3 FW 190	Holland
18-22	23 Dec. 44	3 Me 109 &	
		2 FW 190	E Bonn

Personal Aircraft: P-47C-1-RE, LM: S, P-47D-1-RE, 42-7938, LM: S, presentation a/c HOWLETT-WOODMERE, LONG ISLAND (c. Jul.– 3 Feb. 1944). P-47D-11-RE, 42-75231, LM: S, *Whack!* (Feb. 1944– Jun. 1944). P-47D-25-RE, 42-26641, LM: S (Jun. 1944–Jan. 1945). P-47M-1-RE, 44-21125, LM: S (Jan. 1945). Last two a/c were shadow-shaded medium green and medium grey on upper surfaces. Crew Chief: S/Sgt Jack T. Holleman.

DON S. GENTILE, Piqua, Ohio
336th Fighter Squadron, 4th Fighter Group (Sept. 1942–28 Apr. 1944). *Original Score* 23. *Revised score* 21.8. *Original strafing* 7. *Revised strafing* 6.
Decorations: DSC, SS, DFC, AM, British DFC, Croix de Guerre Belge, Military Order of Italy, Italian Croce Al Merido Di Guerra, Italian Medaglia D'Argenti Al Valor Militaire.
Born 12 Jun. 1920, of Italian immigrants to the USA. Learned to fly while still at high school. Enlisted in RAF Sept. 1940. Trained in Canada and sent to UK Dec. 1941. Assigned 133 'Eagle' Sqdn in Jun. 1942 and flew first operational sortie 22 Jun. 1942. First two victories with RAF on 19 Aug. 1942. Transferred 4 FG Sept. 1942 when 133 Sqdn became 336 FS. Claimed over half total victories in one month—Mar. 1944. Returned USA 28 Apr. 1944 with wingman John Godfrey. Later assigned Wright-Patterson AFB as test pilot. Continued as test pilot until leaving service in Apr. 1946. Re-entered USAF in Dec. 1947. Killed in air accident 28 Jan. 1951.
Victories List

1 & 2	19 Aug. 42	1 Ju 88 &	
		1 FW 190	Dieppe
	16 Dec. 43	$\frac{1}{3}$ Ju 88	
3	5 Jan. 44	1 FW 190	Holland
4 & 5	14 Jan. 44	2 FW 190	Compiégne
6	25 Feb. 44	1 FW 190	SW Germany
7 & 8	3 Mar. 44	1 Do 217 &	
		1 Me 109	Hamburg-Berlin
9-12	8 Mar. 44	$4\frac{1}{2}$ Me 109	Berlin
13	18 Mar. 44	1 FW 190	SW Germany
14 & 15	23 Mar. 44	2 Me 109	Brunswick
16-18	29 Mar. 44	2 FW 190 &	
		1 Me 109	Brunswick
19	1 Apr. 44	1 Me 109	Mannheim
20 & 21	8 Apr. 44	2 FW 190	Brunswick

Personal Aircraft: At least two Spitfire V, one being BL 255. A P-47C and P-47D. P-51B-5-NA, 43-6913, VF: T, *Shangri-La* (late Feb. 1944–13 Apr. 1944).

FREDERICK J. CHRISTENSEN JR, Watertown, Mass.
62nd Fighter Squadron, 56th Fighter Group (27 Aug. 1943–c. Sept. 1944).
Original Score 22. *Revised score* 21½. No strafing credits.
Decorations: DSC, SS, DFC, AM.
Born 17 Oct. 1921. Sent to UK as a replacement pilot summer 1943. Trained at Atcham and assigned 56 FG 26 Aug. 1943 and to 62 FS next day. Rank 2/Lt. Dead stick landing Leiston 27 Dec. 1943. Promoted 1/Lt Jan. 1944. First 8AF pilot to shoot down six e/a on one mission, 7 Jul. 1944. Returned USA Sept. 1944. Nickname "Rat-Top". Colonel in Mass. ANG post-war.
Personal Aircraft: P-47D-10-RE, 42-75207, IM: C, *Rozzi Geth* for girl friend Rosamond Gethro. P-47D-25-RE, 42-26628, LM: C, *Miss Fire* and *Rozzi Geth II* (Jun. 1944–Sept. 1944).

RAY S. WETMORE, Kerman, California

275

370th Fighter Squadron, 359th Fighter Group (1943–1945).
Original score 21. *Revised score* 22.59. *Original strafing* 3½. *Revised strafing* 2.
Decorations: DSC (1 OLC), SS (1 OLC), DFC (5 OLC), AM (12 OLC).
Born 1923. Assigned 359 FG 1943 and came to UK with Group. Promoted Major 1945 and given command of 370 FS. Flew 142 missions totalling 563 combat hours. Served in USAF until killed in flying accident at Otis AFB, Mass, on 14 Feb. 1951.
Personal Aircraft: One P-47D and one P-51B. P-51D-10-NA, 44-14733, CS: L, *Daddy's Girl* (summer 1944–spring 1945). CS: L named for daughter.

HUBERT A. ZEMKE, Missoula, Montana
Hq. 56th Fighter Group (Sept. 1942–Aug. 1944). Hq. 479th Fighter Group (Aug. 1944–30 Oct. 1944).
Original score 19½. *Revised score* 17¾. *Original strafing* 10½. *Revised strafing* 8½.
Born 1914. Brilliant fighter leader. Full Colonel as of 8 May 1943. 1943. DSC for action on 11 Feb. and 6 Mar. 1944. Transferred 479 FG 12 Aug. 1944. 17 air victories with 56 FG flying P-47s; 2½ with 479 FG flying P-51s. Lost 30 Oct. 1944 when P-51 broke up in storm. POW and senior officer Stalag Luft I. Retired from USAF 1967.
Personal Aircraft: P-47C, LM: Z. P-47D-5-RE, LM: Z, *May Tavarish* (Russian characters) (to 3 Oct. 1943). P-47D-15-RE, 42-75864, UN: Z (Jan. 1944–Jun. 1944). P-47D-25-RE, 42-26413, UN: Z, presentation a/c OREGON'S BRITANNIA (early Jun. 1944–Aug. 1944). P-38J, Z (Aug.–Sept. 1944), P-51D-10-NA, J2: Z (Sept.–Oct. 1944).

WALKER H. MAHURIN, Fort Wayne, Indiana
63rd Fighter Squadron, 56th Fighter Group (1941–27 Mar. 1944).
Original score 21. *Revised score* 20¾. No strafing credits.
(1 Japanese bomber in Pacific theatre: 3½ Migs in Korean War).
Decorations: DSC, SS, DFC, AM.
Born 5 Dec. 1918. Enlisted in USAAC 1940. Assigned 56 FG 1941 and came to UK Jan. 1943. Promoted Captain and flight leader May 1943. Awarded 56th's first Silver Star, 10 Oct. 1943. Triple victories on three occasions. Promoted Major 21 Mar. 1944. Shot down by Do 217 rear gunner 27 Mar. 1944. Evaded capture, aided by French patriots and returned to UK 7 May 1944. 85 missions and 192 combat hours with 56 FG. Returned USA and assigned 3rd Air Commando Group in SWPA. Credited with one Dinah bomber. Remained in USAF and flew in Korean War. Shot down in an F-86 and made POW. Nicknamed 'Bud'.
Victories List

1 & 2	17 Aug. 43	2 FW 190	Nr. Eupen
3	9 Sept. 43	1 FW 190	S Beauvais
4, 5 & 6	4 Oct. 43	3 Me 110	Nr. Düren
7 & 8	3 Nov. 43	1 Me 109 & 1 Me 110	Essens & N Juist Isles
9, 10 & 11	26 Nov. 43	3 Me 110	S Oldenburg
12	29 Nov. 43	1 Me 109	Pappenberg
13 & 14	22 Dec. 43	2 Me 109	Hesepe
15	30 Jan. 44	1 Ju 88	S Quackenbruck
16	3 Feb. 44	1 Me 109	S Ruhletwist
17	6 Mar. 44	1 FW 190	Wesendorf
18, 19 & 20	8 Mar. 44	2 FW 190 & 1 Ju 88	Wesendorf
21	27 Mar. 44	1 Do 217	E Chartres

Personal Aircraft: P-47C-5-RE, 41-6334, UN: M (c. Mar. 1943–11 Aug. 1943. Collision over Rumbrugh, Suffolk). P-47D-5-RE, 42-8487, UN: M, presentation a/c SPIRIT OF ATLANTIC CITY, N.J. (Aug. 1943–27 Mar. 1944. Shot down in this). Crew Chief: S/Sgt J. Barnes.

DUANE W. BEESON, Boise, Idaho
334th Fighter Squadron, 4th Fighter Group (Sept. 1942–5 Apr. 1944).

Original score 18. *Revised score* 19½. *Original strafing* 7. *Revised strafing* 4¾.

Born 1922. 71 'Eagle' Sqdn transferee. Highest scoring 4 FG pilot with P-47 12 e/a. Promoted Major shortly before being shot down by flak 5 Apr. 1944. Made POW. Died 13 Feb. 1947.
Personal Aircraft: Spitfire V. P-47C-2-RE, 41-6195, QP: B. P-47D-1-RE, 42-7890, QP: B, *Boise Bee* (to Feb. 1944). P-51B-5-NA, 43-6819, QP: B, *Boise Bee* (Feb. 1944–Apr. 1944).

LEONARD K. CARSON, Clearlake, Iowa
362nd Fighter Squadron, 357th Fighter Group (1943–1945).
Original score 18½. *Strafing* 3½. No revision.
Flight leader in 362 FS. Did not become an ace until autumn 1944. Promoted Captain. Claimed majority of victories during last six months of war. Five FW 190s on 27 Nov. 1944.
Personal Aircraft: Four P-51s. Last being P-51K-5-NT, 44-11622, G4: C, *Nooky Booky IV.*

JOHN F. THORNELL, East Walpole, Mass.
328th Fighter Squadron, 352nd Fighter Group (1943–Aug. 1944).
Original score 18½. *Strafing* 2. No revision.
Amassed all victories during first six months 1944, last being on 21 Jun. 1944. Promoted Captain end Jun. 1944.

Personal Aircraft: P-47D-5-RE, PE: T, *Pattie Ann* (Jul. 1943–Apr. 1944). P-51B-15-NA, 42-106872, PE: T, *Pattie Ann* (Apr. 1944–Aug. 1944). A/c named for niece.

GLENN E. DUNCAN, Houston, Texas
Hq. 353rd Fighter Group (Dec. 1942–7 Jul. 1944 and 22 Apr. 1945–Sept. 1945).
Original score 21½. *Revised score* 19. *Original strafing* 6. *Revised strafing* 7.83.
Born 19 May 1918. Group Executive Officer 353 FG until 25 Nov. 1943 when given command of Group. Promoted Lt Col Nov. 1943. Shot down by flak while strafing 7 Jul. 1944. Evaded capture and worked with Dutch underground movement until Allied armies arrived in spring of 1945. Returned to 353 FG and took command 22 Apr. 1945. All victories in P-47s.
Personal Aircraft: P-47D-5-RE, 42-8634, LH: X *IV, Dove of Peace.* P-47D-15-RE, LH: X *V.* P-47D-22-RE, 42-25506, LH: X *VI, Dove of Peace* (Apr. 44). P-47D-22-RE, 42-25971, LH: X *VII, Dove of Peace* (end Apr. 1944–7 Jul. 1944). P-51D-25-NA, 44-73060, LH: X *VIII, Dove of Peace* (Apr.–Sep. 1945).

JOHN T. GODFREY, Woonsocket, Rhode Island

336th Fighter Squadron, 4th Fighter Group (Sept. 1943–27 Apr. 1944 and 1 Aug. 1944–24 Aug. 1944).
Original score 18. *Original strafing* 18. *Revised strafing* 12.6.
Born 28 Mar. 1922 in Canada. Parents later settled in R.I. Joined RCAF and transferred 8AF in UK, Apr. 1943. Earned fame as wingman Don Gentile. Rank 1/Lt. Returned USA end Apr. 1944. Promoted Captain and on return to 4 FG for second tour, Major. Assumed command 336 FS c. 4 Aug. 1944. Shot down while strafing German a/d 24 Aug. 1944. Made POW. Died 1958.
Personal Aircraft: P-47D, VF: P, *Reggie's Reply* (Nov. 1943–Feb. 1944). P-51B-5-NA, 43-6765, VF: P, *Reggie's Reply* (Feb. 1944–Apr. 1944). P-51D-5-NA, 44-13412, VF: P, *Reggie's Reply* (Aug.1944). A/c named for brother lost at sea through enemy action. Crew Chief S/Sgt L. Krantz.

362nd Fighter Squadron, 357th Fighter Group (1943–fall 1944).
Original score 17½. No strafing credits. No revision.
Born 15 Jan. 1923. Leading ace of 357 FG during summer 1944. Extended combat tour five times. Killed in flying accident 17 Nov. 1954 at Toul, France. England AFB, La, named for him.
Personal Aircraft: P-51B-10-NA, 42-106462, G4: H, *You've Had I* P-51D-5-NA, G4: E, *Missouri Armarda*.

GERALD W. JOHNSON, Owenton, Kentucky
61st Fighter Squadron (1942–18 Feb. 1944) and 63rd Fighter Squadron (19 Feb.–27 Mar. 1944), 56th Group.
Original score 18. No strafing credits. No revision.
Born 10 Jul. 1919. First ace in 56 FG. Took command 63 FS 19 Feb. 1944 and promoted Major. Awarded DSC. Shot down while strafing a road convoy 27 Mar. 1944. Made POW. 88 missions totalling 196 combat hours. Rose to rank of Major-General in USAF.
Personal Aircraft: P-47C-2-RE, HV: D. P-47D-1-RE, 42-7877, HV: D, *In The Mood*, presentation a/c JACKSON COUNTY, MICHIGAN, FIGHTER (c. Aug. 1943–Feb. 1944). P-47D-15-RE, 42-76249, UN: V (Feb. 1944–27 Mar. 1944. Shot down in this a/c).

WALTER C. BECKHAM, De Funiak Springs, Florida
351st Fighter Squadron, 353rd Fighter Group (Oct. 1942–Feb. 1944).
Original score 18. No strafing claims. No revision.
Born 12 May 1916. Leading 8AF ace at one period. Assumed command 351 FS Nov. 1943 and promoted Major. DSC for heroism on 10 Oct. 1943. Lost while strafing German a/d 22 Feb. 1944. Made POW. 57 missions totalling 123 combat hours. Post-war USAF Colonel.
Personal Aircraft: P-47D-5-RE, 42-8476, YJ: X, *Little Demon*. Most, if not all victories obtained with this a/c. Shot down while flying it.

JOHN B. ENGLAND, Caruthersville, Missouri

RALPH K. HOFER, Salem, Missouri

334th Fighter Squadron, 4th Fighter Group (Oct. 1943–2 Jul. 1944). *Original score* 16. *Revised score* 16½. *Original strafing* 11½. *Revised strafing* 14.
Born 22 Jun. 1921. Joined RCAF and transferred to 8AF Jun. 1943. Destroyed an e/a on first mission, 8 Oct. 1943. Killed in action 2 Jul. 1944, Yugoslavia. Rank 1/Lt.
Personal Aircraft: P-47D, QP: K, *Susan III* (Oct. 1943–Jan. 1944). P-47D, QP: L, *The Missouri Kid* (Jan.–Feb. 1944). P-51B-5-NA, 43-6946, QP: L (Feb.–5 Apr. 1944). Lost with another pilot). P-51B-10-NA, 42-106682, QP: L (to 29 Apr. 1944. Lost with another pilot). P-51N-15-NA, 42-106924, QP: L. *Salem Representative* (May–Jun. 1944). (Lost in QP: X, a P-51D).

HENRY W. BROWN, Washington, D.C.
354th Fighter Squadron, 355th Fighter Group (1943–Oct. 1944)
Original score 17½. *Strafing* 14½.
Born 25 Jan. 1923. Highest scoring ace in 355 FG and one of youngest of original pilots. Shot down 3 Oct. 1944 while strafing and made POW. Colonel post-war USAF.
Personal Aircraft: P-47D, WR: Z, *Hun Hunter from Texas*. P-51B-10-NA, 42-106448, WR: Z, *Hun Hunter from Texas* (Apr. 1944–Jun. 1944). P-51D-5-NA, 44-13305, WR: Z, *Hun Hunter from Texas* (Jun. 1944–3 Oct. 1944).

CLARENCE E. ANDERSON, Newcastle, California
363rd Fighter Squadron, 357th Fighter Group (1943–1945).
Original score 16¼. *Strafing* 1. No revision.

Born 13 Jan. 1922. Two tours with 357 FG attaining rank of Captain. 116 missions and 480 combat hours.
Personal Aircraft: P-51B, B6: S (lost Holland with another pilot). P-51B-15-NT, 43-24823, B6: S, *Old Crow*. P-51D-10-NA, 44-14450, B6: S, *Old Crow*.

ROBERT W. FOY, Oswego, New York
363rd Fighter Squadron, 357th Fighter Group (1943–1945).
Original score 17. *Strafing* 3. No revision.
Born 1921. Rose from 2/Lt to Major during service with 357th FG. First victory Berlin on 6 Mar. 1944 Claimed 7 victories on first tour. Captain on return to USA in late summer 1944. Killed in flying accident after war.
Personal Aircraft: P-51B, B6: V, *Reluctant Rebel*. P-51D-20-NA, 44-63621, B6: V, *Little Shrimp*.

WILLIAM T. WHISNER, Shreveport, Louisiana
487th Fighter Squadron, 352nd Fighter Group (1943–1945).

Original score 15½. Strafing 3. No revision. (5½ Mig-15s in Korean War).
Born 17 Oct. 1923. Reached rank of Captain. Flew 137 missions with 352 FG in two tours. Awarded the DFC twice. Was Preddy's wingman at one time. Post-war USAF officer.
Personal Aircraft: P-51B-10-NA, 42-106449, HO: W, *Princess Elizabeth* (Apr. 1944–Jun. 1944). P-51D-10-NA, 44-14237, HO: W, *Moonbeam McSwine* (c. Aug. 1944–1945).

JAMES A. GOODSON, Toronto, Ontario, Canada
336th Fighter Squadron, 4th Fighter Group (Sept. 1942–Jun. 1944).
Original score 15. *Strafing* 15. No revision.
Born 21 Mar. 1921. First victory while flying Spitfire V with 133 Sqdn RAF. Flew first USAAF low-level fighter strafing sortie. Two victories while 'breaking in' 15th AF P-51 group Apr. 1944. Was leading strafing ace at time of loss. Shot down flak 20 Jun. 1944. DSC. In business in France and Belgium after war.
Personal Aircraft: P-47D 42-7959, VF: W. P-51B-5-NA, 43-7059, VF: B (Mar. 1944–Jun. 1944). P-51D-5-NA, 44-13303, VF: B (Jun. 1944). Lost in this a/c.

DONALD H. BOCHKAY, North Hollywood, California

363rd Fighter Squadron, 357th Fighter Group (1944–1945).
Original score 15. *Revised score* 14.84. *Strafing* None.
Born 19 Sept. 1916. Two tours with 357 FG flying 123 missions. Rose to rank of Captain. One of the few pilots to destroy two Me 262s. Post-war USAF.
Personal Aircraft: P-51B-5-NA, 43-6933, B6: F, *Alice in Wonderland.* P-51B, B6: F, *Speedball Alice.* P-51D-15-NA, 44-15422, B6: F (c. Sept. 1944–Feb. 1945). P-51D-20-NA, 44-72244, B6: F (Feb. 1945–May 1945). Both P-51D carried flying ace of spades insignia.

DONALD J. M. BLAKESLEE, Fairport Harbor, Ohio
Hq. 4th Fighter Group.
Original Score 15. *Revised score* 15½. *Original strafing* 6. *Revised strafing* 2.
Born 1918. 133 Eagle Squadron transferee. Brilliant fighter leader. Three air victories with RAF, one while detached 357 FG. DSC. Retired from USAF as Colonel.
Personal Aircraft: Spitfire V, MD: C. P-47C, WD: C. P-47D-1-RE, 42-7863, WD: C. P-51B-5-NA, 43-6437, WD: C (Feb.–Apr. 1944). P-51B-10-NA, 42-106726, WD: C (Apr. 1944–Jun. 1944). P-51D-5-NA, 44-13779, WD: C (Jun.–Aug. 1944).

RICHARD A. PETERSON, Alexandra, Minnesota
364th Fighter Squadron, 357th Fighter Group (1944–1945).
Original score 15. *Revised score* 15½. *Strafing* 3½.
Born 1924. Rose to rank of Major. Majority victories final nine months of war.
Personal Aircraft: P-51D-5-NA, 44-13586, C5: T, *Hurry Home Honey.* P-51D-15-NA, 44-14868, C5: T, *Hurry Home Honey.*

Top Strafing Aces

ELWYN G. RIGHETTI, San Luis Obispo, California
338th Fighter Squadron, 55th Fighter Group (Oct. 1944—Feb. 1945).
HQ 55th Fighter Group (22 Feb. 1945—17 Apr. 1945).
Strafing 27. *Air combat* $7\frac{1}{2}$.
Decorations: DSC, SS, DFC, AM.
Born 1916. Assigned to command 338th FS in Oct. 1944. Lt Col Group
CO 22 Feb. 1945. Crashlanded near airfield N of Dresden after strafing
attack 17 Apr. 1945. Killed by hostile civilians.

Three other pilots were credited with 20 or more ground strafing
victories:
JOSEPH L. THURY, 505 FS, 339 FG: *Strafing* 25. *Air combat* $2\frac{1}{2}$.
WILLIAM J. CULLERTON, 357 FS, 355 FG: *Strafing* 21. *Air combat* 6.
POW 1/45.
JOHN D. LANDERS, 55, 357 and 78 FGs: *Strafing* 20. *Air combat* $8\frac{1}{2}$.

JOSEPH L. THURY

WILLIAM J. CULLERTON

JOHN D. LANDERS

Airfields

The USAAF had some 250 stations in the United Kingdom of which 112 were occupied by the Eighth Air Force. Eight operational airfields were pre-war RAF installations with good buildings, including centrally heated barracks (Bassingbourn, Debden, Duxford, Honington, Horsham St. Faiths, Martlesham, Watton and Wattisham). The remainder were wartime constructions, the majority specifically for the USAAF.

Original plans called for fighter groups to use grass surfaced fields while bombers would operate from those with concrete runways and taxiways. The decision to establish the Fifteenth Air Force in Italy and divert 15 heavy bomb groups from the Eighth Air Force programme, led to the abandonment of some projected sites in Essex, and to a surfeit of airfields in East Anglia by the spring of 1944. In consequence some fighter groups were able to operate from 'hard' fields.

Although grass fields were well drained, mud was often a problem and steel mesh or perforated planking was put down on dispersal points, taxiways and runways. Concrete runways were eventually laid at some of these fighter stations.

Building of airfields was largely carried out by the British although US Army engineer battalions put down runways at a few. All told, expenditure on airfields and the numerous other installations for the USAAF ran to £645,000,000 of which £40,000,000 was provided by the US government. A single bomber airfield cost £990,000 in 1942.

Typical layout is that shown in this aerial view of Hardwick, Norfolk, home of 93rd BG for two and a half years. The flying field occupied an area of approximately 500 acres. Three concrete runways were 50 yds wide, with main (aligned along axis of usual prevailing wind) 2,000 yds and the others 1,400 yds in length. With perimeter track and hardstands, concrete area ran to 20,000 sq. yds. Hardstands were dispersed irregularly off perimeter track to lessen destruction in event of an enemy air attack. Twelve additional hardstands were added after this picture was taken.

Full night flying lighting was available. Facilities were designed to make the station as independent as possible from local services. Standard hangars were 25 ft high by 240 ft long and 120 ft wide. Most airfields completed after 1942 had two, but Hardwick (completed that year) had three (A). Fuel storage at two underground points totalled 144,000 imperial gallons (B). Accommodation for 460 officers and 2,660 men was dispersed in surrounding countryside to lessen casualties in the event of an air raid (C). Other features visible in the photograph are the bomb dump (D) and ammunition storage (E), control tower (F), butts (G), briefing rooms (H), the communal sites [mess halls, etc.] (I), motor transport yard (J), station Hq. (K), and village of Topcroft (L). The name of an airfield was not necessarily its exact location. A complete station usually spread across two or more parishes, in this case chiefly Shelton and Topcroft. Hardwick lay a mile away to the south west. Airfield names had to be distinctive to avoid possible confusion between them.

Fortresses break formation to land in late February sunshine.

Mustangs cross the Stour in winter mists.

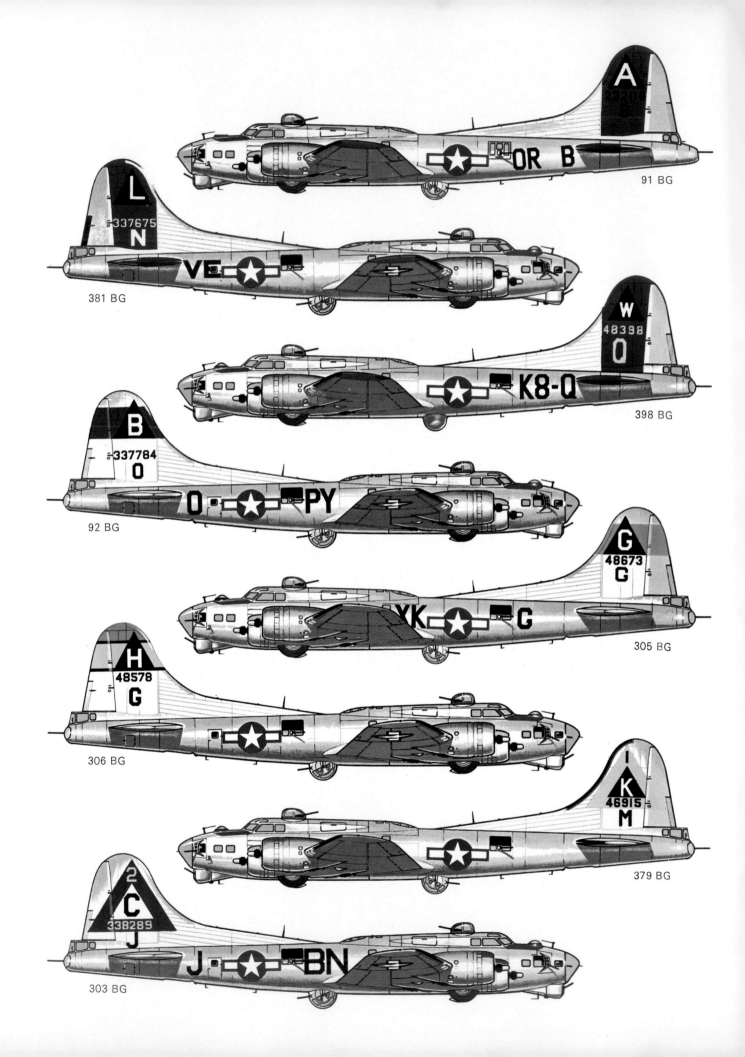

91 BG

381 BG

398 BG

92 BG

305 BG

306 BG

379 BG

303 BG

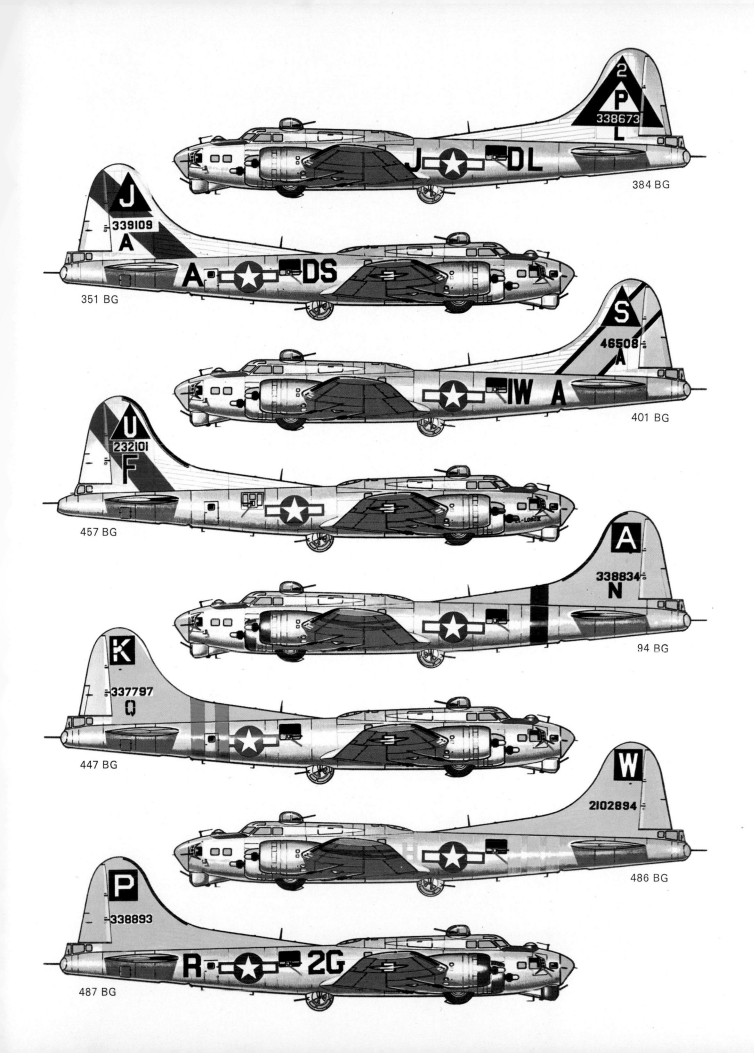

384 BG

351 BG

401 BG

457 BG

94 BG

447 BG

486 BG

487 BG

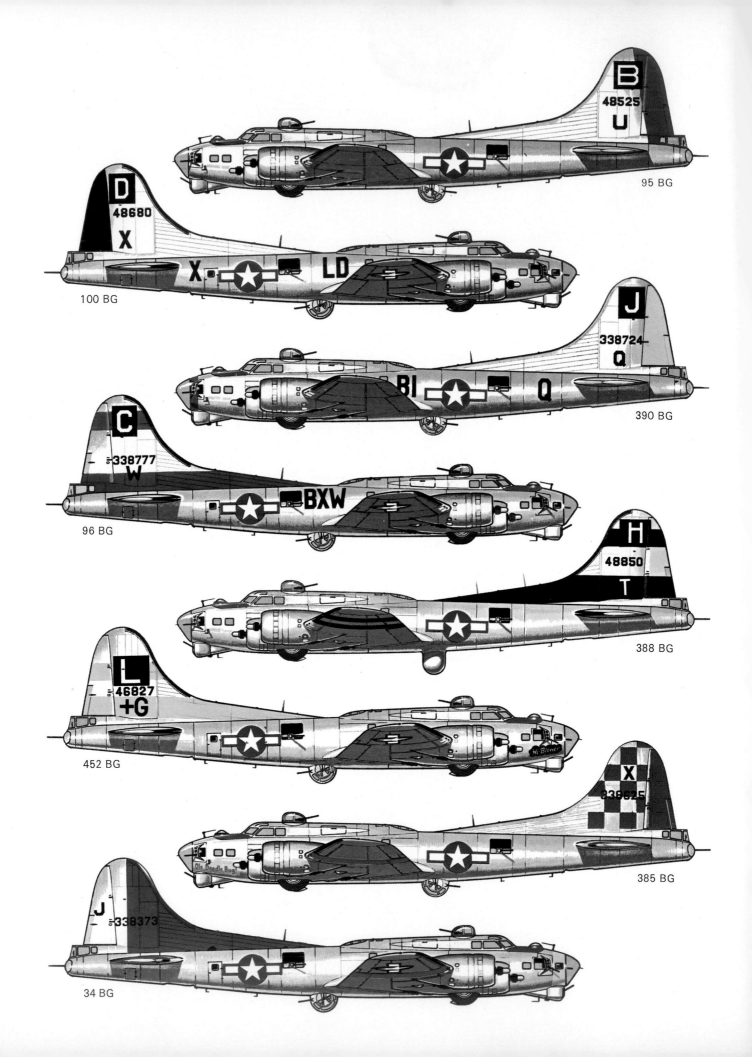

95 BG

100 BG

390 BG

96 BG

388 BG

452 BG

385 BG

34 BG

490 BG

493 BG

381 BG

95 BG

100 BG

390 BG

94 BG

447 BG

486 BG

487 BG

96 BG

388 BG

452 BG

34 BG

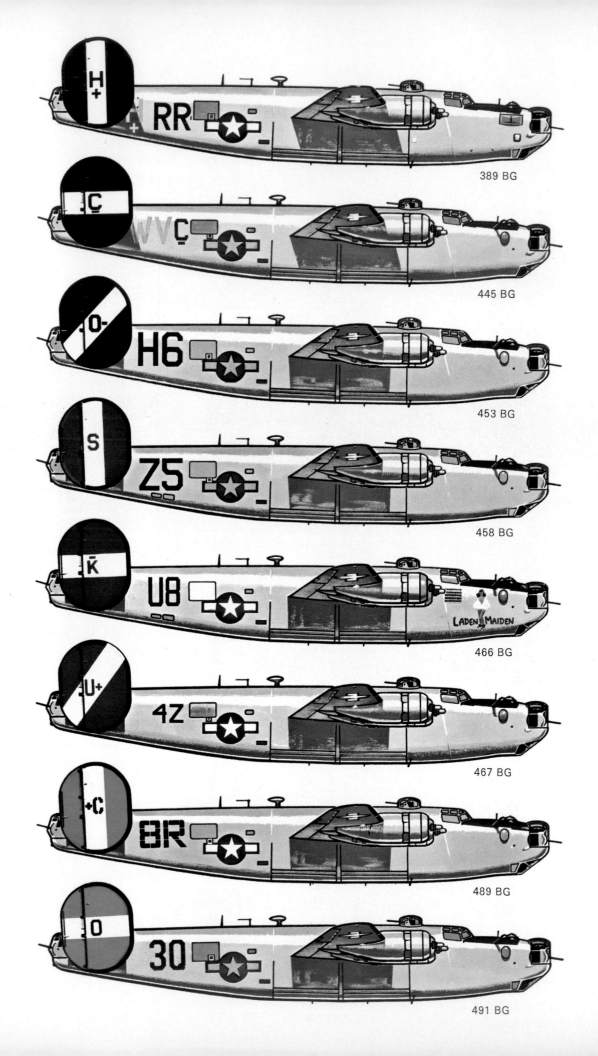

389 BG

445 BG

453 BG

458 BG

466 BG

467 BG

489 BG

491 BG

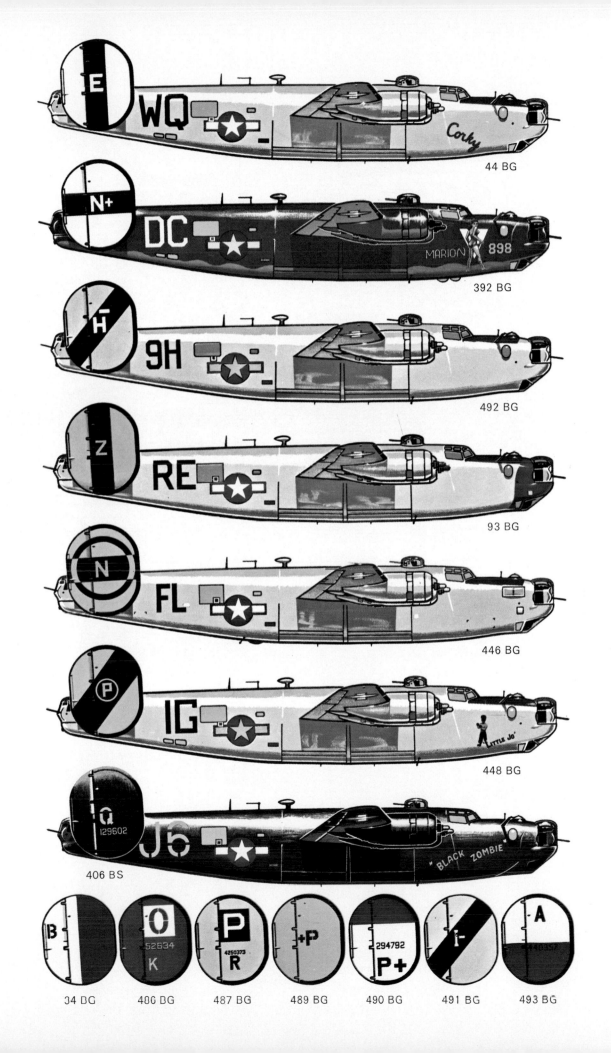

E WQ — *Corky* — 44 BG

N+ DC — MARION 898 — 392 BG

H 9H — 492 BG

Z RE — 93 BG

N FL — 446 BG

P IG — *LITTLE JO* — 448 BG

Q 129602 J6 — "BLACK ZOMBIE" — 406 BS

B — 34 BG

O 52634 K — 486 BG

P 4250373 R — 487 BG

+P — 489 BG

294792 P+ — 490 BG

I — 491 BG

A 448337 — 493 BG

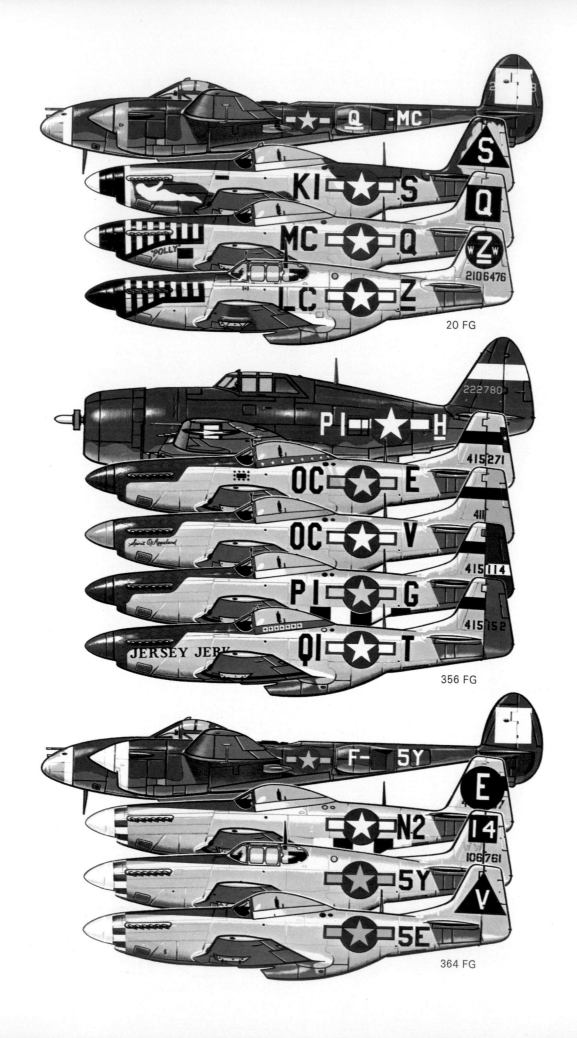

20 FG

356 FG

364 FG

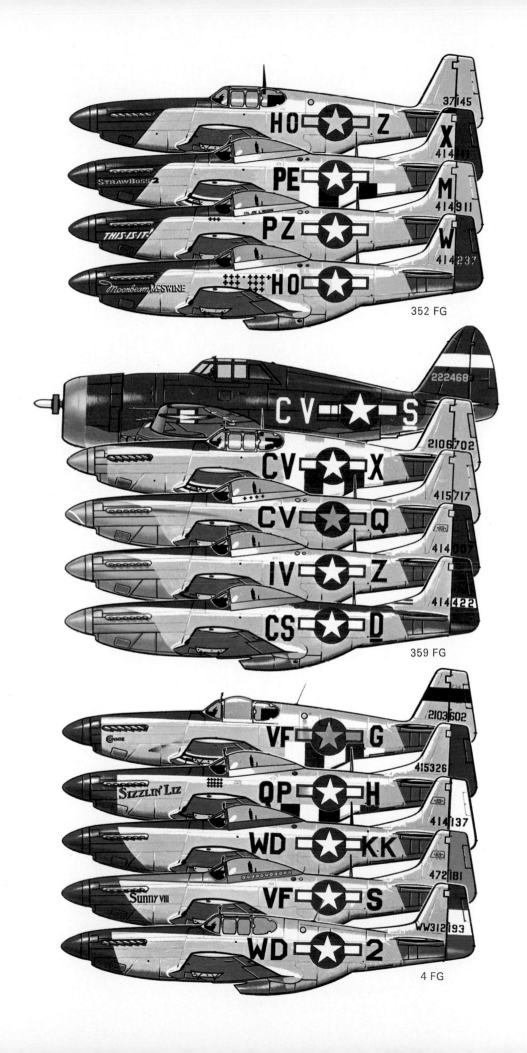

352 FG

359 FG

4 FG

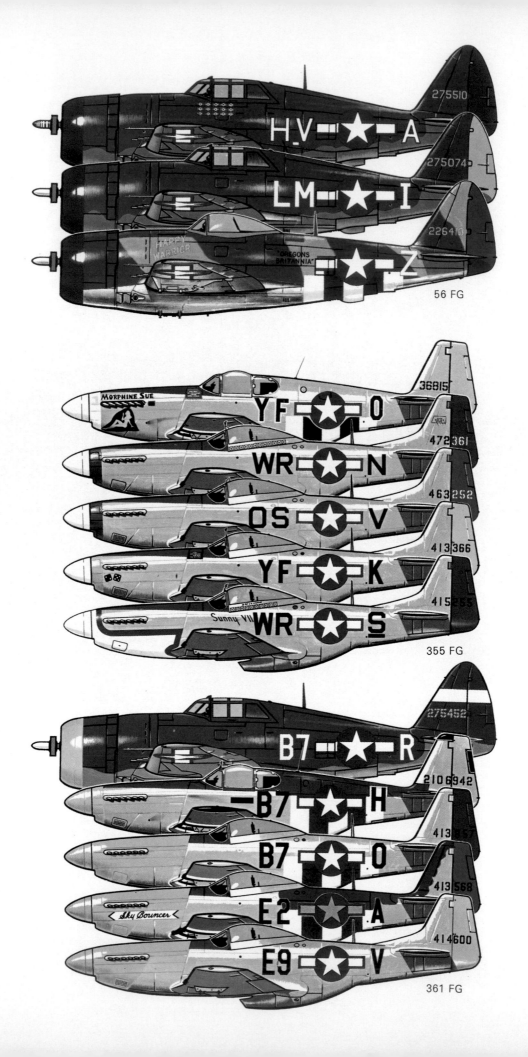

56 FG

355 FG

361 FG

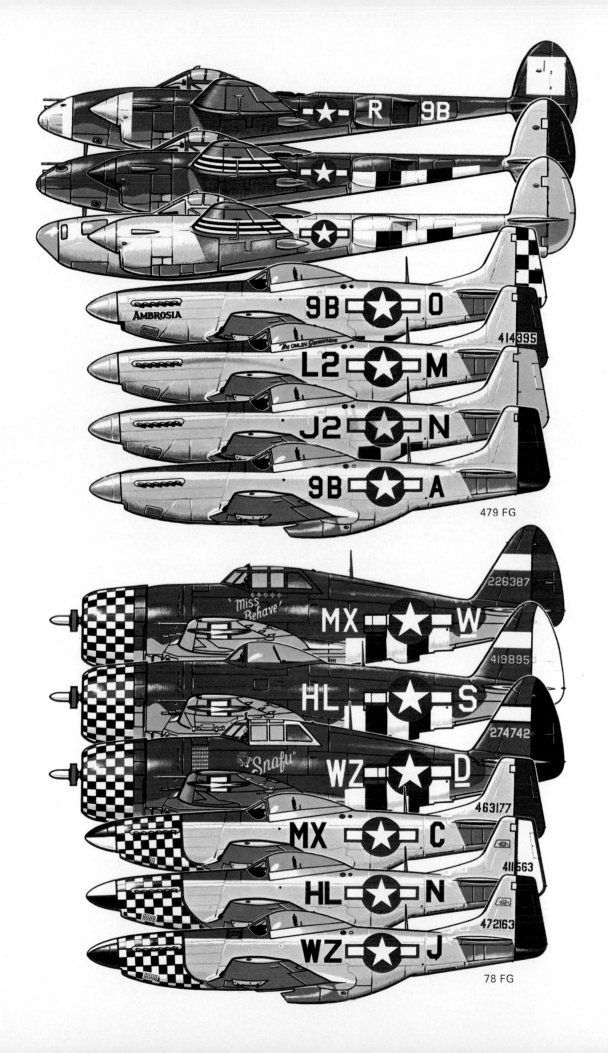

AMBROSIA
R 9B
9B O
The ONLEY Genevieve
L2 M
414395
J2 N
9B A
479 FG

226387
'Miss Behave'
MX W
419895
HL S
274742
"Snafu"
WZ D
463177
MX C
411563
HL N
472163
WZ J
78 FG

339 FG

353 FG

357 FG

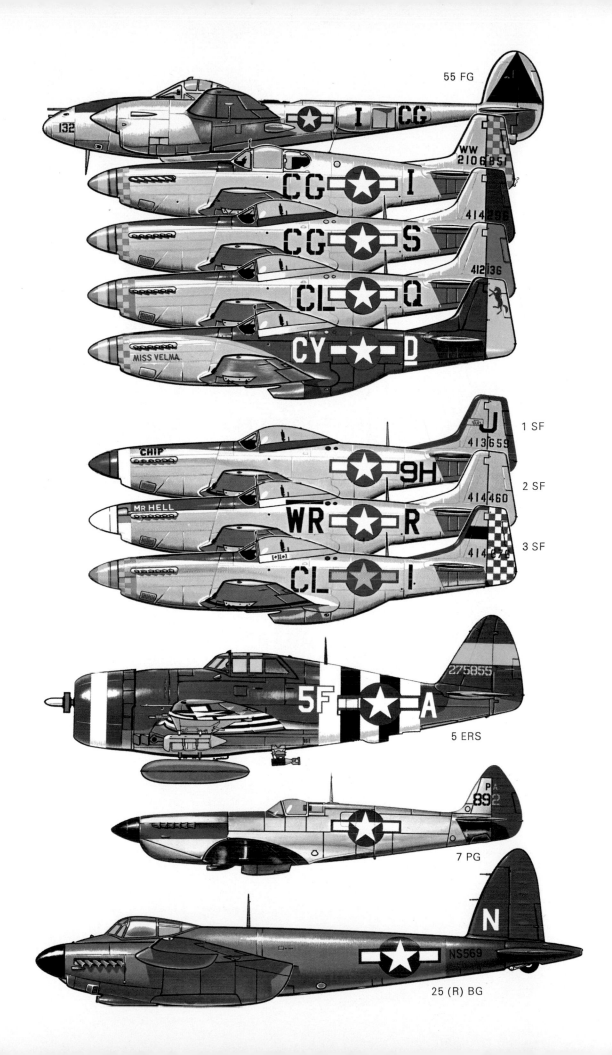

55 FG

132

WW
2106851

CG — ★ — I

414296

CG — ★ — S

412136

CL — ★ — Q

MISS VELMA.

CY — ★ — D

J
413659   1 SF

'CHIP'

★ 9H   2 SF

414460

MR HELL

WR — ★ — R   3 SF

414674

CL — ★ — I

5F ★ A   275855

5 ERS

PA
89   7 PG

N

NS569

25 (R) BG

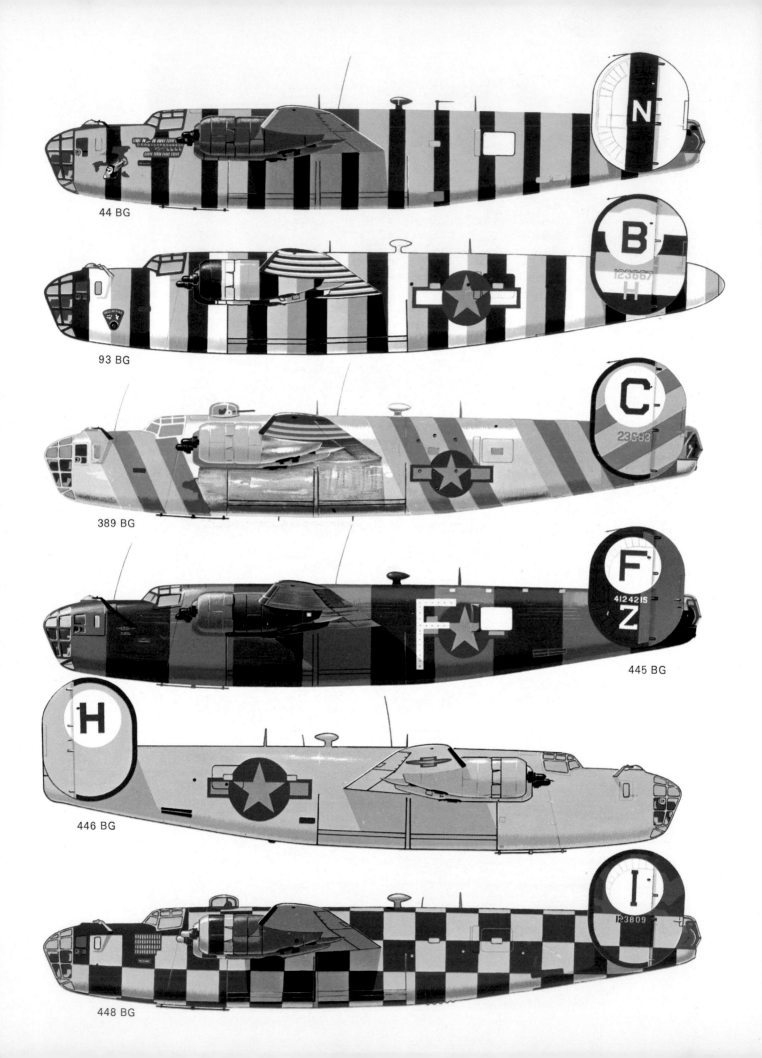

44 BG

93 BG

389 BG

445 BG

446 BG

448 BG

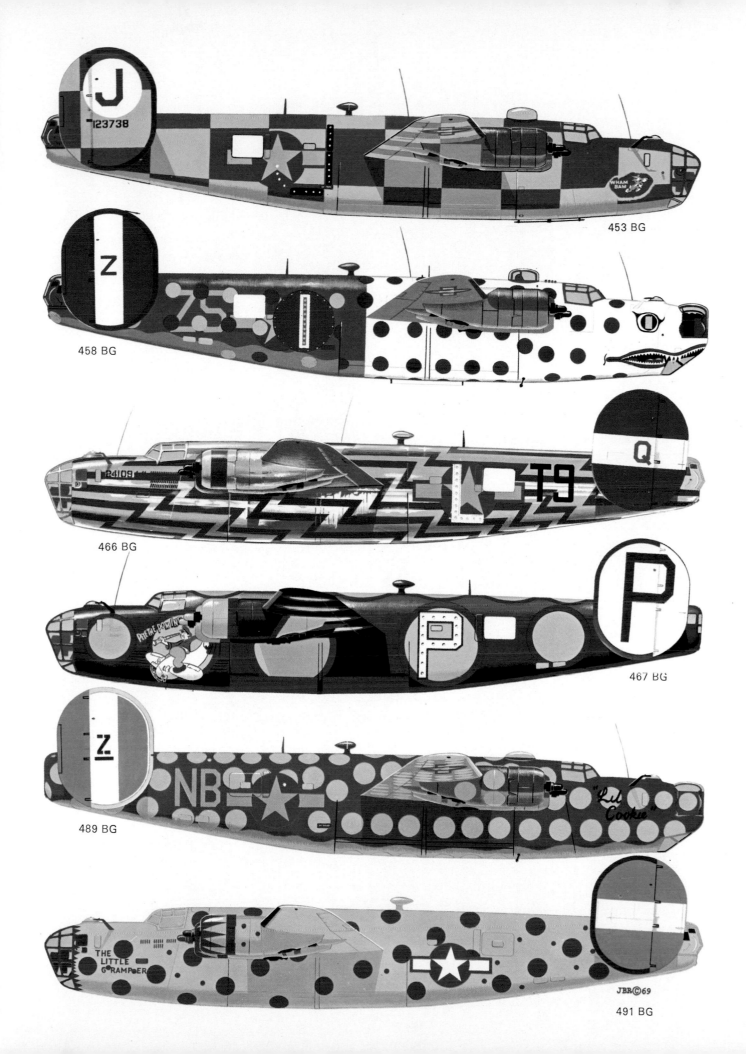

453 BG

458 BG

466 BG

467 BG

489 BG

491 BG

JBR©69

Training took its toll. P-51B, 43-6503 of 496th Fighter Training Group bellied in on a main runway. The 495th Fighter Training Group's P-47C, 41-6538 took a dip in the river Severn near Atcham. A group of RAF men and the lucky pilot survey the wreckage. Both incidents occurred in July 1944. (Photos. Ray Bowers)

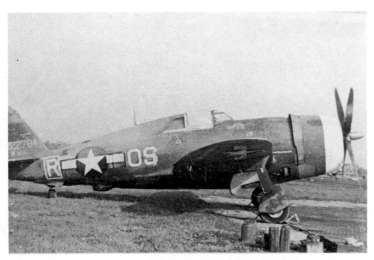

War Weary P-47D used by the 355th Fighter Group OTU. This machine was assigned after VE-day for the purpose of giving pilots P-47 experience in case they were posted to Thunderbolt units in the Pacific theatre. (Photo via Olmstead) P-47D, 42-8532, used by the 389th Bomber Group as a formation monitor. Like most groups, the 389th decked out its support aircraft with markings similar to those carried by its combat aircraft. (Photo Clendenin)

One of the most popular light transports used by Eighth Air Force was the Norduyn UC-64 Norseman. This example, 43-5314, was assigned to AFSC at Stanstead in August 1944. (Photo Holmes)
The Piper L-4Bs originally assigned to the 67th Observation Group eventually found their way to combat groups as headquarter's transport. HL:6⅞ was given a painted mouth and teeth by the 78th Fighter Group.

Aircraft camouflage and markings

While a mass produced aircraft may have distinctive control and flight characteristics which to a pilot distinguishes it from its kin, visually, any individual difference rests with paintwork. This covers general finish, paint for protective purposes and camouflage for concealment; the military nationality markings; individual aircraft identification in the form of a serial number, special tactical recognition markings; unit identification markings; and the unofficial personal decorations bestowed by the men who flew or serviced the machine. All these contributed towards the creation of an individual atmosphere about an aeroplane, a visual extension of an intangible quality that is akin to personality in a human. As this book reveals, many individual aircraft, because of the exploits in which they were involved, became more famous than the men who flew them.

Ultimately, paintwork on Eighth Air Force aircraft came to be amongst the most flamboyant of any air arm in the Second World War. It was subject to frequent change, sometime through necessity, sometime through fancy. Historically a knowledge of this subject serves to identify aircraft in illustrations with their unit, and often enables the date of photographs to be established.

BASIC PAINTWORK
Under this heading comes paint applied at the factory during or after construction, and its variation in the course of an aircraft's life. This can be divided into camouflage and general finish, functional paintwork, serial numbers, and national insignia.

Camouflage and General Finish
Basic camouflage for USAAF combat aircraft at the time of Eighth Air Force's establishment in the UK was dark Olive Drab for upper surfaces and Neutral Gray for undersurfaces. These colours were standardised as Shades 41 and 43 respectively, but there was considerable variation, possibly due to slight deviations in manufacturing process. Certainly varying shades of green and grey could be found on a brand new B-17 or B-24. Olive drab was particularly vulnerable to exposure in sunlight, and with age would fade to a browner hue. This was particularly pronounced on the B-17F and early B-17F models where after nine months service the olive drab had become a purplish-brown. Later camouflage was more durable.

B-17Es of the 97th BG had RAF type camouflage, shadow-shading with light brown and dark green on upper surfaces and pale blue gray undersurfaces. In August 1942 a Technical Order was issued requiring Medium Green (Shade 42) to be applied in irregular blotches along the trailing and leading edges of wings and tail assembly, extending inwards for varying distances up to a fifth of the total width of the surface concerned. B-17s and B-24s of the 44th, 91st, 93rd, 303rd, 305th and 306th BGs in England received this treatment, individual interpretations varying with blotching also on the fuselage in some units. Although Medium Green blotching was specified in a later T.O. it does not appear to have been factory applied to heavy bombers and its use was discontinued on aircraft arriving in England after April 1943. There is no record of medium green blotching on fighter aircraft in England.

The division between the olive drab and grey was not sharp, as a gradual blend was obtained by slight overspray.

In Jan. 1944 camouflage paint was discontinued on most USAAF aircraft as its basic purpose was then deemed of little importance, and a slight improvement in performance was obtained through reduced weight and smoother finish: but a major consideration was the saving in factory man hours. Fabric surfaces were now silver doped.

The first natural metal deliveries from the US arrived in Feb. 1944 and were chiefly B-17Gs and P-38Js. There were some misgivings in bomber units about operating a lone "silver" aircraft in a formation of camouflaged machines due to the likelihood of its attracting action from enemy fighters. Ideally, commanders preferred to operate natural metal aircraft together in small formations until sufficient numbers became available to make them no longer a curiosity. New camouflage finish aircraft continued to arrive at operational stations as replacements up to June 1944, due to delays at depots.

In practise the abandonment of paint finish made little if any difference to the operational performance of combat aircraft in the ETO, and camouflaged machines continued to form part of formations until the last mission of the war—although by then a dwindling minority. Natural metal finish first appeared in England on an early B-26B at Andrews Field in August 1943, and shortly afterwards at Honington on a B-17 used for transport duties. Both were war weary machines from which the camouflage was experimentally removed.

With the impending invasion of the continent SHAEF advised that camouflage was desirable on those aircraft in the tactical air forces likely to be based on the continent. VIII FC units were expected to be in this category and a programme of applying camouflage paint to metal finish fighters was carried out at depots and operational bases commencing May 1944. The paint used appears to have been principally from British sources and the range of colours varied greatly, units being left very much to their own devices. Most common camouflage was a dark green of a somewhat lighter shade than Olive Drab but applied to approximately the same area as with factory paint jobs. There were also schemes involving shadow-shading in green and grey, and dappling in the same colours. Some units simply broke the outline of an aircraft with large irregular patches of olive drab (and in some case insignia blue) on wings, tail and upper fuselage. Undersides were mostly left as bare metal but with the 78th and 357th groups in particular, they were painted a pale blue-grey (Sky) or pale grey. Towards the end of 1944 "in the field" camouflaging of metal finish aircraft was discontinued and some machines were even returned to a bare metal state again. The 56FG, however, continued the practise with individual schemes for each squadron, but it was more unit livery than camouflage. Apart from the 56th, at no time was a fighter group without metal finish aircraft on its strength, although the numbers were often small when replacements were few and the paintshops could cope.

Special camouflage involved gloss black for the undersides of Leaflet Sqdn. B-17s, overall gloss black for the RCM Sqdn. and Carpetbagger B-24s, gloss black having proved better than matt black for escaping searchlight beams. OA-10s of 5ERS were matt white for over sea work. Photographic reconnaissance Lightnings and Spitfires were P.R. blue (an azure shade) during 1943 and 1944.

Black rudder de-icing boots remained unpainted on both camouflaged and natural metal finish aircraft. Propellers were matt black apart from a 4 inch yellow tip to each blade. Propeller bosses were usually black but later natural metal when camouflage was abandoned. Aircraft acquired from the British usually remained in their original camouflage. For fighters this was dark green and ocean grey shadow-shading on upper surfaces and Sky type S undersurfaces. This latter colour was commonly described as duck-egg blue, probably the nearest one can come to an exact description is a pale blue-grey with slight green tinge. Training and communications aircraft were camouflaged dark green and dark earth while undersides were deep yellow. Douglas Boston and Havoc types usually had dark green and dark earth top sides and either black or sky undersides, dependent upon their original role. 67th RG operated a few Havoc I and II on target-towing duties during the summer of 1943 and these retained original RAF night fighter camouflage.

Basic Functional markings
The yellow warning propeller tips mentioned above came under this heading. Other warning markings were in insignia red and included fire extinguisher panel doors, various alert lines and "No step" patches. On natural metal finishes anti-dazzle panels in front of cockpit windows and on the cowlings of multi-engined aircraft, were olive drab, occasionally matt black.

Data panel on left side of fuselage, forward of cockpit, gave a/c type and model, full serial number, crew weights and fuel grade: stencilled in black on both natural metal and camouflage finishes. On night flying aircraft painted black in the UK, the data panel was repainted in white, or yellow and occasionally red.

The serial number of the aircraft was also applied to the vertical tail in abbreviated form as a radio call-sign. Whereas the full serial consisted of a prefix (last two digits of the year in which aircraft was budgeted) followed by a hyphen and number, on the tail the first digit of prefix and the hyphen were omitted. The tail number was painted in yellow (Shade 48) on olive drab, and black on natural metal. In squadron service where unit markings were applied to the vertical tail, the number was often obscured and repainted in another position. When this happened it was not uncommon for the new application to omit the first digit, or occasionally to give the serial in full, less the hyphen. This was particularly common on B-24s where the factory applied tail number was high on the fin. With the Divisional symbols the serial had to be moved down the fin, and with full-colour tail markings, to the upper inner sides of both fins. In some factories manufacturing changes were denoted by painted marks on fuselage or tail. B-17s often had a white X for this purpose which was not removed in operational units despite its insignificance.

National Insignia

When the United States entered the war the national insignia on her military aircraft consisted of a red disc centred on a five pointed white star, the whole set on a dark blue disc. This form was only to be seen on a few visitors that reached the UK prior to mid-May 1942. On May 15th 1942 the insignia was officially changed by the omission of the red disc, to prevent confusion with the Japanese marking. The early Eighth Air Force aircraft arriving in Britain carried the new insignia which officially remained in force for just over a year. On British advice the fuselage insignia was outlined in yellow, a 2 inch thick band to make it more prominent, as was the fashion with the British roundel. Most units going to North Africa with the Twelfth AF had their aircraft so marked but there were serveral exceptions. A few heavy bombers remaining in the UK gained the yellow outline but the practise was never pursued. Only on the fighter aircraft was the yellow outline in general use and P-47s of 4th, 56th and 78th groups all sported it during the spring of 1943. On B-24 aircraft earmarked for bad weather flying, the white star was considered too conspicuous and was dulled with grey.

On June 29th 1943 another change was made; this was the addition of a white rectangle each side of the cocades and the whole outlined in red. This caused problems as the white rectangles when added to the existing cocades obscured unit markings. In the case of newly arrived B-26 groups, a completely fresh national insignia was applied re-positioned forward of the original.

This insignia was short lived for on August 14th 1943 the red outline was changed to blue, again reflecting Pacific theatre associations with the colour red. At this date many Eighth Air Force aircraft had still not received the changes of June 29th due to a busy operational period. Although over a month was allowed for institution of the blue outline some aircraft were still flying off to war with red banded star and bars in the opening months of 1944.

Location of the national insignia was on the upper surface of the left wing and on the lower surface of the right wing, and on both sides of the fuselage between wings and tail. Size and location were stipulated in various TO's but in practise factories selected the most suitable points for positioning. On early P-47s the British advised an additional insignia under the left wing and that both under wing insignia should be of a larger size. This was to aid in recognition owing to the risk of the radial engined fighter being taken for an FW 190.

OPERATIONAL PAINTWORK

This comprises the markings applied to an aircraft by the depots in its theatre of operations or the unit to which it was assigned. To some extent camouflage and markings dealt with under Basic Paintwork also fall under this heading and for convenience have been dealt with under that section.

Special Tactical Markings

The first of these involved the P-47 which, because of its radial configuration, was—as mentioned above—in danger of being mistaken for an FW 190. On February 20th 1943 special identity markings were issued by VIII FC: a 24 inch wide white band around leading edge of engine cowling; a 12 inch wide white band across fin and rudder from leading to trailing edge, and likewise an 18 inch wide white band on both horizontal stabilisers and elevators. It was at this juncture that a 59 inch dia. national insignia was painted under the left wing and the existing insignia under the right wing increased to the same size, while the fuselage insignia was repositioned further forward.

Similar markings were notified for the P-51B when this appeared in

England and was repeatedly "bounced" by P-38 and P-47 pilots eager to shoot down Me109s. The spinner and first 12 inch of engine cowling directly aft, were painted white. A 12 inch wide white band across vertical tail and a 15 inch white band round each horizontal tailplane and wing. With the abandonment of camouflage P-47 and P-51 recognition markings were painted in black. Apart from those aircraft already in combat groups at the time of the initial orders, these special markings were applied at depots where new aircraft were assembled upon delivery from the US. From March 23rd 1944, the white fin and rudder strips on P-51s was discontinued due to its effect of breaking up the outline of the vertical tail, a distinctive recognition feature. The order was not extended to black bands which continued to be applied until the end of 1944. By the spring of 1945 P-51 wing bands were also omitted although it appears that in both the case of P-47 and P-51 new aircraft were leaving the depots both with and without black recognition markings. Further, it was policy of some combat groups to remove all or part of these bands.

In late May 1944, P-47s of the 65th FW's A/S/R squadron were painted with yellow tail bands, similar to the general white bands but wider. A yellow band was also painted round each wing inboard of the weapons bay but due to the location of suspended wing stores in that area, the bands were superseded by yellow wing tips.

The P-38 had no need for painted identification due to its unusual twin-boom configuration. However, with the advent of the unarmed Droop-Snoot there arose a need to conceal its vulnerability and this was achieved by the subterfuge of making other P-38s look like Droop-Snoots. An 8 inch white band was painted round the fuselage at the rear of the Droop-Snoot's perspex nose-piece and also in approximately the same position on normal P-38s. The armed P-38s then had all paint removed from the nose forward of the white band and the exposed metal highly polished to reflect as perspex. From early April most P-38s in the 20th and 55th FGs were so treated.

The best known special recognition markings are the Allies black and white stripes applied to tactical aircraft on the eve of D-Day, June 6th 1944. At first these stripes completely encircled fuselage and wings but after a month they were removed from upper surfaces. In September SHAEF ordered that the stripes be erased on the under-surfaces of the wings too, leaving only the under fuselage portion. After 1944 the remaining stripes were also removed. Amongst Eighth Air Force combat units "Invasion Stripes" adorned only fighter and some reconnaissance aircraft. A number of communications types which were likely to be in the vicinity of the bridgehead also received them, plus a few special duties aircraft. In the first instance fuselage Invasion stripes completely obscured unit code letters on P-38 tail booms and these markings were not repainted. With P-47s and P-51s there was partial obscuring of letters but where this occurred the letter was soon repainted on the stripes in black or white as appropriate: in many cases a letter was part black, part white.

A longitudinally placed yellow stripe on the underside of B-24 fuselages from the spring of 1944 was not a recognition marking in the usual sense. The stripe was actually two narrow bands of yellow along the bottom edge of each bomb door, and allowed an easier visual check on the position of the roller type doors from another aircraft in a formation. This stemmed from a number of incidents when bombs were dropped through closed doors.

There were several special purpose markings having more limited use. The radio controlled Aphrodite B-17s had upper surfaces of wings and tail painted white or in white panels to facilitate observation from "mother" aircraft. Target-towing aircraft in gunnery flights were distinguished with yellow tail tops or a yellow horizontal tail band from the autumn of 1944 although some units apparently ignored the practise.

Radar equipped lead bombers were often identified by distinctive markings but these were of individual unit origin, as were the gaudy formation assembly aircraft.

UNIT IDENTIFICATION MARKINGS

Individual Aircraft Letters

When the Eighth Air Force adopted the British air communication and control system, all aircraft in an operational unit were given a radio call sign based on the phonetic alphabet. Painted on tail or fuselage, this letter also served as a means of visual identification for an aircraft within its squadron or unit. During the early operations of VIII BC, B-17s and B-24s did not display their call-letters although each had one assigned and in use for plane-to-plane and plane-to-base communication. From November 1942 these letters were painted in yellow on tail fins in some units, and later, when squadron codes were introduced, on the fuselage. Not until June 1943 was the use of the radio-call letter regularised as a visual identity marking on heavy bombers when it was specified for the fin 24 inch-28 inches high by 12 inches wide, in yellow. As a rule (but as always one can find exceptions) it was the first marking applied to a new bomber on assignment to a combat unit, and many B-17s and B-24s made their operational debut with only this unit device. With fighter aircraft the radio-call letter was usually only used for plane-to-base communication during non-formation flights, and it served chiefly as visual identification on the fuselage of the aircraft. In fact, far more use was made of identification letters on fighters than with bombers where the tendency was to identify an individual machine by Stateside practise of the last three digits of the serial number. Many fighter pilots flew aircraft with the same individual letter as the initial letter of their surname, and in any case the combination of squadron code letters and individual letter frequently became a familiar cypher that identified the pilot as much as the aircraft.

Where more than 26 aircraft were assigned to a squadron—and many fighter squadrons had 35 or more apiece at VE-day—individual letters were duplicated but the duplicate letter would be distinguished by an adjacent bar sign. With most VIII FC units the bar was painted below the letter, but sometimes above. In the fighter training squadrons where there were very large numbers of aircraft examples existed where a letter was barred both above and below. A bar was occasionally painted in a vertical position aft of an aircraft letter and in the Eighth this was generally the case with B-17s. In B-24 bomb groups when no squadron markings existed, the bar sign came to identify aircraft within the group rather than the squadron. This was achieved by the use of bars above or below a letter to give cover for over seventy aircraft. This was taken a stage further by some groups who used the bar as a form of squadron marking: one squadron had no sign, one had a bar above the letter, one a bar below the letter, and the fourth squadron was identified by the introduction of plus sign before or after the letter. Two B-17 groups also took up this form of squadron identification.

At one period the 4th FG's duplicate plane-in-squadron letters were distinguished by the same letter being repeated beside the first—double letters, e.g. AA, BB, etc. There were a few unusual examples of distinguishing duplicate plane-in-squadron letters, such as the use of the numeral 2 following the letter.

Numerals were used in some fighter Group OTUs from November 1944 as plane-in-squadron identification.

Squadron codes

At the time of the Eighth Air Force's arrival in the UK the USAAF had no authorised form of unit markings on its aircraft. In consequence the Eighth was influenced by the RAF in this matter and the Spitfire fighter groups in training with RAF Fighter Command received squadron code letters and displayed them in the same fashion as their Allies. Squadron codes consisted of a two-letter combination painted to one side of the national insignia, while on the other side appeared the individual aircraft letter. Together—with the squadron codes read first—the three letters gave an aircraft a simple form of visual (and oral) identity within *an air force* and as such is possibly the best form of identity marking to appear on military aircraft. Squadron code letters were extended to the 16 B-17 squadrons in December 1942 and in the spring and summer of 1943 to new B-17 units. In the case of bombers, it is noticeable that many groups had two squadrons with similar combinations, as if a deliberate attempt was being made to confuse enemy intelligence.

By the autumn of 1943 the number of new RAF and USAAF units came near to exhausting possible two-letter combinations so the letters C and I, originally omitted due to confusion with other letters, were brought into use and many new Eighth AF groups were given codes featuring one of these letters. The system was further expanded by introducing numerals (excluding 1) and issuing one letter, one numeral codes. Unit code letters were chiefly issued to squadrons, but special flights and other organisations were also recipients. Only eight long term combat squadrons in the Eighth were never allotted codes. These were those of 388th and 457th BGs. A great many other bomber squadrons never displayed their codes during hostilities, apparently because Wing organisations thought them unnecessary or did not issue details to groups. From the second week in May 1945 codes were painted under the wing of all USAAF aircraft in the UK in an anti-low flying campaign. The 388th and 457th Groups used their wireless transmitter codes for this purpose.

Fighter squadrons made good use of squadron codes throughout hostilities the only exception being the P-38 units which had theirs obscured by D-day stripes and did not repaint them. Positioning on fighters was normally ahead of the national insignia on both sides of fuselage with aircraft letter aft. Normal colours were white on camouflage and black on metal. B-26s also conformed with squadron codes forward of the cocades and the aircraft letter aft: the colour was grey with a bluish tinge. On B-24s—which did not display these markings until mid-March 1944, the normal position was aft of the waist gun windows and the colour grey with bluish tinge on camouflage or black on metal. B-17s, however, did not conform to any particular pattern after the spring of 1943 and in some cases, particularly with 384BG, the squadron codes were split, one letter on either side of the national insignia. The size of letters also varied considerably in B-17 units. Grey with a bluish tinge was the most common colour on camouflage, although yellow, blue and white were also used.

Unit codes used by the Eighth and Ninth Air Forces were complimentary with those of the RAF but a few cases of duplication existed. The symbols 4N used by 833 BS was also carried by a Ninth A.F. fighter squadron, Z5 was used by both an RAF Halifax and a 458th BG B-24 squadron both based in Norfolk. The codes issued to the 1, 31 and 52 FG's were issued to the 56, 78 and 4 FG's respectively, when the former units moved to North Africa. In 1944 when 4th, 31st, 52nd and 78th were all flying P-51s over Germany confusion was only avoided by extensive colour markings.

Squadron colour markings

A bright colour marking was the traditional means of identifying a squadron within its group, and when camouflage was abandoned many units returned to this practice that had been followed during Stateside training. Squadron colour markings were generally unofficial and with bombers the positioning and extent a matter for each individual unit: engine cowlings, propeller bosses, nose and tail bands, tail tips and, in one case, coloured aircraft letters. In the case of fighter aircraft there was official guidance from the late autumn of 1944 when a coloured rudder scheme came into general use. The 56th FG had originated rudder colours in March that year for recognition of squadron formations at a greater distance than was possible with code letters. Some units also used squadron colours as part of the group nose marking.

Group, Wing and Divisional Markings

To aid assemble and marshalling of heavy bomber formations, VIII BC introduced group and bombardment wing identification markings in June 1943. A geometric device was painted on either side of the fin and on the upper surface of the right wing; approximately 80 inches diameter and coloured white. This was the wing—later division—marking, the 1BW having a triangle, 2BW a circle, and 4BW a square. Marauders of the 3BW were not included in this scheme. There was considerable variation in the size and shape of these symbols, particularly with 4BW/3BD where the square was often a rectangle.

The group was identified by a yellow letter superimposed on the symbol. The colour of the letter was changed to insignia blue in July and few aircraft had the yellow marking. Initially the letters E and F were omitted because of the likelihood of confusion, although peculiarly, the more obvious for omission, C and G, were in fact used. Letters were originally assigned in order of numerical designation but later there were some exceptions. Experimentation with group markings was apparently carried out on 92nd BG B-17s to obtain the best form. B-24s of 2BD did not receive their circle group markings until the return from Africa in August 1943. On natural metal aircraft the markings were a white letter on a black symbol. Many original 3BD B-17s had their white square marking dulled to a pale grey. From the spring of 1944 40 CBW Groups carried the group marking under the left wing as well as above the right. Only one change of group letter is known; the 486BG changed from Square O to Square W on conversion to B-17s to avoid confusion with the Square D of 100 BG.

Even these conspicuous markings could not be clearly discerned beyond a mile and as the number of bomb groups doubled and trebled assembly problems increased. Large colour markings appeared to offer a substantial advantage for identification purposes and when camouflage regulations were relaxed in the spring of 1944, 2BD introduced a system utilising the whole of the outer sides of its B-24's vertical tails. Fin and rudder were painted in the Combat Wing colour—white, black, yellow, red, green—and a white or black band in one of three positions identified the group within the wing. The radio call letter (individual aircraft letter) was then painted in the centre of the band, the serial number being repainted on the inner sides of the fins. The circle symbol remained on the upper surface of the right wing. In June 1944 3BD B-24s of 93CBW followed suit with bright full colour tail markings but

285

discontinued the existing group marking on the wing. The next splash of colour appeared on 1CBW B-17s in July but all three groups wore the same red markings. Other 1BD groups did not utilize colour markings until the late summer of that year. The remaining 3BD groups acquired colour markings in the winter of 1944-45 and produced some highly elaborate schemes which required some two months to paint up all their aircraft.

First group identification markings for fighters were introduced in March 1944, and took the form of coloured spinners and bands round the front of engine cowlings. 66 FW groups all had checkerboard designs.

Personal decorations

A warplane was government property but a man who fought in it was apt to consider it "my plane". His appropriation was usually affirmed in paint; plus a nickname, motif, combat record or other decorations. As a fighter pilot was usually assigned to one specific machine in his unit his name and that of the aircraft's crew chief, and servicing personal were usually painted in approximately inch high lettering on the left hand side of the fuselage near the cockpit. Colours, naturally varied, although yellow predominated on camouflaged machines. Quite often the crew information was painted on a small coloured panel. On P-51D and K types the broad canopy frame was a favourite location.

In 1942 and 1943 a bomber crew also retained the same bomber (when available) for their tour and it was common practice for individual names to be painted on the fuselage near their station. Towards the end of hostilities, with more crews than aircraft, and although it was still policy to assign one crew to a particular bomber, a combat tour would take in perhaps a dozen different aircraft. In consequence crew names tended to disappear from B-17s and B-24s.

The majority of aircraft had nicknames, usually wildly individualistic, but in a few cases there was some sort of order: 511 BS had nicknames with a "ball" suffix after its CO; the 834 BS B-24s were named after signs of the zodiac, 368 FS P-47s were characters from the Little Abner strip. Nicknames were a mixed reflection of the contemporary scene, the meaning of many obscure to future generations. Some were disguised obscenities while others were more of a comment than a name. Some were highly original, others like Paper Doll, Patches, Pistol Packin' Mama, appeared in several units. With the name there was often a linking illustration. The female form featured as first favourite and there was some competition as to who could get away with the most daring portrayal. More discerning commanders would periodically attempt a clean-up campaign but any initial success was soon lost. The standard of art-work was often extremely high; a man might spend many hours doing an intricate painting that a few days later might be destroyed in a matter of seconds.

When camouflage was discarded pilots or mechanics embellished aircraft with coloured propeller bosses, wing tips, trim tabs, canopy frames and so on. Authority usually tolerated these decorations provided they did not interfere with identity markings. Before this date such paintwork was scarce. One spot that authority did ignore from the earliest days was wheel discs, and these were often highly decorated.

The combat achievements of an aircraft were often recorded on its fuselage. Bombers had a vertical bomb symbol to represent each mission undertaken. These were usually yellow on camouflage and black on bare metal. Special missions such as D-Day had a large or differently coloured bomb symbol; participation in the Ploesti low-level mission was sometimes indicated by a bomb silhouette in horizontal position. A duck silhouette indicated a decoy diversion mission and a parachute with box attached was a supply mission. Each group had its variations and special symbols; stars above bomb symbols where an aircraft had flown group or squadron lead; a shamrock for a trip to Northern Ireland for modification; a Purple Heart to record the number of missions on which damage had been experienced, and so on. The destruction of enemy fighters was recorded by swastikas, crosses or Nazi flags. These were painted in a row adjacent to the mission symbol, but additionally the "score" of a particular gunner was also painted near his station on many early B-17s and B-24s.

With fighters the pilots score of enemy aircraft destroyed was recorded with flags, cross or swastika symbols, most with no differentiation between air and ground kills. During the later part of 1943 and the first half of 1944, many fighter aircraft carried mission records too. A top hat and stick, or bomb symbol indicated bomber escort, a broom was for a sweep and an umbrella meant top cover. Strafing claims were also recorded with locomotive symbols, sinking ships, and motor vehicles. This mania for symbols lapsed and by the end of 1944

only aircraft victory symbols were displayed on most P-47s and P-51s. The victory symbols were the record of the pilot, not necessarily all achieved in the aircraft displaying them.

Operational Bomb Groups

34th BG

B-24H & J olive and grey factory finish; natural metal. Sqdn codes issued but not displayed. Group markings: S in square. From end June 1944 new colour marking introduced: leading third outer sides tail painted red, remainder white or bare metal. A/c letter in black on rudder. Square S no longer applied to wing of replacement a/c. All red outer sides vertical tail on PFF a/c held at Mendlesham for 93rd CBW. *B-17G*: natural metal. Sqdn codes painted under left wing post VE-day: 4BS-Q6; 7BS-R2; 18BS-8I; 391BS-3L. Coloured nose band: 4BS-white; 7BS-yellow; 18BS-red; 391BS-green. Some a/c had squadron colour bands on fuselage aft of tailplane. Group markings: approximately front half vertical fin red, remainder metal finish. Red band round each horizontal stabiliser, and wing outboard of engines. A/c call-letter in black on rudder. Tail serial in black on red and metal.

44th BG

B-24D, H & J in olive and grey factory finish. Original B-24Ds had medium green blotching on olive drab on wings and tailplane. *B-24H & J* in natural metal from Aptil 1944. *B-24L & M* in natural metal early 1945. RAF type fin flash on many a/c in North Africa July/Aug. 1943. No squadron codes displayed until mid-March 1944: 66BS-WQ, 67BS-NB, 68BS-GJ, 506BS-QK. Group markings: A in circle from end August 1943. From late April 1944 outer sides vertical tail white or bare metal with black vertical band, and a/c letter on band in white. Bar sign above or below individual a/c letter in summer 1943 to differentiate between a/c with same letter. Different signs for each squadron in autumn 1943. 66BS—no sign with letter; 67BS—bar below letter; 68BS—bar above letter; 506BS—plus sign after letters. A/c letter and sign on nose under turret some a/c from late 1943. Group Assembly Ship from early 1944, B-24D *Lemon Drop* alternating yellow and black stripes (see Plate). Most original B-24Ds carried Group "Flying Eightball" insignia on left of nose.

91st BG

B-17F & G in olve and grey factory finish. Medium green blotching on original combat B-17F and early replacements. *B-17G* in natural metal from March 1944. Yellow surround to national insignia on a very few early B-17F. Squadron codes: 322BS—LG; 323BS—OR; 324BS—DF; 401BS—LL: from Dec. 1942 in yellow; forward of national insignia, a/c letter aft. From late July 1943 squadron codes and a/c letter grouped aft national insignia on both sides fuselage. Group markings: A in triangle, from end June 1943. From mid-July 1944, 80 inches wide vertical red band on fin, red tailplane (less elevators) and red wing tips. Tail serial and call letter in black on red, for metal finish a/c; yellow on red for camouflaged a/c. Original B-17F had yellow a/c letter on fin, removed on introduction of fuselage codes: reintroduced August 1943. I not normally used as a/c letter.

92nd BG

B-17E in medium green and brown shadow shading, with pale blue-grey undersides. *B-17F, YB-40, B-17G* in olive and grey factory finish. B-17G in natural metal from March 1944. Squadron codes: 325BS—NV, 326BS—JW, 327BS—UX, 407BS—PY: from January 1943; in grey on camouflage: forward of national insignia on both sides fuselage; a/c letter aft. Group markings: B in triangle. Experimental group markings in June 1943 employed yellow letter on white triangle with dark outline, and white letter on black triangle with white outline. From spring of 1944 Triangle B marking also carried on underside of left wing. From August 1944 48 inches horizontal red band on vertical tail. I not normally used as a/c letter.

93rd BG

B-24D, H & J in olive and grey factory finish. Original B-24D with medium green blotching and many with star of national insignia dulled with light grey. RAF type fin flash (red/white/blue) on fins of B-24D detached North Africa December 1942 and summer 1943. Natural metal B-24H & J from April 1944 and B-24 L & M early 1945. Squadron codes: 328BS—GO, 329BS—RE, 330BS—AG, 409BS—YM; from mid March 1944. Later some codes white on camouflage. A/c letter in yellow on B-24 tail fins from February 1943, some positioned above and some below tail serial. Bar above or below letter distinguished a/c with same call letter in Group. Bar discontinued after coloured tail marking introduced. No plus symbols. Complete alphabet as a/c letters. Group markings: B in circle, from late August 1943. From late April 1944 outer sides vertical stabilisers painted deep yellow with black vertical band, and a/c letter on band in yellow. From late summer 1944 329BS had noses of PFF a/c painted red. In winter 1944/45 several 330BS noses painted with dragon mouth design, and several 409BS a/c with yellow engine cowlings. Some more individualistic variations of these markings existed. First Assembly Ship *Ball of Fire* with alternating yellow, black, white bands (see colour Plate); replacement appeared July 1944, a camouflaged B-24D. Broad yellow band around fuselage aft of wing, yellow nose forward of cockpit. Upper and lower surfaces wings painted yellow from tips inward for 15 feet and with 10 feet thick yellow diagonal band from forward part wing root to trailing edge. Engine cowls and elevators yellow. Normal 93rd tail markings, a/c letter O.

94th BG

B-17F and G in olive and grey factory finish. Natural metal B-17G from March 1944. Squadron codes: 331BS—QE, 332BS—XM, 333BS—TS, 410BS—GL: in grey on camouflage, forward of national insignia both side of fuselage; a/c letter aft. Odd examples of squadron codes on rear fuselage right side. No fuselage squadron codes applied to replacement a/c from late 1944 and existing codes gradually removed. A/c letter retained on rear fuselage. No a/c letter on fin until July 1943. I not normally used as a/c letter. Group markings: A in square, from July 1943. Red wing cheveron (upper right, lower left) from late 1944. All yellow tail, yellow wing tips, and red rear fuselage band from late January 1945; existing tail and wing markings remained. Squadron colours on engine cowlings from late 1944: 331BS—Dark blue, 332BS—red, 333BS—bright green, 410BS—yellow.

95th BG

B-17F & G in olive and grey factory finish. Natural metal B-17G from March 1944. Squadron codes: 334BS—BG, 335BS—OE, 336BS—ET, 412BS—QW; forward of national insignia; a/c letter aft. 412BS in sky blue on camouflage, other squadrons grey. No a/c letter on tail until July 1943. I not normally used as a/c letter. Squadron codes discontinued on new a/c from early spring 1945. Group markings: B in square, from July 1943. From January 1945 red diagonal wing band (upper right; lower left) and broad red band along trailing edge vertical tail. Coloured nose bands from July 1944: 334BS—yellow, 335BS—dark blue, 336BS—bright green, 412BS—red. Some a/c with similar band round tail gun position later in year.

96th BG

B-17F & G in olive and grey factory finish. Metal finish B-17G from March 1944. Squadron codes: 337BS—AW, 338BS—BX, 339BS—QJ, 413BS—MZ; in grey on early camouflaged a/c; increasing use of white in spring 1944. Positioned forward of national insignia with a/c letter aft. From spring of 1944, no uniformity. Common for squadron codes and a/c letter to be grouped together aft of the national insignia, but occasionally forward. Group markings: C in square, from July 1943. From late January 1945 two parallel red bands cordwise on wings (upper right, lower left) and longitudinally across vertical tail. Existing markings remained. From March to November 1944 PFF a/c operated by 413BS did not normally carry Square C marking. No squadron colours.

97th BG

B-17E in medium green and brown shadow shading; pale blue-grey undersides. *B-17F* olive and grey factory finish. Some a/c with yellow surround to national insignia. No squadron codes or a/c letters applied. No group markings. A few 414BS B-17E carried skull and bombs motif (based on squadron insignia) in white on rear entry door. Last two digets of serial, approximately 6 inches high, painted adjacent perspex nose piece in yellow' Individual a/c nicknames mostly yellow.

100th BG

B-17F & G in olive and grey factory finish. Natural metal B-17G from March 1944. Squadron codes: 349BS—XR, 350BS—LN, 351BS—EP, 418BS—LD; in grey on camouflage; forward of national insignia, a/c letter aft. I not normally used as a/c letter. Group markings: D in square from July 1943. Black diagonal wing band (upper right, lower left)

and black rudder from late January 1945. Squadron nose bands from mid July 1944: 349BS—dark blue, 350BS—yellow, 351BS—bright green, 418BS—red.

301st BG

B-17F: Olive and grey factory finish with medium green blotching on some a/c. Yellow surround to national insignia pn a number of a/c. No squadron code, a/c letter or Group markings. Originally a/c mostly B-17F-1-BO & 5-BO.

303rd BG

B-17F & G in olive and grey factory finish. Original B-17F with medium green blotching on wings, tail and fuselage. B-17G with natural metal finish from March 1944. Squadron codes: 358BS—VK, 359BS—BN, 360BS—PU, 427BS—GN; from December 1942 in grey on camouflage; forward of national insignia, a/c letter aft. Squadron codes not applied to many new a/c during 1945. A/c letter below tail serial in yellow from November 1942. Group markings: C in triangle, from July 1943. From August 1944, red band framing Triangle C insignia on both tail and wing. This made whole device a 12 foot equilateral triangle and as a rule entailed repositioning of all existing tail markings. Centre triangle white with black C; serial in yellow on base of red triangle; a/c letter below either black or yellow. Squadron-in-group number at apex of red triangle in yellow: 358BS—1, 359BS—2, 360BS—3, 427BS—4. *Wabash Cannonball*, 42-29947, U (ex-91BG), still with red markings, used as Assembly Ship from July 1944. Later *Vicious Virgin* 42-5341, painted red, white and blue bands on fuselage and wings, for use as weather and tow-target a/c.

305th BG

B-17F & G in olive and grey factory finish. Original B-17F with medium green blotching on wings and tail. Natural metal B-17G from March 1944. Some a/c with yellow surround to national insignia. Many 422 BS a/c with black undersides from autumn 1943. Squadron codes: 364BS—WF, 365BS—XK, 366BS—KY, 422BS—JJ; in grey on camouflaged a/c but later also white; forward national insignia, a/c letter aft. Group markings: G in triangle; also under left wing from spring 1944. From august 1944, bright green 48 inches wide horizontal band across vertical tail; existing marking remained. Many 422BS a/c on leaflet dropping duties had G removed from triangle. 422BS a/c did not carry Triangle G again until squadron reformed in June 1944. C & I not normally used for a/c letter.

306th BG

B-17F & G in olive and grey factory finish. Original B-17F with medium green blotching on wings and tail. Some a/c with yellow surround to national insignia. B-17G in natural metal from March 1944. Squadron codes: 367BS—GY, 368BS—BO, 369BS—WW, 423BS—RD; from December 1942 in grey on camouflage forward of national insignia, a/c letter aft. Letters C, E and I not normally used as a/c letters in early days. From July 1943 a/c had squadron codes on rear fuselage pale grey on white. A/c letters usually omitted from fuselage. Very large a/c letter on fin; a few in pale grey. From late February 1944 squadron codes abandoned and by April 1944 all or most erased. Group markings: H in triangle, from July 1943. Also under left wing from spring of 1944. From August 1944 yellow horizontal band across vertical tail, outlined black on metal finish a/c; existing markings remained. No known squadron markings March-late August 1944 when coloured tip to fin and rudder introduced: 367BS—red, 368BS—white, 369BS—bright green, 423BS—medium blue.

351st BG

B-17F & G in olive and grey factory finish. B-17G in natural metal from March 1944. Squadron codes: 508BS—YB, 509BS—RQ, 510BS—TU, 511BS—DS; in grey on camouflage a/c; forward of national insignia, a/c letter aft. A few early a/c had squadron code split on right side fuselage with first letter aft national insignia and second grouped with a/c letter forward. Many replacement a/c had one letter of squadron code painted into national insignia throughout war. Group markings: J in triangle. In August 1944 red diagonal band across vertical tail, 48 inches wide: existing markings remained. Prior to introduction of Triangle J marking some a/c had yellow a/c letter on fin above serial number. Narrow red bar underlining tail serial on lead a/c, both camouflage and natural metal. From spring 1944 one or two small black triangles at top of rudder served similar purpose. Tow-target and assembly aircraft used late 1944 painted gloss black overall with large Triangle J on tail.

379th BG

B-17F & G in olive and grey factory finish. Natural metal B-17G from March 1944. Squadron codes: 524BS—WA, 525BS—FR, 526BS—

LF, 527BS—FO; in grey on camouflage; forward of national insignia a/c letter aft. A/c letter in yellow also on fin above tail serial prior to introduction of Triangle K marking. From November 1943 squadron codes painted on rear fuselage aft of national insignia in white, a/c letter forward. Two examples in 527BS had medium blue codes in spring 1944. From early September 1944 squadron codes discontinued and those existing eventually erased, although examples could still be seen in early 1945. Group markings: K in triangle, from July 1943. From August 1944, Triangle K on wing and tail framed with yellow band making 12 feet equilateral triangle. In most cases all tail markings repositioned. Camouflaged a/c then had Triangle K insignia white on black as metal finish a/c. Serial in black on base of yellow triangle. Squadron-in-Group number at apex of yellow triangle: 524BS—1, 525BS—2, 526BS—3, 527BS—4, in black. From summer 1944 B-17E *Birmingham Blitkrieg*, 41-9100, used for target towing and painted with broad white stripes.

381st BG

B-17F & G in olive and grey factory finish. Natural metal B-17G from March 1944. Squadron codes: 532BS—VE, 533BS—VP, 534BS—GD, 535BS—MS; in grey on rear fuselage, aft national insignia. Most did not have a/c letter on fuselage, those that did were chiefly in 533BS. Codes in white on camouflage from autumn 1943. Yellow a/c letter on fin above serial prior to group markings. Group markings: L in triangle, from July 1943. From July 1944, red wing tips, red tail-plane less elevators, and 80 inch vertical red band on fin. Triangle L on camouflaged a/c then white on black as with metal finish a/c. A/c letter and serial white on red fin band. In a few cases yellow on red. In summer 1944 target towing B-17 had white, red, white, red, white bands round rear fuselage. Later acquired by 398 BG.

384th BG

B-17F & G in olive and grey factory finish. Natural metal finish B-17G from March 1944. Squadron codes: 544BS—SU, 545BS—JD, 546BS—BK, 547BS—SO; in grey on camouflage. No uniform position: throughout hostilities squadron code split either side of national insignia on many a/c. On left side fuselage first letter of code forward of national insignia, last letter grouped with a/c letter aft. On right side squadron codes aft and a/c letter forward of national insignia was commonest form, but squadron codes also split on right side on some a/c. Grouping of squadron codes with a/c letter forward or aft of national insignia also common from summer 1944. Letter I not normally used as a/c letter. Group markings: P in triangle. From August 1944 black band framing to Triangle P on tail and wings. All tail markings repositioned with black P on white triangle inside black framing triangle, whole device making 12 foot equilateral triangle. Serial in yellow on base of black triangle: squadron-in-group number at apex: 544BS—1, 545BS—2, 546BS—3, 547BS—4. From April 1945 coloured engine cowlings: 544BS—dark blue, 545BS—yellow, 546BS—red, 547BS—white. Fuselage flashes in squadron colours on many a/c after VE-day, also black plane-in group nose numbers. 1 to 72.

385th BG

B-17F & *G* in olive and grey factory finish. Natural metal B-17G from March 1944. Squadron codes issued but not displayed during hostilities. A few PFF a/c inherited from 333BS retained TS codes. Grey a/c letter also on rear fuselage on many original a/c. Group markings: G in square from July 1943. On most original a/c the square was dulled with pale grey. From late 1944 yellow chevron on wing (upper right, lower left). From late February 1945 red cordwise bands around wings and tailplane as other 93CBW groups; red checkerboard design on vertical tail (over camouflage or metal finish). Square G erased: a/c letter high on fin in white on red. Old markings still to be seen up to late March 1945. Squadron colours on prop bosses: 548BS—Blue, 549BS—yellow, 550BS—red, 551BS—bright green. Not general until spring of 1944 although apparently in use in 1943. Under wing squadron codes post VE-day: 548BS—GX, 549BS—XA, 550BS—SG, 551BS—HR.

388th BG

B-17F & G in olive and grey factory finish. B-17G in natural metal from March 1944. No squadron codes used or issued during hostilities. A few early a/c had grey a/c letter on rear fuselage. C and I not normally used as a/c letters. Group markings: H in square. Bar of H generally rather high so that marking appeared to be M at a distance. Square on many early a/c dulled with pale grey. From late January 1945 two parallel black bands cordwise on wings (upper right, lower left) and horizontally on vertical tail. A/c letter obscured and repainted on lower black band in white. 388th was only bomber group in the Eighth AF

that had no form of squadron identification on its aircraft during hostilities. Post VE-day the three letter wireless transmitter codes were painted under the left wing with the a/c letter as a prefix, e.g. A of 561BS was ALHN. Project Aphrodite B-17s administered by the 388th BG at Fersfield during the summer and autumn of 1944 had upper surfaces of wings and tailplane painted white. Extent varied on each a/c. Square H on tails of some a/c.

389th BG

B-24D, H & J in olive and grey factory finish. B-24 H & J in natural metal from April 1944. *B-24 L & M* from early 1945. Squadron codes: 564BS—YO, 565BS—EE, 566BS—RR, 567BS—HP; in pale grey on camouflage: from mid March 1944. Yellow a/c letter on fin from June 1943. From late summer 1944 a/c letter also on fuselage directly aft squadron code, in yellow on both camouflaged and metal finish a/c. Fuselage a/c letter smaller than code letters. Group markings: C in circle, from late August 1943. From late April 1944, outer side vertical tail painted black with white vertical band. A/c letter on band in black. Bar and plus signs used from autumn 1943: 564BS no sign, 565BS bar before a/c letter, 566BS plus after letter, 567BS bar after letter. With all colour tail markings, 565BS—bar above, 566BS—plus below, 567BS bar below. These signs similarly placed with fuselage a/c letter. B24D Assembly Ship natural metal with green and yellow bands (as plate): replacement aircraft camouflaged with small yellow diamond joined to form diagonal bands round fuselage and across wings.

390th BG

B-17F & G in olive and grey factory finish. B-17G in nat ural metal from March 1944. Squadron codes: 568BS—BI, 569BS—CC, 570BS—DI, 571BS—FC; from October 1943 in grey on camouflaged a/c; forward of national insignia, a/c letter aft. Group markings: J in square. From January 1945 a yellow diagonal band across wing (upper right, lower left) and yellow band along trailing edge of vertical tail: existing markings remained. Colour nose bands from July 1944: 568BS—red, 569BS—dark blue, 570BS—yellow, 571BS—bright green.

392nd BG

B-24H & J in olive and grey factory finish. B-24H, J in natural metal from April 1944; *L and M* from early 1945. Squadron codes: 576BS—CI, 577BS—DC, 578BS—EC, 579BS—GC, from mid March 1944 in pale grey on camouflage. Group markings: D in circle, from September 1943. From late April 1944 outer side vertical tail white with black horizontal band on camouflage a/c; black band only on natural metal a/c. A/c letter in white on black band. Bar and plus signs from end 1943: 576BS—no sign, 577BS—plus after a/c letter, 578BS—bar under a/c letter; 579BS—bar above a/c letter. Last three digits of serial on both sides of nose from late spring 1944, yellow on camouflage, black on metal. A/c letter and sign on front nose below turret from winter 1943/44. B-24D Assembly Ship light grey overall with black and white outline painting of B-24 nose section on each side of nose and outline painting of B-24 tail turret area on both sides rear fuselage forward of tail unit.

398th BG

B-17G in natural metal finish. A few camouflaged a/c assigned from other units. Squadron codes: 600BS—N8, 601BS—30, 602BS—K8, 603BS—N7; no uniform positioning. Most squadron codes grouped aft with a/c letter (separated by hyphen) on left side fuselage while on right squadron codes aft and a/c letter forward of national insignia. In some cases all three characters forward of national insignia. Outsize O in most 30 combinations. I not normally used as a/c letter. Group markings: W in triangle. From second week July 1944 red wing tips, red horizontal stabiliser less elevators, and 80 inch vertical red band on fin. Serial and a/c call letter in yellow on red band. A few a/c had black serial and a/c letter; 30-F, 42-102667 and 30M, 42-102565 had black letter W in white triangle with black outline.

401st BG

B-17G in olive and grey factory finish. B-17G in natural metal from March 1944. Squadron codes: 612BS—SC, 613BS—IN, 614BS—IW, 615BS—IY; in yellow, on camouflage. Positioning varied, most 612BS and 614BS had squadron codes grouped aft with a/c letter on left side, a/c letter aft and squadron codes forward of national insignia on right side. 613BS and 615BS had squadron codes forward of national insignia, a/c letter aft, on both sides. There were exceptions. Distinctive Roman I form used by 615BS. Group markings: S in triangle. From August 1944 yellow diagonal band painted on vertical tail, outlined black on metal finish a/c. On camouflaged a/c serial and a/c call letter usually repainted in black on yellow band.

445th BG

B-24H & J in olive and grey factory finish. B-24H & J in natural metal from April 1944, and *B-24L & M* from early 1945. Squadron codes: 700BS—RN, 701BS—MK, 702BS—WV, 703BS—IS; in pale grey on camouflage from March 1944. A/c letter and bar and plus signs on fin in yellow from December 1943. A/c letter and signs also on rear fuselage from March 1944. Grouped with but aft codes on left, grouped with but forward of squadron codes on right: yellow on camouflage, black on metal finish. Group markings: F in circle. From late April 1944 outer side vertical tail black with vertical white band, a/c letter and sign on white band in black. Plus and bar signs: 700BS—none, 701BS—bar above a/c letter, 702BS—bar below a/c letter, 703BS—plus after a/c letter. Some muddled painting of signs and squadron codes in this group. Assembly Ship, B-24D 41-24215 in orange and black bands (see plate). Replacement a/c a metal finish B-24H with large red and black checkers on nose section and horizontal tail, red engine nacelles with black band round cowls, Circle F insignia on rear fuselage.

446th BG

B-24H & J in olive and grey factory finish. B-24H & J in natural metal from April 1944; *B-24L & M* from early 1945. Squadron codes: 704BS—FL, 705BS—HN, 706BS—RT, 707BS—JU; in grey on camouflage from mid-March 1944. Group markings: H in circle. From late April 1944 outer side vertical tail yellow with black horizontal band: a/c letter in yellow on black band; but no plus or bar signs. Previous to this bar signs only, above and below a/c letter, but did not identify squadron (as with 93rd BG). Coloured cowling bands from June 1944: 704BS—red, 705BS—yellow, 706BS—white, 707BS—dark blue. From late summer 1944, 704BS PFF a/c carried large black outline circle superimposed on existing tail markings. First B-24D Assembly Ship *Fearless Freddie* from January 1944, yellow overall (see plate), replacement had similar scheme and same nickname (in blue).

447th BG

B-17G in olive and grey factory finish. Natural metal from March 1944. Squadron codes issued but not displayed during hostilities. A few PFF a/c inherited from 333 BS still retained that unit's codes. Squadron codes underwing from second week May 1945 as follows. 708BS—CQ, 709BS—IE, 710BS—IJ, 711BS—IR. Group markings: K in square. From late 1944 insignia blue cheveron on wing (upper right, lower left). From end January 1945 wing tips and all tail surfaces painted yellow; two parallel medium green bands round rear fuselage. Existing markings remained. Blue wing cheveron no longer applied but existing examples not erased. Coloured engine cowlings from September 1944: 708BS—yellow, 709BS—white, 710BS—red, 711BS—yellow. I not normally used as a/c letter. X, Y, and Z were PFF a/c in all squadrons during 1945.

448th BG

B-24H & J in olive and grey factory finish. B-24H and J in natural metal from April 1944, *B-24L & M* from early 1945. Squadron codes: 712BS—CT, 713BS—IG, 714BS—EI, 715BS—IO; from mid March 1944 in grey on camouflage. Squadron codes abandoned late summer of 1944 and those existing on a/c eventually erased, although examples still to be seen on a few a/c as late as December 1944. Group markings: I in circle. From late April 1944 outer sides vertical tail yellow with diagonal black band: a/c letter on band in yellow within squadron symbol. From December 1943 squadron symbols: 712BS—triangle, 713BS—circle, 714BS—square, 715BS—diamond in yellow outline round a/c letter on fin. Later black on metal, and yellow on black tail band. From late April 1944 a/c letter and squadron symbol also on inner sides of vertical stabilisers; later large size letter only; yellow or black as appropriate. No serial number on inner side fins. Assembly Ship from January 1944 in yellow and black checkerboard (see plate). Replacement a/c maroon and white diagonal bands, fuselage and wings.

452 BG

B-17G in olive and grey factory finish. Natural metal from March 1944. Squadron codes issued but not displayed during hostilities: 728BS—9Z, 729BS—M3, 730BS—6K, 731—7D underwing post VE-day. A few PFF a/c inherited from 413BS retained MZ codes on fuselage. From summer 1944 bar and plus symbol adjacent a/c letter: 728BS—no sign, 729BS—bar before letter, 730BS—plus after letter, 731BS—bar after letter. Group markings: L in square. From end January 1945 two parallel horizontal yellow bands on vertical tail and cordwise on wings. A/c letter on lower yellow tail band in black. Existing markings remained.

453rd BG

B-24H & J in olive and grey factory finish; natural metal from April

1944. *B-24L & M* from early 1945. Squadron codes: 732BS—E3, 733BS—F8, 734BS—E8, 735BS—H6; in grey on camouflage, from mid March 1944. Group markings: J in circle. From late April 1944 outer sides vertical tail painted black with diagonal white band; a/c letter on band in black. Plus and bar signs: 732BS—no sign, 733BS—plus above letter, 734BS—bar after letter, 735BS—bar below letter. Assembly Ship *Wham Bam* (ex-93rd BG) yellow checkerboard over camouflage (see plate).

457th BG

B-17G in olive and grey factory finish; natural metal from March 1944. No squadron codes issued or displayed. Group markings: U in triangle. From August 1944 48 inches wide dark blue diagonal band on vertical tail. Bare metal division left between blue band and a/c letter, serial, and Triangle U. Some early metal finish a/c had rudder and part of fin sprayed olive drab and markings in appropriate colours on this. Coloured prop bosses as means of squadron marking from spring 1944: 748BS—red, 749BS—blue, 750BS—white, 751BS—yellow. Wireless transmitter codes under wing post VE-day: 748BS—RUW, 749BS—JOB, 750BS—PPL, 751BS—MJA. A/c letter as a suffix. I and C not normally used as a/c letters. Last three digits of serial with a/c letter as prefix on nose from summer 1944.

458th BG

B-24H & J in olive and grey factory finish. Natural metal from April 1944. *B-24L & M* from early 1945. Squadron codes: 752BS—7V, 753BS—J4, 754BS—Z5, 755BS—J3 from mid-March 1944 in grey. Group markings: K in circle. From late April 1944 outer sides vertical tail painted red with white vertical band. A/c letter in red on band. Normally no bar signs. Bar signs used previous to full colour tail markings but apparently did not identify squadrons. From early spring 1945 many a/c with last three digits of serial and a/c letter as suffix, on nose; yellow or black as appropriate. First Assembly Ship, 42-40127 *First Sergeant*, normal camouflage with front half fuselage and top of wing white painted. Red and black polka dots on white portion, red and yellow polka dots on camouflage. Circle K insignia on rear fuselage. Replaced in May 1944 by similarly marked a/c (see plate) which crashed in March 1945.

466th BG

B-24H & J in olive and grey factory finish. Natural metal from April 1944. *B-24L & M* from early 1945. Squadron codes: 784BS—T9, 785BS—2U, 786BS—U8, 787BS—6L; from mid March 1944 in grey on camouflage. Group markings; L in circle. From late April 1944 outer sides vertical tail painted red with white horizontal band, a/c letter on band in red. Bar and plus signs adjacent a/c letter: 784BS—no sign. 785BS—plus after letter, 786BS—bar above letter, 787BS—bar below letter. Coloured engine cowl bands from early 1945: 784BS—red, 785BS—dark blue, 786BS—yellow, 787BS—white. First Assembly Ship B-24D 41-24109 (ex-44BG), all camouflage removed and painted red zig-zags all over (see plate). Replacement a/c similarly marked, was coded 6L-Q.

467th BG

B-24H & J in olive and grey factory finish. Natural metal from April 1944. *B-24L & M* early 1945. Squadron codes: 788BS—X7, 789BS—6A, 790BS—Q2, 791BS—4Z, in grey from mid March 1944. Group markings: P in circle. From late April 1944 outer sides vertical tail painted red and white diagonal band; a/c letter on band in red. Bar and plus signs adjacent to a/c letter in appropriate colour: 788BS—no sign, 789BS—bar above letter, 790BS—bar below letter, 791BS—plus after letter. Last three digits of serial on nose most a/c from October 1944 (yellow or black as appropriate). B-24D Assembly Ship *Pete the POM Inspector,* black with yellow discs outlined red (see plate). Replacement a/c a B-24E with very similar markings and same nickname.

482nd BG

B-17F & G, B-24H & J in olive and grey factory finish. *B-17G* and *B-24H, G, J* in natural metal from April 1944. *B-24L* from December 44. Mosquito in RAF night bomber camouflage. Squadron codes: 812BS—MI, 813BS—PC, 814BS—SI; in grey on camouflage from late 1943. Erratic application of codes. Many a/c did not display any during spring and summer 1944, but only a/c letter only on fin. Codes positioned forward of national insignia, a/c letter aft, both sides on B-17. Squadron codes on rear fuselage of B-24. Group markings: none, but at least two a/c carried black triangle on fin as normal 1st Division marking but with no group letter. Some early aircraft retained group insignia of other groups. Early B-24H H2X machine operated with Circle A markings.

486th BG

B-24H & J in olive and grey factory finish, and natural metal. Squadron codes: 832BS—3R, 833BS—4N, 834BS—2S, 835BS—H8; in grey on camouflage. A/c letter also on fuselage forward of national insignia, both sides. Group markings: O in square. *B-17G* in natural metal. Squadron codes as B-24. No uniform positioning but squadron codes commonly aft of national insignia and a/c letter forward. Group markings: W in square. In late 1944 red and blue bands forming chevron on wing with blue band towards tip. From late January 1945 wing tips and complete tail section painted yellow; three parallel bands of yellow round rear fuselage. Existing tail markings remained but at same date squadron codes abandoned and erased. In place nose bands and a/c letter on fuselage (forward national insignia) in squadron colour; 832BS—yellow, 833BS—medium blue, 834BS—red, 835BS—bright green. Yellow letters often edged black.

487th BG

B-24H & J in olive and grey factory finish, and natural metal. Squadron codes: 836BS—2G, 837BS—4F, 838BS—2C, 839BS—R5; in grey on camouflage. A/c letter also on fuselage forward of national insignia. Group markings: P in square. *B-17G* in natural metal. Codes as B-24. No uniform position. Group markings: as B-24. From late 1944 red and yellow band forming chevron on wing, red band towards tip. From late January 1945 wing tips, and complete tail painted yellow. A/c letter on fin obscured and not repainted. Other markings remained. During final two months of war many 839BS a/c had red engine cowlings and a few red chin turrets while many 837BS a/c had yellow cowls. Other squadrons not known to have used any colour markings. Some B-17s had a/c letter repeated on chin turret.

489th BG

B-24H & J in olive and grey factory finish, and natural metal. Squadron codes: 844BS—4R, 845BS—S4, 846BS—8R, 847BS—T4; in grey on rear fuselage. Group markings: W in circle on wing only. Outer side vertical tail bright green with vertical white band and a/c letter on band in black. From August 1944 (when 489 BG assigned 20CBW) outer sides vertical tail painted all yellow with a/c letters on fin in black. Bar and plus signs adjacent a/c letter from May 1944: 844BS—none, 845BS—bar before or below a/c letter, 846BS—plus before letter, 847BS—bar above or after letter. Assembly Ship *Lil' Cookie* B-24H (ex 44BG) camouflaged with yellow polka dots (see plate).

490th BG

B-24H & J in olive and grey factory finish, and natural metal. Squadron codes issued but not displayed during hostilities. Group markings: T in square. From end June 1944 top third of vertical tail painted red remainder white on camouflaged a/c, bare metal on uncamouflaged a/c. A/c letter in black on white or bare metal portion fin. Bar and plus signs adjacent a/c letter: 848BS—bar before letter, 849BS—no sign, 851BS—plus before letter. *B-17G* in natural metal. Squadron codes under wing after VE-day: 848BS—7W, 849BS—W8, 850BS—7Q, 851BS—S3. Group markings: red top to vertical tail, red band cordwise round each wing and tailplane. Squadron signs adjacent tail letters; as B-24. 850BS, when reformed August 1944, used bar after a/c letter. Bar markings in 490th BG were small black rectangles.

491st BG

B-24H & J in olive and grey factory finish, and natural metal. *B-24L & M* from early 1945. Squadron codes: 852BS—3Q, 853BS—T8, 854BS—6X, 855BS—V2, in grey on camouflage. Group markings: Z in circle, on wing only. Outer sides vertical tail painted bright green with horizontal white band and a/c letter on band in black. From late March

1945 outer sides vertical tail white or metal finish with black diagonal bar and band and a/c letter on band in white. (Although re-assigned 14CBW in August 1944, 491BG was at first reluctant to use tail markings of defunct 492BG). Bar and plus signs adjacent a/c letter: 852BS—no sign, 853BS—bar before or below a/c letter, 854BS—bar above or after a/c letter, 855BS—plus after letter. A few 852BS a/c had red cowling collector rings in 1945, and a few 854BS a/c had yellow cowling bands at the same time. First Assembly Ship, *Little Gramper* 42-40722 (ex-389th BG—yellow with red polka dots (see plate), replaced by *Rage in Heaven*, 44-40165, 3Q-G which had alternating green and yellow band on rear fuselage. Destroyed in January 1945 and replaced by similarly marked 44-40101 *Tubarao* with shark mouth design.

492nd BG (original formation)

B-24H & J in olive and grey factory finish, and natural metal. Squadron codes: 856BS—5Z, 857BS—9H, 858BS—9A, 859BS—X4 in grey on camouflage. Group marking*: U in circle. Work had started on painting circle device on vertical tails when new full-colour markings introduced. Outer sides vertical tail white or bare metal with black diagonal band; a/c letter on band in white. Bar and plus signs adjacent a/c letters: 856BS—no sign, 857BS—bar above a/c letter, 858BS—bar below a/c letter, 859BS—plus after letter. No Assembly Ship known.

493rd BG

B-24H & J in olive and grey factory finish, and natural metal. Squadron codes issued but not displayed during hostilities. Group markings: X in square. From late June 1944 bottom third of outer sides vertical tail painted red, remained white or natural metal; a/c letter on fin in black. No squadron markings known for B-24s. *B-17G* in natural metal. Squadron codes under wing post VE-day; 860BS—N6, 861BS—G6, 862BS—8M, 863BS—Q4. Initial letter of squadron call sign used as identity marking and positioned either forward or aft national insignia: 860BS—S, 861BS—P, 862BS—C, 863BS—B. A/c letter on fin only. Group markings: bottom third vertical tail red, red band round each wing and tailplane.

Medium Bomb Groups

332nd BG

B-26B & C in olive and grey factory finish. Squadron codes: 449BS—PN; 450BS—ER; 451BS—SS; 452BS—DR; in grey. A/c letter on early aircraft positioned partly under tailplane, and white bar of new insignia extended over letter.

323rd BG

B-26B & C in olive and grey factory finish, Squadron codes: 453BS—VT; 454BS—RJ; 455BS—YU; 456BS—WT; in grey. A/c letter partly under tail on a few early machines. Fuselage national insignia moved forward on most.

386th BG

B-26B & C in olive and gret factory finish. Squadron Codes: 552BS—RG; 553BS—AN; 554BS—RU; 555BS—YA; in grey. Fuselage national insignia moved forward on original a/c.

387th BG

B-26B & C in olive and grey factory finish. Squadron codes: 556BS—FW; 557BS—KS; 558BS—KX; 559BS—TQ; in grey. Fuselage national insignia moved forward on original a/c.

490th BG made a practice of painting large aircraft letters and signs low on B-17s fins, and repainting serial number above.

Operational Fighter Groups

1st FG

P-38F. Olive and grey factory finish. Yellow surround to fuselage insignia added soon after. Squadron codes: 27FS—HV; 71FS—LM;

94FS—UN. In yellow and grouped with individual a/c letter (separated by hyphen) on glycol cooler housing. Squadron codes usually forward on left side, aft on rear.

4th FG
Spitfire V. Standard RAF day fighter camouflage and markings. Squadron codes: 334FS—XR; 335FS—AV; 336FS—MD; light grey; usually forward of national insignia on left, aft on right.
P-47C and D. Olive and grey factory finish. Serial numbers painted out on some early P-47Cs. Squadron codes: 334FS—QP; 335FS—WD; 336FS—VF. Individual letter repeated underside cowl lip on some a/c. (Early P-47C used in training carried two-digit number forward of national insignia in white.)
P-51B. Olive and grey factory finish. *P-51B, C, D & K* in natural metal finish with some field application of dark green to upper surfaces. Codes as P-47. Double individual a/c letters for a/c with duplicate call-signs, e.g. WD-AA. Group markings: red spinner and 12 inch cowling band, introduced late March 1944. Cowling band extended to approximately 24 inch in December 1944, and swept back and down in January 1945. Rudder colours from October 1944: 334FS—red; 335FS—white (red outline); 336FS—blue (shade varied from bright to dark blue). In 1945 some a/c had canopy frame in squadron colour. Codes often outlined in red at this date. OTU a/c had red, white and blue rudders, horizontal division. Also, numerals as individual a/c identification. Two-seat P-51B a/c (WD-2) painted red overall post VE-day.

14th FG
P-38F and G. Olive and grey factory finish. Yellow surround to fuselage national insignia. Squadron codes: 48FS—ES, 49FS—QU; in grey; on glycol housing with hyphen. Individual a/c letter on rear boom.

20th FG
P-38H and J. Olive and grey factory finish; natural metal finish from February 1944. Squadron codes: 55FS—KI; 77FS—LC; 79FS—MC. Codes not repainted after application of Invasion Stripes. Squadron symbols on vertical tail, from end December 1943: 55FS—triangle; 77FS—circle; 79FS—square. Tail serial obscured but many repainted. Group markings: yellow spinners and 12 inch wide yellow band round engine cowls from late March 1944. Droop Snoot decoy markings early April 1944. *P-51B, C, D & K.* Metal finish with some field application of dark green to wings, tail and fuselage decking during summer 1944. Squadron codes as P-38. Squadron symbols as P-38, on vertical tail in black (approximately 30 inches diameter). A/c letter in white on symbol. Tail serial obscured and few repainted. Group markings: front 12 inches spinner, white; rear, 15 inch, black. First 11 inch cowling directly aft spinner black band, followed by 5 inch white band. In November 1944, additional stripes, seven black and six white, added to extend marking. Sometimes white omitted and effect obtained by black on bare metal. Extended Group marking not over anti-glare panel. OTU a/c had all black spinners, and "WW" war-weary marking often painted (in white) on squadron symbol.

31st FG
Spitfire V. Standard RAF day fighter camouflage and markings. Squadron codes: 307FS—MX; 308FS—HL; 309FS—WZ; light grey; usually forward of national insignia on left, aft on right.

52nd FG
Spitfire V. Standard RAF day fighter camouflage and markings. Squadron codes: 2FS—QP; 4FS—WD; 5FS—VF; light grey; positioned as with 31st FG. a/c.

55th FG
P-38H and J. Olive and grey factory finish; natural metal finish machines from February 1944. Squadron codes: 38FS—CG; 338FS—CL; 343FS—CY. Codes obscured by Invasion Stripes and not repainted. Squadron symbols on vertical tail from end December 1943; 38FS—triangle; 338FS—circle; 343FS—square. No Group colour markings. (Yellow and white checkerboard issued but as far as known not applied to any aircraft.)
P-51B, C, D & K. Metal finish with some field application of camouflage, chiefly dark green. 343FS painted many of its a/c in distinctive pattern; dark green upper surfaces to wings and tail, dark green rear fuselage, swept forward and up to combine with anti-dazzle panel. Squadron codes as P-38. No tail symbols. Group markings: green, yellow, green bands encircling spinner (of equal widths). 12 inch green and yellow checkerboard band round cowling. Green of a darkish shade, had the effect of making Group markings appear yellow and

black from as little as 100 yards away. Rudder colours from October 1944: 338FS—green (shade as nose); 343FS—yellow. 38FS did not adopt a rudder colour until late March 1945 when red was used. Some 343FS P-51s had red rearing stallion motif on rudders or fins in late 1944. This practice never extended to all a/c. From late 1944 2 inch band in squadron colour framed rear of nose checkerboard. OTU P-51B and C had green and yellow checkerboard rudders and numeral individual a/c identification. 3rd Scout Force P-51Ds had 338FS codes, and red and white checkerboard rudders from late 1944.

56th FG
P-47C and early D: olive and grey factory finish; metal finish from *P-47D-21* with much field application of camouflage, May-December 1944. Predominately RAF style grey and green shadow shading, but also full dark green upper surfaces, and more individualistic schemes featuring green and grey mottle: light and dark grey shadow shadings; and full matt black. A special camouflage scheme distinguished each squadron with the arrival of the P-47M in January 1945. 61FS had an all matt black scheme (slight purplish hue); 62FS, dark green and light grey shadow shading; 63FS dark purple blue and sky blue shadow shading. Pattern varied on 62nd and 63rd a/c. Same camouflage schemes applied after VE-day to He111K and FW190A acquired by 61 and 62FS respectively. Undersides on field camouflaged a/c left natural metal, with only known exceptions being a P-47D-28 flown by Gladych which was sky blue, and a few a/c inherited from the 78th FG from December 1944 which were light grey or sky. Squadron codes: 61FS—HV; 62FS—LM; 63FS—UN. A few 61FS and 63FS field camouflaged P-47D had black codes, and one, red. 61FS codes outlined red on some a/c. With P-47M camouflage scheme, 61FS had red letters (usually outlined white), 62FS yellow, and 63FS bare metal. On presentation a/c used by Group, squadron codes usually omitted on port side where inscription painted. Group markings: A 24 inch red cowl band from March 1944. In February 1944 56th FG became first Eighth AF group to use nose colours as identification markings. At that date 61FS painted white portion of cowl red, 62FS yellow, while 63FS retained white cowl. With introduction of VIII FC group nose colour scheme, 61FS painted rudders red and 62FS painted rudders yellow. At same date tail bands removed—this practise continued. 63FS had no special rudder colour until September 1944 when medium blue introduced. On camouflaged P-47Ms, 61FS tail serials red, 62FS yellow and 63FS blue.

78th FG
P-47C and early D in olive and grey factory finish. Metal finish from D-21 models, but most received field applied camouflage: dark green upper surfaces and light blue-grey (Sky) undersurfaces. Some variation in shades, but complete a/c paint job in most cases. White a/c type recognition bands applied to field camouflage a/c; undersurface bands outlined black. Squadron codes: 82FS—MX; 83FS—HL; 84FS—WZ. Individual a/c letter under cowl lip on some P-47C & D in 1943. Group markings: black and white checkerboard, square set, introduced first week April 1944. Checkerboard extended back to cowling shutters, six squares per longitudinal row. Squadron rudder colours in November 1944. 82FS—red; 83FS—white; 84FS—black. White band retained on fin. *P-51D & K.* Natural metal finish. Squadron codes as P-47s. Group markings: black and white checkerboard cowling, usually eight 6 inch squares per longitudinal row, but more under nose where checkerboard extended back to wing root. A 2 inch red line framed rear of checkerboard on most a/c. Spinner half black, half white with longitudinal division that gave flickering effect when spinner revolved. Squadron rudder colours as P-47. 83FS rudders outlined red. P-51B two-seat a/c (MX-Z) painted insignia red overall post VE-day (white codes). CO's a/c post VE-day had black and white checkerboard rudder (WZ-I).

339th FG
P-51B, C, D & K. Original combat a/c metal finish. Few camouflaged a/c. Squadron codes: 503FS—D7; 504FS—5Q; 505FS—6N. Group markings: red, white red ringed spinner (equal width); 12 inch band red and white checkerboard around cowling, 6 inch squares. (Checkerboard framed at rear with thin band in squadron colour on some a/c early 1945. Coloured rudders from November 1944; 503FS—red, 504FS—green (similar 55FG shade); 505FS—yellow). OTU a/c mostly bar above letter. Some early a/c carried flight letter on fin in black.

352nd FG
P-47D olive and grey factory finish. Squadron codes: 328FS—PE; 486FS—PZ; 487FS—HO. *P-51B:* olive and grey factory finish. *P-51B, C, D & K:* natural metal finish with some field application of dark green

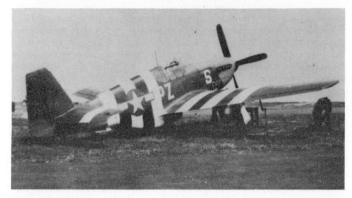

When 'invasion stripes' obscured aircraft letter on 43-6500, ground crew painted a fresh one on the nose.—(Via Morris)

to upper surfaces during summer 1944. Squadron codes as P-47. Individual a/c letter originally on rear fuselage but when obscured by Invasion Stripes in June 1944, the letter was painted on tail fin of many a/c (in white or black as appropriate). This eventually became standard practise and the rear fuselage letter was discontinued. The black fin and rudder stripe usually completely removed. Group markings: Medium blue spinner and 12 inch cowling band introduced in April 1944. Extended back covering anti-glare panel and swept up to cockpit the same month. Shade varied, some early applications much lighter. Squadron rudder colours in November 1944: 328FS—red, 486FS—yellow, 487FS—blue. Prior to this trim tabs in Flight colours on some a/c. Serials white, on blue or red rudders. OTU a/c had numerals for individual identification: a few had blue, yellow, red sectioned rudders, post VE-day.

353rd FG

Early *P-47D* olive and grey factory finish. P-47D-21 onwards in metal finish. A very few a/c received field applied camouflage in dark green, and green and grey shadow shading. Squadron codes: 350FS—LH; 351FS—YJ; 352FS—SX. Group markings: yellow and black checkerboard, diamond set, extending back to cowling shutters early April 1944. Location of checkerboard pattern varied. Group CO's a/c had square set checkerboard similar to 78th FG pattern. Tail bands removed from all surfaces following introduction of checkerboard marking. *P-51B, C, D & K:* metal finish. Only one example of field applied camouflage (green and grey shadow shading) known. Squadron codes as P-47. Late 1944 onwards many a/c had codes outlined yellow. Group markings: black, yellow, black, yellow ringed spinner; black and yellow checkerboard cowling band, square set, three 6 inch squares per longitudinal row. Owing to confusion with 55FG markings, between November 1944 and January 1945 the checkerboard was extended with eight 6 inch squares per row as standard. Checkerboard not uniform. Squadron colours from November 1944: 350FS—yellow; 352FS—black; 351FS—no colour. OTU a/c carried numeral identification.

355th FG

P-47D: olive and grey factory finish. Squadron codes: 354FS—WR; 357FS—OS; 358FS—YF. *P-51B:* olive and grey factory finish. *P-51B, C, D & K:* natural metal finish with high proportion of dark

355th FG's Lt Col Kinnard's last *Man O'War* had swept white nose marking and no rudder colour to distinguish it as CO's aircraft.—(Via Cavanagh)

green field applied camouflage. Squadron codes as P-47. Group markings: white spinner and 12 inch cowl band on both metal finish and camouflaged a/c from late March 1944. In late 1944 Group CO's a/c had white on cowling extended back to cockpit and outlined in red. Later other Group Hq. a/c had similar markings. Some a/c carried a small letter C on fin or rudder to signify use by command pilots. Squadron rudder colours from November 1944: 354FS—red; 357FS—blue; 358FS—yellow. Serials on red or blue in white. Nose bands also painted in squadron colour with only spinner remaining white. OTU a/c had individual letter within black outline square: 2nd Scout Force a/c in 354FS had black bar painted above WR codes and upper half of cowl band in bright green from late November 1944.

356th FG

Early P-47D: olive and grey factory finish. Metal finish from P-47D-21 with most receiving field applied camouflage. Usually complete dark green cover of upper surfaces. Squadron codes: 359FS—OC; 360FS—PI; 361FS—QI. Group markings: no nose band from early April 1944. White nose band painted out and black nose band removed, as appropriate. *P-51D & K:* natural metal finish. Squadron codes as P-47. Group markings: forward part spinner red with four thin blue bands, approximately 9 inch rear spinner blue. Longitudinal rows medium blue diamonds superimposed on 12 inch red nose band and red extension back to windscreen, above exhaust stacks. Squadron rudder colours from December 1944: 359FS—yellow, 360FS—red, 361FS—blue. From February 1945 spinner also painted in squadron colour. Many a/c had canopy framing in squadron colour. CO's P-51 (PI-T) yellow and blue spiral on red spinner, in 1945.

357th FG

P-51B: Olive and grey factory finish. *P-51B, C, D & K:* natural metal with high proportion of field applied camouflage during summer of 1944. A few a/c with limited application of dark green to upper surfaces. At least one example with shadow shading. Most a/c with complete dark green uppers and light blue grey (sky) or medium grey lower surfaces. A few P-51Ds had all camouflage paint removed December 1944 onwards. Squadron codes: 362FS—G4; 363FS—B6; 364FS—C5. Group markings: red, yellow, red ringed spinner (equal widths), 12 inch red and yellow checkerboard band round cowling, 6 inch squares. Squadron rudder colours from November 1944: 363FS—red; 364FS—yellow; 362FS—no colour. OTU a/c had numerals for individual identity.

358th FG

P-47D: olive and grey factory finish. Squadron codes: 365FS—CH; 366FS—IA; 367FS—CP.

359th FG

P-47D: olive and grey factory finish. Metal finish P-47D-21 onwards. Squadron codes: 368FS—CV; 369FS—IV; 370FS—CR. Group markings: bright green 24 inch cowl band from late March 1944. *P-51B:* olive and grey factory finish (few). *P-51B, C, D & K:* metal finish: some field applied dark green camouflage during summer 1944. Squadron codes: 368 & 369FS as P-47; 370FS—CS. Group markings: bright green spinner and 12 inch cowl band. Green cowling marking extended back and swept down in late 1944. Rudder colours from November 1944: 368FS—yellow; 369FS—red; 370FS—dark blue. Flight leaders stripes on fin fillet in flight colours winter 1944/1945. Yellow spiral on some 368FS spinners at VE-day.

361st FG

P-47D: olive and grey factory finish. Metal finish from P-47D-21. Squadron codes: 374FS—B7; 375FS—E2; 376FS—E9. Group markings: 24 inch yellow cowl band from late March 1944. *P-51B,* olive and grey factory finish (few). *P-51B, C, D & K,* metal finish with some field application of dark green camouflage. On a few P-51s camouflaged in June 1944, insignia blue patches applied. Squadron codes as P-47. Group markings: yellow spinner and 12 inch nose band. In July/August 1944 yellow on cowling extended back to windscreen. Squadron rudder colours November 1944: 374FS—red, 375FS—medium blue; 376FS—yellow. Prior to this flight colours on trim tabs of some a/c.

364th FG

P-38J: olive and grey factory finish, and natural metal. Squadron codes: 383FS—N2; 384FS—5Y; 385FS—5E. Codes not repainted when obscured by Invasion Stripes. Squadron symbols on vertical tail: 383FS—circle; 384FS—square; 385FS—triangle. Group markings: white spinners and 12 inch cowling bands: April 1944 Droop-snoot decoy markings. *P-51B, C, D & K* natural metal with some field applied dark green camouflage. Squadron codes as P-38, but painted aft national insignia on both sides of fuselage. No individual a/c letter carried on fuselage. Squadron symbol, as P-38, in black on vertical tail (approximately 30 inch dia.) with individual a/c letter superimposed in white. Group markings: white spinner; 12 inch cowl band divided into 6 inch medium blue and white longitudinal stripes. OTU a/c with numerals for individual identity. 1st Scout Force, 385FS a/c with red outline to tail, red spinner and 12 inch white cowl band.

479th FG

P-38J: olive and grey factory finish; natural metal with some field applied dark green camouflage. Squadron codes: 434FS—L2; 435FS—J2; 436FS—9B. Squadron symbol on vertical tail: 434FS—triangle; 435FS—circle; 436FS—square. Group markings: no colours. Some camouflaged a/c had paint removed from spinners and approx. leading 12 inch of cowl to expose bare metal. In August 1944 tail symbols removed and rudders painted: 434FS—red; 435FS—yellow; 436FS—no colour. On many camouflaged P-38s all paint on fin was removed at same date. Some P-38s inherited from 20th and 364th FGs still retained yellow and white group markings. Individual a/c letter on inner sides of tail fin much smaller than usual on many original P-38s. Droop-snoot decoy markings on many a/c.

P-51B, C, D & K: natural metal finish. Codes as P-38. Group markings: no colours on spinner or cowling. Rudder colours as P-38. 436FS used black and white checkerboard rudders during October 1944, but in November 1944 all 436FS rudders painted black. Tail serials painted over by rudder colours rarely repainted. Most a/c had complete serial and tail bar removed. Two seat P-51B (J2-Q) painted yellow overall post VE-day.

Other Fighter Organisations

495th FG

P-47C & D in factory finished olive and grey and natural metal. Normal fighter markings carried. Squadron codes: 551FS—DQ; 552FS—VM. (These codes in use when OTU squadrons formed in 6 FW in summer 1943. P-38s also coded DQ.) From May 1944, P-47s had cowling band painted in red, yellow, green, etc, but there appears to have been no group or squadron colour markings.

496th FG

P-51B & C, P-38H & J in olive and grey factory finish and natural metal. Normal fighter markings carried. Squadron codes: 554FS—B9; 555FS—C7. Former squadron handled P-38s, latter P-51s. Various spinner and nose colours but no known squadron or group colour markings. Most camouflaged P-38s had tail serial painted out.

65th FW-Hq.

P-47C, D & M, P-51B & D. Natural metal finish. White spinner with broad red spiral: narrow alternating bands red and white around first 12 inch-24 inch of cowling aft spinner. Code JA, J on left side of national insignia, A on right. No individual letter.

66 FW-Hq.

P-47D, P-51D, AT-6. Natural metal finish. Checkerboard cowling with pattern of red, white, yellow and blue squares. P-51 spinner in red, white, yellow and blue segments. No codes.

Other Operational Units

Special Operations Group. 801st BG(P)—492nd BG.

B-24D, H & J in gloss black finish overall. Also many a/c in olive and grey factory finish. *C-47* in olive and grey factory finish. *Mosquito* in RAF night bomber camouflage. *A-26* in gloss black finish overall. No squadron codes displayed during hostilities. Original 492BG squadron codes under wing after VE-day. Codes yellow on black. A/c letter on tail B-24s in yellow. No group markings.

Black finished 406th BS B-24 *Midnite Mistress*, J6:I, piloted by Lt Jack Ophan. New cowl rings on this aircraft were left unpainted.—(Via Holmes)

Special Leaflet Squadron 422BS—858BS—406BS

B-17F & G of 422 BS; olive drab upper surfaces, gloss black lower surfaces. Squadron codes: JJ, forward of national insignia in grey. Usually no letter in triangle on fin. Other markings as 305th BG. 858BS retained 422BS markings on B-17s. B-24s of 858BS and 406BS were mostly black overall. Squadron codes: 406BS-J6. A/c letter on fin in yellow. After VE-day squadron codes displayed under wing in yellow.

Radio Counter Measures Squadron—803BS (P)—36BS

B-17F & G: olive and grey factory finish. Squadron codes: R4, in grey forward of national insignia, a/c letter aft. *B-24H & J* natural metal finish. Squadron codes: R4 in black aft of national insignia. A/c letter in black on fins only.

Air/Sea/Rescue Squadron—5th ERS

P-47D in olive and grey factory finish. Only one metal finish example known. Squadron codes: 5F in white forward of national insignia, a/c letter aft. From May 1944, red, white, blue cowling bands each approx. 15 inch wide; 18 inch yellow band round vertical and each horizontal tail surface; also cordwise on wing inboard of weapon bay. Only two a/c known with wing bands, remainder a/c and replacements had instead approx. 14 inch each wing tip yellow. "WW" markings on fin of all a/c in yellow. *OA-10:* matt white overall. Serial black on fin. No a/c letter, squadron codes or other unit markings carried during hostilities. *B-17G* of 457th BG with airborne lifeboat remained in 457th BG colours.

1st Scouting Force—857BS

Original a/c in normal 385FS, 364FG markings. From late summer 1944 black tail triangle removed; a/c letter on fin in black, red outline band to all tail surfaces. Red spinner and 12 inch white cowling band. Unit given squadron status in March 1945 and 5E codes replaced by 9H, original 857BS code.

2nd Scouting Force

Original a/c in normal 354FS, 355FG markings. From November 1944 upper half cowling nose band painted bright green, lower half remained white. No rudder colours. Black bar above squadron code letters WR.

One of the Boston IIIs (AL 397) used by 15th BS on the 6 Sep. 1942 raid was operated by 1st Wing on communications duties in 1944.—(Barnes)

3rd Scouting Force—862BS
Original a/c in normal 338FS, 55FG markings. From late 1944 red and white checkerboard rudder. Unit given squadron status in Feb. 1945 but no change in markings known.

15th BS
Boston III in RAF day bomber camouflage (dark earth and dark green shadow shading, sky undersides). Aircraft used in early missions were on 266 Squadron strength and carried codes MQ in sky forward of roundel: a/c letter on nose. Serials in black. In late July 1942 the Squadron received Boston III's from RAF, the roundel being painted out and US insignia applied. These were all AL prefix serials: 372, 381, 397, 409, 429, 436, 441, 445, 455, 486, 490-499 (less 496). It was in these aircraft that the Squadron flew its final mission from the UK in September. It is not known if code letters were displayed. These Bostons remained in UK when Squadron moved to North Africa with 12th AF and were used by 8th AF units for target towing and other duties during the following years.

Reconnaissance Groups

7th PG
F-4A and F-5A, B & C: sprayed P.R. blue overall. Tail serials obscured and not repainted. From summer 1943 last three digits of serial painted on outer sides engine cowlings in yellow, approx 9 ins. figures. F-5E in natural metal from late 1944, last three of serial on cowling in black. *Spitfire XI* P.R. blue overall. Serial also on vertical tail of many aircraft in yellow. Some a/c in natural metal finish. From late 1944, serial black. Group markings: longitudinal placed red band on engine cowling from winter 1944/1945, both Spitfire and Lightning. Some a/c with red rudders and red spinners. Squadron codes underwing from post VE-day: 13PS-ES.

25th BG(R)-802nd RG(P)
Mosquito PR XVI in normal RAF P.R. blue finish: serials black. A/c letter on fin in white. 653BS a/c distinguished by white outline circle round a/c letter: 654BS a/c had no marking round a/c letter. In August 1944 vertical tail painted red, existing markings retained. In late September all tail surfaces painted red. This marking necessitated by frequency of misidentification of Mosquito as enemy type. *B-17G* 652BS in normal bomber finishes with a/c letter on tail. Squadron codes underwing post-VE-day: 652BS-YN, 653BS-WX, 654BS-XN(?).

67th RG
Spitfire Vb in normal RAF day fighter camouflage. *L-4B* in olive and grey factory finish. *Boston & Havoc* a/c from RAF in day bomber and night fighter finishes. *A-20B* in olive and grey factory finish. Squadron codes: 12RS-ZM, 107RS-AX, 109RS-VX, 153RS-ZS(?) in light grey forward of national insignia. On some Spitfires the Sky band painted out. Coloured spinners on some a/c summer 1943.

Troop Carrier Groups

60th, 62nd and 64th TCGs
C-47 & 53 in olive and grey factory finish. A/c letter on rear fuselage in yellow. No squadron codes or group markings.

315th TCG
C-47 in olive and grey factory finish. Squadron codes: 34TCS-NM, 43TCS-UA; in yellow; usually forward of national insignia: a/c letter aft.

Miscellaneous Units

1st CCGS
AT-23B, A-35B, A-20B and other a/c types serving Gunnery School at Snettisham had 12-24 ins. top of fin and rudder painted yellow from late 1944. Engine cowlings also often yellow, and on A-35 the projecting undercarriage knuckles.

3rd Gunnery and Tow-Target Flt.
P-47D normal fighter finishes and markings. *Vengeance* and *Lysander* in RAF camouflage and operated with RAF roundels throughout 1944 and into 1945. Unit codes: LJ on all a/c forward national insignia in white.

Eighth Technical Operations
Numerous types a/c in normal finishes. Unit codes: Q3 on fuselage forward of national insignia: white or black as appropriate. Not all a/c assigned to unit carried codes. Underwing markings post VE-day consisted of 8TO followed by a/c letter.

2nd AD Hq.
B-24 a/c operated by Hq. in 1945 metal finish with green rudders.

3rd AD Hq.
B-17G a/c operated by Hq. in 1945 had dark green and yellow checkerboard rudders (3 squares across by 7 high). A/c letter black on fin under serial and on some a/c on fuselage forward of national insignia.

1st CBW
Red equilateral triangle with letter A at apex, L at left, base corner, W at right (letters black): inner white triangle with figure 1 in black. This design on vertical tails UC-64, L-4B and B-17G of Wing Hq. flight.

27th ATG of VIII Air Force Service Command
Various USAAF and RAF a/c types in normal finishes. No squadron codes. From summer of 1944 tip of vertical tail, downwards, narrow black, yellow, black yellow stripes on many ASC a/c.

General notes

Abbreviations

a/c — Aircraft
a/d — Airfield
AD — Air Division
AFSC — Air Force Service Command
ASC — Air Support Command
BC — Bomber Command
BD — Bombardment Division
BG — Bombardment Group
BS — Bombardment Squadron
BW — Bombardment Wing
CC — Composite Command
E/a — Enemy Aircraft
FC — Fighter Command
FD — Fighter Division
FG — Fighter Group
FS — Fighter Squadron
FW — Fighter Wing
GASC — Ground Air Support Command
(H) — Heavy
IP — Initial Point
JG — Jagdgeschwader (Fighter Regiment)
KAS — Killed on Active Service
KIA — Killed in Action
(L) — Light
(M) — Medium
MIA — Missing in Action
MPI — Mean Point of Impact
OG — Observation Group
OS — Observation Squadron
(P) — Provisional
PCBW — Provisional Combat Bomb Wing
PG — Photographic Group
POW — Prisoner of War
PS — Photographic Squadron

RG — Reconnaissance Group
RW — Reconnaissance Wing
WIA — Wounded in Action
ZG — Zerstörergeschwader (Heavy Fighter Regiment)

Unless otherwise stated, all gallonage figures are the US measure (·832 of an Imperial gallon). Bomb and supply weights are given as US tons, i.e. short tons of 2,000 lbs each. The mission function of Group, Wing and Division designations has been omitted in the narrative text. Unlike these organisations, squadron numbers were duplicated and to avoid confusion between fighter and bomber units where this arises, all squadron designations have been given in abbreviated form. A very large number of documents and publications were researched in compiling this book. Space limitations, however, prevent the inclusion of bibliographical notes. Accuracy has been a prime consideration throughout and every effort has been made to cross check details. In many instances, particularly in the matter of statistics, there is conflicting information even in official records.

The source of each photograph in this book is given in brackets at the end of the caption. This is the surname of the person supplying the photo, or the initials of an official organisation. Full names are given in the acknowledgements following.

The full colour illustrations of Eighth Air Force aircraft unit markings, following page 282, are the result of many years research and careful preparation. To ensure maximum accuracy colours were matched with paint fragments from actual aircraft. Markings detail was in many cases obtained by measurement of Eighth Air Force aircraft and is backed by photographic evidence.

The author is considering a possible second volume and would welcome information and material on any aspect of the Eighth Air Force not covered in this volume.

Acknowledgements

This book was born of an idea a quarter of a century ago, when the sky above my home in East Anglia, vibrating to the thunder of the Eighth Air Force, led me to wonder if all would be recorded. Since then many others, sympathetic to my idea, have contributed information and material in varying amounts. Their interest, encouragement and kindness have made possible this book and while I am unable to recall and mention all, I express my sincere appreciation to every one of them.

The response by a number of good friends to my persistent requests has been nothing less than magnificent. I am particularly indebted to Kenn Rust who over the years has constantly encouraged, advised, and provided material. Allan Blue devoted many hours to locating information and material that proved invaluable. Robert Cavanagh, William Hess, Bernard Mallon and John Preston never failed to respond most generously. Others whose assistance is gratefully acknowledged are: Trevor Allen, John Archer, Steve Birdsall, Richard Bateson, Mike Bailey, Mike Bowyer, Alan Blackmore, Peter Corbell, the late Pat Cassidy, Guy and Francis Dufton, A. P. De Jong, Chris Elliott, Ed Ferko, Garry Fry, B. A. Forward, John Furbank, R. Havers, James Hoseason, Harry Holmes, William Larkins, Griff Murphey, Philip Moyes, Dave Menard, Richard Mortimer, Don McLean, Ian McLachlan, Danny Morris, Bob Mikesh, Norman Ottaway, Torbjorn Olausson, George Pennick, Wilda Pettis, Hans Ring, Eric Rhodes, Don Smith, Fred Seggons, Richard Smith, O. Sundgren, Jan v.d.Veer, Alan Wright and Gerrit Zwanenburg.

I am also indebted to the staff of the Imperial War Museum, in particular Edward Hine and Vernon Rigby, for their courtesies over many years. Royal Frey at the Air Force Museum, the officers of the USAF Book and Magazine Section, the Aeronautical Chart & Information Center, and other USAF agencies gave valuable assistance. Boeing, North American, Lockheed, Convair, Martin and Air Pictorial all readily provided material.

Much assistance came from men and women who were part of the Eighth Air Force. Many went to great lengths to obtain and provide the material I required, especially Ray Bowers, William R. Cameron, Tom Goodyear, Jack S. Jenkins, Cass S. Hough, Marion Havelaar. At least one member of every combat group in the Eighth had some part in aiding this project on its way. They are:- Clarence E. Anderson, Henry W. Brown, Donald Bochkay, Walter Beckham, Henry Bjorkman, James Beach, John Bode, Whitney Barnes, Paul Burnett, Ken Blakebrough, Howard R. Cleveland, Gordon R. Closway, Gordon T. Courtenay, E. M. Crosthwait, William C. Clark, T. R. Copeland, C. C. Crandell, Byron B. Calomiris, Don Cannavaro, William B. Duane, Abel L. Dolim, William Duffy, Robert J. Falsey, Russell F. Fisher, Ronald R. Force, Royal D. Frey, James Graham, James A. Goodson, Charles M. Guyler, Jerry Gross, Arnold Gottlieb, John K. Gile, Dorothy Harrison, John W. Hammett, Robert C. Horne, Ed. J. Huntzinger, Allan Heirzberg, John M. Jacobowitz, James N. Kidder, Ward J. Kent, Charles P. London, Isador Lerner, Theodore R. Milton, Frank S. McGlynn, Howard W. Moore, Edward Mikolowski, Dorothy McDonald, Victor C. Magnuson, Joe E. Meehan, Glenn D. Mishler, Joe L. Mason, Albert M. Martino, James J. Mahoney, Claude V. Meconis, Jack H. Omohundro, Merle Olmstead, John G. Oder, Richard Oswald, Ramsey D. Potts, Lawrence L. Prince, Edward Parker, Willard O. Pease, William Ripatte, Robert H. Shafer, Carrol Stewart, Walter T. Stewart, Joe A. Skiera, Albert J. Shower, Arthur Silva, Donald F. Sticker, Robert M. Simpson, Harold Solden, Glenn A. Tessmer, Phillip R. Taylor, John F. Thornell, Joseph L. Thury, Jesse D. Thompson, Atlitio Verna, James A. Verinis, Tom H. Welch, Al J. Winant, Donald F. Winn, Chester S. Weaks, Charles B. Westover, and Hubert Zemke.

On the 'production' side I thank Frank Cheesman for checking proofs, and my wife Jean, for a prodigious amount of typing and the difficult task of indexing. John Rabbets for his magnificient colour plates, and Richard Mortimer, Eric Rhodes and Norman Ottaway for preliminary art work in the early days. Norman Ottaway and Mike Bailey were also responsible for the maps in this volume. Over the years Bruce Robertson advised and helped with many aspects of the manuscript and gave the benefit of his experience. Finally, Alex Vanags of Messrs. Macdonalds for his patience, understanding, and endeavours to see this volume was carefully produced.

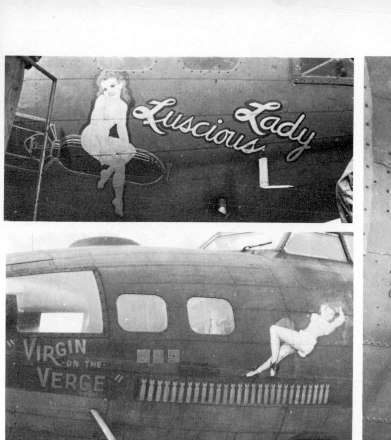

Nose art of the Eighth's Forts and Libs was famous. Favourite decoration was the female form and the paintings were often of a very high standard. This is a typical selection of the girls that kept their smiles despite the sub-zero temperatures they frequented.
The 487th BG had some exceptional artists, notably Sgt Daune Bryers whose spare time was spent embellishing many aircraft at Lavenham (*This Above All, Purty Baby, Tondelayo* and *Classy Chassy*). See Index for details.

Index

This index is divided into sections covering the names of persons, places and aircraft mentioned in this book. In the case of military personnel, airfields and aircraft, additional information is included.

Eighth Air Force Personnel

Other US Persons

Arnold, Henry H., HqAAF 16, 20, 24, 27, 41, 71, 78, 83, 98, 99, 119
Brereton, Lewis H., Hq.9AF 87
Eisenhower, Dwight, 60, 138, 149, 152
Fiske, W. M. L., 10
Hitchcock, Tommy 96, 150
Howard, James H., 354FG, 9AF 105, 119, 121
Hunter, Anothy G., 310BG 265
Kennedy, Joseph Jr., USN 173
Martin, Keith R., 354FG 9AF 96
Quesada, Elwood R., IX TAC 205
Rutherford, Alvord, 319BG 55, 265
Stimson, H. L., 170
Stratemeyer, George, Hq.AAF 36
Terrell, Frederick R., 265
Vandenberg, Hoyt S., 9AF 205
Wade, Kenneth S., 81FG 265
Winant, John G. Ambassador UK 96
Wyler, William, 52

Luftwaffe Personnel

Baer, Heinz, JG1 111
Bartels, Heinz, JG27 196
Galland, Wilhelm, JG26 82
Geisshardt, Fritz, III/JG26 29
Kornatzki, Major, Sturmstaffel 107
Maximowitz, Uff., IV/JG3 137
Mayer, Egon, III/JG2 20, 44, 122
Moritz, Wilhelm, IV/JG3 157, 160
Müller, Friedrich K., JG3 135
Nowotny, Walter, Kommando Nowotny 193, 194
Philipp, Hans, JG1 84
Schall, Lt., Kommando Nowotny 193
Schubert, Fw., 1/JG400 178
Wilcke, Wolf D., JG3 127

British Persons

Bairnsfather, Bruce, 48
Byan, Guy, 208
Churchill, Mary 138
Churchill, Winston 78
Cunningham, Andrew, R.N. 212
Douglas, Sir Sholto, RAF 14
Duke-Woolley, W/C 14, 40
Elizabeth, H.R.H. Princess 208
George VI, H.R.H. King 33
Harris, Sir Arthur, RAF 12
Linney, Anthony, RAF 40
O'Reilly, Thomas 80
Portal, Sir Charles, RAF 78
Richards, A. A. 80
Robb, Sir James, RAF 234
Rosseau, Andre 80
Terrel, Edward, R.N. 212
Trenchard, Lord 27
Wilkinson, R. C., RAF 40
Wolf-Barry, Alex. 44

Bomber Squadrons assigned or attached to Eighth Air Force

4BS 240
7BS 240
15BS 264
18BS 240
32BS 247
34BS 264
36BS 159, 172, 263, 264
37BS 264
66BS 35, 36, 89, 91, 241
67BS 35, 37, 38, 87, 89, 241
68BS 35, 91, 241
84BS 265
85BS 265
86BS 265
95BS 264
97BS 265
322BS 21, 243
323BS 21, 243
324BS 243
325BS 244
326BS 12, 46, 53, 244
327BS 46, 47, 244
328BS 18, 34, 244
329BS 33, 34, 37, 107, 244
330BS 33, 34, 244
331BS 245
332BS 245
333BS 245
334BS 245
335BS 245
336BS 245
337BS 245
338BS 245
339BS 245
340BS 246
341BS 12, 246
342BS 246
349BS 71, 246
350BS 115, 246
351BS 246
352BS 247
353BS 247
358BS 247
359BS 27, 247
360BS 247
364BS 23, 29, 247

365BS 48, 141, 247
366BS 247
367BS 18, 21, 22, 31, 66, 248
368BS 248
369BS 23, 31, 32, 66, 248
379BS 265
380BS 265
381BS 265
391BS 240
401BS 23, 30, 31, 160, 243
406BS 159, 172, 263, 264
407BS 244
409BS 33, 34, 244
410BS 245
412BS 245
413BS 130, 245
414BS 12, 17, 246
418BS 246
422BS 71, 150, 247, 264
423BS 18, 30, 248
427BS 100, 101, 247
428BS 265
432BS 264
437BS 265
438BS 265
439BS 265
440BS 265
441BS 265
442BS 265
443BS 265
444BS 265
449BS 62, 248
450BS 56, 248
451BS 57, 248
452BS 56, 248
453BS 249
454BS 249
455BS 249
456BS 249
506BS 91, 241
508BS 249
509BS 105, 249
510BS 249
511BS 48, 249
524BS 253
525BS 253

526BS 253
527BS 253
532BS 253
533BS 253
534BS 253
535BS 253
544BS 253
545BS 253
546BS 253
547BS 253
548BS 254
549BS 77, 179, 254
550BS 254
551BS 254
552BS 61, 254
553BS 59, 254
554BS 254
555BS 60, 61, 254
556BS 254
557BS 254
558BS 254
559BS 254
560BS 255
561BS 255
562BS 173, 255
563BS 70, 255
564BS 255
565BS 255
567BS 255
568BS 255
569BS 223, 255
570BS 255
571BS 255
576BS 256
577BS 256
578BS 256
579BS 256
600BS 256
601BS 256
602BS 256
603BS 256
612BS 256
613BS 256
614BS 256
615BS 256
652BS(R) 200, 240

653BS(R) 200, 240
654BS(R) 200, 240
700BS 257
701BS 257
702BS 257
703BS 257
704BS 206, 257
705BS 257
706BS 257
707BS 257
708BS 257
709BS 257
710BS 257
711BS 257
712BS 257
713BS 257
714BS 257
715BS 257
728BS 258
729BS 258
730BS 258
731BS 258
732BS 258
733BS 258
734BS 258
735BS 258
748BS 258
749BS 258
750BS 258
751BS 258
752BS 259
753BS 259
754BS 259
755BS 259
784BS 259
785BS 259
786BS 259
787BS 259
788BS 159, 172, 259, 263
789BS 259
790BS 259
791BS 259
803BS(P) 137, 172, 264
812BS 99, 260
813BS 99, 260
814BS 107, 260

832BS 260
833BS 260
834BS 143, 260
835BS 225, 260
836BS 260
837BS 260
838BS 260
839BS 260

844BS 261
845BS 261
846BS 261
847BS 261
848BS 261
849BS 261
850BS 152, 159, 261, 263

851BS 261
852BS 173, 261
853BS 261
854BS 261
855BS 261
856BS 262, 263
857BS 162, 263

858BS 156, 172, 262, 263, 264
859BS 172, 262, 263
860BS 262
861BS 262
862BS 262
863BS 262
2911BS(P) 198

Fighter Squadrons assigned or attached to Eighth Air Force

2FS 14, 241
4FS 14, 241
5FS 14, 241
27FS 7, 11, 13, 238
38FS 92, 123, 170 241
48FS 239
49FS 239
50FS 13, 15, 239
55FS 147, 167, 239
61FS 42, 43, 46, 96, 97, 124, 150, 196, 241
62FS 42, 43, 95, 97, 125, 196, 219, 241
63FS 42, 82, 83, 96, 97, 124, 169, 196, 220, 241
71FS 11, 238
77FS 120, 147, 165, 239
79FS 92, 147, 165, 239
82FS 42, 82, 188, 241

83FS 42, 43, 241
84FS 421
91FS 265
92FS 265
93FS 265
94FS 11, 14, 238
95FS 243
96FS 243
97FS 243
307FS 240
308FS 240
309FS 198, 240
328FS 150, 166, 192, 250
334FS 14, 238
335FS 14, 42, 80, 238
336FS 14, 42, 43, 122, 123, 238
338FS 241
343FS 216 241
345FS 249

346FS 249
347FS 249
350FS 250
351FS 95, 185, 250
352FS 250
354FS 251
357FS 187, 251
358FS 251
359FS 251
360FS 251
361FS 251
362FS 251
363FS 168, 216, 251
364FS 124, 216, 251
365FS 252
366FS 252
367FS 252
368FS 252
369FS 252

370FS 252
374FS 252
375FS 252
376FS 252
383FS 252
384FS 252
385FS 163, 252
434FS 187, 190, 259
435FS 187, 259
436FS 152, 259
486FS 168, 250
487FS 95, 150, 204, 205, 250
503FS 249
504FS 249
505FS 249
551FS 262
552FS 262
554FS 262
555FS 262

Photographic, Observation and Reconnaissance Squadrons assigned or attached to Eighth Air Force

5PS 198, 238
12OS/RS 243
12PS 238
13PS 46, 199, 238, 239

14PS 199, 200, 238, 239
15PS 238
16OS 265
22PS 239

27PS 199, 200, 239
107OS/RS 243
109OS/RS 243
111OS 265

122OS 265
153OS/RS 243
154OS 265

Troop Carrier Squadrons assigned to Eighth Air Force

4TCS 242
7TCS 242
8TCS 242
10TCS 242

11TCS 242
12TCS 242
16TCS 242
17TCS 242

18TCS 242
28TCS 242
34TCS 248
35TCS 242

43TCS 248
51TCS 242

Miscellaneous Squadrons

5ERS 169, 226, 227
18 Weather Sqdn. 200

86ATS 265
87ATS 266

Night Leaflet Sqdn. 153, 179, 264

Radio Counter Measures Sqdn. 264

Groups assigned or attached to Eighth Air Force

1FG 6, 7, 9, 11, 18, 92, 238
3PG 9, 15, 198, 199, 238
4FG 9, 14, 15, 40-46, 79-85, 95, 122, 123, 127, 147, 149, 154, 165-169, 186-189, 194, 220, 221, 227-231, 238
7PG 79, 155, 199, 200, 234, 239
14FG 6, 9, 13-15, 92, 239
17BG 9, 264
20FG 79, 83, 92, 94, 120-124, 147, 149, 154, 170, 171, 188, 191, 192, 216, 217, 239
25BG(R) 172, 176, 200, 224, 240
27ATG 46, 79, 198, 266
31FG 6, 7, 9, 10, 11, 13-15, 240
34BG 143, 155, 156, 229, 240

44BG 9, 19, 20, 33-38, 46, 79, 86-91, 107, 109, 111, 116, 117, 129, 136, 154, 175, 183, 230, 231, 233, 241
52FG 7, 9, 13, 14, 15, 198, 241
55FG 79, 83-85, 92-95, 121, 123, 148-152, 154, 166, 168-171, 186, 188-191, 216-219, 222, 228, 231-233, 241
56FG 41-46, 77, 79, 81-85, 95-97, 119, 120, 122-127, 147-151, 154, 165-167, 169-171, 185, 187-189, 197, 203, 216, 219-221, 227, 230, 231, 233, 242
60TCG 6, 7, 9, 13, 242
62TCG 9, 15, 242

64TCG 9, 13, 242
67RG 9, 15, 46, 79, 198, 243
68OG 9, 15, 265
78FG 41-46, 79-84, 94, 95, 121, 122, 128, 147, 151, 154, 166, 167, 186-190, 193, 203, 220-222, 226, 227, 234, 243, 283, 284, 291
81FG 9, 265
82FG 9, 15, 92, 243
91BG 9, 17, 19-23, 25-32, 46, 49-52, 67, 69, 71, 79, 104, 111, 114, 131, 154, 160, 161, 173, 177, 180, 204, 222, 223, 226, 231, 244
92BG 9, 12, 13, 17, 18, 31, 46, 47, 53, 64, 78, 79, 101-103,

109, 114, 129, 136, 142, 154, 178, 201, 202, 212, 214, 232, 244
93BG 9, 17, 18-20, 33-39, 46, 79, 86-91, 102, 107, 154, 155, 164, 175, 181, 214, 222, 231, 233, 234, 244
94BG 46-49, 51, 53, 65, 66, 68, 74, 79, 105, 121, 135, 139, 141, 154, 159, 179, 231, 232, 234, 245
95BG 46-51, 65, 68, 77, 79, 102, 113, 114, 154, 174, 176, 206, 211, 230, 245
96BG 46-50, 65, 68, 70, 75, 78, 79, 133, 139, 143, 154, 160, 188, 204, 214, 232, 234, 245

97BG 6, 7, 9, 11, 12, 13, 17-20, 25, 33, 246
100BG 68-71, 75-79, 84, 113-116, 139, 141, 142, 154, 178, 189, 204, 206, 208, 209, 214, 225, 232, 234, 246
301BG 9, 13, 17, 18, 19, 247
303BG 9, 17, 19-28, 31, 32, 46, 50, 53, 54, 64, 74, 76, 79, 101, 102, 105, 109, 114, 129, 154, 164, 177, 179, 202, 214, 222, 231, 232, 247
305BG 9, 17, 19, 21-32, 41, 46, 48, 52, 71, 78, 79, 108, 133, 154, 156, 181, 211, 222, 224, 228, 232, 233, 247
306BG 9, 17-32, 46, 49, 66, 70, 78, 79, 103, 109, 117, 129, 208, 222, 232, 234, 248
310BG 9, 15, 265
315TCG 46, 79, 248
319BG 9, 15, 55, 265
320BG 9, 15, 265
322BG 46, 55-62, 79, 248
323RG 46, 57-59, 62, 79, 249
333BG 233
339FG 149, 152, 167, 187, 189, 195, 226, 227, 228, 230, 231, 249
346BG 233
350FG 9, 15, 249
351BG 46-48, 53, 67, 74, 76, 79, 100, 105, 108, 110, 114, 154, 202, 232, 249
352FG 79, 83, 95, 120, 149, 150,

151, 155, 165, 166, 168-171, 184, 186, 191, 192, 195, 203, 204, 205, 216, 219, 228, 250
353FG 46, 79, 81-84, 94, 95, 120-122, 125, 127, 150, 151, 154, 165-167, 170, 186, 187, 189, 190, 194, 195, 220, 222, 227, 232, 233, 250
355FG 79, 83, 95, 122, 147, 149, 152, 155, 165, 166, 170, 176, 187, 189, 195, 224, 230-232, 251
356FG 79, 83, 84, 95, 151, 155, 168, 185, 189, 193, 195, 217, 219, 231, 251
357FG 120-124, 149, 152, 155, 166, 168, 169, 186, 189, 191, 193-195, 216, 222, 228-232, 251
358FG 98, 120, 252
359FG 98, 172, 152, 155, 165, 184, 187, 189, 191-193, 195, 220, 252
361FG 98, 127, 151, 155, 167, 169, 179, 188-190, 193, 195, 203, 219, 228, 232, 252
364FG 123, 149, 155, 171, 190, 191, 203, 219, 225, 229, 252
379BG 46, 49, 50, 52, 65, 71, 78, 79, 104, 106, 110, 134, 139, 141, 154, 157, 162, 208, 222, 231, 232, 253
381BG 46, 52, 53, 63, 64, 69, 75, 78, 79, 102, 114, 131, 132, 143, 154, 155, 201, 223, 227, 253

384BG 46, 52, 59, 66, 67, 78, 79, 103, 104, 109, 114, 115, 134, 135, 139, 145, 154, 161, 164, 183, 209, 229, 232, 253
385BG 53, 54, 68, 70, 73, 76, 79, 109, 114, 115, 135, 136, 142, 143, 155, 179, 210, 211, 225, 230, 254
386BG 46, 50, 57-62, 79, 254
387BG 57, 58, 60-62, 79, 254
388BG 53, 54, 63, 66, 68, 70, 75, 76, 79, 133, 155, 158, 163, 172, 174, 176, 183, 208, 225, 233, 255
389BG 79, 86-91, 103, 110, 131, 143, 153, 155, 157, 202, 222, 225, 227, 232, 255
390BG 53, 66-68, 77-79, 101, 103, 115, 143, 144, 155, 174, 176, 203, 206, 207, 223, 225, 229, 255
392BG 79, 90, 91, 107, 111, 116, 117, 129, 207, 209, 210, 256
398BG 140, 155, 176, 180, 202, 256
401BG 101-103, 105, 108, 141, 143, 144, 155, 174, 183, 204, 256
445BG 102, 110, 115, 128, 155, 178, 179, 182, 256
446BG 102, 105, 136, 137, 139, 142, 155, 180, 228, 232, 257
447BG 102, 105, 136, 137, 139, 142, 155, 180, 228, 232, 257
448BG 109, 129, 133, 135, 155, 175, 222, 223, 224, 233, 257

452BG 107, 128, 133, 155, 158, 180, 181, 188, 206, 207, 211, 225, 228, 258
453BG 140, 144, 155, 222, 258
457BG 139, 155, 178, 180, 226, 258
458BG 110, 146, 155, 156, 202, 259
466BG 128, 130, 132, 155, 175, 177, 207, 259
467BG 129, 133, 135, 155, 156, 164, 172, 202, 203, 206, 225, 227, 231, 259
479FG 152, 184, 187, 188, 190, 196, 197, 203, 217, 229, 259
482BG 73, 74, 79, 104, 105, 113, 117, 118, 155, 209, 260
486BG 140, 143, 153, 155, 172, 225, 260
487BG 140, 141, 155, 172, 181, 182, 201, 231, 260
489BG 144, 145, 155, 157, 172, 174, 175, 179, 233, 261
490BG 144, 155, 172, 214, 225, 228, 261
491BG 144, 145, 155, 172, 182, 206, 261
492BG 141, 142, 155, 156, 160, 163, 172, 174, 175, 262
493BG 155, 159, 178, 183, 211, 262
495FTG 155, 190, 191, 262
496FTG 155, 190, 191, 262
801BG(P) 155, 159, 172, 263
802RG(P) 155, 172, 200, 240

Wings

1BW & CBW 7, 46, 49, 53, 63, 65, 67, 68, 70-72, 76, 78, 81, 82, 105, 110, 143, 162, 216, 243, 244, 246, 247, 248, 249, 253, 256
2BW & CBW 7, 37, 46, 72, 76, 86, 90, 110, 155, 174, 241, 244, 255, 256, 258, 260
3BW 46, 50, 55, 58, 79, 248, 249, 254
4ADW 238, 241, 243
4BW & CBW 13, 46-53, 58, 63, 65-68, 70-72, 76, 101, 104, 110, 135, 136, 142, 179, 201,

212, 245, 246, 254, 255, 257
6FW 7, 46, 238, 239, 240, 241
13CBW 76, 77, 110, 115, 133, 142, 144, 158, 176, 214, 225, 245, 246, 255
14CBW 76, 110, 142, 153, 156, 160, 172, 175, 241, 256, 261, 262
20CBW 110, 153, 172, 174, 175, 179, 223, 244, 257, 261
40CBW 76, 78, 92, 106, 110, 133, 136, 244, 247, 248
41CBW 76, 110, 134, 135, 146, 227, 247, 253

45CBW 76, 110, 115, 133, 140, 142, 157, 158, 184, 214, 225, 245, 255, 258
51TCW 242
65FW 190, 238, 241, 251, 252, 259, 263
66FW 98, 166, 190, 241, 243, 249, 250, 251, 252
67FW 15, 98, 190, 239, 250, 251, 252
92CBW 110, 172, 249, 256, 260
93CBW 110, 225, 240, 254, 261, 262

94CBW 105, 110, 143, 249, 256, 258
95CBW 110, 144, 153, 172, 179, 261
96CBW 110, 141, 156, 174, 259
325RW(R) 239, 240
101PCBW 243, 248, 249, 253
102PCBW 244, 247, 248
103PCBW 247, 253
201PCBW 86, 89, 241, 244, 255
202PCBW 241, 256
401PCBW 245, 254
402PCBW 245, 246, 255
403PCBW 245, 255

Divisions

1FD(P) 243
1BD & AD 72, 73, 75, 77-79, 100, 104, 105, 108-109, 110, 112, 114, 116, 129, 135, 136, 139, 140, 142-144, 156-158, 163, 175, 177, 181, 183, 190,

192, 201-203, 208, 209, 211, 212, 214, 216, 223, 226-229
2BD & AD 72, 75, 78, 79, 91, 104, 105, 108-110, 116, 129, 136, 140, 142-144, 153, 156, 157, 162, 172, 174, 175, 179,

181, 182, 190, 201-203, 208, 211, 212, 214, 222, 225, 227, 229
3BD & AD 72, 73, 75, 77-79, 100, 101, 104, 105, 108-110, 112-114, 116, 129, 135, 136,

139, 140, 142-144, 153, 156-158, 160, 163, 168, 172, 174, 175, 179, 181-183, 190, 191, 201-204, 208, 211, 212, 214, 221, 222, 226-228, 230

Other Eighth Air Force Organisations

1 Base Air Depot 119

1 Combat Crew Gunnery School 155, 190

11 Combat Crew Replacement Center 46, 79, 155

12 Combat Crew Replacement Center 155
Air Technical Section 80, 104, 148
Operational Engineering Section 173

Maintenance and Technical Services 209, 212
2 Air Depot Group 5
1 Strategic Air Depot 155
2 Strategic Air Depot 155
3 Strategic Air Depot 155

4 Strategic Air Depot 155
689 Quartermaster Company 5
1 Scouting Force 163, 227, 293
2 Scouting Force 293
3 Scouting Force 294

Other USAAF Organisations

49FG 222	363FG 123	404FG 163	IXTAC 203, 204, 250
98BG 86, 88	376BG 35	IXBC 86, 87	XIXTAC 203, 252
354FG 95, 96, 119, 124, 127			

Luftwaffe Formations

J.G.1 27, 28, 30, 36, 43, 54, 65, 69, 74, 81, 84, 93, 123, 143
J.G.2 13, 20-22, 26, 30, 43, 44, 74, 81, 122, 166
J.G.3 54, 74, 78, 97, 127, 135, 137, 143, 160, 166, 177-179
J.G.4 178-180

J.G.7 214, 219, 220, 226
J.G.11 54, 69, 74, 81
J.G.26 13, 13, 22, 26, 29, 30, 37, 43, 47, 51, 52, 74, 81, 82, 161, 165, 166
J.G.27 54, 74, 196
J.G.51 54, 74, 78

J.G.52 169
J.G.54 48, 54, 74
J.G.300 74, 160, 177, 179, 194, 226
J.G.301 160, 194, 226
J.G.400 178, 184, 187

Z.G.26 74, 96, 122, 133
Z.G.76 74, 161
Kommando Nowotny 193, 194, 219
Sonderkommando Elbe 225, 226
Luftflotte 3 22

RAF Squadrons

No.71 14
No.107 198

No.121 14, 15
No.133 14, 15, 42

No.226 9, 10
No.303 11

No.601 6

Airfields: United Kingdom

Official name, actual location and alternative name in brackets; county, and USAAF station Number in brackets. See also under appropriate Group numbers.

Alconbury, Hunts. (102) 9, 17, 18, 33, 34, 46, 49, 51, 53, 73, 99, 155, 159, 209
Aldermaston, Berks. (467) 9, 13, 46
Andrews Field (Gt. Saling), Essex (485) 46, 50, 58
Atcham, Shropshire (342) 7, 9, 46, 155
Attlebridge, Norfolk (120) 55, 128, 135, 155, 174, 203

Bassingbourn, Cambs. (121) 9, 20, 25-32, 46, 51-54, 104, 138, 154, 161, 202, 204, 226, 227
Beccles (Ellough), Suffolk (132) 186
Benson, Oxfordshire (RAF) 199
Biggin Hill, Kent (RAF) 14
Bodney, Norfolk (141) 83, 95, 120, 149, 154, 165, 170, 203
Bottisham, Cambs. (374) 98, 151, 154
Bovingdon, Herts. (112 & 341) 5, 9, 14, 46, 47, 80-82, 96, 104, 148, 155, 210
Boxted (Langham) Essex (150) 50, 58, 59, 66, 95, 150, 154, 166, 169, 171, 189, 196, 220, 229, 233
Bradwell Bay, Essex (RAF) 136
Bungay (Flixton), Suffolk (125) 34, 153, 155, 222
Burtonwood, Lancs. 5, 119
Bury St. Edmunds (Rougham) Suffolk (468) 15, 46, 51, 55-57, 62, 65, 66, 72, 106, 121, 154, 202

Chalgrove, Oxfordshire (465)
Cheddington, Herts. (113) 5, 155, 156, 172, 179

Chelveston, Northants (105) 7, 9, 13, 21, 22, 25, 29-32, 41, 46, 48, 118, 141, 153, 154, 211
Chipping Ongar (Willingale), Essex (162) 58, 62, 79
Colerne, Wilts. (RAF) 17

Davidstowe Moor, Cornwall (RAF) 38
Debach, Suffolk (152) 146, 155, 183
Debden, Essex (356) 9, 14, 15, 40-42, 46, 80, 84, 122, 123, 127, 149, 154, 168, 169, 190
Deenethorpe, Northants. (128) 102, 108, 144, 155
Deopham Green, Norfolk (142) 155
Detling, Kent (RAF) 101
Duxford, Cambs. (357) 9, 15, 43, 46, 53, 80, 82, 83, 94, 147, 154, 234

Earls Colne, Essex (358) 46, 50, 51, 58
East Wretham, Norfolk (133) 98, 152, 154
Eglinton, Northern Ireland 9, 14, 15
Exeter, Devon (463) 48, 97
Eye (Brome), Suffolk (134) 144, 155, 172

Farnborough, Hants. (RAF) 11
Feltwell, Norfolk (RAF) 155
Fersfield (Winfarthing), Norfolk (140) 173
Ford, Sussex (RAF) 14, 78, 97
Foulsham, Norfolk (RAF) 65
Fowlmere, Cambs. (378) 149, 152, 154, 166, 167
Framlingham (Parham), Suffolk (153) 46, 51, 53, 66-68, 103, 135, 155, 223

Gatwick, Surrey (RAF) 17
Glatton (Connington), Hunts. (130) 155, 175, 201

Goxhill, Lincs. (345) 7, 9, 11, 41, 46, 81, 83, 155, 162
Grafton Underwood, Northants (106) 5, 9, 11, 12, 17, 46, 47, 52, 154, 209, 229
Great Ashfield, Suffolk (155) 35, 56, 109, 115, 143, 155, 210
Great Dunmow (Little Easton), Essex (164) 79
Great Sampford, Essex (RAF)
Greenham Common, Berks. (486) 84

Halesworth (Holton), Suffolk (365) 81, 83, 95, 97, 122, 126, 144, 149, 155, 166, 220, 226
Hardwick, Norfolk (104) 9, 15, 33, 35, 46, 86, 91, 102, 154
Harrington, Northants (179) 154, 172
Hendon, Midds. 46
Heston, Midds. 266
Hethel, Norfolk (114) 9, 15, 86, 91, 118, 155
High Ercall, Shropshire
Holmsley South, Hants. (455) 33
Honington, Suffolk (375) 22, 46, 56, 123, 149, 155, 162, 165, 171, 234
Horham, Suffolk (119) 9, 15, 46, 51, 57, 102, 113, 154
Horsham St. Faiths, Norfolk (123) 9, 41, 43-46, 55, 81, 146, 155, 174, 202

Ibsley, Hants. 9, 114
Ipswich, Suffolk (RAF) 100

Keevil, Wilts. (471) 9
Kenley, Surrey (RAF) 14
Kimbolton, Hunts. (117) 9, 17, 20, 46, 49, 52, 74, 139, 154, 231
Kings Cliffe, Northants (367) 83, 94, 147, 154, 165, 217
Kirton-in-Lindsey, Lincs. (RAF)
Knettishall, Suffolk (136) 54, 70, 72, 155, 159, 173, 201

Langford Lodge, Northern Ireland (233) 5, 35, 37, 38

Lavenham (Cockfield), Suffolk (137) 140, 155, 172, 181, 201
Leavesden, Herts. (RAF) 21
Leiston (Theberton), Suffolk (373) 97, 98, 123, 124, 149, 152, 154, 168, 191, 196
Little Staughton, Beds. (46)
Little Walden, Essex (165) 154, 203
Llanbedr, Merioneth (RAF) 41, 95
Ludham, Norfolk (RAF) 75
Lyneham, Wilts. (RAF) 175
Manston, Kent (351) 13, 43, 44, 53, 152, 156, 179
Martlesham Heath, Suffolk (369) 94, 154, 217
Maydown, Northern Ireland 15
Membury, Wilts. (466) 9, 15, 46, 198
Mendlesham (Wetheringsett), Suffolk (156) 154, 155, 206, 229
Merston, Sussex (356) 13
Metfield, Suffolk (366) 81, 84, 95, 120, 126, 144, 145, 155, 163, 166, 172, 173
Molesworth, Hunts. (107) 5, 9, 17, 20, 24-26, 30, 32, 46, 47, 101, 105, 129, 154, 202
Mount Farm, Oxfordshire (234) 46, 154, 199

North Pickenham, Norfolk (143) 141, 155, 156, 172, 173, 206
North Weald, Essex (RAF) 62
Nuthampstead, Herts. (131) 83, 85, 92, 140, 154, 180

Old Buckenham, Norfolk (144) 144, 155
Oulton, Norfolk (RAF) 155, 172

Podington, Beds. (109) 9, 46, 142, 154, 178, 201, 212
Polebrook, Northants (110) 7, 9, 11, 12, 17, 46, 53, 108, 114, 154
Portreath, Cornwall (504) 20, 34, 86

Airfields: Continental Europe and North Africa

Place Names, United Kingdom

Place Names: Continental Europe and North Africa

Individual Aircraft Names

Nickname, squadron, group, serial number (where known), code letters (where known).

Alice in Wonderland. P-51B, 363FS/357FG, 43-6966: B6:F
All Hell. P-47C, 61FS/56FG, 41-6235, HV:P
Any Time Annie. B-17F, 422BS/ 305BG, 42-30422, JJ:B 297
Ascend Charlie. B-17F, 571BS/ 390BG, 42-5903, R 72
Aunt Minnie's Bowser. P-38F 27FS/1FG, 41-7622 7
Available Jones. B-17F, 364BS/ 305BG 29

Bad Egg. B-17F, 401BS/91BG, 41-24484, LL:C 29
Bad Penny. B-17F, 322BS/91BG, 41-24480 32
Bay O'Bolts. B-24H, 715BS/ 448BG, 42-7764, B 109
Banshee. B-17F, 369BS/306BG 21, 23
Bat Outa Hell II. B-26B, 387BG 57
Battlin' Botty. B-17G, 614BS/ 401BG 108
Bertie Lee. B-17G, 364BS/305BG, 42-38131 133, 134
Betty A III. P-38J, 383FS/364FG, 42-67978, N2:K 123
Betty and Jim. B-24H, 847BS/ 489BG, 42-84947 144
Big Beautiful Doll. P-51D, 84FS/ 78FG, 44-72258, WZ:I 222
Big Dealer. B-24D, 93BG 35
Birmingham Blitzkrieg. B-17E, 414BS/97BG, 41-9100 (later 379BG) 12, 13, 162
Birmingham Jewell, The. B-17G, 526BS/379BG, 42-97678, LF:J 208
Black Barney. P-38J, 77FS/20FG, 42-67888, LC:B 120
Blazing Heat. B-26B, 553BS/ 386BG, 41-31585, AN:J 59
Bodacious. P-51D, 363FS/357FG, 44-13388, B6:W 191
Boeing's Best. B-17G, 365BS/ 305BG, 42-31342, XK:L 104
Boise Bee. P-51, 334FS/4FG, 43-6819, QP:B

Bomboogie. B-17F, 401BS/91BG, 42-5763, LL:F 29
Bomerang. B-24D, 328BS/93BG, 41-23722, C 18, 89, 90, 91, 102, 129, 130
Boom Town. B-17F, 305BG 23 32
Boulder Buff. B-24J, 858BS/ 492BG, 44-40195, 9A:J 160
Brass Rail Boys. B-17F, 94BG 74
Bugs Bunny. B-17G, 390BG 176
Butcher Shop. B-17E, 340BS/ 97BG 12
Buzzin Bear. B-24D, 67BS/44BG, 41-24229, P 86, 87, 89

Cabin in the Sky. B-17F, 571BS/ 390BG, 42-30338, P 77
Calamity Jane. B-17F, 390BG, 42-30302 66
California Cutie. P-38J, 55FS/ 20FG 170
Cannon Ball. B-17F, 511BS/ 351BG 48
Careful Virgin, The. B-17F, 323BS/91BG, 41-24639, OR:W 32, 173
Carolina Queen. B-17G, 381BG 132, 133
Carter's Little Liver Pills. B-17F, 364BS/305BG 32
Category E. P-47D, 63FS/56FG, 42-75276, UN:Q 229
Chennault's Pappy. B-17F, 306BG 32
Chief Sly II. B-17F, 322BS/91BG, 42-5139, LG:V 26
Chief Wapello. B-24H, 839BS/ 487BG, 42-52618, R5:K 140
Classy Chassy. B-24H, 487BG (later 446BG 298
Constance. P-51D, 383FS/ 364FG, 44-72719, N2:D 225
Contrary Mary. P-51D, 84FS/ 78FG, 44-14251, WZ:I 234
Cookie. P-47D, 351FS/353FG, 42-8395, YJ:S 95
Cripes A'Mighty. P-51s, 352FG, Details: 187, 273

Daddy's Girl. P-51D, 370FS/ 359FG, 44-14733, CS:L 276
Daisy Mae III. P-51D, 376FS/ 361FG, 44-14514, E9:Y 232

Dangerous Dan. B-17F, 524BS/ 379BG, 42-29891, WA:N 50
Delta Rebel II. B-17F, 323BS/ 91BG, 42-5077, OR:T 21, 32, 67
Devil's Own. B-17G, 493BG 183
Dinah Might. B-17G, 452BG, 42-37950, D 107
Doodle Bug. B-24H, 576BS/ 392BG 117
Double Lucky. P-47D, 61FS/ 56FG, 42-76234, HV:P 274
Double Trouble. B-26C, 323BG 62
Dove of Peace. P-47 & P-51, 353FG. Details: 277
Dragon Lady. B-17F, 551BS/ 385BG, 42-30836, V. Photo caption 76
Dry Martini II. B-17F, 364BS/ 305BG 23
Dry Martini 4th. B-17F, 364BS/ 305BG 20, 32, 49
Duchess, The. B-17F, 359BS/ 303BG, 41-24561, BN:T 27, 28, 32, 223

Eagle's Wrath, The. B-17F, 323BS/91BG, 41-24524, OR:Q 32
Easy Aces. B-17F, 94BG 51
Eight Ball. B-17F, 511BS/351BG, 42-3135, DS:P 32
Eight Ball, The. B-17F, 359BS/ 303BG, 41-24635, BN:O 25, 105
El Jeepo. P-47C, 83FS/78FG, 41-6335, HL:B 81
E-rat-icator. B-17G, 730BS/ 452BG, 42-39930, +P 128, 228
Excalibur. B-17F, 91BG 27

Fancy Nancy. B-17G, 612BS/ 401BG, 42-37838 101 (103)
Fancy Nancy IV. B-17G, 612BS/ 401BG, 42-31662, SC:B 157
Fireball. B-17F, 511BS/351BG, 42-29852 48
Flak Bait. B-26B, 449BS/322BG, 41-31773, PN:O 62
Flak Dodger. B-17G, 750BS/ 457BG, 42-97075, V 177
Flak Eater. B-17G, 364BS/305BG, 44-6009, WF:J 177

Flak Happy. B-26B, 452BS/ 322BG 62
Flak Magnet. B-24H, 467BG 177
Flak Wolf. B-17F, 427BS/303BG, 42-3131, GN:U 177
Floose, The. B-17G, 358BS/ 303BG, 42-97298, VK:H 202, 203
Flying Bison. B-17G, 427BS/ 303BG, 42-37875, GN:A 105
Flying Ginny. B-24H, 490BG, 42-94894 155
Foulball. B-17F, 511BS/351BG, 42-3150 48, 49
Fran 2nd. P-51D, 350FS/353FG, 44-15519, LH:H 217
Frenesi. B-17G, 333BS/94BG, 42-39775, TS:K 106, 297

Geezil II. B-17F, 369BS/306BG 32
General Ike. B-17G, 401BS/91BG, 42-97061, LL:B 138, 211
Gentile Annie. P-38J, 79FS/20FG, 42-68165, MC:R 148
Georgia Rebel. B-17F, 535BS/ 381BG, 42-3217, MS:T 63
Geronimo. B-24D, 328BS/93BG, 41-23744 34
GI Wife. B-24J, 487BG 298
Glory Bee. B-24, 606BS/44BG, QK:R+ 233
Golden Gaboon. B-24H, 453BG 144
Great McGinty, The. B-17G, 569BS/390BG, 43-38663, CC:M 223, 229
Greenwich. B-24H, 67BS/44BG, Z 109
Gremlin Gus. B-17, 388BG 174
Gremlin's Sweetheart, The. B-17F, 95BG 297

Half Pint. P-47C, 61FS/56FG 274
Hang The Expense. B-17G, 413BS/96BG, 42-97560, MZ:H 143
Hazee. B-24M, 577BS/392BG 209
Hell's Angels. B-17F, 358BS/ 303BG, 41-24577, VK:D 32, 47, 74, 75, 101
Hell's Angels. B-26B, 555BS/ 386BG, 41-31615, YA:W 61